TEMPUS
SPEEDWAY
YEARBOOK
2004

TEMPUS
SPEEDWAY
YEARBOOK
2004

edited by
ROBERT BAMFORD

TEMPUS

First published 2004

Tempus Publishing Limited
The Mill, Brimscombe Port,
Stroud, Gloucestershire, GL5 2QG
www.tempus-publishing.com

British Library Cataloguing in Publication Data.
A catalogue record for this book is available from the British Library.

ISBN 0 7524 2955 8

Typesetting and origination by Tempus Publishing Limited
Printed in Great Britain by Midway Colour Print, Wiltshire

CONTENTS

ACKNOWLEDGEMENTS

The idea of even contemplating the compilation of a British Speedway yearbook had previously filled me with trepidation, due mainly to the sheer number of meetings staged between March and October. However, having put together a version covering the 2002 season and with the experience gained through the writing of various books in recent years, I was encouraged to have a go at a professionally-bound version by James Howarth at Tempus Publishing. Of course, this would not be at all possible without the great network of enthusiasts scattered around the country and in particular, I would like to thank the following people who have helped in various way throughout the season: Nick Barber, Jo Cooper, Richard Crowley, Chris Durno, Neil Evans, Colin Goddard, Roger Hulbert, Ted Humphrey, Mike Hunter, Jeremy Jackson, Tony Jackson, Dick Jarvis, Roger Last, Tony Lethbridge, Dennis McCleary, Charles McKay, Nigel Meakins, Jayne Moss, Peter Oakes, Robert Peasley, Robbie Perks, Andy Povey, Ray Purvis, Laurence Rogers, John Sampford, Glynn Shailes, George Sheridan, Brett Sparkes, Jan Staechmann, Dave Stallworthy, Barry Stephenson, Norrie Tait, Steve Thorn, Peter Toogood, Malcolm Vasey, Dave Wall, Barry Wallace, Bob Wayte, Bryn Williams and Richard Williams. I am particularly grateful to Matt Jackson and John Weston for help with numerous dates of birth; and indeed to all the riders who were more than helpful with similar information when asked. Statistical genius Mike Moseley has kept me on the straight and narrow as far as the accuracies of averages are concerned and I am deeply indebted for his time and trouble in the cross-checking of my figures. Without the assistance of various photographers, this publication would be much the poorer, so I say a very big and sincere 'thank you' to the following for expertly producing all the images contained herein: main photographic content by Mike Patrick (www.mike-patrick.com); other contributions by Les Aubrey, Steve Brock, Ken Carpenter, Nigel Chanter, Ian Charles, Dave Fairbrother, Eddie Garvey, Phil Hilton, John Hipkiss, Hywel Lloyd and Alan Whale. The internet has also proved invaluable in helping to keep right up with everything in the speedway world, so grateful thanks to all the web-masters for doing such a marvellous job. I also wish to pay tribute to *Speedway Star* magazine, which has been an excellent and invaluable reference point. Finally, for guidance purposes, please note that in the calculation of rider averages, any golden double or tactical joker points are recorded as those normally given for the relevant finishing position, e.g. 1st = 3 points, 2nd = 2 points and 3rd = 1 point. I trust this publication will provide a useful reference, as well as rekindling many happy memories of the 2003 season.

Robert Bamford
31 October 2003

INTRODUCTION

If a theme from the early-1960s television show *That Was The Week That Was* can be applied to a year in speedway, then 'That Was The Season That Was'. It was one that saw young Dane Nicki Pedersen cause a major surprise when he won the World Championship Grand Prix series in the title showdown at Hamar, Norway, while in domestic racing here in the UK, Poole carried all before them as they emerged triumphant in three competitions.

Nicki Pedersen's Grand Prix glory was certainly deserved as he had ridden so consistently well in all the rounds, and it was particularly interesting since the Dane had been sacked by his club boss Nigel Wagstaff at Oxford in mid-season following a disagreement. The bold move by Wagstaff actually did British Speedway a great favour as it brought American Greg Hancock back to the UK scene, and his presence gave a tremendous boost to Oxford. However, despite the success of Pedersen, who had subsequently linked with Eastbourne, it has to be said that the best rider on the world stage was the unlucky Jason Crump. He could, and should, have landed the World Championship, but in heat twenty-four at Hamar he clashed with home star Rune Holta and the Norwegian came down. Crump was excluded and the crown went the way of Pedersen. It was a cruel blow to Crump who headed the Elite League averages with a huge 10.79 figure at Belle Vue, but bad luck really summed up his season on the individual front. He was streets above anybody else in the Elite League Riders' Championship at Coventry on 18 October and comfortably qualified for the final, only to see his bike virtually blow to bits on the start line and hand the title to home star Lee Richardson. Sooner or later Crump has just got to become World Champion – he's far too good a rider not to, and to be fair he really deserves just a little slice of luck.

Sweden came from behind to win the World Cup, seemingly snatching victory from the jaws of defeat and they overcame being 13 points down with just seven heats remaining to emerge as excellent victors ahead of Australia. They did it without the services of Tony Rickardsson, who was suffering from the after-effects of a concussion received in a domestic meeting in his homeland. Poland's Jaroslaw Hampel won the World Under-21 Championship in Kumla, Sweden, but his success was not well received due to his 'team riding' in an earlier heat which ensured that his fellow countryman Rafal Szombierski qualified for a third-place run-off against Swedish youngster Fredrik Lindgren. There was much debate over the actions of Hampel, although this sort of thing had happened on several previous occasions, not least when Bruce Penhall helped his compatriots Dennis Sigalos and the Moran brothers, Kelly and Shawn, in heat nineteen of the Overseas Final at White City in 1982. It surely requires just one referee to exclude a rider, who in his opinion, is not making a bona-fide attempt to race, and it would stop.

Sure, there would be a row and lots of hot air when it first happened, but riders and their advisers would soon get the message.

On the home domestic front, the season undoubtedly belonged to Poole who won a tremendous treble of the Elite League, Knock-Out Cup and British League Cup. If Play-Offs have to decide the Championship, then it is surely only right that the team which actually tops the league goes on to win the Play-Offs, and after all the Pirates did head the league table by 8 clear points. In the Knock-Out Cup, Poole staged the most amazing comeback at a rain-soaked Coventry to claim a narrow two-point aggregate victory. After eight heats the Bees were leading 31-17 and cruising to victory, with the Dorset side all but dead and buried. However, after reducing their deficit to 10 points, heat fourteen saw Coventry's Ryan Fisher lose control and upend Antonio Lindback, with Pirates' guest Mark Loram subsequently coming in as a tactical substitute to replace the Swedish-Brazilian, who was unable to take part in the rerun. Loram and fellow guest Garry Stead duly claimed a 5-1, and as if by magic Poole were back in the fight, with all the riders and management suddenly realizing they could still win on aggregate. And win they did, as Leigh Adams and Tony Rickardsson linked together for a last heat maximum to make the aggregate result Poole 90 Coventry 88. Needless to say the Bees were stunned, and will never quite know how the Knock-Out Cup slipped from their grasp. Thus Coventry earned nothing in terms of silverware from the season, one in which they were always chasing Poole, but never quite making it. It was, however, fitting that the Bees should race against the Pirates for both the league title and the Knock-Out Cup, since they were clearly the best two sides in the top flight.

The British League Cup further served to emphasise Poole's dominance as they defeated Eastbourne 56-34 at Wimborne Road, making up a 6-point deficit from the first leg within the opening two races. Despite rain for most of the day, the Poole track stood up well and the Pirates went to town to complete their trophy hat-trick with great gusto. The British League Cup competition was something new for 2003 which brought together all the Elite and Premier League sides. The Elite League was supposed to 'weaken' its teams by having no Grand Prix riders taking part, although in the event the rules appeared to be very flexible to say the least. One cynic remarked that 'The rules of the British League Cup were that there weren't any', and sometimes supporters could be excused if they agreed with that sentiment. Poole used rider replacement for Lukas Dryml at Newport; Leigh Adams took part in a couple of matches, as did Jason Crump for Belle Vue and Mikael Max had several outings for Wolverhampton. It also appeared that riders could be drafted in from all over Europe, much to the confusion of the paying public. Then there were some riders who appeared for more than one team in the competition, but nobody seemed to get too excited about it, although great emphasis was placed on the point that Craig Boyce was cup-tied. Young Daniel King was also reported to be cup-tied too, yet this didn't seem to apply to anyone else. As far as the averages went, these could not be published in the match programmes; with the result that one supporter of a Premier League side calculated that by converting the Elite League averages to their lower-league equivalent, his team were meeting visitors whose averages totalled nearly 70 points! If the competition is to be carried on, a set of rules that every team abides by must be introduced. The idea of an inter-league cup is good, and has of course been tried before, but if you don't have steadfast rules the whole thing degenerates and that is clearly not good for the sport.

Poole created their own special piece of speedway history on Monday 15 September, when they tracked two teams on the same evening. Their first side raced at home to Oxford in the Knock-Out Cup semi-final, while the British League Cup team took part in their last group match at Wolverhampton! Perhaps most important was the fact that neither Poole line-up was packed out with guest riders. However, when the Pirates had previously raced at Oxford on 29 August in an Elite League match, due to Grand Prix commitments and injuries, they could only track one of their declared team, namely Krzysztof Kasprzak. The rest of the side was made up by a combination of five guests, including British League Cup teamster Craig Boyce, with the rider replacement facility utilized for Tony Rickardsson. This unsatisfactory situation was brought about due to the restaging of the Scandinavian Grand Prix at the Ullevi Stadium and the necessity to complete the league fixtures before the cut-off date for the Play-Offs.

Another idea that had been tried in the past was the 'doubling up' between riders from the Premier League to the Elite League. Riders such as Tom Owen (Newcastle and Newport) successfully did this in the mid-1970s; it was more widely implemented when reintroduced in 2002, and in 2003 we also had 'doubling down'. It can be rightly said that the 'doubling up' was a success since both Charlie Gjedde (Swindon and Oxford) and Chris Harris (Trelawny and Peterborough) were to do exceptionally well in the higher sphere of racing. The experience must have done both riders the world of good and there were others too who benefited from the system.

Peterborough, who were tough nuts to crack on their home circuit, finished in third spot in the Elite League, although they relied too heavily on Aussie Ryan Sullivan, who rode in great discomfort due to injuries for much of the season. Dane Hans Andersen was another to suffer from injuries, while the Pole 'Pepe' Protasiewicz came on in leaps and bounds, although club promoter Mick Horton has already indicated that neither will feature in his team for 2004. Oxford, who were taken over by Nigel Wagstaff when he moved from King's Lynn to Cowley for 2003, came on well and the signing of Greg Hancock was a master stroke. The sacking of Nicki Pedersen would have had an adverse affect on most sides, but Oxford recovered quickly, thanks in no small way to the enthusiasm and professionalism of the American racer. Pedersen was soon snapped up by Eastbourne, who themselves released Joe Screen to Belle Vue, so the decision of Nigel Wagstaff could certainly be seen as being beneficial to three of the sides in the Elite League. Wagstaff, like the bosses at Poole, was always prepared to make changes in order to strengthen within the rules. Oxford brought in Andy Smith and Matej Ferjan from the cold, although the latter didn't last long, while Poole introduced the exciting Swedish-Brazilian Antonio Lindback. He proved an instant hit with the fans, making a sensational debut for the Pirates in a home British League Cup match against Exeter when he registered a paid 21-point maximum!

At Wolverhampton, it was very much the mixture as before, and at Belle Vue and Ipswich the season is perhaps best forgotten. Belle Vue had the brilliance of Jason Crump of course, but were never really settled as the two Americans Josh Larsen and Chris Manchester came and went without adding anything to the Aces, while at Ipswich they relied almost entirely on Scott Nicholls. It must be said, however, that Scotty did the Witches and his country proud, and it was pleasing to see him being very positive in his thinking, believing himself to be as good as anyone else on the track, particularly in world events, and he gave of his best at all times. England can certainly be proud of his contribution to their cause, while Ipswich too can be proud of a rider who kept their flag flying throughout a difficult campaign. Jaroslaw Hampel should have perhaps progressed more than he did, and Chris Slabon, although showing great potential, never seemed fully at home in British racing. If rumours are true that Chris Louis is to join his father, John, in the promotion for 2004, then that is a step in the right direction for the Suffolk club who could soon return to former glories.

In the Premier League Edinburgh were deserving winners of the Championship and it was good to see the Scottish club succeed. No effort has ever been spared to keep the Monarchs in speedway and the promoters must be congratulated for putting together such a potent side. In Frede Schott they possessed the league's top rider, who maintained a huge average throughout and finished with a mammoth 10.76 figure to his name. Rory Schlein can look back on his first full season in the Premier League with much satisfaction and there appears to be a great career ahead in the shale-shifting game for the popular young Australian. Of course, veteran Peter Carr was there as always, posting a 9.07 average, and like good wine, he seems to get better with age. An interesting point is that Frede Schott missed several matches after suffering a nasty collarbone injury while guesting for Swindon, although happily this didn't derail Edinburgh's title charge.

Sheffield finished in the runner-up position after the Isle of Wight missed out on their opportunity to leapfrog the Tigers when suffering a surprise home defeat at the hands of Arena-Essex in the final match of the season. However, the Islanders can look back with much satisfaction at defeating Sheffield in the final of the Knock-Out Cup. The Isle of Wight owed much to Aussie Adam Shields for their success, and he was another rider to benefit greatly from 'doubling up' with Eastbourne. There were many teams in the Premier League who could be described as being pretty equal in terms of strength, and this made for interesting and close racing. Trelawny were excellent on their home strip – surely one of the best in the sport – and with Matej Zagar and Chris Harris leading their attack, racing of the highest order was always guaranteed when the boys from Cornwall went on their travels. Sadly, a cloud hangs over the Tigers at present as they have to vacate their picturesque Clay Country Moto Parc home. It is hoped they can find a new venue soon, and equally important that when they do they can again construct a superb racing circuit.

Swindon were always challenging, and had a top man in Dane Charlie Gjedde, whose racing was invariably of the highest class, and Newcastle also had a fearsome Danish duo in Kenneth Bjerre and Bjarne Pedersen, the latter 'doubling down' when other commitments would allow. Arena-Essex benefited from being able to utilize the services of Joonas Kylmakorpi or David Ruud, and after finishing the season strongly it would appear the Hammers are giving serious thought to joining the Elite League. Berwick enjoyed a good season, but it ended on a very sad note when Argentinian Carlos Villar, who had proven to be a crowd-pleasing thrill-maker, suffered a crash which has left him paralysed from the waist down. This was cruel luck for the twenty-eight-year-old, although typically, everyone in the sport was keen to do their utmost to help as he tried to come to terms with his terrible injuries.

Exeter kept going thanks to the sterling efforts of Tony Lethbridge and Brian James while promoter Colin Hill battled against ill health. The Falcons were, as usual, hard to beat around the sweeping bends of their County Ground circuit, although it looks like they will spend just one more year at the venue before having to relocate elsewhere. King's

Lynn stepped down from the Elite League and put together a useful side, led by 'old boy' Tomas Topinka and heat-leader partners Shane Parker and Davey Watt. The 'Stars' nickname was returned to favour and the team enjoyed a good campaign, although injuries spoiled their chances of success. Having impressed greatly the previous season, mainly in the Conference League, young Edward Kennett showed maturity beyond his sixteen years and burst straight to the top of the Rye House scoring with an average in excess of 8 points per match. Sadly, the son of the former Hackney and Eastbourne rider Dave Kennett suffered a nasty knee injury in July, but returned late in the term at Conference level to show it had not affected him in any way, emphasising the point by signing off with a 9-point haul in the prestigious Ace of Herts Championship. Hull unfortunately finished the season with the wooden spoon, although in hindsight the June decision to dispense with Neil Collins and Lee Dicken didn't help their cause. Both Bjorn G. Hansen and Jimmy Jansson had spells in the side, before Emil Kramer was recruited for the last few weeks of the season and did a grand job. Since the Vikings had used Kramer towards the end of the 2002 campaign, one is left to wonder why they didn't retain him from the start of 2003. There had been doubts about Hull running, and Nigel Wordsworth, together with Paul Hodder who joined him in August, must be congratulated for keeping the sport alive in the city.

So last, but by no means least, we come to the Conference League where Mildenhall, under Graham Drury, put together a side that from day one was capable of winning the Championship, which is just what they did. The Fen Tigers' boss had his critics for the way in which he put his team together, always with winning in mind, and there have been many comments regarding the 'spirit of the rules' within Conference League racing. But what exactly is the spirit of the rules? Having compiled a set of rules, it does seem rather pointless to then have a spirit within them. Rye House chased Mildenhall all the way and were always a team worth watching, and in Len Silver they have the sort of promoter who always gives the public what they want. They, of course, were one of a number of clubs from the Premier and Elite Leagues who ran Conference League racing alongside their main team, and these tracks are to be congratulated for doing their bit for the sport. At the present time it looks as though Wolverhampton may not compete in the future, but it is also understood that their promotion is looking for an alternative venue to stage Conference racing.

Surely everything possible must be done to encourage the Conference League in order to ensure the future of the sport. There is of course a problem, insofar as it is so important in these times to win, and it follows that if you don't win then the support isn't there. However, everything must be done to encourage and market Conference League racing, otherwise speedway is going nowhere.

One cannot leave a review of 2003 without going back to the British League Cup, where but two days before the second-leg of the final at Poole, Peterborough raced their outstanding match and lost to Arena-Essex. As a result, the victorious Hammers actually topped the group, but with the cut-off date being sometime back in September, they didn't qualify for the quarter-final stage. Things like this, no matter what may be said or written, must not be allowed to happen for the overall good of the sport.

Glynn Shailes
31 October 2003

ABBREVIATIONS

GENERAL

AL	Amateur League
BSPA	British Speedway Promoters Association
BLC	British League Cup
CL	Conference League
CLKOC	Conference League Knock-Out Cup
CT	Conference Trophy
DNA	Did Not Arrive
DNR	Did Not Ride
EL	Elite League
ELKOC	Elite League Knock-Out Cup
FIM	Fédération Internationale de Motorcyclisme
KOC	Knock-Out Cup
PL	Premier League
PLKOC	Premier League Knock-Out Cup
R/R	Rider Replacement

LEAGUE TABLES

Mts	Matches
Won	Won
Drn	Drawn
Lst	Lost
For	For
Agn	Against
Pts	Points
Bon	Bonus
Tot	Total

AVERAGES TABLES

Mts	Matches
Rds	Rides
Pts	Points
Bon	Bonus
Tot	Total
Avge	Average
Max	Maximums

SCORE TABLES

DNA	Did Not Arrive
DNR	Did Not Ride
(R)	Replay
R/R	Rider Replacement

RACE POSITIONS

ex	Excluded
f	Fell
n.s.	Non-starter
rem	Remounted
ret	Retired

RACE SCORES TABLES

F	Fell
M	Excluded, 2 minutes
n	Non-starter
R	Retired
X	Excluded
T	Excluded, tapes

SKY SPORTS ELITE LEAGUE 2003

RACING DIARY OF THE SEASON

MARCH

15 Coventry kick-off with a narrow 46-44 victory over Oxford in a challenge match, inspired by a paid 14 return from Lee Richardson.

16 Warm and sunny weather is the order of the day as Dean Barker celebrates his Testimonial at Eastbourne, with the benefit man himself taking glory in the final from Martin Dugard, Leigh Adams and Lee Richardson. The day also sees a second Testimonial, as Peter Karlsson's big event ends in a 50-40 success for Wolverhampton against visiting Swedish side Kaparna, with the meeting's leading player heading the scoring on a paid 12-point tally. Following the main match, a knock-out contest (featuring semi-finals and a final) for a GM engine results in victory for Joonas Kylmakorpi from Mikael Max (formerly known as Mikael Karlsson), Peter Karlsson and Jaroslaw Hampel.

17 Belle Vue swing into action with a challenge match against Premier League outfit Hull, with the Aces storming to a 64-26 win, led by a 15-point full house from Jason Crump, plus a paid maximum (14+1) from fellow Aussie Jason Lyons.

19 Poole gain a 49-41 success over Peterborough in the first leg of a challenge, inspired by 12+1 points from former Oxford man Lukas Drmyl.

20 New acquisition Paul Hurry nets 13+1 points as Ipswich open for business with a big 57-32 victory over Swedish tourists Kaparna.

21 Oxford easily defeat Kaparna 55-35, with super Dane Nicki Pedersen scorching to a five-ride maximum.

22 A hard-fought match results in a 48-42 victory for Coventry over Ipswich at Brandon in the first Elite League match of the year, with both Billy Hamill and Lee Richardson hitting 10-point tallies for the Bees.

23 Peterborough beat Poole 48-42 in the second-leg of their challenge, but it's victory for the visitors on aggregate by 91 points to 89.

24 Led by a brilliant 13+1 points from Carl Stonehewer, Belle Vue comfortably polish off King's Lynn in an inter-league challenge. A nail-biting challenge match at Wolverhampton ends in a 46-44 success for visiting Coventry, for whom Billy Hamill tops the scoring on 13 points.

25 In front of the cameras, Eastbourne clinch a hard-fought 47-42 Elite League success over Wolverhampton.

26 More league action as Poole are unable to stop the powerful Coventry combination from claiming a 47-43 victory at Wimborne Road.

27 Ipswich stage their first home league fixture of the campaign, but they are caught cold as visiting Poole atone for the previous night's slip-up with a 50-40 win.

28 Challenge-match action sees new-look Oxford suffer a 48-42 home defeat at the hands of Coventry. Peterborough begin their league campaign, claiming a comfortable 53-37 success over 2002 Champions Wolverhampton, with Ryan Sullivan flying to a superb paid maximum (14+1).

29 Coventry collect another win, seeing off Peterborough 51-39 in their second home league match of the season. Eastbourne gain a 50-40 league victory over Ipswich at Arlington,

but the undoubted star of the show has to be top Witch Scott Nicholls, who simply oozes class as he cruises to a six-ride maximum.

31 Despite leading 43-41 going into the last heat, Belle Vue end up suffering a 46-44 league reverse at the hands of Oxford, as Nicki Pedersen and Todd Wiltshire gain a somewhat unexpected 5-1 over the Aussie duo of Jason Crump and Jason Lyons to secure the league points. Wolverhampton dash to a 53-37 win over Peterborough, aided no end by a paid full house (14+1) from Mikael Max. With the scores tied on aggregate, that man Max defeats Hans Andersen in a run-off, thereby giving Wolves all three league points. Amazingly, with the month at an end, a full quota of twenty meetings had gone ahead as scheduled at Elite League level, without the dreaded wet stuff playing havoc!

APRIL

2 Poole open the month by racing to a 49-40 league victory over Ipswich, led by big points from their heat-leader trio of Leigh Adams (11+1), Tony Rickardsson (11) and Lukas Dryml (10+1).

3 One day on and Ipswich quickly make amends for their loss at Poole by defeating Peterborough 48-42 in a British League Cup (Group A) clash at Foxhall Heath.

4 A powerful display sees Oxford hammer Wolverhampton 58-32 in the league, inspired by maximums from Nicki Pedersen (13+2) and Sebastian Ulamek (12). Staying with league action, Peterborough suffer a 47-43 reverse at home to the solid Coventry septet.

5 Inspired by a battling 10 points from Dean Barker, Eastbourne end Coventry's winning run with a 47-43 success at Arlington in a tense Elite League encounter.

7 It's another last-heat decider, and another home defeat for Belle Vue, as Coventry grab a 47-43 success, and return to winning ways in a pulsating league fixture. Wolverhampton are held to a 45-45 draw by Poole in a nail-biting league match at Monmore Green.

9 Coventry win again, with a 48-42 Brandon success over Eastbourne also netting them the all-important league bonus point. Inspired by 14 points from Ryan Sullivan, Peterborough scorch to a 53-37 Elite League victory over Belle Vue. Poole defeat Oxford 51-39 in the third league match of the evening, their main points coming from Lukas Dryml (13) and David Ruud (11+2).

10 Chris Slabon and Scott Nicholls card 13 points apiece as Ipswich eke out a narrow 47-43 success over Wolverhampton in the league.

11 Solid scoring paves the way as Oxford beat Belle Vue 51-39 in the Elite League, led by Nicki Pedersen (12) and Todd Wiltshire (10+2). Peterborough stage their second home league match in three days, and it's another victory, by 47 points to 43 over Poole.

12 Coventry consolidate their position on top of the Elite League table, courtesy of a 50-40 success over Belle Vue at Brandon, as flying reserve Stuart Robson nets a tally of 15+1 points. The Arlington faithful witness a nail-biter, but it's the homesters who come through to defeat Oxford 47-43 in a league encounter.

14 Compounding a nightmare start to the season, Belle Vue suffer their sixth successive league defeat, and their third at home, losing 49-41 at the hands of Eastbourne, despite a brilliant 18-point full house from Jason Crump. Amazingly, Peterborough stage their third home Elite League match in six days, racing to a 59-31 win over Oxford, with their main contributor being Piotr Protasiewicz (14). It's British League Cup (Group E) action at Wolverhampton, and the homesters have little difficulty in defeating Somerset 57-33, led ably by maximums from 'Sudden' Sam Ermolenko and David Howe (11+1).

16 Belle Vue's losing sequence continues in a league match at Poole, as the home team comfortably win 54-36, their major points coming from Lukas Dryml (13+1), Tony Rickardsson (12) and maximum-man Leigh Adams (12).

18 A morning start sees Todd Wiltshire (12+2) and Nicki Pedersen (12) score well, as Oxford kick-off the Good Friday programme with a hard-fought 46-44 success over high-flying Coventry. In spite of Krzysztof Kasprzak being stranded in bank-holiday traffic and David Ruud withdrawing after one ride through food poisoning, Poole canter to a 56-34 victory over Eastbourne in the Knock-Out Cup, with Leigh Adams plundering a second successive maximum (14+1) for the club. With 15+1 points from seven starts, Scott Nicholls can't stop Ipswich from suffering a 47-43 home loss in an afternoon league clash against Peterborough. Thanks to a solid team performance, Belle Vue finally claim a victory, defeating Wolverhampton 49-41 in the Knock-Out Cup, with Jason Crump (12) and the recently returned American Chris Manchester (9+3) leading the way. Mark Loram suffers a broken arm as Eastbourne defeat Poole 40-32 in the second-leg of their Knock-Out Cup tie, the match being abandoned after twelve heats as England's last World Champion is taken to hospital. David Norris (10+1) is the leading man in the home camp, but it's the Pirates who edge through to the next round on aggregate. Every home man scores well as Peterborough thrash Ipswich 62-28 to complete a quick-fire Elite League double, their leading players being Gary Havelock (12+2), Ryan Sullivan (11) and Hans Andersen (10+2). For the Witches, Scott Nicholls follows up his marathon morning session with another seven-ride stint earning 16 points.

19 Coventry quickly return to winning ways in the league, avenging their Good Friday loss at Cowley, with a 49-41 success over the Silver Machine outfit.

20 With a 1 p.m. start, Peterborough waste no time to swamp Wolverhampton 58-32 in a league fixture. David Norris and Joe Screen hit five-ride and four-ride full houses respectively, as Eastbourne race to a 55-34 British League Cup (Group D) win over the Isle of Wight.

21 Easter Monday action sees Coventry defeat Peterborough 52-38 in the Knock-Out Cup. The last action of the Easter programme results in a 57-33 Knock-Out Cup victory for Wolverhampton over Belle Vue, as the homesters move safely through to the next round. Jason Crump unfortunately misses the match for the Aces, due to a previously booked Polish Extra League commitment for Torun.

23 Oxford scamper to a 51-38 victory over Ipswich in the league. British League Cup (Group E) action at Wimborne Road sees Poole eke out a 52-38 success over a dogged Trelawny, led by a five-ride maximum from dazzling Dane Bjarne Pedersen.

26 Eastbourne are pushed all the way by bottom-of-the-table Belle Vue, before winning their Elite League encounter 47-43.

28 Belle Vue's league clash with Poole becomes the first rain-off of the year at Elite level, the meeting called off at 10.30 a.m. There is league action at Wolverhampton, however, as the home boys claim a hard-fought 49-41 victory over Ipswich.

29 Led by a 14-point tally from World Champion Tony Rickardsson, Poole edge home 46-44 against a dogged Peterborough side in the Elite League.

MAY

2 Rain is the only winner, as Oxford's eagerly-awaited league clash with Eastbourne is washed out.

3 David Norris top scores with 14 points as Eastbourne entertain and beat Peterborough 55-35 in the league.

4 A waterlogged track sadly ends any hopes of staging the Alan Wilkinson Benefit at Belle Vue.

5 Ipswich suffer a 49-41 home reverse at the hands of Oxford in the Knock-Out Cup, with Sebastian Ulamek hitting a 12-point maximum for the victors. Poole have little difficulty in thrashing Eastbourne 60-30 in a one-sided league affair, thanks largely to unbeaten tallies from Leigh Adams (15) and Tony Rickardsson (13+2). Wolverhampton defeat Belle Vue 48-42 in an entertaining league clash, despite the 'never-say-die' efforts of Jason Crump (15) for the Aces.

8 Peterborough claim a comfortable 52-38 Elite League success over Eastbourne, with lively reserve Chris Harris netting 13+2 points.

9 Oxford oust Ipswich from the Knock-Out Cup, easily winning the second-leg of the tie 55-35, with Todd Wiltshire romping to a full 15-pointer.

10 High-flying Coventry defeat Peterborough 52-38, but the victory is marred by a badly broken collarbone suffered by Swedish ace Andreas Jonsson in the first running of heat fifteen. After successive away defeats, Eastbourne are caught out at home, with Leigh Adams racing to a magical six-ride maximum as Poole grab a 46-43 league success.

12 The Sky cameras are at Ipswich for the Elite League encounter against Coventry, but with the track greasy from afternoon rain only one heat is completed before the meeting is abandoned. There's no change of fortune for Belle Vue, who suffer their tenth league defeat out of ten, as Peterborough collect a 48-42 success at Kirky Lane. Bespectacled Peter Karlsson weighs in with a paid maximum (13+2), helping Wolverhampton to a 53-37 victory over Oxford in the league.

14 Poole comfortably defeat Wolverhampton 58-32 in a league encounter, thereby consolidating third spot in the table.

17 Coventry edge to a 48-42 success over 2002 Premier League Champions Sheffield in a terrific British League Cup (Group B) clash at Brandon, with Billy Hamill completing a paid maximum (14+1).

18 Eastbourne clinch a 52-37 victory over Swindon in the British League Cup (Group D).

19 The rains return to wipe out the day's two Elite League fixtures – Belle Vue v. Ipswich, and Wolverhampton v. Coventry.

21 Poole entertain, and defeat Workington 56-37 in an inter-league challenge, with Leigh Adams (15), Lukas Dryml (14+1) and Craig Boyce (11+1) unbeaten.

22 A 47-43 Elite League victory for Ipswich means yet another loss for beleaguered Belle Vue.

23 Poole win 49-41 at Oxford, and cruise to the head of the Elite League table. A brace of 5-1s in the last two heats give Peterborough a 52-38 success over Coventry in the Knock-Out Cup, leaving the sides locked together on 90 points apiece.

24 Coventry beat Midlands rivals Wolverhampton 49-41 to jump a single point ahead of Poole at the top of the league. Eastbourne comfortably win 54-36 against Ipswich in the league.

25 Sunday evening action at Kirky Lane sees Belle Vue gain a much-needed 55-35 victory over Coventry in the British League Cup (Group B), although the result is subsequently amended as William Lawson's inclusion in the Aces side is deemed ineligible, with his 4 points being deducted from their score.

26 In front of a Sky TV audience, Coventry extend their lead in the league table, comprehensively defeating Ipswich 54-36. Peterborough ease to a 53-37 win versus Belle Vue, as the Manchester outfit complete the unenviable record of having lost each and every one of their first dozen league matches.

29 Ipswich beat Eastbourne 49-41 in an Elite League match at Foxhall Heath, but the star of the show is undoubtedly Eagles reserve Adam Shields, who nets a wonderful seven-ride paid maximum (20+1).

30 In the British League Cup (Group D), it's a comprehensive 53-37 success for Oxford over Premier League Reading, with Travis McGowan unbeaten (14+1). More BLC action at the East of England Showground results in a narrow 45-44 Group A victory for Peterborough against Ipswich.

31 Coventry have no trouble in conclusively beating a weakened Belle Vue side 53-36 in the British League Cup (Group B).

JUNE

2 After twelve successive league defeats, Belle Vue at last collect a victory, coming from behind to defeat Poole 45-44, as Jason Crump establishes a new track record for the Kirky Lane raceway. Wolverhampton eke out a 48-42 league win against Eastbourne, helped no end by Peter Karlsson's five-ride full house.

4 Poole race to a tenth successive home victory, comfortably seeing off Ipswich 57-33 in an Elite League encounter, and returning to the top of the table in the process.

5 Ipswich suffer their second loss in two days, going down 50-40 to Wolverhampton in the league at home.

9 Despite sunny weather, basement club Belle Vue's home league encounter against Ipswich is postponed, due to their landlords being unable to start removing the stock-car safety fence in time for sufficient track preparation to begin. Before the Sky cameras, Eastbourne are beaten 46-44 by Coventry at Arlington in a thrilling league tussle, as the Bees return to the head of the table. Peter Karlsson nets a paid maximum (13+2) as Wolverhampton ease to a 53-37 league victory over Peterborough at Monmore Green.

11 Oxford clinch a 48-42 Elite League win against Peterborough, but it's the Panthers who gain the bonus point to consolidate their third position in the table. Poole have to work hard to defeat Belle Vue 46-44, their victory hoisting them back to the top of the league standings.

12 A difficult campaign for Ipswich continues, as they suffer a humiliating 57-33 home reverse at the hands of Peterborough.

15 Coventry return to pole position in the league, courtesy of a narrow 47-43 success over Oxford at Brandon.

16 Honours are even as Belle Vue and Eastbourne draw 45-45 in the Elite League at Kirky Lane. Wolverhampton deny Poole the opportunity of returning to top spot in the league, winning 46-44 in a hard-fought encounter at Monmore Green.

18 The ding-dong battle at the top continues as Poole again move to the head of the table, courtesy of a convincing 53-37 success over Peterborough.

20 Third-placed Peterborough dig deep to claim a hard-fought 48-42 win over leaders Poole. Amid shambolic scenes, Oxford's Elite League clash with Wolverhampton is abandoned without a wheel turning, due to an over-watered section of the track which wouldn't dry out despite concerted efforts by track staff.

21 Poole consolidate their table-topping position with a stirring 47-43 success at the home of their nearest challengers Coventry. Further improving the Pirates' situation, Leigh Adams then defeats Billy Hamill in a run-off for the bonus point. A fired-up Eastbourne comfortably dispatch Oxford 52-38 in the league at Arlington.

23 Jason Crump rips to a five-ride maximum as basement club Belle Vue record only their second league victory of the season, defeating Oxford 49-41. Following their recent home thrashing at the hands of Peterborough, there's a marked improvement as Ipswich beat Eastbourne 47-43 in a pulsating league encounter. A solid team effort sees Wolverhampton through to a 51-39 win over deposed league leaders Coventry.

25 The East of England Showground serves up some wheel-to-wheel racing as Peterborough claim a 54-36 league success over Oxford, with Piotr Protasiewicz netting a fabulous 17 points. Table-topping Poole are made to work extremely hard by Wolverhampton, eventually claiming a 47-43 victory at Wimborne Road.

27 Local-derby fare sees Oxford defeat Swindon 50-40 in the British League Cup (Group D), with both Andy Smith (15) and Jan Staechmann (9+3) recording maximums. The day's other meeting between Peterborough and King's Lynn, also in the BLC, is washed out by late-afternoon rain.

28 Coventry easily wrap up a 59-31 win over Stoke in the British League Cup (Group B), as Billy Janniro (14+1), Billy Hamill (12) and Stuart Robson (11+4) remain undefeated by an opponent.

30 Rain wins the day as both scheduled matches are called off – Belle Vue v. Coventry (EL) and Wolverhampton v. Poole (BLC).

JULY

2 It's mighty close, but Poole extend their advantage at the top of the table, thanks to a hard-earned 46-44 success over a new-look Oxford – complete with Andy Smith, Greg Hancock and Matej Ferjan on board.

4 Oxford's revamped line-up does the business at Cowley, comfortably defeating Coventry 52-38 in the league as Todd Wiltshire hits a five-ride maximum.

5 All roads lead to Eastbourne for the Championship of Great Britain, and it's Scott Nicholls who successfully defends his title, defeating the home-track trio of Dean Barker, David Norris and Joe Screen in the final.

7 Jason Crump scores the lot (15), as Belle Vue make it three home league victories on the trot, beating second-in-the-table Peterborough 47-43. No surprises at Monmore Green, as Wolverhampton race to a 60-30 league win over beleaguered Ipswich, with David Howe carding a 12-point full house.

8 Great Britain claim a 57-33 success against Sweden in an Under-21 international at Wolverhampton, with David Howe brilliantly netting full points (15).

9 Leigh Adams sets a new track record as his paid maximum (14+1) helps Poole defeat Coventry 52-38 in the league at Wimborne Road.

10 British League Cup (Group A) action sees Ipswich beat near-neighbours King's Lynn 53-37, thereby moving to the head of their sector.

11 Oxford claim a 50-40 success over the Isle of Wight in the British League Cup (Group D), despite visitor Adam Shields' sensational 17 points. More British League Cup (Group A) fare results in a narrow 47-45 success for Peterborough over local rivals King's Lynn.

12 Billy Janniro (15) and Stuart Robson (13+2) remain unbeaten, as Coventry complete their British League Cup (Group B) fixtures with a comfortable 56-35 victory over Hull.

14 Belle Vue ease to a 55-35 success against Sheffield in the British League Cup (Group B). The result is academic for the visitors, however, as they move through to the quarter-final stage. Test-match action at Eastbourne results in a 47-43 triumph for the Rest of the World against Great Britain, with Leigh Adams plundering a five-ride maximum for the victors.

16 Tony Rickardsson cards a paid maximum (14+1), as Poole continue to march ahead at the top of the league, although they are made to work hard before winning 47-43 against an Eastbourne side including returnee Mark Loram. Coventry hold a 36-30 lead at Wolverhampton when the skies open and the meeting is abandoned after heat eleven with the result inconclusive.

17 A season of woe for Ipswich continues, as Oxford race to a 51-39 league success at Foxhall Heath.

18 Oxford again defeat Ipswich in the league, this time by a 58-32 scoreline at Cowley. Ryan Sullivan bags a full 15-pointer as Peterborough overwhelm Eastbourne 56-34 in Elite League action.

19 Coventry end their run of four successive league defeats by scoring a 48-42 success over Belle Vue at Brandon. With Eastbourne holding a 46-38 lead against Wolverhampton, heavy rain aborts the proceedings after heat fourteen, with the result standing.

21 Oxford are pushed all the way in a thrilling league encounter, before finally defeating Eastbourne 47-43. The match is marred, however, by an eleventh-heat crash which leaves Mark Loram suffering a dislocated ankle. Another close match sees Wolverhampton eke out a 47-43 victory over Belle Vue in the league at Monmore Green.

23 Poole suffer their first postponement of the year, with their Four-Team Tournament against Eastbourne, Ipswich and Peterborough falling victim to persistent drizzle. Only four heats of Belle Vue's British League Cup (Group B) match against Stoke are completed, before rain brings proceedings to a premature close.

24 Despite numerous injuries, Poole increase their lead in the league, thanks to a comprehensive 51-39 success at Ipswich, with Leigh Adams unbeaten (13+2).

25 Oxford's league match against Peterborough is a lunchtime postponement victim, due to heavy rainfall.

26 The rains again win the day, as Eastbourne's attractive league encounter with Poole is called off.

28 Exactly seventy-five years since first opening, Belle Vue produce a stirring performance to defeat league leaders Poole 47-43, with the win lifting the Aces off the foot of the table. The day's other league fixture between Wolverhampton and Eastbourne is called off due to heavy evening rain.

30 In the British League Cup (Group E), Poole romp to a 58-32 victory over Exeter, with Antonio Lindback scorching to a sensational seven-ride paid maximum (19+2) on his Pirates' debut.

31 Things don't improve for basement club Ipswich as Coventry cruise to a 54-36 league success at the Witches' den.

AUGUST

1 The month opens on a wet note, as Oxford's Elite League encounter against Belle Vue is called off in the morning.

2   A lighting failure abruptly ends Eastbourne's British League Cup (Group D) match against Oxford after fourteen heats, with the Eagles holding an unassailable 46-38 lead.

3   Belle Vue plays host to a benefit pairs meeting in aid of former star Alan Wilkinson, with the duo of Jon Armstrong (16) and Lee Smethills (10) netting 26 points to emerge on top of the pile.

6   Peterborough swamp Ipswich 62-28 and jump into second position in the league, with Ryan Sullivan paid for the lot (14+1). Poole come from behind to defeat Newport 49-41 in an exciting British League Cup (Group E) encounter by the seaside.

7   A gutsy performance sees Ipswich hang on to defeat a spirited Rye House 46-44 in the British League Cup (Group A) at Foxhall Heath.

11   Early-season league pacesetters Coventry suffer a 47-43 home reverse at the hands of league leaders Poole, as Leigh Adams plunders maximum points (15) for the Pirates. Wolverhampton post a 53-37 league success over Eastbourne, with brothers Mikael Max (16+2) and Peter Karlsson (14+1) notching paid maximums.

13   Belle Vue gain a 49-41 victory over Wolverhampton to claim the aggregate league bonus point.

14   Bottom-of-the-table Ipswich battle hard to gain their first league success since 23 June, defeating Coventry 46-44 in a close tussle at Foxhall Heath.

15   It's edge-of-the-seat league fare at Cowley, with Oxford finally beating Eastbourne 46-44 for their fifth league win on the bounce as they chase a place in the top four and the all-important Play-Offs.

16   Maximum points from Lee Richardson (15) see Coventry through to a 49-41 league victory against Wolverhampton. Despite Jason Crump's brilliant 15-point maximum for Belle Vue, solid-scoring Eastbourne race to a 56-34 league win over the Manchester outfit at Arlington.

18   Jason Crump hits another full house (12) as Belle Vue comfortably see off Ipswich 56-34, leaving the Witches six points adrift at the foot of the league standings. A strong showing sees Wolverhampton garner a 54-36 victory against Oxford at Monmore Green.

20   A gripping league contest eventually results in a 48-42 win for Peterborough over visiting Coventry. The victory takes the Panthers above the Bees into second place in the table. A last-heat mechanical breakdown for Magnus Zetterstrom results in Poole suffering a 46-44 home reverse at the hands of Wolverhampton in a closely fought British League Cup (Group E) match.

21   Ipswich gain a welcome 52-38 success over Arena-Essex in the British League Cup (Group A).

22   Oxford and Eastbourne fight out a 45-45 draw in an entertaining British League Cup (Group D) clash at Cowley. Peterborough suffer a surprise home defeat to Premier League Rye House in the British League Cup (Group A), going down 46-44 in a last-heat decider. The result puts the visiting Rockets on top of the table as they make sure of a place in the quarter-finals.

24   Belle Vue have little difficulty in dispatching Hull 55-35 in the British League Cup (Group B), helped on their way by maximums from former Viking Neil Collins (12+3) and long-time Ace Jason Lyons (12). Joonas Kylmakorpi hits a 15-point full house as Eastbourne power to a 60-30 victory against beleaguered Reading in the British League Cup (Group D).

25   Bank-holiday lunchtime action sees Oxford narrowly defeat Peterborough 46-44 in a

pulsating league encounter. Coventry jump back to second place in the Elite League table, courtesy of a 51-38 win over Eastbourne at Brandon. Poole eventually claim a 51-39 success over a spirited Somerset outfit in the British League Cup (Group E), with Magnus Zetterstrom zipping to a super maximum (15). Mikael Max romps to full points (15) in the first match of a double feature at Monmore Green, as the homesters beat Newport 54-36 in the British League Cup (Group E). The second match, also in the BLC, sees the Wolves wallop Exeter 65-25, with five men remaining unbeaten: Adam Skornicki (14+1), Mikael Max (12), Magnus Karlsson (11+4), Sam Ermolenko (11+1) and Graham Jones (10+2).

27　An estimated crowd of 5,000 turn out at Poole as the Pirates' all-time leading points scorer Craig Boyce celebrates his Testimonial. A great night of racing ends with Jason Crump taking victory in the grand final ahead of Leigh Adams, Billy Hamill and Tony Rickardsson.

28　At Foxhall Heath, Ipswich suffer a 49-41 defeat at the hands of visiting Oxford as they remain firmly rooted to the foot of the league table.

29　Oxford pile up the points to defeat a makeshift Poole side 62-28 in a one-sided league affair at Cowley.

SEPTEMBER

1　The Kirkmanshulme Lane track record is broken by Joe Screen and then Jason Crump as Belle Vue beat Ipswich 51-37 in the league. 'Crumpie' underlines his class by also completing his third successive maximum (15) for the Aces. A competitive league derby results in a 49-41 success for Wolverhampton against second-in-the-table Coventry.

3　Lee Richardson plunders a paid maximum (14+1) as Coventry scorch to a 61-29 win against Peterborough in the first-leg of the Knock-Out Cup quarter-final replay. Charlie Gjedde is paid for the lot (14+1), as Oxford romp to a huge 62-28 league victory over Wolverhampton, displacing the visitors in fourth position in the process. Four-team fare at Wimborne Road sees Scandinavia hit a total of 33 points to take the honours from Team Great Britain (26), home side Poole (21) and the Premier League (19).

4　Ipswich claim a 46-44 success against Belle Vue in their final league match of a difficult season, this in spite of Jason Crump's fourth successive maximum (15) for the Aces. The victory represents only the Witches' sixth victory in their twenty-eight-match programme as they finish last in the table.

8　The Sky Sports cameras are in Manchester to screen the action as Belle Vue defeat Coventry 47-43 in a tight encounter. The result gives the visitors the bonus point and clinches second spot in the Elite League table for the Bees. Eastbourne storm to a 61-29 victory over a depleted Peterborough team, with Nicki Pedersen (15) and Dean Barker (10+2) posting unbeaten tallies. In the British League Cup (Group E), Wolverhampton register a 60-27 win against Trelawny, aided no end by full houses from Mikael Max (15) and Sam Ermolenko (14+1).

10　Belle Vue's important league encounter with Wolverhampton falls victim to heavy overnight rain. The postponement ruins Wolves' hopes of finishing inside the top four, thereby denying them of a place in the Play-Offs for the Championship. That leaves Poole, Coventry, Peterborough and Oxford to go for glory in the chase for the title. In the Knock-Out Cup, Coventry complete a huge aggregate quarter-final replay victory over Peterborough by winning the second-leg 46-44 at the East of England Showground.

12   Oxford defeat visiting Belle Vue 52-38 in their final league fixture of the twenty-eight-match programme, making it five league successes on the trot for the Silver Machine outfit.

13   First-placed Poole complete their league programme with a narrow 47-43 victory at Eastbourne.

15   Despite Jason Lyons' classy maximum (15), a shock result sees Belle Vue suffer a 46-44 home reverse at the hands of Premier League Stoke in the British League Cup (Group B). It's not all bad news for the Aces, however, as they finish as runners-up in the sector to reach the quarter-finals. Poole stride to a 56-34 success against Oxford in the first-leg of the Knock-Out Cup semi-final. Meanwhile, Poole's 'second side' go down 56-37 at Wolverhampton in the British League Cup (Group E). The result leaves a final table showing Wolves in first spot ahead of the Pirates as both sides qualify for the quarter-final stage. The Elite League Play-Offs begin at Brandon, with Coventry cruising into the final courtesy of a 60-30 win against Peterborough. With the Bees on fire, the track record is twice bettered, firstly by 15-point maximum-man Andreas Jonsson (58.3 seconds) and then by Lee Richardson, whose time of 57.4 seconds amazingly knocks a full second off the pre-meeting best time for the 303-metre circuit.

22   Despite unbeaten tallies from Mikael Max (15) and David Howe (12+3), Wolverhampton are made to sweat by Premier League Champions-elect Edinburgh before registering a 47-42 victory in the first-leg of their British League Cup quarter-final clash. In the Elite League Play-Off semi-final, Poole survive some nerve-jangling moments to defeat Oxford 48-42, thereby moving through to a final encounter against Coventry.

24   Belle Vue claim a 49-41 first-leg success over Premier Leaguers Rye House in the British League Cup quarter-final, with Jason Lyons hitting a four-ride full house (12).

25   Home favourite Scott Nicholls emerges triumphant for the second successive year in the Ipswich-staged 16-Lap Classic, as Shane Parker and Kim Jansson fill second and third positions respectively.

27   Having won at Premier League Sheffield two nights previously, Eastbourne move comfortably through to the British League Cup semi-finals with a 59-31 victory, aided by unbeaten performances from Joonas Kylmakorpi (15) and Dean Barker (9+3).

29   The final domestic match of the season results in a 51-39 win for Belle Vue against Wolverhampton, with the Elite League's top man Jason Crump scorching to yet another maximum (12). Despite maximum points from Coventry's Andreas Jonsson (15), the Championship chase sees Poole take a major step towards the ultimate glory with a 45-44 success at the Brandon home of the Bees in the first-leg of the Play-Off final.

OCTOBER

1   Poole's scheduled British League Cup quarter-final second-leg tie against Workington is postponed at 5.30 p.m. after a day of heavy rain. Eastbourne take a big stride towards a place in the semi-finals of the British League Cup by winning 46-43 at Wolverhampton in their first-leg encounter.

6   In front of a crowd reputed to be of around 6,000, Poole clinch the Elite League Championship courtesy of a 55-35 victory over Coventry in the second-leg of the Play-Off final, with both Tony Rickardsson (15) and Ales Dryml (12+3) remaining unbeaten for the jubilant Pirates.

8   Poole march into the last four of the British League Cup thanks to a 57-33 win against

Workington in the second-leg of their quarter-final tie. Knock-Out Cup action sees Wolverhampton eke out a hard-fought 48-41 success over Midlands rivals Coventry in the first-leg of the semi-final.

10 Oxford defeat Poole 46-44 in the second-leg of their Knock-Out Cup semi-final clash, but it's Poole who continue on their merry way, winning 100-80 on aggregate as they chase a glorious treble.

11 Coventry beat Wolverhampton 50-40 in an incident-packed Knock-Out Cup semi-final second-leg at Brandon Stadium, thereby claiming a final spot against Poole by just 3 points on aggregate.

12 At Arlington, a 51-42 semi-final second-leg success sees Eastbourne safely through to the final of the British League Cup.

13 The Poole bandwagon rolls on as they win 49-41 at Belle Vue in the first-leg of the British League Cup semi-final.

15 Poole complete the job against Belle Vue in the British League Cup semi-final, although they are made to work very hard for a narrow 46-44 victory.

17 Pairs action at Peterborough sees Sean Wilson (15) and Paul Lee (6) glean a 21-point total to come out on top, with Andy Smith (16) and Danny Norton (4) a single point behind in second place.

18 With leading qualifying-round scorer Jason Crump's engine unfortunately blowing up on the start line in the final, home-track riders Lee Richardson and Andreas Jonsson race to first and second places respectively in the Elite League Riders' Championship at Coventry, with Scott Nicholls of Ipswich in third spot.

19 Eastbourne gain a first-leg 48-42 advantage over Poole in the British League Cup final as Leigh Adams nets an immaculate 15-point maximum for the treble-chasing Pirates.

20 Mikael Max records a round dozen points to retain the Ladbroke Olympique title at Wolverhampton, with brother Peter Karlsson in second spot (11) and Leigh Adams (10) taking third place courtesy of a run-off victory over Sam Ermolenko and Billy Janniro.

23 Poole host the first-leg of the Knock-Out Cup final against Coventry and in a closely-fought tie they narrowly come out on top with a 46-42 advantage.

25 In the second-leg of the Knock-Out Cup final Coventry open up a big early lead, but a determined Poole fightback restricts the Bees to a 46-44 win on the night as the Pirates take the coveted trophy by two points on aggregate and complete a magical league and cup double.

27 The outstanding Group A match of the British League Cup is completed with a makeshift Peterborough side suffering a 47-43 reverse at the hands of visiting Arena-Essex, despite a brilliant six-ride maximum from Gary Havelock (18). The result leaves Arena-Essex on top of the group table, although they didn't qualify for the quarter-final stage of the competition as they were only lying in third position at the time of the cut-off date, having completed seven of their eight matches.

29 Poole overcome their 6-point first-leg deficit within the first two heats before going on to beat Eastbourne 56-34 in the British League Cup final, thereby completing a superb trophy treble.

SKY SPORTS ELITE LEAGUE TABLE

	Mts	Won	Drn	Lst	For	Agn	Pts	Bon	Tot
Poole	28	20	1	7	1335	1182	41	11	52
Coventry	28	17	0	11	1295	1224	34	10	44
Peterborough	28	16	0	12	1325	1195	32	8	40
Oxford	28	16	0	12	1295	1224	32	8	40
Wolverhampton	28	14	1	13	1248	1265	29	6	35
Eastbourne	28	12	1	15	1261	1250	25	8	33
Belle Vue	28	9	1	18	1219	1298	19	5	24
Ipswich	28	6	0	22	1088	1428	12	0	12

SKY SPORTS ELITE LEAGUE PLAY-OFFS

SEMI-FINALS

Coventry	60	Peterborough	30
Poole	48	Oxford	42

FINAL

Coventry	44	Poole	45	
Poole	55	Coventry	35	(Poole won 100-79 on aggregate)

KNOCK-OUT CUP RESULTS

ROUND ONE

Poole	56	Eastbourne	34	
Eastbourne	40	Poole	32	(Poole won 88-74 on aggregate)

Belle Vue	49	Wolverhampton	41	
Wolverhampton	57	Belle Vue	33	(Wolverhampton won 98-82 on aggregate)

Coventry	52	Peterborough	38	
Peterborough	52	Coventry	38	(Coventry and Peterborough drew 90-90 on aggregate)

Ipswich	41	Oxford	49	
Oxford	55	Ipswich	35	(Oxford won 104-76 on aggregate)

REPLAY

Coventry	61	Peterborough	29	
Peterborough	44	Coventry	46	(Coventry won 107-73 on aggregate)

SEMI-FINALS

| Poole | 56 | Oxford | 34 | |
| Oxford | 46 | Poole | 44 | (Poole won 100-80 on aggregate) |

| Wolverhampton | 48 | Coventry | 41 | |
| Coventry | 50 | Wolverhampton | 40 | (Coventry won 91-88 on aggregate) |

FINAL

| Poole | 46 | Coventry | 42 | |
| Coventry | 46 | Poole | 44 | (Poole won 90-88 on aggregate) |

BRITISH LEAGUE CUP TABLES AND RESULTS

GROUP A

	Mts	Won	Drn	Lst	For	Agn	Pts	Bon	Tot
Arena-Essex	8	5	0	3	385	336	10	3	13
Rye House	8	5	0	3	368	340	10	3	13
Ipswich	8	4	0	4	364	354	8	3	11
King's Lynn	8	4	0	4	345	376	8	1	9
Peterborough	8	2	0	6	327	383	4	0	4

NOTE: Although Arena-Essex topped the group, they did not qualify for the quarter-final stage of the competition as they were only lying in third position at the time of the cut-off date, having completed seven of their eight matches.

GROUP B

	Mts	Won	Drn	Lst	For	Agn	Pts	Bon	Tot
Sheffield	8	6	0	2	376	346	12	2	14
Belle Vue	8	5	0	3	390	327	10	3	13
Coventry	8	4	1	3	382	334	9	4	13
Stoke	8	2	1	5	336	384	5	1	6
Hull	8	2	0	6	314	407	4	0	4

GROUP C

	Mts	Won	Drn	Lst	For	Agn	Pts	Bon	Tot
Workington	8	5	1	2	383	338	11	3	14
Edinburgh	8	5	1	2	374	348	11	3	14
Glasgow	8	4	0	4	350	369	8	3	11
Berwick	8	3	0	5	360	362	6	1	7
Newcastle	8	2	0	6	335	385	4	0	4

GROUP D

	Won	Won	Drn	Lst	For	Agn	Pts	Bon	Tot
Eastbourne	8	5	2	1	393	322	12	4	16
Isle of Wight	8	4	2	2	366	353	10	2	12
Oxford	8	4	1	3	366	343	9	2	11
Swindon	8	3	2	3	359	355	8	2	10
Reading	8	0	1	7	306	417	1	0	1

GROUP E

	Mts	Won	Drn	Lst	For	Agn	Pts	Bon	Tot
Wolverhampton	10	8	0	2	526	374	16	5	21
Poole	10	7	0	3	470½	432½	14	3	17
Newport	10	5	1	4	464½	435½	11	3	14
Exeter	10	5	0	5	422	481	10	2	12
Trelawny	10	4	1	5	452	450	9	2	11
Somerset	10	0	0	10	369	531	0	0	0

QUARTER-FINALS

| Wolverhampton | 47 | Edinburgh | 42 | |
| Edinburgh | 39 | Wolverhampton | 51 | (Wolverhampton won 98-81 on aggregate) |

| Belle Vue | 49 | Rye House | 41 | |
| Rye House | 42 | Belle Vue | 48 | (Belle Vue won 97-83 on aggregate) |

| Sheffield | 43 | Eastbourne | 47 | |
| Eastbourne | 59 | Sheffield | 31 | (Eastbourne won 106-74 on aggregate) |

| Workington | 40 | Poole | 50 | |
| Poole | 57 | Workington | 33 | (Poole won 107-73 on aggregate) |

SEMI-FINALS

| Wolverhampton | 43 | Eastbourne | 46 | |
| Eastbourne | 51 | Wolverhampton | 42 | (Eastbourne won 97-85 on aggregate) |

| Belle Vue | 41 | Poole | 49 | |
| Poole | 46 | Belle Vue | 44 | (Poole won 95-85 on aggregate) |

FINAL

| Eastbourne | 48 | Poole | 42 | |
| Poole | 56 | Eastbourne | 34 | (Poole won 98-82 on aggregate) |

BELLE VUE MAUN MOTORS/REDMERE ACES

ADDRESS: Greyhound Stadium, Kirkmanshulme Lane, Gorton, Manchester.

PROMOTERS: John Perrin, John Hall & George Carswell.

NOTE: John Hall retired in October, with Jim Lynch subsequently taking over his position.

TRACK LENGTH: 285 metres.

FIRST MEETING: 28 July 1928.

YEARS OF OPERATION: 1928 Open; 1988-90 British League; 1991-94 British League Division One; 1995-96 British Premier League; 1997 British Elite League & British Amateur League; 1998-03 British Elite League.

PREVIOUS VENUE: Zoological Gardens, Hyde Road, Manchester.

YEARS OF OPERATION: 1929 English Dirt-track League; 1930 Northern League; 1931 Northern League & Southern League; 1932-33 National League; 1934 National League & Reserve League; 1935-36 National League; 1937 National League & Provincial League; 1938 National League Division One; 1939 National League Division One & National League Division Two; 1940-45 Open; 1946 National League; 1947-56 National League Division One; 1957-64 National League; 1965-67 British League; 1968-69 British League Division One & British League Division Two; 1970-74 British League Division One; 1975-87 British League.

CLUB HONOURS

LEAGUE CHAMPIONS: 1930, 1931, 1933, 1934, 1935, 1936, 1963, 1970, 1971, 1972, 1982, 1993.

NOTE: The Division Two side were also crowned League Champions in 1968 and 1969.

KNOCK-OUT CUP WINNERS: 1931, 1972, 1973, 1975.

NOTE: The Division Two side also won their Knock-Out Cup competition in 1969.

NATIONAL TROPHY WINNERS: 1933, 1934, 1935, 1936, 1937, 1946, 1947, 1949, 1958.

ACU CUP WINNERS: 1934, 1935, 1936, 1937, 1946.

BRITISH SPEEDWAY CUP WINNERS: 1939.

BRITANNIA SHIELD WINNERS: 1957, 1958, 1960.

INTER-LEAGUE KNOCK-OUT CUP WINNERS: 1975.

PREMIERSHIP WINNERS: 1983.

LEAGUE CUP WINNERS: 1983.

FOUR-TEAM CHAMPIONS: 1992.

RIDER ROSTER 2003

BROADHURST, Wayne   b. 28 February 1967, Minsterley, Shropshire.

BRITISH CAREER: (1987) Coventry; (1988) Coventry, Stoke; (1989) Coventry; (1999) Stoke, Workington; (2000) Stoke; (2001) Wolverhampton, Stoke; (2002) Mildenhall; (2003) Mildenhall, Wolverhampton, Poole (BLC), Belle Vue (BLC).

BURROWS, Mark   b. 10 June 1964, Sheffield, South Yorkshire.

BRITISH CAREER: (1984) Scunthorpe, Sheffield; (1985) Scunthorpe, Edinburgh;

(1986) Edinburgh; (1987) Middlesbrough; (1992) Glasgow, Middlesbrough; (1993) Middlesbrough; (1994) Buxton, Cleveland, Middlesbrough, Belle Vue, Coventry; (1995) Buxton, Long Eaton, Middlesbrough, Hull; (1996) Buxton; (1997-01) Stoke; (2002) Stoke, Belle Vue; (2003) Stoke (CT), Wimbledon, Coventry (BLC), Wolverhampton (BLC), Eastbourne (BLC), Belle Vue (BLC).

CAMPBELL, Barry b. 26 August 1979, Glasgow, Scotland.
BRITISH CAREER: (1995) Linlithgow, Swindon; (1996) Linlithgow, Edinburgh; (1997) Edinburgh, Lathallan; (1998) Edinburgh; (1999) Belle Vue, Workington; (2000-01) Workington; (2003) Edinburgh, Armadale (CT), Reading, Swindon (CL), Belle Vue (BLC).

COLLINS, Neil b. 15 October 1961, Partington, Greater Manchester.
BRITISH CAREER: (1978) Ellesmere Port; (1979) Nottingham, Workington, Sheffield; (1980) Edinburgh, Sheffield; (1981) Edinburgh, Cradley Heath, Belle Vue; (1982-83) Leicester; (1984-88) Sheffield; (1989-90) Wolverhampton; (1991) Belle Vue; (1992) Glasgow; (1993-94) Long Eaton; (1995) Sheffield; (1996) Belle Vue; (1997) Glasgow; (1998) Stoke; (1999-00) Swindon; (2001) Belle Vue, Workington; (2002) Somerset; (2003) Hull, Peterborough (BLC & CL 4 Team Champs), Belle Vue.

CRUMP, Jason b. 6 August 1975, Bristol, Avon.
BRITISH CAREER: (1991) Poole; (1992) Peterborough; (1993) Swindon; (1994-95) Poole; (1996-97) Peterborough; (1998) Oxford; (1999) Peterborough; (2000-01) King's Lynn; (2002-03) Belle Vue.

DERBYSHIRE, Lee b. 3 December 1981, Stockport, Greater Manchester.
BRITISH CAREER: (2002) Buxton; (2003) Buxton, Hull, King's Lynn, Belle Vue (BLC).

DRYML, Ales b. 19 October 1979, Pardubice, Czech Republic.
BRITISH CAREER: (2000-02) Oxford; (2003) Belle Vue, Poole.

FELTON, Dean b. 18 August 1969, Wolverhampton, West Midlands.
BRITISH CAREER: (1994) Buxton, Oxford, Ipswich; (1995-96) Buxton; (1997) Buxton, Stoke, Edinburgh, Skegness, Long Eaton, Shuttle Cubs; (1998) Stoke; (1999) Berwick, Glasgow; (2000) Buxton, Berwick; (2001) Stoke, Buxton, Edinburgh, Berwick; (2002) Carmarthen; (2003) Carmarthen, Belle Vue (BLC), Poole (BLC), Eastbourne (BLC), Wolverhampton (BLC).

HOLLINGWORTH, Robert b. 31 December 1955, Boston, Lincolnshire.
BRITISH CAREER: (1973) Berwick; (1974) Boston; (1975) Boston, Hull, King's Lynn, Poole, Wolverhampton; (1976) Boston, Wolverhampton, White City; (1977) Boston, Wolverhampton; (1978) Edinburgh & Wolverhampton; (1979) Boston, King's Lynn; (1980-81) Boston, Coventry; (1982) Boston, King's Lynn; (1983) Scunthorpe; (1984) Boston; (1985) Mildenhall; (1986) Boston; (1999) King's Lynn (CL); (2000-02) Boston; (2003) Boston, Belle Vue (BLC), Poole (BLC).

HUGHES, Danny b. 2 September 1983, Manchester.
BRITISH CAREER: (1999) Workington; (2000) Buxton & Belle Vue; (2001) Buxton, Newport (CL); (2002) Newport (CL), Stoke, Workington, Edinburgh; (2003) Newport (CL & PL), Belle Vue (BLC), Stoke (CT).

JACKSON, Andrew b. 12 July 1975, Manchester.
BRITISH CAREER: (2002) Wolverhampton (CT), Carmarthen, Newport (CL); (2003) Wolverhampton (CL), Sheffield (CL), Mildenhall (CT), Belle Vue (BLC), Swindon (CL), Trelawny (CT), Newcastle (CL).

BELLE VUE ACES: back row, left to right: Carl Stonehewer, Craig Watson, Jason Crump, Joe Screen. On bike: Steve Johnston. Front, kneeling: Neil Collins. Jason Lyons.

JOHNSTON, Steve   b. 12 October 1971, Kalgoorlie, Australia.
BRITISH CAREER: (1992) Sheffield; (1993) Sheffield, Long Eaton; (1994-96) Long
Eaton; (1997) Ipswich; (1998-02) Oxford; (2003) Belle Vue.

JONES, Graham   b. 5 May 1963, Oswestry, Shropshire.
BRITISH CAREER: (1984-87) Stoke; (1988) Stoke, Belle Vue, Reading, Sheffield,
Wolverhampton, King's Lynn, Ipswich; (1989-93) Wolverhampton; (1994)
Middlesbrough; (1995) Hull; (1996) Hull, Middlesbrough; (2003) Wolverhampton
(CL & BLC), Stoke (CT), Coventry (BLC), Belle Vue (BLC), Eastbourne (BLC),
Poole (BLC).

LARSEN, Josh   b. 12 May 1972, Anaheim, California, USA.
BRITISH CAREER: (1992-93) Arena-Essex; (1995) Arena-Essex; (1996) London; (1997)
Bradford; (1999) Eastbourne; (2003) Belle Vue.

LAWSON, William   b. 27 February 1987, Auchterader, Perthshire, Scotland.
BRITISH CAREER: (2002) Newcastle (CL); (2003) Newcastle (PL & CL), Belle Vue
(BLC).

LEMON, Mark   b. 12 February 1973, Brainsdale, Victoria, Australia.
BRITISH CAREER: (1990) Poole; (1991) Poole, Middlesbrough; (1992) Long Eaton,
Middlesbrough; (1996) Oxford; (1997-98) Poole; (1999) Eastbourne, Hull; (2000)
Oxford; (2002) Oxford; (2003) Somerset, Belle Vue.

LYONS, Jason   b. 15 June 1970, Mildura, Victoria, Australia.
BRITISH CAREER: (1990-91) Glasgow; (1992-03) Belle Vue.

MANCHESTER, Chris   b. 28 June 1973, St Louis, Missouri, USA.
BRITISH CAREER: (1994-97) Belle Vue; (1999) Belle Vue; (2003) Belle Vue, Somerset.

OLSEN, Jesper   b. 10 February 1967, Valby, Denmark.
BRITISH CAREER: (1991) Eastbourne; (1992) Mildenhall, Glasgow; (1993-95)
Glasgow; (1996) Middlesbrough; (1997-02) Newcastle; (2003) Belle Vue.

PRIEST, Luke   b. 18 June 1985, Birmingham, West Midlands.
BRITISH CAREER: (2000) Ashfield, Owlerton; (2001) Sheffield (CL), Boston; (2002)
Sheffield (CL), Wolverhampton (CT); (2003) Sheffield (CL & PL), Stoke (CT &
PL), Workington, Exeter, Newport (BLC), Arena-Essex, Wolverhampton (BLC),
Belle Vue (BLC).

SCHLEIN, Rory   b. 1 September 1984, Darwin, Northern Territory, Australia.
BRITISH CAREER: (2001) Edinburgh, Berwick, Glasgow, Newport, Sheffield (CL &
PL), Trelawny, Newcastle; (2002) Edinburgh, Sheffield (CL); (2003) Edinburgh,
Belle Vue.

SCREEN, Joe   b. 27 November 1972, Chesterfield, Derbyshire.
BRITISH CAREER: (1989-93) Belle Vue; (1994-97) Bradford; (1998) Belle Vue; (1999)
Hull; (2000-02) Eastbourne; (2003) Eastbourne, Belle Vue.

STONEHEWER, Carl   b. 16 May 1972, Manchester.
BRITISH CAREER: (1988-89) Belle Vue; (1990) Wolverhampton; (1991-93) Belle Vue;
(1994) Peterborough; (1995-96) Long Eaton; (1997) Long Eaton, King's Lynn,
Peterborough, Coventry, Eastbourne; (1998) Sheffield; (1999-02) Workington;
(2003) Workington, Belle Vue.

WATSON, Craig   b. 6 August 1976, Sydney, New South Wales, Australia.
BRITISH CAREER: (1997-99) Newport; (2000-01) Poole; (2002) Newport; (2003)
Newport, Belle Vue.

WRIGHT, James   b. 13 June 1986, Stockport, Greater Manchester.
   BRITISH CAREER: (2002) Buxton; (2003) Buxton, Belle Vue (BLC), Newcastle (PL), Workington, Stoke (PL), Hull, King's Lynn.

SKY SPORTS ELITE LEAGUE

(*Denotes bonus-point victory)

No	DATE	OPPONENTS	H/A	RESULT	JOHNSTON	LARSON	LYONS	DRYML	CRUMP	OLSEN	STONEHEWER	WATSON	MANCHESTER	SCREEN	COLLINS	OTHERS
1	31/3	Oxford	H	L44-46	4+2(4)	9(4)	12(5)	0(4)	13(5)	0(3)	6(5)	–	–	–	–	–
2	7/4	Coventry	H	L43-47	2+1(4)	5(4)	13+1(6)	1(3)	17(6)	2(3)	3+2(4)	–	–	–	–	–
3	9/4	Peterborough	A	L37-53	4(4)	4+2(5)	4(4)	3(4)	15(6)	2(3)	–	5(4)	–	–	–	–
4	11/4	Oxford	A	L39-51	5(4)	4+2(4)	11+1(5)	3(4)	10(6)	1(3)	–	–	–	–	–	5(4)
5	12/4	Coventry	A	L40-50	1(3)	2(4)	12+2(6)	6+2(5)	16+1(6)	0(2)	–	3(4)	–	–	–	–
6	14/4	Eastbourne	H	L41-49	7(4)	3(4)	1(4)	0(3)	18(6)	–	5(4)	–	7(5)	–	–	–
7	16/4	Poole	A	L36-54	5(5)	1+1(4)	6+1(4)	6+1(4)	11(5)	–	–	3(4)	4+1(4)	–	–	–
8	26/4	Eastbourne	A	L43-47	8+1(5)	0(3)	13+1(6)	1(3)	15(6)	–	–	5(4)	1(3)	–	–	–
9	5/5	Wolverhampton	A	L42-48	10(5)	R/R	10+1(6)	0(3)	15(6)	–	–	6+3(6)	1(4)	–	–	–
10	11/5	Peterborough	H	L42-48	8+1(5)	R/R	7+1(5)	3+1(3)	14(5)	–	9+1(7)	–	1(5)	–	–	–
11	22/5	Ipswich	A	L43-47	12+1(6)	R/R	4+1(3)	1(5)	15+1(6)	––	11+1(7)	–	0(3)	–	–	–
12	26/5	Peterborough	A	L37-53	3(5)	R/R	10(6)	8+1(6)	14+1(6)	–	–	2(4)	0(3)	–	–	–
13	2/6	Poole	H	W45-44	11+2(6)	R/R	14+1(6)	1+1(4)	11+1(5)	––	-	5(5)	3+2(4)	–	–	–
14	11/6	Poole	A	L44-46	9+1(6)	–	R/R	11+1(6)	19(7)	–	-	3+1(4)	2+1(3)	–	–	0(4)
15	16/6	Eastbourne	H	D45-45	10+1(6)	–	R/R	1(3)	17(6)	–	6+2(5)	2(3)	9(6)	–	–	–
16	23/6	Oxford	H	W49-41	8+1(5)	–	2(4)	10+1(5)	15(5)	–	6(4)	6+1(4)	2+1(3)	–	–	–
17	7/7	Peterborough	H	W47-43	11(5)	–	6(4)	5(5)	15(5)	–	6+3(4)	3+1(4)	1(3)	–	–	–
18	19/7	Coventry	A	L42-48	6(4)	–	7+2(5)	3(4)	17(6)	–	–	2(3)	0(3)	7(5)	–	–
19	21/7	Wolverhampton	A	L43-47	6(4)	–	9+1(5)	1+1(3)	13(5)	–	–	7(4)	2(5)	5+2(4)	–	–
20	28/7	Poole	H	W47-43*	8(5)	–	6(4)	–	14(5)	–	3+1(4)	7+1(5)	–	9(4)	0(3)	–
21	13/8	Wolverhampton	H	W49-41*	1(4)	–	8(4)	–	13(5)	–	7(4)	–	–	8+3(5)	4(4)	8(4)
22	16/8	Eastbourne	A	L34-56	7+1(6)	–	6+1(5)	–	15(5)	–	–	0(3)	–	5(5)	0(3)	1(3)
23	18/8	Ipswich	H	W56-34*	11+1(5)	–	4(4)	–	12(4)	–	6(4)	9+3(5)	–	8+1(4)	6+1(4)	–
24	1/9	Ipswich	H	W51-37	7+1(4)	–	7+3(4)	–	15(5)	–	0(4)	9(5)	–	11+1(5)	2+1(3)	–
25	4/9	Ipswich	A	L44-46*	8+1(5)	–	7(4)	–	15(5)	–	5+1(4)	3(5)	–	6(4)	0(3)	–
26	8/9	Coventry	H	W47-43	4+1(4)	–	8(4)	–	12+2(5)	–	7+1(4)	–	–	10(5)	3(4)	3+1(4)
27	12/9	Oxford	A	L38-52	1(4)	–	3(3)	–	14+2(6)	–	3(4)	7(4)	–	10(6)	0(3)	–
28	29/9	Wolverhampton	H	W51-39*	6+1(4)	–	11+1(5)	–	12(4)	–	8+2(5)	–	–	6+2(4)	4+1(4)	4(4)

DETAILS OF OTHER RIDERS:

Match No. 4: Adam Shields 5(4); Match No. 14: Mark Lemon 0(4); Match No. 21: Rory Schlein 8(4); Match No. 22: Rory Schlein 1(3); Match No. 26: Rusty Harrison 3+1(4); Match No. 28: Rory Schlein 4(4).

ELITE LEAGUE AVERAGES

Rider	Mts	Rds	Pts	Bon	Tot	Avge	Max
Jason Crump	28	152	402	8	410	10.79	8 Full
Joe Screen	11	51	85	9	94	7.37	–
Jason Lyons	26	121	201	18	219	7.24	–
Steve Johnston	28	131	183	17	200	6.11	–
Carl Stonehewer	16	73	91	14	105	5.75	–
Craig Watson	19	80	87	10	97	4.85	–
Rory Schlein	3	11	13	0	13	4.73	–
Josh Larsen	8	32	28	5	33	4.13	–
Ales Dryml	19	77	64	9	73	3.79	–
Neil Collins	9	31	19	3	22	2.84	–
Chris Manchester	14	54	33	5	38	2.81	–
Jesper Olsen	5	14	5	0	5	1.43	–
Mark Lemon	1	4	0	0	0	0.00	–
Guests	2	8	8	1	9	4.50	–

BRITISH LEAGUE CUP

(*Denotes bonus-point/aggregate victory)

No	DATE	OPPONENTS	H/A	RESULT	JOHNSTON	DRYML	STONEHEWER	LYONS	WRIGHT	HUGHES	MANCHESTER	JONES	WATSON	COLLINS	SCREEN	OTHERS
1	3/4	Sheffield	A	L42-50	8(5)	8+1(5)	10+2(5)	10+1(5)	1(3)	1(3)	–	–	–	–	–	4+3(4)
2	25/5	Coventry	H	W51-35	12+2(5)	5+1(4)	6+1(4)	14(5)	–	–	9(4)	5(4)	–	–	–	4(4)
3	31/5	Coventry	A	L36-53	11+1(6)	9(6)	–	–	–	0(3)	3+1(4)	–	9(5)	–	–	4+1(6)
4	14/7	Sheffield	H	W55-35*	12+1(5)	5+2(4)	–	6(4)	–	–	11+1(5)	5(4)	9+2(4)	7+2(4)	–	–
5	30/7	Stoke	A	W55-35	–	–	8(4)	–	3+2(4)	–	–	5+1(4)	–	7+1(4)	14+1(5)	18+1(9)
6	20/8	Hull	A	W52-38	14(5)	–	13+1(5)	–	1+1(4)	–	6+2(4)	–	–	7+2(4)	8+1(4)	3(4)
7	24/8	Hull	H	W55-35*	–	–	12+1(5)	12(4)	–	–	6+1(4)	–	–	12+3(5)	10+1(4)	3(8)
8	15/9	Stoke	H	L44-46*	–	–	–	15(5)	3(4)	0(4)	12+1(5)	–	–	7(4)	7(4)	0(4)
9	24/9	Rye House	H	W49-41	11+1(5)	–	–	12(4)	2(5)	–	–	–	–	5+1(4)	9+2(5)	10+3(8)
10	27/9	Rye House	A	W48-42*	10(4)	–	–	11(5)	–	–	–	–	–	4+1(4)	11+2(5)	12+3(12)
11	13/10	Poole	H	L41-49	6(4)	–	–	13+1(6)	1+1(3)	–	–	–	–	1+1(3)	13(6)	7+2(8)
12	15/10	Poole	A	L44-46	–	–	–	15+1(6)	1(3)	–	–	6(4)	–	1+1(3)	–	21+1(14)

NOTE: The home match against Coventry originally ended in a 55-35 victory on track; however, the points scored by William Lawson were subsequently deducted from Belle Vue's total, as his inclusion in the side was deemed ineligible.

DETAILS OF OTHER RIDERS:

Match No. 1: Jesper Olsen 4+3(4); Match No. 2: William Lawson 4(4); Match No. 3: Danny Norton 0(3); Dean Felton 4+1(3); Match No. 5: Dean Felton 4(4); Jason Crump 14+1(5); Match No. 6: Barry Campbell 3(4); Match No. 7: Robert Hollingworth 2(4); Andrew Jackson 1(4); Match No. 8: Lee Derbyshire 0(4); Match No. 9: Rory Schlein 8+3(4); Wayne Broadhurst 2(4); Match No. 10: Rory Schlein 7+1(4); Mark Burrows 4+1(4); Wayne Broadhurst 1+1(4); Match No. 11: Rory Schlein 5+2(5); Mark Burrows 2(3); Match No. 12: Jason Crump 15+1(6); Rory Schlein 6(5); Luke Priest 0(3).

GOLDEN DOUBLE RIDES:

Match No. 1: Jason Lyons' total includes 4 points from a golden double ride.

BRITISH LEAGUE CUP AVERAGES

Rider	Mts	Rds	Pts	Bon	Tot	Avge	Max
Jason Crump	2	11	29	2	31	11.27	1 Paid
Jason Lyons	9	44	106	3	109	9.91	3 Full
Joe Screen	7	33	72	7	79	9.58	1 Paid
Carl Stonehewer	5	23	49	5	54	9.39	—
Steve Johnston	8	39	84	5	89	9.13	—
Chris Manchester	6	26	47	6	53	8.15	—
Craig Watson	3	13	24	2	26	8.00	—
Neil Collins	9	35	51	12	63	7.20	1 Paid
Rory Schlein	4	18	26	6	32	7.11	—
Jesper Olsen	1	4	4	3	7	7.00	—
Ales Dryml	4	19	27	4	31	6.53	—
Graham Jones	3	12	15	1	16	5.33	—
Dean Felton	2	7	8	1	9	5.14	—
Mark Burrows	2	7	6	1	7	4.00	—
Barry Campbell	1	4	3	0	3	3.00	—
James Wright	7	26	12	4	16	2.46	—
Wayne Broadhurst	2	8	3	1	4	2.00	—
Robert Hollingworth	1	4	2	0	2	2.00	—
Andrew Jackson	1	4	1	0	1	1.00	—
Danny Hughes	3	10	1	0	1	0.40	—
Lee Derbyshire	1	4	0	0	0	0.00	—
Danny Norton	1	3	0	0	0	0.00	—
Luke Priest	1	3	0	0	0	0.00	—

NOTE: (1) The figures for Jason Lyons include one golden double ride (4 points), modified to normal score i.e. 2 points. (2) William Lawson's record in the home match against Coventry has been omitted as his inclusion in the side was deemed ineligible.

KNOCK-OUT CUP

No	DATE	OPPONENTS	H/A	RESULT	CRUMP	LARSEN	JOHNSTON	DRYML	LYONS	MANCHESTER	WATSON	STONEHEWER
1	18/4	Wolverhampton	H	W49-41	12(5)	6+2(4)	3(4)	3+1(3)	8(4)	9+3(5)	8+1(5)	—
2	21/4	Wolverhampton	A	L33-57	—	8(5)	6(4)	1+1(3)	9(5)	6(6)	0(3)	3+1(4)

OTHER MEETINGS

17 March: Inter-League Challenge

Belle Vue 64 (Jason Crump 15; Jason Lyons 14+1; Carl Stonehewer 12+1; Jon Armstrong 9+3; Steve Johnston 9+2; James Wright 5; Ales Dryml R/R) Hull 26.

24 March: Inter-League Challenge

Belle Vue 58 (Carl Stonehewer 13+1; Jason Crump 12; Craig Watson 10+2; Jason Lyons 10+1; Steve Johnston 6+1; Ales Dryml 5+1; James Wright 2) King's Lynn 32.

23 July: British League Cup

Belle Vue 13 (James Wright 6; Joe Screen 3; George Stancl 2; Ales Dryml 1+1; Neil Collins 1; Jason Lyons 0; Graham Jones 0) Stoke 11 – meeting abandoned after heat four.

19 September: Conference Challenge

Weymouth 40 Belle Vue Colts 49 (James Wright 11+1; Lee Smart 11+1; Paul Burnett 8+2; Luke Priest 7; Danny Hughes 6+1; John Oliver 4+2; Daniel Hodgson 2).

INDIVIDUAL MEETING

6 August: Junior Championship

1st Richard Hall 15; 2nd James Wright 14; 3rd Lee Derbyshire 12; John Branney 11; Paul Burnett 10; Paul Sharples 9; Tom Brown 8; Benji Compton 7; John Oliver 6; Chris Hunter 6; Lawrence Needs 5; Phil Knowles 5; Carl Downs 3; David Hartley 2; Ben Warburton 1; Karl Langley 1; Andrew Jackson (res) 1.

PAIRS MEETING

3 August: Alan Wilkinson Benefit

1st Jon Armstrong (16) & Lee Smethills (10) 26; 2nd Joe Screen (20) & Dean Felton (6) 26; 3rd Carl Stonehewer (14) & Aidan Collins (9) 23; Rusty Harrison (13) & Adam Allott (8) 21; Ricky Ashworth (17) & David Hartley (2) 19; Steve Johnston (18) & Paul Sharples (0) 18; Lee Howard (res) 2.

COVENTRY VICTOR CHANDLER BEES

ADDRESS: Brandon Stadium, Rugby Road, Brandon, nr Coventry, Warwickshire.
PROMOTER: Colin Pratt.

NOTE: Martin Ochiltree relinquished his position as co-promoter in May 2003.

TRACK LENGTH: 303 metres.

FIRST MEETING: 29 September 1928.

YEARS OF OPERATION: 1928 Open; 1929-31 Southern League; 1932-33 National League; 1934 Open; 1936 Open; 1948 National League Division Three; 1949-56 National League Division Two; 1957-64 National League; 1965-67 British League; 1968-74 British League Division One; 1975-90 British League; 1991-94 British League Division One; 1995-96 British Premier League; 1997-03 British Elite League.

CLUB HONOURS

LEAGUE CHAMPIONS: 1953, 1968, 1978, 1979, 1987, 1988.
KNOCK-OUT CUP WINNERS: 1967.
PAIRS CHAMPIONS: 1978 (Shared with Cradley Heath).
LEAGUE CUP WINNERS: 1981, 1985, 1987.
PREMIERSHIP WINNERS: 1986.
CRAVEN SHIELD WINNERS: 1997, 2000.

RIDER ROSTER 2003

BOAST, Peter   b. 11 April 1964, Louth, Lincolnshire.
  BRITISH CAREER: (1994) Mildenhall; (1995) Mildenhall, Sheffield, Wolverhampton, Swindon; (1996) Mildenhall, Sheffield (1997) Sheffield; (1998) Skegness/Norfolk, Sheffield; (1999) Sheffield, King's Lynn (CL); (2000-02) Boston; (2003) Boston, Coventry (BLC), Hull.

BUNYAN, Jason   b. 9 March 1979, Milton Keynes, Buckinghamshire.
  BRITISH CAREER: (1995) Poole; (1996) Eastbourne (CL); (1997) Oxford, Isle of Wight, Peterborough (AL); (1998) Isle of Wight; (1999-01) Ipswich; (2002) Reading; (2003) Coventry, Stoke (BLC).

BURROWS, Mark   b. 10 June 1964, Sheffield, South Yorkshire.
  BRITISH CAREER: (1984) Scunthorpe, Sheffield; (1985) Scunthorpe, Edinburgh; (1986) Edinburgh; (1987) Middlesbrough; (1992) Glasgow, Middlesbrough; (1993) Middlesbrough; (1994) Buxton, Cleveland, Middlesbrough, Belle Vue, Coventry; (1995) Buxton, Long Eaton, Middlesbrough, Hull; (1996) Buxton; (1997-01) Stoke; (2002) Stoke, Belle Vue; (2003) Stoke (CT), Wimbledon, Coventry (BLC), Wolverhampton (BLC), Eastbourne, Belle Vue (BLC).

DOWNS, Carl   b. 13 November 1983, Coventry, Warwickshire.
  BRITISH CAREER: (1999) King's Lynn (CL); (2000) Boston, Peterborough (CL), Sheffield (CL); (2001) Newport (CL), Mildenhall; (2002) King's Lynn (CL); (2003) Oxford (CL & BLC), Coventry (BLC), Stoke (CT), Isle of Wight.

FISHER, Ryan   b. 7 September 1983, Norco, California, USA.
  BRITISH CAREER: (2002-03) Coventry.

HALL, Richard   b. 23 August 1984, Northallerton, North Yorkshire.
  BRITISH CAREER: (2001) Newcastle; (2002) Newcastle (PL & CL), Trelawny, Glasgow; (2003) Sheffield (CL & PL), Stoke (PL), Coventry (BLC), Hull (BLC), Newport (PL), Boston (KOC & CT), Exeter, Reading, Workington, Somerset.

HAMILL, Billy   b. 23 May 1970, Arcadia, California, USA.
  BRITISH CAREER: (1990-95) Cradley Heath; (1996) Cradley Heath/Stoke; (1997) Belle Vue; (1998-03) Coventry.

HOLLOWAY, Malcolm   b. 22 December 1956, Stratton St Margaret, Wiltshire.
  BRITISH CAREER: (1977) Swindon, Oxford; (1978-79) Milton Keynes, Swindon; (1980-83) Swindon; (1984-88) Reading; (1989) Mildenhall, Reading; (1996) Swindon (CL); (2000) Somerset, Reading; (2001-02) Somerset, Swindon (CT), Mildenhall (CL); (2003) Swindon (CL), Trelawny (CT & PL), Coventry (BLC).

JAMES, Scott   b. 25 May 1984, Adelaide, South Australia.
  BRITISH CAREER: (2002) Workington, Mildenhall; (2003) Mildenhall, Workington, Somerset (KOC), Coventry (BLC).

JANNIRO, Billy   b. 30 July 1980, Vallejo, California, USA.
  BRITISH CAREER: (2001-03) Coventry.

JONES, Graham   b. 5 May 1963, Oswestry, Shropshire.
  BRITISH CAREER: (1984-87) Stoke; (1988) Stoke, Belle Vue, Reading, Sheffield, Wolverhampton, King's Lynn, Ipswich; (1989-93) Wolverhampton; (1994) Middlesbrough; (1995) Hull; (1996) Hull, Middlesbrough; (2003) Wolverhampton (CL & BLC), Stoke (CT), Coventry (BLC), Belle Vue (BLC), Eastbourne (BLC), Poole (BLC).

COVENTRY BEES: back row, left to right: Stuart Robson, Jason Bunyan, Ryan Fisher, Billy Janniro. Front row, kneeling: Lee Richardson, Billy Hamill, Andreas Jonsson.

JONSSON, Andreas *b. 3 September 1980, Hallstavik, Sweden.*
> BRITISH CAREER: (1998–99) Coventry; (2001–03) Coventry.

RICHARDSON, Lee *b. 25 April 1979, Hastings, Sussex.*
> BRITISH CAREER: (1995) Reading; (1996) Reading (CL), Poole; (1997–98) Reading; (1999) Poole; (2000–03) Coventry.

ROBSON, Stuart *b. 8 November 1976, Sunderland, Tyne & Wear.*
> BRITISH CAREER: (1993) Newcastle; (1994) Newcastle, Edinburgh; (1995) Coventry; (1996) Coventry, Middlesbrough; (1997) Hull; (1998–02) Coventry; (2003) Coventry, Newcastle.

SPEIGHT, David *b. 21 March 1980, Bradford, West Yorkshire.*
> BRITISH CAREER: (2000) Owlerton; (2001) Sheffield (CL), Exeter, Stoke; (2002) Hull, Sheffield (CL), Wolverhampton (CT); (2003) Sheffield (CL), Coventry (BLC).

THOMPSON, Mark *b. 8 July 1979, Orsett, Essex.*
> BRITISH CAREER: (1996) Sittingbourne, Linlithgow, Mildenhall, Eastbourne (CL); (1997) Anglian Angels; (1998) Mildenhall, Newport, Stoke; (1999) King's Lynn (CL); (2000–01) Mildenhall; (2002) King's Lynn (CL), Mildenhall, Arena-Essex, Workington, Stoke; (2003) Boston, Stoke (PL), Newport (BLC), Somerset, Peterborough (BLC), Coventry (BLC), King's Lynn, Arena-Essex.

SKY SPORTS ELITE LEAGUE

(* Denotes bonus-point victory)

No	DATE	OPPONENTS	H/A	RESULT	HAMILL	JANNIRO	RICHARDSON	FISHER	JONSSON	ROBSON	BUNYAN	OTHERS
1	22/3	Ipswich	H	W48-42	10(5)	7+1(4)	10(5)	7+1(4)	5(4)	9+2(5)	0(3)	—
2	26/3	Poole	A	W47-43	11+1(5)	6+1(4)	11(5)	6(4)	6(4)	6+2(5)	1+1(3)	–
3	29/3	Peterborough	H	W51-39	11+2(5)	5+1(4)	10+2(5)	7+3(4)	9(4)	9+1(5)	0(3)	–
4	4/4	Peterborough	A	W47-43*	6+1(4)	7+1(4)	11(5)	3+1(4)	10(5)	4(4)	6+2(4)	–
5	5/4	Eastbourne	A	L43-47	7+1(5)	5+1(4)	12(5)	6+1(4)	7(4)	5+1(5)	1+1(3)	–
6	7/4	Belle Vue	A	W47-43	8+2(5)	9+3(5)	R/R	8(5)	13+1(6)	9+1(6)	0(3)	–
7	9/4	Eastbourne	H	W48-42*	9(5)	8+2(5)	4+1(3)	7(4)	7(4)	11+2(6)	2(3)	–
8	12/4	Belle Vue	H	W50-40*	8+2(4)	9+3(5)	–	0(1)	9+1(5)	15+1(7)	2+1(4)	7+1(4)
9	18/4	Oxford	A	L44-46	8(4)	4+1(4)	11(6)	R/R	13+1(6)	6(6)	2+1(4)	–
10	19/4	Oxford	H	W49-41*	10(5)	7+2(4)	11+2(5)	3(4)	7(4)	8+4(5)	3(3)	–
11	10/5	Peterborough	H	W52-38	8+3(4)	10+1(5)	8(4)	4+1(4)	12(4)	9+2(6)	1+1(3)	–
12	24/5	Wolverhampton	H	W49-41	10+1(5)	6+2(4)	10+1(4)	4+1(4)	–	9+2(5)	1+1(3)	9(5)
13	26/5	Ipswich	H	W54-36	16(6)	5(5)	15(6)	2(2)	R/R	13+2(7)	3+2(4)	–
14	9/6	Eastbourne	A	W46-44	13(5)	3+2(4)	13+1(5)	–	6+2(4)	3(4)	3(3)	5+1(5)
15	15/6	Oxford	H	W47-43	10(4)	6+1(4)	7+2(5)	3+3(4)	13(5)	6+1(4)	2(4)	–
16	21/6	Poole	H	L43-47	11+1(5)	R/R	10(5)	–	10(5)	4+1(5)	3+1(5)	5+1(5)
17	23/6	Wolverhampton	A	L39-51	15(7)	6+1(6)	R/R	–	12+1(6)	4(4)	2+1(4)	0(3)
18	4/7	Oxford	A	L38-52	R/R	6(5)	–	1(3)	10+3(7)	7+1(5)	2+1(4)	12+1(6)
19	9/7	Poole	A	L38-52	–	9+4(5)	0(1)	10+1(7)	9(6)	2(3)	0(3)	8(5)
20	19/7	Belle Vue	H	W48-42	12(5)	R/R	6(4)	8+3(7)	11+2(6)	7+2(5)	4+1(3)	–
21	31/7	Ipswich	A	W54-36*	9(5)	R/R	12(4)		12+1(5)	12+3(6)	1(5)	8+2(5)
22	11/8	Poole	H	L43-47	9(6)	R/R	13+2(6)	9+1(5)	–	4+2(4)	1+1(3)	7(6)
23	14/8	Ipswich	A	L44-46*	5(4)	8+2(5)	14(5)	8(5)	–	3+1(4)	1(3)	5(4)

SKY SPORTS ELITE LEAGUE continued

No	DATE	OPPONENTS	H/A	RESULT	HAMILL	JANNIRO	RICHARDSON	FISHER	JONSSON	ROBSON	BUNYAN	OTHERS
24	16/8	Wolverhampton	H	W49-41	12+1(5)	4+1(4)	15(5)	4(5)	–	6(4)	0(3)	8(4)
25	20/8	Peterborough	A	L42-48*	12+2(6)	4+1(4)	14(5)	1(3)	–	5+2(5)	2(3)	4(4)
26	25/8	Eastbourne	H	W51-38*	14(5)	6+2(4)	7+1(4)	8+1(5)	11+2(6)	3(4)	2(3)	–
27	1/9	Wolverhampton	A	L41-49*	11+2(6)	7+1(4)	7(5)	3(3)	7(6)	3(3)	3+1(3)	–
28	8/9	Belle Vue	A	L43-47*	7+2(5)	17+1(7)	9+1(6)	3(3)	R/R	4(5)	3(4)	–

NOTE: Andreas Jonsson is not credited with a full maximum from the home match against Peterborough on 10 May, as he was unable to take his place in a rerun of heat fifteen.

DETAILS OF OTHER RIDERS:

Match No. 8: Lukas Dryml 7+1(4); Match No. 12: Lukas Dryml 9(5); Match No. 14: Scott Robson 5+1(5); Match No. 16: Craig Watson 5+1(5); Match No. 17: Rusty Harrison 0(3); Match No. 18: Lukas Dryml 12+1(6); Match No. 19: Steve Johnston 8(5); Match No. 21: Joonas Kylmakorpi 8+2(5); Match No. 22: Joe Screen 7(6); Match No. 23: Sam Ermolenko 5(4); Match No. 24: Sebastian Ulamek 8(4); Match No. 25: Dean Barker 4(4).

ELITE LEAGUE AVERAGES

Rider	Mts	Rds	Pts	Bon	Tot	Avge	Max
Lee Richardson	24	113	240	13	253	8.96	2 Full
Billy Hamill	26	130	262	21	283	8.71	–
Andreas Jonsson	21	105	199	14	213	8.11	–
Billy Janniro	24	109	164	35	199	7.30	–
Stuart Robson	28	137	186	33	219	6.39	–
Ryan Fisher	23	94	115	17	132	5.62	–
Jason Bunyan	28	96	51	16	67	2.79	–
Guests	12	56	78	6	84	6.00	–

BRITISH LEAGUE CUP

(*Denotes bonus-point victory)

No	DATE	OPPONENTS	H/A	RESULT	HAMILL	BUNYAN	FISHER	ROBSON	JANNIRO	JAMES	HALL	OTHERS
1	8/5	Sheffield	A	L43-47	15+1(6)	4+1(4)	5(3)	5(4)	12+2(5)	1(3)	1(5)	–
2	17/5	Sheffield	H	W48-42*	14+1(5)	4(4)	6+1(4)	6+2(4)	13+1(5)	2(3)	3+1(5)	–
3	25/5	Belle Vue	A	L35-51	–	1(4)	9+1(5)	13(6)	9(6)	–	2(3)	1(6)
4	31/5	Belle Vue	H	W53-36*	15(5)	6(4)	7+1(4)	11+2(5)	8+1(4)	4(4)	2+1(4)	–
5	7/6	Stoke	A	D45-45	–	9(4)	3(4)	15+1(6)	13+1(6)	1(3)	0(4)	4+1(3)
6	28/6	Stoke	H	W59-31*	12(4)	8+1(4)	8+1(4)	11+4(5)	14+1(5)	4(4)	2+1(4)	–
7	2/7	Hull	A	L43-47	–	6(4)	15(6)	12(6)	3(4)	–	4(3)	3+1(7)
8	12/7	Hull	H	W56-35*	–	6+1(4)	9(4)	13+2(5)	15(5)	–	9+1(5)	4+1(7)

NOTE: The away match at Belle Vue originally ended in a 35-55 defeat on track; however, the points scored by William Lawson were subsequently deducted from the Aces' total, as his inclusion in their side was deemed ineligible.

DETAILS OF OTHER RIDERS:

Match No. 3: Malcolm Holloway 0(3); David Speight 1(3); Match No. 5: Mark Burrows 4+1(3); Match No. 7: Peter Boast 2+1(3); Mark Thompson 1(4); Match No. 8: Graham Jones 3+1(4); Carl Downs 1(3).

BRITISH LEAGUE CUP AVERAGES

Rider	Mts	Rds	Pts	Bon	Tot	Avge	Max
Billy Hamill	4	20	56	2	58	11.60	2 Full; 1 Paid
Stuart Robson	8	41	86	11	97	9.46	2 Paid
Billy Janniro	8	40	87	6	93	9.30	1 Full; 1 Paid
Ryan Fisher	8	34	62	4	66	7.76	–
Mark Burrows	1	3	4	1	5	6.67	–
Jason Bunyan	8	32	44	3	47	5.88	–
Peter Boast	1	3	2	1	3	4.00	–
Graham Jones	1	4	3	1	4	4.00	–
Richard Hall	8	33	23	4	27	3.27	–
Scott James	5	17	12	0	12	2.82	–
Carl Downs	1	3	1	0	1	1.33	–
David Speight	1	3	1	0	1	1.33	–
Mark Thompson	1	4	1	0	1	1.00	–
Malcolm Holloway	1	3	0	0	0	0.00	–

KNOCK-OUT CUP

(* Denotes aggregate victory)

No	DATE	OPPONENTS	H/A	RESULT	HAMILL	JANNIRO	RICHARDSON	FISHER	JONSSON	ROBSON	BUNYAN	OTHERS
1	21/4	Peterborough	H	W52-38	17(6)	6+4(5)	15+1(6)	2+1(4)	R/R	11+1(6)	1(3)	–
2	23/5	Peterborough	A	L38-52	15+2(7)	5(7)	8(3)	4(4)	R/R	6+2(6)	0(3)	–
3	3/9	Peterborough (R)	H	W61-29	8+2(4)	7+2(4)	14+1(5)	6+1(4)	12(5)	8+3(4)	6+2(4)	–
4	10/9	Peterborough (R)	A	W46-44*	9+1(4)	6+1(4)	5+1(4)	4(4)	–	10+1(5)	7+1(5)	5+2(4)
5	8/10	Wolverhampton	A	L41-48	–	8(4)	10(5)	4+1(4)	13(5)	3+2(4)	2(4)	1(4)
6	11/10	Wolverhampton	H	W50-40*	–	9+1(4)	11+1(5)	2+1(4)	10+1(5)	7+3(4)	4(4)	7(4)
7	23/10	Poole	A	L42-46	R/R	14(6)	10+1(6)	8(5)	7+1(6)	1(4)	2(3)	–
8	25/10	Poole	H	W46-44	–	7+2(4)	7+1(5)	10+1(6)	12(5)	1(3)	2(3)	7+1(4)

(R) = Replay

DETAILS OF OTHER RIDERS:

Match No. 4: Dean Barker 5+2(4); Match No. 5: Joe Screen 1(4); Match No. 6: Todd Wiltshire 7(4); Match No. 8: Mikael Max 7+1(4).

OTHER MEETINGS

15 March: Challenge

Coventry 46 (Lee Richardson 13+1; Stuart Robson 11+1; Andreas Jonsson 9+1; Ryan Fisher 5; Billy Hamill 4; Billy Janniro 4; Jason Bunyan 0) Oxford 44.

24 March: Challenge

Wolverhampton 44 Coventry 46 (Billy Hamill 13; Lee Richardson 9+1; Andreas Jonsson 8; Billy Janniro 6+1; Stuart Robson 6+1; Ryan Fisher 4+1; Jason Bunyan 0).

28 March: Challenge

Oxford 42 Coventry 48 (Andreas Jonsson 12; Lee Richardson 9; Ryan Fisher 8+2; Billy Hamill 5+2; Jason Bunyan 5+2; Billy Janniro 5; Stuart Robson 4+1).

12 May: Elite League

Ipswich 2 Coventry 4 (Billy Hamill 3; Billy Janniro 1; Lee Richardson DNR; Ryan Fisher DNR; Jason Bunyan DNR; Stuart Robson DNR; Andreas Jonsson R/R) – meeting abandoned after heat one.

16 July: Elite League

Wolverhampton 30 Coventry 36 (Billy Hamill 11; Andreas Jonsson 10+2; Billy Janniro 6+1; Ryan Fisher 6+1; Jason Bunyan 2; Stuart Robson 1; Lee Richardson R/R) – meeting abandoned after heat eleven.

15 September: Elite League Play-Off semi-final

Coventry 60 (Andreas Jonsson 15; Billy Janniro 13+1; Lee Richardson 12; Billy Hamill 7+4; Ryan Fisher 6+3; Jason Bunyan 4+1; Stuart Robson 3) Peterborough 30.

29 September: Elite League Play-Off final (first-leg)

Coventry 44 (Andreas Jonsson 15; Jason Bunyan 7+1; Lee Richardson 7; Billy Hamill 6+1; Billy Janniro 4+1; Stuart Robson 4+1; Ryan Fisher 1+1) Poole 45.

6 October: Elite League Play-Off final (second-leg)

Poole 55 Coventry 35 (Andreas Jonsson 13; Billy Janniro 6+1; Ryan Fisher 6+1; Lee Richardson 4; Joe Screen 3; Stuart Robson 2; Jason Bunyan 1+1) – Poole won 100-79 on aggregate.

EASTBOURNE CINQUE PORTS HOLIDAYS EAGLES

ADDRESS: Arlington Stadium, Arlington Road West, Hailsham, East Sussex.
PROMOTERS: Terry Russell & Jon Cook.
TRACK LENGTH: 275 metres.
FIRST MEETING: September 1928.
YEARS OF OPERATION: 1928-37 Open; 1938 Sunday Dirt-track League; 1939 Open; 1946 Open; 1947 National League Division Three; 1948-53 Open; 1954-57 Southern Area League; 1958 Open; 1959 Southern Area League; 1960-63 Open; 1964 Metropolitan League; 1965 Training; 1969-74 British League Division Two; 1975-78 National League; 1979-84 British League; 1985-90 National League; 1991-94 British League Division One; 1995 British Premier League; 1996 British Premier League & British Conference League; 1997-03 British Elite League.

CLUB HONOURS

LEAGUE CHAMPIONS: 1938, 1947, 1959, 1971, 1977, 1986, 1987, 1995, 2000.
KNOCK-OUT CUP WINNERS: 1975, 1977, 1978, 1985, 1986, 1987, 1994, 1997, 2002.
PREMIERSHIP WINNERS: 1995, 1996.

RIDER ROSTER 2003

BARKER, Dean *b 2 August 1970, Isleworth, Middlesex.*
BRITISH CAREER: (1986) Eastbourne; (1987-88) Eastbourne, Cradley Heath; (1989) Eastbourne; (1990-92) Oxford; (1993-95) Eastbourne; (1997) Eastbourne; (1999-03) Eastbourne.

BARRETT, Wayne *b. 22 March 1968, Redruth, Cornwall.*
BRITISH CAREER: (1984) Weymouth; (1986-87) Poole; (1997) St Austell, Newport; (1998) St Austell; (1999-00) St Austell, Exeter; (2001) Trelawny, Boston; (2002) Boston, Wimbledon, Trelawny; (2003) Wimbledon, Eastbourne (BLC).

BURROWS, Mark *b. 10 June 1964, Sheffield, South Yorkshire.*
BRITISH CAREER: (1984) Scunthorpe, Sheffield; (1985) Scunthorpe, Edinburgh; (1986) Edinburgh; (1987) Middlesbrough; (1992) Glasgow, Middlesbrough; (1993) Middlesbrough; (1994) Buxton, Cleveland, Middlesbrough, Belle Vue, Coventry; (1995) Buxton, Long Eaton, Middlesbrough, Hull; (1996) Buxton; (1997-01) Stoke; (2002) Stoke, Belle Vue; (2003) Stoke (CT), Wimbledon, Coventry (BLC), Wolverhampton (BLC), Eastbourne (BLC), Belle Vue (BLC).

COURTNEY, Scott *b. 3 January 1983, Middlesbrough, Cleveland.*
BRITISH CAREER: (1999) Glasgow, Linlithgow; (2000) Glasgow, Ashfield; (2001) Glasgow, Buxton, Mildenhall, Trelawny, Arena-Essex, Newcastle; (2002) Arena-Essex, Rye House (CL); (2003) Poole, Eastbourne (BLC), Rye House (CL).

CUNNINGHAM, Glenn *b. 10 June 1975, Bristol, Avon.*
BRITISH CAREER: (1991-92) Oxford; (1993-96) Swindon; (1997) Reading; (1998) Peterborough; (1999) Swindon; (2000) Peterborough, Belle Vue; (2001) Newport; (2002) Somerset; (2003) Somerset, Eastbourne.

FELTON, Dean *b. 18 August 1969, Wolverhampton, West Midlands.*
BRITISH CAREER: (1994) Buxton, Oxford, Ipswich; (1995-96) Buxton; (1997) Buxton, Stoke, Edinburgh, Skegness, Long Eaton, Shuttle Cubs; (1998) Stoke; (1999) Berwick, Glasgow; (2000) Buxton, Berwick; (2001) Stoke, Buxton, Edinburgh, Berwick; (2002) Carmarthen; (2003) Carmarthen, Belle Vue (BLC), Poole (BLC), Eastbourne (BLC), Wolverhampton (BLC).

GIFFARD, Daniel *b. 10 November 1984, Eastbourne, East Sussex.*
BRITISH CAREER: (2000) Rye House; (2001) Rye House, Reading, Berwick, Newport; (2002) Isle of Wight, Rye House (CL & PL), Edinburgh; (2003) Wimbledon, Eastbourne (BLC), Somerset, Stoke.

JONES, Graham *b. 5 May 1963, Oswestry, Shropshire.*
BRITISH CAREER: (1984-87) Stoke; (1988) Stoke, Belle Vue, Reading, Sheffield, Wolverhampton, King's Lynn, Ipswich; (1989-93) Wolverhampton; (1994) Middlesbrough; (1995) Hull; (1996) Hull, Middlesbrough; (2003) Wolverhampton (CL & BLC), Stoke (CT), Coventry (BLC), Belle Vue (BLC), Eastbourne (BLC), Poole (BLC).

KENNETT, Edward *b. 28 August 1986, Hastings, Sussex.*
BRITISH CAREER: (2001) Rye House, Mildenhall; (2002-03) Rye House (CL & PL), Eastbourne.

KYLMAKORPI, Joonas *b. 14 February 1980, Seinajoki, Finland.*
BRITISH CAREER: (2001) Eastbourne; (2002) Ipswich; (2003) Arena-Essex, Eastbourne.

EASTBOURNE EAGLES: back row, left to right: Mark Loram, Nicki Pedersen, Dean Barker, Joonas Kylmakorpi, Olli Tyrvainen (Team Manager). On bike: David Norris. Front, kneeling: Glenn Cunningham, Adam Shields.

LJUNG, Peter   *b. 30 October 1982, Vaxjo, Sweden.*
BRITISH CAREER: (2003) Eastbourne, Reading.

LORAM, Mark   *b. 12 January 1971, Malta.*
BRITISH CAREER: (1987) Hackney; (1988) Hackney, King's Lynn, Belle Vue, Reading, Swindon; (1989) Ipswich; (1990-94) King's Lynn; (1995-96) Exeter; (1997) Bradford; (1998) Wolverhampton; (1999-00) Poole; (2001) Peterborough; (2002-03) Eastbourne.

NORRIS, David   *b. 20 August 1972, Eastbourne, East Sussex.*
BRITISH CAREER: (1988-89) Eastbourne; (1990-92) Ipswich; (1993) Ipswich, Eastbourne; (1994) Eastbourne; (1995) Reading; (1996-03) Eastbourne.

OSTERGAARD, Ulrich   *b. 19 April 1981, Odense, Denmark.*
BRITISH CAREER: (2003) Eastbourne (BLC).

PARSONS, Joel   *b. 24 July 1985, Broken Hill, New South Wales, Australia.*
BRITISH CAREER: (2003) Reading, Eastbourne (BLC), Rye House (CL & PL), Newport (PL), Wimbledon (CT), Arena-Essex, Peterborough (BLC), Hull.

READ, Matt   *b. 5 August 1981, Maidstone, Kent.*
BRITISH CAREER: (1997) Anglian Angels, King's Lynn; (1998-99) Arena-Essex; (2000) Arena-Essex, Reading; (2002) Isle of Wight; (2003) Eastbourne (BLC), Somerset.

ROBSON, Scott   *b. 15 August 1971, Sunderland, Tyne & Wear.*
BRITISH CAREER: (1987-92) Berwick; (1993-94) Newcastle; (1995-96) Middlesbrough; (1997) Hull; (1998) Eastbourne, Berwick; (1999-00) Coventry; (2001) Berwick; (2002) Rye House; (2003) Rye House, Eastbourne.

SCREEN, Joe   *b. 27 November 1972, Chesterfield, Derbyshire.*
BRITISH CAREER: (1989-93) Belle Vue; (1994-97) Bradford; (1998) Belle Vue; (1999) Hull; (2000-02) Eastbourne; (2003) Eastbourne, Belle Vue.

SHIELDS, Adam   *b. 8 February 1977, Kurri-Kurri, New South Wales, Australia.*
BRITISH CAREER: (2000-02) Isle of Wight; (2003) Isle of Wight, Eastbourne.

STEAD, Garry   *b. 5 January 1972, Holmfirth, Yorkshire.*
BRITISH CAREER: (1990-92) Stoke; (1993) Newcastle; (1994) Newcastle, Bradford; (1995) Bradford; (1996) Sheffield; (1997) Bradford; (1998) Wolverhampton; (1999-02) Hull; (2003) Hull, Eastbourne.

STEPHENS, Seemond   *b. 9 August 1967, St Austell, Cornwall.*
BRITISH CAREER: (1998) St Austell, Exeter, Sheffield, Swindon; (1999) Eastbourne, Swindon, St Austell; (2000-01) Exeter; (2002) Trelawny, Exeter; (2003) Exeter, Eastbourne.

TATUM, Neville   *b. 21 July 1965, Epsom, Surrey.*
BRITISH CAREER: (1984-85) Canterbury; (1986) Wimbledon; (1987) Wimbledon, Coventry; (1988) Coventry; (1989-90) Wimbledon; (1991) Eastbourne, Ipswich; (1992) Peterborough, Eastbourne; (1993) Arena-Essex; (1996) Eastbourne, London; (1997) Oxford, Ipswich, King's Lynn; (1998-99) Isle of Wight; (2000) Stoke; (2002) Somerset; (2003) Eastbourne (BLC).

SKY SPORTS ELITE LEAGUE

(* Denotes bonus-point victory)

No	DATE	OPPONENTS	H/A	RESULT	LORAM	BARKER	NORRIS	KYLMAKORPI	SCREEN	SHIELDS	LJUNG	STEPHENS	STEAD	PEDERSEN	CUNNINGHAM	OTHERS
1	25/3	Wolverhampton	H	W47-42	11+1(5)	8+2(4)	7(4)	1(4)	12(5)	8+1(5)	0(3)	–	–	–	–	–
2	29/3	Ipswich	H	W50-40	7+1(4)	10+3(5)	12(5)	4+1(4)	8(4)	9+3(5)	0(3)	–	–	–	–	–
3	5/4	Coventry	H	W47-43	8+1(5)	10(5)	5(4)	6+1(4)	8(4)	9(5)	–	–	–	–	–	1(3)
4	9/4	Coventry	A	L42-48	15+1(6)	8+1(5)	8+1(6)	3+1(3)	4+1(4)	4(3)	–	0(3)	–	–	–	–
5	12/4	Oxford	H	W47-43	6+1(4)	10+2(5)	6(4)	6(4)	11+1(5)	7+1(5)	–	1(3)	–	–	–	–
6	14/4	Belle Vue	A	W49-41	11+1(5)	7+3(4)	10+1(5)	2+2(4)	10(4)	–	–	–	3(3)	–	–	6+2(5)
7	26/4	Belle Vue	H	W47-43*	R/R	12+1(5)	6(6)	7+1(5)	9+1(6)	8+2(4)	–	–	–	–	–	5+2(4)
8	3/5	Peterborough	H	W55-35	–	7+1(4)	14(5)	7+3(4)	10+2(5)	7+1(4)	–	–	–	–	–	10+1(8)
9	5/5	Poole	A	L30-60	–	7+1(6)	5(5)	1(3)	3+1(4)	2+1(3)	–	–	–	–	–	12+1(9)
10	8/5	Peterborough	A	L38-52*	–	3(4)	4+1(3)	10(6)	3(4)	5(4)	–	–	2(3)	–	–	11+1(6)
11	10/5	Poole	H	L43-46	–	7+1(4)	4+2(5)	7(4)	7(4)	8+3(6)	–	–	6+2(3)	–	–	4+2(4)
12	24/5	Ipswich	H	W54-36	–	5+2(4)	8(4)	5(4)	13(5)	5(4)	–	–	–	–	–	18+4(9)
13	29/5	Ipswich	A	L41-49*	–	1(3)	3(2)	5+1(6)	9+1(6)	20+1(7)	1(3)	–	–	–	–	2(3)
14	2/6	Wolverhampton	A	L42-48	–	5+2(4)	R/R	14(7)	5(5)	6+2(5)	–	–	–	–	–	12+3(9)
15	9/6	Coventry	H	L44-46	–	14+1(6)	13(6)	6+1(4)	5(4)	2+2(3)	0(3)	–	–	–	–	4+2(4)
16	16/6	Belle Vue	A	D45-45	–	3+2(4)	8(4)	10+2(5)	10+1(5)	–	–	–	–	–	–	14+1(12)
17	21/6	Oxford	H	W52-38	R/R	13+2(6)	9(5)	–	10(5)	7+2(5)	–	–	–	–	–	13+2(9)
18	23/6	Ipswich	A	L43-47*	R/R	7+2(5)	10+1(6)	15(7)	11+3(6)	–	–	–	–	–	–	0(6)
19	16/7	Poole	A	L43-47	5+2(4)	4(4)	7(5)	3(4)	–	8(4)	–	–	12+2(6)	4(3)	–	–
20	18/7	Peterborough	A	L34-56	6(5)	9+1(6)	4+1(4)	0(3)	–	2+1(3)	–	–	12(6)	–	–	1(3)
21	19/7	Wolverhampton †	H	W46-38	9+1(4)	6+1(4)	5+1(4)	8+1(5)	–	–	–	–	12(5)	–	–	6+2(6)
22	21/7	Oxford	A	L43-47*	2+2(3)	8+2(5)	9+2(6)	3(3)	–	9+1(4)	–	–	11(6)	1+1(3)	–	–
23	11/8	Wolverhampton	A	L37-53	R/R	9(6)	6+3(6)	12+1(6)	–	3+1(3)	–	–	6(6)	1(3)	–	–
24	15/8	Oxford	A	L44-46*	R/R	2+1(3)	13+2(7)	8+2(6)	–	7+1(5)	–	–	13+1(6)	–	–	1+1(3)
25	16/8	Belle Vue	H	W56-34*	R/R	9+2(5)	12+3(6)	9+3(5)	–	11+1(5)	–	–	12+1(5)	3+2(4)	–	–
26	25/8	Coventry	A	L38-51	9+1(5)	5+2(4)	2(3)	8(4)	–	7+1(6)	–	–	–	–	–	7(8)
27	8/9	Peterborough	H	W61-29*	7+1(4)	10+2(4)	11+1(5)	9+1(4)	–	7(4)	–	–	15(5)	2+1(4)	–	–
28	13/9	Poole	H	L43-47	7(5)	8+1(4)	6+2(4)	10+2(6)	–	–	–	–	9(5)	2+2(3)	–	1+1(3)

† Meeting abandoned after fourteen heats, with the result standing

DETAILS OF OTHER RIDERS:

Match No. 3: Leigh Lanham 1(3); Match No. 6: Davey Watt 6+2(5); Match No. 7: Leigh Lanham 5+2(4); Match No. 8: Davey Watt 5+1(4); Lee Richardson 5(4); Match No. 9: Lee Richardson 10+1(6); Frank Smart 2(3); Match No. 10: Todd Wiltshire 11+1(6); Match No. 11: Jason Lyons 4+2(4); Match No. 12: Todd Wiltshire 11+1(5); Davey Watt 7+3(4); Match No. 13: Billy Janniro 2(3); Match No. 14: Billy Janniro 10+2(6); Frank Smart 2+1(3); Match No. 15: Todd Wiltshire 4+2(4); Match No. 16: Billy Janniro 9+1(5); Simon Stead 5(4); Ricky Ashworth 0(3); Match No. 17: Sam Ermolenko 10+2(5); Chris Manchester 3(4); Match No. 18: Shaun Tacey 0(3); Edward Kennett 0(3); Match No. 20: Scott Robson 1(3); Match No. 21: Davey Watt 4+2(3); Scott Robson 2(3); Match No. 24: Scott Robson 1+1(3); Match No. 26: Jason Lyons 6(5); Adrian Rymel 1(3); Match No. 28: Matt Read 1+1(3).

ELITE LEAGUE AVERAGES

Rider	Mts	Rds	Pts	Bon	Tot	Avge	Max
Nicki Pedersen	9	50	102	4	106	8.48	1 Full
Mark Loram	13	59	103	13	116	7.86	–
Dean Barker	28	128	207	38	245	7.66	1 Paid
Joe Screen	18	85	148	11	159	7.48	–
Adam Shields	23	102	161	25	186	7.29	1 Paid
David Norris	27	129	207	21	228	7.07	–
Joonas Kylmakorpi	27	124	179	23	202	6.52	–
Garry Stead	3	9	11	2	13	5.78	–
Glenn Cunningham	6	20	13	6	19	3.80	–
Matt Read	1	3	1	1	2	2.67	–
Scott Robson	3	9	4	1	5	2.22	–
Seemond Stephens	2	6	1	0	1	0.67	–
Peter Ljung	4	12	1	0	1	0.33	–
Edward Kennett	1	3	0	0	0	0.00	–
Guests	24	99	123	23	146	5.90	–

BRITISH LEAGUE CUP

(* Denotes bonus point/aggregate victory)

No	DATE	OPPONENTS	H/A	RESULT	LORAM	GIFFARD	NORRIS	STEAD	BARKER	READ	SCREEN	PARSONS	LJUNG	KYLMAKORPI	OSTERGAARD	OTHERS
1	31/3	Reading	A	W51-42	13(5)	0(4)	15(5)	5+1(4)	11+1(4)	5(4)	–	–	–	–	–	2(4)
2	20/4	Isle of Wight	H	W55-34	–	–	15(5)	7+2(4)	12+1(5)	0(4)	12(4)	6(4)	–	–	–	3+1(4)
3	22/4	Isle of Wight	A	D45-45*	–	0(3)	–	4+1(4)	7(4)	6+2(5)	13(5)	–	5+2(4)	10(5)	–	–
4	18/5	Swindon	H	W52-37	–	–	12(5)	–	14(5)	4(4)	10(4)	2+1(4)	4+2(4)	–	–	6+1(4)
5	2/8	Oxford	H	W46-38	–	–	7(4)	5+1(4)	10(4)	6+2(4)	–	–	–	10(4)	2+1(4)	6+1(4)
6	22/8	Oxford	A	D45-45*	–	–	11+1(5)	–	9(4)	8+2(5)	–	0(3)	–	11(5)	6+1(4)	0(4)
7	24/8	Reading	H	W60-30*	–	–	9(3)	–	11(4)	5+3(5)	–	6+1(4)	–	15(5)	7+2(5)	7+2(4)
8	7/9	Swindon	A	L39-51*	–	–	8(5)	7+2(5)	7+2(4)	–	–	–	–	6(4)	8+3(6)	3+1(5)
9	25/9	Sheffield	A	W47-43	13(5)	–	–	–	3+1(3)	7+2(6)	–	2+1(3)	–	8+1(4)	–	14+4(9)
10	27/9	Sheffield	H	W59-31*	–	–	10+1(4)	–	9+3(4)	7(5)	–	4+1(4)	–	15(5)	8+3(5)	6(3)
11	1/10	Wolverhampton	A	W46-43	–	–	7+1(4)	–	9+2(4)	–	–	0(3)	1+1(4)	12+1(5)	5(5)	12+1(5)
12	12/10	Wolverhampton	H	W51-42*	–	–	14(5)	–	7+1(4)	–	–	4+1(4)	–	11+1(5)	2(4)	13+4(8)
13	19/10	Poole	H	W48-42	–	–	13(5)	–	10+1(5)	2+1(4)	–	–	–	7+2(4)	3+2(4)	13+2(8)
14	29/10	Poole	A	L34-56	–	–	4+1(4)	–	5+1(5)	2(3)	–	–	–	11+2(6)	3+1(3)	9+2(9)

DETAILS OF OTHER RIDERS:

Match No. 1: Wayne Barrett 2(4); Match No. 2: Scott Courtney 3+1(4); Match No. 4: Edward Kennett 6+1(4); Match No. 5: Graham Jones 6+1(4); Match No. 6: Glenn Cunningham 0(4); Match No. 7: Glenn Cunningham 7+2(4); Match No. 8: Wayne Barrett 2(2); Dean Felton 1+1(3); Match No. 9: Adam Shields 10+2(5); Mark Burrows 4+2(4); Match No. 10: Adam Shields 6(3); Match No. 11: Adam Shields 12+1(5); Match No. 12: Adam Shields 9+2(4); Wayne Barrett 4+2(4); Match No. 13: Adam Shields 8(4); Neville Tatum 5+2(4); Match No. 14: Adam Shields 7+1(6); Neville Tatum 2+1(3).

BRITISH LEAGUE CUP AVERAGES

Rider	Mts	Rds	Pts	Bon	Tot	Avge	Max
Joe Screen	3	13	35	0	35	10.77	1 Full
Mark Loram	2	10	26	0	26	10.40	–
David Norris	12	54	125	4	129	9.56	2 Full
Joonas Kylmakorpi	11	52	116	7	123	9.46	2 Full
Dean Barker	14	59	124	13	137	9.29	2 Paid
Adam Shields	6	27	52	6	58	8.59	–
Graham Jones	1	4	6	1	7	7.00	–
Edward Kennett	1	4	6	1	7	7.00	–
Garry Stead	5	21	28	7	35	6.67	–
Mark Burrows	1	4	4	2	6	6.00	–
Neville Tatum	2	7	7	3	10	5.71	–
Ulrich Ostergaard	9	40	44	13	57	5.70	–
Matt Read	11	49	52	12	64	5.22	–
Peter Ljung	3	12	10	5	15	5.00	–
Glenn Cunningham	2	8	7	2	9	4.50	–
Joel Parsons	8	29	24	5	29	4.00	–
Scott Courtney	1	4	3	1	4	4.00	–
Wayne Barrett	3	10	8	2	10	4.00	–
Dean Felton	1	3	1	1	2	2.67	–
Daniel Giffard	2	7	0	0	0	0.00	–

KNOCK-OUT CUP

No	DATE	OPPONENTS	H/A	RESULT	LORAM	BARKER	NORRIS	KYLMAKORPI	SCREEN	SHIELDS	STEAD
1	18/4	Poole	A	L34-56	8(6)	4+1(4)	9+1(6)	2(3)	7+1(5)	3(3)	1+1(3)
2	18/4	Poole †	H	W40-32	7(3)	5+2(4)	10+1(4)	6+2(3)	5(3)	5+1(4)	2+1(3)

† Meeting abandoned after twelve heats, with the result standing

OTHER MEETINGS

28 June: Home Counties Cup

Rye House 44 Eastbourne 43 (Adam Shields 15; Joe Screen 11; David Norris 8+2; Ulrich Ostergaard 5; Matt Read 2; James Cockle 2; Cameron Woodward 0).

14 July: Test Match

Great Britain 43 (Scott Nicholls 13; Dean Barker 12+2; David Howe 7; Joe Screen 4+3; David Norris 4+1; Chris Harris 2; Danny Bird 1) Rest Of The World 47 (Leigh Adams 15; Joonas Kylmakorpi 10; Mikael Max 9; Ryan Fisher 5+1; Billy Janniro 4+2; Adam Skornicki 2; Sebastian Tresarrieu 2).

INDIVIDUAL MEETING

16 March: Dean Barker Testimonial
　　(Qualifying scores: Leigh Adams 10; Martin Dugard 10; Dean Barker 9; David Norris 8; Joe
　　Screen 8; Mark Loram 7; Scott Nicholls 7; Lee Richardson 6; Billy Janniro 6; Adam Shields 6;
　　Ryan Fisher 5; Paul Hurry 4; Shane Parker 3; Leigh Lanham 3; Peter Ljung 2; Danny Bird 1; Matt
　　Read (res) 0; Daniel Giffard (res) DNR); First Semi-Final: 1st Richardson; 2nd Adams; 3rd Norris;
　　4th Screen; Second Semi-Final: 1st Barker; 2nd Dugard; 3rd Nicholls; 4th Loram; Final:
　　1st Barker; 2nd Dugard; 3rd Adams; 4th Richardson.

IPSWICH EVENING STAR WITCHES

ADDRESS: Foxhall Heath Stadium, Foxhall Road, Ipswich, Suffolk.
PROMOTER: John Louis.
TRACK LENGTH: 300 metres.
FIRST MEETING: 25 October 1950.
YEARS OF OPERATION: 1950-51 Open; 1952-53 Southern League; 1954-56 National League
　　Division Two; 1957-58 National League; 1959 Southern Area League; 1960-62 National
　　League; 1964 Metropolitan League; 1965 Open; 1969-71 British League Division Two;
　　1972-74 British League Division One; 1975-88 British League; 1989-90 National
　　League; 1991-94 British League Division One; 1995-96 British Premier League;
　　1997-03 British Elite League

NOTE: Ipswich also took part in the 1997 British Amateur League, sharing their fixtures with King's Lynn
and riding under the banner of 'Anglian Angels'.

CLUB HONOURS

KNOCK-OUT CUP WINNERS: 1970, 1971, 1976, 1978, 1981, 1984, 1998.
LEAGUE CHAMPIONS: 1975, 1976, 1984, 1998.
PAIRS CHAMPIONS: 1976, 1977.
INTER-LEAGUE KNOCK-OUT CUP WINNERS: 1977.
FOUR-TEAM CHAMPIONS: 1991.
CRAVEN SHIELD WINNERS: 1998.

RIDER ROSTER 2003

BALDWIN, Carl　　*b. 4 July 1964, Ipswich, Suffolk.*
　　BRITISH CAREER: (1980) Mildenhall, Hull; (1981) Mildenhall; (1982-84) Mildenhall,
　　Ipswich; (1985) Mildenhall; (1986) Peterborough, King's Lynn; (1987) Peterborough,
　　Boston; (1988-89) Milton Keynes; (2002) Ipswich, Arena-Essex, Mildenhall; (2003)
　　Mildenhall, Ipswich (BLC).

BIRD, Danny   *b. 16 November 1979, Guildford, Surrey.*
BRITISH CAREER: (1998-01) Isle of Wight; (2002-03) Isle of Wight, Ipswich.

BOXALL, Steve   *b. 16 May 1987, Canterbury, Kent.*
BRITISH CAREER: (2002) Rye House (CL); (2003) Rye House (CL), Ipswich (BLC),
Reading (BLC), King's Lynn.

BOYCE, Craig   *b. 2 August 1967, Sydney, New South Wales, Australia.*
BRITISH CAREER: (1988-90) Poole; (1991) Oxford; (1992-94) Poole; (1995) Swindon;
(1996-98) Poole; (1999) Oxford; (2000) King's Lynn; (2001-02) Ipswich; (2003) Poole
(BLC), Oxford, Ipswich.

ERIKSSON, Freddie   *b. 23 April 1981, Stockholm, Sweden.*
BRITISH CAREER: (2001-02) King's Lynn; (2003) Ipswich.

HAMPEL, Jaroslaw   *b. 17 April 1982, Lodz, Poland.*
BRITISH CAREER: (2000-03) Ipswich.

HOWE, Ben   *b. 6 December 1974, Crawley, Sussex.*
BRITISH CAREER: (1991-96) Ipswich; (1997) Ipswich, Poole; (1998) King's Lynn; (1999)
Ipswich, Hull; (2000) Newport; (2002) Newport; (2003) Ipswich (BLC), Mildenhall.

HURRY, Paul   *b. 9 April 1975, Canterbury, Kent.*
BRITISH CAREER: (1991) Arena-Essex; (1992-93) Peterborough; (1994-95) Arena-Essex;
(1996) London; (1997) King's Lynn; (1998-99) Oxford; (2000) Eastbourne; (2001-02)
Wolverhampton; (2003) Ipswich.

JANSSON, Kim   *b. 30 October 1981, Gothenburg, Sweden.*
BRITISH CAREER: (2002) Ipswich; (2003) Ipswich.

KING, Daniel   *b. 14 August 1986, Maidstone, Kent.*
BRITISH CAREER: (2001) Peterborough (CL); (2002) Peterborough (CL), Swindon (CT);
(2003) Peterborough (CL), Ipswich (BLC), Reading, Mildenhall, Arena-Essex.

LANHAM, Leigh   *b. 15 August 1977, Ipswich, Suffolk.*
BRITISH CAREER: (1993) Ipswich, Arena-Essex; (1994-96) Ipswich; (1997) Exeter,
Bradford, King's Lynn; (1998-99) Arena-Essex; (2001) Arena-Essex; (2002-03) Arena-
Essex, Ipswich.

MADSEN, Tom P.   *b. 24 November 1977, Esbjerg, Denmark.*
BRITISH CAREER: (1999) Berwick; (2000-02) King's Lynn; (2003) Ipswich, King's Lynn.

NERMARK, Daniel   *b. 30 July 1977, Karlstad, Sweden.*
BRITISH CAREER: (2001-02) Wolverhampton; (2003) Ipswich.

NICHOLLS, Scott   *b. 16 May 1978, Ipswich, Suffolk.*
BRITISH CAREER: (1994) Peterborough; (1995-98) Ipswich; (1999-00) Poole; (2001-03)
Ipswich.

SLABON, Chris   *b. 21 February 1981, Wroclaw, Poland.*
BRITISH CAREER: (2002-03) Ipswich.

WRIGHT, Matthew   *b. 19 November 1985, Harlow, Essex.*
BRITISH CAREER: (2002) Boston, Mildenhall, Carmarthen, Wimbledon; (2003)
Mildenhall, Ipswich (BLC), Arena-Essex (BLC), Reading, Peterborough (BLC).

IPSWICH WITCHES: back row, left to right: Danny Bird, Paul Hurry, Daniel Nermark, Jaroslaw Hampel. On bike: Scott Nicholls. Front, kneeling: Chris Slabon, Tom P. Madsen.

SKY SPORTS ELITE LEAGUE

No	DATE	OPPONENTS	H/A	RESULT	HAMPEL	SLABON	HURRY	NERMARK	NICHOLLS	LANHAM	MADSAM	BIRD	ERIKSSON	BOYCE	JANSSON	OTHERS
1	22/3	Coventry	A	L42-48	7+1(5)	5+2(4)	5(4)	2+1(4)	13(5)	4+2(4)	6(4)	–	–	–	–	–
2	27/3	Poole	H	L40-50	14(6)	5+2(4)	10(5)	3+1(4)	6(4)	–	1(4)	1(3)	–	–	–	–
3	29/3	Eastbourne	A	L40-50	7+1(6)	1(3)	4+1(4)	5+1(4)	18(6)	–	2+1(3)	3(4)	–	–	–	–
4	2/4	Poole	A	L40-49	9(5)	3(4)	7(5)	2+2(4)	13+2(6)	–	2+1(3)	4+1(3)	–	–	–	–
5	10/4	Wolverhampton	H	W47-43	R/R	13(6)	–	5(5)	13(5)	2+1(3)	8+3(6)	–	–	–	–	6+3(5)
6	18/4	Peterborough	H	L43-47	R/R	7(5)	9+1(7)	3+1(4)	15+1(7)	–	4(3)	5+1(4)	–	–	–	–
7	18/4	Peterborough	A	L28-62	R/R	4(6)	1+1(5)	6(6)	16(7)	–	0(3)	1(3)	–	–	–	–
8	23/4	Oxford	A	L38-51	–	9(6)	1+1(3)	3(4)	15(6)	–	3+2(4)	6(5)	–	–	–	1+1(3)
9	28/4	Wolverhampton	A	L41-49	R/R	4+1(5)	4+1(5)	11(6)	17(6)	4(5)	1+1(3)	–	–	–	–	–
10	22/5	Belle Vue	H	W47-43	8+2(5)	8+2(4)	3+1(4)	9(4)	12(5)	3(4)	4(4)	–	–	–	–	–
11	24/5	Eastbourne	A	L36-54	10+1(7)	5+1(5)	R/R	9(7)	8(5)	–	1(3)	3(3)	–	–	–	–
12	26/5	Coventry	A	L36-54	1+1(4)	9(6)	2(2)	6(5)	14(6)	1+1(4)	3(3)	–	–	–	–	–
13	29/5	Eastbourne	H	W49-41	9+1(6)	5+1(5)	R/R	8+1(5)	13+2(5)	–	7(6)	7+1(3)	–	–	–	–
14	4/6	Poole	A	L33-57	7(6)	1+1(3)	–	9(5)	12(6)	–	2+2(3)	2(4)	–	–	–	0(3)
15	5/6	Wolverhampton	H	L40-50	R/R	9+2(6)	3+2(4)	8+1(6)	14(7)	–	2+1(3)	4(4)	–	–	–	–
16	12/6	Peterborough	H	L33-57	–	3+2(4)	2(3)	–	11(5)	4(5)	–	–	2(4)	–	–	11+2(9)
17	23/6	Eastbourne	H	W47-43	8+1(5)	4(4)	6(4)	7+2(5)	14(5)	3+1(3)	–	–	5+1(4)	–	–	–
18	7/7	Wolverhampton	A	L30-60	1(5)	R/R	6(6)	7+2(6)	14(6)	–	0(3)	2(4)	–	–	–	–
19	17/7	Oxford	H	L39-51	–	R/R	2+2(4)	4(4)	16(6)	4+1(4)	–	–	6(5)	–	–	7+2(7)
20	18/7	Oxford	A	L32-58	–	R/R	3+1(4)	2(4)	14(6)	–	–	–	2+1(5)	–	–	11+1(11)
21	24/7	Poole	H	L39-51	11+1(6)	–	–	1(3)	11+2(6)	–	–	9(4)	1(3)	3(4)	3(4)	–
22	31/7	Coventry	H	L36-54	7(5)	–	–	1(3)	14(6)	5(4)	–	–	2(4)	5(5)	2+2(3)	–
23	6/8	Peterborough	A	L28-62	–	–	–	7+1(6)	R/R	–	–	3(3)	0(4)	5(6)	9(7)	4+1(4)
24	14/8	Coventry	H	W46-44	10+1(5)	–	–	5+1(4)	14(5)	9+1(7)	–	–	3+1(4)	5+1(4)	0(0)	–
25	18/8	Belle Vue	A	L34-56	R/R	–	–	4(6)	15+1(6)	9(6)	–	–	0(3)	6+1(6)	–	0(3)
26	28/8	Oxford	H	L41-49	R/R	–	8(6)	9+2(5)	14+1(6)	–	–	4(4)	–	2+1(4)	4+1(5)	–
27	1/9	Belle Vue	A	L37-51	R/R	–	1+1(2)	5+1(6)	12+1(7)	9(4)	–	–	–	5+2(6)	5+2(4)	–
28	4/9	Belle Vue	H	W46-44	7+1(5)	–	R/R	3+1(4)	10+2(5)	–	–	14(6)	–	1+1(3))	11+3(7)	–

DETAILS OF OTHER RIDERS:

Match No. 5: Bjarne Pedersen 6+3(5); Match No. 8: Chris Manchester 1+1(3); Match No. 14: Adam Shields 0(3); Match No. 16: Steve Johnston 10+1(6); Davey Watt 1+1(3); Match No. 19: Steve Johnston 7+2(7); Match No. 20: Steve Johnston 8+1(7); Davey Watt 3(4); Match No. 23: Steve Johnston 4+1(4); Match No. 25: Ricky Ashworth 0(3).

ELITE LEAGUE AVERAGES

Rider	Mts	Rds	Pts	Bon	Tot	Avge	Max
Scott Nicholls	27	155	358	12	370	9.55	1 Full; 1 Paid
Jaroslaw Hampel	15	81	116	11	127	6.27	–
Kim Jansson	7	30	34	8	42	5.60	–
Chris Slabon	17	80	95	14	109	5.45	–

Rider	Mts	Rds	Pts	Bon	Tot	Avge	Max
Daniel Nermark	27	129	144	18	162	5.02	–
Danny Bird	15	56	66	3	69	4.93	–
Leigh Lanham	12	53	57	7	64	4.83	–
Paul Hurry	18	77	77	12	89	4.62	–
Tom P. Madsen	15	55	46	11	57	4.15	–
Craig Boyce	8	38	32	6	38	4.00	–
Freddie Eriksson	10	40	23	3	26	2.60	–
Guests	10	45	40	10	50	4.44	–

BRITISH LEAGUE CUP

(* Denotes bonus-point victory)

No	DATE	OPPONENTS	H/A	RESULT	SLABON	MADSEN	JANSSON	NERMARK	HURRY	KING	HOWE	BIRD	WRIGHT	ERIKSSON	HAMPEL	OTHERS
1	3/4	Peterborough	H	W48-42	9+2(5)	5+1(4)	5+2(4)	6+1(4)	11(5)	7(4)	5+2(4)	–	–	–	–	–
2	12/4	Rye House	A	L44-46	3+1(4)	4+1(4)	–	12(5)	–	10(6)	4+1(3)	11(5)	–	–	–	0(3)
3	30/5	Peterborough	A	L44-45*	7+1(5)	7+2(4)	7+2(4)	8+1(5)	–	7+2(6)	2+1(3)	6(3)	–	–	–	–
4	31/5	King's Lynn	A	L41-48	11+1(6)	11+1(5)	6+3(5)	6(4)	–	5(4)	–	–	1(3)	–	–	1(3)
5	10/7	King's Lynn	H	W53-37*	–	–	7+2(4)	10(4)	14(5)	6+1(5)	–	11+1(5)	0(3)	5+2(4)	–	–
6	25/7	Arena-Essex	A	L36-54	–	–	8(6)	8(4)	8+1(5)	3+1(3)	1(3)	–	–	7+3(6)	–	1(3)
7	7/8	Rye House	H	W46-44*	–	–	7+1(4)	5(4)	12+1(5)	1(4)	3(4)	13+1(5)	–	5+2(4)	–	–
8	21/8	Arena-Essex	H	W52-38	–	–	–	10+1(4)	12+2(5)	8+1(6)	0(3)	–	1(3)	7+2(4)	14(5)	–

DETAILS OF OTHER RIDERS:

Match No. 2: Carl Baldwin 0(3); Match No. 4: James Horton 1(3); Match No. 6: Steve Boxall 1(3).

BRITISH LEAGUE CUP AVERAGES

Rider	Mts	Rds	Pts	Bon	Tot	Avge	Max
Jaroslaw Hampel	1	5	14	0	14	11.20	–
Paul Hurry	5	25	57	4	61	9.76	–
Danny Bird	4	18	41	2	43	9.56	–
Daniel Nermark	8	34	65	3	68	8.00	–
Tom P. Madsen	4	17	27	5	32	7.53	–
Kim Jansson	6	27	40	10	50	7.41	–
Freddie Eriksson	4	18	24	9	33	7.33	–
Chris Slabon	4	20	30	5	35	7.00	–
Daniel King	8	38	47	5	52	5.47	–
Ben Howe	6	20	15	4	19	3.80	–
Steve Boxall	1	3	1	0	1	1.33	–
James Horton	1	3	1	0	1	1.33	–
Matthew Wright	3	9	2	0	2	0.89	–
Carl Baldwin	1	3	0	0	0	0.00	–

KNOCK-OUT CUP

No	DATE	OPPONENTS	H/A	RESULT	HAMPEL	SLABON	HURRY	NERMARK	NICHOLLS	BIRD	MADSEN	OTHERS
1	5/5	Oxford	H	L41-49	5+1(4)	10+1(5)	4+2(4)	5(4)	12(5)	2+1(3)	3(5)	–
2	9/5	Oxford	A	L35-55	7+1(5)	7+1(5)	8(5)	2+1(3)	6(5)	4+1(4)	1+1(3)	–

OTHER MEETINGS

20 March: International Club Challenge

Ipswich 57 (Paul Hurry 13+1; Scott Nicholls 12+1; Chris Slabon 8+1; Jaroslaw Hampel 7+1; Daniel Nermark 6+1; Danny Bird 6; Tom P. Madsen 5+3) Kaparna 32 (Peter Karlsson 10; Ryan Sullivan 9; Kim Jansson 3+1; Tomasz Gapinski 3+1; Joonas Kylmakorpi 3; Sebastian Bengtsson 3; Magnus Karlsson 1).

12 May: Elite League

Ipswich 2 (Jaroslaw Hampel 2; Tom P. Madsen 0; Danny Bird 0; Paul Hurry DNR; Daniel Nermark DNR; Scott Nicholls DNR; Chris Slabon R/R) Coventry 4 – meeting abandoned after heat one.

INDIVIDUAL MEETING

25 September: 16-Lap Classic

Qualifying scores: Scott Nicholls 11; David Howe 11; Joe Screen 10; Leigh Lanham 7; Steve Johnston 7; Shane Parker 5; Kim Jansson 5; Brett Woodifield 5; Adam Skornicki 5; Chris Harris 3; Carl Stonehewer 3; Daniel King 0; Final: 1st Parker (14); 2nd Jansson (12); 3rd Lanham (10); 4th Nicholls (8+2); 5th Johnston (6+2); 6th Woodifield (4); 7th Screen (2+2); 8th Howe (0+2); Overall Result: 1st Nicholls 21; 2nd Parker 19; 3rd Jansson 17; Lanham 17; Johnston 15; Screen 14; Howe 13; Woodifield 9.

OXFORD SILVER MACHINE

NOTE: The information below relates only to the main Oxford team. For details of the second side, please refer to the Conference League section.

ADDRESS: Oxford Stadium, Sandy Lane, Cowley, Oxford.

PROMOTER: Nigel Wagstaff.

TRACK LENGTH: 297 metres.

FIRST MEETING: 8 April 1939.

YEARS OF OPERATION: 1939–41 Open; 1949–50 National League Division Three; 1951–52 National League Division Two; 1953 Southern League; 1954–56 National League Division Two; 1957–64 National League; 1965–67 British League; 1968–74 British League Division One; 1975 British League; 1976–83 National League; 1984–90 British League; 1991–92 British League Division One; 1993–94 British League Division Two; 1995–97 British Premier League; 1998–03 British Elite League.

CLUB HONOURS

LEAGUE CHAMPIONS: 1950, 1964, 1985, 1986, 1989, 2001.
NATIONAL TROPHY (DIVISION THREE) WINNERS: 1950.
NATIONAL TROPHY WINNERS: 1964.
BRITANNIA SHIELD WINNERS: 1964.
KNOCK-OUT CUP WINNERS: 1985, 1986 (Shared with Cradley Heath).
LEAGUE CUP WINNERS: 1986 (Shared with Cradley Heath).
PREMIERSHIP WINNERS: 1987.
GOLD CUP WINNERS: 1989.
FOUR-TEAM CHAMPIONS: 1994, 1996.

RIDER ROSTER 2003

ANDREWS, Darren   b. 19 January 1977, Banbury, Oxfordshire.
  BRITISH CAREER: (1993) Coventry & Oxford; (1994) Coventry, Oxford, Mildenhall; (1995) Sittingbourne; (1996) Reading (CL); (1997) Berwick, Hull, Long Eaton, Oxford (PL & AL), Isle of Wight; (2000) St Austell; (2001) Rye House; (2002) Mildenhall, Hull; (2003) Oxford (CL & BLC), Carmarthen (CT).
BOYCE, Craig   b. 2 August 1967, Sydney, New South Wales, Australia.
  BRITISH CAREER: (1988-90) Poole; (1991) Oxford; (1992-94) Poole; (1995) Swindon; (1996-98) Poole; (1999) Oxford; (2000) King's Lynn; (2001-02) Ipswich; (2003) Poole (BLC), Oxford, Ipswich.
COOK, Joe   b. 24 December 1983, King's Lynn, Norfolk.
  BRITISH CAREER: (2002) King's Lynn (CL), Arena-Essex, Newport (PL), Isle of Wight; (2003) Stoke (PL & CT), Oxford (CL & BLC).
DOWNS, Carl   b. 13 November 1983, Coventry, Warwickshire.
  BRITISH CAREER: (1999) King's Lynn (CL); (2000) Boston, Peterborough (CL), Sheffield (CL); (2001) Newport (CL), Mildenhall; (2002) King's Lynn (CL); (2003) Oxford (CL & BLC), Coventry (BLC), Stoke (CT), Isle of Wight.
FERJAN, Matej   b. 5 January 1977, Ljubljana, Slovenia.
  BRITISH CAREER: (1998) Belle Vue; (1999) Poole; (2000) Ipswich; (2001) Peterborough, Belle Vue; (2002) Belle Vue; (2003) Oxford.
GJEDDE, Charlie   b. 28 December 1979, Holstebro, Denmark.
  BRITISH CAREER: (1998) Swindon; (1999) Coventry, Wolverhampton; (2001) Reading; (2002) Swindon; (2003) Swindon, Oxford.
HANCOCK, Greg   b. 3 June 1970, Whittier, California, USA.
  BRITISH CAREER: (1989-95) Cradley Heath; (1996) Cradley Heath, Stoke; (1997-01) Coventry; (2003) Oxford.
IVERSEN, Niels-Kristian   b. 20 June 1982, Esbjerg, Denmark.
  BRITISH CAREER: (2001) King's Lynn; (2003) Newport, Oxford
  NOTE: Iversen also rode for King's Lynn in 2002, but only in a challenge match.
JANKOWSKI, Lukasz   b. 7 December 1982, Leszno, Poland.
  BRITISH CAREER: (2002) King's Lynn; (2003) Oxford (BLC).
KLINGBERG, Niklas   b. 6 February 1973, Varing, Sweden.
  BRITISH CAREER: (1994-96) Belle Vue; (1998) Belle Vue; (2001) King's Lynn; (2003) Oxford.

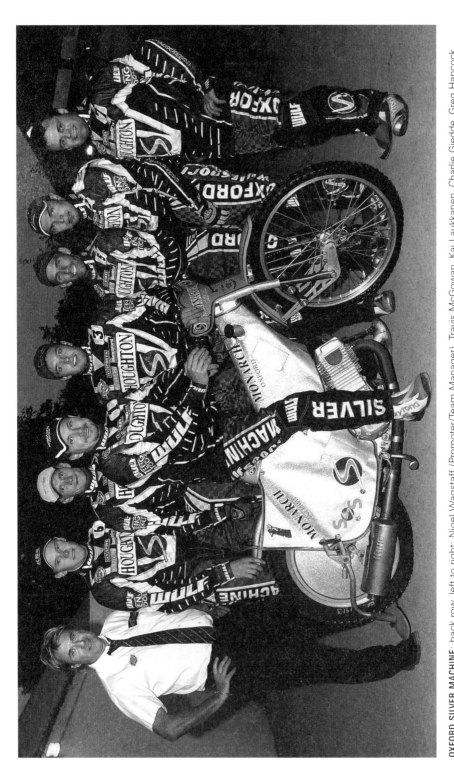

OXFORD SILVER MACHINE: back row, left to right: Nigel Wagstaff (Promoter/Team Manager), Travis McGowan, Kaj Laukkanen, Charlie Gjedde, Greg Hancock, Sebastian Ulamek, Andy Smith. Front, on bike: Todd Wiltshire.

KOLENKO, Jernej   *b. 20 November 1982, Ljubljana, Slovenia.*
BRITISH CAREER: (2002) King's Lynn; (2003) Oxford.

KRAMER, Emil   *b. 14 November 1977, Mariestad, Sweden.*
BRITISH CAREER: (2002) King's Lynn, Hull; (2003) Oxford (BLC), Hull.

LAUKKANEN, Kaj   *b. 8 April 1975, Seinajoki, Finland.*
BRITISH CAREER: (1995-96) Long Eaton; (1998) Glasgow; (1999-02) Belle Vue; (2003) Oxford.

McGOWAN, Travis   *b. 13 January 1981, Mildura, Victoria, Australia.*
BRITISH CAREER: (1999-00) King's Lynn; (2002) King's Lynn; (2003) Oxford.

MASTERS, Steve   *b. 6 December 1970, Eastbourne, East Sussex.*
BRITISH CAREER: (1989-91) Eastbourne; (1992-93) Swindon; (1994) Swindon, Cradley Heath, Reading, Poole; (1995) Poole; (1996-97) Swindon; (1998) Swindon, Isle of Wight; (1999) Swindon; (2000) King's Lynn; (2001) Newport; (2002) Trelawny; (2003) Trelawny, Oxford.

NORTON, Danny   *b. 27 August 1986, Hull, East Yorkshire.*
BRITISH CAREER: (2001-02) Peterborough (CL); (2003) Peterborough (CL & BLC), Armadale (CT), Swindon (PL), Reading, Mildenhall (KOC & CT), Poole (BLC), Oxford (BLC).

PEDERSEN, Nicki   *b. 2 April 1977, Odense, Denmark.*
BRITISH CAREER: (1998) Newcastle; (1999-00) Wolverhampton; (2001-02) King's Lynn; (2003) Oxford.

SCARBORO, Ricky   *b. 31 July 1966, Grunby, Lincolnshire.*
BRITISH CAREER: (1999) Mildenhall, King's Lynn (CL); (2000) Boston; (2001) Boston, Newport (PL); (2002) Boston, King's Lynn (CL); (2003) Oxford (CL & BLC), Stoke (CT), Newport (PL).

SMITH, Andy   *b. 25 May 1966, York, North Yorkshire.*
BRITISH CAREER: (1982-88) Belle Vue; (1989-90) Bradford; (1991) Swindon; (1992-95) Coventry; (1996) Bradford; (1997) Coventry; (1998) Belle Vue, Swindon; (1999-01) Belle Vue; (2003) Oxford (EL & CL).

STAECHMANN, Jan   *b. 5 June 1966, Kolding, Denmark.*
BRITISH CAREER: (1985-90) Wolverhampton; (1991-94) Long Eaton; (1995-96) Hull; (1997) Peterborough; (1998-99) Oxford; (2000) Oxford, Belle Vue; (2001-02) Stoke; (2003) Stoke, Oxford.

TOMICEK, Lubos   *b. 14 March 1986, Prague, Czech Republic.*
BRITISH CAREER: (2003) Oxford (BLC).

ULAMEK, Sebastian   *b. 20 November 1975, Czestochowa, Poland.*
BRITISH CAREER: (2000) Wolverhampton; (2002) King's Lynn; (2003) Oxford.

WILTSHIRE, Todd   *b. 26 September 1968, Bankstown, Sydney, New South Wales, Australia.*
BRITISH CAREER: (1988) Wimbledon, Ipswich; (1989) Wimbledon; (1990-91) Reading; (1998-01) Oxford; (2003) Oxford.

SKY SPORTS ELITE LEAGUE

(* Denotes bonus-point victory)

No	DATE	OPPONENTS	H/A	RESULT	WILTSHIRE	McGOWAN	ULAMEK	KLINGBERG	PEDERSEN	KOLENKO	GJEDDE	STAECHMANN	BOYCE	HANCOCK	SMITH	FERJAN	LAUKKANEN	OTHERS
1	31/3	Belle Vue	A	W46-44	9+1(5)	5+2(4)	3+1(4)	6+1(4)	11+1(5)	2+2(3)	10(5)							
2	4/4	Wolverhampton	H	W58-32	13+1(5)	2+1(4)	12(4)	8+2(4)	13+2(5)	1(4)	9(4)							
3	9/4	Poole	A	L39-51	10(7)	5+1(5)	R/R	3(4)	15(6)	1(3)	5(5)							
4	11/4	Belle Vue	H	W51-39*	10+2(5)	6(4)	7(4)	6(4)	12(5)	4(3)	6+2(5)							
5	12/4	Eastbourne	A	L43-47	11+1(5)	3+1(4)	-	4+1(4)	11(5)	-	7+2(5)							6+1(4)
6	14/4	Peterborough	A	L31-59	13(6)	0(4)	3(5)	R/R	10(6)	3(3)		2+1(3)						
7	18/4	Coventry	H	W46-44	12+2(5)	8+2(5)	8(5)	R/R	12(5)	1(3)		5+1(7)						
8	19/4	Coventry	A	L41-49	12+1(6)	3+2(3)	8+1(4)	-	9+1(6)	-	4(3)		5(5)					0(3)
9	23/4	Ipswich	H	W51-38	8+3(5)	8+2(4)	6+1(4)	-	13(5)	0(3)		7+2(5)	9+2(4)					
10	12/5	Wolverhampton	A	L37-53*	10(6)	4+1(4)	0(3)	-	8+2(6)	1(3)	3(3)		11(5)					3+1(3)
11	23/5	Poole	H	L41-49	9+1(6)	7+1(5)	4+1(3)	-	11(6)	-	3(3)		4(4)					
12	11/6	Peterborough	H	W48-42	15(6)	5+1(5)	11+1(6)	-	R/R	-	10+3(6)	0(3)	7+2(4)	9+1(5)		10(5)		
13	15/6	Coventry	A	L43-47	10(6)	1+1(3)	6+1(4)	-	15+1(6)	-	3(3)		6+1(5)	8+1(5)	0(3)	1(4)		2(3)
14	21/6	Eastbourne	A	L38-52	7+1(6)	1(4)	R/R	-	17(6)	-			3+1(4)	12+1(5)	4+2(4)	9(4)		0(4)
15	23/6	Belle Vue	A	L41-49	9+1(6)	2(3)	5(4)	-	14+1(6)	-		3+2(4)	5(4)	9+1(4)	5+1(4)	7+2(4)		
16	25/6	Peterborough	A	L36-54	10(6)	1+1(3)	8(6)	-	10+2(5)	-	10+2(5)		5+1(4)	14(5)	4+1(4)	1(4)		1(3)
17	2/7	Poole	A	L44-46	6+1(4)	2+1(3)	2+2(4)	-			15(6)			16(6)				
18	4/7	Coventry	H	W52-38*	15(5)	5+1(4)	10(4)				9+2(4)			9+1(6)	0(3)	0(3)		
19	17/7	Ipswich	A	W51-39*	10+1(5)	10(4)	-				1(4)			12(5)	3+2(5)	0(3)		4+1(4)
20	18/7	Ipswich	H	W58-32	9+1(5)	7+1(4)	14(5)				7+1(4)				3(5)			
21	21/7	Eastbourne	A	W47-43	7+1(5)	1(3)	10(4)				10+1(5)			11+3(5)	3+1(4)			
22	15/8	Eastbourne	H	W46-44	R/R	4(4)	10(6)				9+1(5)							7+3(6)
23	18/8	Wolverhampton	A	L36-54	7(4)	5(6)	R/R				12+1(6)			13+1(5)	10+2(5)			
24	25/8	Peterborough	H	W46-44	6(3)	12+2(7)	R/R				11+1(6)			10+1(5)	1(3)	2(4)		
25	28/8	Ipswich	A	W49-41*	13(5)	10(5)	-							13+1(5)	8(4)		2+1(4)	
26	29/8	Poole	H	W62-28*	13(5)	10+2(5)					13(5)			16(6)		2+1(4)	6+1(5)	10+2(5)
27	3/9	Wolverhampton	H	W62-28*	11+3(5)	16+2(7)	R/R				14+1(5)			13+1(5)		7(5)	10+1(7)	
28	12/9	Belle Vue	H	W52-38*	11(5)	3+1(4)	7+2(4)				7+1(4)			10+1(5)		6+1(4)	10+2(5)	

DETAILS OF OTHER RIDERS:

Match No. 5: Adam Skornicki 6+1(4); Niels-Kristian Iversen 1(3); Match No. 8: Jamie Smith 0(3); Match No. 10: Leigh Lanham 3+1(3); Match No. 13: Steve Masters 2(3); Match No. 14: Niels-Kristian Iversen 10(6); Henning Bager 0(4); Match No. 15: Niels-Kristian Iversen 3+1(3); Match No. 16: Niels-Kristian Iversen 1(3); Steve Masters 1(3); Match No. 19: Kenneth Bjerre 4+1(4); Match No. 22: Ryan Fisher 7+3(6); Match No. 25: Ryan Fisher 6(3); Scott Robson 4+1(4); Match No. 26: Billy Hamill 10+2(5).

ELITE LEAGUE AVERAGES

Rider	Mts	Rds	Pts	Bon	Tot	Avge	Max
Greg Hancock	11	56	123	10	133	9.50	–
Nicki Pedersen	15	83	181	10	191	9.20	1 Paid
Todd Wiltshire	27	142	276	21	297	8.37	1 Full
Charlie Gjedde	19	89	164	16	180	8.09	1 Paid
Sebastian Ulamek	19	83	134	10	144	6.94	1 Full
Craig Boyce	9	39	55	7	62	6.36	–
Travis McGowan	28	120	146	26	172	5.73	–
Niklas Klingberg	6	23	27	4	31	5.39	–
Andy Smith	11	45	46	10	56	4.98	–
Kaj Laukkanen	5	22	23	3	26	4.73	–
Matej Ferjan	7	27	28	2	30	4.44	–
Niels-Kristian Iversen	4	15	15	1	16	4.27	–
Jan Staechmann	7	29	21	8	29	4.00	–
Jernej Kolenko	8	25	13	2	15	2.40	–
Steve Masters	2	6	3	0	3	2.00	–
Guests	9	36	40	9	49	5.44	–

NOTE: The figures for Niels-Kristian Iversen include one match as a guest.

BRITISH LEAGUE CUP

(*Denotes bonus-point victory)

No	DATE	OPPONENTS	H/A	RESULT	ULAMEK	STAECHMANN	McGOWAN	SMITH	SCARBORO	WILTSHIRE	KOLENKO	ANDREWS	TOMICEK	OTHERS
1	18/3	Isle of Wight	A	L43-47	10+2(6)	13+2(6)	3(3)	8+1(4)	0(3)	–	–	–	–	9(8)
2	10/4	Swindon	A	L37-48	–	2+2(3)	12+3(6)	11(5)	–	12(6)	0(3)	0(3)	–	4(4)
3	26/5	Reading	A	W50-40	10+1(4)	7+2(4)	11+1(5)	–	1(4)	15(5)	5+1(4)	1(4)	–	–
4	30/5	Reading	H	W53-37*	14(5)	9+2(4)	14+1(5)	7(4)	5+2(5)	–	4(4)	0(3)	–	–
5	27/6	Swindon	H	W50-40	11(4)	9+3(4)	10+1(5)	15(5)	1+1(4)	–	2+1(4)	–	2(4)	–
6	11/7	Isle of Wight	H	W50-40*	13(5)	6+2(4)	8(4)	10+2(5)	–	–	5+1(4)	1(3)	7+3(5)	–
7	2/8	Eastbourne	A	L38-46	–	–	11+1(5)	9(5)	–	13+1(5)	1(3)	–	3+1(4)	1(6)
8	22/8	Eastbourne	H	D45-45	–	–	11(5)	9(5)	2(3)	–	–	–	3+1(4)	20+2(13)

NOTE: The away match at Swindon originally ended in a 41-48 defeat on track; however, the points scored by Lukasz Jankowski were subsequently deducted from Oxford's total, as his inclusion in the side was deemed ineligible.

DETAILS OF OTHER RIDERS:

Match No. 1: Niklas Klingberg 8(5); Joe Cook 1(3); Match No. 2: Lukasz Jankowski 4(4); Match No. 7: Danny Norton 1(3); Carl Downs 0(3); Match No. 8: Emil Kramer 7+1(5) Matej Ferjan 7(4); Niels-Kristian Iversen 6+1(4).

BRITISH LEAGUE CUP AVERAGES

Rider	Mts	Rds	Pts	Bon	Tot	Avge	Max
Todd Wiltshire	3	16	40	1	41	10.25	1 Full
Sebastian Ulamek	5	24	58	3	61	10.17	–
Jan Staechmann	6	25	46	13	59	9.44	1 Paid
Travis McGowan	8	38	80	7	87	9.16	1 Paid
Andy Smith	7	33	69	3	72	8.73	1 Full
Matej Ferjan	1	4	7	0	7	7.00	–
Niels-Kristian Iversen	1	4	6	1	7	7.00	–
Niklas Klingberg	1	5	8	0	8	6.40	–
Emil Kramer	1	5	7	1	8	6.40	–
Lubos Tomicek	4	17	15	5	20	4.71	–
Jernej Kolenko	6	22	17	3	20	3.64	–
Ricky Scarboro	5	19	9	3	12	2.53	–
Joe Cook	1	3	1	0	1	1.33	–
Danny Norton	1	3	1	0	1	1.33	–
Darren Andrews	4	13	2	0	2	0.62	–
Carl Downs	1	3	0	0	0	0.00	–

NOTE: Lukasz Jankowski's record in the away match at Swindon has been omitted as his inclusion in the side was deemed ineligible.

KNOCK-OUT CUP

(* Denotes aggregate victory)

No	DATE	OPPONENTS	H/A	RESULT	WILTSHIRE	McGOWAN	BOYCE	ULAMEK	PEDERSEN	KOLENKO	GJEDDE	LAUKKANEN	HANCOCK	SMITH
1	5/5	Ipswich	A	W49-41	6+2(5)	3+1(4)	7+1(4)	12(4)	13(5)	1(3)	7+2(5)	–	–	–
2	9/5	Ipswich	H	W55-35*	15(5)	5+1(4)	4(4)	9(4)	12+1(5)	0(3)	10+2(5)	–	–	–
3	15/9	Poole	A	L34-56	3(4)	3(3)	–	4+1(4)	–	1+1(3)	6(6)	13(6)	4+1(4)
4	10/10	Poole	H	W46-44	11+1(5)	5+2(4)	–	7+1(4)	–	8(4)	1+1(3)	8+3(5)	6+1(5)

OTHER MEETINGS

15 March: Challenge

Coventry 46 Oxford 44 (Nicki Pedersen 13; Charlie Gjedde 7+2; Todd Wiltshire 7+1; Niklas Klingberg 6; Sebastian Ulamek 5; Travis McGowan 4; Jernej Kolenko 2).

21 March: International Club Challenge

Oxford 55 (Nicki Pedersen 15; Niklas Klingberg 9+1; Todd Wiltshire 9; Sebastian Ulamek 7+2; Jan Staechmann 7+2; Travis McGowan 6+2; Jernej Kolenko 2) Kaparna 35 (Jaroslaw Hampel 11; Ryan Sullivan 11; Peter Karlsson 6; Kim Jansson 3+1; Sebastian Bengtsson 2+1; Tomasz Gapinski 2; Norvy Brandin 0).

28 March: Challenge

Oxford 42 (Niklas Klingberg 12; Nicki Pedersen 11+1; Charlie Gjedde 9+2; Todd Wiltshire 5; Sebastian Ulamek 5; Jernej Kolenko 0; Travis McGowan R/R) Coventry 48.

22 September: Elite League Play-Off semi-final

Poole 48 Oxford 42 (Greg Hancock 10; Sebastian Ulamek 7+2; Andy Smith 7+1; Todd Wiltshire 7; Kaj Laukkanen 5; Charlie Gjedde 4; Travis McGowan 2+1).

PETERBOROUGH EUROPRESS PANTHERS

NOTE: The information below relates only to the main Peterborough team. For details of the second side, please refer to the Conference League section.

ADDRESS: East of England Showground, Alwalton, Peterborough.

PROMOTERS: Mick Horton & Jim Lynch, with the former assuming full control at the end of September 2003.

TRACK LENGTH: 336 metres.

FIRST MEETING: 12 June 1970.

YEARS OF OPERATION: 1970-74 British League Division Two; 1975-90 National League; 1991-94 British League Division Two; 1995-96 British Premier League; 1997 British Elite League; 1998 British Premier League; 1999-03 British Elite League.

CLUB HONOURS

FOUR-TEAM CHAMPIONS: 1977, 1978, 1988, 1989, 1992, 1997, 1998.
LEAGUE CHAMPIONS: 1992, 1998, 1999.
KNOCK-OUT CUP WINNERS: 1992, 1999, 2001.
PREMIERSHIP WINNERS: 1993.
PAIRS CHAMPIONS: 1998.
CRAVEN SHIELD WINNERS: 1999.

RIDER ROSTER 2003

ANDERSEN, Hans N. *b. 3 November 1980, Odense, Denmark.*
　　BRITISH CAREER: (2001-02) Poole; (2003) Peterborough.

BARNEY, Ian *b. 15 February 1961, Stamford, Lincolnshire.*
　　BRITISH CAREER: (1980-92) Peterborough; Also (1982-84) Eastbourne; (1983) Cradley Heath; (1985) King's Lynn; (1987) King's Lynn; (1988) King's Lynn, Wolverhampton, Swindon; (1990) Exeter; (1991) Sheffield; (1992) Mildenhall, Milton Keynes; (1993) Long Eaton; (1994) Peterborough, Coventry; (2000-01) Peterborough (CL); (2002) Peterborough (CL), King's Lynn (CL); (2003) Peterborough (BLC).

BJERRE, Kenneth *b. 24 May 1984, Esbjerg, Denmark.*
　　BRITISH CAREER: (2002) Newcastle; (2003) Newcastle, Peterborough.

CLARKE, Steve *b. 14 January 1984, Aylesbury, Buckinghamshire.*
　　BRITISH CAREER: (2002) King's Lynn (CL), Wolverhampton (CT); (2003) Wolverhampton (CL), Peterborough (CL & BLC).

COLLINS, Neil *b. 15 October 1961, Partington, Greater Manchester.*
　　BRITISH CAREER: (1978) Ellesmere Port; (1979) Nottingham, Workington, Sheffield; (1980) Edinburgh, Sheffield; (1981) Edinburgh, Cradley Heath, Belle Vue; (1982-83) Leicester; (1984-88) Sheffield; (1989-90) Wolverhampton; (1991) Belle Vue; (1992) Glasgow; (1993-94) Long Eaton; (1995) Sheffield; (1996) Belle Vue; (1997) Glasgow; (1998) Stoke; (1999-00) Swindon; (2001) Belle Vue, Workington; (2002) Somerset; (2003) Hull, Peterborough (BLC & CL 4 Team Champs), Belle Vue.

DART, Tony   b. 2 September 1979, Ashford, Kent.
   BRITISH CAREER: (2003) Mildenhall, King's Lynn, Peterborough (BLC), Isle of Wight (KOC).
FRY, Paul   b. 25 October 1964, Ledbury, Hereford & Worcester.
   BRITISH CAREER: (1984) Newcastle, Cradley Heath, Arena-Essex; (1986-87) Cradley
   Heath; (1988) Stoke; (1989-90) Long Eaton; (1991) King's Lynn; (1992-96) Exeter;
   (1997-98) Newport; (1999) Stoke; (2000-02) Swindon; (2003) Swindon, Peterborough.
HARRIS, Chris   b. 28 November 1982, Truro, Cornwall.
   BRITISH CAREER: (1998) St Austell; (1999-00) Exeter; (2001) Trelawny; (2002-03)
   Trelawny, Peterborough.
HAVELOCK, Gary   b. 4 November 1968, Yarm, Cleveland.
   BRITISH CAREER: (1985) Middlesbrough, King's Lynn, Wolverhampton; (1986)
   Middlesbrough, Bradford; (1987-88) Bradford; (1990-97) Bradford; (1998) Eastbourne,
   Poole; (1999-02) Poole; (2003) Peterborough.
HAWKINS, Ritchie   b. 9 November 1983, Peterborough, Cambridgeshire.
   BRITISH CAREER: (2000) Sheffield (CL); (2001) Swindon, Sheffield (CL); (2002)
   Swindon (PL & CT); (2003) Swindon (PL & CL), Peterborough (BLC).
HORTON, James   b. 22 June 1985, Slough, Berkshire.
   BRITISH CAREER: (2001-02) Peterborough (CL); (2003) Peterborough (CL & BLC),
   Boston (CT), Trelawny (PL & CT).
McCABE, Shane   b. 3 May 1974, Townsville, Queensland, Australia.
   BRITISH CAREER: (2002) Peterborough (CL), Edinburgh, Somerset, Trelawny, Rye
   House, Newport, Stoke; (2003) King's Lynn, Boston, Peterborough (CL, ELKOC &
   BLC), Somerset.
NORTON, Danny   b. 27 August 1986, Hull, East Yorkshire.
   BRITISH CAREER: (2001-02) Peterborough (CL); (2003) Peterborough (CL & BLC),
   Armadale (CT), Swindon (PL), Reading, Mildenhall (KOC & CT), Poole (BLC) &
   Oxford (BLC).
PAINTER, Rob   b. 23 June 1978, Whipps Cross, Walthamstow, London.
   BRITISH CAREER: (2001) Newport (CL), Boston; (2002) Peterborough (CL); (2003)
   Peterborough (CL & BLC) & Newport (CL).
PARKER, Shane   b. 29 April 1970, Adelaide, South Australia, Australia.
   BRITISH CAREER: (1990-94) Ipswich; (1995-96) Middlesbrough; (1997-98) King's Lynn;
   (1999) Hull; (2000) King's Lynn, Belle Vue; (2001-02) Peterborough; (2003) King's
   Lynn, Peterborough.
PARSONS, Joel   b. 24 July 1985, Broken Hill, New South Wales, Australia.
   BRITISH CAREER: (2003) Reading, Eastbourne (BLC), Rye House (CL & PL), Newport
   (PL), Wimbledon (CT), Arena-Essex, Peterborough (BLC), Hull.
PROTASIEWICZ, Piotr   b. 25 January 1975, Zielona Gora, Poland.
   BRITISH CAREER: (1998) King's Lynn; (2002-03) Peterborough.
PURCHASE, James   b. 21 October 1987, Southampton, Hampshire.
   BRITISH CAREER: (2003) Oxford (CL), Peterborough (CL & BLC).
SADLER, Nigel   b. 17 September 1978, Blackwood, Adelaide, South Australia.
   BRITISH CAREER: (1997) Skegness/Isle of Wight; (1998-01) Peterborough; (2002) Rye
   House; (2003) Rye House, Peterborough.
SULLIVAN, Ryan   b. 20 January 1975, Melbourne, Victoria, Australia.
   BRITISH CAREER: (1994-97) Peterborough; (1998) Poole; (1999-03) Peterborough.

PETERBOROUGH PANTHERS: back row, left to right: Mick Horton (Co-Promoter), Hans Andersen, Piotr Protasiewicz, Ryan Sullivan, Gary Havelock, Jim Lynch (Co-Promoter/Team Manager). On bike: Shane Parker. Front, kneeling: Chris Harris, Nigel Sadler.

THOMPSON, Mark   *b. 8 July 1979, Orsett, Essex.*
BRITISH CAREER: (1996) Sittingbourne, Linlithgow, Mildenhall, Eastbourne (CL); (1997) Anglian Angels; (1998) Mildenhall, Newport, Stoke; (1999) King's Lynn (CL); (2000-01) Mildenhall; (2002) King's Lynn (CL), Mildenhall, Arena-Essex, Workington, Stoke; (2003) Boston, Stoke (PL), Newport (BLC), Somerset, Peterborough (BLC), Coventry (BLC), King's Lynn, Arena-Essex.

WERNER, Brent   *b. 15 April 1974, Los Angeles, California, USA.*
BRITISH CAREER: (1995-97) Long Eaton; (1998) Newcastle; (1999-00) Workington; (2001) Eastbourne; (2002) Rye House; (2003) Rye House, Peterborough.

WRIGHT, Matthew   *b. 19 November 1985, Harlow, Essex.*
BRITISH CAREER: (2002) Boston, Mildenhall, Carmarthen, Wimbledon; (2003) Mildenhall, Ipswich (BLC), Arena-Essex (BLC), Reading, Peterborough (BLC).

SKY SPORTS ELITE LEAGUE

(* Denotes bonus-point victory)

No	DATE	OPPONENTS	H/A	RESULT	SULLIVAN	PARKER	HAVELOCK	ANDERSEN	PROTASIEWICZ	BJERRE	HARRIS	WERNER	SADLER	FRY	OTHERS
1	28/3	Wolverhampton	H	W53-37	14+1(5)	8(4)	8+4(5)	8(4)	5(4)	2(3)	8+2(5)	-	-	-	-
2	29/3	Coventry	A	L39-51	17(6)	1(3)	4(4)	4+1(4)	2(3)	2(4)	9+1(6)	-	-	-	-
3	31/3	Wolverhampton	A	L37-53	10+1(6)	6+2(5)	4(4)	11(6)	1(3)	4+1(3)	-	1(3)	-	-	-
4	4/4	Coventry	H	L43-47	12(6)	3+2(4)	5+2(4)	11(5)	6(4)	3(3)	-		3(4)	-	-
5	9/4	Belle Vue	H	W53-37	14(5)	3(4)	6+1(4)	7(4)	9+2(5)	6(4)	8(4)	-	-	-	-
6	11/4	Poole	H	W47-43	12(5)	5+1(4)	3+2(4)	9+1(4)	8+2(5)	7(5)	3+1(3)	-	-	-	-
7	14/4	Oxford	H	W59-31	10(4)	5(4)	7+3(4)	10+2(5)	14(5)	-	9+1(4)	-	4+2(4)	-	-
8	18/4	Ipswich	A	W47-43	14(6)	1(3)	8+1(5)	7+1(4)	7+2(4)	-	9+1(5)	-	-	-	1(3)
9	18/4	Ipswich	H	W62-28*	11(4)	5+2(4)	12+2(5)	10+2(5)	8+1(4)	-	8+1(4)	-	8+1(4)	-	-
10	20/4	Wolverhampton	H	W58-32	14(5)	7+2(4)	10+1(5)	5+1(4)	9+2(4)	-	10+1(4)	-	3+1(4)	-	-
11	30/4	Poole	A	L44-46*	11(5)	6+2(5)	8(5)	9+3(6)	R/R	1(3)	9+1(6)	-	-	-	-
12	3/5	Eastbourne	A	L35-55	16(6)	2+1(5)	7+1(6)	R/R	-	8(6)	-	-	-	-	2+1(7)
13	8/5	Eastbourne	H	W52-38	R/R	9(5)	10+1(6)	7(4)	9+2(5)	-	13+2(7)	-	4+1(4)	-	-
14	10/5	Coventry	A	L38-52	-	2+2(4)	3(3)	7+2(5)	14(6)	-	4(4)	-	-	-	8(8)
15	11/5	Belle Vue	A	W48-42*	-	2(3)	2+1(4)	6+1(4)	10(4)	15(7)	4+1(3)	-	-	-	9+1(5)
16	26/5	Belle Vue	H	W53-37	8(3)	8+4(5)	3+2(4)	9(4)	10(4)	11+3(7)	-	-	-	4(3)	-
17	9/6	Wolverhampton	A	L37-53*	4(3)	1(3)	3+1(3)	7+1(6)	11(5)	9+2(6)	-	-	-	2(4)	-
18	11/6	Oxford	A	L42-48*	15(6)	2+1(5)	0(2)	11+1(6)	9+1(4)	5(4)	0(3)	-	-	-	-
19	12/6	Ipswich	A	W57-33	12(4)	9+2(7)	R/R	7(4)	13(5)	8+1(5)	8+2(5)	-	-	-	-
20	18/6	Poole	A	L37-53	12(6)	2(4)	3+2(4)	R/R	15(7)	-	4+1(6)	-	-	1(3)	-
21	20/6	Poole	H	W48-42	14(5)	4(5)	-	R/R	-	-	6+3(5)	-	11(7)	-	13(8)
22	25/6	Oxford	H	W54-36	6(4)	10+3(6)	10(5)	R/R	17(6)	-	6+1(5)	-	5+4(4)	-	-
23	7/7	Belle Vue	A	L43-47*	-	6+2(6)	3(4)	R/R	8(6)	19(7)	-	-	-	-	7+1(7)
24	18/7	Eastbourne	H	W56-34	15(5)	9+2(6)	11(4)	-	11+3(5)	8+2(5)	2(4)	-	-	-	0(1)
25	6/8	Ipswich	H	W62-28*	14+1(5)	12+3(6)	-	-	R/R	-	14+2(6)	-	9+1(5)	2+1(4)	11(4)
26	20/8	Coventry	H	W48-42	11(5)	2(3)	11+2(6)	0(3)	11(4)	7+1(5)	6(4)	-	-	-	-
27	25/8	Oxford	A	L44-46*	7(5)	6+1(6)	2(3)	9+1(4)	13(5)	-	7+3(4)	-	-	-	0(3)
28	8/9	Eastbourne	A	L29-61	8+1(6)	10(6)	4+1(5)	-	R/R	-	-	-	-	-	7+1(13)

DETAILS OF OTHER RIDERS:

Match No. 8: Phil Morris 1(3); Match No. 12: Adam Skornicki 1(4); Frank Smart 1+1(3); Match No. 14: Scott Nicholls 8(5); Paul Clews 0(3); Match No. 15: Joe Screen 9+1(5); Match No. 21: Lee Richardson 12(5); Craig Watson 1(3); Match No. 23: Joe Screen 6(4); Kevin Little 1+1(3); Match No. 24: David Howe 0(1); Match No. 25: Simon Stead 11(4); Match No. 27: Craig Watson 0(3); Match No. 28: Leigh Lanham 6(5); Mark Lemon 1+1(4); Tom P. Madsen 0(4).

ELITE LEAGUE AVERAGES

Rider	Mts	Rds	Pts	Bon	Tot	Avge	Max
Ryan Sullivan	24	120	281	4	285	9.50	2 Full; 2 Paid
Piotr Protasiewicz	23	107	220	15	235	8.79	–
Hans N. Andersen	20	91	154	17	171	7.52	–
Chris Harris	21	97	147	24	171	7.05	–
Kenneth Bjerre	16	77	115	10	125	6.49	–
Gary Havelock	25	108	147	27	174	6.44	–
Nigel Sadler	8	36	47	10	57	6.33	–
Shane Parker	28	129	146	32	178	5.52	–
Paul Fry	4	14	9	1	10	2.86	–
Brent Werner	1	3	1	0	1	1.33	–
Guests	16	59	58	4	62	4.20	–

BRITISH LEAGUE CUP

No	DATE	OPPONENTS	H/A	RESULT	ANDERSEN	PARKER	BJERRE	HAVELOCK	HORTON	NORTON	HARRIS	THOMPSON	COLLINS	McCABE	OTHERS
1	3/4	Ipswich	A	L42-48	11(6)	8+2(4)	8(4)	13(5)	1(4)	0(4)	–	–	–	–	1(3)
2	30/5	Ipswich	H	W45-44	–	14+1(5)	12+1(5)	–	0(4)	2(5)	14(5)	2(3)	–	–	1(3)
3	11/7	King's Lynn	H	W47-45	R/R	14(6)	–	17(6)	1(4)	3+1(5)	–	–	9+2(5)	3(4)	–
4	16/7	King's Lynn	A	L43-47	–	14(5)	11(5)	8(4)	0(1)	6+1(4)	–	–	2(4)	2(7)	–
5	26/7	Rye House †	A	L36-42	–	12+1(5)	12(4)	–	–	1(4)	–	–	10+1(5)	0(3)	1(6)
6	22/8	Rye House	H	L44-46	R/R	15+1(6)	–	12+1(5)	0(4)	3(6)	14(6)	–	–	–	0(3)
7	12/9	Arena-Essex	A	L27-64	–	10(7)	–	10(6)	3(5)	3+1(2)	–	–	–	–	1(9)
8	27/10	Arena-Essex	H	L43-47	–	–	–	18(6)	–	–	13(6)	3(3)	–	–	9+1(15)

† Meeting abandoned after thirteen heats, with the result standing.

DETAILS OF OTHER RIDERS:

Match No. 1: Rob Painter 1(3); Match No. 2: Ian Barney 1(3); Match No. 5: Joel Parsons 1(5); Steve Clarke 0(1); Match No. 6: Steve Clarke 0(3); Match No. 7: Tony Dart 1(5); Steve Clarke 0(4); Paul Fry R/R; Match No. 8: Paul Fry 6+1(5); Ritchie Hawkins 1(3); Matthew Wright 1(4); James Purchase 1(3).

GOLDEN DOUBLE RIDES:

Match No. 7: Gary Havelock's total includes 2 points from a golden double ride; Match No. 8: Chris Harris' total includes 2 points from a golden double ride.

BRITISH LEAGUE CUP AVERAGES

Rider	Mts	Rds	Pts	Bon	Tot	Avge	Max
Kenneth Bjerre	4	18	43	1	44	9.78	1 Full
Gary Havelock	6	32	77	1	78	9.75	1 Full
Shane Parker	7	38	87	5	92	9.68	1 Paid
Chris Harris	3	17	40	0	40	9.41	–
Hans N. Andersen	1	6	11	0	11	7.33	–
Neil Collins	3	14	21	3	24	6.86	–
Paul Fry	1	5	6	1	7	5.60	–
Mark Thompson	2	6	5	0	5	3.33	–
Danny Norton	7	30	18	3	21	2.80	–
Shane McCabe	3	14	5	0	5	1.43	–
Ian Barney	1	3	1	0	1	1.33	–
Ritchie Hawkins	1	3	1	0	1	1.33	–
Rob Painter	1	3	1	0	1	1.33	–
James Purchase	1	3	1	0	1	1.33	–
Matthew Wright	1	4	1	0	1	1.00	–
James Horton	6	22	5	0	5	0.91	–
Tony Dart	1	5	1	0	1	0.80	–
Joel Parsons	1	5	1	0	1	0.80	–
Steve Clarke	3	8	0	0	0	0.00	–

NOTE: Gary Havelock's figures include one golden double ride (2 points), modified to normal score i.e. 1 point;
Chris Harris' figures include one golden double ride (2 points), modified to normal score i.e. 1 point.

KNOCK-OUT CUP

No	DATE	OPPONENTS	H/A	RESULT	SULLIVAN	PARKER	HAVELOCK	ANDERSEN	PROTASIEWICZ	McCABE	SADLER	HARRIS	FRY	OTHERS
1	21/4	Coventry	A	L38-52	–	2+1(4)	9(6)	8+2(5)	–	0(3)	4(3)	1(3)	–	14(6)
2	23/5	Coventry	H	W52-38	11+1(5)	7+2(5)	5+1(4)	8(4)	12+2(5)	–	–	5+2(4)	4(3)	–
3	3/9	Coventry (R)	A	L29-61	9+1(7)	2(4)	0(3)	3(5)	R/R	–	1+1(4)	14(7)	–	–
4	10/9	Coventry (R)	H	L44-46	16(6)	7+1(6)	13(7)	R/R	–	–	–	–	–	8(11)

(R) = Replay

DETAILS OF OTHER RIDERS:

Match No. 1: Lukas Dryml 14(6); Match No. 4: Adam Shields 4(5); Leigh Lanham 3(3); Travis McGowan 1(3).

OTHER MEETINGS

19 March: Challenge (first-leg)

Poole 49 Peterborough 41 (Hans N. Andersen 11+1; Ryan Sullivan 10; Chris Harris 5+1; Kenneth Bjerre 5+1; Shane Parker 4+1; Gary Havelock 4+1; Piotr Protasiewicz 2+1).

23 March: Challenge (second-leg)

Peterborough 48 (Piotr Protasiewicz 10+1; Ryan Sullivan 10; Hans N. Andersen 9; Nigel Sadler 7+1; Shane Parker 4+3; Gary Havelock 4+2; Chris Harris 4+1) Poole 42 – Poole won 91-89 on aggregate.

15 September: Elite League Play-Off semi-final

Coventry 60 Peterborough 30 (Ryan Sullivan 6+1; Kenneth Bjerre 6+1; Gary Havelock 5+1; Piotr Protasiewicz 5; Shane Parker 4; Scott Robson 3; Hans N. Andersen 1).

PAIRS MEETING

17 October: Super 2s Best Pairs

1st Sean Wilson (15) & Paul Lee (6) 21; 2nd Andy Smith (16) & Danny Norton (4) 20; =3rd Gary Havelock (18) & Barrie Evans (1) 19 and Niels-Kristian Iversen (15) & Ben Wilson (4) 19; Ricky Ashworth (12) & Ritchie Hawkins (5) 17; Carl Stonehewer (13) & Tommy Allen (4) 17; David Howe (12) & Luke Priest (1) 13.

POOLE MERIDIAN LIFTS PIRATES

ADDRESS: Poole Stadium, Wimborne Road, Poole, Dorset.
PROMOTERS: Pete Ansell, Matt Ford & Mike Golding.
TRACK LENGTH: 299.1 metres.
FIRST MEETING: 26 April 1948.
YEARS OF OPERATION: 1948-51 National League Division Three; 1952-55 National League Division Two; 1956 National League Division One; 1957 Open; 1958-59 National League; 1960-63 Provincial League; 1964 Provincial League & Metropolitan League; 1965-67 British League; 1968-74 British League Division One; 1975-84 British League; 1985-90 National League; 1991-94 British League Division One; 1995-96 British Premier League; 1997-03 British Elite League.

CLUB HONOURS

LEAGUE CHAMPIONS: 1951, 1952, 1955, 1961, 1962, 1969, 1989, 1990, 1994, 2003.
NATIONAL TROPHY (DIVISION TWO) WINNERS: 1952, 1955.
KNOCK-OUT CUP WINNERS: 1990, 2003.
FOUR-TEAM CHAMPIONS: 1994.
CRAVEN SHIELD WINNERS: 2001 & 2002.
BRITISH LEAGUE CUP WINNERS: 2003.

RIDER ROSTER 2003

ADAMS, Leigh   b. 28 April 1971, Mildura, Victoria, Australia.
BRITISH CAREER: (1989) Poole; (1990-92) Swindon; (1993-95) Arena-Essex; (1996) London;

(1997-98) Swindon; (1999-00) King's Lynn; (2001-02) Oxford; (2003) Poole.

ASHWORTH, Ricky   b. 17 August 1982, Salford, Greater Manchester.
BRITISH CAREER: (2001) Sheffield (CL); (2002) Sheffield (PL & CL); (2003) Sheffield (PL), Poole.

BOYCE, Craig   b. 2 August 1967, Sydney, New South Wales, Australia.
BRITISH CAREER: (1988-90) Poole; (1991) Oxford; (1992-94) Poole; (1995) Swindon; (1996-98) Poole; (1999) Oxford; (2000) King's Lynn; (2001-02) Ipswich; (2003) Poole (BLC), Oxford, Ipswich.

BROADHURST, Wayne   b. 28 February 1967, Minsterley, Shropshire.
BRITISH CAREER: (1987) Coventry; (1988) Coventry, Stoke; (1989) Coventry; (1999) Stoke, Workington; (2000) Stoke; (2001) Wolverhampton, Stoke; (2002) Mildenhall; (2003) Mildenhall, Wolverhampton, Poole (BLC), Belle Vue (BLC).

CAMBRIDGE, Matt   b. 14 May 1981, Rugby, Warwickshire.
BRITISH CAREER: (2000) Sheffield (CL); (2001-02) Sheffield (CL), Exeter; (2003) Newport (PL & CL), Wimbledon, Poole (BLC).

COMPTON, André   b. 15 May 1977, Dewsbury, West Yorkshire.
BRITISH CAREER: (1993) Bradford, Newcastle; (1994) Stoke, Newcastle, Buxton; (1995-96) Buxton; (1997) Newcastle, Berwick; (1998-99) Sheffield; (2000) Peterborough, Newcastle; (2001) Newcastle; (2002) Newcastle, Poole; (2003) Sheffield, Poole.

COURTNEY, Scott   b. 3 January 1983, Middlesbrough, Cleveland.
BRITISH CAREER: (1999) Glasgow, Linlithgow; (2000) Glasgow, Ashfield; (2001) Glasgow, Buxton, Mildenhall, Trelawny, Arena-Essex, Newcastle; (2002) Arena-Essex, Rye House (CL); (2003) Poole, Eastbourne (BLC), Rye House (CL).

DAVIDSSON, Daniel   b. 17 March 1983, Motala, Sweden.
BRITISH CAREER: (2003) Poole (BLC).

DRYML, Ales   b. 19 October 1979, Pardubice, Czech Republic.
BRITISH CAREER: (2000-02) Oxford; (2003) Belle Vue, Poole.

DRYML, Lukas   b. 16 April 1981, Pardubice, Czech Republic.
BRITISH CAREER: (2000-02) Oxford; (2003) Poole.

ELKINS, Justin   b. 27 August 1974, Salisbury, Wiltshire.
BRITISH CAREER: (1990) Poole; (1991) Rye House, Exeter; (1992) Swindon; (1993) Poole; (1994) Poole, Reading, Coventry, Exeter; (1995) Peterborough, Poole; (1996) Ryde, Eastbourne (PL & CL); (1997) Long Eaton; (1998) Reading; (1999) Reading, Edinburgh; (2000) Poole, Arena-Essex; (2001) Hull, Workington, Exeter; (2002) Isle of Wight, Wimbledon, Newport (PL); (2003) Poole (BLC).

FELTON, Dean   b. 18 August 1969, Wolverhampton, West Midlands.
BRITISH CAREER: (1994) Buxton, Oxford, Ipswich; (1995-96) Buxton; (1997) Buxton, Stoke, Edinburgh, Skegness, Long Eaton, Shuttle Cubs; (1998) Stoke; (1999) Berwick, Glasgow; (2000) Buxton, Berwick; (2001) Stoke, Buxton, Edinburgh, Berwick; (2002) Carmarthen; (2003) Carmarthen, Belle Vue (BLC), Poole (BLC), Eastbourne (BLC), Wolverhampton (BLC).

HOLLINGWORTH, Robert   b. 31 December 1955, Boston, Lincolnshire.
BRITISH CAREER: (1973) Berwick; (1974) Boston; (1975) Boston, Hull, King's Lynn, Poole, Wolverhampton; (1976) Boston, Wolverhampton, White City; (1977) Boston, Wolverhampton; (1978) Edinburgh, Wolverhampton; (1979) Boston, King's Lynn; (1980-81) Boston, Coventry; (1982) Boston, King's Lynn; (1983) Scunthorpe; (1984) Boston;

(1985) Mildenhall; (1986) Boston; (1999) King's Lynn (CL); (2000-02) Boston; (2003) Boston, Belle Vue (BLC), Poole (BLC).

JONES, Graham b. 5 May 1963, Oswestry, Shropshire.
BRITISH CAREER: (1984-87) Stoke; (1988) Stoke, Belle Vue, Reading, Sheffield, Wolverhampton, King's Lynn & Ipswich; (1989-93) Wolverhampton; (1994) Middlesbrough; (1995) Hull; (1996) Hull, Middlesbrough; (2003) Wolverhampton (CL & BLC), Stoke (CT), Coventry (BLC), Belle Vue (BLC), Eastbourne (BLC) & Poole (BLC).

KASPRZAK, Krzysztof b. 18 July 1984, Leszno, Poland.
BRITISH CAREER: (2003) Poole.

LANGLEY, Karl b. 2 June 1981, Whitehaven, Cumbria.
BRITISH CAREER: (2002) Workington; (2003) Newcastle (CL), Armadale (CLKOC), Mildenhall, Poole (BLC).

LINDBACK, Antonio b. 5 May 1985, Rio De Janeiro, Brazil.
BRITISH CAREER: (2003) Poole.

NORTON, Danny b. 27 August 1986, Hull, East Yorkshire.
BRITISH CAREER: (2001-02) Peterborough (CL); (2003) Peterborough (CL & BLC), Armadale (CT), Swindon (PL), Reading, Mildenhall (KOC & CT), Poole (BLC), Oxford (BLC).

PEDERSEN, Bjarne b. 12 July 1978, Ryrde, Denmark.
BRITISH CAREER: (2000-01) Newcastle; (2002) Poole; (2003) Poole, Newcastle.

PEGLER, Scott b. 3 August 1973, Exeter, Devon.
BRITISH CAREER: (1989-90) Exeter; (1992-94) Exeter; (1995) Exeter, Devon; (1996) Swindon (PL & CL); (1997) Newport (PL); (1998) Newport (PL & CL); (1999) Newport (PL); (2000-02) Newport (CL); (2003) Newport (CL), Poole (BLC).

PRIMMER, Tony b. 11 April 1966, Maitland, New South Wales, Australia.
BRITISH CAREER: (1988) Wimbledon, Milton Keynes; (1989) Milton Keynes; (1990) Eastbourne; (1991) Oxford; (2002) Trelawny; (2003) Poole (BLC).

RICKARDSSON, Tony b. 17 August 1970, Grytas, Sweden.
BRITISH CAREER: (1991-94) Ipswich; (1997-98) Ipswich; (1999) King's Lynn; (2001-03) Poole.

RUUD, David b. 21 January 1980, Gislaved, Sweden.
BRITISH CAREER: (2001) Poole; (2003) Poole, Arena-Essex.

TAYLOR, Craig b. 31 January 1974, Dudley, West Midlands.
BRITISH CAREER: (1993) Wolverhampton; (1994) Stoke, Wolverhampton, Cradley Heath, Berwick; (1995) Stoke, Wolverhampton, Long Eaton, Belle Vue; Cradley Heath, Oxford; (1996) Buxton, Wolverhampton; (1997) Stoke, Wolverhampton; (1998) Berwick, Stoke; (1999) Wolverhampton; (2000) Newport; (2001) Buxton; (2002) Carmarthen; (2003) Carmarthen, Poole (BLC).

WALKER, Simon b. 19 February 1980, Bristol, Avon.
BRITISH CAREER: (2001) Newport (CL); (2002) Newport (CL), Arena-Essex, Swindon (CT), Trelawny; (2003) Swindon (CL), Trelawny (CT), Reading, Somerset (BLC), Poole (BLC), Exeter (BLC), Newport.

WARWICK, Dan b. 21 November 1983, Poole, Dorset.
BRITISH CAREER: (2002) Newport (CL), Reading; (2003) Newport (CL & PL), Poole (BLC), Exeter.

POOLE PIRATES: back row, left to right: Mike Golding (Co-Promoter), Davey Watt, Bjarne Pedersen, Scott Courtney, Krzysztof Kasprzak, Neil Middleditch (Team Manager), Andre Compton, Leigh Adams, Matt Ford (Co-Promoter). On bike: Tony Rickardsson. Front, kneeling: David Ruud, Craig Boyce.

WATT, Davey   b. *6 January 1978, Townsville, Queensland, Australia.*
  BRITISH CAREER: (2001) Isle of Wight; (2002) Newcastle; (2003) King's Lynn, Poole.
WOODWARD, Cameron   b. *8 January 1985, Mildura, Victoria, Australia.*
  BRITISH CAREER: (2003) Poole (BLC).
ZETTERSTROM, Magnus   b. *9 December 1971, Eskilstuna, Sweden.*
  BRITISH CAREER: (1996) Poole; (1998–99) Poole; (2000) Peterborough; (2001) Poole; (2002) Poole, Peterborough; (2003) Poole (BLC).

SKY SPORTS ELITE LEAGUE

(* Denotes bonus-point victory)

No	DATE	OPPONENTS	H/A	RESULT	ADAMS	KASPRZAK	L-DRYML	PEDERSEN	RICKARDSSON	RUUD	COMPTON	WATT	OTHERS
1	26/3	Coventry	H	L43-47	11+1(6)	5(4)	6(4)	3(4)	12(5)	5(4)	1+1(3)	–	–
2	27/3	Ipswich	A	W50-40	11+1(5)	0(3)	5(4)	8(4)	12(5)	8(5)	–	6+2(4)	–
3	2/4	Ipswich	H	W49-40*	11+1(5)	1(4)	10+1(4)	8+1(4)	11(5)	5+2(4)	–	3(4)	–
4	7/4	Wolverhampton	A	D45-45	13(6)	R/R	7+1(4)	5+1(4)	14(6)	4+1(5)	2(5)	–	–
5	9/4	Oxford	H	W51-39	8(4)	5+1(4)	13(5)	4+1(4)	9+2(5)	11+2(5)	1(3)	–	–
6	11/4	Peterborough	A	L43-47	14+1(6)	1+1(3)	13(5)	1(4)	5(4)	3+1(4)	–	6+1(4)	–
7	16/4	Belle Vue	H	W54-36	12(4)	–	13+1(5)	4+1(4)	12(5)	7+1(5)	6+1(4)	–	0(3)
8	30/4	Peterborough	H	W46-44	11+2(5)	4(4)	7+1(4)	4(4)	14(5)	3(4)	3+1(4)	–	–
9	5/5	Eastbourne	H	W60-30	15(5)	R/R	9(4)	7(5)	13+2(5)	6+2(5)	–	10+4(6)	–
10	10/5	Eastbourne	A	W46-43*	18(6)	4+2(4)	6(4)	7+1(4)	10+2(5)	0(4)	–	–	1(3)
11	14/5	Wolverhampton	H	W58-32*	8+2(4)	5+2(4)	11+1(5)	10+3(5)	9(4)	13+1(6)	–	–	2(3)
12	23/5	Oxford	A	W49-41*	9+1(4)	5(4)	11+1(5)	5(4)	12+2(5)	6+1(4)	–	1+1(4)	–
13	2/6	Belle Vue	A	L44-45*	7+1(4)	3(3)	5(4)	8+2(5)	10(5)	3(4)	8+3(5)	–	–
14	4/6	Ipswich	H	W57-33	8(4)	9(5)	11+3(5)	6(4)	13(5)	8+1(4)	2(3)	–	–
15	11/6	Belle Vue	H	W46-44	8(4)	3(5)	9+1(5)	6+1(4)	14(5)	6+2(4)	–	–	0(3)
16	16/6	Wolverhampton	A	L44-46	17(6)	0(3)	11+1(5)	2+1(3)	6+2(6)	0(3)	–	8(4)	–
17	18/6	Peterborough	H	W53-37	12+1(5)	6+1(4)	6(4)	5(4)	14+1(5)	5+2(4)	–	–	5+3(4)
18	20/6	Peterborough	A	L42-48*	13+1(6)	4+2(5)	10+1(7)	–	9(5)	R/R	–	3(3)	3+3(4)
19	21/6	Coventry	A	W47-43*	12(5)	9(6)	–	–	11(5)	R/R	–	0(3)	15+3(11)
20	25/6	Wolverhampton	H	W47-43*	11(5)	8+1(6)	10(4)	3+1(3)	13(5)	1+1(4)	–	–	1(3)
21	2/7	Oxford	H	W46-44	14(5)	3(6)	14+2(6)	R/R	–	–	–	–	15+3(14)
22	9/7	Coventry	H	W52-38	14+1(5)	–	11+1(5)	R/R	13+1(5)	3(5)	–	–	11+2(10)
23	16/7	Eastbourne	H	W47-43	9+2(5)	6+1(6)	–	R/R	14+1(5)	–	–	–	18+3(14)
24	24/7	Ipswich	A	W51-39*	13+2(5)	–	R/R	–	–	–	–	8+3(6)	30+3(19)
25	28/7	Belle Vue	A	L43-47	9(5)	–	R/R	10(5)	–	–	–	3+2(5)	21+5(15)
26	11/8	Coventry	A	W47-43*	15(5)	11+1(5)	7(5)	4+1(4)	–	1(3)	–	4(4)	5+1(4)
27	29/8	Oxford	A	L28-62	–	4(4)	–	–	R/R	–	–	–	24+3(27)
28	13/9	Eastbourne	A	W47-43*	13+1(5)	–	–	2+1(4)	13+1(5)	–	–	–	19(16)

DETAILS OF OTHER RIDERS:

Match No. 7: Scott Courtney 0(3); Match No. 10: Ricky Ashworth 1(3); Match No. 11: Pavel Ondrasik 2(3); Match No. 15: Dan Warwick 0(3); Match No. 17: Olly Allen 5+3(4); Match No. 18: Steve Johnston 3+3(4) ; Match No. 19: Mikael Max 12+3(6); Steve Johnston 3(5); Match No. 20: Brent Werner 1(3); Match No. 21: Craig Watson 7+1(5); Scott Nicholls 6+1(4); Andrew Appleton

2+1(5); Match No. 22: Steve Masters 6+1(5); Glenn Cunningham 5+1(5); Match No. 23: Charlie Gjedde 9+1(5); Matej Ferjan 6+1(5); Brent Werner 3+1(4); Match No. 24: Sam Ermolenko 16+2(6); Jason Lyons 7(5); Craig Watson 5+1(5); Brent Werner 2(3); Match No. 25: Scott Nicholls 12+2(6); Daniel Nermark 6+3(5); Pavel Ondrasik 3(4); Match No. 26: Jason Lyons 5+1(4); Match No. 27: Craig Boyce 8(7); Adam Shields 8(7); Daniel Nermark 5+1(5); Tony Atkin 2+1(4); Steve Masters 1+1(4); Match No. 28: Jason Lyons 8(4); Antonio Lindback 7(4); Andrew Moore 3(4); Ricky Ashworth 1(4).

ELITE LEAGUE AVERAGES

Rider	Mts	Rds	Pts	Bon	Tot	Avge	Max
Leigh Adams	27	134	316	18	334	9.97	4 Full; 2 Paid
Tony Rickardsson	23	115	263	14	277	9.63	3 Paid
Lukas Dryml	22	103	205	15	220	8.54	–
Antonio Lindback	1	4	7	0	7	7.00	–
Bjarne Pedersen	21	86	112	15	127	5.91	–
Davey Watt	11	47	52	13	65	5.53	–
David Ruud	20	86	98	17	115	5.35	–
Krzysztof Kasprzak	21	92	96	12	108	4.70	–
André Compton	7	27	23	6	29	4.30	–
Scott Courtney	1	3	0	0	0	0.00	–
Dan Warwick	1	3	0	0	0	0.00	–
Guests	31	143	163	29	192	5.37	1 Paid

BRITISH LEAGUE CUP

(* Denotes bonus-point/aggregate victory)

No	DATE	OPPONENTS	H/A	RESULT	BOYCE	WATT	L.DRYML	RUUD	PEDERSEN	PRIMMER	COMPTON	WARWICK	WOODWARD	LINDBACK	ZETTERSTROM	OTHERS
1	15/4	Trelawny	A	W51-40	11(5)	8+2(4)	7+1(4)	9+2(5)	8+1(4)	4+1(4)	–	–	–	–	–	4+1(4)
2	23/4	Trelawny	H	W52-38*	–	–	12(5)	8+2(4)	15(5)	4(4)	9+1(4)	1+1(4)	3(4)	–	–	–
3	1/6	Newport	A	W47½-42½	8(5)	15(6)	R/R	–	13½(6)	6(5)	–	2+1(4)	3+2(4)	–	–	–
4	30/7	Exeter	H	W58-32	14+1(5)	–	10+2(4)	–	10(4)	3(4)	–	2+1(3)	–	19+2(7)	–	0(3)
5	1/8	Somerset	A	W50-39	14+1(5)	8(4)	–	13+1(5)	–	4(4)	–	–	2(5)	–	9+2(4)	0(3)
6	4/8	Exeter	A	L31-59	8(6)	1+1(3)	–	–	–	4(4)	–	2+1(3)	2+1(4)	–	9(6)	5+1(4)
7	6/8	Newport	H	W49-41*	–	–	–	–	8(6)	10+2(4)	–	1(3)	–	14(5)	–	16+1(11)
8	20/8	Wolverhampton	H	L44-46	4(4)	–	–	9(4)	14(5)	3(4)	–	0(3)	–	13+1(6)	–	1+1(4)
9	25/8	Somerset	H	W51-39*	13(5)	–	–	–	10(4)	6+1(5)	–	1+1(4)	–	15(5)	–	6(8)
10	15/9	Wolverhampton	A	L37-56	10(6)	–	–	–	–	2(3)	–	–	–	19(6)	–	6+2(15)
11	27/9	Workington	A	W50-40	11+2(6)	9+2(4)	–	–	–	5(4)	–	–	8(4)	14(5)	–	3+1(7)
12	8/10	Workington	H	W57-33*	9+1(4)	–	–	14(5)	–	4+1(4)	–	–	10+1(4)	12+2(5)	–	8+1(8)
13	13/10	Belle Vue	A	W49-41	3(4)	11(5)	–	6+1(5)	11(4)	–	–	–	7+1(4)	11(5)	–	0(3)
14	15/10	Belle Vue	H	W46-44*	7+1(5)	2+2(3)	–	10(5)	8+1(5)	–	–	–	6+2(4)	11(4)	–	2+1(4)
15	19/10	Eastbourne	A	L42-48	–	–	–	3(3)	10(6)	4(5)	–	–	–	7(4)	–	18(12)
16	29/10	Eastbourne	H	W56-34*	9+1(4)	–	–	6+1(4)	15(5)	5(4)	–	–	–	4+2(4)	12(5)	5+3(4)

NOTE: Lukas Dryml is not credited with a paid maximum in the home match versus Exeter, as he missed a programmed ride (in heat 5) through a two-minute exclusion.

DETAILS OF OTHER RIDERS:

Match No. 1: Scott Courtney 4+1(4); Match No. 4: Simon Walker 0(3); Match No. 5: Simon Walker 0(3); Match No. 6: Graham Jones 5+1(4); Match No. 7: Leigh Adams 12(5); Craig Taylor 3(4); Dean Felton 1+1(3); Match No. 8: Danny Norton 1+1(4); Match No. 9: Scott Pegler 5(4); Justin Elkins 1(4); Match No. 10: Daniel Davidsson 5+1(5); Wayne Broadhurst 1+1(4); Robert Hollingworth 0(3); Matt Cambridge 0(3); Match No. 11: Daniel Davidsson 3+1(4); Karl Langley 0(3); Match No. 12: Daniel Davidsson 7+1(4); Scott Pegler 1(4); Match No. 13: Wayne Broadhurst 0(3); Match No. 14: Scott Pegler 2+1(4); Match No. 15: Leigh Adams 15(5); Ricky Ashworth 2(4); Scott Pegler 1(3); Match No. 16: Ricky Ashworth 5+3(4).

GOLDEN DOUBLE RIDES:

Match No. 10: Magnus Zetterstrom's total includes 6 points from a golden double ride.

BRITISH LEAGUE CUP AVERAGES

Rider	Mts	Rds	Pts	Bon	Tot	Avge	Max
André Compton	2	8	19	3	22	11.00	1 Paid
Leigh Adams	2	10	27	0	27	10.80	1 Full
Magnus Zetterstrom	11	56	136	5	141	10.07	1 Full
Lukas Dryml	3	13	29	3	32	9.85	–
Bjarne Pedersen	9	44	104½	2	106½	9.68	2 Full
Antonio Lindback	7	31	61	8	69	8.90	1 Paid
David Ruud	10	44	88	7	95	8.64	–
Davey Watt	7	29	54	7	61	8.41	–
Craig Boyce	13	64	121	7	128	8.00	2 Paid
Graham Jones	1	4	5	1	6	6.00	–
Daniel Davidsson	3	13	15	3	18	5.54	–
Ricky Ashworth	2	8	7	3	10	5.00	–
Scott Courtney	1	4	4	1	5	5.00	–
Tony Primmer	14	60	62	3	65	4.33	–
Craig Taylor	1	4	3	0	3	3.00	–
Cameron Woodward	5	20	11	3	14	2.80	–
Dean Felton	1	3	1	1	2	2.67	–
Scott Pegler	4	15	9	1	10	2.67	–
Dan Warwick	6	21	8	5	13	2.48	–
Danny Norton	1	4	1	1	2	2.00	–
Wayne Broadhurst	2	7	1	1	2	1.14	–
Justin Elkins	1	4	1	0	1	1.00	–
Matt Cambridge	1	3	0	0	0	0.00	–
Robert Hollingworth	1	3	0	0	0	0.00	–
Karl Langley	1	3	0	0	0	0.00	–
Simon Walker	2	6	0	0	0	0.00	–

NOTE: Magnus Zetterstrom's figures include one golden double ride (6 points), modified to normal score i.e. 3 points.

KNOCK-OUT CUP

(* Denotes aggregate victory)

No	DATE	OPPONENTS	H/A	RESULT	ADAMS	KASPRZAK	L.DRYML	PEDERSEN	RICKARDSSON	RUUD	WATT	LINDBACK	A.DRYML	OTHERS
1	18/4	Eastbourne	H	W56-34	14+1(5)	R/R	8+1(4)	9+2(5)	12+2(5)	3(1)	10+2(7)	–	–	–
2	18/4	Eastbourne †	A	L32-40*	8+1(3)	0(3)	3(4)	4+1(3)	9(4)	4(3)	4+1(4)	–	–	–
3	15/9	Oxford	H	W56-34	12+2(5)	–	–	8+3(4)	13+1(5)	–	1+1(4)	8(4)	7+1(4)	7+1(4)
4	10/10	Oxford	A	L44-46*	17(6)	–	–	2(4)	9(5)	–	2(3)	3(3)	4+1(4)	7+2(5)
5	23/10	Coventry	H	W46-42	12+1(5)	–	–	3+1(4)	13+1(5)	–	–	2+2(4)	5(4)	11+2(8)
6	25/10	Coventry	A	L44-46*	12+2(6)	–	–	8+1(5)	12+1(6)	–	–	1(2)	2(3)	9+1(8)

† Meeting abandoned after twelve heats, with the result standing

DETAILS OF OTHER RIDERS:

Match No. 3: David Norris 7+1(4); Match No. 4: Mark Loram 7+2(5); Match No. 5: Mark Loram 8(4); Garry Stead 3+2(4); Match No. 6: Mark Loram 6(5); Garry Stead 3+1(3).

OTHER MEETINGS

19 March: Challenge (first-leg)

    Poole 49 (Lukas Dryml 12+1; Bjarne Pedersen 9+2; Tony Rickardsson 8; Leigh Adams 7; Krzysztof Kasprzak 6; David Ruud 4+1; Davey Watt 3+1) Peterborough 41.

23 March: Challenge (second-leg)

    Peterborough 48 Poole 42 (Leigh Adams 14+1; Tony Rickardsson 10; Lukas Dryml 6; Bjarne Pedersen 5+1; Krzysztof Kasprzak 3; David Ruud 2+1; André Compton 2+1) – Poole won 91-89 on aggregate.

21 May: Inter-League Challenge

    Poole 56 (Leigh Adams 15; Lukas Dryml 14+1; Craig Boyce 11+1; David Ruud 7+2; Tony Primmer 6; Cameron Woodward 3+1; Dan Warwick 0) Workington 37.

7 June: Inter-League Challenge

    Workington 46 Poole 44 (Craig Boyce 13+1; Bjarne Pedersen 12; Cameron Woodward 6+1; Daniel Nermark 5+1; Daniel Davidsson 5; Tony Primmer 3; Dan Warwick 0).

3 September: Four-Team Tournament

    Scandinavia 33 (Tony Rickardsson 9; Magnus Zetterstrom 9; David Ruud 8; Antonio Lindback 7); Team Great Britain 26 (David Norris 9; Dean Barker 8; Joe Screen 6; Andrew Appleton 3); Poole 21 (Leigh Adams 11; Bjarne Pedersen 7; Daniel Nermark 3; Craig Boyce 0); Premier League 19 (Steve Masters 8; Craig Watson 5; Adrian Rymel 4; Mark Lemon 2).

22 September: Elite League Play-Off semi-final

    Poole 48 (Leigh Adams 14; Ales Dryml 9+1; Bjarne Pedersen 7+3; Antonio Lindback 7; Tony Rickardsson 7; Dean Barker 2; Brent Werner 2) Oxford 42.

29 September: Elite League Play-Off final (first-leg)

    Coventry 44 Poole 45 (Tony Rickardsson 11; Todd Wiltshire 9; Leigh Adams 7+2; Bjarne Pedersen 6; Davey Watt 4+3; Antonio Lindback 4; Ales Dryml 4).

6 October: Elite League Play-Off final (second-leg)

    Poole 55 (Tony Rickardsson 15; Ales Dryml 12+3; Leigh Adams 11+2; Mark Loram 8; Bjarne Pedersen 5; Antonio Lindback 4+1; Davey Watt 0) Coventry 35 – Poole won 100-79 on aggregate.

INDIVIDUAL MEETING

27 August: Craig Boyce Testimonial

Qualifying scores: Leigh Adams 10; Tony Rickardsson 10; Billy Hamill 10; Jason Crump 9; Joe Screen 8; Scott Nicholls 8; Craig Boyce 7; Greg Hancock 7; Stuart Robson 5; Steve Johnston 4; Sean Wilson 4; Travis McGowan 4; Shane Parker 3; Craig Watson 2; Todd Wiltshire 2; Sam Ermolenko 2; Jason Lyons 1; Lee Herne 0; Semi-Final: 1st Crump; 2nd Hamill; 3rd Nicholls; 4th Screen; Final: 1st Crump; 2nd Adams; 3rd Hamill; 4th Rickardsson.

WOLVERHAMPTON PARRYS INTERNATIONAL WOLVES

NOTE: The information below relates only to the main Wolverhampton team. For details of the second side, please refer to the Conference League section.

ADDRESS: Monmore Green Stadium, Sutherland Avenue, Wolverhampton, West Midlands.
PROMOTERS: Chris Van Straaten, John Woolridge & Terry Gough.
TRACK LENGTH: 264 metres.
FIRST MEETING: 30 May 1928.
YEARS OF OPERATION: 1928-30 Open; 1950 Open; 1951 National League Division Three; 1952 Southern League; 1953-54 National League Division Two; 1961-64 Provincial League; 1965-67 British League; 1968-74 British League Division One; 1975-80 British League; 1981 National League; 1984-90 British League; 1991-94 British League Division One; 1995-96 British Premier League; 1997-03 British Elite League.

CLUB HONOURS

LEAGUE CHAMPIONS: 1963, 1991, 1996, 2002.
PREMIERSHIP WINNERS: 1992, 1997.
GOLD CUP WINNERS: 1992.
KNOCK-OUT CUP WINNERS: 1996.

RIDER ROSTER 2003

ALLEN, Olly   b. 27 May 1982, Norwich, Norfolk.
BRITISH CAREER: (1997) Peterborough (AL); (1998) Mildenhall, Norfolk, Peterborough, Arena-Essex; (1999-01) Swindon; (2002) Swindon, Peterborough; (2003) Swindon, Wolverhampton.
BRAIDFORD, Steve   b. 31 December 1985, Maidstone, Kent.
BRITISH CAREER: (2002) Wolverhampton (CT), Isle of Wight, Wimbledon; (2003) Wolverhampton (CL & BLC), King's Lynn (BLC).
BROADHURST, Wayne   b. 28 February 1967, Minsterley, Shropshire.
BRITISH CAREER: (1987) Coventry; (1988) Coventry, Stoke; (1989) Coventry;

(1999) Stoke, Workington; (2000) Stoke; (2001) Wolverhampton, Stoke; (2002) Mildenhall; (2003) Mildenhall, Wolverhampton, Poole (BLC), Belle Vue (BLC).

BURROWS, Mark   *b. 10 June 1964, Sheffield, South Yorkshire.*
BRITISH CAREER: (1984) Scunthorpe, Sheffield; (1985) Scunthorpe, Edinburgh; (1986) Edinburgh; (1987) Middlesbrough; (1992) Glasgow, Middlesbrough; (1993) Middlesbrough; (1994) Buxton, Cleveland, Middlesbrough, Belle Vue, Coventry; (1995) Buxton, Long Eaton, Middlesbrough, Hull; (1996) Buxton; (1997-01) Stoke; (2002) Stoke, Belle Vue; (2003) Stoke (CT), Wimbledon, Coventry (BLC), Wolverhampton (BLC), Eastbourne (BLC), Belle Vue (BLC).

CARTER, Wayne   *b. 19 December 1970, Halifax, West Yorkshire.*
BRITISH CAREER: (1989) Mildenhall, Wolverhampton; (1990) Wolverhampton; (1991) Wolverhampton, Middlesbrough; (1992) Wolverhampton; (1993) Middlesbrough; (1994-95) Wolverhampton; (1996) Belle Vue, Middlesbrough; (1997) Skegness, Isle of Wight, Peterborough, Belle Vue, Wolverhampton, Bradford; (1998-99) Isle of Wight; (2000) Wolverhampton; (2001) Belle Vue, Berwick; (2002) Coventry, Newcastle; (2003) Wolverhampton (BLC), Edinburgh.

ERMOLENKO, Sam   *b. 23 November 1960, Maywood, California, USA.*
BRITISH CAREER: (1983-84) Poole; (1986-95) Wolverhampton; (1996) Sheffield; (1997) Belle Vue; (1998) Wolverhampton; (1999) Hull; (2000-01) Wolverhampton; (2002) Belle Vue; (2003) Wolverhampton.

FELTON, Dean   *b. 18 August 1969, Wolverhampton, West Midlands.*
BRITISH CAREER: (1994) Buxton, Oxford, Ipswich; (1995-96) Buxton; (1997) Buxton, Stoke, Edinburgh, Skegness, Long Eaton, Shuttle Cubs; (1998) Stoke; (1999) Berwick, Glasgow; (2000) Buxton, Berwick; (2001) Stoke, Buxton, Edinburgh, Berwick; (2002) Carmarthen; (2003) Carmarthen, Belle Vue (BLC), Poole (BLC), Eastbourne (BLC), Wolverhampton (BLC).

FINLOW, Rob   *b. 27 May 1984, Bromsgrove, Hereford & Worcester.*
BRITISH CAREER: (1999) Newport (CL); (2000) Newport (CL), Buxton; (2001) Newport (CL & PL); (2002) Newport (CL & PL), Wolverhampton (CT), Somerset; (2003) Wolverhampton (CL & BLC), Somerset, Stoke (KOC), Buxton (CT).

GRIEVES, James   *b. 28 September 1974, Paisley, Scotland.*
BRITISH CAREER: (1991-95) Glasgow; (1996-97) Wolverhampton; (1998) Wolverhampton, Berwick; (1999) Edinburgh; (2000-02) Glasgow; (2003) Glasgow, Wolverhampton.

HOWE, David   *b. 1 March 1982, Leicester, Leicestershire.*
BRITISH CAREER: (1997) Peterborough (AL); (1998) Peterborough, Norfolk; (1999-01) Peterborough; (2002-03) Wolverhampton.

JENSEN, Jesper B.   *b. 14 October 1977, Esbjerg, Denmark.*
BRITISH CAREER: (1997-03) Wolverhampton.

JONES, Graham   *b. 5 May 1963, Oswestry, Shropshire.*
BRITISH CAREER: (1984-87) Stoke; (1988) Stoke, Belle Vue, Reading, Sheffield, Wolverhampton, King's Lynn, Ipswich; (1989-93) Wolverhampton; (1994) Middlesbrough; (1995) Hull; (1996) Hull, Middlesbrough; (2003) Wolverhampton (CL & BLC), Stoke (CT), Coventry (BLC), Belle Vue (BLC), Eastbourne (BLC), Poole (BLC).

WOLVERHAMPTON WOLVES: back row, left to right: Olly Allen, Peter Karlsson, Peter Adams (Team Manager), David Howe, Sam Ermolenko. On bike: Mikael Karlsson. Front, kneeling: Adam Skornicki, Chris Neath.

KARLSSON, Magnus *b. 28 December 1981, Gullspang, Sweden.*
BRITISH CAREER: (2002) Edinburgh; (2003) Edinburgh, Wolverhampton.

KARLSSON, Peter *b. 17 December 1969, Gullspang, Sweden.*
BRITISH CAREER: (1990) Wolverhampton; (1992-97) Wolverhampton; (1999) Wolverhampton; (2000) Peterborough; (2001) King's Lynn, Belle Vue; (2002-03) Wolverhampton.

LINDGREN, Fredrik *b. 15 September 1985, Orebro, Sweden.*
BRITISH CAREER: (2003) Wolverhampton.

MAX, Mikael *(formerly Mikael Karlsson)* *b. 21 August 1973, Gullspang, Sweden.*
BRITISH CAREER: (1993-94) Wolverhampton; (1996-99) Wolverhampton; (2001-03) Wolverhampton.

NEATH, Chris *b. 29 January 1982, Worcester, Hereford & Worcester.*
BRITISH CAREER: (1998-99) Newport (CL & PL); (2000-01) Newport; (2002-03) Swindon, Wolverhampton.

PRIEST, Luke *b. 18 June 1985, Birmingham, West Midlands.*
BRITISH CAREER: (2000) Ashfield, Owlerton; (2001) Sheffield (CL), Boston; (2002) Sheffield (CL), Wolverhampton (CT); (2003) Sheffield (CL & PL), Stoke (CT & PL), Workington, Exeter, Newport (BLC), Arena-Essex, Wolverhampton (BLC), Belle Vue (BLC).

SKORNICKI, Adam *b. 22 October 1976, Wolsztyn, Poland.*
BRITISH CAREER: (2000-03) Wolverhampton.

STEAD, Simon *b. 25 April 1982, Sheffield, South Yorkshire.*
BRITISH CAREER: (1997) Peterborough (AL); (1998) Peterborough (PL), Buxton; (1999-01) Sheffield; (2002) Sheffield, Peterborough; (2003) Workington, Wolverhampton.

STEVENS, Jaye *b. 8 February 1982, Newcastle, New South Wales, Australia.*
BRITISH CAREER: (2003) Wolverhampton (BLC).

SKY SPORTS ELITE LEAGUE

(* Denotes bonus-point victory)

No	DATE	OPPONENTS	H/A	RESULT	MAX	HOWE	ERMOLENKO	SKORNICKI	P. KARLSSON	NEATH	ALLEN	GRIEVES	M. KARLSSON	STEAD	OTHERS
1	25/3	Eastbourne	A	L42-47	14+1(6)	5(4)	5(4)	5+2(4)	9+1(6)	2(3)	2+2(3)	–	–	–	–
2	28/3	Peterborough	A	L37-53	6+1(5)	6(5)	3(4)	5(4)	12+1(6)	2(3)	3(3)	–	–	–	–
3	31/3	Peterborough	H	W53-37*	14+1(5)	R/R	5+1(4)	8+1(5)	10+2(5)	13+1(7)	–	3+1(4)	–	–	–
4	4/4	Oxford	A	L32-58	9(6)	R/R	5(5)	4+1(5)	9(6)	–	2+2(3)	3+1(5)	–	–	–
5	7/4	Poole	H	D45-45	10(5)	R/R	5(4)	10(5)	8+2(5)	8+1(7)	–	4+1(4)	–	–	–
6	10/4	Ipswich	A	L43-47	14(6)	R/R	2+1(3)	6+1(5)	15+2(6)	–	5(5)	1(4)	–	–	–
7	20/4	Peterborough	A	L32-58	3(4)	5(5)	8+3(6)	1(3)	13(6)	0(3)	2+1(3)	–	–	–	–
8	28/4	Ipswich	H	W49-41*	11(5)	3+2(4)	7+1(4)	6(4)	10+2(5)	–	–	9+2(5)	3+1(3)	–	–
9	5/5	Belle Vue	H	W48-42	9+2(5)	6+1(4)	8+1(4)	5+1(4)	12(5)	6(4)	2+1(4)	–	–	–	–
10	12/5	Oxford	H	W53-37	14(5)	7+2(4)	7+1(4)	4(4)	13+2(5)	5+1(4)	3+1(4)	–	–	–	–

SKY SPORTS ELITE LEAGUE continued

No	DATE	OPPONENTS	H/A	RESULT	MAX	HOWE	ERMOLENKO	SKORNICKI	P. KARLSSON	NEATH	ALLEN	GRIEVES	M. KARLSSON	STEAD	OTHERS
11	14/5	Poole	A	L32-58	10(6)	2+1(4)	2(4)	1(3)	8(5)	3+1(4)	6+1(5)	–	–	–	–
12	24/5	Coventry	A	L41-49	12+3(6)	10(6)	1(5)	R/R	13(6)	0(3)	–	5(4)	–	–	–
13	2/6	Eastbourne	H	W48-42*	14+1(6)	7+1(5)	4+1(5)	R/R	15(5)	5(5)	–	3+2(4)	–	–	–
14	5/6	Ipswich	A	W50-40	11+2(5)	5(4)	9(4)	9+1(4)	12+1(5)	–	–	4+2(5)	0(3)	–	–
15	9/6	Peterborough	H	W53-37	11(4)	R/R	11(5)	6+3(6)	13+2(5)	11+2(7)	1(4)	–	–	–	–
16	16/6	Poole	H	W46-44	12(5)	6+4(4)	3+1(4)	5+1(3)	11+2(5)	8(6)	–	–	–	–	1(3)
17	23/6	Coventry	H	W51-39*	9(5)	8+1(4)	6+1(4)	7(5)	8+1(4)	–	–	7+2(4)	–	6+1(4)	–
18	25/6	Poole	A	L43-47	8+2(5)	9+1(5)	2(3)	7(4)	11+2(6)	–	2(3)	–	–	4+1(4)	–
19	7/7	Ipswich	H	W60-30*	12+1(5)	12(4)	8+1(4)	6+1(4)	10+3(5)	8+1(4)	–	4+1(4)	–	–	–
20	19/7	Eastbourne †	A	L38-46	4+3(4)	–	11(5)	R/R	9(4)	0(3)	–	–	–	–	14+1(12)
21	21/7	Belle Vue	H	W47-43	11(5)	–	5+1(4)	2(3)	13+1(5)	0(3)	9+2(6)	–	–	–	7+1(4)
22	11/8	Eastbourne	H	W53-37*	16+2(6)	R/R	2(5)	7(5)	14+1(5)	2(3)	–	–	12+1(6)	–	–
23	13/8	Belle Vue	A	L41-49	8(5)	–	3(4)	3(4)	13(6)	1(3)	–	–	5+3(4)	–	8+1(4)
24	16/8	Coventry	A	L41-49	8(5)	–	3+1(3)	4+1(4)	9+1(6)	2+1(3)	10+2(5)	–	–	–	5+1(4)
25	18/8	Oxford	H	W54-36	17(6)	R/R	11+4(6)	9+1(4)	–	–	5+1(5)	–	8+1(5)	–	4+1(4)
26	1/9	Coventry	H	W49-41	17(6)	R/R	6+1(5)	8(5)	10+2(5)	0(3)	–	–	8+2(6)	–	–
27	3/9	Oxford	A	L28-62	6(7)	R/R	8(6)	3+1(4)	4(5)	–	–	–	3(4)	4(4)	–
28	29/9	Belle Vue	A	L39-51	12(5)	3+1(4)	4+1(4)	8+1(5)	5+1(4)	2(4)	–	–	–	–	5(4)

† Meeting abandoned after fourteen heats, with the result standing

DETAILS OF OTHER RIDERS:

Match No. 16: Steve Masters 1(3); Match No. 20: Brent Werner 8+1(7); Daniel Nermark 6(5); Match No. 21: Daniel Nermark 7+1(4); Match No. 23: Kenneth Bjerre 8+1(4); Match No. 24: Daniel Nermark 5+1(4); Match No. 25: Lee Richardson 4+1(4); Match No. 28: Fredrik Lindgren 5(4).

ELITE LEAGUE AVERAGES

Rider	Mts	Rds	Pts	Bon	Tot	Avge	Max
Peter Karlsson	27	141	289	29	318	9.02	1 Full; 3 Paid
Mikael Max	28	148	302	19	321	8.68	2 Paid
Simon Stead	7	33	47	9	56	6.79	–
David Howe	15	66	94	14	108	6.55	1 Full
Adam Skornicki	25	106	139	16	155	5.85	–
Sam Ermolenko	28	122	154	20	174	5.70	–
James Grieves	9	40	43	11	54	5.40	–
Olly Allen	12	48	47	13	60	5.00	–
Fredrik Lindgren	1	4	5	0	5	5.00	–
Chris Neath	20	82	78	8	86	4.20	–
Magnus Karlsson	5	18	11	2	13	2.89	–
Guests	7	31	39	5	44	5.68	–

BRITISH LEAGUE CUP

(* Denotes bonus-point/aggregate victory)

No	DATE	OPPONENTS	H/A	RESULT	NEATH	CARTER	HOWE	ERMOLENKO	BRAIDFORD	JONES	SKORNICKI	FINLOW	ALLEN	P. KARLSSON	MAX	OTHERS
1	30/3	Newport	A	L39-51	9(5)	4+2(4)	3(1)	9(5)	3(6)	11(6)	–	–				0(3)
2	8/4	Trelawny	A	L42-48	–	1+1(3)	–	8+2(6)	–	7+1(4)	3+1(4)	2(3)	7+1(4)	14(6)	–	–
3	14/4	Somerset	H	W57-33	–	5+1(4)	11+1(4)	15(5)	6(4)	5+2(4)	13+1(5)	2+1(4)	–	–	–	–
4	23/5	Somerset	A	W57-33*	–	–	10+1(4)	13+1(5)	2+1(4)	6+2(4)	–	3(4)	10+2(4)	–	13+1(5)	–
5	20/8	Poole	A	W46-44	–	–	–	12(5)	–	9+1(5)	10+1(5)	2(4)	–	–	–	13+6(11)
6	25/8	Exeter	A	W50-40	–	–	–	13(5)	–	5(4)	7+2(4)	1+1(4)	–	–	12(4)	12+2(9)
7	25/8	Newport	H	W54-36*	–	–	–	12+1(5)	–	9+1(5)	6(4)	3+1(4)	–	–	15(5)	9+2(7)
8	25/8	Exeter	H	W65-25*	–	–	–	11+1(4)	–	10+2(4)	14+1(5)	3+2(4)	–	–	12(4)	15+5(9)
9	8/9	Trelawny	H	W60-27*	–	–	–	14+1(5)	–	11+1(5)	8(4)	1(2)	–	–	15(5)	11+5(8)
10	15/9	Poole	H	W56-37*	–	–	–	11(5)	–	7+1(4)	9+2(4)	5+1(4)	14(5)	–	–	10+4(8)
11	22/9	Edinburgh	H	W47-42	–	–	12+3(5)	7(4)	–	0(1)	–	0(4)	–	–	15(5)	13+2(11)
12	26/9	Edinburgh	A	W51-39*	8+1(4)	–	6(4)	12+2(5)	–	8+1(7)	–	0(1)	–	–	15(5)	2(4)
13	1/10	Eastbourne	H	L43-46	5+2(4)	–	11(5)	5(4)	–	6+2(5)	10(5)	–	–	–	–	6+2(7)
14	12/10	Eastbourne	A	L42-51	6+3(4)	–	15+1(6)	8(5)	–	–	5+2(4)	–	–	–	–	8(11)

DETAILS OF OTHER RIDERS:

Match No. 1: Jaye Stevens 0(3); Match No. 5: Jesper B. Jensen 6+2(4); Simon Stead 4+2(4); Wayne Broadhurst 3+2(3); Match No. 6: Magnus Karlsson 11+1(5); Wayne Broadhurst 1+1(4); Match No. 7: Magnus Karlsson 7+1(4); Wayne Broadhurst 2+1(3); Match No. 8: Magnus Karlsson 11+4(5); Wayne Broadhurst 4+1(4); Match No. 9: James Grieves 7+4(4); Mark Burrows 4+1(4); Match No. 10: Simon Stead 7+3(4); Dean Felton 3+1(4); Match No. 11: James Grieves 8+1(4); Mark Burrows 5+1(7); Match No. 12: Mark Burrows 2(4); Match No. 13: Fredrik Lindgren 5+2(4); Mark Burrows 1(3); Match No. 14: Fredrik Lindgren 7(4); Mark Burrows 1(4); Luke Priest 0(3).

GOLDEN DOUBLE RIDES:

Match No. 14: David Howe's total includes 6 points from a golden double ride.

BRITISH LEAGUE CUP AVERAGES

Rider	Mts	Rds	Pts	Bon	Tot	Avge	Max
Mikael Max	7	33	97	1	98	11.88	6 Full
Peter Karlsson	2	11	28	0	28	10.18	–
Olly Allen	2	8	17	3	20	10.00	1 Paid
James Grieves	2	8	15	5	20	10.00	–
Magnus Karlsson	3	14	29	6	35	10.00	1 Paid
David Howe	7	29	65	6	71	9.79	2 Paid
Sam Ermolenko	14	68	150	8	158	9.29	1 Full; 2 Paid
Adam Skornicki	10	44	85	10	95	8.64	1 Paid
Jesper B. Jensen	1	4	6	2	8	8.00	–
Chris Neath	4	17	28	6	34	8.00	–
Simon Stead	2	8	11	5	16	8.00	–
Graham Jones	13	58	94	14	108	7.45	1 Paid
Fredrik Lindgren	2	8	12	2	14	7.00	–

Rider	Mts	Rds	Pts	Bon	Tot	Avge	Max
Wayne Carter	3	11	10	4	14	5.09	–
Wayne Broadhurst	4	14	10	5	15	4.29	–
Dean Felton	1	4	3	1	4	4.00	–
Steven Braidford	3	14	11	1	12	3.43	–
Rob Finlow	11	38	22	6	28	2.95	–
Mark Burrows	5	22	13	2	15	2.73	–
Luke Priest	1	3	0	0	0	0.00	–
Jaye Stevens	1	3	0	0	0	0.00	–

NOTE: David Howe's figures include one golden double ride (6 points), modified to normal score i.e. 3 points.

KNOCK-OUT CUP

(* Denotes aggregate victory)

No	DATE	OPPONENTS	H/A	RESULT	MAX	HOWE	ERMOLENKO	SKORNICKI	P. KARLSSON	GRIEVES	ALLEN	NEATH	LINDGREN	OTHERS
1	18/4	Belle Vue	A	L41-49	13(6)	3(4)	6+1(4)	5(4)	12+2(6)	0(3)	–	–	–	2+1(3)
2	21/4	Belle Vue	H	W57-33*	13+1(5)	8+2(4)	11+2(5)	7+1(4)	9+2(4)	–	5(4)	4+1(4)	–	–
3	8/10	Coventry	H	W48-41	13(5)	6(4)	5+1(4)	3+2(4)	9+1(5)	–	–	5(3)	7+1(5)	–
4	11/10	Coventry	A	L40-50	12(6)	9+2(6)	3(3)	3(3)	6+2(4)	–	–	3(3)	4+1(5)	–

DETAIL OF OTHER RIDERS:

Match No. 1: Lee Dicken 2+1(3).

OTHER MEETINGS

16 March: Peter Karlsson Testimonial

Wolverhampton 50 (Peter Karlsson 11+1; Mikael Max 10+1; David Howe 7+1; Adam Skornicki 7; Daniel Nermark 6+4; Sam Ermolenko 6+1; Magnus Karlsson 3+1) Kaparna 40 (Jaroslaw Hampel 10+1; Ryan Sullivan 10; Tony Rickardsson 7+1; Joonas Kylmakorpi 6+1; Kim Jansson 3; Rafal Dobrucki 2; Tomasz Gapinski 2). Run-off for GM engine: First Semi-Final: 1st Kylmakorpi; 2nd Hampel; 3rd Rickardsson; 4th Sullivan; Second Semi-Final: 1st Max; 2nd P. Karlsson; 3rd Nermark; 4th Howe; Final: 1st Kylmakorpi; 2nd Max; 3rd P. Karlsson; 4th Hampel.

24 March: Challenge

Wolverhampton 44 (Mikael Max 14+1; Peter Karlsson 13+1; Sam Ermolenko 7; David Howe 5+2; Magnus Karlsson 3+2; James Grieves 2; Adam Skornicki 0) Coventry 46.

8 July: Under-21 International

Great Britain 57 (David Howe 15; Simon Stead 11+1; Andrew Moore 8+1; Chris Neath 8+1; Edward Kennett 7+3; Ricky Ashworth 7; James Brundle 1+1) Sweden 33 (Antonio Lindback 12; Daniel Davidsson 7+2; Peter Ljung 6; Fredrik Lindgren 5; Jonas Davidsson 1+1; Mattias Nilsson 1+1; Erik Andersson 1).

16 July: Elite League

Wolverhampton 30 (Simon Stead 6+2; Sam Ermolenko 6+1; David Howe 6; Mikael Max 5; Peter Karlsson 5; Chris Neath 2+1; Adam Skornicki 0) Coventry 36 – meeting abandoned after heat eleven.

INDIVIDUAL MEETING

20 October: Ladbroke Olympique

    1st Mikael Max 12; 2nd Peter Karlsson 11; 3rd Leigh Adams (after run-off) 10; Sam Ermolenko 10; Billy Janniro 10; David Howe 9; Charlie Gjedde 9; Adam Skornicki 9; Scott Nicholls 8; Stefan Danno 8; Magnus Karlsson 8; Fredrik Lindgren 6; Jan Staechmann 4; Norbert Magosi 3; Richard Juul 2; Chris Neath 1; Dean Felton (res) 0.

PREMIER LEAGUE 2003

RACING DIARY OF THE SEASON

MARCH

15 Berwick open up with a challenge against Swedish tourists Valsarna, and there is bad news in the home camp as popular Dane Claus Kristensen receives ligament damage to his right ankle in a heavy track spill. The match results in a 47-43 victory for the visitors, with Sam Ermolenko topping their scoring on 14 points. Workington also open up, beating Newcastle 50-40 in the first British League Cup (Group C) fixture, with Carl Stonehewer heading their victory charge on a 13-point total.

16 Up in Scotland, Glasgow take to the track at 1 p.m. with a challenge fixture against Valsarna, but the Tigers are no match for their Swedish opponents, suffering a 52-38 reverse. At Newport, the home side drop behind from the start, and try as they might, cannot get on level terms as Reading claim a 46-44 victory in the M4 Trophy. Unfortunately, the Racers lose Phil Morris after a heat-five crash, their inspirational skipper suffering a knock to the knee. Newcastle stage the return leg of their British League Cup (Group C) encounter against Workington, only just managing to eke out a 46-43 victory, helped enormously by 13 points from Danish sensation Kenneth Bjerre. Sheffield begin their season with a thriller against Stoke in the first-leg of the Easy-Rider/Pirtek Cup, the meeting going right to the wire, before ending all-square at 45-45.

17 Reading, minus the injured Phil Morris, open their twenty-ninth season of track action at Smallmead, with Newport supplying dogged opposition as the sides fight out a 45-45 draw in the M4 Trophy.

18 British League Cup (Group D) action is the order of the day as the Isle of Wight gain a thrilling 47-43 victory over Elite-League opponents Oxford, spearheaded by 13 points from brilliant Aussie Adam Shields. King's Lynn start with a challenge match against Swedish tourists Kaparna, and the Saddlebow Road raceway serves up a real cracker as the homesters narrowly win 46-44.

19 Following a traumatic winter, Somerset get back to the business of track action with a 51-39 win over Kaparna.

20 Swindon begin their fifty-fifth successive season of action at Blunsdon, with a pulsating 45-45 draw against Newport in the M4 Trophy. Sheffield hosts the Steel City Championship, and it's a victory for Workington's Chris Collins in the grand final from Trevor Harding, Ben Wilson and James Brundle.

22 Utilizing the rider-replacement facility for Claus Kristensen, Berwick clinch a narrow 47-43 victory over Newcastle in the first-leg of the Tyne-Tweed Trophy, with the fast-starting Paul Bentley leading the way on 14+2 points. Unfortunately, the Bandits suffer misfortune during the match when Czech favourite Adrian Rymel suffers a broken shoulder in a twelfth-heat spill. Workington get down to Knock-Out Cup business, with the first-leg of their preliminary-round tie against King's Lynn. The away side supply dogged resistance, restricting the Comets to a 46-43 victory as Carl Stonehewer tops the Derwent Park scoreboard on 12+1 points. Stoke become the sixth team to face Swedish touring side Kaparna, and although the visitors track a makeshift line-up, it's a cracking meeting, with the Potters narrowly winning 47-43.

23 Queensway Meadows is bathed in glorious sunshine as Newport defeat Swindon 50-40 in the M4 Trophy. Having lost at home the previous week, Glasgow make a better fist of it against their old rivals from Edinburgh, but the first-leg of the Spring Trophy still ends in a 46-44 defeat, despite a 17-point haul from George Stancl, and 15+1 from James Grieves. The second-leg of the Tyne-Tweed Trophy ends with Newcastle claiming a last-heat 5-1 for a 46-44 success over Berwick, but it's the Bandits who win narrowly on aggregate by 91 points to 89. The meeting is somewhat marred by a heat-eleven pile-up which leaves home rider Mick Powell suffering from a dislocated shoulder and three broken ribs.

24 Exeter begin another season of racing at their County Ground home by defeating Trelawny 54-39 in a British League Cup (Group E) encounter. Having first faced each other in 1971, Reading take on old rivals Swindon in the penultimate match for the M4 Trophy, with honours eventually ending even at 45-45 in a thrilling match.

25 Trelawny make a flying start to their third season at the Clay Country Moto Parc, blasting to a 63-27 success over Exeter in the British League Cup (Group E), inspired by a trio of maximum men in Matej Zagar (13+2), Steve Masters (13+2) and Chris Harris (12).

26 Hull charge to a 55-35 challenge-match win over Newcastle, led by tallies of a dozen apiece from Shaun Tacey and Garry Stead. King's Lynn hit Rye House for a 60-36 thrashing in the first-leg of the A10 Trophy at Saddlebow Road, with Shane Parker racing to a 15-point maximum, and Tomas Topinka also paid for the lot on 13+2. For the beleaguered Rockets, Scott Robson tops the pile on 11 points, with team manager John Sampford three times experimenting with the new tactical-joker golden double rule allowing a rider to gain extra points without having to go from a fifteen-metre handicap.

27 Sheffield turn on the power to defeat Hull 55-35 in a British League Cup (Group B) encounter at the Owlerton raceway. Swindon reveal top form to beat Reading 55-35 in the last match of the M4 Trophy, with Charlie Gjedde (15) and Olly Allen (11+1) attaining unbeaten scores. The result puts the homesters on top of the table, courtesy of a superior race-points difference; however, with all three teams finishing up with five points on the board, it is agreed to try and rerun the competition at a later date if fixtures (and weather) would allow.

28 Edinburgh cruise to a 53-37 win over old rivals Glasgow in the second-leg of the Spring Cup, thereby securing aggregate victory by 99 points to 81, with both Frede Schott and Peter Carr recording four-ride maximums for the Monarchs. In spite of wet weather, the Oak Tree Arena serves up its usual level of terrific racing, although Somerset suffer a 47-43 reverse at the hands of Exeter in a British League Cup (Group E) encounter. Premier League action is the order of the day at Purfleet, as Arena-Essex grab a 49-42 victory over highly-fancied Isle of Wight.

29 Despite injuries to key riders, patched-up Berwick manage to eke out a 47-42 victory over a determined Glasgow septet in the British League Cup (Group C). Rye House open their season with the second-leg of the A10 Trophy against King's Lynn, and despite racing to a 53-39 success, they lose 99-89 on aggregate. Workington and Edinburgh play out a 45-45 British League Cup (Group C) draw at Derwent Park, with the match marred by a frightening heat-eight crash that leaves visiting reserve Derek Sneddon suffering a broken left femur after being catapulted over the safety fence. That apart, Simon Stead is in breathtaking form for the Comets on his way to 12+1 points, with team-mate Carl Stonehewer leading him home for a last heat 5-1 to leave the sides all-square. Stoke defeat Sheffield 52-38 to lift the Easy-Rider/Pirtek Cup by an aggregate score of 97-83.

30   Newport defeat top-flight Champions Wolverhampton 51-39 in a British League Cup
     (Group E) encounter at Queensway Meadows, with vital contributions made by Frank
     Smart (12+2), Craig Watson (12+1) and Niels-Kristian Iversen (11). Glasgow suffer
     another setback as they lose 53-37 to Workington in the British League Cup (Group C)
     at their superfast Ashfield raceway. Newcastle race to a commanding 52-38 challenge-
     match success over Hull.

31   The last day of the month sees Seemond Stephens (13+1) and Michael Coles (13) lead the
     way as Exeter claim a 50-40 win over Newport in the British League Cup (Group E). At
     Smallmead, Reading lose 51-42 to higher-sphere opponents Eastbourne in the British
     League Cup (Group D), with Andrew Appleton having a great night to register 17 points,
     his tally including a winning golden double ride in the eighth heat. For the Eagles, both
     David Norris (15) and Dean Barker (11+1) show their class with unbeaten performances,
     while 2000 World Champion Mark Loram weighs in with 13. Incredibly, that means thirty-
     six fixtures have been raced at Premier League level during March, without a single rain-off!

APRIL

1   It had to happen sometime, although the timing was uncanny, as the Isle of Wight's league
     fixture against Arena-Essex becomes the first rained-off meeting of the season. It's dry in
     Cornwall, however, as Trelawny and Newport end up all-square at 45-45 in the British
     League Cup (Group E).

2   Solid-scoring Hull grab a 49-41 success over Stoke in the British League Cup (Group B).

3   Headed by top performances from guest Simon Stead (13), plus Scott Smith (12+1) and
     maximum-man André Compton (11+1), Sheffield fly the Premier League flag with a
     marvellous 50-42 victory over Belle Vue in the British League Cup (Group B). The British
     League Cup (Group D) action continues at Blunsdon as Swindon are held to a 45-45
     draw by the Isle of Wight in an exciting encounter.

4   Edinburgh cruise to a 53-37 victory over Berwick in the British League Cup (Group C),
     their scoring headed by Magnus Karlsson (12+1) and Frede Schott (12), with guest and
     former Monarch Kevin Little (12+2) proving best for the Bandits. Somerset suffer a
     second successive home defeat in the British League Cup (Group E), going down 49-42
     at the hands of Trelawny. Arena-Essex go on the rampage to thrash Exeter 63-27 in a
     Premier League match, with every member of the side paid for at least nine points thus:
     Leigh Lanham (13+1), Jason King (9+3), Kelvin Tatum (9+2), Henning Bager (9), Lee
     Herne (8+2), Joonas Kylmakorpi (8+2) and Andy Galvin (7+2). Interestingly, despite the
     score, Jason King is the only Hammer to register a maximum.

5   Berwick take Newcastle to the cleaners in the British League Cup (Group C), romping to
     a 62-30 success, with Michal Makovsky blasting to a five-ride maximum. League activity
     is on the menu at Rye House, and it's the homesters who claim a hard-fought
     48-42 success over Reading, with Brent Werner netting 10+2 points, and teenage
     sensation Edward Kennett scoring 9+2. Workington have little difficulty in defeating
     Glasgow 55-35 in the British League Cup (Group C). Stoke celebrate thirty years of racing
     at Loomer Road with a grand individual meeting, and fittingly it's long-serving Potter
     Paul Pickering who takes victory in the final from Robbie Kessler, Garry Stead and Jamie
     Smith. King's Lynn and Sheffield engage in an outstanding Premier League encounter at
     Saddlebow Road, with the homesters just shading it 46-44, thanks to a last heat 4-2 from
     their leading duo of maximum-man Shane Parker (15) and Tomas Topinka (11).

6   Newport thrash Somerset 61-35 in a Knock-Out Cup tie, with both Craig Watson (15) and Niels-Kristian Iversen (14+1) going through the card unbeaten for the Wasps. Following six previous losses, Glasgow finally win their first match of the season, beating Berwick 50-41 in the British League Cup (Group C). Newcastle slump to a 48-42 reverse against visiting Edinburgh in the British League Cup (Group C).

7   Exeter ease to a 54-36 win over Somerset in the British League Cup (Group E). Reading edge a narrow 46-44 league victory over Arena-Essex, thanks only to a last-heat 'fiver' from maximum-man Andrew Appleton (15) and skipper Phil Morris (10+1).

8   In the British League Cup (Group D), the Isle of Wight gain a comfortable 56-34 success over Reading, their scoring topped by maximum points from Danny Bird (15), while Ray Morton weighs in with 13+1. In the same competition (Group E), Trelawny pull off something of a surprise result, beating Wolverhampton 48-42, thanks to scintillating performances from Chris Harris (14) and Matej Zagar (13).

9   Hull slip to a surprise 46-44 defeat at the hands of visiting Somerset in the Premier League. King's Lynn ease through the preliminary round of the Knock-Out Cup, defeating Workington 52-43 for a 6-point overall win on aggregate, with maximum-man Tom P. Madsen (12), plus Tomas Topinka (13), Davey Watt (11) and Trevor Harding (10+3) hitting the main points for the Stars.

10 Sheffield brush King's Lynn aside by 57 points to 33 in the Premier League, led by a 15-point full house from André Compton. In the British League Cup (Group D), Swindon produce a solid team effort to defeat top-flighters Oxford 48-37, with Charlie Gjedde's brilliant 12-point haul at the top of the pile. The match actually finishes with a 48-41 scoreline on the night, but is subsequently amended as Lukasz Jankowski is deemed ineligible to ride for Oxford, his 4-point tally being deducted from their score.

11 Premier League action sees Arena-Essex have little difficulty in beating Reading 56-34, as Joonas Kylmakorpi hits a paid maximum (14+1). Edinburgh race to a 53-39 success over Workington in the British League Cup (Group C). Knock-Out Cup action at Somerset sees the Rebels lose 49-43 to Newport, despite the brave efforts of Mark Lemon (15).

12 Berwick inflict the first defeat of the season on Edinburgh, winning 52-38 in the British League Cup (Group C), thanks largely to a paid maximum from guest Davey Watt (11+1), plus major contributions from Paul Bentley (14) and Michal Makovsky (10+1). A tight British League Cup (Group A) clash at Hoddesdon ends in a 46-44 success for Rye House against Elite League Ipswich. Derwent Park throws up another thriller as Workington grab a 45-44 league win over Sheffield. Stoke overwhelm Hull 54-36 in the British League Cup (Group B), thanks to unbeaten tallies from Jan Staechmann (15) and Alan Mogridge (14+1), plus a 10-point haul from Paul Pickering.

13 Newport dig deep to overcome Trelawny 46-44 in the British League Cup (Group E), with Frank Smart (11) and Tony Atkin (10+1) leading their scoring, while Chris Harris produces a star performance in collecting a 15-point maximum for the visitors. Glasgow take victory for the second successive British League Cup (Group C) match at Ashfield, beating Newcastle 50-39.

14 Led by a dozen points from Michael Coles, and 11+1 from Seemond Stephens, Exeter open their Premier League account with a 49-41 win over Swindon. Newcastle suffer a second successive home loss, going down 46-44 at the hands of Glasgow in the British League Cup (Group C). There's more British League Cup (Group D) action at Smallmead as Reading lose 50-40 to the Isle of Wight, with the leading lights on the night being

home man Andrew Appleton (13), plus the visiting duo of Danny Bird (14) and maximum-man Adam Shields (13+2).

15 British League Cup (Group D) action sees the Isle of Wight defeat Swindon 49-41. In further British League Cup (Group E) fare, Trelawny go down to a 51-40 defeat at home to Elite League Poole.

16 Hull defeat King's Lynn 50-40 in the Premier League, with Garry Stead speeding to a full 15-point maximum for the Vikings.

17 Swindon survive a late rally from Trelawny to win an exciting Premier League encounter 48-42.

18 The first meeting of a hectic Good Friday results in a 46-44 win for Rye House in a Knock-Out Cup tie at Arena-Essex. Workington round off their home British League Cup (Group C) campaign with a 50-40 win against Berwick, their main points on the night supplied by the unbeaten Carl Stonehewer (14+1). Thanks to major contributions from Sean Wilson (13) and Ricky Ashworth (11), Sheffield claim a 50-40 success over Stoke in the British League Cup (Group B). Edinburgh secure a 47-43 win over Newcastle in the British League Cup (Group C). The Oak Tree Arena serves up another classic, but Somerset lose again, going down 48-42 to Swindon in the Premier League.

19 Berwick fail to stop Workington from winning 48-42 at Shielfield Park, the victorious visitors possessing three big players in paid-maximum scorer Simon Stead (14+1), plus Carl Stonehewer (14) and flying reserve Blair Scott (11+2). Thrilling Knock-Out Cup action sees Arena-Essex avenge their home defeat with a 46-44 success at Rye House, thereby leaving the sides all-square at 90 points apiece on aggregate. At Stoke, it's super action all the way in the British League Cup (Group B), as Sheffield grab a narrow 46-44 win, despite a five-ride maximum from home man and ex-Tiger Robbie Kessler.

20 At Queensway Meadows, Newport ease to a 49-41 league victory over Reading, with visiting skipper Phil Morris suffering a nasty arm injury in a heat-thirteen spill. Glasgow collect their fourth win in a row, defeating arch rivals Edinburgh 50-40 in the British League Cup (Group C). More British League Cup (Group C) activity at Brough Park results in Newcastle's first victory of the month, as they see off Berwick 51-39.

21 Bank Holiday action sees Exeter cruise to a 59-31 success over King's Lynn in an 11 a.m. Premier League encounter, with Michael Coles (14+1) unbeaten by an opponent. Despite the absence of Phil Morris, Reading wallop successive 5-1s in the last four races to defeat Hull 50-40 in an exciting Premier League fixture.

22 The Isle of Wight grab a 45-45 draw with Eastbourne in a thrilling British League Cup (Group D) match at Smallbrook Stadium, thanks to a last-heat 4-2 from Adam Shields and Danny Bird. There's terrific stuff at the Clay Country Moto Parc as visiting King's Lynn clinch a 46-44 league victory over Trelawny, thanks to a 4-2 from Tomas Topinka and Shane Parker in the final race.

23 Claus Kristensen returns for Berwick, as they secure a 50-40 league success at Hull. King's Lynn race to their second league win in two days, narrowly beating Arena-Essex 48-42 at Saddlebow Road, the bulk of their points coming courtesy of a four-ride full house from Davey Watt, plus double-figure tallies from Tomas Topinka (11+1) and Shane Parker (11).

24 Rain threatens to scupper the British Under-21 Championship at Sheffield, but the meeting goes ahead in difficult conditions, and eventually results in a third successive title for the all-action Simon Stead, who takes the 'A' final from Olly Allen, Edward Kennett

and Andrew Appleton. The 'B' final is won by Chris Harris ahead of Aidan Collins, Jamie Smith and Richie Hawkins.

25   Rain is the only victor as the three scheduled meetings are all postponed, namely Somerset v. Rye House, and Arena-Essex v. King's Lynn in the Premier League, plus Edinburgh v. Glasgow in the final British League Cup match of Group C.

26   Berwick suffer a humiliating 53-37 home league reverse at the hands of Sheffield. Rye House rack up a comfortable 55-35 league win over Exeter, their main men being teenager Edward Kennett (14+2) and the ever-battling Scott Robson (13+2). Workington overcome an early deficit to beat Newcastle 49-40 in the league at Derwent Park. King's Lynn complete a hat-trick of league victories in the space of five days, comfortably defeating Hull 58-32, with Shane Parker netting 13 points, while Davey Watt claims his second successive 12-point maximum. With heavy rain falling from darkened skies at Loomer Road, the Premier League fixture between Stoke and Somerset is abandoned after just one heat. The race results in a 5-1 advantage to the visitors, with home skipper Paul Pickering taking a hefty fall and suffering injuries to his leg and posterior.

27   Newport collect their second home league win, beating Rye House 51-39 at a slick Queensway Meadows. Possessing a high-scoring trio in four-ride maximum-man James Grieves, plus George Stancl (14) and veteran Les Collins (11+2), Glasgow get their Premier League campaign off to a flying start by defeating Stoke 50-40. Workington complete a quick-fire league double over Newcastle, winning a close encounter 46-44 at Brough Park.

28   Reading's mouth-watering British League Cup (Group D) fixture against arch-rivals Swindon unfortunately falls victim to persistent rain at lunchtime. An exciting see-saw battle sees Exeter finally clinch a 48-42 league victory over a determined Isle of Wight, thanks largely to a penultimate-heat 5-1 from Lee Smethills and Krister Marsh.

29   Danny Bird plunders a four-ride maximum as the Isle of Wight easily gain revenge over Exeter, winning 54-35 in the league. Trelawny's British League Cup (Group E) encounter with Somerset is called off due to early-evening rain.

30   Hull suffer another home loss, going down 48-42 to Edinburgh in a closely fought Premier League encounter. It's a second rain-off in two nights for Somerset, as their scheduled league fixture at King's Lynn provides only one winner.

MAY

1   The Championship of Great Britain semi-final is hosted by Swindon, and in a terrific finish, it's Danny Bird who emerges on top for a second successive year, with the home duo of Paul Fry and Chris Neath gleefully occupying the other podium positions.

2   Three league matches go by the wayside, thanks to bucketloads of rainfall, namely Edinburgh v. Exeter, Somerset v. Hull and Arena-Essex v. Trelawny.

3   Problems at Berwick, as the visiting Exeter riders fail to contest the league clash from the eighth heat onwards, due to worsening conditions created by rain. Just the home men contest four further races, as the meeting continues on until reaching the point of no return at heat twelve, with the Bandits claiming a 51-17 success. The day's other two meetings are called off due to inclement weather, namely Workington v. Rye House (Premier League) and Stoke v. Coventry (British League Cup Group B).

4   With the skies unloading torrents of the wet stuff, Glasgow's league clash with Hull is postponed. Newport defeat Workington 49-41 in a thriller of a league encounter at

Queensway Meadows. Newcastle suffer another home reverse, going down 47-43 at the hands of Premier League table-toppers King's Lynn.

5   Rye House overcome an early deficit to earn a 50-40 league success over Workington, helped no end by a captain's performance from David Mason (11+2). Knock-Out Cup action sees Reading claim a narrow first-leg 51-45 success over a battling Trelawny septet. Seemond Stephens grabs a 12-point maximum, as Exeter are made to work extremely hard in defeating Arena-Essex 46-44 in an exciting league fixture at the County Ground.

6   Danny Bird nets a full 15 points as the Isle of Wight demolish Stoke 54-35 in a one-sided league affair at Smallbrook Stadium. Similarly, Trelawny romp to a 55-35 Premier League success over Arena-Essex, their points spree led by five-ride maximum-man Chris Harris.

7   Hull bring their four-match losing run to an end, courtesy of a relatively easy 56-34 league victory over Reading. Table-topping King's Lynn lose out in the final three heats as Swindon come from behind to snatch a 46-44 win at Saddlebow Road.

8   Sheffield make it another success for the lower league with a battling 47-43 victory over top-flight Coventry in the British League Cup (Group B). League action at Swindon sees the homesters comprehensively defeat Berwick 57-33, with Chris Neath plundering a first-ever maximum (12) for the Robins. The result is subsequently amended as Lee Smethills is deemed ineligible to appear for the Bandits, his 7 points on the night being deducted from their score.

9   League activity sees Edinburgh thrash reigning Champions Sheffield 62-28 on a track made heavy by rain. At the Oak Tree Arena, Somerset are held to a 45-45 draw by Berwick in the league. In the third league match of the evening, Arena-Essex turn up the power to wallop Newport 65-24, with Henning Bager setting a new track record for the tight Purfleet circuit in the opening heat.

10   Berwick narrowly defeat Glasgow 52-46 in the Knock-Out Cup, with the Tigers staying in the hunt throughout due to astute use of the tactical-joker golden double facility. Derwent Park serves up another exciting encounter, as Workington just edge home 46-44 against a determined Edinburgh in the league. Rye House claim an untroubled 55-35 success over King's Lynn in the British League Cup (Group A), the visitors losing skipper Trevor Harding to a knee injury in a second-heat pile-up. Mick Powell is a non-arrival for Newcastle in their Knock-Out Cup tie at Stoke, but despite this the homesters cannot gain anything more than a 51-44 success.

11   Newport scrape to a 47-43 Knock-Out Cup win over a dogged Exeter septet, thanks only to a final heat 5-1 from Craig Watson and Frank Smart. Rain washes out Glasgow's second-leg Knock-Out Cup tie against Berwick after fourteen heats, but with the score standing at 42-42, it's the visitors who progress through on aggregate. Newcastle battle their way to a 50-40 win over Stoke in the second-leg of their Knock-Out Cup tie, thereby progressing to the next round by just 3 points overall.

12   Exeter complete the job they started the afternoon before, defeating Newport 50-43 for an aggregate success and a safe passage to the quarter-finals of the Knock-Out Cup. Reading are made to work extremely hard before securing a 47-43 win over Stoke in the Premier League.

13   Both Danny Bird (15) and Adam Shields (13+2) are unbeaten, as the Isle of Wight race to a convincing 54-38 win over Swindon in the first-leg of their Knock-Out Cup clash. Trelawny have no difficulty in thrashing Reading 65-30, thereby progressing safely to the quarter-final stage of the Knock-Out Cup.

14   Rain wins the day, as both scheduled meetings are called off: Hull v. Sheffield (Knock-Out
      Cup) and King's Lynn v. Ipswich (British League Cup).

15   Yorkshire rivals Sheffield and Hull battle it out in the Knock-Out Cup at Owlerton, with
      the home side restricted to a 56-43 success, thanks to clever usage of the tactical-joker
      golden double rules by Vikings team manager John Bailey. The Isle of Wight cruise
      through to the next stage of the Knock-Out Cup, courtesy of a second-leg 51-49 win at
      Swindon, the score looking closer than it might have done due to several tactical-joker
      golden double outings from the Robins.

16   With rain falling, Edinburgh's Knock-Out Cup tie versus King's Lynn only sees four heats
      completed, before deteriorating conditions lead to a halt. Thanks to continuous showers,
      the evening's other two meetings are called off: Somerset v. Rye House (Premier League)
      and Arena-Essex v. Ipswich (British League Cup).

17   The elements conspire to ruin the entire programmes of events, with the Stars of Tomorrow
      called off at Berwick, plus three league fixtures: Rye House v. Edinburgh, Workington v.
      King's Lynn and Stoke v. Newport.

18   Newport's league encounter with Edinburgh is called off after heavy morning rainstorms.
      With the Tigers leading 43-35, Glasgow's league engagement against King's Lynn is
      abandoned, but with thirteen heats completed, at least the result stands. With Bjarne
      Pedersen back in a Newcastle race-jacket, the Diamonds claim a hard-fought 48-41
      success over Sheffield in the league, the stylish Dane's contribution being 14 points.

19   Unlucky Edinburgh lose the third match of their Southern tour to rain, as a late
      downpour leaves Reading's circuit in no fit state to race. There's no such problem in
      Devon, as Exeter wallop Rye House 62-27 in a one-sided league fixture at the County
      Ground.

20   The Isle of Wight eclipse Hull 59-30 in the Premier League, with Danny Bird romping
      to his fourth successive home maximum (15). Trelawny trounce Rye House
      60½-29½ in a one-sided PL affair at the Clay Country Moto Parc, with both Pavel
      Ondrasik (14+1) and Matej Zagar (10+2) unbeaten.

21   Despite drizzle, Hull's league meeting against Swindon goes the distance, with the Vikings
      edging a 48-42 success. King's Lynn are not so fortunate, however, as their league
      encounter with Stoke is washed away by evening rain.

22   Swindon's eagerly-awaited British League Cup clash versus Eastbourne is unfortunately
      called off amid heavy showers just after 6.30 p.m. Following a delayed start, Sheffield power
      to a 61-29 league victory over Newcastle, with André Compton scooping a four-ride full
      house.

23   Frede Schott reels off five straight wins as Edinburgh overhaul Hull 57-33 in Premier
      League action at Armadale. Somerset are emphatically beaten 57-33 around their own
      patch by top-flight Wolverhampton in the British League Cup (Group E), with Olly Allen
      landing a paid maximum (10+2) for the victorious visitors. In the Knock-Out Cup replay,
      Arena-Essex dominate proceedings to gain a 55-40 first-leg success over Rye House.

24   Solid scoring gives Berwick the league points against Workington, 51-39 being the result,
      with Carlos Villar starring on 11+1 points from five starts. The returning Paul Pickering
      nets a maximum (13+2), as Stoke run up a 57-32 victory over Rye House, with Jan
      Staechmann (15) also unbeaten by an opponent.

25   Niels-Kristian Iversen plunders a paid maximum (14+1), and establishes a new track
      record as Newport swamp Exeter 56-34 in the British League Cup (Group E). The

Hoddesdon faithful are stunned as Stoke carry on from the previous evening, thundering to 54-35 PL success against an out-of-sorts Rye House septet. James Grieves and George Stancl claim a last heat 5-1 as Glasgow complete a hat-trick of league wins at Ashfield, overcoming 2002 Champions Sheffield 47-42.

26 Bank Holiday morning action sees Exeter storm to a 53-37 league win against Cornish rivals Trelawny, with fast-starting Seemond Stephens zipping to a 15-point maximum. Afternoon racing is the order of the day at Rye House, as the homesters again go down, losing 46-44 at the hands of Arena-Essex to exit the Knock-Out Cup. Workington also compete in the afternoon and it's another thriller at Derwent Park, with the Comets just shading their league encounter 46-44 against Berwick, thanks to a 4-2 in the last race. The final meeting of the day starts at the conventional time of 7.30 p.m. and Todd Wiltshire blasts through the card for an unbeaten tally (15), as Oxford claim a 50-40 victory at Reading in the British League Cup (Group D).

27 A full-blooded scrap at Smallbrook Stadium sees the Isle of Wight edge out Newport 45-44, in a terrific advert for Premier League racing. Trelawny coast to a 59-31 victory against Somerset in the British League Cup (Group E), with both Matej Zagar (14+1) and Emiliano Sanchez (12) remaining undefeated.

28 Hull lose 48-41 at home to Sheffield in the Knock-Out Cup, as the visiting Tigers move safely through to the next round. King's Lynn romp to a 62-34 Knock-Out Cup success over Edinburgh, with three men unbeaten in Davey Watt (15), Shane Parker (14+1) and Tomas Topinka (11+1).

29 With visiting number one Charlie Gjedde missing after his mechanic, Neil Ferguson, is involved in a road traffic accident, Sheffield claim a 54-36 league win over unlucky Swindon, as Ricky Ashworth helps himself to a paid maximum (12+3).

30 Edinburgh's wretched luck with the weather continues, but at least they reach the magical twelfth heat before their league encounter against Arena-Essex is halted, due to fog! At the time of the abandonment, the Monarchs were leading 40-32. New acquisition Matt Read shines, netting 12+2 points as Somerset beat Exeter 48-42 in the Premier League.

31 A solid team performance takes Berwick to a 53-37 league success over Arena-Essex. Charlie Gjedde clocks a new track record as a Swindon rider wins each of the first nine heats, but a big fightback from Rye House eventually restricts the Robins to a narrow 45½-44½ victory in a pulsating league encounter at Hoddesdon. The league action continues as Workington race to a 50-40 win against Hull in another entertaining evening at Derwent Park. In the British League Cup (Group A), it's another great night for the lower league as King's Lynn beat Ipswich 48-41. A Youth International between Great Britain and Germany is staged after the main match, but only reaches heat seven before being abandoned as Shane Waldron is taken to hospital after alarmingly looping at the gate. At the time of the stoppage, the Under-16 Lions are leading 24-18. Stoke crash to a 46-44 reverse against a compact Glasgow septet in an exciting league tussle at Loomer Road.

JUNE

1 Newport entertain Poole in the British League Cup (Group E), and in a close encounter, it's the Pirates who sneak a 47½-42½ success. A 47-43 home defeat at the hands of high-flying Edinburgh keeps Newcastle firmly rooted at the foot of the league table. Swindon ease to a 50-40 league win against Sheffield at a sunny Blunsdon. Glasgow maintain their 100 per cent league record, the Tigers' 48-42 victory over Arena-Essex being their fifth on the trot.

2   Despite Seemond Stephens' maximum (15), Exeter are caught out by a determined Berwick outfit, who collect a 46-44 win at the County Ground. Meanwhile, there's another away triumph at Smallmead, with Edinburgh beating Reading 50-40, and jumping up to top spot in the league, although only on race-points difference from a trio of teams in Berwick, Workington and Exeter.

3   The Isle of Wight are untroubled as they collect a 54-36 league success over Somerset. Trelawny are equally comfortable victors, beating Berwick 53-37 in the Premier League, with Steve Masters plundering a rare paid maximum (13+2).

4   Hull claim a 49-41 league win against a dogged Rye House outfit. King's Lynn take over at the top of the league table, courtesy of an emphatic 54-38 success over visiting Trelawny.

5   There's another change at the head of the league table as Swindon romp to a 55-35 win against Stoke, with guest Chris Harris charging to a five-ride full house. It's a classic at Owlerton, as Sean Wilson's 15-point maximum helps Sheffield to a 49-40 league triumph over Workington.

6   In the Knock-Out Cup, Frede Schott takes the chequered flag in all five of his rides as Edinburgh overcome King's Lynn 59-37, but it's the Norfolk outfit that progress through on aggregate. A tight battle ensues at the Oak Tree Arena, with Glasgow finally losing their first league match, 46-44, at the hands of a determined Somerset side. Arena-Essex fail to get their British League Cup (Group A) campaign underway, their home match against Peterborough being postponed, due to the Elite League outfit being unable to field a team within the regulations of the competition.

7   Berwick claim first position in the league with a narrow 46-44 success over a dogged King's Lynn side, for whom Shane Parker nets a fabulous 18-point maximum. Rye House finally end their eight-match losing streak by defeating Glasgow 49-39 in the league. Workington remain unbeaten at home with a hard-fought 46-44 win over Poole in an inter-league challenge fixture. With a large crowd present, the Loomer Road circuit serves up a cracker as Stoke hold Coventry to a 45-45 draw in the British League Cup (Group B).

8   Newport recover from an early deficit to beat reigning Champions Sheffield 50-40 in an exciting league match. The day's other two scheduled league meetings are unfortunately rained-off – Newcastle v. Stoke and Glasgow v. Workington.

9   Exeter's much-anticipated British League Cup (Group E) clash versus Poole is called off, due to large amounts of the dreaded wet stuff.

10 Trelawny defeat Swindon 48-42 in the league, and with the sides level at 90 points apiece on aggregate, Chris Harris wins a restarted run-off for the bonus.

11 Inspired by Carl Stonehewer's paid maximum (14+1), Workington win 46-44 at Hull, and with the additional bonus point, the Cumbrian outfit jump to the head of the league table. King's Lynn pull away in the latter stages to defeat Rye House 49-41 in the British League Cup (Group A).

12 Despite a power failure, a large pre-British Grand Prix crowd witnesses some thrilling action, with Swindon beating Glasgow 49-41 to take over first position in the Premier League standings. Ricky Ashworth plunders 19 points as Sheffield clinch a 47-42 victory in the battle of the 'big-guns' against the Isle of Wight, with Adam Shields scorching to a six-ride maximum for the visitors.

13 A last heat 5-1 gives Newport a slender 45-44 league success over visiting Glasgow in an incident-packed meeting. Frede Schott nets an unbeaten 15 points as power-packed Edinburgh comfortably win their seventh league match in eight starts, defeating Stoke

55-35 at Armadale. Individual action sees David Ruud dash to victory in the Somerset Open Championship, the Swede finishing ahead of Adam Shields, Michael Coles and Craig Boyce in the final.

15 At Newport, New Year Classic victor David Howe adds the Welsh Open Championship to his collection, winning the final ahead of Adam Shields, Craig Watson and Niels-Kristian Iversen. In the league, Sheffield's 46-44 success at Rye House puts them on top of the table, with skipper Sean Wilson romping to a paid maximum (17+1). Jan Staechmann races to a five-ride full house, as Stoke see off Berwick for a 53-37 league victory.

16 Seemond Stephens speeds to maximum points (15), as Exeter return to winning ways, decisively beating Hull 58-32 in the league. Kenneth Bjerre lands his first maximum of the season (15), as Newcastle claim a 48-42 league victory against Berwick. Reading's season of woe continues, with the Isle of Wight grabbing a 46-44 win at Smallmead.

17 The Isle of Wight surge on, emphatically defeating Rye House 61-29 in the league at Smallbrook Stadium, with both Danny Bird (15) and Adam Shields (13+2) remaining unbeaten. Trelawny have little difficulty in recording a 53-37 win over visiting Hull at the wonderful Clay Country Moto Parc.

18 Challenge-match action sees Hull defeat Banga's Boys (a team fronted by Paul Bentley) 51-39, with former Viking Joe Screen blistering to a full 18-pointer for the composite side. King's Lynn grab a 49-41 success over a spirited Newcastle in the league at Saddlebow Road.

19 Sheffield are in the comfort zone as they beat Berwick 53-36 to retain top spot in the league, with Ricky Ashworth scorching to a paid maximum (13+2) from the difficult number two berth. Swindon retain second spot behind the South Yorkshiremen, thanks to a 50-42 win over a determined Newcastle outfit.

20 Despite a high-tempo start, Edinburgh only claim a 50-40 British League Cup (Group C) success against Glasgow, with George Stancl subsequently beating Frede Schott in a run-off for the bonus point. That leaves Workington as group winners, with the Monarchs likely to join them in the quarter-finals as one of the best runners-up. Foot-of-the-table fare sees Somerset grab a narrow 47-43 victory over Newcastle in yet another Oak Tree Arena thriller. Following three weeks of inactivity, the roar of the speedway is again heard in Purfleet as Arena-Essex defeat Workington 52-38 in a Premier League fixture.

21 Knock-Out Cup action at Shielfield Park results in a 55-42 win for Berwick against battling Trelawny, for whom Chris Harris plunders 20 points – his tally including extra points gained from tactical joker and golden double rides. Rye House race to their biggest success of the year thus far, winning 57-33 against lowly Somerset in a league fixture. Individual action is on the menu at Workington, with Carl Stonehewer victorious in the Cumberland Open Championship, ahead of Frede Schott, Rusty Harrison and Kauko Nieminen.

22 Newport's unbeaten home league record goes, as the Isle of Wight triumph 47-43 at Queensway Meadows. At Ashfield, Glasgow are pushed all the way before emerging with a 46-44 victory over Trelawny in the league. Staying with league action, Stoke recover from a first-heat reverse to pull away and defeat Somerset 55-35, led by full maximums from Jan Staechmann (15) and guest Chris Neath (12), plus a paid one from Alan Mogridge (9+3). Torrential mid-morning rain unfortunately leads to the postponement of Newcastle's KOC quarter-final tie versus Arena-Essex.

23 In the Knock-Out Cup quarter-final, Exeter work hard to establish a 53-42 advantage over the c in the County Ground-staged first-leg. Meanwhile, in the British League Cup (Group D), Reading and Swindon play out a gripping 45-45 draw at Smallmead, with Pole Janusz Kolodziej providing plenty of entertainment on his Racers debut.

24 The Isle of Wight ease into the Knock-Out Cup semi-final, defeating Exeter 61-34 in a match marred by serious back injuries suffered by Falcons linchpin Michael Coles. Further KOC action at Trelawny sees the homesters also make the semis, comfortably beating Berwick 61-34, with Matej Zagar plundering a paid full score (14+1).

25 Tomas Topinka (11+1) stays unbeaten as King's Lynn race to a 52-37 success over Stoke in the league.

26 Amid dusty conditions, Sheffield claim a narrow 50-48 win in the Knock-Out Cup against battling King's Lynn, with Shane Parker hitting a remarkable paid 21 points for the Stars, his score aided considerably by a brace of tactical joker/golden double outings. Despite power cuts in and around the Blunsdon area, Swindon record a 49-41 league victory over Arena-Essex, the meeting being completed largely due to the efforts of stadium manager Brian Ludgate in getting a newly-installed generator to perform efficiently.

27 Knock-Out Cup quarter-final activity results in a 55-41 first-leg win for Arena-Essex against Newcastle, with Leigh Lanham gleaning a full 15-pointer. Somerset are undone as Adam Shields powers to a paid maximum (14+1) to help the Isle of Wight gain a 53-37 success at the Oak Tree Arena. The win, and all-important bonus point, takes the Islanders to the head of the Premier League table, above Sheffield and Swindon. Edinburgh's wretched luck with the weather continues, with their scheduled league match against Berwick washed out by bucketloads of evening rain.

28 Berwick race to an untroubled 53-37 league victory over new-look Hull, for whom Bjorn G. Hansen nets 8 points on his club debut. In the Home Counties Cup, Rye House claim a hard-fought 44-43 win against Elite League Eastbourne, with Adam Shields going through the card (15) for the visitors. Workington maintain their unbeaten home league record, comfortably seeing off Exeter by a 50-39 scoreline.

29 Following their home defeat at the hands of the Isle of Wight, Newport get back to winning ways, coming from behind to defeat Newcastle 50-40, with Craig Watson storming to a paid maximum (14+1). Glasgow romp to their biggest win of the season, defeating Exeter 60-30 in a one-sided league encounter. Shoulder-to-shoulder racing is the order of the day as Stoke are beaten 46-44 by Reading in exciting league fare at Loomer Road.

30 Despite the absence of Michael Coles, Exeter easily race to a 55-35 league success against Somerset at their pacy County Ground home. Smallmead serves up a Premier League classic, with Reading finally edging a 47-43 win over a dogged Workington septet.

JULY

1 The Isle of Wight stay first in the league, courtesy of a 55-35 win against Workington, with both Adam Shields (15) and Danny Bird (13+2) unbeaten by an opponent. Trelawny overpower Stoke to register a 55-34 success in league fare at the picturesque Clay Country Moto Parc.

2 It's a victory for the Premier League over higher opposition as Hull defeat Coventry 47-43 in the British League Cup (Group B) at Craven Park. A dramatic Knock-Out Cup night at Saddlebow Road results in a 49-48 win for visiting Sheffield against King's Lynn,

as the Tigers progress to the semi-final by just 3 points on aggregate. The annual Thursday-night league clash between Glasgow and Newport at Ashfield sees the homesters triumph 52-38, with George Stancl in maximum mood (12). Sheffield grind out a 49-41 league win against battling Arena-Essex to keep up their title push. Both Paul Fry (17+1) and Olly Allen (12) are unbeaten, as Swindon romp to a 60-30 victory over Somerset. The win sees them move into second position in the league, as they depose Sheffield by virtue of a superior race-points difference.

4   An excellent Armadale scrap ends in a 49-40 league triumph for Edinburgh against Newport, with the amazing Frede Schott gleaning a full tally from five starts. The Oak Tree Arena serves up a cracker, as Somerset grab a last-heat 5-1 to gain a 46-45 league victory over visiting Reading. The third league match of the day sees Arena-Essex untroubled in defeating Hull 53-36 at Purfleet.

6   Maximums from Craig Watson (15) and Niels-Kristian Iversen (14+1) help Newport to an easy 59-31 win against a patched-up Somerset outfit in the British League Cup (Group E). A 54-36 scoreline gives Workington their biggest home league victory of the campaign, with luckless Rye House on the receiving end. Basement club Newcastle gain a morale-boosting 57-33 success over Exeter, as both Kenneth Bjerre (15) and Kevin Little (12) net full maximums. Remaining in touch with the pace-setters, Glasgow record their eighth consecutive home league win, beating Hull 51-39. A thrilling contest ends in a 46-44 success for Stoke against Swindon, with the Robins moving to top spot in the league, courtesy of the aggregate bonus point.

7   A solid performance gives Exeter a 55-35 win over Edinburgh, as new Falcon Scott Smith makes his home debut. A great display sees Rye House defeat Trelawny 52-38 in the league, as sixteen-year-old Edward Kennett gleans an incredible 15+2 points. Reading's Smallmead Stadium plays host as the Great Britain Under-21 side claim a 49-41 victory over their Swedish counterparts, with Olly Allen storming to a 15-point maximum.

8   The Isle of Wight jump back to the top of the Premier League table, thanks to a 50-40 win against Reading. At the Clay Country Moto Parc, Trelawny suffer a 46-44 reverse at the hands of Edinburgh in a thrilling league encounter.

9   Hull have no answers as visiting Sheffield score a 51-39 success in the British League Cup (Group B), inspired by Sean Wilson's five-ride maximum. King's Lynn swamp league-leaders the Isle of Wight 58-32, with both Davey Watt (15) and Shane Parker (14+1) notching undefeated tallies.

10   Sheffield romp to a 57-33 success over Newport in the league, with both Sean Wilson (14+1) and Ricky Ashworth (12+3) unbeaten by an opponent. Charlie Gjedde's 15-point maximum helps Swindon register a 52-38 win against local rivals Reading in the British League Cup (Group D).

11   Edinburgh claim a 48-42 success in an entertaining league encounter against Swindon at Armadale. Lee Herne comes up trumps with a paid maximum (13+2), as Arena-Essex polish off Somerset by a 56-34 scoreline in the league.

12   Flying reserve David Meldrum nets 19 points as Berwick narrowly beat Swindon 47-43 in the league. Rye House are held to a thrilling 45-45 draw in the league by Newport, with the sensational Edward Kennett thundering to a six-ride paid maximum (17+1) for the Rockets. Carl Stonehewer plunders a full 15-pointer as Workington romp to a 56-34 league victory against Glasgow. Home skipper Paul Pickering piles up a 16-point tally as Stoke narrowly defeat King's Lynn 46-44 in the league at Loomer Road.

13 Newport are unable to stop Berwick from claiming a somewhat surprising 46-44 success in the league at Queensway Meadows. The Ashfield racing strip serves up some cracking league action, with Glasgow narrowly defeating Swindon 46-44, although the match is marred by a last-race crash which sees Swindon guest (and the Premier League's top man) Frede Schott sustain a broken collarbone, with Glasgow's James Grieves suffering a nasty hand injury. Newcastle move off the foot of the Premier League table thanks to a comfortable 52-38 victory over Somerset, with William Lawson impressively recording 12+2 points for the Diamonds.

14 Exeter are in the comfort zone as they see off Workington by a 59-30 scoreline in the league. Reading's troubled year continues, as Kenneth Bjerre's 15-point maximum helps Newcastle to a 49-40 success in the league at Smallmead.

15 The Isle of Wight consolidate their position at the head of the league table, courtesy of a 51-39 victory over a spirited Newcastle outfit. Trelawny are always in front, as they claim a couple of league points, winning 52-38 against Workington.

16 Individual fare at Hull sees Vikings veteran Paul Thorp romp to a 15-point maximum prior to heading home Garry Stead, Paul Bentley and Chris Manchester in the final of the Mid-Summer Showdown. In the British League Cup (Group A), King's Lynn become the latest PL side to beat Elite opposition, as they narrowly see off Peterborough 47-43.

17 André Compton's paid maximum (14+1) helps Sheffield to an emphatic 56-34 victory over Rye House, and with the additional bonus point, the homesters take over at the top of the league. Amid worsening conditions, Swindon's league match against Exeter is halted after fourteen heats, with the Robins holding an unassailable 48-36 advantage, which takes them up to second spot in the table.

18 Leigh Lanham hits 17 points as Arena-Essex sweep to a 53-36 win over league-leaders Sheffield. Edinburgh win their seventh home league match out of seven, narrowly beating Workington 48-42, with Peter Carr blasting to a 15-point full house. British League Cup (Group E) action results in a 48-42 success for Newport at Somerset, as Niels-Kristian Iversen completes a wonderful maximum (15) for the Wasps.

19 Workington host the Premier League Pairs Championship for a fifth successive year, and for a fourth time it proves to their advantage, as Carl Stonehewer and Simon Stead defeat the Newport duo of Frank Smart and Niels-Kristian Iversen in the final.

20 In a lunchtime league match, Berwick secure a 49-41 win over old rivals Edinburgh. Craig Watson goes through the card (15), as Newport race to 61-29 victory against Exeter. Challenge-match action sees Rye House record their highest tally of the season, as they thump Reading 60-30, with Brent Werner in maximum mood (15). Glasgow lose their unbeaten home league record, as rain curtails their match against Workington after twelve heats, with the Comets leading 38-34. Newcastle's resurgence continues as they defeat Trelawny 52-38 in the league, with Kenneth Bjerre establishing a new track record on his way to a full 15 points. Injury-hit Stoke are unable to prevent Arena-Essex from gaining a 48-44 win in the league at Loomer Road.

21 Exeter are caught cold, as a determined Glasgow septet gain a 46-44 league success at the County Ground. Continuing on the league theme, Reading secure a 48-42 win against visiting Rye House. The match is marred by Edward Kennett's spectacular fifth-heat crash, with the talented youngster unfortunately suffering a serious knee injury.

22 The Isle of Wight depose league-leaders Sheffield, thanks to a 49-42 success over the West Yorkshire side at Smallbrook Stadium. Chris Harris (14+1), Pavel Ondrasik (13+2) and

Matej Zagar (11+1) notch paid maximums as Trelawny canter to a 59-31 league victory over Glasgow.

23 Newport overcome an early deficit to win 48-41 in an incident-packed league match at Hull. Maximums from Davey Watt (18) and Shane Parker (14+1) lead King's Lynn to a comfortable 52-37 win over Edinburgh.

24 Sheffield thunder to a huge 64-26 victory against Somerset in the league, helped no end by paid maximums from Sean Wilson (14+1), André Compton (14+1) and Ricky Ashworth (11+1). Keeping the league at boiling point, Swindon move to the head of the table by defeating Edinburgh 51-39, with the in-form Charlie Gjedde netting a paid full house (14+1).

25 At Armadale, the prestigious Scottish Open Championship results in victory for the amazing Sam Ermolenko ahead of Carl Stonehewer, George Stancl and Kevin Little. Glenn Cunningham hits a paid maximum (14+1), as Somerset grab an emphatic 58-32 success over Stoke in league competition at the Oak Tree Arena. Arena-Essex race their first British League Cup (Group A) match, and it's a great start as they overcome Elite-League Ipswich 54-36.

26 Berwick's Stars of Tomorrow event sees Craig Branney emerge victorious from Benji Compton, James Wright and Carl Shield. Despite rain, Rye House's British League Cup (Group A) clash against Peterborough reaches heat thirteen, with the homesters gaining a 42-36 success over their Elite-League opponents. Workington suffer their first home defeat of the season, as visiting Trelawny claim a narrow 46-44 league victory. The other meeting of the day between Stoke and Exeter is called off in mid-morning, due to a waterlogged circuit.

27 Blunsdon Stadium plays host to the Premier League Four-Team Championship, and Swindon make full use of their home advantage to win their semi-final on 15 points from Glasgow (12), Edinburgh (10) and the Isle of Wight (10). The second semi-final sees Newport hit 15 points to finish ahead of Trelawny (13), King's Lynn (11) and Arena-Essex (9). A thrilling final then results in victory for Swindon (25), ahead of Trelawny (22), Newport (21) and Glasgow (4), with Charlie Gjedde brilliantly taking his record for the day to five wins out of five for the triumphant Robins.

28 Exeter suffer their second successive home league reverse, as Sheffield move back to the top of the table with a marginal 46-44 win. Kenneth Bjerre romps to a five-ride maximum as Newcastle defeat Arena-Essex 49-41 in the Knock-Out Cup, but it's the Hammers who go through to the semi-final stage on aggregate. Reading's difficult season continues as Berwick come from behind to gain a 49-41 success in the league at Smallmead.

29 The top-of-the-table clash between the Isle of Wight and Swindon sadly falls victim to sweeping afternoon rain. Trelawny race to a convincing 57-33 success over title-chasing Sheffield, with Pavel Ondrasik going through the card unbeaten (10+2).

30 King's Lynn's Premier League clash with Glasgow is postponed due to a waterlogged track. Bottom-club Hull suffer another home loss, going down 46-44 at the hands of the Isle of Wight. In stark contrast, the win once again sees the Islanders move to the head of the table. Stoke are swamped 55-35 at home by Belle Vue in the British League Cup (Group B), as both Joe Screen (14+1) and Jason Crump (14+1) net paid maximums for the Aces.

31 Sheffield take over at the top of the league, courtesy of a 52-38 victory against a battling Glasgow outfit. The fans pour through the Blunsdon turnstiles for Leigh Adams'

Testimonial, and it's the beneficiary man himself who races to victory in the final from Jason Lyons, Joe Screen and Travis McGowan.

AUGUST

1   Edinburgh collect a 49-44 league success over Trelawny, with Magnus Karlsson impressively completing a four-ride full house for the Monarchs. Craig Boyce is paid for the lot (14+1), as Poole have little difficulty in registering a 50-39 victory at Somerset in the British League Cup (Group E). The third and final match of the evening sees Arena-Essex defeat Newcastle 52-38 in the league at their tight Purfleet raceway.

2   Rye House record their first league win since 7 July, overcoming Newcastle 49-41, thanks to some solid teamwork. A close league encounter at Shielfield Park results in a 48-42 victory for Berwick over Trelawny. A brilliant golden-double victory from Simon Stead helps Workington come from behind to beat the Isle of Wight 50-43 in an entertaining league match at Derwent Park. In their quest for league honours, Sheffield pull further ahead in pole position, courtesy of a 48-42 victory at Stoke.

3   In a fine advert for the Premier League, Newport determinedly overcome an 8-point deficit to defeat Arena-Essex 47-42 at a sunny Queensway Meadows. Glasgow get back to winning ways at Ashfield, narrowly seeing off Berwick 47-42 in league fare, with guest Simon Stead collecting a paid maximum (14+1). Newcastle race to a 54-36 success over the title-chasing Isle of Wight at Brough Park, with Islanders skipper Ray Morton unfortunately suffering a broken wrist in a tenth-heat spill.

4   Roger Lobb sweeps to a paid full house (13+2), helping Exeter score a big win for the so-called lower division as they swamp Poole 59-31 in the British League Cup (Group E). Sheffield's league aspirations take a jolt at Smallmead, with Reading claiming an impressive 47-42 victory.

5   The Isle of Wight defeat Edinburgh 48-42 in a hard-fought contest to maintain second spot in the league. Trelawny claim a 51-39 league success against a plucky Reading side, for whom Pole Janusz Kolodziej stars with 13-points.

6   Hull suffer a ninth successive league defeat, going down 48-42 at home to Newcastle. King's Lynn race to a 50-40 win over Arena-Essex in the British League Cup (Group A) at Saddlebow Road. Edinburgh become the first side to attain five away wins in the league, leaving it to the last heat before claiming a 46-44 success at Somerset.

7   Sheffield extend their lead at the top of the league to four points, thanks to a handsome 55-35 victory against Stoke.

8   Edinburgh complete a quick-fire double over Somerset to move into third position in the league standings. Full maximums for Magnus Karlsson (15) and Rory Schlein (12) are the main feature of the Monarchs' 55-35 success. In the British League Cup (Group A), it's a 49-41 win for Arena-Essex against Rye House.

9   Rye House stage a Premier League international, and it's Australia who gain a 47-43 success over England in an enthralling encounter. Claus Kristensen roars back to form with 20+1 points from seven starts (although it's not classed as a paid maximum due to his missing of a programmed ride), as Berwick hammer Somerset 58-32 in a one-sided league meeting at Shielfield Park. A ding-dong battle finally sees Workington grab a narrow 47-43 league win against a battling Swindon side at Derwent Park. With new signings Rob Grant and Australian Scott Smith on board, Stoke romp to a 60-32 victory over Hull in the league.

10 Craig Watson scorches to a 15-point maximum, but Newport are made to work hard before claiming a 48-42 league success over basement-club Hull. Newcastle pull away to inflict a 53-37 defeat on Swindon, with super-Dane Kenneth Bjerre flying to his fifth full league maximum (15) of the year. Premier League fare sees Glasgow race to a comfortable 59-31 win against a depleted Reading outfit at Ashfield Stadium.

11 Terrific league action sees a dogged Glasgow side come from behind to snatch a 45-45 draw at Reading. Seemond Stephens' home consistency proves fruitful as he hits 14 points to take victory in the prestigious Westernapolis at Exeter, with Chris Harris and Mark Simmonds sharing second place on 11 points apiece.

12 In the Knock-Out Cup semi-final, Trelawny gain a hard-fought first-leg 49-43 advantage over the Isle of Wight at the Clay Country Moto Parc.

13 After eleven successive league defeats, Hull claim an overdue 50-39 success against Exeter, helped no end by paid maximums from Paul Thorp (14+1) and Garry Stead (14+1). A powerful performance takes King's Lynn to a 57-32 victory over Newport in the league at Saddlebow Road.

14 Sean Wilson romps to an 18-point maximum as Sheffield extend their lead at the head of the league standings with a 51-39 win over Exeter. Swindon remain in contention at the right end of the league, courtesy of a 52-37 success against Workington, with Olly Allen carding a paid maximum (14+1).

15 Edinburgh's league-title challenge continues with a comfortable 60-30 win over Reading, as guest Shane Parker (15) and the evergreen Peter Carr (11+1) net maximums. Gripping league action at the Oak Tree Arena finally ends with honours even, as Somerset and Workington draw 46-46. With a 56-34 scoreline, and a full 15-pointer from Leigh Lanham, it's a comfortable win for Arena-Essex against King's Lynn in the British League Cup (Group A).

16 Remaining in the league's top five teams, Berwick coast to a 53-37 success over Reading at Shielfield Park. In the British League Cup (Group A), Rye House comprehensively defeat local rivals Arena-Essex 53-37. Workington surge to a 53-37 win against King's Lynn in the league at Derwent Park. Stoke overcome an early setback to overwhelm Exeter 55-35 in the league, with Jan Staechmann plundering an unbeaten tally (14+1).

18 Following seven successive league losses, Exeter return to winning form by beating Newcastle 53-37. Reading gain their first victory in six outings, easily seeing off Somerset by a 54-36 scoreline at Smallmead.

19 The Isle of Wight remain second in the league, courtesy of a 52-40 success against battling King's Lynn. A last-heat 5-1 gives Trelawny a sensational 47-46 victory over a determined Newcastle septet at the Moto Parc.

20 Beleaguered Hull lose 52-38 at the hands of visiting Belle Vue in the British League Cup (Group B). King's Lynn achieve a 48-42 win against a spirited Rye House side in typically thrilling Saddlebow Road league action.

21 Both Sean Wilson (18) and Andrew Moore (14+1) net maximums as top-of-the-table Sheffield power to a 58-32 league success over depleted Reading. Swindon's title aspirations take a jolt as Olly Allen crashes out in the opening heat, with the Isle of Wight going on to grab a 47-43 victory at Blunsdon.

22 Frede Schott roars back into action with a maximum (15) as powerful Edinburgh romp to a 63-27 league win over Exeter, with Rory Schlein (13+2) and Peter Carr (11+1) also unbeaten by an opponent.

23 Berwick comfortably race to a 55-35 league victory against Glasgow, as Claus Kristensen chalks up a paid full house (11+1). King's Lynn canter to a 65-25 success over Exeter in the league, with four men unbeaten in the home camp – Trevor Harding (12+3), Davey Watt (12), Shane Parker (12) and Tomas Topinka (11+1). Thanks to a last-heat 5-1, Stoke force a dramatic 45-45 draw with visiting Workington in pulsating league action at Loomer Road. Arena-Essex are beaten 48-45 at home by Edinburgh as the solid Scottish side move up to second place in the league standings.

24 Glasgow take full advantage of Kenneth Bjerre's first-race crash to defeat Newcastle 61-28 in the league, with Christian Henry (12+3) and guest Simon Stead (12) knocking up fine maximums. Newport are caught cold as local-rivals Swindon storm to a 50-40 league success at Queensway Meadows.

25 Bank Holiday morning action sees Exeter fail to contain Elite League Wolverhampton in the British League Cup (Group E), with Mikael Max hitting a full house (12) as his side wins 50-40. It's afternoon delight for Rye House as they race to a 49-41 win against King's Lynn in an enthralling league tussle. Bjarne Pedersen garners a five-ride maximum (15) as Newcastle race to a 53-37 victory against Glasgow in the league. Workington triumph 54-35 against Stoke in a rather one-sided league meeting at Derwent Park. The clash of the M4 rivals ends in a 48-42 success for Swindon at Reading, as the Robins hoist themselves back into the title chase.

26 There's high tension and dramatic scenes at Smallbrook Stadium as the Isle of Wight defeat Trelawny 54-45 to claim an aggregate victory and a place in the Knock-Out Cup final.

27 Trelawny quickly recover from their KOC exit to grab a 50-40 league win at Hull. King's Lynn romp to a 58-32 league success against Workington, aided no end by a paid maximum from Tom P. Madsen (13+2).

28 Swindon jump back to second spot in the league, courtesy of a comfortable 56-34 defeat of Hull, with both Charlie Gjedde (14+1) and guest Simon Stead (12) unbeaten by an opponent. Sheffield's league match versus Trelawny is unfortunately called off following persistent rainfall.

29 Edinburgh displace Swindon in the league standings, thanks to a 55-34 victory over Rye House as Frede Schott cards his fifth full maximum (15) of the campaign. Somerset are soundly beaten 52-38 by visiting King's Lynn in the league. Continuous rain forces Arena-Essex to postpone their eagerly awaited Knock-Out Cup semi-final tie with Sheffield.

30 Paul Bentley (15) and David Meldrum (13+2) remain unbeaten as Berwick go on the rampage to defeat Rye House 67-23 in the league. By a 59-31 scoreline, Workington defeat visiting Newport, with Simon Stead hitting a stylish full house (15). Stoke suffer a 46-44 reverse at the hands of title-chasing Edinburgh in an absorbing league encounter at Loomer Road.

31 Craig Watson scorches to a magnificent six-ride maximum (18), as Newport gain a 48-41 league success over a gritty Stoke outfit. Newcastle's good home form continues with a 53-37 win against basement-side Hull. Edinburgh make it eight league wins on the trot and dash to the top of the standings as they register a 55-37 victory at the home of arch-rivals Glasgow, with Rory Schlein (13+2), Frede Schott (12) and Peter Carr (12) netting maximums. Rare Sunday-evening fare at Reading sees the Racers finally overhaul Exeter 49-41 in a thrilling league encounter, with guest Craig Watson carding a paid maximum (14+1).

SEPTEMBER

1   Exeter quickly gain revenge over Reading, winning 57-33 in the return league fixture at the County Ground. Rye House captain David Mason notches a paid full house (11+4), as his side race to an emphatic 62-27 victory over Berwick in a heated league match at Hoddesdon.

2   Exciting Frenchman Sebastian Tresarrieu lands a paid maximum (14+1), as the Isle of Wight keep their title hopes alive with a narrow 47-43 success against battling Berwick. Trelawny comfortably defeat Somerset 52-38 in the league at their wonderful Clay Country Moto Parc home.

3   In a stirring display, Hull come from behind to post a morale-boosting 47-43 league victory over Yorkshire rivals Sheffield. Tomas Topinka reels off a maximum (12) and sets a new track record as King's Lynn record a 59-31 win against Glasgow in the league at Saddlebow Road.

4   Sean Wilson nets a paid full score (17+1), as Sheffield gain a 57-41 advantage over Arena-Essex in the first-leg of the Knock-Out Cup semi-final. League activity sees Swindon beat Rye House 49-41 in the twenty-ninth meeting of a busy season at Blunsdon.

5   Armadale plays host to the Motor Show 2, as Peter Carr celebrates a speedway career spanning twenty-five years. A four-team tournament results in victory for the Aces (21) from the Diamonds (20), the Motors (16) and the Tigers (14). Following the main event, a knock-out contest (featuring semi-finals and a final) results in victory for Steve Johnston ahead of Rory Schlein, Joe Screen and Ross Brady. Somerset go down 46-44 to visiting Newport in typically entertaining fare at the Oak Tree Arena, with Niels-Kristian Iversen hitting maximum points (15) for the victorious Wasps. Arena-Essex grab a last-heat 5-1 to snatch a 46-44 victory over gallant Berwick in a thrilling league fixture at the compact Thurrock raceway.

6   Stoke's Premier League match against Trelawny falls victim to heavy afternoon rain. Berwick dominate proceedings to hammer Newcastle 63-27 in the league, with Paul Bentley (15+3) and Claus Kristensen (15) unbeaten for the Bandits. Rye House narrowly defeat basement-club Hull 47-43 in the league at Hoddesdon, as the visitors gain only their second bonus point of a difficult season. Workington record their biggest victory of the campaign, outpacing lowly Somerset 60-30, with full-house tallies from Simon Stead (15), Rusty Harrison (14+1) and Carl Stonehewer (10+2).

7   Newport seal a 52-38 win against King's Lynn, making it three league victories in eight days for the Wasps. George Stancl plunders a faultless league maximum (15), as Glasgow clock up a 55-35 success over Somerset. Newcastle hang on to beat a determined Rye House 46-44, with Bjarne Pedersen's full house (15) paving the way to the league points. Super-guest Simon Stead (15) and Charlie Gjedde (13+2) post maximums as Swindon gain an excellent 51-39 win over top-flight club Eastbourne in the British League Cup (Group D). The result is academic for the Eagles, however, as they top the group on sixteen points and qualify for the quarter-finals.

8   Rain wins the day at Exeter as the Falcons' league match against Stoke is postponed just after the scheduled starting time. Reading's season of struggle continues as they go down 50-40 to visiting Newport in the league, with both Niels-Kristian Iversen (15) and Craig Watson (14+1) remaining unbeaten for the Wasps.

9   Maximums from Danny Bird (15) and Adam Shields (13+2) help the title-chasing Isle of Wight to a 54-36 league win against Glasgow. Trelawny crush Exeter 62-28 in a league encounter, with Czech ace Pavel Ondrasik hitting a perfect five-ride full house (15).

10   Hull and Glasgow end all-square at 45-45 in an exciting league clash at Craven Park. Further league fare sees King's Lynn defeat a dogged Reading side 49-41 at the Norfolk Arena.

11   Sheffield lose the bonus point, but the Steel City team still jump up to top spot in the league with a 55-34 victory over Trelawny.

12   A double dose of action firstly sees Arena-Essex cruise to a 60-30 success against Stoke in the league, with Kelvin Tatum MBE recording maximum points (12). The second match results in an even bigger 64-27 win for the Hammers against top-flight Peterborough in the British League Cup (Group A), as Joonas Kylmakorpi (15) and Leigh Lanham (13+2) get into the maximum mood. Table-topping Sheffield show no mercy as they romp to a 53-37 victory at Somerset, aided by paid maximums from guest Brent Werner (14+1) and club skipper Sean Wilson (13+2). Cutting-edge action at the sharp end of the league sees Edinburgh claim a significant 53-36 triumph over the Isle of Wight.

13   Maximums from Simon Stead (15) and Carl Stonehewer (14+1) see Workington through to a comfortable 56-34 win against Arena-Essex in the league. Having lost at Edinburgh the previous evening, the Isle of Wight's Championship aspirations are further dented with a 52-39 reverse at Berwick. The result does the Bandits a power of good though, as they move up to third spot in the table. Meanwhile, Edinburgh leap back to first position in the Premier League standings with a tenth successive victory – their 47-43 success at Rye House led by inspirational Dane Frede Schott's latest maximum (14+1) of a remarkable campaign. Having lost Scott Smith to a third-heat accident, Stoke subsequently go down 47-43 to visiting Newcastle in league action at Loomer Road.

14   Edinburgh's glorious league run finally ends as they suffer a 50-40 defeat at Newport, with the Welsh outfit also claiming the vital bonus point. The super Ashfield raceway serves up a thriller, with the Isle of Wight suffering their third league loss in three days as solid-scoring Glasgow triumph 47-43. Kenneth Bjerre makes his first home appearance in five weeks and his five-ride maximum helps Newcastle to a 52-38 victory over Arena-Essex in the league.

15   Depleted Exeter claim a 48-42 league success against Newport at the County Ground. Beleaguered Reading lose their fourth successive league match, going down 48-42 to visiting Trelawny.

16   Cracking league action at the Clay Country Moto Parc sees Trelawny gain a 48-42 victory over a dogged Isle of Wight septet.

17   Hull pick up only their seventh league win of a difficult campaign, beating Arena-Essex 50-40 at Craven Park. Davey Watt (14+1) and Tomas Topinka (11+1) remain unbeaten as King's Lynn romp to a 60-30 league victory against Berwick.

18   Sheffield return to the head of the league table with their sixteenth successive home win as they beat Hull 58-32, helped by paid maximums from Andrew Moore (13+2) and Ricky Ashworth (12+3). Swindon gain their fifth league victory on the trot as they convincingly see off King's Lynn by a 52-37 scoreline.

19   Scottish derby action results in Edinburgh quickly returning to top spot in the Premier League standings, courtesy of a 56-34 triumph over the 'auld enemy' Glasgow. Somerset secure a rare league win, beating Trelawny 46-44 in a thriller at the Oak Tree Arena. Knock-Out Cup semi-final fare sees Arena-Essex defeat Sheffield 55-43, but it's insufficient for an aggregate success as the Tigers go through to face the Isle of Wight in the final.

20   Heavy rain forces the postponement of Workington's league clash against Reading. Due

to difficult track conditions caused by an afternoon downpour, Berwick's league fixture with Newport is abandoned following a shared opening heat. American Brent Werner zooms to a 15-point maximum as Rye House defeat Arena-Essex 48-42 in gripping league activity. With Stoke leading 34-26 after ten heats, their league encounter with the Isle of Wight is abandoned due to persistent rainfall.

21 Newport post a 48-42 league victory over battling Trelawny. Amid poor conditions brought about by steady drizzle, Glasgow claim a 47-43 success against a spirited Rye House outfit at Ashfield.

22 Reading's league fixture with King's Lynn falls victim to rain less than half-an-hour before the scheduled starting time. Exeter's season ends drearily with a 46-44 league loss at the hands of visiting Stoke.

23 The Isle of Wight beat Trelawny 53-40 to remain in the higher echelons of the Premier League table.

24 Hull raise their hopes of avoiding the wooden spoon with a 49-41 win against Stoke. Individual action at King's Lynn sees Simon Stead card maximum points (15) to triumph ahead of Davey Watt (14) and Tomas Topinka (13) in the Pride of the East event.

25 Rare Thursday-night racing at Brough Park results in a 50-40 victory for Newcastle over Reading in the league, with Kenneth Bjerre riding unbeaten (13+2). Sheffield suffer their first home loss in five years, going down 47-43 to Eastbourne in the first-leg of the British League Cup quarter-final. Swindon are held to a 45-45 draw by a battling Newport side in the penultimate league match of the season at Blunsdon.

26 With Peter Carr absent through illness, Edinburgh suffer a 51-39 reverse to visiting Wolverhampton in the British League Cup quarter-final. Mikael Max bags a five-ride full house (15) for the victorious Wolves as they motor into the semi-finals. Somerset defeat Hull 52-38 to condemn the Vikings to finishing in the unwanted cellar position in the table. With torrential rain falling, Arena-Essex's league match against Glasgow is abandoned after twelve heats, with the Hammers holding an unassailable 49-23 lead.

27 Berwick move into third spot in the league table courtesy of a crushing 58-32 success over Stoke. Rye House fight hard, but cannot prevent top-flight Belle Vue from claiming a 48-42 win and a place in the last four of the British League Cup. Injury-hit Workington are unable to stop Elite Leaguers Poole from collecting a 50-40 victory at Derwent Park in the first-leg of their British League Cup quarter-final clash.

28 At Sheffield, home-man Sean Wilson saves his best until last to lift the Premier League Riders' Championship for the second time in his career, with Adam Shields, Carl Stonehewer and Craig Watson filling the other podium positions respectively.

29 Newcastle's league fixture versus Newport falls victim to heavy afternoon rain. Super individual action at Smallmead sees Charlie Gjedde race to victory in the rerun final of the Euphony Classic, ahead of Travis McGowan and Danny Bird.

30 Still in with a chance of winning the league title, the Isle of Wight keep their hopes alive by defeating Swindon 50-40.

OCTOBER

1 Twelve-point maximums from Tomas Topinka, Shane Parker and Adam Allott help King's Lynn to a 48-point total and victory over Swindon (32) and Hull (28) in a three-team tournament at Saddlebow Road. Wednesday-night action at the Oak Tree Arena results in a 48-42 success for visiting Arena-Essex in the league.

2   Helped by unbeaten tallies from Sean Wilson (15) and guest Paul Pickering (10+2), Sheffield romp to a 58-32 victory over Champions-elect Edinburgh. Guest Chris Harris plunders a wonderful paid full house (12+3) as Swindon complete their home league fixtures with a comfortable 51-39 win over M4 rivals Reading.

3   Edinburgh move to within grasping distance of the League Championship by swamping Berwick 60-30, with maximums from Frede Schott (14+1), Peter Carr (14+1) and Rory Schlein (11+1). The Triangle Trophy at Hull results in victory for the White Wizards (39) from the Red Raiders (38) and the Blue Bombers (31). Contrasting fortunes, however, see Sam Ermolenko plunder a paid full house (11+1) for the runners-up, while Blue-Bombers representative Billy Hamill unfortunately suffers a broken collarbone in a third-heat crash. Arena-Essex claim a 51-42 success over a gritty Swindon side, thereby moving inside the top ten in the league standings.

4   Stoke's league match against Newport is called off in mid-afternoon due to a waterlogged circuit. Rye House triumph 50-40 against the Isle of Wight, with the result ending any lingering hopes the visitors held of claiming the league title as Edinburgh are declared Champions for the first time since their formation in 1948. Workington end their league campaign with a comprehensive 56-34 victory over beleaguered Reading.

5   Classy Australian Mark Lemon wins the Frank Smart Farewell Meeting at Newport, with fellow antipodeans Craig Watson, Davey Watt and Adam Shields following him home in the final. Amid damp conditions Glasgow entertain Edinburgh in the first-leg of the Scottish Cup, with the newly crowned League Champions making light of the weather to win 54-36, aided by Peter Carr's umpteenth career maximum (12) for the Monarchs. Newcastle's league match against Stoke is abandoned after twelve heats due to rain, with the Diamonds holding a match-winning 43-29 advantage at the time.

7   Smallbrook Stadium hosts the first-leg of the Knock-Out Cup final, with the Isle of Wight gaining a hard-fought 49-44 win against a battling Sheffield outfit. The picturesque Clay Country Moto Parc stages its last meeting after seven wonderful seasons of racing, and fittingly, Chris Harris thunders to maximum points (15) as Trelawny defeat Newport 47-43 in a keenly contested league match.

8   Shane Parker (15) and Tomas Topinka (13+2) remain unbeaten as King's Lynn race to a convincing 59-31 league victory against Somerset.

10 At Armadale, Frede Schott clocks a new track record of 55.6 seconds, and also posts a 12-point maximum as Championship-winners Edinburgh beat a dogged Newcastle 48-42 in their last-but-one home league match. Somerset plays host to the Graeme Gordon Testimonial, with Scott Nicholls taking victory in the final from Magnus Zetterstrom, Mark Lemon and Craig Boyce. Arena-Essex claim a 53-37 success over Rye House in an entertaining Premier League encounter.

11 Popular Cornishman Chris Harris takes all the accolades at Berwick's prestigious Bordernapolis meeting, winning the final in fine style from Leigh Adams, Joe Screen and Claus Kristensen.

12 With Dane Mads Korneliussen replacing the departed Frank Smart, Newport complete their home league programme by defeating Somerset 50-39. Individual fare at Glasgow results in Carl Stonehewer winning the final of the Ashfield Classic ahead of James Grieves, Rory Schlein and Magnus Karlsson. Stoke suffer a 49-42 reverse at the hands of a sharper Trelawny side in league activity at Loomer Road.

13 Exeter stage Michael Coles' Twenty-Year Testimonial Meeting, with Leigh Adams taking

victory in the final from Mark Lemon, Leigh Lanham and Chris Harris. Kenneth Bjerre storms to a full house (15) as Newcastle defeat Newport 57-33 to complete their league schedule for the year.

14   The scores are close throughout, but Stoke finally come through to defeat Newport 46-44 in superb Premier League action at Loomer Road.

16   Sheffield are restricted to a narrow 47-46 victory as the Isle of Wight make sure of an aggregate Knock-Out Cup final success with a gutsy second-leg performance at Owlerton.

17   By defeating King's Lynn 52-38, Champions Edinburgh complete a magnificent 100 per cent home league record. Somerset finish a tough league campaign in style at the Oak Tree Arena, beating Rye House 50-40, with guest Craig Watson plundering a full house (15). Kelvin Tatum MBE bags a maximum as Arena-Essex cruise to a 54-36 league success against Trelawny.

18   Berwick end their league programme with a 48-41 win against Newport, but the match is marred by an horrific second-heat spill which leaves popular Argentinian Carlos Villar with crippling spinal injuries. Stoke complete their league fixtures with a 47-43 loss at the hands of an Isle of Wight side who are still chasing a second-place finish to go with their KOC success.

19   Hotly-contested challenge match action at Newport results in a narrow 46-44 victory for the Lions over the Kangaroos. A waterlogged Newcastle circuit leaves no option but to postpone the George English Memorial Trophy.

20   Reading come from behind to snatch a dramatic 44-44 draw against King's Lynn in the final meeting of an injury-ravaged season for the Racers.

21   Rain is the only winner as the Isle of Wight's final league match against Arena-Essex is postponed.

23   The Northern Riders' Championship results in a scintillating home victory for Sean Wilson, with Gary Havelock, Sam Ermolenko and Adam Shields following the Sheffield man home in the final.

24   Frede Schott romps to maximum points (15) as Edinburgh retain the Scottish Cup, winning the second-leg against Glasgow 54-36. Arena-Essex record their sixth league victory on the bounce, comfortably defeating a depleted King's Lynn side 55-35.

25   Brent Werner wins a run-off to take the Ace of Herts Championship at Rye House, with Steve Masters having to settle for the runner-up spot after falling in the title decider.

26   David Howe wins his third individual meeting of the year at Newport, taking victory in the final of the Prince of Wales Trophy ahead of Craig Watson, Niels-Kristian Iversen and Chris Harris. William Lawson streaks clear to win the final of the restaged George English Memorial Trophy at Newcastle, with Rory Schlein, Carl Stonehewer and Richard Juul following the young Scot home. Mark Lemon tallies a dozen points to win the Pride of the Potteries at Stoke, with Carl Stonehewer (having made the dash down from the earlier meeting at Newcastle) finishing second after defeating Ricky Ashworth in a run-off.

28   The league season ends with a shock result as Arena-Essex produce a late spurt to win 47-44 on the Isle of Wight. The defeat is the Islanders' first home league loss since September 2000 and denies them second place in the final table.

31   Edinburgh celebrate their tremendous season with a Champions Farewell challenge fixture that sees the All-Blues beat the All-Golds 48-42.

PREMIER LEAGUE TABLE

	Mts	Won	Drn	Lst	For	Agn	Pts	Bon	Tot
Edinburgh	34	26	0	8	1653	1393	52	14	66
Sheffield	34	22	0	12	1655	1397	44	13	57
Isle of Wight	34	22	0	12	1603	1463	44	12	56
Swindon	34	20	1	13	1598½	1451½	41	12	53
Berwick	34	20	1	13	1563	1465	41	12	53
King's Lynn	34	19	1	14	1598	1448	39	13	52
Arena-Essex	34	19	0	15	1609	1421	38	13	51
Trelawny	34	19	0	15	1599½	1470½	38	12	50
Workington	34	19	2	13	1551	1489	40	9	49
Newport	34	17	2	15	1504	1546	36	8	44
Newcastle	34	17	0	17	1525	1518	34	9	43
Glasgow	34	17	2	15	1479	1529	36	7	43
Exeter	34	13	0	21	1435	1592	26	5	31
Rye House	34	12	1	21	1441	1612	25	5	30
Stoke	34	10	1	23	1443	1597	21	3	24
Reading	34	9	2	23	1404	1653	20	2	22
Somerset	34	9	2	23	1357	1705	20	2	22
Hull	34	8	1	25	1395	1663	17	2	19

KNOCK-OUT CUP RESULTS

PRELIMINARY ROUND

| Workington | 46 | King's Lynn | 43 | |
| King's Lynn | 52 | Workington | 43 | (King's Lynn won 95-89 on aggregate) |

| Newport | 61 | Somerset | 35 | |
| Somerset | 43 | Newport | 49 | (Newport won 110-78 on aggregate) |

ROUND ONE

| Arena-Essex | 44 | Rye House | 46 | |
| Rye House | 46 | Arena-Essex | 44 | (Arena-Essex and Rye House drew 90-90 on aggregate) |

| Reading | 51 | Trelawny | 45 | |
| Trelawny | 65 | Reading | 30 | (Trelawny won 110-81 on aggregate) |

| Berwick | 52 | Glasgow | 46 | |
| Glasgow | 42 | Berwick | 42 | (Berwick won 94-88 on aggregate) |

| Stoke | 51 | Newcastle | 44 | |
| Newcastle | 50 | Stoke | 40 | (Newcastle won 94-91 on aggregate) |

| Newport | 47 | Exeter | 43 | |
| Exeter | 50 | Newport | 43 | (Exeter won 93-90 on aggregate) |

| Isle of Wight | 54 | Swindon | 38 | |
| Swindon | 49 | Isle of Wight | 51 | (Isle of Wight won 105-87 on aggregate) |

| Sheffield | 56 | Hull | 43 | |
| Hull | 41 | Sheffield | 48 | (Sheffield won 104-84 on aggregate) |

| King's Lynn | 62 | Edinburgh | 34 | |
| Edinburgh | 59 | King's Lynn | 37 | (King's Lynn won 99-93 on aggregate) |

REPLAY

| Arena-Essex | 55 | Rye House | 40 | |
| Rye House | 44 | Arena-Essex | 46 | (Arena-Essex won 101-84 on aggregate) |

ROUND TWO

| Berwick | 55 | Trelawny | 42 | |
| Trelawny | 61 | Berwick | 34 | (Trelawny won 103-89 on aggregate) |

| Exeter | 53 | Isle of Wight | 42 | |
| Isle of Wight | 61 | Exeter | 34 | (Isle of Wight won 103-87 on aggregate) |

| Sheffield | 50 | King's Lynn | 48 | |
| King's Lynn | 48 | Sheffield | 49 | (Sheffield won 99-96 on aggregate) |

| Arena-Essex | 55 | Newcastle | 41 | |
| Newcastle | 49 | Arena-Essex | 41 | (Arena-Essex won 96-90 on aggregate) |

SEMI-FINALS

| Trelawny | 49 | Isle of Wight | 43 | |
| Isle of Wight | 54 | Trelawny | 45 | (Isle of Wight won 97-94 on aggregate) |

| Sheffield | 57 | Arena-Essex | 41 | |
| Arena-Essex | 55 | Sheffield | 43 | (Sheffield won 100-96 on aggregate) |

FINAL

| Isle of Wight | 49 | Sheffield | 44 | |
| Sheffield | 47 | Isle of Wight | 46 | (Isle of Wight won 95-91 on aggregate) |

ARENA-ESSEX AF STOCKTAKING HAMMERS

ADDRESS: Arena-Essex Raceway, A1306 Arterial Road, Thurrock, Essex.
PROMOTER: Ronnie Russell.
TRACK LENGTH: 252 metres.
FIRST MEETING: 5 April 1984.
YEARS OF OPERATION: 1984-90 National League; 1991 British League Division Two;
    1992-94 British League Division One; 1995 British Premier League; 1996 British
    Conference League; 1997-03 British Premier League.

CLUB HONOURS

LEAGUE CHAMPIONS: 1991.
KNOCK-OUT CUP WINNERS: 1991.
FOUR-TEAM CHAMPIONS: 1991.

RIDER ROSTER 2003

BAGER, Henning   *b. 18 February 1981, Esbjerg, Denmark.*
    BRITISH CAREER: (2001) Glasgow; (2002) Peterborough, Isle of Wight; (2003) Arena-
    Essex.
CLEMENT, James   *b. 29 August 1985, Crawley, West Sussex.*
    BRITISH CAREER: (2003) Wimbledon, Arena-Essex (BLC).
FERROW, Alan   *b. 28 April 1982, Ashington, Northumberland.*
    BRITISH CAREER: (2003) Trelawny (CT), Arena-Essex, Newport (PL).
GALVIN, Andy   *b. 13 November 1965, Whitstable, Kent.*
    BRITISH CAREER: (1982-83) Crayford; (1984) Hackney, Wimbledon; (1985) Hackney;
    (1986) Hackney, Reading; (1987) Hackney; (1988) Hackney, Swindon, Cradley Heath,
    Sheffield, Ipswich; (1989-90) Hackney; (1991-93) Arena-Essex; (2001-03) Arena-Essex.
HERNE, Lee   *b. 27 March 1980, Ipswich, Suffolk.*
    BRITISH CAREER: (2000) Newport (PL & CL); Swindon, Workington, Isle of Wight,
    Reading; (2001) Trelawny, Somerset, Stoke, Arena-Essex; (2002-03) Arena-Essex.
KING, Daniel   *b. 14 August 1986, Maidstone, Kent.*
    BRITISH CAREER: (2001) Peterborough (CL); (2002) Peterborough (CL), Swindon (CT);
    (2003) Peterborough (CL), Ipswich (BLC), Reading, Mildenhall, Arena-Essex.
KING, Jason   *b. 13 April 1985, Maidstone, Kent.*
    BRITISH CAREER: (2000) Peterborough (CL); (2001) Peterborough (CL), Newport (PL),
    Newcastle; (2002) Swindon (PL & CT), Peterborough (CL & ELKOC); (2003) Arena-
    Essex, Peterborough (CL).
KYLMAKORPI, Joonas   *b. 14 February 1980, Seinajoki, Finland.*
    BRITISH CAREER: (2001) Eastbourne; (2002) Ipswich; (2003) Arena-Essex, Eastbourne
LANHAM, Leigh   *b. 15 August 1977, Ipswich, Suffolk.*
    BRITISH CAREER: (1993) Ipswich, Arena-Essex; (1994-96) Ipswich; (1997) Exeter,
    Bradford, King's Lynn; (1998-99) Arena-Essex; (2001) Arena-Essex; (2002-03) Arena-
    Essex, Ipswich.

ARENA-ESSEX HAMMERS: back row, left to right: Jason King, Lee Herne, Joonas Kylmakorpi, Henning Bager, Andy Galvin, Leigh Lanham, Ronnie Russell (Promoter/Team Manager). Front, on bike: Kelvin Tatum MBE.

PARSONS, Joel   b. 24 July 1985, Broken Hill, New South Wales, Australia.
BRITISH CAREER: (2003) Reading, Eastbourne (BLC), Rye House (CL & PL), Newport (PL), Wimbledon (CT), Arena-Essex, Peterborough (BLC), Hull.

PRIEST, Luke   b. 18 June 1985, Birmingham, West Midlands.
BRITISH CAREER: (2000) Ashfield, Owlerton; (2001) Sheffield (CL), Boston; (2002) Sheffield (CL), Wolverhampton (CT); (2003) Sheffield (CL & PL), Stoke (CT & PL), Workington, Exeter, Newport (BLC), Arena-Essex, Wolverhampton (BLC), Belle Vue (BLC).

RUUD, David   b. 21 January 1980, Gislaved, Sweden.
BRITISH CAREER: (2001) Poole; (2003) Poole, Arena-Essex.

TATUM MBE, Kelvin   b. 8 February 1964, Epsom, Surrey.
BRITISH CAREER: (1983-84) Wimbledon; (1985-90) Coventry; (1991) Berwick; (1992-93) Bradford; (1994) Arena-Essex; (1995) Poole, Eastbourne; (1996) London; (1997) Belle Vue, Peterborough; (1998) Poole; (1999) Eastbourne; (2002-03) Arena-Essex.

THOMPSON, Mark   b. 8 July 1979, Orsett, Essex.
BRITISH CAREER: (1996) Sittingbourne, Linlithgow, Mildenhall, Eastbourne (CL); (1997) Anglian Angels; (1998) Mildenhall, Newport, Stoke; (1999) King's Lynn (CL); (2000-01) Mildenhall; (2002) King's Lynn (CL), Mildenhall, Arena-Essex, Workington, Stoke; (2003) Boston, Stoke (PL), Newport (BLC), Somerset, Peterborough (BLC), Coventry (BLC), King's Lynn, Arena-Essex.

WRIGHT, Matthew   b. 19 November 1985, Harlow, Essex.
BRITISH CAREER: (2002) Boston, Mildenhall, Carmarthen, Wimbledon; (2003) Mildenhall, Ipswich (BLC), Arena-Essex (BLC), Reading, Peterborough (BLC).

PREMIER LEAGUE

(* Denotes bonus-point victory)

No	DATE	OPPONENTS	H/A	RESULT	TATUM	HERNE	KYLMAKORPI	BAGER	LANHAM	GALVIN	J. KING	RUUD	D. KING	OTHERS
1	28/3	Isle of Wight	H	W49-42	6(2)	5(4)	6+1(4)	11+2(5)	13(5)	6+2(5)	2(5)	–	–	–
2	4/4	Exeter	H	W63-27	9+2(4)	8+2(4)	8+2(5)	9(4)	13+1(5)	7+2(4)	9+3(4)	–	–	–
3	7/4	Reading	A	L44-46	11(4)	2(4)	11(5)	5+1(4)	10(5)	0(3)	5+1(5)	–	–	–
4	11/4	Reading	H	W56-34*	7+1(4)	6+1(4)	14+1(5)	10+1(5)	11(4)	6+1(4)	2(4)	–	–	–
5	23/4	King's Lynn	A	L42-48	11(5)	2+1(3)	13+1(6)	4+2(4)	11+1(6)	0(3)	1(3)	–	–	–
6	5/5	Exeter	A	L44-46*	8(4)	2+1(4)	11+1(5)	2(4)	14(5)	2(3)	5+1(5)	–	–	–
7	6/5	Trelawny	A	L35-55	8(5)	0(4)	–	9+1(5)	11(6)	1(3)	6+1(4)	–	–	–
8	9/5	Newport	H	W65-24	9+3(5)	7+3(4)	14+1(5)	10(4)	12(4)	4(4)	9+1(4)	–	–	–
9	30/5	Edinburgh †	A	L32-40	3(3)	0(2)	13(5)	6+3(5)	5(5)	2(3)	3(3)	–	–	–
10	31/5	Berwick	A	L37-53	6(5)	0(3)	17(6)	3(4)	8(6)	2(3)	1+1(3)	–	–	–
11	1/6	Glasgow	A	L42-48	10+1(6)	1(3)	17(6)	2(5)	10(5)	2(4)	0(1)	–	–	–
12	20/6	Workington	H	W52-38	6+1(5)	5+3(4)	7+1(4)	8+1(4)	13(5)	0(1)	13(7)	–	–	–
13	26/6	Swindon	A	L41-49	6+1(4)	2+1(3)	–	3(4)	10+1(5)	–	6(5)	13(6)	–	1(1)
14	3/7	Sheffield	A	L41-49	7+1(5)	4+1(3)	14+1(6)	4+2(4)	10(6)	–	2+1(3)	–	–	0(3)
15	4/7	Hull	H	W53-36	1+1(3)	8+2(6)	12+1(5)	9(4)	14(5)	–	8+3(4)	–	–	1(3)
16	11/7	Somerset	H	W56-34	9+2(4)	13+2(5)	7(5)	7+1(4)	10+1(5)	–	6+2(4)	–	–	4+1(3)
17	18/7	Sheffield	H	W53-36*	11+2(6)	10+1(5)	–	8+1(5)	17(6)	–	5+1(5)	R/R	–	2+1(3)

PREMIER LEAGUE continued

No	DATE	OPPONENTS	H/A	RESULT	TATUM	HERNE	KYLMAKORPI	BAGER	LANHAM	GALVIN	J. KING	RUUD	D. KING	OTHERS
18	20/7	Stoke	A	W48-44	8+1(4)	7+2(5)	13+1(5)	5+3(4)	12(5)	–	2(4)	–	1(3)	–
19	1/8	Newcastle	H	W52-38	7+1(4)	8+1(5)	10+2(5)	9+2(4)	14(5)	–	4+1(4)	–	0(3)	–
20	3/8	Newport	A	L42-47*	8(4)	8+2(5)	–	5+2(4)	10(5)	–	0(3)	9(5)	2+2(4)	–
21	23/8	Edinburgh	H	L45-48	6(5)	6+3(7)	17+1(6)	R/R	12+1(5)	–	2+1(4)	–	2(3)	–
22	5/9	Berwick	H	W46-44	13(5)	3(4)	14(5)	R/R	12+2(5)	–	3(7)	–	–	1+1(4)
23	12/9	Stoke	H	W60-30*	12(4)	7+4(4)	12+1(5)	6+2(4)	14(5)	–	9(5)	–	–	0(3)
24	13/9	Workington	A	L34-56	7(5)	1(3)	–	3+1(5)	12(6)	–	2(3)	9+1(5)	–	0(3)
25	14/9	Newcastle	A	L38-52*	–	2+2(4)	–	2+1(4)	13(6)	–	3+2(4)	11(5)	–	7+1(7)
26	17/9	Hull	A	L40-50*	–	2+1(4)	–	7+2(6)	16(7)	–	10+1(6)	R/R	2+1(3)	3(4)
27	20/9	Rye House	A	L42-48	7+1(5)	4+2(4)	12+2(6)	2(3)	14(6)	–	2(3)	–	1+1(3)	–
28	26/9	Glasgow ‡	H	W49-23*	10(4)	4+3(5)	9(3)	8+3(4)	8(3)	–	6+2(3)	–	4+2(4)	–
29	1/10	Somerset	A	W48-42*	15+1(6)	5(5)	R/R	5+1(4)	13+2(6)	–	6+1(5)	–	4+1(4)	–
30	3/10	Swindon	H	W51-42*	9+2(5)	7+2(5)	R/R	12+1(6)	14+1(6)	–	7(4)	–	2+1(4)	–
31	10/10	Rye House	H	W53-37*	8(4)	8+1(4)	14(5)	7+2(4)	12+2(5)	–	4+1(5)	–	0(3)	–
32	17/10	Trelawny	H	W54-36	12(4)	5(4)	12(5)	7+2(4)	10(5)	–	4(4)	–	4+1(4)	–
33	24/10	King's Lynn	H	W55-35*	9(4)	4+2(4)	10(5)	11+3(5)	10(4)	–	7+1(4)	–	4+2(4)	–
34	28/10	Isle of Wight	A	W47-44*	R/R	5+2(6)	16+1(6)	7+2(5)	17(7)	–	0(3)	–	2+1(3)	–

† Meeting abandoned after twelve heats, with the result standing.

‡ Meeting abandoned after twelve heats, with the result standing.

DETAILS OF OTHER RIDERS:

Match No. 13: Joel Parsons 1(1); Match No. 14: Ben Warburton 0(3); Match No. 15: James Cockle 1(3); Match No. 16: Joel Parsons 4+1(3); Match No. 17: Joel Parsons 2+1(3); Match No. 22: Mark Thompson 1+1(4); Match No. 23: Matthew Wright 0(3); Match No. 24: Luke Priest 0(3); Match No. 25: David Meldrum 7+1(4); Alan Ferrow 0(3); Match No. 26: Lee Dicken 3(4).

GOLDEN DOUBLE RIDES:

Match No. 21: Joonas Kylmakorpi's figures include 6 points from one golden double ride; Match No. 34: Joonas Kylmakorpi's figures include 6 points from one golden double ride.

PREMIER LEAGUE AVERAGES

Rider	Mts	Rds	Pts	Bon	Tot	Avge	Max
Joonas Kylmakorpi	25	128	297	18	315	9.84	2 Paid
Leigh Lanham	34	177	405	12	417	9.42	1 Full
David Ruud	4	21	42	1	43	8.19	–
Kelvin Tatum	31	137	259	21	280	8.18	2 Full
Henning Bager	32	140	206	42	248	7.09	–
Lee Herne	34	141	161	45	206	5.84	1 Paid
Joel Parsons	3	7	7	2	9	5.14	–
Jason King	34	140	154	25	179	5.11	1 Paid
Andy Galvin	12	40	32	5	37	3.70	–
Daniel King	13	45	28	12	40	3.56	–
Mark Thompson	1	4	1	1	2	2.00	–
James Cockle	1	3	1	0	1	1.33	–

Rider	Mts	Rds	Pts	Bon	Tot	Avge	Max
Alan Ferrow	1	3	0	0	0	0.00	–
Luke Priest	1	3	0	0	0	0.00	–
Ben Warburton	1	3	0	0	0	0.00	–
Matthew Wright	1	3	0	0	0	0.00	–
Guests	2	8	10	1	11	5.50	–

NOTE: The figures for Joonas Kylmakorpi include two golden double rides (12 points), modified to normal score i.e. 6 points.

BRITISH LEAGUE CUP

(* Denotes bonus-point victory)

No	DATE	OPPONENTS	H/A	RESULT	KYLMAKORPI	BAGER	TATUM	J. KING	LANHAM	PARSONS	HERNE	D. KING	RUUD	WRIGHT	OTHERS
1	25/7	Ipswich	H	W54-36	12+2(5)	3+1(4)	12(4)	2+1(4)	14(5)	2+1(3)	9+2(5)	–	–	–	–
2	6/8	King's Lynn	A	L40-50	R/R	7+2(5)	11(6)	2+1(4)	13(6)	–	4+1(5)	3(4)	–	–	–
3	8/8	Rye House	H	W49-41	9+2(5)	5+3(4)	9(4)	0(3)	14(5)	–	8+3(5)	4(4)	–	–	–
4	15/8	King's Lynn	H	W56-34*	–	9+1(4)	12+1(5)	4+2(4)	15(5)	–	10+2(5)	–	6+1(4)	0(3)	–
5	16/8	Rye House	A	L37-53	–	4+1(4)	7(5)	1(3)	10+1(6)	–	5(4)	–	9+1(5)	1+1(3)	–
6	21/8	Ipswich	A	L38-52*	12+1(6)	5+3(5)	4(4)	0(3)	12(6)	–	4(3)	–	–	–	1(3)
7	12/9	Peterborough	H	W64-27	15(5)	7+1(4)	10+1(4)	11+2(5)	13+2(5)	–	6+1(4)	–	–	2(3)	–
8	27/10	Peterborough	A	W47-43*	10+1(5)	6+1(5)	R/R	3+2(4)	12(5)	–	7+1(5)	9+3(6)	–	–	–

DETAILS OF OTHER RIDERS:

Match No. 6: James Clement 1(3).

BRITISH LEAGUE CUP AVERAGES

Rider	Mts	Rds	Pts	Bon	Tot	Avge	Max
Leigh Lanham	8	43	103	3	106	9.86	1 Full; 1 Paid
Joonas Kylmakorpi	5	26	58	6	64	9.85	1 Full
Kelvin Tatum	7	32	65	2	67	8.38	1 Full
David Ruud	2	9	15	2	17	7.56	–
Lee Herne	8	36	53	10	63	7.00	–
Henning Bager	8	35	46	13	59	6.74	–
Daniel King	3	14	16	3	19	5.43	–
Jason King	8	30	23	8	31	4.13	–
Joel Parsons	1	3	2	1	3	4.00	–
Matthew Wright	3	9	3	1	4	1.78	–
James Clement	1	3	1	0	1	1.33	–

KNOCK-OUT CUP

(* Denotes aggregate victory)

No	DATE	OPPONENTS	H/A	RESULT	TATUM	HERNE	LANHAM	BAGER	KYLMAKORPI	GALVIN	J. KING	RUUD	D. KING	OTHERS
1	18/4	Rye House	H	L44-46	8(5)	5+2(5)	16+1(6)	10+2(6)	R/R	2(4)	3+1(4)	–	–	–
2	19/4	Rye House	A	W46-44	10+1(4)	2+1(4)	14(5)	5+1(4)	8+2(5)	5+1(4)	2(4)	–	–	–
3	23/5	Rye House (R)	H	W55-40	9+1(4)	6(4)	13+1(5)	6+1(4)	11(5)	4(4)	6+1(4)	–	–	–
4	26/5	Rye House (R)	A	W46-44*	12(4)	4+1(4)	12+1(5)	3+1(4)	12(5)	2+1(5)	1(3)	–	–	–
5	27/6	Newcastle	H	W55-41	9+2(5)	6(4)	15(5)	6(4)	–		4+1(4)	6(4)		9(4)
6	28/7	Newcastle	A	L41-49*	11(5)	7+2(5)	13(6)	6+3(6)	R/R	–	2+1(4)		2+1(4)	–
7	4/9	Sheffield	A	L41-57	12+1(6)	2(5)	17(6)	R/R	7+1(4)	–	3+1(7)		0(2)	–
8	19/9	Sheffield	H	W55-43	11(4)	6+2(4)	13+1(5)	6+3(4)	12+1(5)	–	5+2(5)		2+1(3)	–

(R) = Replay

DETAILS OF OTHER RIDERS:

Match No. 5: Joel Parsons 9(4).

GOLDEN DOUBLE/TACTICAL JOKER RIDES:

Match No. 7: Leigh Lanham's total includes 6 points from a tactical joker ride and 2 points from a golden double outing; Joonas Kylmakorpi's total includes 4 points from a tactical joker ride; Kevin Tatum's total includes 4 points from a tactical joker ride.

BERWICK 3tmobile.net BANDITS

ADDRESS: Shielfield Park, Tweedmouth, Berwick-upon-Tweed, Northumberland.
PROMOTER: Peter Waite.
TRACK LENGTH: 368 metres.
FIRST MEETING: 18 May 1968.
YEARS OF OPERATION: 1968-74 British League Division Two; 1975-80 National League; 1995 Demonstration; 1996 British Conference League; 1997 British Premier League & British Amateur League; 1998-03 British Premier League.

PREVIOUS VENUE: Berrington Lough Stadium, nr. Ancroft, Northumberland.
YEARS OF OPERATION: 1982-90 National League; 1991 British League Division One; 1992 British League Division Two; 1993 Open; 1994 British League Division Three; 1995 British Academy League.

CLUB HONOURS

KNOCK-OUT CUP WINNERS: 1980, 1989, 1995.
GOLD CUP WINNERS: 1991.
LEAGUE CHAMPIONS: 1994, 1995.
FOUR-TEAM CHAMPIONS: 2002.

RIDER ROSTER 2003

BENTLEY, Paul   *b. 18 January 1968, Newcastle-upon-Tyne, Tyne & Wear.*
BRITISH CAREER: (1987) Newcastle; (1988-91) Middlesbrough; (1992) Coventry; (1993) Bradford; (1994) Middlesbrough; (1995-96) Coventry; (1997) Newcastle; (1998) Hull; (1999) Glasgow; (2000) Berwick; (2001) Hull; (2002-03) Berwick.

FRANC, Josef   *b. 18 January 1979, Kutna Hora, Czech Republic.*
BRITISH CAREER: (2001) Berwick; (2003) Berwick.

GRANT, Rob   *b. 10 June 1984, Newcastle-upon-Tyne, Tyne & Wear.*
BRITISH CAREER: (1999) Linlithgow; (2000) Ashfield, Newcastle; (2001) Newcastle; (2002) Newcastle, Boston, Stoke; (2003) Berwick, Sheffield (CL), Stoke.

KRISTENSEN, Claus   *b. 11 June 1977, Holstebro, Denmark.*
BRITISH CAREER: (1999) Berwick; (2000-01) Swindon; (2002-03) Berwick.

MAKOVSKY, Michal   *b. 6 April 1976, Hradec Kralove, Czech Republic.*
BRITISH CAREER: (2001-03) Berwick.

MELDRUM, David   *b. 6 October 1977, Berwick-upon-Tweed, Northumberland.*
BRITISH CAREER: (1994-95) Berwick; (1996) Berwick, Eastbourne (CL); (1997) Berwick (PL & AL); (1998) Berwick, Buxton; (1999-01) Berwick; (2002) Somerset, Wimbledon, Edinburgh; (2003) Berwick.

RYMEL, Adrian   *b. 30 October 1975, Koprivnice, Czech Republic.*
BRITISH CAREER: (2001-03) Berwick.

SHIELD, Carl   *b. 27 June 1979, Bishop Auckland, County Durham.*
BRITISH CAREER: (2002) Newcastle (CL), Sheffield (PLKOC); (2003) Berwick, Newcastle (CL), Armadale, Edinburgh.

VILLAR, Carlos   *b. 13 January 1975, Coronel Pringles, Argentina.*
BRITISH CAREER: (2003) Berwick.

PREMIER LEAGUE

(* Denotes bonus-point victory)

No	DATE	OPPONENTS	H/A	RESULT	BENTLEY	FRANC	KRISTENSEN	RYMEL	MAKOVSKY	GRANT	VILLAR	MELDRUM	OTHERS
1	23/4	Hull	A	W50-40	13+2(6)	6+1(4)	7(4)	7(4)	12+1(5)	0(3)	5+1(4)	–	–
2	26/4	Sheffield	H	L37-53	13(6)	R/R	5(5)	5+1(5)	9+1(6)	1(3)	4+2(5)	–	–
3	3/5	Exeter †	H	W51-17	8(3)	8+1(4)	8(3)	8+1(3)	8+2(4)	–	4+2(3)	7+3(4)	–
4	8/5	Swindon	A	L26-57	7+1(6)	–	2(3)	4+2(4)	10+1(6)	–	2(4)	1(3)	7(4)
5	9/5	Somerset	A	D45-45	5+1(4)	7+2(4)	7+1(5)	2+1(4)	11(5)	–	5+1(4)	8(4)	–
6	24/5	Workington	H	W51-39	7(4)	4+1(4)	4+1(3)	8+2(5)	11+1(5)	–	11+1(5)	6+2(4)	–
7	26/5	Workington	A	L44-46*	8(5)	7+1(4)	6+1(4)	9+1(5)	7+1(4)	–	4+3(4)	3+1(4)	–
8	31/5	Arena-Essex	H	W53-37	10(5)	9+2(4)	6+1(4)	4(4)	11+1(5)	–	6+2(4)	7+2(4)	–
9	2/6	Exeter	A	W46-44*	7(4)	3(5)	11(4)	6(4)	6+3(5)	–	3(3)	10+1(5)	–
10	3/6	Trelawny	A	L37-53	3(4)	4+1(3)	7(6)	1(3)	11+1(6)	–	4+1(3)	7+3(5)	–
11	7/6	King's Lynn	H	W46-44	8+1(4)	–	3+1(3)	8+2(5)	5+1(4)	–	6+1(5)	8(5)	8+3(4)
12	15/6	Stoke	A	L37-53	10+2(6)	4(3)	1(3)	4+2(5)	7+1(6)	–	4(3)	7+2(4)	–
13	16/6	Newcastle	A	L42-48	6+1(5)	6+1(5)	2(3)	7+1(4)	5(4)	–	3(3)	13+1(6)	–
14	19/6	Sheffield	A	L36-53	1(3)	9+2(5)	2+1(3)	6+1(5)	10+1(6)	–	0(2)	8+2(6)	–
15	28/6	Hull	H	W53-37*	12+1(6)	7+1(5)	12(6)	7(4)	7+1(4)	–	R/R	8+3(5)	–

BERWICK BANDITS: back row, left to right: Carlos Villar, Michal Makovsky, Claus Kristensen, Adrian Rymel, David Meldrum, Peter Waite (Promoter/Team Manager). Front, on bike: Paul Bentley.

PREMIER LEAGUE continued

No	DATE	OPPONENTS	H/A	RESULT	BENTLEY	FRANC	KRISTENSEN	RYMEL	MAKOVSKY	GRANT	VILLAR	MELDRUM	OTHERS
16	12/7	Swindon	H	W47-43	3+2(4)	3+2(5)	2(3)	12+1(6)	8(5)	–	R/R	19(7)	–
17	13/7	Newport	A	W46-44	8+1(5)	10+1(6)	4(3)	12(6)	5+1(4)	–	R/R	7+3(6)	–
18	20/7	Edinburgh	H	W49-41	11+1(5)	10+2(5)	3+2(4)	12+1(6)	7+1(4)	–	R/R	6+1(6)	–
19	28/7	Reading	A	W49-41	11+2(5)	17+2(7)	4+1(3)	9(5)	5(4)	–	R/R	3(6)	–
20	2/8	Trelawny	H	W48-42	8+2(6)	R/R	11+1(7)	8+2(5)	8+2(5)	–	7+2(4)	6+2(4)	–
21	3/8	Glasgow	A	L42-47	7+1(5)	R/R	5(5)	15+1(6)	7+2(5)	–	3+1(5)	5+1(4)	–
22	9/8	Somerset	H	W58-32*	13+1(5)	8+3(5)	20+1(7)	R/R	6+2(4)	–	0(4)	11(5)	–
23	16/8	Reading	H	W53-37*	10+1(5)	2+1(3)	14+2(7)	R/R	9(4)	–	8+3(7)	10+1(5)	–
24	23/8	Glasgow	H	W55-35*	5+2(4)	12+1(5)	11+1(4)	4+1(4)	7(4)	–	9+1(5)	7+2(4)	–
25	30/8	Rye House	H	W67-23	15(5)	R/R	9+3(6)	11+1(4)	12+2(5)	–	7+2(6)	13+2(5)	–
26	1/9	Rye House	A	L27-62*	4(3)	–	9(6)	3(5)	1(4)	–	1(3)	8(5)	1+1(4)
27	2/9	Isle of Wight	A	L43-47	12(6)	R/R	5(4)	9+1(6)	7(4)	–	7+4(6)	3+1(4)	–
28	5/9	Arena-Essex	A	L44-46*	6(4)	–	9+1(5)	6+1(5)	5+3(4)	–	2+2(2)	5+2(4)	11(5)
29	6/9	Newcastle	H	W63-27*	15+3(6)	R/R	15(5)	7+1(5)	12+1(5)	–	3+1(4)	11(5)	–
30	13/9	Isle of Wight	H	W52-39*	9+2(5)	5+2(4)	10(5)	5+4(4)	8+1(4)	–	7+3(4)	8+1(4)	–
31	17/9	King's Lynn	A	L30-60	4(4)	11(6)	1(4)	8(5)	3+1(4)	–	2+2(4)	1(3)	–
32	27/9	Stoke	H	W58-32*	13+1(5)	6+2(4)	13+1(6)	7+2(4)	12+2(5)	–	1(3)	6+1(4)	–
33	3/10	Edinburgh	A	L30-60	10+1(6)	1(4)	8(6)	1+1(4)	R/R	–	2(3)	8(7)	–
34	18/10	Newport	H	W48-41*	3+1(4)	9+2(5)	13+1(6)	4+1(4)	11+1(5)	–	0(1)	8+2(4)	–

† Meeting abandoned after twelve heats, with the result standing.

NOTE: The away match at Swindon originally ended in a 33-57 defeat on track; however, the points scored by guest Lee Smethills were subsequently deducted from Berwick's total, as his inclusion in the side was deemed ineligible.

DETAILS OF OTHER RIDERS:

Match No. 4: Lee Smethills 7(4); Match No. 11: Ricky Ashworth 8+3(4); Match No. 26: Andrew Moore 1+1(4); Match No. 28: Brent Werner 11(5).

PREMIER LEAGUE AVERAGES

Rider	Mts	Rds	Pts	Bon	Tot	Avge	Max
Michal Makovsky	33	153	263	35	298	7.79	–
Paul Bentley	34	163	285	30	315	7.73	1 Full; 1 Paid
David Meldrum	32	151	238	39	277	7.34	1 Paid
Josef Franc	24	109	168	31	199	7.30	–
Claus Kristensen	34	155	249	20	269	6.94	1 Full; 1 Paid
Adrian Rymel	32	147	219	32	251	6.83	–
Carlos Villar	29	113	120	35	155	5.49	–
Rob Grant	2	6	1	0	1	0.67	–
Guests	3	13	20	4	24	7.38	–

NOTES: (1) Claus Kristensen is not credited with a paid maximum in the home match versus Somerset, as he missed a programmed ride (in heat eight) when replaced by fellow reserve Carlos Villar. (2) Adrian Rymel is not credited with a paid maximum in the home match against Rye House due to a two-minute exclusion in heat nine. (3) The figures for guests do not include Lee Smethills' record at Swindon as his appearance was deemed ineligible.

BRITISH LEAGUE CUP

(* Denotes bonus-point victory)

No	DATE	OPPONENTS	H/A	RESULT	BENTLEY	FRANC	RYMEL	MAKOVSKY	GRANT	SHIELD	VILLAR	OTHERS
1	29/3	Glasgow	H	W47-42	10+1(5)	6+3(4)	–	8+1(4)	4+1(4)	2(3)	–	17+2(9)
2	4/4	Edinburgh	A	L37-53	8(5)	3(4)	–	2(4)	2(3)	3+1(3)	–	19+4(11)
3	5/4	Newcastle	H	W62-30	12+2(5)	7+2(4)	–	15(5)	9+1(5)	1(3)	–	18+4(8)
4	6/4	Glasgow	A	L41-50	8+1(5)	6(4)	–	8(4)	2(4)	1(3)	–	16+2(10)
5	12/4	Edinburgh	H	W52-38	14(5)	4+1(4)	–	10+1(5)	5(4)	4+1(4)	–	15+1(8)
6	18/4	Workington	A	L40-50	12(6)	6+1(4)	–	5(4)	2(3)	–	1(3)	14+3(10)
7	19/4	Workington	H	L42-48	4(4)	7(4)	–	8+1(4)	5+2(4)	–	2+1(4)	16+2(10)
8	20/4	Newcastle	A	L39-51*	R/R	10+1(6)	5(5)	10+1(7)	5(4)	–	0(3)	9(5)

DETAILS OF OTHER RIDERS:

Match No. 1: Andrew Appleton 11+2(5); Shaun Tacey 6(4); Match No. 2: Kevin Little 12+2(6); Neil Collins 7+2(5); Match No. 3:
Seemond Stephens 11(4); Neil Collins 7+4(4); Match No. 4: Davey Watt 13(6); Neil Collins 3+2(4); Match No. 5: Davey Watt 11+1(4);
Henning Bager 4(4); Match No. 6: Andrew Appleton 12+3(6); Seemond Stephens 2(4); Match No. 7: Andrew Appleton 9+1(5);
Seemond Stephens 7+1(5); Match No. 8: Paul Pickering 9(5).

GOLDEN DOUBLE RIDES:

Match No. 4: Davey Watt's figures include 2 points from one golden double ride.

BRITISH LEAGUE CUP AVERAGES

Rider	Mts	Rds	Pts	Bon	Tot	Avge	Max
Paul Bentley	7	35	68	4	72	8.23	–
Michal Makovsky	8	37	66	4	70	7.57	1 Full
Josef Franc	8	34	49	8	57	6.71	–
Rob Grant	8	31	34	4	38	4.90	–
Adrian Rymel	1	5	5	0	5	4.00	–
Carl Shield	5	16	11	2	13	3.25	–
Carlos Villar	3	10	3	1	4	1.60	–
Guests	15	71	123	18	141	7.94	1 Paid

NOTE: The figures for guests include one golden double ride (2 points), modified to normal score i.e. 1 point.

KNOCK-OUT CUP

(* Denotes aggregate victory)

No	DATE	OPPONENTS	H/A	RESULT	BENTLEY	MELDRUM	MAKOVSKY	RYMEL	KRISTENSEN	VILLAR	FRANC	OTHERS
1	10/5	Glasgow	H	W52-46	11(5)	5+1(4)	8+2(4)	9+1(5)	7(4)	4+3(3)	8+1(5)	–
2	11/5	Glasgow †	A	D42-42*	7(4)	6+2(4)	7+1(4)	5(3)	2(3)	4(4)	11+1(6)	–
3	21/6	Trelawny	H	W55-42	7+1(4)	8+1(4)	8+2(4)	12+1(5)	11+1(5)	–	8+3(5)	1+1(3)
4	24/6	Trelawny	A	L34-61	7(5)	3+1(4)	8(5)	15+1(7)	0(2)	R/R	1+1(6)	–

† Meeting abandoned after fourteen heats, with the result standing.

DETAILS OF OTHER RIDERS:

Match No. 3: Richard Hall 1+1(3).

GOLDEN DOUBLE/TACTICAL JOKER RIDES:

Match No. 4: Adrian Rymel's total includes 4 points from a golden double ride and 4 points from a tactical joker outing; Paul Bentley's total includes 2 points from a tactical joker ride.

OTHER MEETINGS

15 March: International Club Challenge

Berwick 43 (Paul Bentley 14; Michal Makovsky 8+2; Claus Kristensen 7+1; Adrian Rymel 5; Adam Skornicki 4; Josef Franc 3+2; Carl Shield 1+1; Rob Grant 1) Valsarna 47 (Sam Ermolenko 14; Davey Watt 10+2; Bjorn G. Hansen 8+2; Stefan Danno 4+1; Peter I. Karlsson 4; Arnt Forland 4; Steven Andersen 3; Jesper Olsen 0).

22 March: Tyne-Tweed Trophy (first-leg)

Berwick 47 (Paul Bentley 14+2; Michal Makovsky 13+1; Adrian Rymel 7+1; Josef Franc 6+2; Rob Grant 6; Carl Shield 1; Claus Kristensen R/R) Newcastle 43.

23 March: Tyne-Tweed Trophy (second-leg)

Newcastle 46 Berwick 44 (Josef Franc 12+1; Michal Makovsky 12; Davey Watt 10; Rob Grant 7+2; Paul Bentley 3; Carl Shield 0; Adrian Rymel R/R) – Berwick won 91-89 on aggregate.

20 September: Premier League

Berwick 3 (David Meldrum 2; Josef Franc 1+1; Michal Makovsky DNR; Adrian Rymel DNR; Paul Bentley DNR; Claus Kristensen DNR; Carlos Villar DNR) Newport 3 – meeting abandoned after heat one.

INDIVIDUAL MEETINGS

26 July: Stars of Tomorrow

(Qualifying scores:- James Wright 11; Craig Branney 11; Benji Compton 10; Carl Shield 9; Steven Jones 7; Gary Flint 7; John Branney 7; John Morrison 4; Scott Nettleship 3; Alan McGreevy 1; John MacPhail 1; Robert Connon 1; Alan Ferrow 0). First Semi-Final: 1st Wright; 2nd Compton; 3rd J. Branney; 4th Jones. Second Semi-Final: 1st C. Branney; 2nd Shield; 3rd Morrison; 4th Flint. Final: 1st C. Branney; 2nd Compton; 3rd Wright; 4th Shield.

11 October: Bordernapolis

(Qualifying scores: Joe Screen 12; Chris Harris 11; Leigh Adams 10; Claus Kristensen 7; Paul Bentley 6; Steve Johnston 5; Scott Nicholls 5; Josef Franc 5; David Meldrum 3; Adrian Rymel 2; Carlos Villar 2). First Semi-Final: 1st Adams; 2nd Screen; 3rd Nicholls; 4th Bentley. Second Semi-Final: 1st Kristensen; 2nd Harris; 3rd Franc; 4th Johnston. Final: 1st Harris; 2nd Adams; 3rd Screen; 4th Kristensen.

EDINBURGH FULFILMENT FACTORY MONARCHS

NOTE: The information below relates only to the main Edinburgh team. For details of the second side, please refer to the Conference League section.

ADDRESS: Armadale Stadium, Bathgate Road, Armadale, West Lothian.

PROMOTERS: John Campbell & Alex Harkess.

TRACK LENGTH: 280 metres.

FIRST MEETING: 4 April 1997.

YEARS OF OPERATION: 1997–03 British Premier League.

PREVIOUS VENUES AS 'MONARCHS':

(1) Old Meadowbank Stadium, Clockmill Road, Edinburgh.
YEARS OF OPERATION: 1948–54 National League Division Two; 1957 Training; 1959 Open; 1960–64 Provincial League; 1965–67 British League; 1998 Demonstration.

(2) Cliftonhill Stadium, Main Street, Coatbridge, Lanarkshire.
YEARS OF OPERATION: 1968–69 British League Division One (Team rode as 'Coatbridge Monarchs').

(3) Powderhall Stadium, Beaverhall Road, Edinburgh.
YEARS OF OPERATION: 1977–90 National League; 1991–94 British League Division Two; 1995 British Premier League.

(4) Shawfield Stadium, Glasgow Road, Rutherglen, Glasgow.
YEARS OF OPERATION: 1996 British Premier League (Team rode under the name of 'Scottish Monarchs').

CLUB HONOURS

QUEEN'S CUP WINNERS: 1953.
FOUR-TEAM CHAMPIONS: 1981, 1993.
KNOCK-OUT CUP WINNERS: 1981, 1997, 1999.
PAIRS CHAMPIONS: 1986.
PREMIERSHIP WINNERS: 1998.
LEAGUE CHAMPIONS: 2003.

RIDER ROSTER 2003

CAMPBELL, Barry   *b. 26 August 1979, Glasgow, Scotland.*
BRITISH CAREER: (1995) Linlithgow, Swindon; (1996) Linlithgow, Edinburgh; (1997) Edinburgh, Lathallan; (1998) Edinburgh; (1999) Belle Vue, Workington; (2000–01) Workington; (2003) Edinburgh, Armadale (CT), Reading, Swindon (CL), Belle Vue (BLC).

CARR, Peter   *b. 22 January 1963, Preston, Lancashire.*
BRITISH CAREER: (1979) Ellesmere Port, Halifax; (1980) Ellesmere Port, Belle Vue, Birmingham, Hull; (1981) Ellesmere Port, Belle Vue; (1982–84) Belle Vue; (1985–88) Sheffield; (1989–90) Newcastle; (1991–93) Sheffield; (1994–95) Belle Vue; (1997–03) Edinburgh.

EDINBURGH MONARCHS: back row, left to right: Peter Carr, Theo Pijper, Matthew Wethers, Rory Schlein. On bike: Frede Schott. Front, kneeling: Wayne Carter, Magnus Karlsson.

CARTER, Wayne b. 19 December 1970, Halifax, West Yorkshire.
BRITISH CAREER: (1989) Mildenhall, Wolverhampton; (1990) Wolverhampton; (1991) Wolverhampton, Middlesbrough; (1992) Wolverhampton; (1993) Middlesbrough; (1994–95) Wolverhampton; (1996) Belle Vue, Middlesbrough; (1997) Skegness, Isle of Wight, Peterborough, Belle Vue, Wolverhampton, Bradford; (1998–99) Isle of Wight; (2000) Wolverhampton; (2001) Belle Vue, Berwick; (2002) Coventry, Newcastle; (2003) Wolverhampton (BLC), Edinburgh.

KARLSSON, Magnus b. 28 December 1981, Gullspang, Sweden.
BRITISH CAREER: (2002) Edinburgh; (2003) Edinburgh, Wolverhampton (BLC).

PIJPER, Theo b. 11 February 1980, Rinsumageest, Holland.
BRITISH CAREER: (2002–03) Edinburgh.

SCHLEIN, Rory b. 1 September 1984, Darwin, Northern Territory, Australia.
BRITISH CAREER: (2001) Edinburgh, Berwick, Glasgow, Newport, Sheffield (CL & PL), Trelawny, Newcastle; (2002) Edinburgh, Sheffield (CL); (2003) Edinburgh, Belle Vue.

SCHOTT, Frede b. 28 December 1970, Kolding, Denmark.
BRITISH CAREER: (1990) Edinburgh; (1991) Edinburgh, Berwick; (1992–96) Belle Vue; (2002–03) Edinburgh.

SHIELD, Carl b. 27 June 1979, Bishop Auckland, County Durham.
BRITISH CAREER: (2002) Newcastle (CL), Sheffield (PLKOC); (2003) Berwick, Newcastle (CL), Armadale (CT), Edinburgh.

SNEDDON, Derek b. 27 July 1982, Falkirk, Scotland.
BRITISH CAREER: (1998) Hull; (1999) Linlithgow, Isle of Wight; (2000) Ashfield, Edinburgh; (2001) Edinburgh, Glasgow; (2002) Newcastle; (2003) Edinburgh.

WETHERS, Matthew b. 30 May 1985, Modbury, South Australia.
BRITISH CAREER: (2003) Armadale (CT), Wolverhampton (CL), Edinburgh.

PREMIER LEAGUE

(* Denotes bonus-point victory)

No	DATE	OPPONENTS	H/A	RESULT	SCHOTT	PIJPER	CARR	SCHLEIN	KARLSSON	CAMPBELL	CARTER	SHIELD	WETHERS	OTHERS
1	30/4	Hull	A	W48-42	11(5)	5(4)	10+1(5)	9(4)	7(4)	0(3)	6+2(5)	–	–	–
2	9/5	Sheffield	H	W62-28	14+1(5)	7+3(4)	6+1(4)	11(4)	10+3(5)	6+1(4)	8+2(4)	–	–	–
3	10/5	Workington	A	L44-46	13(5)	5(4)	4+1(5)	6(4)	7(4)	1+1(3)	8+2(5)	–	–	–
4	23/5	Hull	H	W57-33*	15(5)	7+1(4)	11+3(5)	10+1(4)	8(4)	1(4)	5+1(4)	–	–	–
5	30/5	Arena-Essex †	H	W40-32	8(3)	4+1(4)	11+1(4)	6+1(3)	7(3)	–	3+1(4)	1+1(3)	–	–
6	1/6	Newcastle	A	W47-43	14(5)	5+1(4)	9+1(5)	6+1(4)	5+1(4)	–	8+1(5)	0(3)	–	–
7	2/6	Reading	A	W50-40	14(5)	6+1(4)	10(4)	3+2(4)	10+1(5)	–	5+1(5)	–	2+2(3)	–
8	13/6	Stoke	H	W55-35	15(5)	7+1(4)	13+1(5)	5+2(4)	7(4)	2+1(4)	6+2(4)	–	–	–
9	4/7	Newport	H	W49-40	15(5)	5(4)	8+2(5)	6+1(4)	7(4)	–	6+2(4)	–	2+1(4)	–
10	7/7	Exeter	A	L35-55	12(6)	1(4)	11(5)	5+1(5)	3(4)	–	1+1(3)	–	2(3)	–
11	8/7	Trelawny	A	W46-44	13(5)	3+1(4)	11+2(5)	8+1(4)	7(4)	–	1(4)	–	3+1(4)	–
12	11/7	Swindon	H	W48-42	11(4)	6+1(4)	10+2(5)	7+1(4)	5(4)	1+1(3)	8+2(6)	–	–	–
13	18/7	Workington	H	W48-42*	–	5(4)	15(5)	10(5)	6+3(4)	–	4+1(4)	–	3+2(4)	5(4)
14	20/7	Berwick	A	L41-49	–	6(6)	8(4)	8(5)	4+1(4)	–	0(3)	–	1(3)	14(5)
15	23/7	King's Lynn	A	L37-52	–	9+1(5)	6+2(5)	7+1(7)	R/R	–	1+1(3)	–	3+3(4)	11(6)

PREMIER LEAGUE continued

No	DATE	OPPONENTS	H/A	RESULT	SCHOTT	PIJPER	CARR	SCHLEIN	KARLSSON	CAMPBELL	CARTER	SHIELD	WETHERS	OTHERS
16	24/7	Swindon	A	L39-51	–	6+3(4)	4+1(5)	7+1(5)	10(5)	–	0(3)	–	2+2(3)	10(6)
17	1/8	Trelawny	H	W49-44*	–	8+1(5)	5+2(5)	9(5)	12(4)	–	3+1(3)	–	3+1(4)	9+1(4)
18	5/8	Isle of Wight	A	L42-48	–	4+1(4)	R/R	8+3(7)	9(6)	–	1(3)	–	2(3)	18(7)
19	6/8	Somerset	A	W46-44	–	3(4)	9(5)	6+1(4)	8+2(5)	–	2+1(3)	–	3+1(3)	15+1(6)
20	8/8	Somerset	H	W55-35*	–	7+2(6)	9+3(4)	12(4)	15(5)	–	1(3)	–	5+1(4)	6(4)
21	15/8	Reading	H	W60-30*	–	5+2(4)	11+1(4)	10+1(5)	9+1(4)	–	5+1(4)	–	5+1(4)	15(5)
22	22/8	Exeter	H	W63-27*	15(5)	11+1(5)	11+1(4)	13+2(5)	7+2(4)	–	4+2(4)	–	2(3)	–
23	23/8	Arena-Essex	A	W48-45*	14(5)	14+1(7)	9(4)	3+2(4)	5+2(4)	–	2+1(3)	–	–	1(3)
24	29/8	Rye House	H	W55-34	15(5)	10+1(5)	10+1(4)	11+3(5)	4+1(4)	–	5(4)	–	0(3)	–
25	30/8	Stoke	A	W46-44*	10(4)	10+2(6)	10+1(5)	7(5)	6+3(4)	–	2+2(3)	–	1+1(3)	–
26	31/8	Glasgow	A	W55-37	12(4)	12(7)	12(4)	13+2(5)	4+2(4)	–	1(3)	–	1(3)	–
27	12/9	Isle of Wight	H	W53-36*	11+2(5)	7+1(4)	11+1(4)	10+3(5)	9(4)	–	3(4)	–	2+1(4)	–
28	13/9	Rye House	A	W47-43*	14+1(5)	6+1(4)	7(4)	9+1(5)	7+1(4)	–	3+1(4)	–	1+1(4)	–
29	14/9	Newport	A	L40-50	13(6)	1(4)	8+1(5)	10+1(5)	6+1(4)	–	1(3)	–	1+1(3)	–
30	19/9	Glasgow	H	W56-34*	8+1(4)	8+2(4)	11(4)	11+2(5)	9+1(5)	–	5(4)	–	4+2(4)	–
31	2/10	Sheffield	A	L32-58*	6+1(4)	8+2(6)	4(4)	9(6)	3(4)	–	0(3)	–	2+1(3)	–
32	3/10	Berwick	H	W60-30*	14+1(5)	8+1(4)	14+1(5)	11+1(4)	7+1(4)	–	4(4)	–	2+1(4)	–
33	10/10	Newcastle	H	W48-42*	12(4)	6(4)	8+1(4)	7(5)	10+1(5)	–	1+1(3)	–	4(5)	–
34	17/10	King's Lynn	H	W52-38	14(5)	6+1(4)	12+1(5)	6+1(4)	6+3(4)	–	3(3)	–	5+1(5)	–

† Meeting abandoned after twelve heats, with the result standing.

DETAILS OF OTHER RIDERS:

Match No. 13: George Stancl 5(4); Match No. 14: Shane Parker 14(5); Match No. 15: Olly Allen 11(6); Match No. 16: Carl Stonehewer 10(6); Match No. 17: Shane Parker 9+1(4); Match No. 18: Craig Watson 18(7); Match No. 19: Carl Stonehewer 15+1(6); Match No. 20: Kevin Little 6(4); Match No. 21: Shane Parker 15(5); Match No. 23: Craig Branney 1(3).

PREMIER LEAGUE AVERAGES

Rider	Mts	Rds	Pts	Bon	Tot	Avge	Max
Frede Schott	25	119	313	7	320	10.76	7+3
Peter Carr	33	150	308	32	340	9.07	2+5
Rory Schlein	34	158	279	36	315	7.97	1+3
Magnus Karlsson	33	140	239	30	269	7.69	2+0
Theo Pijper	34	154	221	33	254	6.60	–
Wayne Carter	34	127	116	29	145	4.57	–
Matthew Wethers	25	90	61	24	85	3.78	–
Barry Campbell	6	21	11	4	15	2.86	–
Carl Shield	2	6	1	1	2	1.33	–
Guests	10	50	104	2	106	8.48	1+0

NOTE: Peter Carr is not credited with a paid maximum in the home match versus Somerset, as he missed a programmed ride (in heat five) through a two-minute exclusion.

BRITISH LEAGUE CUP

(* Denotes bonus-point victory)

No	DATE	OPPONENTS	H/A	RESULT	SCHOTT	PIJPER	CARR	SCHLEIN	KARLSSON	CAMPBELL	SNEDDON	CARTER	WETHERS	OTHERS
1	29/3	Workington	A	D45-45	11(5)	4+1(4)	11(5)	8+3(4)	5+1(4)	2+2(5)	4(3)	–	–	–
2	4/4	Berwick	H	W53-37	12(5)	8+1(4)	8+1(4)	4(4)	12+1(5)	4+1(4)	–	–	–	5(4)
3	6/4	Newcastle	A	W48-42	14(5)	3+2(4)	11+1(5)	2+1(4)	7(4)	1(3)	–	–	–	10+1(5)
4	11/4	Workington	H	W53-39*	14(5)	6+1(4)	12+1(5)	5+2(4)	9(4)	2(4)	–	–	–	5+1(4)
5	12/4	Berwick	A	L38-52*	13+1(6)	7+1(6)	5+2(4)	6+2(5)	2(2)	1(3)	–	–	–	4(4)
6	18/4	Newcastle	H	W47-43*	8+1(5)	5+2(4)	10(4)	4+1(4)	13(5)	2(3)	–	5+3(5)	–	–
7	20/4	Glasgow	A	L40-50	15(6)	0(3)	13+1(6)	1(4)	7(5)	2(3)	–	2+1(3)	–	–
8	20/6	Glasgow	H	W50-40	12(5)	4+1(4)	12+1(5)	7(4)	7(4)	–	–	5+1(5)	3(3)	–
9	22/9	Wolverhampton	A	L42-47	9(6)	5+2(4)	7+1(5)	12+2(6)	4+1(3)	–	–	3+1(3)	2+2(3)	–
10	26/9	Wolverhampton	H	L39-51	11(6)	4+3(5)	R/R	12+1(7)	5+1(5)	–	–	5(4)	2+2(3)	–

DETAILS OF OTHER RIDERS:

Match No. 2: David McAllan 5(4); Match No. 3: Lee Smethills 10+1(5); Match No. 4: Lee Smethills 5+1(4); Match No. 5: Steffen Mell 4(4).

BRITISH LEAGUE CUP AVERAGES

Rider	Mts	Rds	Pts	Bon	Tot	Avge	Max
Frede Schott	10	54	119	2	121	8.96	–
Peter Carr	9	43	89	8	97	9.02	–
Magnus Karlsson	10	41	71	4	75	7.32	–
Rory Schlein	10	46	61	12	73	6.35	–
Theo Pijper	10	42	46	14	60	5.71	–
Derek Sneddon	1	3	4	0	4	5.33	–
Wayne Carter	5	20	20	6	26	5.20	–
Matthew Wethers	3	9	7	4	11	4.89	–
Barry Campbell	7	25	14	3	17	2.72	–
Guests	4	17	24	2	26	6.12	–

KNOCK-OUT CUP

No	DATE	OPPONENTS	H/A	RESULT	SCHOTT	PIJPER	CARR	SCHLEIN	KARLSSON	SHIELD	CARTER	WETHERS
1	28/5	King's Lynn	A	L34-62	12+1(6)	4(4)	4(4)	6+1(5)	6(4)	0(3)	2+1(4)	–
2	6/6	King's Lynn	H	W59-37	15(5)	6(4)	11(4)	6+1(4)	10+1(5)	–	9+3(5)	2(3)

GOLDEN DOUBLE/TACTICAL JOKER RIDES:

Match No. 1: Frede Schott's total includes 4 points from a tactical joker ride and 4 points from a golden double outing; Theo Pijper's total includes 2 points from a tactical joker ride; Magnus Karlsson's total includes 2 points from a tactical joker ride.

OTHER MEETINGS

23 March: Spring Trophy (first-leg)

Glasgow 44 Edinburgh 46 (Peter Carr 10+1; Frede Schott 9+1; Rory Schlein 7+1; Theo Pijper 6+1; Magnus Karlsson 6+1; Derek Sneddon 6+1; Barry Campbell 2+1).

28 March: Spring Trophy (second-leg)

Edinburgh 53 (Frede Schott 12; Peter Carr 12; Theo Pijper 8+2; Derek Sneddon 8+2; Rory Schlein 7+2; Magnus Karlsson 6; Barry Campbell 0) Glasgow 37 – Edinburgh won 99-81 on aggregate.

16 May: Knock-Out Cup First Round, (first-leg)

Edinburgh 15 (Wayne Carter 4+1; Frede Schott 3; Magnus Karlsson 3; Peter Carr 2; Rory Schlein 1+1; Barry Campbell 1+1; Theo Pijper 1) King's Lynn 9 – meeting abandoned after heat four.

5 September: Motor Show 2 – Peter Carr 25 Year Benefit

The Aces 21 (Frede Schott 9; Joe Screen 6; Les Collins 4; Wayne Carter 2); The Diamonds 20 (Carl Stonehewer 6; Rory Schlein 6; Kevin Little 4; Martin Dixon 4); The Motors 16 (Steve Johnston 8; Christian Henry 4; Peter Carr 3; Magnus Karlsson 1); The Tigers 14 (James Grieves 6; Ross Brady 4; André Compton 2; Trent Leverington 1; Jamie Robertson 1). Individual Knock-Out: First Semi-Final: 1st Schlein; 2nd Screen; 3rd Stonehewer; 4th Schott. Second Semi-Final: 1st Johnston; 2nd Brady; 3rd Robertson; 4th Collins. Final: 1st Johnston; 2nd Schlein; 3rd Screen; 4th Brady.

5 October: Scottish Cup (first-leg)

Glasgow 36 Edinburgh 54 (Frede Schott 14; Peter Carr 12; Rory Schlein 10+2; Magnus Karlsson 7+1; Theo Pijper 5; Blair Scott 4; Matthew Wethers 2+1).

24 October: Scottish Cup (second-leg)

Edinburgh 54 (Frede Schott 15; Rory Schlein 10+1; Magnus Karlsson 8+1; Matthew Wethers 7+1; Wayne Carter 5+1; Peter Carr 5; Lee Smethills 4) Glasgow 36 – Edinburgh won 108-72 on aggregate.

31 October: Champions Farewell Challenge

All-Golds 42 (Frede Schott 11; Matthew Wethers 7+2; Barry Campbell 7; Magnus Karlsson 6+2; Sean Stoddart 6+2; Kristian Lund 4+1; Andrew Tully 1+1) All-Blues 48 (Mark Loram 12+1; Rory Schlein 10+2; Peter Carr 9+1; Gary Beaton 9; Craig Branney 6; Keith Maben 2; Wayne Carter 0).

INDIVIDUAL MEETING

25 July: Scottish Open Championship

(Qualifying scores: Sam Ermolenko 15; Carl Stonehewer 13; Kevin Little 12; Rusty Harrison 10; Magnus Karlsson 9; George Stancl 8; Matej Zagar 7; Kevin Doolan 7; Emiliano Sanchez 7; Peter Carr 6; David Meldrum 6; Theo Pijper 6; Christian Henry 5; Matthew Wethers (res) 4; Joe Screen 2; Wayne Carter 1; Barry Campbell (res) 1; Rory Schlein 0; Semi-Final: 1st Little; 2nd Stancl; 3rd Karlsson; 4th Harrison. Final: 1st Ermolenko; 2nd Stonehewer; 3rd Stancl; 4th Little.

EXETER FALCONS

ADDRESS: County Ground Stadium, St Thomas, Exeter, Devon.
PROMOTER: Colin Hill.
TRACK LENGTH: 396 metres.
FIRST MEETING: 9 March 1929.
YEARS OF OPERATION: 1929-31 Open; 1934 Open; 1947-51 National League Division
    Three; 1952-53 Southern League; 1954-55 National League Division Two; 1957-58
    Open; 1960 Open; 1961-64 Provincial League; 1965-67 British League; 1968-74 British
    League Division One; 1975-79 British League; 1980-83 National League; 1984 British
    League; 1985-90 National League; 1991-94 British League Division Two; 1995-03
    British Premier League.
    NOTE: Exeter also ran a second team in the 1995 British Academy League, the 1996 British Conference
    League and the 1997 British Amateur League. The team of 1995-96 rode as 'Devon Demons', whereas in
    1997 the fixtures were shared with Newport, under the banner of 'Western Warriors'.

CLUB HONOURS

LEAGUE CHAMPIONS: 1948, 1974, 2000.
NATIONAL TROPHY (DIVISION THREE) WINNERS: 1951.
KNOCK-OUT CUP WINNERS: 1962, 1983.
YOUNG SHIELD WINNERS: 1997.

RIDER ROSTER 2003

BLACKMAN, Corey   b. 30 April 1977, Perth, Western Australia.
    BRITISH CAREER: (2002) Carmarthen, Reading, Edinburgh, Glasgow, Exeter,
    Wolverhampton (CT), Sheffield (CL), Trelawny; (2003) Exeter, Carmarthen.
BRANNEY, John   b. 7 November 1985, Whitehaven, Cumbria.
    BRITISH CAREER: (2002) Rye House (CL), Newcastle (CL); (2003) Newcastle (CL),
    Wimbledon (CT), Mildenhall (CT), King's Lynn, Exeter, Newport (PL), Buxton (CT).
CANDY, Paul   b. 4 February 1980, Basingstoke, Hampshire.
    BRITISH CAREER: (2003) Carmarthen, Somerset, Exeter.
COLES, Michael   b. 11 August 1965, Exeter, Devon.
    BRITISH CAREER: (1982-83) Exeter; (1984) Exeter, Weymouth; (1985-87) Exeter; (1988)
    Mildenhall; (1989-93) Edinburgh; (1994) Belle Vue; (1995) Oxford; (1996) Exeter;
    (1997) Exeter, King's Lynn; (1998-03) Exeter.
COMPTON, Benji   b. 17 September 1986, Tenerife, Spain.
    BRITISH CAREER: (2002) Newcastle (CL); (2003) Sheffield (CL & PL), Swindon (PL),
    Hull (BLC), Mildenhall (KOC), Exeter.
HALL, Richard   b. 23 August 1984, Northallerton, North Yorkshire.
    BRITISH CAREER: (2001) Newcastle; (2002) Newcastle (PL & CL), Trelawny, Glasgow;
    (2003) Sheffield (CL & PL), Stoke (PL), Coventry (BLC), Hull (BLC), Newport (PL),
    Boston (KOC & CT), Exeter, Reading, Workington, Somerset.

LOBB, Roger   *b. 20 April 1978, Shepton Mallet, Somerset.*
BRITISH CAREER: (1995) Devon; (1996) Devon, Reading (CL), Exeter; (1997) Western Warriors, Reading, Newport (PL), Exeter; (1998) St Austell, Newport (CL), Exeter; (1999) Arena-Essex; (2000) Exeter; (2002-03) Exeter.

MACKAY, Brendon   *b. 14 August 1980, Darwin, Northern Territory, Australia.*
BRITISH CAREER: (2001-02) Reading; (2003) Somerset, Trelawny (CT), Newport (BLC), Exeter (BLC), Mildenhall

MARSH, Krister   *b. 23 March 1976, Hereford, Hereford & Worcester.*
BRITISH CAREER: (1995) Devon; (1996) Swindon (CL & PL), Sheffield, London; (1997) Oxford (AL & PL), Reading; (1998) Reading; (1999) Swindon; (2000) Reading, Newcastle; (2001) Newport, Swindon, Exeter; (2002-03) Exeter.

MASON, Karl   *b. 4 March 1986, Hillingdon, London.*
BRITISH CAREER: (2001) Buxton, Mildenhall, Somerset; (2002) Newport (CL), Reading; (2003) Newport (CL & PL), Exeter (BLC).

POWELL, Ben   *b. 29 November 1984, Helensvale, Gold Coast, Queensland, Australia.*
BRITISH CAREER: (2002) Sheffield (CL), Edinburgh, Trelawny, Glasgow; (2003) Carmarthen, Exeter.

PRIEST, Luke   *b. 18 June 1985, Birmingham, West Midlands.*
BRITISH CAREER: (2000) Ashfield, Owlerton; (2001) Sheffield (CL), Boston; (2002) Sheffield (CL), Wolverhampton (CT); (2003) Sheffield (CL & PL), Stoke (CT & PL), Workington, Exeter, Newport (BLC), Arena-Essex, Wolverhampton (BLC), Belle Vue (BLC).

SIMMONDS, Mark   *b. 10 May 1971, Truro, Cornwall.*
BRITISH CAREER: (1989-96) Exeter; (1997) Isle of Wight; (1998-03) Exeter.

SIMMONS, Nick   *b. 24 July 1981, Leamington Spa, Warwickshire.*
BRITISH CAREER: (1997) Shuttle Cubs, Ryde; (1998) Newport (CL & PL), Isle of Wight, Exeter; (1999) Isle of Wight, Stoke, Newport (CL); (2000) Arena-Essex; (2001) Newport (PL & CL), Somerset; (2002) Isle of Wight; (2003) Stoke, Reading, Mildenhall, Workington, King's Lynn, Exeter.

SMETHILLS, Lee   *b. 30 March 1982, Bolton, Greater Manchester.*
BRITISH CAREER: (1998) Mildenhall; (1999) Workington, Rye House, Buxton, Belle Vue, Newcastle; (2000) Workington, Buxton; (2001) Workington; (2002) Hull, Belle Vue; (2003) Exeter.

SMITH, Scott A.   *b. 29 September 1972, Sheffield, South Yorkshire.*
BRITISH CAREER: (1990-95) Cradley Heath; (1996-99) Sheffield; (2000) Berwick; (2001-02) Sheffield; (2003) Sheffield, Exeter.

STEPHENS, Seemond   *b. 9 August 1967, St Austell, Cornwall.*
BRITISH CAREER: (1998) St Austell, Exeter, Sheffield, Swindon; (1999) Eastbourne, Swindon, St Austell; (2000-01) Exeter; (2002) Trelawny, Exeter; (2003) Exeter, Eastbourne.

WALKER, Simon   *b. 19 February 1980, Bristol, Avon.*
BRITISH CAREER: (2001) Newport (CL); (2002) Newport (CL), Arena-Essex, Swindon (CT), Trelawny; (2003) Swindon (CL), Trelawny (CT), Reading, Somerset (BLC), Poole (BLC), Exeter (BLC), Newport.

WARWICK, Dan   *b. 21 November 1983, Poole, Dorset.*
BRITISH CAREER: (2002) Newport (CL), Reading; (2003) Newport (CL & PL), Poole (BLC), Exeter.

EXETER FALCONS: back row, left to right: Michael Coles, Corey Blackman, Tony Lethbridge (Team Manager), Seemond Stephens, Krister Marsh. On bike: Mark Simmonds. Front, kneeling: Roger Lobb, Lee Smethills.

PREMIER LEAGUE

(* Denotes bonus-point victory)

No	DATE	OPPONENTS	H/A	RESULT	SIMMONS	LOBB	STEPHENS	MARSH	COLES	SMETHILLS	BLACKMAN	SMITH	OTHERS
1	4/4	Arena-Essex	A	L27-63	12(6)	0(3)	3(4)	1(4)	8(6)	2+1(4)	1(3)	–	–
2	14/4	Swindon	H	W49-41	9+1(4)	7+2(4)	11+1(5)	2+1(4)	12(5)	4(4)	4+3(4)	–	–
3	21/4	King's Lynn	H	W59-31	9+1(4)	5+2(4)	12+2(5)	8+1(4)	14+1(5)	7+1(4)	4+1(4)	–	–
4	26/4	Rye House	A	L35-55	3(3)	0(4)	9+1(6)	4(4)	9+1(6)	10+1(5)	0(3)	–	–
5	28/4	Isle of Wight	H	W48-42	8(4)	5(4)	9+1(5)	5+1(4)	12(5)	7(4)	2+1(4)	–	–
6	29/4	Isle of Wight	A	L35-54	5(4)	R/R	8+1(6)	4+3(5)	10(6)	7+2(5)	1(4)	–	–
7	3/5	Berwick†	A	L17-51	2(2)	0(2)	8(3)	0(2)	1(2)	6(3)	0(2)	–	–
8	5/5	Arena-Essex	H	W46-44	3+3(4)	8(5)	12(4)	6+1(4)	8(5)	7+1(5)	2(3)	–	–
9	19/5	Rye House	H	W62-27*	14(5)	8+3(4)	13(5)	8+2(4)	6(4)	8+1(4)	5+2(4)	–	–
10	26/5	Trelawny	H	W53-37	5+1(4)	8(4)	15(5)	5+2(4)	11+1(5)	5+1(4)	4+1(4)	–	–
11	30/5	Somerset	A	L42-48	6+1(5)	2(3)	4+1(4)	6+1(4)	17(6)	6+1(5)	1(3)	–	–
12	2/6	Berwick	H	L44-46	7(4)	3+1(4)	15(5)	2(4)	9(5)	7+1(5)	1(3)	–	–
13	16/6	Hull	H	W58-32	8(4)	3(4)	15(5)	10+2(5)	12+2(5)	8+2(4)	2(3)	–	–
14	28/6	Workington	A	L39-50	7+2(6)	4(4)	7(4)	4(4)	–	6+2(4)	0(2)	–	11(5)
15	29/6	Glasgow	A	L30-60	2(4)	2(4)	8(6)	5(4)	–	1(3)	0(3)	–	12(6)
16	30/6	Somerset	H	W55-35*	13(5)	2+1(4)	17(6)	9+2(6)	R/R	9+2(5)	5+2(4)	–	–
17	6/7	Newcastle	A	L33-57	7+2(6)	4(4)	6(5)	9(6)	–	6+1(5)	1(3)	0(0)	–
18	7/7	Edinburgh	H	W55-35	11(4)	5+1(5)	13+1(5)	7+3(4)	–	8+2(4)	4+2(4)	7(4)	–
19	14/7	Workington	H	W59-30*	9(4)	7+1(4)	14(5)	9+3(5)	–	10+3(5)	3+2(3)	7(4)	–
20	17/7	Swindon ‡	A	L36-48	R/R	4(5)	14(6)	7+1(5)	–	4+2(4)	–	6+2(5)	1(3)
21	20/7	Newport	A	L29-61	–	1(5)	5(5)	6+1(4)	–	2(3)	–	3+1(4)	12(9)
22	21/7	Glasgow	H	L44-46	–	4+2(4)	11(5)	4+1(5)	–	5+1(4)	–	9(4)	11+1(8)
23	28/7	Sheffield	H	L44-46	7(4)	1(3)	9(5)	9+1(6)	–	11+1(5)	–	7+1(4)	0(3)
24	13/8	Hull	A	L39-50*	6(5)	7+2(5)	7+1(5)	6+2(4)	–	8+1(4)	–	5+1(4)	0(3)
25	14/8	Sheffield	A	L39-51	8+1(6)	6(5)	2(3)	1(3)	–	6(4)	–	14(6)	2(3)
26	16/8	Stoke	A	L35-55	11(6)	3(4)	7+1(6)	6+1(4)	–	2(3)	–	5(4)	1(3)
27	18/8	Newcastle	H	W53-37	6+1(4)	14+1(6)	12(5)	8+1(4)	–	6(4)	–	7+3(4)	0(3)
28	22/8	Edinburgh	A	L27-63	6(5)	3+1(5)	8(6)	4(4)	–	5+1(4)	–	0(3)	1+1(3)
29	23/8	King's Lynn	H	L25-65	2(2)	3(4)	9(6)	2(4)	–	6+1(6)	–	3+1(4)	0(4)
30	31/8	Reading	A	L41-49	–	4+1(3)	6+1(4)	8+1(6)	–	5(4)	–	3+1(4)	15+1(9)
31	1/9	Reading	H	W57-33*	R/R	16(6)	14+1(6)	7+3(5)	–	10+2(5)	–	7+2(5)	3+1(3)
32	9/9	Trelawny	A	L28-62	–	1(3)	6(5)	6(4)	–	1+1(3)	–	6+1(6)	8(9)
33	15/9	Newport	H	W48-42	R/R	11+1(6)	–	6+2(5)	–	10+1(5)	–	12(6)	9+2(8)
34	22/9	Stoke	H	L44-46	R/R	8(6)	–	8+1(5)	–	7+1(5)	–	6+2(5)	15+2(9)

† Meeting abandoned after twelve heats, with the result standing.

‡ Meeting abandoned after fourteen heats, with the result standing.

DETAILS OF OTHER RIDERS:

Match No. 14: Rory Schlein 11(5); Match No. 15: Rory Schlein 12(6); Ben Powell 1(3); Match No. 21: Paul Fry 12(6); Ben Powell 0(3); Match No. 22: Paul Fry 10(5); Ben Powell 1+1(3); Match No. 23: Karl Mason 0(3); Match No. 24: Benji Compton 0(3); Match No. 25: Richard Hall 2(3); Match No. 26: Luke Priest 1(3); Match No. 27: Paul Candy 0(3); Match No. 28: John Branney 1+1(3); Match No. 29: Brendon Mackay 0(4); Match No. 30: Graeme Gordon 13(6); Dan Warwick 2+1(3); Match No. 31: Nick Simmons 3+1(3); Match

No. 32: Brent Werner 8(6); Brendon Mackay 0(3); Match No. 33: Michal Makovsky 7+1(5); Nick Simmons 2+1(3); Match No. 34: Paul Fry 12+1(6); Nick Simmons 3+1(3).

PREMIER LEAGUE AVERAGES

Rider	Mts	Rds	Pts	Bon	Tot	Avge	Max
Michael Coles	13	65	129	5	134	8.25	1 Paid
Seemond Stephens	32	160	309	12	321	8.03	4 Full
Mark Simmonds	26	114	186	13	199	6.98	–
Lee Smethills	34	145	212	34	246	6.79	–
Scott A. Smith	18	76	107	15	122	6.42	–
Krister Marsh	34	149	192	37	229	6.15	–
Roger Lobb	33	140	159	19	178	5.09	–
Nick Simmons	3	9	8	3	11	4.89	–
Dan Warwick	1	3	2	1	3	4.00	–
Corey Blackman	19	63	40	14	54	3.43	–
John Branney	1	3	1	1	2	2.67	–
Richard Hall	1	3	2	0	2	2.67	–
Ben Powell	3	9	2	1	3	1.33	–
Luke Priest	1	3	1	0	1	1.33	–
Paul Candy	1	3	0	0	0	0.00	–
Benji Compton	1	3	0	0	0	0.00	–
Brendon Mackay	2	7	0	0	0	0.00	–
Karl Mason	1	3	0	0	0	0.00	–

BRITISH LEAGUE CUP

(* Denotes bonus-point victory)

No	DATE	OPPONENTS	H/A	RESULT	SIMMONS	LOBB	STEPHENS	MARSH	COLES	SMETHILLS	BLACKMAN	SMITH	OTHERS
1	24/3	Trelawny	H	W54-39	12(5)	2(4)	10(4)	5+2(4)	12+2(5)	10+1(4)	3+2(4)	–	–
2	25/3	Trelawny	A	L27-63	4+1(4)	1(3)	2+1(4)	4(4)	10(6)	6+1(6)	0(3)	–	–
3	28/3	Somerset	A	W47-43	7(4)	1+1(4)	9(5)	4(3)	16(6)	8+1(5)	2+1(3)	–	–
4	31/3	Newport	H	W50-40	8+1(4)	3+1(4)	13+1(5)	0(3)	13(5)	7(4)	6+2(5)	–	–
5	7/4	Somerset	H	W54-36*	8+1(4)	9+2(5)	11(4)	3(4)	13(5)	5+1(4)	5+2(4)	–	–
6	25/5	Newport	A	L34-56	3(4)	3(4)	8(5)	4+2(5)	12(6)	2(3)	2+1(3)	–	–
7	30/7	Poole	A	L32-58	8(6)	5+1(4)	9+1(6)	2(4)	–	4+2(4)	–	2+1(3)	2+1(3)
8	4/8	Poole	H	W59-31*	12+2(5)	13+2(5)	13+1(5)	7+1(4)	–	7+1(4)	–	7+2(4)	0(3)
9	25/8	Wolverhampton	H	L40-50	–	11+1(6)	12(5)	5+1(4)	–	4+2(4)	–	2+2(4)	6+1(7)
10	25/8	Wolverhampton	A	L25-65	–	2+1(4)	3+2(6)	9(6)	–	3(5)	–	R/R	8+1(9)

DETAILS OF OTHER RIDERS:

Match No. 7: Karl Mason 2+1(3); Match No. 8: Simon Walker 0(3); Match No. 9: Tony Atkin 6+1(4); Brendon Mackay 0(3); Match No. 10: Tony Atkin 6(5); Luke Priest 2+1(4).

BRITISH LEAGUE CUP AVERAGES

Rider	Mts	Rds	Pts	Bon	Tot	Avge	Max
Michael Coles	6	33	76	2	78	9.45	–
Seemond Stephens	10	49	90	6	96	7.84	–
Mark Simmonds	8	36	62	5	67	7.44	–
Lee Smethills	10	43	56	9	65	6.05	–
Scott A. Smith	3	11	11	5	16	5.82	–
Roger Lobb	10	43	50	9	59	5.49	1 Paid
Krister Marsh	10	41	43	6	49	4.78	–
Corey Blackman	6	22	18	8	26	4.73	–
Karl Mason	1	3	2	1	3	4.00	–
Luke Priest	1	4	2	1	3	3.00	–
Brendon Mackay	1	3	0	0	0	0.00	–
Simon Walker	1	3	0	0	0	0.00	–
Guests	2	9	12	1	13	5.78	–

KNOCK-OUT CUP

(* Denotes aggregate victory)

No	DATE	OPPONENTS	H/A	RESULT	SIMMONS	LOBB	STEPHENS	MARSH	COLES	SMETHILLS	BLACKMAN
1	11/5	Newport	A	L43-47	6(4)	3+1(4)	13(5)	4(4)	9(5)	8+3(5)	0(3)
2	12/5	Newport	H	W50-43*	4(4)	4+1(4)	11+1(5)	4(4)	12+1(5)	9(4)	6+3(4)
3	23/6	Isle of Wight	H	W53-42	6(4)	7(4)	14(5)	7+1(5)	9(5)	7+1(4)	3(3)
4	24/6	Isle of Wight	A	L34-61	9(5)	0(3)	7(5)	9+1(6)	6(4)	2+1(3)	1(4)

GOLDEN DOUBLE/TACTICAL JOKER RIDES:

Match No. 4: Mark Simmonds' total includes 4 points from a tactical joker ride; Seemond Stephens' total includes 4 points from a tactical joker ride; Michael Coles' total includes 2 points from a tactical joker ride and 0 points from a golden double outing.

INDIVIDUAL MEETINGS

11 August: Westernapolis
    1st Seemond Stephens 14; =2nd Chris Harris 11 & Mark Simmonds 11; Michal Makovsky 10; Krister Marsh 10; Scott A. Smith 9; Mark Lemon 9; Craig Watson 9; Lee Smethills 8; Paul Hurry 7; Garry Stead 7; David Meldrum 5; Roger Lobb 5; Graeme Gordon 3; Mario Jirout 1; Paul Candy 1; Matej Zagar 0.

13 October: Michael Coles' 20 Years Of Speedway
    (Qualifying scores: Leigh Adams 12; Chris Harris 10; Danny Bird 9; Mark Lemon 8; Leigh Lanham 8; Krister Marsh 8; Lee Smethills 7; Andrew Appleton 6; Jason Crump 6; Jason Bunyan 5; Shaun Tacey 5; Glenn Cunningham 4; Pavel Ondrasik 3; Scott A. Smith 2; Steve Bishop 2; Tom Brown (res) 1; Graeme Gordon 0; Malcolm Holloway (res) 0) Semi-Final: 1st Lemon; 2nd Lanham; 3rd Bird; 4th Marsh. Final: 1st Adams; 2nd Lemon; 3rd Lanham; 4th Harris.

GLASGOW TIGERS

ADDRESS: Ashfield Stadium, 404 Hawthorn Street, Possilpark, Glasgow.
PROMOTERS: Alan Dick & Stewart Dickson.
TRACK LENGTH: 302 metres.
FIRST MEETING: 19 April 1949.
YEARS OF OPERATION: 1949-52 National League Division Two; 1953 Open; 1999-03 British Premier League.

> NOTES: (1) Between 1949-53, the track was home to 'Ashfield Giants'; (2) Ashfield Stadium also played host to a second team in the 2000 British Conference League, under the banner of 'Lightning Ashfield Giants'.

PREVIOUS VENUES AS 'TIGERS':

(1) White City Stadium, Paisley Road West, Ibrox, Glasgow.
YEARS OF OPERATION: 1928-29 Open; 1930-31 Northern League; 1939 Union Cup; 1940 Open; 1945 Open; 1946 Northern League; 1947-53 National League Division Two; 1954 Northern Shield; 1956 Open; 1964 Provincial League; 1965-67 British League; 1968 British League Division One (NOTE: Glasgow first acquired the 'Tigers' moniker in 1946).

(2) Hampden Park, Mount Florida, Glasgow.
YEARS OF OPERATION: 1969-72 British League Division One.

(3) Cliftonhill Stadium, Main Street, Coatbridge, Lanarkshire.
YEARS OF OPERATION: 1973 British League Division One; 1974 British League Division Two; 1975-77 National League (Team rode as 'Coatbridge Tigers' throughout their stay at this venue).

(4) Blantyre Sports Stadium, Glasgow Road, Blantyre, Nr. Glasgow.
YEARS OF OPERATION: 1977-81 National League (Coatbridge moved to Blantyre midway through the 1977 season, reverting back to the name of 'Glasgow Tigers').

(5) Craighead Park, Forrest Street, Blantyre, Nr. Glasgow.
YEARS OF OPERATION: 1982-86 National League.

(6) Derwent Park, Workington, Cumbria.
YEAR OF OPERATION: 1987 National League (Began year as 'Glasgow Tigers', before becoming 'Workington Tigers').

(7) Shawfield Stadium, Glasgow Road, Rutherglen, Glasgow.
YEARS OF OPERATION: 1988-90 National League; 1991-94 British League Division Two; 1995 British Premier League; 1997-98 British Premier League (NOTE: In 1996, Shawfield Stadium was used by the 'Scottish Monarchs', who took part in the British Premier League).

CLUB HONOURS

NATIONAL SERIES WINNERS: 1990.
LEAGUE CHAMPIONS: 1993, 1994.
KNOCK-OUT CUP WINNERS: 1993, 1994.

RIDER ROSTER 2003

BEATON, Gary   b. 20 August 1986, Glasgow, Scotland.
BRITISH CAREER: (2002) Newport (CL), Newcastle (CL); (2003) Wolverhampton (CL),
Armadale, Newcastle (CL), Glasgow.

BRADY, Ross   b. 17 February 1981, Winchburgh, Broxburn, Scotland.
BRITISH CAREER: (1997) Lathallan, Peterborough (AL); (1998) Mildenhall, Peterborough
(PL), Berwick; (1999-00) Edinburgh; (2001) King's Lynn, Hull; (2002) Hull; (2003)
Glasgow, Sheffield (CL & PL).

COLLINS, Les   b. 24 May 1958, Partington, Greater Manchester.
BRITISH CAREER: (1975) Crewe, Belle Vue; (1976) Stoke, Belle Vue; (1977-79) Belle Vue;
(1980-83) Leicester; (1984-85) Sheffield; (1986) Edinburgh, King's Lynn; (1987) Edinburgh;
(1988) Edinburgh, Sheffield, King's Lynn, Belle Vue; (1989-95) Edinburgh; (1996)
Cradley/Stoke; (1997) Stoke; (1999-01) Glasgow; (2002) Workington; (2003) Glasgow.

DOOLAN, Kevin   b. 30 November 1980, Mildura, Victoria, Australia.
BRITISH CAREER: (1999-00) Belle Vue; (2002) Berwick; (2003) Glasgow.

GRIEVES, James   b. 28 September 1974, Paisley, Scotland.
BRITISH CAREER: (1991-95) Glasgow; (1996-97) Wolverhampton; (1998) Wolverhampton,
Berwick; (1999) Edinburgh; (2000-02) Glasgow; (2003) Glasgow, Wolverhampton.

HENRY, Christian   b. 20 February 1981, Sydney, New South Wales, Australia.
BRITISH CAREER: (2000) Edinburgh, Ashfield; (2001-02) Edinburgh; (2003) Glasgow.

LEVERINGTON, Trent   b. 13 May 1980, Brisbane, Queensland, Australia.
BRITISH CAREER: (2003) Glasgow, Armadale, Wolverhampton (CL).

McALLAN, David   b. 20 June 1980, Edinburgh, Scotland.
BRITISH CAREER: (1996) Berwick; (1997) Berwick (PL & AL), Sheffield; (1998) Berwick,
Newcastle; (1999) Edinburgh, Linlithgow; (2000) Ashfield, Stoke; (2001) Berwick,
Boston, Stoke, Workington, Glasgow, Edinburgh, Newcastle; (2002) Glasgow, Sheffield
(CL); (2003) Glasgow, Boston.

ROBERTSON, Jamie   b. 8 October 1986, Berwick-upon-Tweed, Northumberland
BRITISH CAREER: (2002) Newcastle (CL); (2003) Newcastle (PL & CL), Glasgow.

STANCL, George   b. 19 August 1975, Prague, Czech Republic.
BRITISH CAREER: (1994-95) Sheffield; (1996-99) Wolverhampton; (2000) Coventry;
(2002-03) Glasgow.

PREMIER LEAGUE

(* Denotes bonus-point victory)

No	DATE	OPPONENTS	H/A	RESULT	STANCL	HENRY	GRIEVES	BRADY	COLLINS	McALLAN	LEVERINGTON	DOLAN	OTHERS
1	27/4	Stoke	H	W50-40	14(5)	3+1(4)	12(4)	0(3)	11+2(5)	7+1(5)	3(4)	–	–
2	18/5	King's Lynn †	H	W43-35	11(4)	6+1(5)	10(4)	R/R	6(4)	6+2(5)	4+3(4)	–	–
3	25/5	Sheffield	H	W47-42	12+1(5)	3+1(4)	13(5)	–	5(4)	7+1(5)	2(3)	5+1(4)	–
4	31/5	Stoke	A	W46-44*	12(5)	R/R	12+1(5)	–	3(4)	4+2(6)	5(5)	10+1(5)	–
5	1/6	Arena-Essex	H	W48-42	10(5)	R/R	11(5)	–	9+1(4)	6+3(6)	5+2(5)	7+1(5)	–
6	6/6	Somerset	A	L44-46	16+1(6)	R/R	6+2(4)	–	5(4)	2(4)	5+2(6)	10+1(6)	–
7	7/6	Rye House	A	L39-49	13+2(6)	R/R	11(6)	–	7(5)	2+1(4)	1(3)	5+1(6)	–

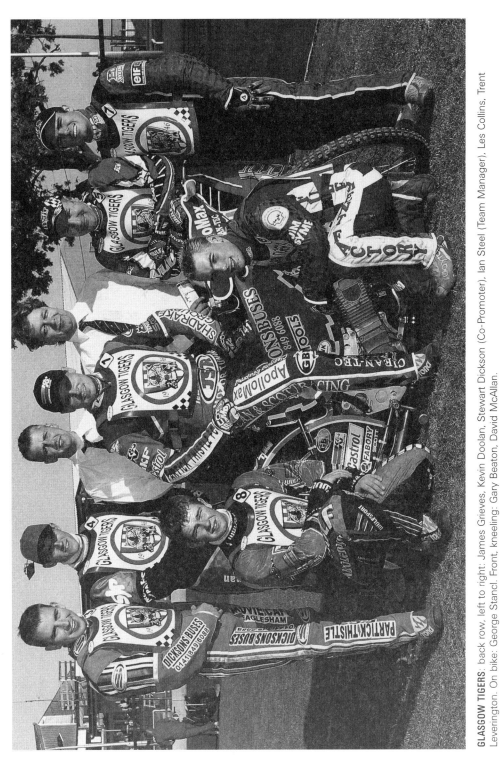

GLASGOW TIGERS: back row, left to right: James Grieves, Kevin Doolan, Stewart Dickson (Co-Promoter), Ian Steel (Team Manager), Les Collins, Trent Leverington. On bike: George Stancl. Front, kneeling: Gary Beaton, David McAllan.

PREMIER LEAGUE continued

No	DATE	OPPONENTS	H/A	RESULT	STANCL	HENRY	GRIEVES	BRADY	COLLINS	MCALLAN	LEVERINGTON	DOLAN	OTHERS
8	12/6	Swindon	A	L41-49	15(6)	R/R	12+1(6)	–	3(4)	1(3)	3+1(5)	7+2(6)	–
9	13/6	Newport	A	L44-45	11+1(6)	R/R	4(2)	–	6(4)	10+1(7)	1+1(4)	12+2(7)	–
10	22/6	Trelawny	H	W46-44	6(5)	5+1(4)	10(4)	–	12(5)	8+2(5)	1(3)	4+1(4)	–
11	29/6	Exeter	H	W60-30	11+3(5)	9(4)	12+2(5)	–	9+1(4)	7(4)	4+1(4)	8+1(4)	–
12	3/7	Newport	H	W52-38*	12(4)	6+1(4)	11(5)	–	9(5)	4+1(4)	6+2(4)	4+2(4)	–
13	6/7	Hull	H	W51-39	7+1(4)	6(4)	12(5)	–	11+2(5)	4+2(4)	5+1(4)	6+1(4)	–
14	12/7	Workington	A	L34-56	11(6)	0(3)	12+1(6)	–	4+1(4)	0(3)	1(3)	6(5)	–
15	13/7	Swindon	H	W46-44	10+1(5)	3(4)	11(4)	–	5(4)	4+1(4)	4+3(5)	9+1(4)	–
16	20/7	Workington ‡	H	L34-38	6(3)	5(3)	–	–	5+1(3)	3(4)	6+2(4)	2+2(3)	7+1(4)
17	21/7	Exeter	A	W46-44*	14+1(6)	11(5)	–	–	1+1(4)	0(3)	4+1(4)	5+1(3)	11+1(5)
18	22/7	Trelawny	A	L31-59	8+1(5)	5(5)	–	–	1(3)	0(3)	4+2(4)	3+1(4)	10(6)
19	31/7	Sheffield	A	L38-52	8(5)	1(3)	–	–	3(5)	1+1(3)	3(3)	6+1(5)	16+1(6)
20	3/8	Berwick	H	W47-42	9(4)	4(4)	–	–	7+1(5)	6+2(4)	3(4)	4+1(4)	14+1(5)
21	10/8	Reading	H	W59-31	14(5)	12(5)	–	–	6+1(4)	6+2(4)	4+2(4)	9+2(4)	8+1(4)
22	11/8	Reading	A	D45-45*	13(5)	6(3)	–	–	5(4)	3+1(4)	2+1(5)	11+2(6)	5(3)
23	23/8	Berwick	A	L35-55	13+1(6)	8(5)	–	–	2(3)	0(3)	0(3)	6+1(5)	6+1(5)
24	24/8	Newcastle	H	W61-28	10+1(5)	12+3(5)	–	–	5+2(4)	9+2(5)	5+2(3)	8+1(4)	12(4)
25	25/8	Newcastle	A	L37-53*	14(6)	4(4)	5+1(4)	–	9(6)	3+1(4)	1+1(3)	1+1(3)	–
26	31/8	Edinburgh	H	L37-55	1(3)	8+1(5)	7(5)	–	12+2(6)	4+1(4)	1+1(3)	4+2(4)	–
27	3/9	King's Lynn	A	L31-59	13(6)	4(5)	2(4)	–	0(3)	0(3)	5+1(5)	7(4)	–
28	7/9	Somerset	H	W55-35*	15(5)	R/R	10+1(5)	–	12(5)	7+1(6)	5+3(5)	6(4)	–
29	9/9	Isle of Wight	A	L36-54	10+1(5)	2(4)	8(5)	–	9(6)	2+1(3)	1+1(3)	4+2(4)	–
30	10/9	Hull	A	D45-45*	8+1(5)	8(4)	3(4)	–	12+1(5)	1+1(3)	8+2(5)	5+2(4)	–
31	14/9	Isle of Wight	H	W47-43	11+1(5)	9+2(4)	6+1(4)	–	3+1(4)	6(4)	5+2(4)	7+1(5)	–
32	19/9	Edinburgh	A	L34-56	13(6)	1(3)	11(6)	–	2(4)	1(3)	1(3)	5(5)	–
33	21/9	Rye House	H	W47-43	10(4)	3+1(4)	15(5)	–	12(5)	–	–	4+1(4)	3(8)
34	26/9	Arena-Essex ¶	A	L23-49	10(4)	0(3)	8(4)	–	0(3)	–	–	4+1(4)	1(6)

† Meeting abandoned after thirteen heats, with the result standing.

‡ Meeting abandoned after twelve heats, with the result standing.

¶ Meeting abandoned after twelve heats, with the result standing.

DETAILS OF OTHER RIDERS:

Match No. 16: Davey Watt 7+1(4); Match No. 17: Tomas Topinka 11+1(5); Match No. 18: Davey Watt 10(6); Match No. 19: Simon Stead 16+1(6); Match No. 20: Simon Stead 14+1(5); Match No. 21: Peter Carr 8+1(4); Match No. 22: Olly Allen 5(3); Match No. 23: Chris Harris 6+1(5); Match No. 24: Simon Stead 12(4); Match No. 33: Blair Scott 3(5); Gary Beaton 0(3); Match No. 34: Jamie Robertson 1(2); Aidan Collins 0(4).

GOLDEN DOUBLE RIDES:

Match No. 26: Les Collins' figures include 4 points from a golden double ride.

PREMIER LEAGUE AVERAGES

Rider	Mts	Rds	Pts	Bon	Tot	Avge	Max
George Stancl	34	170	371	17	388	9.13	2 Full
James Grieves	25	116	234	10	244	8.41	2 Full
Kevin Doolan	32	143	194	37	231	6.46	–
Les Collins	34	147	209	17	226	6.15	–
Christian Henry	27	110	144	12	156	5.67	1 Paid
David McAllan	32	132	124	30	154	4.67	–
Trent Leverington	32	127	108	37	145	4.57	–
Jamie Robertson	1	2	1	0	1	2.00	–
Gary Beaton	1	3	0	0	0	0.00	–
Ross Brady	1	3	0	0	0	0.00	–
Guests	11	51	92	6	98	7.69	1 Full; 1 Paid

NOTE: The figures for Les Collins include one golden double ride (4 points), modified to normal score i.e. 2 points.

BRITISH LEAGUE CUP

(* Denotes bonus-point victory)

No	DATE	OPPONENTS	H/A	RESULT	STANCL	HENRY	COLLINS	BRADY	GRIEVES	McALLAN	LEVERINGTON	DOLAN	OTHERS
1	29/3	Berwick	A	L42-47	9(4)	2+1(4)	9(5)	2+1(4)	12(5)	7+1(5)	1(3)	–	–
2	30/3	Workington	H	L37-53	–	6+1(5)	7+1(6)	2(3)	14(6)	3(3)	0(3)	–	5(4)
3	5/4	Workington	A	L35-55	10(4)	2(4)	8+1(6)	1(3)	12(6)	0(3)	2+1(4)	–	–
4	6/4	Berwick	H	W50-41*	13(5)	3(4)	7(4)	6+1(4)	13+1(5)	7+1(5)	1(3)	–	–
5	13/4	Newcastle	H	W50-39	12+1(5)	5(4)	10+1(4)	2(4)	13+1(5)	5+1(4)	3(4)	–	–
6	14/4	Newcastle	A	W46-44*	14+2(6)	1(3)	6+1(5)	–	7(5)	3(3)	0(2)	–	15(6)
7	20/4	Edinburgh	H	W50-40	13(5)	5(4)	5+1(3)	–	10+1(5)	4(4)	8+3(5)	–	5+1(4)
8	20/6	Edinburgh	A	L40-50*	13+1(6)	4+1(4)	3(4)	–	–	4+1(3)	0(3)	2+1(4)	14+1(6)

DETAILS OF OTHER RIDERS:

Match No. 2: Rory Schlein 5(4); Match No. 6: Andrew Moore 15(6); Match No. 7: Andrew Moore 5+1(4); Match No. 8: Michael Coles 14+1(6).

BRITISH LEAGUE CUP AVERAGES

Rider	Mts	Rds	Pts	Bon	Tot	Avge	Max
George Stancl	7	35	84	4	88	10.06	–
James Grieves	7	37	81	3	84	9.08	–
Les Collins	8	37	55	5	60	6.49	–
David McAllan	8	30	33	4	37	4.93	–
Christian Henry	8	32	28	3	31	3.88	–
Ross Brady	5	18	13	2	15	3.33	–
Kevin Doolan	1	4	2	1	3	3.00	–
Trent Leverington	8	27	15	4	19	2.81	–
Guests	4	20	39	2	41	8.20	–

KNOCK-OUT CUP

No	DATE	OPPONENTS	H/A	RESULT	STANCL	HENRY	BRADY	GRIEVES	COLLINS	McALLAN	LEVERINGTON	OTHERS
1	10/5	Berwick	A	L46-52	15+2(5)	3(4)	0(4)	17(5)	7(5)	1(3)	3(4)	–
2	11/5	Berwick †	H	D42-42	12(4)	5+1(5)	R/R	10+1(4)	10(5)	2+1(6)	3+1(4)	–

† Meeting abandoned after 14 heats, with the result standing

GOLDEN DOUBLE/TACTICAL JOKER RIDES:

Match No. 1: George Stancl's total includes 6 points from a tactical joker ride; James Grieves' total includes 6 points from a tactical joker ride; Les Collins' total includes 4 points from a tactical joker ride and 0 points from a golden double outing.

OTHER MEETINGS

16 March: International Club Challenge

Glasgow 38 (James Grieves 15+1; George Stancl 13+1; Ross Brady 5; Les Collins 4+1; David McAllan 1; Christian Henry 0; Trent Leverington 0) Valsarna 52 (Peter I. Karlsson 13+1; Stefan Danno 11; Bjorn G. Hansen 10+1; Davey Watt 7+1; Steven Andersen 6+2; Arnt Forland 5+2; Bohumil Brhel R/R).

23 March: Spring Trophy (first-leg)

Glasgow 44 (George Stancl 17; James Grieves 15+1; Les Collins 5; Ross Brady 3+1; Christian Henry 2; David McAllan 1+1; Trent Leverington 1) Edinburgh 46.

28 March: Spring Trophy (second-leg)

Edinburgh 53 Glasgow 37 (James Grieves 13+2; George Stancl 10+1; Ross Brady 6; Les Collins 3+1; David McAllan 3; Trent Leverington 1+1; Christian Henry 1) – Edinburgh won 99-81 on aggregate.

5 October: Scottish Cup (first-leg)

Glasgow 36 (James Grieves 12; Kevin Doolan 7+1; George Stancl 5; Les Collins 5; David McAllan 4+1; Christian Henry 2; Kauko Nieminen 1) Edinburgh 54.

24 October: Scottish Cup (second-leg)

Edinburgh 54 Glasgow 36 (Carl Stonehewer 13; Kevin Doolan 9+1; Les Collins 5+2; Rusty Harrison 4; David McAllan 3+1; Christian Henry 2; Kevin Little 0) – Edinburgh won 108-72 on aggregate.

INDIVIDUAL MEETING

12 October: City Of Glasgow Ashfield Classic

(Qualifying scores: Carl Stonehewer 14; Rory Schlein 14; James Grieves 13; Magnus Karlsson 11; George Stancl 10; Paul Bentley 8; Les Collins 8; Adrian Rymel 7; Rusty Harrison 6; Kevin Doolan 6; Ricky Ashworth 5; Garry Stead 5; Kevin Little 5; Emiliano Sanchez 4; Kristian Lund 3; David Meldrum 1). Semi-Final: 1st Karlsson; 2nd Grieves; 3rd Stancl; 4th Bentley. Final: 1st Stonehewer; 2nd Grieves; 3rd Schlein; 4th Karlsson.

HULL VIKINGS

ADDRESS: Craven Park Stadium, Poorhouse Lane, Preston Road, Kingston upon Hull, East Yorkshire.

PROMOTERS: Nigel Wordsworth & Paul Hodder.
NOTE: Paul Hodder joined as co-promoter in August 2003 and subsequently took over full control three months later.

TRACK LENGTH: 346 metres.

FIRST MEETING: 5 April 1995.

YEARS OF OPERATION: 1995-98 British Premier League; 1999 British Elite League; 2000-03 British Premier League.

PREVIOUS VENUE AS 'VIKINGS': The Boulevard Stadium, Airlie Street, Kingston upon Hull, East Yorkshire.
YEARS OF OPERATION: 1971-73 British League Division Two; 1974 British League; 1975-81 British League.

CLUB HONOURS

INTER-LEAGUE KNOCK-OUT CUP WINNERS: 1976.
PREMIER TROPHY WINNERS: 2000.
KNOCK-OUT CUP WINNERS: 2001.
PREMIERSHIP WINNERS: 2002.

RIDER ROSTER 2003

BISHOP, Steve   b. 28 November 1963, Bristol, Avon.
BRITISH CAREER: (1981) Swindon, Canterbury; (1982-83) Swindon, Exeter; (1984) Stoke, Exeter; (1985) Exeter; (1986) Exeter, Swindon; (1987) Arena-Essex; (1988) Poole, Long Eaton; (1989) Long Eaton, Exeter; (1990) Exeter; (1995) Oxford; (1997-98) St Austell; (1999) Swindon; (2000-02) Somerset; (2003) Somerset, Hull.

BOAST, Peter   b. 11 April 1964, Louth, Lincolnshire
BRITISH CAREER: (1994) Mildenhall; (1995) Mildenhall, Sheffield, Wolverhampton, Swindon; (1996) Mildenhall, Sheffield (1997) Sheffield; (1998) Skegness, Norfolk, Sheffield; (1999) Sheffield, King's Lynn (CL); (2000-02) Boston; (2003) Boston, Coventry (BLC), Hull.

BRANNEY, Craig   b. 31 July 1982, Whitehaven, Cumbria.
BRITISH CAREER: (2000) Ashfield; (2001) Workington, Buxton, Isle of Wight, Newport (PL); (2002) Newcastle (CL), Hull; (2003) Newcastle (PL & CL), Armadale (CT), Workington, Swindon (PL), Hull, Somerset.

CARTWRIGHT, Simon   b. 2 November 1978, Northallerton, North Yorkshire.
BRITISH CAREER: (1996) Owlerton; (1997) Belle Vue (AL & EL); (1998) Hull, Norfolk; (1999-00) Sheffield; (2001) Stoke, Glasgow; (2002) Berwick; (2003) Hull.

COLLINS, Neil   b. 15 October 1961, Partington, Greater Manchester.
BRITISH CAREER: (1978) Ellesmere Port; (1979) Nottingham, Workington, Sheffield; (1980) Edinburgh, Sheffield; (1981) Edinburgh, Cradley Heath, Belle Vue; (1982-83) Leicester; (1984-88) Sheffield; (1989-90) Wolverhampton; (1991) Belle Vue; (1992) Glasgow; (1993-94) Long Eaton; (1995) Sheffield; (1996) Belle Vue; (1997) Glasgow;

(1998) Stoke; (1999–00) Swindon; (2001) Belle Vue, Workington; (2002) Somerset; (2003) Hull, Peterborough (BLC & 4 Team Champs), Belle Vue.

COMPTON, Benji   *b. 17 September 1986, Tenerife, Spain.*
BRITISH CAREER: (2002) Newcastle (CL); (2003) Sheffield (CL & PL), Swindon (PL), Hull (BLC), Mildenhall (KOC), Exeter.

DERBYSHIRE, Lee   *b. 3 December 1981, Stockport, Greater Manchester.*
BRITISH CAREER: (2002) Buxton; (2003) Buxton, Hull, King's Lynn, Belle Vue (BLC).

DICKEN, Lee   *b. 24 August 1978, Hull, East Yorkshire.*
BRITISH CAREER: (1994) Buxton; (1995) Hull, Stoke, Peterborough; (1996) Hull, Owlerton, Sheffield; (1997–98) Hull; (1999) Hull, Exeter; (2000) Hull; (2001) Hull, Arena-Essex; (2002) Newport, Wolverhampton; (2003) Hull, Newcastle.

EVANS, Barrie   *b. 16 April 1984, King's Lynn, Norfolk.*
BRITISH CAREER: (1999) Mildenhall; (2000) Arena-Essex, Mildenhall; (2001) Arena-Essex, Mildenhall, Exeter; (2002) Newport, Rye House (CL); (2003) Hull, Rye House (CL).

HALL, Richard   *b. 23 August 1984, Northallerton, North Yorkshire.*
BRITISH CAREER: (2001) Newcastle; (2002) Newcastle (PL & CL), Trelawny, Glasgow; (2003) Sheffield (CL & PL), Stoke (PL), Coventry (BLC), Hull (BLC), Newport (PL), Boston (KOC & CT), Exeter, Reading, Workington, Somerset.

HANSEN, Bjorn G.   *b. 25 June 1980, Drammen, Norway.*
BRITISH CAREER: (2002) King's Lynn; (2003) Hull.

JANSSON, Jimmy   *b. 16 September 1980, Eskilstuna, Sweden.*
BRITISH CAREER: (2003) Hull.

KRAMER, Emil   *b. 14 November 1977, Mariestad, Sweden.*
BRITISH CAREER: (2002) King's Lynn, Hull; (2003) Oxford (BLC), Hull.

PARSONS, Joel   *b. 24 July 1985, Broken Hill, New South Wales, Australia.*
BRITISH CAREER: (2003) Reading, Eastbourne (BLC), Rye House (CL & PL), Newport (PL), Wimbledon (CT), Arena-Essex, Peterborough (BLC), Hull.

PICKERING, Michael   *b. 28 October 1982, Hull, East Yorkshire.*
BRITISH CAREER: (1998) Buxton; (2000) Buxton; (2002) Newport (CL); (2003) Hull, Newcastle (CL).

STEAD, Garry   *b. 5 January 1972, Holmfirth, Yorkshire.*
BRITISH CAREER: (1990–92) Stoke; (1993) Newcastle; (1994) Newcastle, Bradford; (1995) Bradford; (1996) Sheffield; (1997) Bradford; (1998) Wolverhampton; (1999–02) Hull; (2003) Hull, Eastbourne (BLC).

TACEY, Shaun   *b. 27 November 1974, Norwich, Norfolk.*
BRITISH CAREER: (1992) Ipswich; (1993) Ipswich, Arena-Essex; (1994–96) Coventry; (1997) King's Lynn, Isle of Wight, Bradford, Coventry; (1998–00) Coventry; (2001–02) Arena-Essex; (2003) Hull.

THORP, Paul   *b. 9 September 1964, Macclesfield, Cheshire.*
BRITISH CAREER: (1980) Birmingham; (1981) Birmingham, Scunthorpe, Workington; (1982–83) Berwick, Birmingham; (1984–85) Stoke, Wolverhampton; (1986) Stoke, Sheffield, Belle Vue; (1987–88) Belle Vue; (1989–92) Bradford; (1993) Newcastle; (1994) Bradford; (1995–96) Hull; (1997) Belle Vue; (1998) Hull; (1999) Hull, Stoke; (2000–03) Hull.

WRIGHT, James   *b. 13 June 1986, Stockport, Greater Manchester.*
BRITISH CAREER: (2002) Buxton; (2003) Buxton, Belle Vue (BLC), Newcastle (PL), Stoke (PL), Workington, Hull, King's Lynn.

HULL VIKINGS: back row, left to right: Shaun Tacey, Lee Dicken, John Bailey (Team Manager), Simon Cartwright, Barrie Evans. On bike: Garry Stead. Front, kneeling: Paul Thorp. Neil Collins.

PREMIER LEAGUE

(* Denotes bonus-point victory)

No	DATE	OPPONENTS	H/A	RESULT	TACEY	DICKEN	THORP	COLLINS	STEAD	CARTWRIGHT	EVANS	HANSEN	PICKERING	JANSSON	KRAMER	BISHOP	OTHERS
1	9/4	Somerset	H	L44-46	12+2(6)	3(3)	8(4)	4(4)	12+2(6)	4+1(4)	1(3)	–	–	–	–	–	–
2	16/4	King's Lynn	H	W50-40	7(5)	5+2(4)	8(4)	7(4)	15(5)	7+2(5)	1(4)	–	–	–	–	–	–
3	21/4	Reading	A	L40-50	8+1(5)	4+1(4)	8+1(4)	7+2(4)	9(5)	3(5)	1+1(3)	–	–	–	–	–	–
4	23/4	Berwick	H	L40-50	5(5)	1+1(4)	7+1(4)	6+1(4)	10+1(5)	7+1(5)	4(3)	–	–	–	–	–	–
5	26/4	King's Lynn	A	L32-58	7+1(5)	0(3)	6(4)	8+2(6)	10(6)	0(3)	1(3)	–	–	–	–	–	–
6	30/4	Edinburgh	H	L42-48	7(5)	5(4)	5+1(4)	7+1(4)	12(5)	4+1(4)	2(4)	–	–	–	–	–	–
7	7/5	Reading	H	W56-34*	10(4)	6+2(4)	13(5)	8+2(4)	12+2(5)	4(4)	3+2(4)	–	–	–	–	–	–
8	20/5	Isle of Wight	A	L30-59	7(6)	2+1(3)	4(4)	4+1(5)	12(6)	1(3)	0(3)	–	–	–	–	–	–
9	21/5	Swindon	H	W48-42	4+1(2)	5+2(4)	11(5)	8+2(4)	10(5)	9+1(6)	1(4)	–	–	–	–	–	–
10	23/5	Edinburgh	A	L33-57	–	1+1(3)	8(6)	6+1(5)	9+1(6)	5(4)	0(4)	–	–	–	–	–	4(3)
11	31/5	Workington	A	L40-50	5+1(3)	3(4)	10(6)	5(4)	11+2(6)	4(4)	2+1(3)	–	–	–	–	–	–
12	4/6	Rye House	H	W49-41	11(4)	5(4)	12(5)	3(4)	12+1(5)	5+3(5)	1(3)	–	–	–	–	–	–
13	11/6	Workington	H	L44-46	9+1(5)	5+2(4)	9+1(5)	7+1(4)	6+1(4)	1+1(4)	7+1(4)	–	–	–	–	–	–
14	16/6	Exeter	A	L32-58	6(6)	4(4)	7(5)	2(3)	12(6)	1(3)	0(3)	–	–	–	–	–	–
15	17/6	Trelawny	A	L37-53	3(4)	3(3)	15(6)	4+1(4)	8(6)	0(3)	4+1(4)	–	–	–	–	–	–
16	28/6	Berwick	A	L37-53	10+1(6)	–	5(5)	–	9+1(6)	3(4)	1(3)	8(5)	1+1(2)	–	–	–	–
17	4/7	Arena-Essex	A	L36-53	8+2(6)	–	12+2(6)	–	9+1(5)	2(3)	0(3)	2(4)	–	–	–	–	3(3)
18	6/7	Glasgow	A	L39-51	6+1(5)	–	8+1(6)	–	9+1(5)	3(3)	0(3)	12+1(5)	–	–	–	–	1(3)
19	23/7	Newport	H	L41-48	7+2(4)	–	9(5)	–	10(5)	1(4)	11(7)	0(2)	–	–	–	–	3+1(3)
20	30/7	Isle of Wight	H	L44-46	5+1(4)	–	11(5)	–	9(5)	4+1(4)	6+3(5)	–	–	–	–	–	9(7)
21	6/8	Newcastle	H	L42-48	4(4)	–	14+1(6)	–	10+1(6)	2(3)	5+2(4)	–	–	–	–	–	7+1(7)
22	9/8	Stoke	A	L32-60	2(5)	–	14(5)	–	9(6)	6(4)	–	–	–	0(4)	–	–	1(6)
23	10/8	Newport	A	L42-48	8+2(4)	–	8+1(5)	–	6(4)	10(5)	7+2(5)	–	1(3)	2(4)	–	–	–
24	13/8	Exeter	H	W50-39	4(4)	–	14+1(5)	–	14+1(5)	6+1(4)	7(5)	–	–	1(3)	–	–	4+1(4)
25	27/8	Trelawny	H	L40-50	12(5)	–	10(6)	–	8(6)	4+1(3)	3+1(4)	–	–	0(3)	–	–	3(3)
26	28/8	Swindon	A	L34-56	1+1(3)	–	10(5)	–	9+1(6)	2+1(4)	1+1(3)	–	–	–	–	–	11+1(9)
27	31/8	Newcastle	A	L37-53	3(4)	–	11(6)	–	11+2(6)	6(5)	0(3)	–	–	–	–	–	6+1(7)
28	3/9	Sheffield	H	W47-43	8+2(4)	–	12+1(5)	–	7+1(5)	8+2(5)	4+4(4)	–	–	–	–	–	8+1(7)
29	6/9	Rye House	A	L43-47*	1(3)	–	13(6)	–	6+1(4)	2(3)	7(5)	–	–	–	–	–	14+1(9)
30	10/9	Glasgow	H	D45-45	6+2(4)	–	13(5)	–	8+1(4)	3+1(4)	6(5)	–	–	–	–	–	9(8)
31	17/9	Arena-Essex	H	W50-40	8+2(4)	–	13(5)	–	7+1(4)	4(4)	2(4)	–	–	–	12(5)	4+2(4)	–
32	18/9	Sheffield	A	L32-58	5+2(5)	–	6(5)	–	4+1(4)	4+1(4)	0(3)	–	–	–	11(5)	2(4)	–
33	24/9	Stoke	H	W49-41	5(4)	–	13+1(5)	–	6(4)	7+1(4)	5+3(4)	–	–	–	11(5)	2+1(4)	–
34	26/9	Somerset	A	L38-52	2(3)	–	9+1(6)	–	7(4)	4+1(4)	2+1(3)	–	–	–	8(6)	6+1(4)	–

DETAILS OF OTHER RIDERS:

Match No. 10: Kevin Doolan 4(3); Match No. 17: Richard Hall 3(3); Match No. 18: Benji Compton 1(3); Match No. 19: Craig Branney 3+1(3); Match No. 20: Paul Bentley 9(4); Richard Hall 0(3); Match No. 21: Scott Robson 5(4); Joel Parsons 2+1(3); Match No. 22: Lee Derbyshire 1(3); James Wright 0(3); Match No. 24: Craig Branney 4+1(4); Match No. 25: Danny Norton 3(3); Match No. 26: Glenn Cunningham 8(6); Craig Branney 3+1(3); Match No. 27: Chris Manchester 5+1(4); Richard Hall 1(3); Match No. 28: Chris Manchester 5+1(4); Benji Compton 3(3); Match No. 29: Chris Neath 14+1(6); Peter Boast 0(3); Match No. 30: Jan Staechmann 9(5); Benji Compton 0(3).

GOLDEN DOUBLE RIDES:

Match No. 22: Paul Thorp's figures include 6 points from one golden double ride.

PREMIER LEAGUE AVERAGES

Rider	Mts	Rds	Pts	Bon	Tot	Avge	Max
Paul Thorp	34	173	333	13	346	8.00	1 Paid
Emil Kramer	4	21	42	0	42	8.00	–
Garry Stead	34	175	318	23	341	7.79	1 Full; 1 Paid
Neil Collins	15	63	86	14	100	6.35	–
Shaun Tacey	33	146	206	25	231	6.33	–
Bjorn G. Hansen	4	16	22	1	23	5.75	–
Craig Branney	3	10	10	3	13	5.20	–
Lee Dicken	15	55	52	12	64	4.65	–
Simon Cartwright	34	136	136	20	156	4.59	–
Steve Bishop	4	16	14	4	18	4.50	–
Joel Parsons	1	3	2	1	3	4.00	–
Barrie Evans	33	125	95	23	118	3.78	–
Michael Pickering	2	5	2	1	3	2.40	–
Benji Compton	3	9	4	0	4	1.78	–
Richard Hall	3	9	4	0	4	1.78	–
Lee Derbyshire	1	3	1	0	1	1.33	–
Jimmy Jansson	4	14	3	0	3	0.86	–
Peter Boast	1	3	0	0	0	0.00	–
James Wright	1	3	0	0	0	0.00	–
Guests	13	52	74	7	81	6.23	–

NOTE: The figures for Paul Thorp include one golden double ride (6 points), modified to normal score i.e. 3 points.

BRITISH LEAGUE CUP

No	DATE	OPPONENTS	H/A	RESULT	TACEY	DICKEN	THORP	COLLINS	STEAD	CARTWRIGHT	EVANS	HANSEN	COMPTON	JANSSON	BRANNEY	OTHERS
1	27/3	Sheffield	A	L35-55	9(6)	2(4)	6(4)	8+1(5)	7(4)	2(4)	1(3)	–	–	–	–	–
2	2/4	Stoke	H	W49-41	9(5)	5+1(4)	9(4)	7(4)	8(5)	6(4)	5+1(4)	–	–	–	–	–
3	12/4	Stoke	A	L36-54	9+1(6)	4+3(4)	5+1(4)	6+1(4)	9(6)	3+1(3)	0(3)	–	–	–	–	–
4	2/7	Coventry	H	W47-43	7(4)	–	12+1(5)	–	4(4)	8(4)	5+2(4)	8+2(5)	3+1(4)	–	–	–
5	9/7	Sheffield	H	L39-51	5+2(4)	–	9+1(5)	–	9(6)	1+1(3)	4(3)	10+1(6)	–	–	–	1+1(3)
6	12/7	Coventry	A	L35-56	6+1(6)	–	7+2(5)	–	8+1(6)	4(4)	2+2(3)	6+1(4)	2(3)	–	–	–
7	20/8	Belle Vue	H	L38-52	6(6)	–	14(5)	–	8(6)	2+2(4)	2+2(3)	–	–	1+1(3)	5(3)	–
8	24/8	Belle Vue	A	L35-55	6+1(4)	–	11(6)	–	7(6)	2+1(4)	4+3(4)	–	–	2(3)	3(3)	–

DETAILS OF OTHER RIDERS:

Match No. 5: Richard Hall 1+1(3).

GOLDEN DOUBLE RIDES:

Match No. 5: Garry Stead's figures include 2 points from one golden double ride.

BRITISH LEAGUE CUP AVERAGES

Rider	Mts	Rds	Pts	Bon	Tot	Avge	Max
Paul Thorp	8	38	73	5	78	8.21	–
Bjorn G. Hansen	3	15	24	4	28	7.47	–
Neil Collins	3	13	21	2	23	7.08	–
Shaun Tacey	8	41	57	5	62	6.05	–
Garry Stead	8	43	59	1	60	5.58	–
Craig Branney	2	6	8	0	8	5.33	–
Lee Dicken	3	12	11	4	15	5.00	–
Barrie Evans	8	27	23	10	33	4.89	–
Simon Cartwright	8	30	28	5	33	4.40	–
Benji Compton	2	7	5	1	6	3.43	–
Richard Hall	1	3	1	1	2	2.67	–
Jimmy Jansson	2	6	3	1	4	2.67	–

NOTE: The figures for Garry Stead include one golden double ride (2 points), modified to normal score i.e. 1 point.

KNOCK-OUT CUP

No	DATE	OPPONENTS	H/A	RESULT	STEAD	DICKEN	TACEY	COLLINS	THORP	CARTWRIGHT	EVANS
1	15/5	Sheffield	A	L43-56	16+1(6)	1+1(2)	3(4)	7(5)	9(4)	7+1(5)	0(4)
2	28/5	Sheffield	H	L41-48	8+1(5)	3+1(4)	10(4)	3+2(4)	8+1(5)	6(5)	3(3)

GOLDEN DOUBLE/TACTICAL JOKER RIDES:

Match No. 1: Garry Stead's total includes 6 points from a tactical joker ride and 2 points from a golden double outing; Paul Thorp's total includes 6 points from a tactical joker ride; Neil Collins' total includes 4 points from a tactical joker ride.

OTHER MEETINGS

17 March: Inter-League Challenge

Belle Vue 64 Hull 26 (Neil Collins 7; Garry Stead 6; Shaun Tacey 5; Simon Cartwright 4; Paul Thorp 2+1; Barrie Evans 2; Lee Dicken 0).

26 March: Challenge

Hull 55 (Shaun Tacey 12; Garry Stead 12; Paul Thorp 9+1; Simon Cartwright 7; Neil Collins 6+2; Lee Dicken 5+1; Barrie Evans 4+3) Newcastle 35.

30 March: Challenge

Newcastle 52 Hull 38 (Lee Dicken 11+2; Paul Thorp 11; Shaun Tacey 6; Garry Stead 5; Simon Cartwright 5; Neil Collins 0; Carl Shield 0).

18 June: Challenge

Hull 51 (Neil Collins 10+1; Paul Thorp 9; Shaun Tacey 8+2; Lee Dicken 7+3; Garry Stead 7; Barrie Evans 6+2; Simon Cartwright 4+1) Banga's Boys 39 (Joe Screen 18; Jan Staechmann 12+1; Paul Bentley 6+1; Carlos Villar 1; Lee Smethills 1; James Wright 1; Benji Compton 0).

25 June: Conference Four-Team Tournament

Hull 19 (David Chadburn 7; Benji Compton 5; Phil Pickering 4; Michael Pickering 3), Buxton 29,

Scunthorpe 25 (Richard Hall 12; Robert Hollingworth 7; Richie Dennis 5; Andrew Blackburn 1; Michael Mitchell 0), Wolverhampton 23.

1 October: Three-Team Tournament

King's Lynn 48, Swindon 32, Hull 28 (Garry Stead 10; Paul Thorp 8; Lee Dicken 6+1; Barrie Evans 3+1; Simon Cartwright 1; John Oliver 0).

3 October: Triangle Trophy

White Wizards 39 (Sean Wilson 11; Shaun Tacey 9; Gary Havelock 8; Sebastian Alden 6+1; Lee Dicken 5+3; Jimmy Jansson 0), Red Raiders 38, (Sam Ermolenko 11+1; Paul Thorp 9; Robert Eriksson 6; Carl Stonehewer 5+1; Lee Smethills 5; Barrie Evans 2), Blue Bombers 31 (Garry Stead 9+1; Simon Cartwright 7; Kristian Lund 6+1; Neil Collins 4; Danny Norton 3+1; David Baker 2+2; Billy Hamill 0); Triangle Trophy: 1st Thorp; 2nd Wilson; 3rd Stead; 4th Ermolenko.

INDIVIDUAL MEETING

16 July: Mid-Summer Showdown

(Qualifying scores: Paul Thorp 15; Garry Stead 13; Paul Bentley 10; Chris Manchester 10; Ricky Ashworth 10; Kevin Doolan 8; Simon Cartwright 8; Ray Morton 8; Shaun Tacey 7; Paul Pickering 6; Bjorn G. Hansen 6; Scott Smith 5; Lee Dicken 5; Les Collins 4; Barrie Evans 2; Ross Brady 2; Michael Pickering (res) 0); Final: 1st Thorp; 2nd Stead; 3rd Bentley; 4th Manchester.

ISLE OF WIGHT WIGHTLINK ISLANDERS

ADDRESS: Smallbrook Stadium, Ashey Road, Ryde, Isle of Wight.
PROMOTERS: Dave Pavitt & Martin Newnham.
TRACK LENGTH: 380 metres.
FIRST MEETING: 13 May 1996.
YEARS OF OPERATION: 1995 Demonstration; 1996 British Conference League; 1997 British Amateur League & British Premier League; 1998-03 British Premier League.

CLUB HONOURS

YOUNG SHIELD WINNERS: 1998, 2001.
PAIRS CHAMPIONS: 2002.
KNOCK-OUT CUP WINNERS: 2003.

RIDER ROSTER 2003

BIRD, Danny   b. 16 November 1979, Guildford, Surrey.
BRITISH CAREER: (1998-01) Isle of Wight; (2002-03) Isle of Wight, Ipswich.
DART, Tony   b. 2 September 1979, Ashford, Kent.
BRITISH CAREER: (2003) Mildenhall, King's Lynn, Peterborough (BLC), Isle of Wight (KOC).

ISLE OF WIGHT ISLANDERS: back row, left to right: Jed Stone (Team Manager), Chris Mills, Glen Phillips, Gary Phelps, Sebastian Tresarrieu. On bike: Ray Morton. Front, kneeling: Danny Bird, Adam Shields.

DOWNS, Carl   b. 13 November 1983, Coventry, Warwickshire.
> BRITISH CAREER: (1999) King's Lynn (CL); (2000) Boston, Peterborough (CL), Sheffield (CL); (2001) Newport (CL), Mildenhall; (2002) King's Lynn (CL); (2003) Oxford (CL & BLC), Coventry (BLC), Stoke (CT), Isle of Wight.

JOHNSON, Chris   b. 13 October 1987, Chichester, Sussex.
> BRITISH CAREER: (2003) Oxford (CL), Trelawny (CT), Isle of Wight.

LEE, Nick   b. 3 January 1983, Swindon, Wiltshire.
> BRITISH CAREER: (2002) Swindon (CT); (2003) Swindon (CL), Isle of Wight.

MILLS, Chris   b. 29 March 1983, Chelmsford, Essex.
> BRITISH CAREER: (2001) Arena-Essex; (2002) King's Lynn (CL), Wimbledon; (2003) Isle of Wight, Oxford (CL).

MORTON, Ray   b. 19 June 1968, Peckham, London.
> BRITISH CAREER: (1985-87) King's Lynn; (1988) Wimbledon, King's Lynn; (1989-90) Wimbledon; (1991-92) Reading; (1993) Poole; (1994-95) Reading; (1996) Reading, Hull; (1998) Isle of Wight; (1999) Hull; (2000-03) Isle of Wight.

PHELPS, Gary   b. 30 March 1977, Swindon, Wiltshire.
> BRITISH CAREER: (1996) Swindon (CL); (1997) M4 Raven Sprockets, Swindon; (1998) Norfolk, Isle of Wight; (1999) Workington, Berwick, King's Lynn (CL), St Austell, Edinburgh, Newcastle, Isle of Wight; (2000) Arena-Essex, St Austell, Isle of Wight, Workington; (2001) Trelawny, Somerset; (2002) Somerset, Isle of Wight; (2003) Isle of Wight.

PHILLIPS, Glen   b. 22 November 1982, Farnborough, Kent.
> BRITISH CAREER: (1999) Exeter, King's Lynn (CL); (2000) Isle of Wight, Somerset; (2001) Isle of Wight; (2002) Wimbledon, Reading; (2003) Isle of Wight.

SHIELDS, Adam   b. 8 February 1977, Kurri-Kurri, New South Wales, Australia.
> BRITISH CAREER: (2000-02) Isle of Wight; (2003) Isle of Wight, Eastbourne.

TRESARRIEU, Mathieu   b. 2 March 1986, Bordeaux, France.
> BRITISH CAREER: (2002) Isle of Wight (Young Shield only); (2003) Isle of Wight.

TRESARRIEU, Sebastian   b. 10 January 1981, Bordeaux, France.
> BRITISH CAREER: (2001-03) Isle of Wight.

TRESARRIEU, Stephane   b. 27 February 1975, Bordeaux, France.
> BRITISH CAREER: (2003) Isle of Wight.

PREMIER LEAGUE

(* Denotes bonus-point victory)

No	DATE	OPPONENTS	H/A	RESULT	BIRD	PHILLIPS	MORTON	SEB. TRESARRIEU	SHIELDS	PHELPS	MILLS	M. TRESARRIEU	OTHERS
1	28/3	Arena-Essex	A	L42-49	7+1(5)	3+2(4)	10(6)	1+1(2)	17(6)	3+1(4)	1+1(3)	–	–
2	28/4	Exeter	A	L42-48	12+1(5)	3(3)	9(4)	4(4)	10+1(6)	4+1(5)	0(3)	–	–
3	29/4	Exeter	H	W54-35*	12(4)	8+2(5)	13+1(5)	3(4)	8+1(4)	2+1(4)	8(4)	–	–
4	6/5	Stoke	H	W54-35	15(5)	5+1(4)	13+1(5)	4+1(4)	10+1(4)	5+1(4)	2+1(4)	–	–
5	20/5	Hull	H	W59-30	15(5)	7+1(4)	11+1(4)	8(4)	9+1(5)	3+1(4)	6(4)	–	–
6	27/5	Newport	H	W45-44	7(4)	3(3)	11(5)	6+1(4)	13(5)	3(5)	2+1(5)	–	–
7	3/6	Somerset	H	W54-36	9(3)	3+1(4)	10+1(4)	10+1(5)	12+1(5)	7+1(5)	3+1(4)	–	–
8	12/6	Sheffield	A	L42-47	9+1(6)	2(4)	6+1(4)	4(4)	18(6)	3(4)	0(2)	–	–

PREMIER LEAGUE continued

No	DATE	OPPONENTS	H/A	RESULT	BIRD	PHILLIPS	MORTON	SEB. TRESARRIEU	SHIELDS	PHELPS	MILLS	M. TRESARRIEU	OTHERS
9	16/6	Reading	A	W46-44	11(4)	2(4)	13+1(5)	2(4)	12+1(5)	2+1(3)	4+1(5)	–	–
10	17/6	Rye House	H	W61-29	15(5)	7+1(4)	8+1(4)	10+1(4)	13+2(5)	3(3)	5+3(5)	–	–
11	22/6	Newport	A	W47-43*	15(6)	3(4)	9+1(4)	3(3)	12+2(5)	5+1(5)	0(3)	–	–
12	27/6	Somerset	A	W53-37*	13+1(5)	5+1(4)	4+2(4)	8(4)	14+1(5)	4(3)	5+1(5)	–	–
13	1/7	Workington	H	W55-35	13+2(5)	6+1(4)	9+1(4)	6+1(4)	15(5)	4+1(4)	2+1(4)	–	–
14	8/7	Reading	H	W50-40*	14(5)	4+1(4)	9(5)	2(4)	10+1(4)	5(4)	6+2(4)	–	–
15	9/7	King's Lynn	A	L32-58	8(6)	4+3(6)	4+1(4)	R/R	10(6)	0(3)	6+1(5)	–	–
16	15/7	Newcastle	H	W51-39	12(5)	5+1(4)	9+1(4)	7+2(4)	12+1(5)	1+1(3)	5+2(5)	–	–
17	22/7	Sheffield	H	W49-42*	9(5)	1(3)	10+1(5)	11+1(4)	–	6+1(6)	–	–	12+1(7)
18	30/7	Hull	A	W46-44*	10(5)	4+1(4)	12(5)	9+1(4)	5(2)	2(5)	–	4+1(5)	–
19	2/8	Workington	A	L43-50*	8(5)	1(3)	10(5)	7+2(4)	–	6+1(5)	–	2+1(4)	9(4)
20	3/8	Newcastle	A	L36-54	9(4)	4+1(5)	3(3)	5(5)	–	3+1(3)	–	0(4)	12(6)
21	5/8	Edinburgh	H	W48-42	13(5)	4+1(4)	–	8+2(4)	8(4)	3+2(4)	–	3(4)	9+1(5)
22	19/8	King's Lynn	H	W52-40	14(5)	5+1(4)	–	6+1(4)	11+2(5)	3+1(4)	–	4+1(4)	9+1(4)
23	21/8	Swindon	A	W47-43	7+1(4)	3+2(4)	–	6(4)	13(5)	5+2(5)	–	–	13+2(8)
24	2/9	Berwick	H	W47-43	10+1(5)	6(4)	–	14+1(5)	5(4)	3(4)	0(3)	–	9+3(5)
25	9/9	Glasgow	H	W54-36	15(5)	3(4)	–	6+1(4)	13+2(5)	5(4)	3+1(4)	–	9+1(4)
26	12/9	Edinburgh	A	L36-53	8+1(6)	1+1(3)	–	1(4)	13(6)	0(3)	3(3)	–	10(5)
27	13/9	Berwick	A	L39-52	14+1(6)	0(5)	–	0(2)	15(6)	3(4)	1(5)	–	6(2)
28	14/9	Glasgow	A	L43-47*	13+1(6)	1(3)	–	1(3)	14+1(6)	3+1(3)	0(4)	–	11(5)
29	16/9	Trelawny	A	L42-48	5(5)	1(3)	–	8+1(5)	13(6)	2+1(3)	4(3)	–	9+2(5)
30	23/9	Trelawny	H	W53-40*	13+1(5)	2(4)	–	9+1(4)	12+1(5)	6+1(5)	2(3)	–	9+2(4)
31	30/9	Swindon	H	W50-40*	9+1(5)	5+2(4)	–	7+1(4)	14(5)	4+2(4)	3(4)	–	8+1(4)
32	4/10	Rye House	A	L40-50*	8+2(6)	2+1(3)	–	5(4)	10+1(6)	3(3)	–	–	12+2(8)
33	18/10	Stoke	A	W47-43*	11+1(5)	4(4)	–	9(4)	14(5)	2+1(4)	–	–	7+3(8)
34	28/10	Arena-Essex	H	L44-47	10+1(6)	9+2(5)	R/R	6(5)	12(5)	4(5)	–	–	3+2(4)

DETAILS OF OTHER RIDERS:

Match No. 17: Craig Watson 10(4); Tony Dart 2+1(3); Match No. 19: Davey Watt 9(4); Match No. 20: Davey Watt 12(6); Match No. 21: Frank Smart 9+1(5); Match No. 22: Craig Watson 9+1(4); Match No. 23: Craig Watson 11+1(5); Nick Lee 2+1(3); Match No. 24: Jan Staechmann 9+3(5); Match No. 25: Paul Pickering 9+1(4); Match No. 26: Seemond Stephens 10(5); Match No. 27: Seemond Stephens 6(2); Match No. 28: Adrian Rymel 11(5); Match No. 29: Michal Makovsky 9+2(5); Match No. 30: Paul Pickering 9+2(4); Match No. 31: Jan Staechmann 8+1(4); Match No. 32: Steve Masters 10+1(5); Carl Downs 2+1(3); Match No. 33: Chris Neath 4+2(4); Stephane Tresarrieu 3+1(4); Match No. 34: Chris Johnson 3+2(4).

GOLDEN DOUBLE RIDES:

Match No. 1: Adam Shields' total includes 4 points from one golden double ride; Match No. 27: Gary Phelps' total includes 2 points from one golden double ride.

PREMIER LEAGUE AVERAGES

Rider	Mts	Rds	Pts	Bon	Tot	Avge	Max
Adam Shields	31	156	365	20	385	9.87	2 Full; 3 Paid
Danny Bird	34	171	373	17	390	9.12	5 Full; 1 Paid

Rider	Mts	Rds	Pts	Bon	Tot	Avge	Max
Ray Morton	20	89	183	14	197	8.85	1 Paid
Sebastian Tresarrieu	33	131	196	20	216	6.60	2 Paid
Chris Johnson	1	4	3	2	5	5.00	–
Glen Phillips	34	134	126	27	153	4.57	–
Gary Phelps	34	137	116	24	140	4.09	–
Tony Dart	1	3	2	1	3	4.00	–
Carl Downs	1	3	2	1	3	4.00	–
Nick Lee	1	3	2	1	3	4.00	–
Stephane Tresarrieu	1	4	3	1	4	4.00	–
Chris Mills	24	94	71	16	87	3.70	–
Mathieu Tresarrieu	5	21	13	3	16	3.05	–
Guests	16	71	145	15	160	9.01	–

NOTE: The figures for Adam Shields include one golden double ride (4 points), modified to normal score i.e. 2 points; the figures for Gary Phelps include one golden double ride (2 points), modified to normal score i.e. 1 point.

BRITISH LEAGUE CUP

(* Denotes bonus-point victory)

No	DATE	OPPONENTS	H/A	RESULT	BIRD	SEB. TRESARRIEU	MORTON	PHILLIPS	SHIELDS	PHELPS	MILLS	STE. TRESARRIEU	OTHERS
1	18/3	Oxford	H	W47-43	9+1(5)	5+2(4)	9(4)	3+2(4)	13(5)	3(4)	5+3(4)	–	–
2	3/4	Swindon	A	D45-45	15+1(6)	2(3)	–	2(3)	15+1(6)	2(3)	2+2(5)	–	7(4)
3	8/4	Reading	H	W56-34	15(5)	3+2(4)	13+1(5)	6(4)	9+2(4)	4+1(4)	6(4)	–	–
4	14/4	Reading	A	W50-40*	14(5)	8(4)	4+1(4)	7+2(4)	13+2(5)	3+1(5)	1(3)	–	–
5	15/4	Swindon	H	W49-41*	9(4)	6+1(4)	11+2(5)	6(4)	10+1(5)	0(3)	7+1(5)	–	–
6	20/4	Eastbourne	A	L34-55	3+1(5)	2+2(3)	9(5)	7+1(5)	10(6)	3(3)	0(3)	–	–
7	22/4	Eastbourne	H	D45-45	14+1(6)	1+1(4)	7+1(4)	0(3)	15(6)	–	6+1(4)	2+2(3)	–
8	11/7	Oxford	A	L40-50	9(6)	2(4)	R/R	2(4)	17(6)	4+1(4)	6+1(6)	–	–

DETAILS OF OTHER RIDERS:

Match No. 2: Niels-Kristian Iversen 7(4).

BRITISH LEAGUE CUP AVERAGES

Rider	Mts	Rds	Pts	Bon	Tot	Avge	Max
Adam Shields	8	43	102	6	108	10.05	1 Paid
Danny Bird	8	42	88	4	92	8.76	1 Full
Ray Morton	6	27	53	5	58	8.59	–
Stephane Tresarrieu	1	3	2	2	4	5.33	–
Sebastian Tresarrieu	8	30	29	8	37	4.93	–
Glen Phillips	8	31	33	5	38	4.90	–
Chris Mills	8	34	33	8	41	4.82	–
Gary Phelps	7	26	19	3	22	3.38	–
Guests	1	4	7	0	7	7.00	–

KNOCK-OUT CUP

(* Denotes aggregate victory)

No	DATE	OPPONENTS	H/A	RESULT	BIRD	PHILLIPS	MORTON	SEB. TRESARRIEU	SHIELDS	MILLS	PHELPS	M. TRESARRIEU	STE. TRESARRIEU	OTHERS
1	13/5	Swindon	H	W54-38	15(5)	3+1(4)	9+1(4)	5(4)	13+2(5)	3+1(4)	6+1(4)	–	–	–
2	15/5	Swindon	A	W51-49*	10(5)	4(4)	10(4)	2+1(4)	15(5)	4+1(4)	6+1(4)	–	–	–
3	23/6	Exeter	A	L42-53	12+1(5)	3(5)	9(5)	5+1(4)	9(4)	2+1(3)	2(4)	–	–	–
4	24/6	Exeter	H	W61-34*	12(5)	8+1(4)	13+2(5)	9+1(4)	8+1(4)	7+1(5)	4+1(3)	–	–	–
5	12/8	Trelawny	A	L43-49	5(4)	0(3)	–	5+1(4)	12+1(5)	–	6(4)	3+3(5)	–	12(5)
6	26/8	Trelawny	H	W54-45*	12+1(5)	7(4)	–	8+2(4)	9+2(5)	1(3)	8+1(5)	–	–	9+1(4)
7	7/10	Sheffield	H	W49-44	7+1(5)	8(4)	–	8+1(4)	12+1(5)	–	5+1(5)	–	–	9(7)
8	16/10	Sheffield	A	L46-47*	6+2(5)	4(4)	–	5(4)	17(5)	–	0(3)	–	2(5)	12(4)

DETAILS OF OTHER RIDERS:

Match No. 5: Craig Watson 12(5); Match No. 6: Paul Pickering 9+1(4); Match No. 7: Paul Pickering 9(4); Tony Dart 0(3); Match No. 8: Paul Pickering 12(4).

GOLDEN DOUBLE/TACTICAL JOKER RIDES:

Match No. 3: Danny Bird's total includes 4 points from a tactical joker ride; Ray Morton's total includes 4 points from a tactical joker ride; Sebastian Tresarrieu's total includes 2 points from a tactical joker ride; Glen Phillips' total includes 0 points from a golden double ride; Match No. 5: Craig Watson's total includes 4 points from a tactical joker ride; Match No. 8: Adam Shields' total includes 6 points from a tactical joker ride.

OTHER MEETINGS

20 September: Premier League

Stoke 34 Isle Of Wight 26 (Danny Bird 8; Adam Shields 8; Paul Thorp 3; Sebastian Tresarrieu 3; Gary Phelps 3; Chris Mills 1+1; Glen Phillips 0) – meeting abandoned after heat ten.

KING'S LYNN LILLEVILLA LOG CABINS STARS

ADDRESS: Norfolk Arena, Saddlebow Road, King's Lynn, Norfolk.
PROMOTERS: Buster Chapman & Laurence Rogers.
TRACK LENGTH: 342 metres.
FIRST MEETING: 23 May 1965.
YEARS OF OPERATION: 1965 Open; 1966–67 British League; 1968–74 British League Division One; 1975–90 British League; 1991–94 British League Division One; 1995 British Premier League; 1996 Training; 1997–02 British Elite League; 2003 British Premier League.

CLUB HONOURS

KNOCK-OUT CUP WINNERS: 1977, 2000.
INTER-LEAGUE KNOCK-OUT CUP WINNERS: 1978, 1980.

RIDER ROSTER 2003

ALLOTT, Adam *b. 19 March 1983, Stockport, Greater Manchester.*
BRITISH CAREER: (1998) Norfolk, Buxton; (1999) Buxton, Sheffield; (2000) Sheffield, Owlerton; (2001) Sheffield; (2002) Sheffield (CL), Swindon, Somerset; (2003) Buxton, Stoke (BLC), King's Lynn.

BOXALL, Steve *b. 16 May 1987, Canterbury, Kent.*
BRITISH CAREER: (2002) Rye House (CL); (2003) Rye House (CL), Ipswich (BLC), Reading (BLC), King's Lynn.

BRAIDFORD, Steven *b. 31 December 1985, Maidstone, Kent.*
BRITISH CAREER: (2002) Wolverhampton (CT), Isle of Wight, Wimbledon; (2003) Wolverhampton (CL & BLC), King's Lynn (BLC).

BRANNEY, John *b. 7 November 1985, Whitehaven, Cumbria.*
BRITISH CAREER: (2002) Rye House (CL), Newcastle (CL); (2003) Newcastle (CL), Wimbledon (CT), Mildenhall (CT), King's Lynn, Exeter, Newport (PL), Buxton (CT).

BRUNDLE, James *b. 15 December 1986, King's Lynn, Norfolk.*
BRITISH CAREER: (2002) King's Lynn (CL), Mildenhall; (2003) King's Lynn (PL), Mildenhall.

DART, Tony *b. 2 September 1979, Ashford, Kent.*
BRITISH CAREER: (2003) Mildenhall, King's Lynn, Peterborough (BLC), Isle of Wight (KOC).

DERBYSHIRE, Lee *b. 3 December 1981, Stockport, Greater Manchester.*
BRITISH CAREER: (2002) Buxton; (2003) Buxton, Hull, King's Lynn, Belle Vue (BLC).

HARDING, Trevor *b. 1 November 1986, Perth, Western Australia.*
BRITISH CAREER: (2002) Sheffield (CL), Carmarthen; (2003) King's Lynn, Boston.

HODGSON, Daniel *b. 21 January 1982, Bradford, West Yorkshire.*
BRITISH CAREER: (1998) Buxton; (1999) King's Lynn (CL); (2000) Buxton, Hull; (2001) Somerset, Sheffield (PL), Newport (CL); (2003) Carmarthen, King's Lynn (BLC).

JAROS, Jan *b. 11 November 1984, Prague, Czech Republic.*
BRITISH CAREER: (2003) King's Lynn (BLC).

McCABE, Shane *b. 3 May 1974, Townsville, Queensland, Australia.*
BRITISH CAREER: (2002) Peterborough (CL), Edinburgh, Somerset, Trelawny, Rye House, Newport, Stoke; (2003) King's Lynn, Boston, Peterborough (CL, ELKOC & BLC), Somerset.

MADSEN, Tom P. *b. 24 November 1977, Esbjerg, Denmark.*
BRITISH CAREER: (1999) Berwick; (2000-02) King's Lynn; (2003) Ipswich, King's Lynn.

MALLETT, Darren *b. 25 May 1986, Boston, Lincolnshire.*
BRITISH CAREER: (2001) Somerset, Boston; (2002) Boston; (2003) Boston, King's Lynn.

MELL, Steffen *b. 12 June 1978, Teterow, Germany.*
BRITISH CAREER: (2001) Trelawny; (2002) Berwick; (2003) King's Lynn, Newcastle.

OLIVER, John *b. 22 July 1987, Melbourne, Victoria, Australia.*
BRITISH CAREER: (2003) Carmarthen (CL), Buxton, King's Lynn.

PARKER, Shane *b. 29 April 1970, Adelaide, South Australia.*
BRITISH CAREER: (1990-94) Ipswich; (1995-96) Middlesbrough; (1997-98) King's Lynn; (1999) Hull; (2000) King's Lynn, Belle Vue; (2001-02) Peterborough; (2003) King's Lynn, Peterborough.

KING'S LYNN STARS: back row, left to right: Laurence Rogers (Co-Promoter/Team Manager), Adam Allott, Darren Mallett, Davey Watt, James Brundle. On bike: Trevor Harding. Front, kneeling: Shane Parker, Tomas Topinka.

ROLPH, Darren   *b. 17 May 1982. Braintree, Essex.*
BRITISH CAREER: (2003) Boston, King's Lynn.

SCHUTZBACH, Sirg   *b. 23 July 1980, Ravensburg, Germany.*
BRITISH CAREER: (2003) King's Lynn.

SIMMONS, Nick   *b. 24 July 1981, Leamington Spa, Warwickshire.*
BRITISH CAREER: (1997) Shuttle Cubs, Ryde; (1998) Newport (CL & PL), Isle of Wight, Exeter; (1999) Isle of Wight, Stoke, Newport (CL); (2000) Arena-Essex; (2001) Newport (PL & CL), Somerset; (2002) Isle of Wight; (2003) Stoke, Reading, Mildenhall, Workington, King's Lynn, Exeter.

SUCHANEK, Tomas   *b. 7 April 1984, Pardubice, Czech Republic.*
BRITISH CAREER: (2003) King's Lynn (BLC).

THOMPSON, Mark   *b. 8 July 1979, Orsett, Essex.*
BRITISH CAREER: (1996) Sittingbourne, Linlithgow, Mildenhall, Eastbourne (CL); (1997) Anglian Angels; (1998) Mildenhall, Newport, Stoke; (1999) King's Lynn (CL); (2000-01) Mildenhall; (2002) King's Lynn (CL), Mildenhall, Arena-Essex, Workington, Stoke; (2003) Boston, Stoke (PL), Newport (BLC), Somerset, Peterborough (BLC), Coventry (BLC), King's Lynn, Arena-Essex.

TOPINKA, Tomas   *b. 5 June 1974, Prague, Czech Republic.*
BRITISH CAREER: (1993-95) King's Lynn; (1996) Oxford; (1997-98) King's Lynn; (1999) Ipswich; (2001) Belle Vue; (2002) Coventry; (2003) King's Lynn.

WATT, Davey   *b. 6 January 1978, Townsville, Queensland, Australia.*
BRITISH CAREER: (2001) Isle of Wight; (2002) Newcastle; (2003) King's Lynn, Poole.

WRIGHT, James   *b. 13 June 1986, Stockport, Greater Manchester.*
BRITISH CAREER: (2002) Buxton; (2003) Buxton, Belle Vue (BLC), Newcastle (PL), Stoke (PL), Workington, Hull, King's Lynn.

PREMIER LEAGUE

(* Denotes bonus-point victory)

No	DATE	OPPONENTS	H/A	RESULT	TOPINKA	MELL	WATT	PARKER	BRUNDLE	HARDING	MALLETT	ALLOTT	MADSEN	DERBYSHIRE	OTHERS
1	5/4	Sheffield	H	W46-44	11(5)	0(3)	9(4)	15(5)	2(4)	9(6)	–	–	–	–	0(3)
2	10/4	Sheffield	A	L33-57	9(5)	1+1(3)	11(5)	9(6)	1(4)	0(3)	2+1(4)	–	–	–	–
3	16/4	Hull	A	L40-50	11+2(6)	–	10(5)	14(6)	0(3)	4+1(4)	0(3)	1+1(3)	–	–	–
4	21/4	Exeter	A	L31-59	10+1(6)	–	4+1(4)	12(6)	3(4)	0(3)	2(4)	0(3)	–	–	–
5	22/4	Trelawny	A	W46-44	11+1(5)	–	8(4)	12(5)	5+2(5)	9+1(5)	0(3)	1(4)	–	–	–
6	23/4	Arena-Essex	H	W48-42	11+1(5)	–	12(4)	11(5)	3(4)	8+1(6)	1(3)	2+1(3)	–	–	–
7	26/4	Hull	H	W58-32*	–	–	12(4)	13(5)	6+1(4)	8+2(5)	5+1(4)	5+1(4)	–	–	9(4)
8	4/5	Newcastle	A	W47-43	16+1(6)	–	12(5)	8+1(4)	0(3)	5+1(5)	2(3)	4(4)	–	–	–
9	7/5	Swindon	H	L44-46	11(5)	–	11+1(5)	7(4)	7(5)	4+1(4)	4+2(4)	0(3)	–	–	–
10	18/5	Glasgow †	A	L35-43	9+1(5)	–	12(5)	13(5)	1(4)	0(2)	0(2)	0(3)	–	–	–
11	4/6	Trelawny	H	W54-38*	11(5)	–	13+1(5)	8+1(4)	–	12+1(6)	0(1)	6+1(4)	–	–	4+2(5)
12	7/6	Berwick	A	L44-46	15+2(6)	–	5(4)	18(6)	–	3+1(4)	R/R	2(5)	–	–	1(5)
13	18/6	Newcastle	H	W49-41*	12(5)	–	11(4)	–	7+1(5)	4(4)	–	6+1(4)	9(5)	–	0(3)
14	25/6	Stoke	H	W52-37	11+1(4)	–	12(5)	–	3+1(4)	4+2(4)	–	2(4)	14(5)	–	6(4)
15	9/7	Isle of Wight	H	W58-32	10+1(4)	–	15(5)	14+1(5)	4(4)	5+1(4)	–	6+2(4)	–	–	4+2(5)

PREMIER LEAGUE continued

No	DATE	OPPONENTS	H/A	RESULT	TOPINKA	MELL	WATT	PARKER	BRUNDLE	HARDING	MALLETT	ALLOTT	MADSEN	DERBYSHIRE	OTHERS
16	12/7	Stoke	A	L44-46*	10+1(5)	–	10(5)	13(5)	5+1(5)	4+2(3)		2+1(4)	–	–	0(3)
17	23/7	Edinburgh	H	W52-37	7+2(4)	–	18(6)	14+1(5)	0(0)	R/R		11+1(5)	–	–	2(7)
18	13/8	Newport	H	W57-32	12+2(5)	–	10(4)	13+1(5)	6+1(4)	8+3(4)	–	6+1(4)	–	2+1(4)	–
19	16/8	Workington	A	L37-53	10+1(6)	–	4+1(4)	14(6)	0(3)	3(4)	–	5+1(4)	–	–	1(3)
20	19/8	Isle of Wight	A	L40-52*	12(6)	–	9+2(5)	12(6)	1(4)	3+2(3)	–	1+1(3)	–	–	2(3)
21	20/8	Rye House	H	W48-42	9+1(5)	–	10(5)	–	7+2(4)	4+1(4)	–	7+1(5)	11(4)	0(3)	–
22	23/8	Exeter	H	W65-25*	11+1(4)	–	12(4)	12(4)	7+3(4)	12+3(5)	–	7+1(5)	–	4+1(4)	–
23	25/8	Rye House	A	L41-49	14(6)	–	13+1(6)	–	0(3)	0(3)	–	6+1(4)	8(5)	–	0(3)
24	27/8	Workington	H	W58-32*	13+1(5)	–	10(4)	–	2+1(4)	8+3(4)	–	12+2(5)	13+2(5)	–	0(3)
25	29/8	Somerset	A	W52-38	13+1(5)	–	9(4)	9(3)	4(4)	7+2(5)	–	6(5)	–	–	4+1(4)
26	3/9	Glasgow	H	W59-31*	12(4)	–	11(4)	–	10+2(5)	6+1(4)	4(4)	7+3(5)	9(4)	–	–
27	7/9	Newport	A	L38-52*	–	–	7(4)	11(6)	5(4)	0(3)	1+1(3)	4(4)	–	–	10(6)
28	10/9	Reading	H	W49-41	12+1(5)	–	14(5)	–	7+1(5)	2+1(4)	1(4)	4(4)	9(3)	–	–
29	17/9	Berwick	H	W60-30*	11+1(4)	–	14+1(5)	13+1(5)	4+2(4)	9+1(4)	3(4)	6+1(4)	–	–	–
30	18/9	Swindon	A	L37-52	5+1(5)	–	13(6)	9(4)	2(4)	5+1(5)	2+1(4)	1+1(3)	–	–	–
31	8/10	Somerset	H	W59-31*	13+2(5)	–	14(5)	15(5)	–	R/R	5(5)	9+2(5)	–	3+2(5)	–
32	17/10	Edinburgh	A	L38-52*	–	–	R/R	9(6)	–	–	4(4)	7+1(6)	–	1(3)	17(11)
33	20/10	Reading	A	D44-44*	–	–	R/R	9(5)	–	–	2+1(3)	7(5)	–	–	26+3(18)
34	24/10	Arena-Essex	A	L35-55	–	–	R/R	–	–	–	–	10(7)	–	–	25+1(23)

† Meeting abandoned after thirteen heats, with the result standing.

DETAILS OF OTHER RIDERS:

Match No. 1: Shane McCabe 0(3); Match No. 7: Olly Allen 9(4); Match No. 11: Chris Mills 4+2(5); Match No. 12: Chris Mills 1(5); Match No. 13: Tony Dart 0(3); Match No. 14: Chris Mills 6(4); Match No. 15: Mark Thompson 4+2(4); Match No. 16: Mark Thompson 0(3); Match No. 17: Tony Dart 2(5); John Oliver 0(2); Match No. 19: John Branney 1(3); Match No. 20: Joel Parsons 2(3); Match No. 23: Darren Rolph 0(3); Match No. 24: James Wright 0(3); Match No. 25: Nick Simmons 4+1(4); Match No. 27: Steve Masters 10(6); Match No. 32: James Grieves 16(7); David McAllan 1(4); Match No. 33: Chris Harris 13(6); Chris Schramm 10+2(7); Graeme Gordon 3+1(5); Match No. 34: Brent Werner 17(7); Mark Lemon 6+1(6); Graeme Gordon 1(4); Steve Boxall 1(3); Mark Thompson 0(3).

GOLDEN DOUBLE RIDES:

Match No. 20: Shane Parker's total includes 4 points from a golden double ride.

PREMIER LEAGUE AVERAGES

Rider	Mts	Rds	Pts	Bon	Tot	Avge	Max
Tom P. Madsen	7	31	73	2	75	9.68	1 Paid
Tomas Topinka	29	146	322	26	348	9.53	1 Full; 4 Paid
Davey Watt	31	144	335	8	343	9.53	5 Full; 1 Paid
Shane Parker	26	131	305	6	311	9.50	4 Full; 2 Paid
Trevor Harding	29	120	146	32	178	5.93	1 Paid
Adam Allott	32	135	153	25	178	5.27	–
Nick Simmons	1	4	4	1	5	5.00	–
James Brundle	28	110	102	18	120	4.36	–
Lee Derbyshire	5	19	10	4	14	2.95	–
Darren Mallett	18	62	38	7	45	2.90	–

Rider	Mts	Rds	Pts	Bon	Tot	Avge	Max
Mark Thompson	3	10	4	2	6	2.40	–
Steve Boxall	1	3	1	0	1	1.33	–
John Branney	1	3	1	0	1	1.33	–
Steffen Mell	2	6	1	1	2	1.33	–
Tony Dart	2	8	2	0	2	1.00	–
Shane McCabe	1	3	0	0	0	0.00	–
John Oliver	1	2	0	0	0	0.00	–
Darren Rolph	1	3	0	0	0	0.00	–
James Wright	1	3	0	0	0	0.00	–
Guests	14	73	99	6	105	5.75	–

NOTE: The figures for Shane Parker include one golden double ride (4 points), modified to normal score i.e. 2 points.

BRITISH LEAGUE CUP

(* Denotes bonus-point victory)

No	DATE	OPPONENTS	H/A	RESULT	TOPINKA	SCHUTZBACH	WATT	MALLETT	ALLOTT	BRUNDLE	HARDING	THOMPSON	SUCHANEK	JAROS	OTHERS
1	10/5	Rye House	A	L35-55	13(6)	0(3)	12(6)	0(4)	9(5)	1(5)	0(1)	–	–	–	–
2	31/5	Ipswich	H	W48-41	9+1(4)	–	12+2(5)	3(4)	7(4)	2+1(4)	5(5)	–	–	–	10(4)
3	11/6	Rye House	H	W49-41	12+2(5)	–	13(5)	–	8+1(4)	7(4)	4+3(5)	1+1(3)	–	–	4(4)
4	10/7	Ipswich	A	L37-53	14(6)	–	12+1(6)	–	4(4)	3+2(4)	1(3)	3(4)	0(3)	–	–
5	11/7	Peterborough	A	L45-47	17+1(6)	–	11(6)	–	4(4)	4+1(3)	1+1(3)	1+1(3)	7+2(5)	–	–
6	16/7	Peterborough	H	W47-43*	10+1(5)	–	12(5)	–	10+1(5)	9+4(6)	R/R	1(4)	–	5+2(5)	–
7	6/8	Arena-Essex	H	W50-40	–	–	10(4)	–	12+1(6)	5(4)	6+3(4)	–	4+1(4)	–	13+1(8)
8	15/8	Arena-Essex	A	L34-56	12(6)	–	13(6)	–	3(4)	1+1(3)	3+1(4)	–	–	0(4)	2+1(3)

DETAILS OF OTHER RIDERS:

Match No. 2: Andrew Moore 10(4); Match No. 3: Olly Allen 4(4); Match No. 7: Jan Staechmann 13+1(5); Daniel Hodgson 0(3); Match No. 8: Steven Braidford 2+1(3).

GOLDEN DOUBLE RIDES:

Match No. 1: Davey Watt's total includes 0 points from a golden double ride; Match No. 5: Tomas Topinka's total includes 4 points from a golden double ride.

BRITISH LEAGUE CUP AVERAGES

Rider	Mts	Rds	Pts	Bon	Tot	Avge	Max
Tomas Topinka	7	38	85	5	90	9.47	1 Paid
Davey Watt	8	43	95	3	98	9.12	–
Adam Allott	8	36	57	3	60	6.67	–
James Brundle	8	33	32	9	41	4.97	–
Tomas Suchanek	3	12	11	3	14	4.67	–
Trevor Harding	7	25	20	8	28	4.48	–
Steven Braidford	1	3	2	1	3	4.00	–
Jan Jaros	2	9	5	2	7	3.11	–

Rider	Mts	Rds	Pts	Bon	Tot	Avge	Max
Mark Thompson	4	14	6	2	8	2.28	–
Darren Mallett	2	8	3	0	3	1.50	–
Daniel Hodgson	1	3	0	0	0	0.00	–
Sirg Schutzbach	1	3	0	0	0	0.00	–
Guests	3	13	27	1	28	8.61	–

NOTE: The figures for Tomas Topinka include one golden double ride (4 points), modified to normal score i.e. 2 points;

The figures for Davey Watt include one golden double ride (0 points).

KNOCK-OUT CUP

(* Denotes aggregate victory)

No	DATE	OPPONENTS	H/A	RESULT	TOPINKA	MELL	WATT	McCABE	PARKER	BRUNDLE	HARDING	MADSEN	MALLETT	ALLOTT	OTHERS
1	22/3	Workington	A	L43-46	10(5)	7(4)	8(4)	4+1(4)	9+1(5)	3(4)	2+1(4)	–	–	–	–
2	9/4	Workington	H	W52-43*	13(5)	0(3)	11(5)	–	–	6+1(4)	10+3(6)	12(4)	0(3)	–	–
3	28/5	Edinburgh	H	W62-34	11+1(4)	–	15(5)	–	14+1(5)	4+1(4)	6+1(4)	–	5+2(4)	7+1(4)	–
4	6/6	Edinburgh	A	L37-59*	12(6)	–	14(5)	–	–	–	3(6)	6(4)	R/R	2(5)	0(5)
5	26/6	Sheffield	A	L48-50	5(4)	–	14+1(5)	–	20+1(6)	4+2(5)	0(3)	–	–	4(4)	1(3)
6	2/7	Sheffield	H	L48-49	11(5)	–	12(5)	–	10(4)	7+1(5)	3+1(4)	–	–	5(4)	0(3)

DETAILS OF OTHER RIDERS:

Match No. 4: William Lawson 0(5); Match No. 5: Chris Collins 1(3); Match No. 6: Matthew Wright 0(3).

GOLDEN DOUBLE/TACTICAL JOKER RIDES:

Match No. 4: Tomas Topinka's total includes 6 points from a tactical joker ride; Davey Watt's total includes 6 points from a tactical joker ride; Tom P. Madsen's total includes 0 points from a tactical joker ride; Match No. 5: Shane Parker's total includes 6 points from a tactical joker ride and 4 points from a golden double outing; Davey Watt's total includes 6 points from a tactical joker ride; Tomas Topinka's total includes 0 points from a tactical joker ride.

OTHER MEETINGS

18 March: International Club Challenge

King's Lynn 46 (Davey Watt 12; Shane Parker 12; Tomas Topinka 8; James Brundle 5+2; Trevor Harding 5; Sirg Schutzbach 3+2; Shane McCabe 1; Steffen Mell 0) Kaparna 44 (Joonas Kylmakorpi 10+3; Rafal Dobrucki 10; Tomasz Gapinski 10; Jim Jansson 6; Magnus Karlsson 4+2; Sebastian Bengtsson 3+3; Norvy Brandin 1).

24 March: Inter-League Challenge

Belle Vue 58 King's Lynn 32 (Tomas Topinka 9; Davey Watt 8+1; Shane Parker 6; James Brundle 3+1; Trevor Harding 2+2; Steffen Mell 2; Tom P. Madsen 2).

26 March: A10 Trophy (first-leg)

King's Lynn 60 (Shane Parker 15; Tomas Topinka 13+2; Davey Watt 11; Trevor Harding 7+2; James Brundle 6+1; Shane McCabe 4+1; Steffen Mell 4) Rye House 36.

29 March: A10 Trophy (second-leg)

Rye House 53 King's Lynn 39 (Tomas Topinka 14; Davey Watt 14; Trevor Harding 7; Steffen Mell 2+1; Shane McCabe 1; James Brundle 1; Sirg Schutzbach 0; Shane Parker R/R) – King's Lynn won 99-89 on aggregate.

16 May: Knock-Out Cup First Round (first-leg)

Edinburgh 15 King's Lynn 9 (Davey Watt 3; Trevor Harding 3; Tomas Topinka 2; Shane Parker 1; Adam Allott 0; James Brundle 0; Darren Mallett 0) – meeting abandoned after heat four.

31 May: Youth International

Great Britain 24 (Richie Dennis 5; Jamie Westacott 5; Harland Cook 5; Lee Smart 3+2; Chris Johnson 3+2; Shane Waldron 3; Lewis Bridger 0) Germany 18 (Alexander Lieschke 5; Kevin Woelbert 4; Tobias Busch 3; Richard Speiser 2+2; Stefan Kurtz 2; Frank Facher 1; Soenke Peterson 1) – meeting abandoned after heat seven.

1 October: Three-Team Tournament

King's Lynn 48 (Tomas Topinka 12; Shane Parker 12; Adam Allott 12; James Brundle 6+2; Darren Mallett 3+1; Carl Wilkinson 3+1) Swindon 32, Hull 28.

INDIVIDUAL MEETING

24 September: Pride Of The East

1st Simon Stead 15; 2nd Davey Watt 14; 3rd Tomas Topinka 13; Craig Watson 12; Adam Allott 9; Chris Harris 9; Leigh Lanham 9; Shane Parker 7; Charlie Gjedde 7; James Brundle 6; Trevor Harding 5; Andrew Appleton 5; Jonas Davidsson 4; Olly Allen 3; Darren Mallett (res) 1; Darren Rolph (res) 1; Steve Masters 0; Jamie Smith 0; John Oliver (res) 0.

NEWCASTLE KBS DIAMONDS

NOTE: The information below relates only to the main Newcastle team. For details of the second side, please refer to the Conference League section.

ADDRESS: Brough Park Stadium, The Fossway, Byker, Newcastle upon Tyne, Tyne & Wear.
PROMOTERS: George English, Dave Rowland & Darryl Illingworth.
TRACK LENGTH: 300 metres.
FIRST MEETING: 17 May 1929.
YEARS OF OPERATION: 1929 English Dirt-track League; 1930 Open; 1938-39 National League Division Two; 1945 Open; 1946 Northern League; 1947-51 National League Division Two; 1961-64 Provincial League; 1965-67 British League; 1968-70 British League Division One; 1975-83 National League; 1984 British League; 1986-87 National League; 1989-90 National League; 1991-94 British League Division Two; 1997-03 British Premier League.

NOTE: Although Newcastle have predominantly used 'Diamonds' as a nickname, there were three seasons when they ran with an alternative, namely 'Brough' in 1946, 'Magpies' in 1949 and 'Federation Specials' in 1986.

CLUB HONOURS

LEAGUE CHAMPIONS: 1964, 1976, 1982, 1983, 2001.
FOUR-TEAM CHAMPIONS: 1976, 1982, 1983.

KNOCK-OUT CUP WINNERS: 1976, 1982.
SUPERNATIONAL WINNERS: 1982, 1983.
GOLD CUP WINNERS: 1991, 1992.

RIDER ROSTER 2003

BJERRE, Kenneth   b. 24 May 1984, Esbjerg, Denmark.
BRITISH CAREER: (2002) Newcastle; (2003) Newcastle, Peterborough.
BRANNEY, Craig   b. 31 July 1982, Whitehaven, Cumbria.
BRITISH CAREER: (2000) Ashfield; (2001) Workington, Buxton, Isle of Wight, Newport
(PL); (2002) Newcastle (CL), Hull; (2003) Newcastle (PL & CL), Armadale (CT),
Workington, Swindon (PL), Hull, Somerset.
DICKEN, Lee   b. 24 August 1978, Hull, East Yorkshire.
BRITISH CAREER: (1994) Buxton; (1995) Hull, Stoke, Peterborough; (1996) Hull,
Owlerton, Sheffield; (1997-98) Hull; (1999) Hull, Exeter; (2000) Hull; (2001) Hull,
Arena-Essex; (2002) Newport, Wolverhampton; (2003) Hull, Newcastle.
JUUL, Richard   b. 30 October 1970, Copenhagen, Denmark.
BRITISH CAREER: (1991-94) Newcastle; (1995) Wolverhampton; (1997) Newcastle,
Berwick; (1998) Stoke; (1999) Wolverhampton; (2000) Glasgow, Isle of Wight; (2001-03)
Newcastle.
KNUDSEN, Rune   b. 15 August 1983, Helsingor, Denmark.
BRITISH CAREER: (2003) Newcastle.
LAWSON, William   b. 27 February 1987, Auchterader, Perthshire, Scotland.
BRITISH CAREER: (2002) Newcastle (CL); (2003) Newcastle (PL & CL), Belle Vue (BLC).
LITTLE, Kevin   b. 24 September 1972, Edinburgh, Scotland.
BRITISH CAREER: (1989) Glasgow, Berwick; (1990-91) Berwick; (1992) Bradford; (1993)
Edinburgh; (1994) Edinburgh, Berwick; (1995) Berwick, Belle Vue, Edinburgh,
Coventry; (1996) Coventry; (1997) Berwick; (1998-00) Edinburgh; (2001-03)
Newcastle.
LUND, Kristian   b. 8 August 1984, Outrup, Denmark.
BRITISH CAREER: (2003) Newcastle.
MELL, Steffen   b. 12 June 1978, Teterow, Germany.
BRITISH CAREER: (2001) Trelawny; (2002) Berwick; (2003) King's Lynn, Newcastle.
PEDERSEN, Bjarne   b. 12 July 1978, Ryrde, Denmark.
BRITISH CAREER: (2000-01) Newcastle; (2002) Poole; (2003) Poole, Newcastle.
POWELL, Mick   b. 24 September 1969, Brisbane, Queensland, Australia.
BRITISH CAREER: (1989-90) Edinburgh; (1991-95) Glasgow; (1996) Scottish Monarchs;
(1997-98) Glasgow; (1999) Glasgow, Berwick; (2000-01) Workington; (2002) Glasgow;
(2003) Newcastle.
ROBERTSON, Jamie   b. 8 October 1986, Berwick-upon-Tweed, Northumberland.
BRITISH CAREER: (2002) Newcastle (CL); (2003) Newcastle (PL & CL), Glasgow.
ROBSON, Stuart   b. 8 November 1976, Sunderland, Tyne & Wear.
BRITISH CAREER: (1993) Newcastle; (1994) Newcastle, Edinburgh; (1995) Coventry;
(1996) Coventry, Middlesbrough; (1997) Hull; (1998-02) Coventry; (2003) Coventry,
Newcastle.

NEWCASTLE DIAMONDS: back row, left to right: Stuart Robson, Steffen Mell, Craig Branney, Richard Juul. On bike: Kevin Little. Front, kneeling: Jamie Robertson, Kenneth Bjerre.

WRIGHT, James   *b. 13 June 1986, Stockport, Greater Manchester.*
    BRITISH CAREER: (2002) Buxton; (2003) Buxton, Belle Vue (BLC), Newcastle (PL), Stoke (PL), Workington, Hull, King's Lynn.

PREMIER LEAGUE

(* Denotes bonus-point victory)

No	DATE	OPPONENTS	H/A	RESULT	BJERRE	JUUL	LUND	LITTLE	POWELL	BRANNEY	ROBERTSON	MELL	PEDERSEN	LAWSON	ROBSON	DICKEN	OTHERS
1	26/4	Workington	A	L40-49	12(6)	1(3)	6(4)	10+1(6)	6(4)	5+2(4)	0(3)	-	-	-	-	-	
2	27/4	Workington	H	L44-46	12+1(5)	5+1(4)	4(4)	10+1(5)	6+1(4)	0(3)	7+3(4)	-	-	-	-	-	
3	4/5	King's Lynn	H	L43-47	11(5)	3+2(4)	5(4)	9+1(5)	5+2(4)	3+1(3)	7(5)	-	-	-	-	-	
4	18/5	Sheffield	H	W48-41	6+1(4)	7+2(5)	-	9+1(4)	-	-	0(2)	4+2(4)	14(5)	8(6)	-	-	
5	22/5	Sheffield	A	L29-61	8(7)	4(6)	-	R/R	-	-	-	1(4)	11(6)	3(3)	-	-	2+2(4)
6	1/6	Edinburgh	H	L43-47	13(5)	7+3(4)	-	9(4)	-	1+1(4)	1+1(3)	-	-	7+1(5)	5(5)	-	
7	16/6	Berwick	H	W48-42	15(5)	4+1(4)	-	11(4)	-	1(3)	6(5)	1(4)	-	-	10+1(5)	-	
8	18/6	King's Lynn	A	L41-49	15(6)	4+2(4)	-	6+1(5)	-	2(3)	3+1(3)	3+1(3)	-	-	8+2(6)	-	
9	19/6	Swindon	A	L42-50	19(6)	6+2(5)	-	3+1(4)	-	2(3)	2+1(3)	0(3)	-	-	10(6)	-	
10	20/6	Somerset	A	L43-47	16(6)	6+1(5)	-	4+2(4)	-	0(3)	3(3)	2(3)	-	-	12+1(6)	-	
11	29/6	Newport	A	L40-50	-	2(4)	-	9(5)	-	-	0(3)	-	10+1(5)	4+1(6)	-	7+1(4)	8(3)
12	6/7	Exeter	H	W57-33	15(5)	4(4)	-	12(4)	-	-	5+2(4)	-	-	5+1(4)	12+2(5)	4+1(4)	
13	13/7	Somerset	H	W52-38*	8(4)	R/R	-	12(6)	-	-	6+2(5)	-	-	12+2(6)	8+2(4)	6+2(5)	
14	14/7	Reading	A	W49-40	15(5)	R/R	-	13(5)	-	-	4(5)	-	-	4(6)	10+1(5)	3(4)	
15	15/7	Isle of Wight	A	L39-51	13+1(6)	R/R	-	10(6)	-	-	2(4)	-	-	4+1(4)	8(6)	2+1(4)	
16	20/7	Trelawny	H	W52-38	15(5)	R/R	-	14(6)	-	-	6(5)	-	-	7+1(5)	7(4)	3(5)	
17	1/8	Arena-Essex	A	L38-52	-	4+2(4)	-	11(6)	-	-	1+1(3)	-	-	7(5)	13(6)	2+2(3)	
18	2/8	Rye House	A	L41-49	-	2(4)	-	9+1(5)	-	-	2(3)	-	-	1+1(3)	13+2(6)	2+1(3)	12(6)
19	3/8	Isle of Wight	H	W54-36*	-	6+2(4)	-	12+1(5)	-	-	1(2)	-	-	11+1(6)	13+1(5)	3+1(4)	8+2(4)
20	6/8	Hull	A	W48-42	-	5+1(4)	-	6+1(4)	-	-	-	-	-	9+1(6)	13(5)	7+1(4)	8+1(8)
21	10/8	Swindon	H	W53-37*	15(5)	5+1(4)	-	6+1(4)	-	4+2(4)	-	-	11+2(5)	4+1(4)	-	8+2(4)	-
22	18/8	Exeter	A	L37-53*	11+2(6)	1(3)	-	3(5)	-	2+1(3)	-	-	15(6)	0(3)	-	5(4)	
23	19/8	Trelawny	A	L46-47*	11+1(5)	6+1(4)	-	6+3(4)	-	1+1(3)	-	-	-	4(4)	10+1(5)	8(5)	
24	24/8	Glasgow	A	L28-61	0(0)	0(3)	-	8(6)	-	-	0(3)	-	14(6)	2(5)	-	4(7)	
25	25/8	Glasgow	H	W53-37	-	3+1(4)	-	9+1(4)	-	-	1(3)	-	15(5)	7(4)	-	7+2(5)	11+1(5)
26	31/8	Hull	H	W53-37*	-	9+3(5)	-	8(5)	-	4+1(4)	-	-	-	6+3(4)	10(4)	7+1(4)	9(4)
27	6/9	Berwick	A	L27-63	2(1)	5+2(5)	-	7(6)	-	1(4)	-	-	-	0(4)	11(6)	1+1(4)	
28	7/9	Rye House	H	W46-44	-	5(4)	-	6(4)	-	5+1(4)	-	-	15(5)	3+2(4)	-	4+1(4)	8(5)
29	13/9	Stoke	A	W47-43	-	6+3(5)	-	R/R	-	6+2(4)	-	-	-	3+1(4)	16(6)	9+1(7)	7(5)
30	14/9	Arena-Essex	H	W52-38	15(5)	4+1(4)	-	8(4)	-	3+1(4)	-	-	-	7(4)	10+1(5)	5+1(4)	
31	25/9	Reading	H	W50-40*	13+2(5)	R/R	-	8(4)	-	5(5)	-	-	14(5)	4+2(5)	-	6+3(6)	
32	5/10	Stoke †	H	W43-29*	9(3)	R/R	-	12(5)	-	1(4)	-	-	-	5+1(4)	7(3)	9+1(5)	
33	10/10	Edinburgh	A	L42-48	10(5)	3(4)	-	11+1(5)	-	2(3)	-	-	-	3+1(4)	9+1(5)	4(4)	
34	13/10	Newport	H	W57-33*	15(5)	5+1(4)	-	9+1(4)	-	4+3(4)	-	-	-	8+2(5)	7+3(4)	9+1(4)	-

† Meeting abandoned after twelve heats, with the result standing.

DETAILS OF OTHER RIDERS:

Match No. 5: James Wright 2+2(4); Match No. 11: Chris Harris 8(3); Match No. 17: Olly Allen 0(3); Match No. 18: Craig Watson 12(6); Match No. 19: Chris Harris 8+2(4); Match No. 20: George Stancl 8+1(5); Malcolm Holloway 0(3); Match No. 25: Sean Wilson 11+1(5); Match No. 26: Simon Stead 9(4); Match No. 28: Paul Bentley 8(5); Match No. 29: Sean Wilson 7(5).

GOLDEN DOUBLE RIDES:

Match No. 1: Kenneth Bjerre's total includes 0 points from a golden double ride; Match No. 9: Kenneth Bjerre's total includes 4 points from a golden double ride; Match No. 22: Kevin Little's total includes 0 points from a golden double ride.

PREMIER LEAGUE AVERAGES

Rider	Mts	Rds	Pts	Bon	Tot	Avge	Max
Bjarne Pedersen	9	48	119	3	122	10.17	2 Full
Kenneth Bjerre	25	120	292	8	300	10.00	7 Full; 1 Paid
Stuart Robson	22	112	222	18	240	8.57	–
Kevin Little	32	153	280	18	298	7.79	1 Full
Mick Powell	3	12	17	3	20	6.67	–
Lee Dicken	24	107	125	24	149	5.57	–
Richard Juul	28	117	122	32	154	5.26	–
William Lawson	27	123	138	23	161	5.24	–
Kristian Lund	3	12	15	0	15	5.00	–
James Wright	1	4	2	2	4	4.00	–
Jamie Robertson	20	71	57	11	68	3.83	–
Craig Branney	20	72	52	16	68	3.78	–
Steffen Mell	6	21	11	3	14	2.67	–
Guests	10	43	71	4	75	6.98	–

NOTE: The figures for Kenneth Bjerre include two golden double rides (4 points), modified to normal score i.e. 2 points; the figures for Kevin Little include one golden double ride (0 points).

BRITISH LEAGUE CUP

No	DATE	OPPONENTS	H/A	RESULT	BJERRE	JUUL	KNUDSEN	LITTLE	POWELL	BRANNEY	ROBERTSON	LAWSON	LUND	OTHERS
1	15/3	Workington	A	L40-50	10(6)	3(4)	0(2)	8(5)	14(6)	2+1(3)	3+1(3)	–	–	–
2	16/3	Workington	H	W46-43	13(5)	6+2(4)	1(4)	12(5)	6(4)	5+2(4)	3+2(4)	–	–	–
3	5/4	Berwick	A	L30-62	14(6)	2+1(5)	1(4)	5(5)	–	–	4(3)	2+1(4)	–	2+1(3)
4	6/4	Edinburgh	H	L42-48	12(5)	6+1(4)	3+1(4)	10(5)	–	–	4+1(5)	0(3)	–	7(4)
5	13/4	Glasgow	A	L39-50	13(6)	7+2(4)	–	10(6)	–	–	1+1(3)	1(3)	0(3)	7+1(5)
6	14/4	Glasgow	H	L44-46	12(5)	6+1(4)	–	6(4)	–	–	9(5)	1(3)	4+3(4)	6+1(5)
7	18/4	Edinburgh	A	L43-47	14+1(6)	7+1(5)	–	14+2(6)	R/R	–	0(2)	3(5)	5(4)	–
8	20/4	Berwick	H	W51-39	17(6)	9+2(6)	–	13+1(5)	–	1(4)	6+2(4)	–	R/R	5(5)

DETAILS OF OTHER RIDERS:

Match No. 3: Lee Dicken 2+1(3); Match No. 4: Rusty Harrison 7(4); Match No. 5: Andrew Appleton 7+1(5); Match No. 6: Scott Robson 6+1(5); Match No. 8: Lee Dicken 5(5).

GOLDEN DOUBLE RIDES:

Match No. 3: Kenneth Bjerre's total includes 4 points from a golden double ride.

BRITISH LEAGUE CUP AVERAGES

Rider	Mts	Rds	Pts	Bon	Tot	Avge	Max
Kenneth Bjerre	8	45	103	1	104	9.24	–
Mick Powell	2	10	20	0	20	8.00	–
Kevin Little	8	41	78	3	81	7.90	–
Richard Juul	8	36	46	10	56	6.22	–
Jamie Robertson	8	29	30	7	37	5.10	–
Kristian Lund	3	11	9	3	12	4.36	–
Craig Branney	3	11	8	3	11	4.00	–
William Lawson	5	18	7	1	8	1.78	–
Rune Knudsen	4	14	5	1	6	1.71	–
Guests	5	22	27	3	30	5.45	–

NOTE: Kenneth Bjerre's figures include one golden double ride (4 points), modified to normal score i.e. 2 points.

KNOCK-OUT CUP

(* Denotes aggregate victory)

No	DATE	OPPONENTS	H/A	RESULT	BJERRE	JUUL	POWELL	LITTLE	LUND	BRANNEY	ROBERTSON	MELL	ROBSON	LAWSON	DICKEN	OTHERS
1	10/5	Stoke	A	L44-51	16(6)	5+1(4)	DNA	11+1(5)	3(4)	1(3)	8+2(5)	–	–	–	–	–
2	11/5	Stoke	H	W50-40*	14(5)	6+1(4)	–	7(4)	–	4+2(3)	5+1(5)	3+1(4)	11+1(5)	–	–	–
3	27/6	Arena-Essex	A	L41-55	14+1(6)	3+1(4)	–	5(4)	–	–	0(3)	1(3)	11+1(5)	7+1(5)	–	–
4	28/7	Arena-Essex	H	W49-41	15(5)	5(4)	–	–	–	–	3+1(4)	–	12+2(5)	7+1(4)	0(3)	7(4)

DETAILS OF OTHER RIDERS:

Match No. 4: Scott Robson 7(4).

GOLDEN DOUBLE/TACTICAL JOKER RIDES:

Match No. 1: Kevin Little's total includes 6 points from a tactical joker ride; Kenneth Bjerre's total include 4 points from a golden double ride; Match No. 3: Kenneth Bjerre's total includes 4 points from a tactical joker ride and 4 points from a golden double outing; Stuart Robson's total includes 4 points from a tactical joker ride; Kevin Little's total includes 0 points from a tactical joker ride.

OTHER MEETINGS

22 March: Tyne-Tweed Trophy (first-leg)

Berwick 47 Newcastle 43 (Kenneth Bjerre 13; Kevin Little 7; Rune Knudsen 6+1; Jamie Robertson 6+1; Mick Powell 5; Richard Juul 4; Craig Branney 2+1).

23 March: Tyne-Tweed Trophy (second-leg)

Newcastle 46 (Kenneth Bjerre 13; Kevin Little 10+1; Jamie Robertson 6+3; Richard Juul 6+2; Mick Powell 5; William Lawson 4+2; Rune Knudsen 2+1) Berwick 44 – Berwick won 91-89 on aggregate.

26 March: Challenge

Hull 55 Newcastle 35 (Kenneth Bjerre 14; Kevin Little 10+1; Josef Franc 6; Richard Juul 3; Jamie Robertson 2+1; Rune Knudsen 0; William Lawson 0).

30 March: Challenge

Newcastle 52 (Kenneth Bjerre 13; Kevin Little 11; Michal Makovsky 10; Richard Juul 7+2; Rune Knudsen 5+1; Jamie Robertson 3+2; William Lawson 3+1) Hull 38.

INDIVIDUAL MEETING

26 October: George English Memorial Trophy

(Qualifying scores: Carl Stonehewer 11; Richard Juul 9; Rory Schlein 8; William Lawson 8; Lee Dicken 7; Craig Branney 2; Jamie Robertson 2; John Branney 1; Steven Jones 0); Final: 1st Lawson; 2nd Schlein; 3rd Stonehewer; 4th Juul.

NEWPORT WASPS

NOTE: The information below relates only to the main Newport team. For details of the second side, please refer to the Conference League section.

ADDRESS: Hayley Stadium, Plover Close, Longditch Road, Queensway Meadows, Newport, Gwent, South Wales.
PROMOTER: Tim Stone.
TRACK LENGTH: 285 metres.
FIRST MEETING: 4 May 1997.
YEARS OF OPERATION: 1997-03 British Premier League.

PREVIOUS VENUE: Somerton Park, Newport, Gwent, South Wales.
YEARS OF OPERATION: 1964 Provincial League; 1965-67 British League; 1968-74 British League Division One; 1975-76 British League; 1977 National League
NOTE: Newport did not use a nickname from 1973-76 inclusive, and in 1977 they were known as 'Dragons'.

CLUB HONOURS

PREMIER NATIONAL TROPHY WINNERS: 1999

RIDER ROSTER 2003

ATKIN, Tony   b. 8 April 1966, Chester, Cheshire.
BRITISH CAREER: (1986) Stoke; (1994) Wolverhampton; (1995) Bradford; (1996) Sheffield, Wolverhampton, Buxton; (1997) Stoke; (1999-02) Stoke; (2003) Newport.

NEWPORT WASPS: back row, left to right: Carl Wilkinson, Frank Smart, Niels Kristian Iversen, Tony Atkin. On bike: Craig Watson. Front, kneeling: Matt Cambridge, Chris Schramm.

BRANNEY, John   *b. 7 November 1985, Whitehaven, Cumbria.*
   BRITISH CAREER: (2002) Rye House (CL), Newcastle (CL); (2003) Newcastle (CL),
   Wimbledon (CT), Mildenhall (CT), King's Lynn, Exeter, Newport (PL), Buxton (CT).
CAMBRIDGE, Matt   *b. 14 May 1981, Rugby, Warwickshire.*
   BRITISH CAREER: (2000) Sheffield (CL); (2001-02) Sheffield (CL), Exeter; (2003)
   Newport (PL & CL), Wimbledon, Poole (BLC).
FERROW, Alan   *b. 28 April 1982, Ashington, Northumberland.*
   BRITISH CAREER: (2003) Trelawny (CT), Arena-Essex, Newport (PL).
HALL, Richard   *b. 23 August 1984, Northallerton, North Yorkshire.*
   BRITISH CAREER: (2001) Newcastle; (2002) Newcastle (PL & CL), Trelawny, Glasgow;
   (2003) Sheffield (CL & PL), Stoke (PL), Coventry (BLC), Hull (BLC), Newport (PL),
   Boston (KOC & CT), Exeter, Reading, Workington, Somerset.
HUGHES, Danny   *b. 2 September 1983, Manchester.*
   BRITISH CAREER: (1999) Workington; (2000) Buxton, Belle Vue; (2001) Buxton,
   Newport (CL); (2002) Newport (CL), Stoke, Workington, Edinburgh; (2003) Newport
   (CL & PL), Belle Vue (BLC), Stoke (CT).
IVERSEN, Niels-Kristian   *b. 20 June 1982, Esbjerg, Denmark.*
   BRITISH CAREER: (2001) King's Lynn; (2003) Newport, Oxford (Note: Niels also rode
   for King's Lynn in 2002, but only in a challenge match).
KORNELIUSSEN, Mads   *b. 15 June 1983, Aalborg, Denmark.*
   BRITISH CAREER: (2003) Newport.
MACKAY, Brendon   *b. 14 August 1980, Darwin, Northern Territory, Australia.*
   BRITISH CAREER: (2001-02) Reading; (2003) Somerset, Trelawny (CT), Newport (BLC),
   Exeter (BLC), Mildenhall.
MASON, Karl   *b. 4 March 1986, Hillingdon, London.*
   BRITISH CAREER: (2001) Buxton, Mildenhall, Somerset; (2002) Newport (CL), Reading;
   (2003) Newport (CL & PL), Exeter (BLC).
PARSONS, Joel   *b. 24 July 1985, Broken Hill, New South Wales, Australia.*
   BRITISH CAREER: (2003) Reading, Eastbourne (BLC), Rye House (CL & PL), Newport
   (PL), Wimbledon (CT), Arena-Essex, Peterborough (BLC), Hull.
PRIEST, Luke   *b. 18 June 1985, Birmingham, West Midlands.*
   BRITISH CAREER: (2000) Ashfield, Owlerton; (2001) Sheffield (CL), Boston; (2002)
   Sheffield (CL), Wolverhampton (CT); (2003) Sheffield (CL & PL), Stoke (CT & PL),
   Workington, Exeter, Newport (BLC), Arena-Essex, Wolverhampton (BLC), Belle Vue
   (BLC).
SCARBORO, Ricky   *b. 31 July 1966, Grunby, Lincolnshire.*
   BRITISH CAREER: (1999) Mildenhall, King's Lynn (CL); (2000) Boston; (2001) Boston,
   Newport (PL); (2002) Boston, King's Lynn (CL); (2003) Oxford (CL & BLC), Stoke
   (CT), Newport (PL).
SCHRAMM, Chris   *b. 30 May 1984, Maldon, Essex.*
   BRITISH CAREER: (2000) Peterborough (CL), Berwick, Arena-Essex; (2001) Peterborough
   (EL & CL), Isle of Wight, Reading; (2002) Reading, Peterborough (CL); (2003)
   Newport (PL), Wimbledon (CT), Peterborough (CL), Oxford (CL).
SMART, Frank   *b. 27 October 1969, Perth, Western Australia, Australia.*
   BRITISH CAREER: (1990-91) Exeter; (1992) Milton Keynes, Exeter; (1993) Exeter;
   (1997-98) Exeter; (1999) Newport; (2000) Swindon; (2002-03) Newport.

THOMPSON, Mark b. 8 July 1979, Orsett, Essex.
BRITISH CAREER: (1996) Sittingbourne, Linlithgow, Mildenhall, Eastbourne (CL); (1997) Anglian Angels; (1998) Mildenhall, Newport, Stoke; (1999) King's Lynn (CL); (2000-01) Mildenhall; (2002) King's Lynn (CL), Mildenhall, Arena-Essex, Workington, Stoke; (2003) Boston, Stoke (PL), Newport (BLC), Somerset, Peterborough (BLC), Coventry (BLC), King's Lynn, Arena-Essex.

WALKER, Simon b. 19 February 1980, Bristol, Avon.
BRITISH CAREER: (2001) Newport (CL); (2002) Newport (CL), Arena-Essex, Swindon (CT), Trelawny; (2003) Swindon (CL), Trelawny (CT), Reading, Somerset (BLC), Poole (BLC), Exeter (BLC), Newport.

WARWICK, Dan b. 21 November 1983, Poole, Dorset.
BRITISH CAREER: (2002) Newport (CL), Reading; (2003) Newport (CL & PL), Poole (BLC), Exeter.

WATSON, Craig b. 6 August 1976, Sydney, New South Wales, Australia.
BRITISH CAREER: (1997-99) Newport; (2000-01) Poole; (2002) Newport; (2003) Newport, Belle Vue.

WILKINSON, Carl b. 16 May 1981, Boston, Lincolnshire.
BRITISH CAREER: (1997) Peterborough (AL); (1998) Norfolk; (1999) King's Lynn (CL); (2000) Boston, Newcastle, Glasgow; (2001) Boston, Newport (PL); (2002-03) Newport (PL & CL).

WILLIAMS, Stuart b. 7 May 1965, Bristol, Avon.
BRITISH CAREER: (1985) Reading; (1986) Exeter; (2002) Carmarthen, Somerset; (2003) Reading (M4 Trophy only), Newport.

PREMIER LEAGUE

(* Denotes bonus-point victory)

No	DATE	OPPONENTS	H/A	RESULT	SMART	WILKINSON	IVERSEN	ATKIN	WATSON	SCHRAMM	PARSONS	MASON	HUGHES	KORNELIUSSEN	OTHERS
1	20/4	Reading	H	W49-41	11+2(5)	4+1(4)	11(4)	6+2(4)	14(5)	3(5)	–	–	–	–	0(3)
2	27/4	Rye House	H	W51-39	13(5)	4+1(4)	11(4)	5+3(4)	12+2(5)	5(5)	–	–	–	–	1+1(3)
3	4/5	Workington	H	W49-41	13+1(5)	4(4)	9+2(4)	7(4)	10+1(5)	4+2(5)	–	–	–	–	2(3)
4	9/5	Arena-Essex	A	L24-65	9(6)	0(3)	4(6)	4+1(4)	3(5)	2+1(3)	2(3)	–	–	–	–
5	27/5	Isle of Wight	A	L44-45	9(5)	3+2(4)	12+1(5)	4+1(4)	10(5)	4+1(4)	–	2(3)	–	–	–
6	8/6	Sheffield	H	W50-40	12+3(6)	6+3(5)	R/R	11+1(5)	–	4(4)	–	–	3(4)	–	14(6)
7	13/6	Glasgow	H	W45-44	5+1(3)	4(4)	14(5)	5+2(4)	12+1(5)	2(5)	3+1(4)	–	–	–	–
8	22/6	Isle of Wight	H	L43-47	–	6+2(4)	11(5)	6+3(4)	10(5)	3+2(4)	3(4)	–	–	–	4(4)
9	29/6	Newcastle	H	W50-40	8+2(5)	6+1(4)	5+1(4)	9+1(5)	14+1(5)	5+1(4)	–	–	3(3)	–	–
10	3/7	Glasgow	A	L38-52	7+1(5)	3+2(4)	5+2(5)	7(4)	14(6)	0(3)	2+1(3)	–	–	–	–
11	4/7	Edinburgh	A	L40-49	6+1(4)	0(3)	14(6)	3+1(4)	13(6)	2(3)	2(4)	–	–	–	–
12	10/7	Sheffield	A	L33-57	2(3)	0(3)	7+3(6)	11(6)	10(5)	3+1(4)	–	–	–	–	0(3)
13	12/7	Rye House	D	D45-45*	7+1(4)	1+1(3)	12+4(6)	7(4)	15(6)	2+1(4)	–	–	–	–	1(3)
14	13/7	Berwick	H	L44-46	14+1(6)	1(3)	9+1(5)	6(4)	11+1(6)	2+1(3)	1(3)	–	–	–	–
15	20/7	Exeter	H	W61-29	9+1(4)	7+3(4)	11+1(5)	10+2(4)	15(5)	7+2(4)	–	–	–	–	2(4)
16	23/7	Hull	A	W48-41	6(4)	5+1(4)	15(6)	7+2(4)	11+1(5)	0(3)	–	–	–	–	4+1(4)
17	3/8	Arena-Essex	H	W47-42	11+4(6)	3(3)	–	5+1(5)	17(6)	5+1(3)	0(3)	–	–	–	6(4)

PREMIER LEAGUE continued

No	DATE	OPPONENTS	H/A	RESULT	SMART	WILKINSON	IVERSEN	ATKIN	WATSON	SCHRAMM	PARSONS	MASON	HUGHES	KORNELIUSSEN	OTHERS
18	10/8	Hull	H	W48-42*	7+1(4)	3+1(4)	12+1(5)	5+1(4)	15(5)	–	–	–	–	–	6+1(8)
19	13/8	King's Lynn	A	L32-57	1+1(4)	9(6)	13+1(6)	2+2(4)	5(4)	–	–	–	–	–	2(6)
20	24/8	Swindon	H	L40-50	3(4)	7(4)	11+1(6)	7+3(5)	11(5)	–	–	0(3)	–	–	1(3)
21	30/8	Workington	A	L31-59	8(6)	1(4)	–	5+1(4)	6(4)	2+1(3)	–	–	–	–	9+1(8)
22	31/8	Stoke	H	W48-41	11(6)	9+2(5)	R/R	6+2(5)	18(6)	4+1(6)	–	–	–	–	0(2)
23	5/9	Somerset	A	W46-44	6+3(4)	8(4)	15(5)	1(4)	12+1(5)	3+1(4)	–	–	–	–	1(4)
24	7/9	King's Lynn	H	W52-38	10+2(5)	4+3(4)	11(4)	5(4)	12(5)	7(5)	–	–	–	–	3(3)
25	8/9	Reading	A	W50-40*	9(4)	4+1(4)	15(5)	3(4)	14+1(5)	4+1(5)	–	–	–	–	1+1(3)
26	14/9	Edinburgh	H	W50-40*	10+1(5)	4+2(4)	–	6(4)	12(5)	6+1(5)	2+1(3)	–	–	–	10+1(4)
27	15/9	Exeter	A	L42-48*	5+1(5)	5(4)	16(6)	4+1(4)	9(5)	3(3)	–	–	–	–	0(3)
28	21/9	Trelawny	H	W48-42	8+1(4)	5+2(4)	12(5)	4+1(4)	13(5)	6+2(5)	–	0(3)	–	–	–
29	25/9	Swindon	A	D45-45	8+3(5)	2+1(3)	13+1(6)	3+1(4)	10+2(6)	8(3)	1(3)	–	–	–	–
30	7/10	Trelawny	A	L43-47*	5+1(4)	R/R	13(5)	6+1(5)	12+2(6)	5+2(6)	2(4)	–	–	–	–
31	12/10	Somerset	H	W50-39*	–	–	9+1(5)	8+1(4)	13(5)	3+2(4)	–	5+1(4)	–	8+2(4)	4+1(4)
32	13/10	Newcastle	A	L33-57	–	–	9+1(6)	8(4)	10(5)	1(4)	–	1(3)	0(3)	4+1(5)	–
33	14/10	Stoke	A	L44-46*	–	–	15+1(6)	4+1(4)	14+2(6)	5+2(4)	–	0(3)	–	4+1(4)	2(3)
34	18/10	Berwick	A	L41-48	–	–	5(4)	11+1(6)	15(5)	1(4)	–	2(3)	–	6+3(5)	1+1(3)

DETAILS OF OTHER RIDERS:

Match No. 1: Matt Cambridge 0(3); Match No. 2: Stuart Williams 1+1(3); Match No. 3: Stuart Williams 2(3); Match No. 6: Adam Shields 14(6); Match No. 8: Michael Coles 4(4); Match No. 12: Ben Warburton 0(3); Match No. 13: Dan Warwick 1(3); Match No. 15: Dan Warwick 2(4); Match No. 16: Richard Hall 4+1(4); Match No. 17: Chris Neath 6(4); Match No. 18: Tom Brown 4+1(4); Dan Warwick 2(4); Match No. 19: Joe Cook 1(3); Richard Hall 1(3); Match No. 20: Tom Brown 1(3); Match No. 21: Chris Neath 8+1(5); John Branney 1(3); Match No. 22: Ricky Scarboro 0(2); Match No. 23: Richard Hall 1(4); Match No. 24: Richard Hall 3(3); Match No. 25: Brendon Mackay 1+1(3); Match No. 26: Brent Werner 10+1(4); Match No. 27: Simon Walker 0(3); Match No. 31: Richard Hall 4+1(4); Match No. 33: Luke Priest 2(3); Match No. 34: Alan Ferrow 1+1(3).

PREMIER LEAGUE AVERAGES

Rider	Mts	Rds	Pts	Bon	Tot	Avge	Max
Craig Watson	33	172	392	15	407	9.47	4 Full; 2 Paid
Niels-Kristian Iversen	29	150	319	22	341	9.09	2 Full
Frank Smart	29	136	233	32	265	7.79	–
Tony Atkin	34	146	201	36	237	6.49	1 Paid
Mads Korneliussen	4	18	22	7	29	6.44	–
Carl Wilkinson	29	113	118	29	147	5.20	–
Chris Schramm	31	127	111	26	137	4.31	–
Richard Hall	5	18	13	2	15	3.33	–
Alan Ferrow	1	3	1	1	2	2.67	–
Brendon Mackay	1	3	1	1	2	2.67	–
Joel Parsons	8	27	15	3	18	2.67	–
Luke Priest	1	3	2	0	2	2.67	–
Stuart Williams	2	6	3	1	4	2.67	–

Rider	Mts	Rds	Pts	Bon	Tot	Avge	Max
Karl Mason	8	26	13	1	14	2.15	–
Danny Hughes	4	13	6	0	6	1.85	–
Dan Warwick	3	11	5	0	5	1.82	–
John Branney	1	3	1	0	1	1.33	–
Matt Cambridge	1	3	0	0	0	0.00	–
Ricky Scarboro	1	2	0	0	0	0.00	–
Simon Walker	1	3	0	0	0	0.00	–
Ben Warburton	1	3	0	0	0	0.00	–
Guests	8	33	48	3	51	6.18	–

BRITISH LEAGUE CUP

(* Denotes bonus-point victory)

No	DATE	OPPONENTS	H/A	RESULT	SMART	WILKINSON	IVERSEN	ATKIN	WATSON	SCHRAMM	CAMBRIDGE	MASON	WARWICK	OTHERS
1	30/3	Wolverhampton	H	W51-39	12+2(5)	4+1(4)	11(4)	7+3(4)	12+1(5)	–	4(4)	1(4)	–	–
2	31/3	Exeter	A	L40-50	9(5)	1+1(4)	9+2(6)	7+2(4)	10(5)	4(3)	0(3)	–	–	–
3	1/4	Trelawny	A	D45-45	12(5)	4+1(4)	11(5)	4(4)	8(4)	6+2(5)	0(3)	–	–	–
4	13/4	Trelawny	H	W46-44*	11(5)	0(4)	9+2(5)	10+1(4)	6(4)	2+1(3)	–	–	–	8(5)
5	25/5	Exeter	H	W56-34*	13+1(5)	3+1(4)	14+1(5)	6+1(4)	9(4)	11+3(5)	–	–	–	0(3)
6	1/6	Poole	H	L42½-47½	12(5)	2+1(3)	7(5)	8+1(4)	8½+1(6)	5+1(4)	–	0(3)	–	–
7	6/7	Somerset	H	W59-31	10+1(4)	6+2(4)	14+1(5)	6+1(4)	15(5)	6+1(4)	–	–	2+1(4)	–
8	18/7	Somerset	A	W48-42*	10(4)	3+1(4)	15(5)	8+2(4)	9(5)	3+1(5)	–	0(3)	–	–
9	6/8	Poole	A	L41-49	14(7)	4+2(5)	R/R	8+3(6)	7+2(6)	–	–	–	4(3)	4+1(3)
10	25/8	Wolverhampton	A	L36-54	9+1(5)	1+1(3)	13+1(6)	5+2(4)	7(6)	–	–	1(3)	–	0(3)

DETAILS OF OTHER RIDERS:

Match No. 4: Barrie Evans 8(5); Match No. 5: Mark Thompson 0(3); Match No. 9: Brendon Mackay 4+1(3); Match No. 10: Luke Priest 0(3).

BRITISH LEAGUE CUP AVERAGES

Rider	Mts	Rds	Pts	Bon	Tot	Avge	Max
Niels-Kristian Iversen	9	46	103	7	110	9.57	1 Full; 2 Paid
Frank Smart	10	50	112	5	117	9.36	–
Tony Atkin	10	42	69	16	85	8.10	–
Craig Watson	10	50	91½	4	95½	7.64	1 Full
Brendon Mackay	1	3	4	1	5	6.67	–
Chris Schramm	7	29	37	9	46	6.34	–
Carl Wilkinson	10	39	28	11	39	4.00	–
Dan Warwick	3	10	6	1	7	2.80	–
Matt Cambridge	3	10	4	0	4	1.60	–
Karl Mason	3	10	2	0	2	0.80	–
Luke Priest	1	3	0	0	0	0.00	–
Mark Thompson	1	3	0	0	0	0.00	–
Guest	1	5	8	0	8	6.40	–

KNOCK-OUT CUP

(* Denotes aggregate victory)

No	DATE	OPPONENTS	H/A	RESULT	SMART	WILKINSON	IVERSEN	ATKIN	WATSON	SCHRAMM	CAMBRIDGE	MASON	OTHERS
1	6/4	Somerset	H	W61-35	9+1(4)	8+1(4)	14+1(5)	8+2(4)	15(5)	5(4)	2(4)	–	–
2	11/4	Somerset	A	W49-43*	11+2(5)	4+1(4)	6+1(4)	7+1(4)	14(5)	7+1(4)	–	0(2)	–
3	11/5	Exeter	H	W47-43	12+2(5)	4+1(4)	6(4)	6+1(4)	13(5)	4+1(4)	–	–	2+2(4)
4	12/5	Exeter	A	L43-50	11(5)	3+1(4)	5+2(4)	11+1(4)	9+1(5)	4+1(5)	–	0(3)	–

DETAILS OF OTHER RIDERS:

Match No. 3: Joel Parsons 2+2(4).

GOLDEN DOUBLE/TACTICAL JOKER RIDES:

Match No. 4: Tony Atkin's total includes 6 points from a tactical joker ride.

OTHER MEETINGS

16 March: M4 Trophy (first-leg)

Newport 44 (Frank Smart 14; Craig Watson 11+1; Tony Atkin 9+1; Niels-Kristian Iversen 7+1; Carl Wilkinson 2+1; Chris Schramm 1; Matt Cambridge 0) Reading 46.

17 March: M4 Trophy (second-leg)

Reading 45 Newport 45 (Craig Watson 15; Niels-Kristian Iversen 13; Frank Smart 8+2; Chris Schramm 4+1; Tony Atkin 2; Matt Cambridge 2; Carl Wilkinson 1) – Reading won 91-89 on aggregate.

20 March: M4 Trophy (first-leg)

Swindon 45 Newport 45 (Craig Watson 14; Niels-Kristian Iversen 9+1; Frank Smart 7; Tony Atkin 7; Chris Schramm 3; Matt Cambridge 3; Carl Wilkinson 2+2).

23 March: M4 Trophy (second-leg)

Newport 50 (Craig Watson 13; Frank Smart 10+1; Tony Atkin 10; Chris Schramm 5+1; Carl Wilkinson 5; Niels-Kristian Iversen 4+1; Matt Cambridge 3+1) Swindon 40 – Newport won 95-85 on aggregate.

M4 TROPHY TABLE

Team	Mts	Won	Drn	Lst	For	Agn	Pts	Bon	Tot
Swindon	4	1	2	1	185	175	4	1	5
Newport	4	1	2	1	184	176	4	1	5
Reading	4	1	2	1	171	189	4	1	5

NOTE: With all three sides finishing level on 5 points, it was decided to replay the competition, although in the event this never took place.

20 September: Premier League

Berwick 3 Newport 3 (Frank Smart 3; Carl Wilkinson 0; Niels-Kristian Iversen DNR; Tony Atkin DNR; Craig Watson DNR; Chris Schramm DNR; Richard Hall DNR) – meeting abandoned after heat one.

19 October: Challenge

Lions 46 (David Howe 13; Chris Harris 11+1; Chris Neath 10; Lee Smethills 5+1; Chris Schramm 4+1; Tony Atkin 3+2) Kangaroos 44 (Craig Watson 16; Mark Lemon 13; Rusty Harrison 7; Lee Herne 4+2; Ben Powell 4+1; Scott Smith R/R).

INDIVIDUAL MEETINGS

5 January: New Year Classic

(Qualifying scores: David Howe 15; Brent Werner 14; Leigh Lanham 11; Shaun Tacey 10; Carl Wilkinson 9; Michael Coles 7; Chris Neath 7; Neil Collins 6; Robbie Kessler 5; Roger Lobb 3; Les Collins 3; Paul Clews 0; Dan Warwick (res) 0; Danny Hughes (res) 0) Final: 1st Howe; 2nd Lanham; 3rd Tacey; 4th Werner.

15 June: Welsh Open Championship

(Qualifying scores: Niels-Kristian Iversen 13; Craig Watson 12; Adam Shields 11; David Howe 11; Carl Stonehewer 10; Steve Johnston 10; Mark Lemon 10; Chris Harris 8; Simon Stead 7; Sam Ermolenko 6; Leigh Lanham 6; Paul Fry 5; Scott Smith 5; George Stancl 4; Carl Wilkinson 2; Michael Coles 0) Final: 1st Howe; 2nd Shields; 3rd Watson; 4th Iversen.

5 October: Frank Smart Farewell

(Qualifying scores: Davey Watt 11; Craig Watson 11; Adam Shields 10; Mark Lemon 9; Tony Atkin 9; Frank Smart 8; Niels-Kristian Iversen 6; Chris Schramm 5; Emil Lindqvist 5; Carl Wilkinson 4; Shane Parker 3; Nigel Sadler 3; Chris Harris 3; Scott Pegler 3; Karl Mason (res) 3; Tom Brown (res) 2; Martin Dixon 0; Paul Fry 0) Semi-Final: 1st Shields; 2nd Lemon; 3rd Smart; 4th Atkin; Final: 1st Lemon; 2nd Watson; 3rd Watt; 4th Shields.

26 October: Prince Of Wales Trophy

(Qualifying scores: David Howe 13; Chris Harris 12; Craig Watson 11; Niels-Kristian Iversen 11; Kristian Lund 10; Chris Neath 9; Jan Staechmann 7; Emiliano Sanchez 6; Scott Smith 5; Mads Korneliussen 5; Karl Mason 1; Tom Brown 0) Final: 1st Howe; 2nd Watson; 3rd Iversen; 4th Harris.

READING EUPHONY RACERS

ADDRESS: Smallmead Stadium, Bennet Road, Smallmead, Reading, Berkshire.
PROMOTERS: Pat Bliss & Chris Shears.
TRACK LENGTH: 307 metres.
FIRST MEETING: 28 April 1975.
YEARS OF OPERATION: 1975-90 British League; 1991-94 British League Division One; 1995-03 British Premier League

NOTE: Reading also ran a second team in the 1996 British Conference League and the 1997 British Amateur League. The 1996 side ran as 'Reading Ravens', whereas in 1997, the fixtures were shared with Swindon, under the banner of 'M4 Raven Sprockets'.

PREVIOUS VENUE: Reading Greyhound Stadium, Oxford Road, Tilehurst, Reading, Berkshire.
YEARS OF OPERATION: 1968-70 British League Division Two; 1971-73 British League Division One.

CLUB HONOURS

LEAGUE CHAMPIONS: 1980, 1990, 1992, 1997.
KNOCK-OUT CUP WINNERS: 1990, 1998.
PREMIERSHIP WINNERS: 1991, 1993.
BSPA CUP WINNERS: 1992.
FOUR-TEAM CHAMPIONS: 1993.

RIDER ROSTER 2003

APPLETON, Andrew   b. 18 June 1982, Reading, Berkshire.
    BRITISH CAREER: (1997) Oxford (AL); (1998) Newport (CL & PL), Arena-Essex,
    Edinburgh; (1999) Newport (PL & CL); (2000) Newport; (2001) Oxford; (2002)
    Oxford, Reading; (2003) Reading.
BOXALL, Steve   b. 16 May 1987, Canterbury, Kent.
    BRITISH CAREER: (2002) Rye House (CL); (2003) Rye House (CL), Ipswich (BLC),
    Reading (BLC), King's Lynn.
CAMPBELL, Barry   b. 26 August 1979, Glasgow, Scotland.
    BRITISH CAREER: (1995) Linlithgow, Swindon; (1996) Linlithgow, Edinburgh; (1997)
    Edinburgh, Lathallan; (1998) Edinburgh; (1999) Belle Vue, Workington; (2000-01)
    Workington; (2003) Edinburgh, Armadale (CT), Reading, Swindon (CL), Belle Vue (BLC).
CLEWS, Paul   b. 19 July 1979, Coventry, Warwickshire.
    BRITISH CAREER: (1995) Coventry; (1996) Peterborough (CL & PL), Coventry, Oxford,
    Anglian Angels; (1997) Skegness, Isle of Wight, Peterborough (AL), Coventry; (1998)
    Peterborough; (1999-03) Reading.
COLLYER, Peter   b. 2 December 1981, Frimley Green, Camberley, Surrey.
    BRITISH CAREER: (1999) Reading, Glasgow, Rye House, Newcastle; (2002) Wimbledon,
    Carmarthen, Reading; (2003) Wimbledon, Reading (BLC).
COLVIN, Shane   b. 4 February 1982, Hastings, East Sussex.
    BRITISH CAREER: (1997) Oxford (AL), Ryde, M4 Raven Sprockets; (1998) Newport
    (CL); (1999) Reading, Mildenhall; (2000) Reading, Mildenhall, Ashfield; (2001)
    Reading, Newport (CL), Trelawny; (2002) Carmarthen, Wolverhampton (CLKOC),
    Workington, Reading; (2003) Reading.
DAVIDSSON, Jonas   b. 7 August 1984, Motala, Sweden.
    BRITISH CAREER: (2003) Reading.
FLINT, Gary   b. 5 May 1982, Ashington, Durham.
    BRITISH CAREER: (1999) Berwick, Linlithgow, St Austell; (2000) Ashfield, Berwick;
    (2001) Buxton, Newcastle, Exeter, Sheffield (PL), Berwick; (2002) Newcastle (CL),
    Somerset, Rye House (PL), Isle of Wight, Glasgow; (2003) Buxton, Sheffield (CL),
    Reading, Stoke (CT).
HALL, Richard   b. 23 August 1984, Northallerton, North Yorkshire.
    BRITISH CAREER: (2001) Newcastle; (2002) Newcastle (PL & CL), Trelawny, Glasgow;
    (2003) Sheffield (CL & PL), Stoke (PL), Coventry (BLC), Hull (BLC), Newport (PL),
    Boston (KOC & CT), Exeter, Reading, Workington, Somerset.

READING RACERS: back row, left to right: Ivan Shears (Team Manager), Paul Clews, Andrew Appleton, Jonas Davidsson, Daniel King. On bike: Phil Morris. Front, kneeling: Scott Smith, Shane Colvin.

KING, Daniel   b. 14 August 1986, Maidstone, Kent.
  BRITISH CAREER: (2001) Peterborough (CL); (2002) Peterborough (CL), Swindon (CT); (2003) Peterborough (CL), Ipswich (BLC), Reading, Mildenhall, Arena-Essex.

KOLODZIEJ, Janusz   b. 27 May 1984, Tarnow, Poland.
  BRITISH CAREER: (2003) Reading (BLC).

LJUNG, Peter   b. 30 October 1982, Vaxjo, Sweden.
  BRITISH CAREER: (2003) Eastbourne, Reading.

MORRIS, Phil   b. 10 September 1975, Newport, Gwent, Wales.
  BRITISH CAREER: (1991-96) Reading; (1997) Stoke; (1998-03) Reading.

NORTON, Danny   b. 27 August 1986, Hull, East Yorkshire.
  BRITISH CAREER: (2001-02) Peterborough (CL); (2003) Peterborough (CL & BLC), Armadale (CT), Swindon (PL), Reading, Mildenhall (KOC & CT), Poole (BLC), Oxford (BLC).

PARSONS, Joel   b. 24 July 1985, Broken Hill, New South Wales, Australia.
  BRITISH CAREER: (2003) Reading, Eastbourne (BLC), Rye House (CL & PL), Newport (PL), Wimbledon (CT), Arena-Essex, Peterborough (BLC), Hull.

SIMMONS, Nick   b. 24 July 1981, Leamington Spa, Warwickshire.
  BRITISH CAREER: (1997) Shuttle Cubs, Ryde; (1998) Newport (CL & PL), Isle of Wight, Exeter; (1999) Isle of Wight, Stoke, Newport (CL); (2000) Arena-Essex; (2001) Newport (PL & CL), Somerset; (2002) Isle of Wight; (2003) Stoke, Reading, Mildenhall, Workington, King's Lynn, Exeter.

SMITH, Scott   b. 4 February 1980, Brisbane, Queensland, Australia.
  BRITISH CAREER: (2001-02) Newport; (2003) Reading, Stoke.

WALKER, Simon   b. 19 February 1980, Bristol, Avon.
  BRITISH CAREER: (2001) Newport (CL); (2002) Newport (CL), Arena-Essex, Swindon (CT), Trelawny; (2003) Swindon (CL), Trelawny (CT), Reading, Somerset (BLC), Poole (BLC), Exeter (BLC), Newport.

WILLIAMS, Stuart   b. 7 May 1965, Bristol, Avon.
  BRITISH CAREER: (1985) Reading; (1986) Exeter; (2002) Carmarthen, Somerset; (2003) Reading (M4 Trophy only), Newport.

WRIGHT, Matthew   b. 19 November 1985, Harlow, Essex.
  BRITISH CAREER: (2002) Boston, Mildenhall, Carmarthen, Wimbledon; (2003) Mildenhall, Ipswich (BLC), Arena-Essex (BLC), Reading, Peterborough (BLC).

PREMIER LEAGUE

(* Denotes bonus-point victory)

No	DATE	OPPONENTS	H/A	RESULT	MORRIS	CLEWS	DAVIDSSON	APPLETON	SMITH	KING	COLVIN	PARSONS	NORTON	KOLODZIEJ	LJUNG	OTHERS
1	5/4	Rye House	A	L42-48	7+1(4)	4+1(4)	7+1(5)	10(5)	8(5)	–	5(4)	1(4)	–	–	–	–
2	7/4	Arena-Essex	H	W46-44	10+1(5)	4+1(4)	4+1(4)	15(5)	2+1(4)	3(4)	8(4)	–	–	–	–	–
3	11/4	Arena-Essex	A	L34-56	14(6)	0(3)	10+1(6)	2+1(4)	4(4)	3(4)	1+1(3)	–	–	–	–	–
4	20/4	Newport	A	L41-49	3+1(4)	5+1(4)	2(3)	15+1(6)	5+1(5)	10+1(5)	1+1(3)	–	–	–	–	–
5	21/4	Hull	H	W50-40	–	4+1(4)	4+2(4)	17(6)	4+1(4)	7+2(4)	3+1(3)	–	–	–	–	11+1(5)
6	7/5	Hull	A	L34-56	–	9(6)	1+1(3)	6(4)	9+1(6)	–	1(3)	0(3)	–	–	–	8(5)
7	12/5	Stoke	H	W47-43	–	6+1(4)	5+1(4)	14(5)	8(5)	6+1(6)	0(3)	–	–	–	–	8(4)
8	2/6	Edinburgh	H	L40-50	–	7+1(5)	5(4)	11(5)	7(5)	–	5+1(4)	–	–	–	–	5+1(7)

PREMIER LEAGUE continued

No	DATE	OPPONENTS	H/A	RESULT	MORRIS	CLEWS	DAVIDSSON	APPLETON	SMITH	KING	COLVIN	PARSONS	NORTON	KOLODZIEJ	LJUNG	OTHERS
9	16/6	Isle of Wight	H	L44-46	–	7+2(4)	3+3(4)	8+1(5)	15(6)	1(3)	5+1(4)	–	–	–	–	5+1(4)
10	29/6	Stoke	A	W46-44*	R/R	9+2(5)	–	–	11+1(6)	0(4)	–	–	–	–	–	26+3(15)
11	30/6	Workington	H	W47-43	R/R	4+2(5)	–	14+1(6)	10(5)	4+2(4)	–	5(4)	–	–	–	10+1(6)
12	4/7	Somerset	A	L45-46	–	6+1(4)	6+2(4)	9+1(5)	3(4)	–	–	–	–	–	–	21+1(13)
13	8/7	Isle of Wight	A	L40-50	R/R	5+2(5)	–	14(7)	10(7)	–	1+1(3)	–	–	–	–	10+1(8)
14	14/7	Newcastle	H	L40-49	–	10+1(6)	4(4)	0(1)	8+2(6)	–	–	6+1(4)	–	–	–	12(9)
15	21/7	Rye House	H	W48-42	–	10+1(5)	12(5)	R/R	5+1(5)	–	–	–	0(3)	–	–	21+4(12)
16	28/7	Berwick	H	L41-49	–	6+2(5)	–	10(6)	3+1(4)	–	–	2(3)	1(3)	–	–	19+1(9)
17	4/8	Sheffield	H	W47-42	–	6+1(4)	12+1(5)	3+1(4)	–	–	–	–	1(3)	10+2(5)	–	15+2(9)
18	5/8	Trelawny	A	L39-51	–	1+1(3)	3+1(4)	8+1(6)	–	–	–	2(3)	2+1(3)	13(6)	–	10(5)
19	10/8	Glasgow	A	L31-59	–	2(4)	6(5)	12(6)	–	–	–	–	1(3)	–	–	10+1(12)
20	11/8	Glasgow	H	D45-45	–	5+1(4)	4+1(4)	14(5)	–	–	–	3(4)	2+1(4)	10(5)	–	7(4)
21	15/8	Edinburgh	A	L30-60	–	4(4)	5+2(5)	3(4)	–	–	–	–	0(3)	10+1(6)	–	8(8)
22	16/8	Berwick	A	L37-53	–	5+1(5)	1(3)	9+1(6)	–	–	–	–	1(3)	16(6)	–	5+1(7)
23	18/8	Somerset	H	W54-36*	–	5+1(4)	8+1(4)	10+1(5)	–	–	–	–	1(4)	13+1(5)	–	17(9)
24	21/8	Sheffield	A	L32-58	–	6+1(6)	R/R	5(6)	–	–	–	–	0(3)	–	–	21+4(15)
25	25/8	Swindon	H	L42-48	–	2+1(4)	8+2(4)	3(4)	–	–	–	–	0(3)	–	12+2(6)	17+1(9)
26	31/8	Exeter	H	W49-41	R/R	7+4(5)	16+1(6)	9(5)	–	2(5)	–	–	1(4)	–	–	14+1(5)
27	1/9	Exeter	A	L33-57	R/R	4+1(6)	1(4)	13(7)	–	1(3)	–	–	0(3)	–	–	14+1(7)
28	8/9	Newport	H	L40-50	–	5+2(5)	9+1(6)	11+1(7)	–	–	–	1+1(3)	–	–	R/R	14+3(9)
29	10/9	King's Lynn	A	L41-49	–	5+3(4)	13+1(6)	9+2(6)	–	–	–	–	2(3)	–	R/R	12+2(11)
30	15/9	Trelawny	A	L42-48	–	4+2(5)	10+1(5)	11(6)	–	–	–	–	–	–	R/R	17+2(14)
31	25/9	Newcastle	A	L40-50	R/R	7+2(5)	8+1(5)	9+2(7)	–	–	–	–	1(3)	–	–	15(10)
32	2/10	Swindon	A	L39-51	–	3+1(4)	10(6)	8(4)	–	–	–	–	1(3)	–	5+2(3)	14(10)
33	4/10	Workington	A	L34-56	–	2+1(5)	1(5)	16+1(7)	–	–	–	–	1(3)	–	R/R	14(10)
34	20/10	King's Lynn	H	D44-44	R/R	6(5)	16+1(6)	4+2(5)	–	–	–	–	0(3)	–	–	18+1(11)

DETAILS OF OTHER RIDERS:

Match No. 5: Glenn Cunningham 11+1(5); Match No. 6: James Grieves 8(5); Match No. 7: Garry Stead 8(4); Match No. 8: Danny Bird 5+1(4); Peter Collyer 0(3); Match No. 9: Glenn Cunningham 5+1(4); Match No. 10: Danny Bird 15(6); Chris Mills 9+2(6); Jason Bunyan 2+1(3); Match No. 11: Danny Bird 10+1(6); Match No. 12: Paul Pickering 12(5); Aidan Collins 8(5); Simon Walker 1+1(3); Match No. 13: Garry Stead 9+1(5); Nick Simmons 1(3); Match No. 14: Paul Pickering 8(4); Chris Mills 4(5); Match No. 15: Rusty Harrison 11+2(6); Chris Schramm 10+2(6); Match No. 16: Paul Pickering 15+1(6); Aidan Collins 4(3); Match No. 17: Chris Schramm 8+1(5); Garry Stead 7+1(4); Match No. 18: Garry Stead 10(5); Match No. 19: Rusty Harrison 9+1(6); Adam Allott 1(3); Barry Campbell 0(3); Match No. 20: Rusty Harrison 7(4); Match No. 21: Garry Stead 7(5); Craig Branney 1(3); Match No. 22: Garry Stead 5+1(4); Gary Flint 0(3); Match No. 23: Paul Pickering 11(4); Adam Allott 6(5); Match No. 24: Garry Stead 11(6); Adam Allott 8+3(5); Richard Hall 2+1(4); Match No. 25: Garry Stead 13(6); James Brundle 4+1(3); Match No. 26: Craig Watson 14+1(5); Match No. 27: Mark Lemon 14+1(7); Match No. 28: Garry Stead 8+1(5); James Brundle 6+2(4); Match No. 29: Nigel Sadler 9(7); Chris Schramm 3+2(4); Match No. 30: Chris Neath 14+1(6); Matthew Wright 2(3); Tommy Allen 1+1(5); Match No. 31: Paul Pickering 15(7); James Brundle 0(3); Match No. 32: Garry Stead 10+2(6); Chris Mills 2+2(4); Match No. 33: Garry Stead 11(7); Craig Branney 3(3); Match No. 34: Paul Pickering 16+1(7); Tommy Allen 2(4).

GOLDEN DOUBLE RIDES:

Match No. 21: Janusz Kolodziej's total includes 0 points from a golden double ride.

PREMIER LEAGUE AVERAGES

Rider	Mts	Rds	Pts	Bon	Tot	Avge	Max
Peter Ljung	2	9	17	4	21	9.33	–
Janusz Kolodziej	6	33	72	4	76	9.21	–
Phil Morris	4	19	34	3	37	7.79	–
Andrew Appleton	32	170	302	17	319	7.51	1 Full
Jonas Davidsson	29	133	194	26	220	6.62	–
Scott Smith	16	81	112	9	121	5.98	–
Paul Clews	34	155	175	42	217	5.60	–
Daniel King	8	34	34	6	40	4.71	–
Shane Colvin	11	39	32	5	37	3.79	–
Joel Parsons	8	28	20	2	22	3.14	–
Richard Hall	1	4	2	1	3	3.00	–
Simon Walker	1	3	1	1	2	2.67	–
Matthew Wright	1	3	2	0	2	2.67	–
Nick Simmons	1	3	1	0	1	1.33	–
Danny Norton	19	60	16	3	19	1.27	–
Barry Campbell	1	3	0	0	0	0.00	–
Peter Collyer	1	3	0	0	0	0.00	–
Gary Flint	1	3	0	0	0	0.00	–
Guests	49	240	390	35	425	7.08	1 Paid

NOTE: Janusz Kolodziej's figures include one golden double ride (0 points).

BRITISH LEAGUE CUP

No	DATE	OPPONENTS	H/A	RESULT	MORRIS	CLEWS	DAVIDSSON	APPLETON	SMITH	COLLYER	COLVIN	PARSONS	KOLODZIEJ	OTHERS
1	31/3	Eastbourne	H	L42-51	8+1(5)	3+2(4)	4+2(4)	17(6)	5(4)	2+1(3)	3+1(4)	–	–	–
2	8/4	Isle of Wight	A	L34-56	9(6)	4+4(4)	1(4)	13(6)	6(4)	–	1(3)	0(3)	–	–
3	14/4	Isle of Wight	H	L40-50	7(5)	4+2(4)	5+2(5)	13(6)	3(4)	–	4+1(3)	4+1(3)	–	–
4	26/5	Oxford	H	L40-50	–	2+1(4)	1+1(3)	13(6)	3+1(4)	–	4(3)	7+3(4)	–	10+1(6)
5	30/5	Oxford	A	L37-53	–	0(3)	5+2(4)	12(6)	6+1(5)	–	4(4)	3+2(3)	–	7+1(5)
6	23/6	Swindon	H	D45-45	–	3+1(4)	–	9+1(5)	9(4)	–	2(1)	4+2(7)	8+1(5)	10+1(4)
7	10/7	Swindon	A	L38-52	–	6+2(5)	4+1(4)	7+1(4)	7(5)	–	–	0(3)	–	14+3(9)
8	24/8	Eastbourne	A	L30-60	R/R	1(3)	1(5)	–	7+1(7)	–	–	–	–	21+1(15)

DETAILS OF OTHER RIDERS:

Match No. 4: Garry Stead 10+1(6); Match No. 5: Garry Stead 7+1(5); Match No. 6: Paul Pickering 10+1(4); Match No. 7: Paul Pickering 10+2(5); Aidan Collins 4+1(4); Match No. 8: Brent Werner 14+1(7); Adam Allott 4(4); Steve Boxall 3(4).

GOLDEN DOUBLE RIDES:

Match No. 1: Andrew Appleton's total includes 6 points from a golden double ride.

BRITISH LEAGUE CUP AVERAGES

Rider	Mts	Rds	Pts	Bon	Tot	Avge	Max
Andrew Appleton	7	39	81	2	83	8.51	–
Janusz Kolodziej	1	5	8	1	9	7.20	–
Phil Morris	3	16	24	1	25	6.25	–
Scott Smith	8	37	46	3	49	5.30	–
Paul Clews	8	31	23	12	35	4.52	–
Joel Parsons	6	23	18	8	26	4.52	–
Shane Colvin	6	18	18	2	20	4.44	–
Peter Collyer	1	3	2	1	3	4.00	–
Jonas Davidsson	7	29	21	8	29	4.00	–
Steve Boxall	1	4	3	0	3	3.00	–
Guests	7	35	59	7	66	7.54	–

NOTES: (1) Andrew Appleton's figures include one golden double ride (6 points) modified to normal score i.e. 3 points;

(2) Scott Smith's figures include one match as a guest after he had been released.

KNOCK-OUT CUP

No	DATE	OPPONENTS	H/A	RESULT	SMITH	CLEWS	DAVIDSSON	APPLETON	PARSONS	COLVIN	KING	OTHERS
1	5/5	Trelawny	H	W51-45	4+2(4)	5(4)	6+2(4)	11(5)	5(4)	6+2(4)	–	14(5)
2	13/5	Trelawny	A	L30-65	6(5)	0(4)	–	7(4)	1+1(3)	3+1(4)	1(4)	12(6)

DETAILS OF OTHER RIDERS:

Match No. 1: Danny Bird 14(5); Match No. 2: Garry Stead 12(6).

GOLDEN DOUBLE/TACTICAL JOKER RIDES:

Match No. 2: Garry Stead's total includes 2 points from a tactical joker ride and 4 points from a golden double outing; Andrew Appleton's total includes 4 points from a tactical joker ride.

OTHER MEETINGS

16 March: M4 Trophy (first-leg)

Newport 44 Reading 46 (Scott Smith 12; Shane Colvin 8+3; Andrew Appleton 7+2; Jonas Davidsson 7+1; Paul Clews 6+2; Phil Morris 3; Stuart Williams 3).

17 March: M4 Trophy (second-leg)

Reading 45 (Shane Colvin 10+1; Glenn Cunningham 8; Paul Clews 7+3; Jonas Davidsson 7+1; Scott Smith 7+1; Andrew Appleton 6; Stuart Williams 0) Newport 45 – Reading won 91-89 on aggregate.

24 March: M4 Trophy (first-leg)

Reading 45 (Andrew Appleton 12; Shane Colvin 11+1; Phil Morris 8+1; Paul Clews 5+2; Scott Smith 5; Jonas Davidsson 2+1; Daniel Giffard 2+1) Swindon 45.

27 March: M4 Trophy (second-leg)

Swindon 55 Reading 35 (Phil Morris 10; Jonas Davidsson 7+1; Andrew Appleton 6+1; Scott Smith 6; Shane Colvin 5+2; Paul Clews 1+1; Daniel Giffard 0) – Swindon won 100-80 on aggregate.

M4 TROPHY TABLE

Team	Mts	Won	Drn	Lst	For	Agn	Pts	Bon	Tot
Swindon	4	1	2	1	185	175	4	1	5
Newport	4	1	2	1	184	176	4	1	5
Reading	4	1	2	1	171	189	4	1	5

NOTE: With all three sides finishing level on 5 points, it was decided to replay the competition, although in the event this never took place.

9 June: Conference Challenge

Reading 46 (Shane Colvin 15; Tom Brown 9+1; Peter Collyer 8; Jamie Westacott 7+1; Simon Paget 5; Carl Warwick 2+1; Matt Tutton 0) Swindon 47.

7 July: Under-21 International

Great Britain 49 (Olly Allen 15; Andrew Appleton 10+3; Simon Stead 7+1; Andrew Moore 7; Daniel King 6+2; Ricky Ashworth 4+1; Daniel Giffard 0) Sweden 41 (Jonas Davidsson 9+2; Daniel Davidsson 9; Erik Andersson 6+2; Antonio Lindback 6+1; Fredrik Lindgren 5+1; Mattias Nilsson 5; Peter Ljung 1).

20 July: Challenge

Rye House 60 Reading 30 (Andrew Moore 10; Scott Smith 8+2; Jonas Davidsson 6+2; Paul Clews 4+1; Joel Parsons 2; Chris Mills 0; Phil Morris R/R).

4 August: Conference Challenge

Reading 63 (Lee Smart 12+2; Peter Collyer 11+3; Luke Priest 11+1; Matt Tutton 9+2; Jamie Westacott 9+2; Danny Norton 8; Carl Warwick 3) Carmarthen 25.

18 August: Conference Challenge

Reading 38 (Danny Norton 12; Jamie Westacott 9+1; Tom Brown 8+1; Dan Warwick 5+1; Matt Tutton 4+1; Carl Warwick R/R) Swindon 39.

INDIVIDUAL MEETING

29 September: Euphony Classic

(Qualifying scores: Danny Bird 15; Charlie Gjedde 13; Mark Lemon 11; Travis McGowan 10; Emiliano Sanchez 9; Brent Werner 9; Andrew Appleton 8; Jonas Davidsson 7; Garry Stead 6; Nigel Sadler 6; Armando Castagna 6; Paul Clews 6; Paul Pickering 5; Sebastian Bengtsson 4; Rusty Harrison 3; Glenn Cunningham 2) Final: 1st Gjedde; 2nd McGowan; 3rd Bird; 4th Lemon.

RYE HOUSE SILVER SKI ROCKETS

NOTE: The information below relates only to the main Rye House team. For details of the second side, please refer to the Conference League section.

ADDRESS: Rye House Stadium, Rye Road, Hoddesdon, Hertfordshire.

PROMOTER: Len Silver.

TRACK LENGTH: 271 metres.

FIRST MEETING: 3 August 1958.

YEARS OF OPERATION: 1958 Open; 1959 Southern Area League; 1960–66 Open & Training; 1967 Training; 1969–73 Open & Training; 1974 British League Division Two; 1975–90 National League; 1991–93 British League Division Two; 1999–01; British Conference League; 2002–03 British Premier League. (NOTE: In 1999, Rye House staged their home matches at Eastbourne, King's Lynn and Mildenhall.)

PREVIOUS VENUE: Hoddesdon Stadium, Rye Road, Hoddesdon, Hertfordshire.
YEARS OF OPERATION: 1935 Open & Training; 1936-37 Open; 1938 Sunday Dirt-track League; 1939-43 Open; 1945-53 Open; 1954-57 Southern Area League.

NOTE: Rye House first acquired the 'Rockets' moniker in 1974, having previously been known as 'Roosters' in 1955 and 'Red Devils' from 1960-73.

CLUB HONOURS

KNOCK-OUT CUP WINNERS: 1979.
LEAGUE CHAMPIONS: 1980.

RIDER ROSTER 2003

COURTNEY, Mark   b. 25 March 1961, Braintree, Essex.
BRITISH CAREER: (1978) Barrow; (1979) Middlesbrough; (1980-81) Middlesbrough, Leicester; (1982-83) Leicester; (1984) Belle Vue; (1985) King's Lynn; (1986) Middlesbrough, Belle Vue; (1987) Newcastle; (1988-90) Berwick; (1991) Glasgow; (1992) Rye House; (1993) Middlesbrough; (2000) Glasgow; (2001) Glasgow, Trelawny; (2002-03) Rye House.

KENNETT, Edward   b. 28 August 1986, Hastings, Sussex.
BRITISH CAREER: (2001) Rye House, Mildenhall; (2002-03) Rye House (CL & PL), Eastbourne.

MASON, David   b. 20 December 1976, Crawley, West Sussex.
BRITISH CAREER: (1995) Sittingbourne, Reading, Arena-Essex, Swindon, Poole, Oxford; (1996) Sittingbourne, London, Reading; (1997) Arena-Essex; (1998) Newport, Stoke, Arena-Essex, Mildenhall; (1999) Swindon, Rye House; (2000) Rye House, Arena-Essex, Poole; (2001-03) Rye House.

ORCHARD, Johnny   b. 22 February 1969, Truro, Cornwall.
BRITISH CAREER: (2003) Trelawny (CT), Rye House (PL).

PARSONS, Joel   b. 24 July 1985, Broken Hill, New South Wales, Australia.
BRITISH CAREER: (2003) Reading, Eastbourne (BLC), Rye House (CL & PL), Newport (PL), Wimbledon (CT), Arena-Essex, Peterborough (BLC), Hull.

ROBSON, Scott   b. 15 August 1971, Sunderland, Tyne & Wear.
BRITISH CAREER: (1987-92) Berwick; (1993-94) Newcastle; (1995-96) Middlesbrough; (1997) Hull; (1998) Eastbourne, Berwick; (1999-00) Coventry; (2001) Berwick; (2002) Rye House; (2003) Rye House, Eastbourne.

SADLER, Nigel   b. 17 September 1978, Blackwood, Adelaide, South Australia.
BRITISH CAREER: (1997) Skegness, Isle of Wight; (1998-01) Peterborough; (2002) Rye House; (2003) Rye House, Peterborough.

WERNER, Brent   b. 15 April 1974, Los Angeles, California, USA.
BRITISH CAREER: (1995-97) Long Eaton; (1998) Newcastle; (1999-00) Workington; (2001) Eastbourne; (2002) Rye House; (2003) Rye House, Peterborough.

WOODIFIELD, Brett   b. 15 March 1976, Gawler, South Australia.
BRITISH CAREER: (1997) Skegness, Isle of Wight, Peterborough; (1998) Peterborough; (1999) Ipswich; (2000) Peterborough; (2001) Trelawny; (2003) Rye House.

RYE HOUSE ROCKETS: back row, left to right: Len Silver (Promoter), Brent Werner, Nigel Sadler, John Sampford (Team Manager), Brett Woodifield, Scott Robson. On bike: David Mason. Front, kneeling: Edward Kennett, Mark Courtney.

PREMIER LEAGUE

(* Denotes bonus-point victory)

No	DATE	OPPONENTS	H/A	RESULT	SADLER	WOODIFIELD	ROBSON	COURTNEY	WERNER	MASON	KENNETT	PARSONS	OTHERS
1	5/4	Reading	H	W48-42	8(5)	7+1(4)	8(4)	3(4)	10+2(5)	–	9+2(5)	–	3(3)
2	26/4	Exeter	H	W55-35	6(4)	R/R	13+2(6)	9(5)	6(4)	6+2(4)	14+2(6)	1(1)	–
3	27/4	Newport	A	L39-51	9(6)	R/R	4+1(5)	8(6)	6(4)	2+1(4)	10(5)	–	–
4	5/5	Workington	H	W50-40	10+1(5)	R/R	5+2(4)	9(5)	7+1(4)	11+2(6)	8+1(6)	–	–
5	19/5	Exeter	A	L27-62	10(6)	2+1(4)	7+1(5)	0(3)	5+1(6)	1(3)	2+1(3)	–	–
6	20/5	Trelawny	A	L29½-60½	9½(6)	1+1(3)	9(6)	2(4)	4+1(5)	4+1(4)	–	–	0(2)
7	24/5	Stoke	A	L32-57	8(6)	3+1(4)	7(5)	1+1(3)	9(6)	3(3)	–	1(3)	–
8	25/5	Stoke	H	L35-54	9(6)	2(3)	11+1(6)	3+1(3)	6(5)	4+1(4)	–	0(3)	–
9	31/5	Swindon	H	L44½-45½	–	8+3(5)	6+1(4)	2(3)	6½+2(5)	3(3)	5+2(4)	–	14(6)
10	4/6	Hull	A	L41-49	6(5)	1+1(3)	11+2(6)	2(3)	12+1(6)	3(3)	6+1(4)	–	–
11	7/6	Glasgow	H	W49-39	5+1(4)	5+1(4)	11+1(5)	5+1(4)	9(5)	7+1(4)	7+1(4)	–	–
12	15/6	Sheffield	H	L44-46	4+2(4)	2+1(3)	5+1(4)	5+1(4)	10(5)	11+2(6)	7+1(4)	–	–
13	17/6	Isle of Wight	A	L29-61	8(6)	0(3)	10(6)	1(3)	4(5)	1+1(3)	5(4)	–	–
14	21/6	Somerset	H	W57-33	13(5)	5+3(4)	12+1(5)	4(4)	–	6+1(4)	9(4)	–	8+1(4)
15	6/7	Workington	A	L36-54	5+1(4)	2(4)	6+1(5)	1(3)	10+1(6)	1+1(3)	11(5)	–	–
16	7/7	Trelawny	H	W52-38	5+1(4)	6+1(4)	4+1(4)	6+2(4)	13(5)	3+1(3)	15+2(6)	–	–
17	12/7	Newport	H	D45-45	6+1(5)	7(4)	2+1(4)	3(3)	6+1(5)	4(3)	17+1(6)	–	–
18	17/7	Sheffield	A	L34-56	11(6)	1+1(3)	1+1(3)	0(3)	12(6)	5+2(5)	4(4)	–	–
19	21/7	Reading	A	L42-48*	8(4)	4(4)	11+2(5)	3(3)	11(6)	2(6)	3(2)	–	–
20	2/8	Newcastle	H	W49-41	6+1(4)	3(4)	8+1(5)	6+1(4)	12(5)	8+1(4)	–	–	6(4)
21	20/8	King's Lynn	A	L42-48	16+1(6)	6+1(5)	6(4)	1(3)	3(4)	1+1(3)	–	–	9+2(5)
22	25/8	King's Lynn	H	W49-41*	9+3(6)	5(4)	14(6)	8+1(5)	8(5)	5+1(4)	R/R	–	–
23	29/8	Edinburgh	A	L34-55	8(6)	3+1(4)	8(5)	2(3)	10+1(5)	1+1(3)	–	–	2+2(4)
24	30/8	Berwick	A	L23-67	8(6)	0(3)	7(6)	1(3)	5(5)	1+1(3)	–	–	1(4)
25	1/9	Berwick	H	W62-27	5+1(4)	5+2(4)	16+1(6)	10+1(5)	15+2(6)	11+4(5)	R/R	–	–
26	4/9	Swindon	A	L41-49	5+1(5)	9+2(6)	17(7)	3(4)	7+2(7)	0(1)	R/R	–	–
27	6/9	Hull	H	W47-43	8+1(5)	3+2(4)	11+1(6)	11+2(6)	12(6)	–	R/R	2+1(3)	–
28	7/9	Newcastle	A	L44-46*	4+1(5)	5+1(5)	15+1(6)	0(3)	9+1(5)	R/R	–	–	11(6)
29	13/9	Edinburgh	H	L43-47	10+1(6)	10+3(6)	14(7)	1+1(3)	6+2(5)	–	R/R	2(3)	–
30	20/9	Arena-Essex	H	W48-42	4+2(4)	9(6)	8+2(4)	1(3)	15(5)	4+1(3)	–	–	7+1(5)
31	21/9	Glasgow	A	L43-47*	5(4)	8+2(4)	7(5)	6+2(4)	4+2(4)	5(4)	–	–	8+1(5)
32	4/10	Isle of Wight	H	W50-40	7+2(4)	8+1(5)	11(5)	–	14(5)	3(4)	–	0(3)	7+1(4)
33	10/10	Arena-Essex	A	L37-53	3(3)	3+2(4)	1+1(3)	8(6)	7(5)	6(4)	–	–	9(6)
34	17/10	Somerset	A	L40-50*	6+1(5)	4+1(3)	4(4)	3(3)	10+1(6)	1+1(3)	–	–	12+1(6)

DETAILS OF OTHER RIDERS:

Match No. 1: Lee Smethills 3(3); Match No. 6: Johnny Orchard 0(2); Match No. 9: Frede Schott 14(6); Match No. 14: Chris Neath 8+1(4); Match No. 20: Chris Neath 6(4); Match No. 21: Andrew Moore 9+2(5); Match No. 23: Kevin Little 2+2(4); Match No. 24: Ricky Ashworth 1(4); Match No. 28: Paul Pickering 11(6); Match No. 30: Chris Neath 7+1(5); Match No. 31: Rusty Harrison 8+1(5); Match No. 32: Chris Neath 7+1(4); Match No. 33: Paul Thorp 9(6); Match No. 34: Chris Neath 12+1(6).

PREMIER LEAGUE AVERAGES

Rider	Mts	Rds	Pts	Bon	Tot	Avge	Max
Edward Kennett	16	72	132	14	146	8.11	1 Paid
Scott Robson	34	171	290	26	316	7.39	–
Brent Werner	33	171	283½	21	304½	7.12	1 Full
Nigel Sadler	33	164	244½	22	266½	6.50	–
Brett Woodifield	31	126	137	33	170	5.40	–
David Mason	30	112	123	27	150	5.36	1 Paid
Mark Courtney	33	125	128	14	142	4.54	–
Joel Parsons	6	16	6	1	7	1.75	–
Johnny Orchard	1	2	0	0	0	0.00	–
Guests	13	62	97	9	106	6.84	–

BRITISH LEAGUE CUP

(* Denotes bonus-point victory)

No	DATE	OPPONENTS	H/A	RESULT	SADLER	WOODIFIELD	ROBSON	COURTNEY	WERNER	MASON	KENNETT	OTHERS
1	12/4	Ipswich	H	W46-44	5(4)	5+1(4)	13(5)	3+1(4)	10(5)	1(3)	9+3(5)	–
2	10/5	King's Lynn	H	W55-35	6(4)	6+2(4)	12+1(5)	7(4)	8+1(4)	6+3(4)	10(5)	–
3	11/6	King's Lynn	A	L41-49*	12(5)	9+1(5)	7+1(4)	2+1(4)	6+1(4)	1+1(3)	4+1(5)	–
4	26/7	Peterborough †	H	W42-36	4+2(4)	10(4)	7+2(4)	2+1(2)	5(3)	11+2(5)	–	3+1(4)
5	7/8	Ipswich	A	L44-46	13(6)	13+1(6)	14+2(6)	3(3)	1(3)	0(3)	–	0(3)
6	8/8	Arena-Essex	A	L41-49	4(4)	3+1(3)	8+2(6)	3(3)	12(6)	2(3)	–	9(5)
7	16/8	Arena-Essex	H	W53-37*	14+1(6)	8+1(5)	4(4)	9+2(5)	13+2(6)	5+1(4)	R/R	–
8	22/8	Peterborough	A	W46-44*	9(5)	9+1(5)	12(5)	3+2(3)	7(4)	3+3(4)	–	3+2(4)
9	24/9	Belle Vue	A	L41-49	2+1(4)	11+2(6)	16(7)	3+2(3)	8(6)	1+1(4)	R/R	–
10	27/9	Belle Vue	H	L42-48	1(3)	10+2(6)	9(5)	0(3)	8+1(4)	2+1(4)	–	12(5)

† Meeting abandoned after thirteen heats, with the result standing.

DETAILS OF OTHER RIDERS:

Match No. 4: Paul Bentley 3+1(4); Match No. 5: Chris Neath 0(3); Match No. 6: Chris Neath 9(5); Match No. 8: Andrew Moore 3+2(4); Match No. 10: Paul Thorp 12(5).

BRITISH LEAGUE CUP AVERAGES

Rider	Mts	Rds	Pts	Bon	Tot	Avge	Max
Scott Robson	10	51	102	8	110	8.63	–
Brett Woodifield	10	48	84	12	96	8.00	–
Brent Werner	10	45	78	5	83	7.38	–
Edward Kennett	3	15	23	4	27	7.20	–
Nigel Sadler	10	45	70	4	74	6.58	–
Mark Courtney	10	34	35	9	44	5.18	–
David Mason	10	37	32	12	44	4.76	–
Guests	5	21	27	3	30	5.71	–

KNOCK-OUT CUP

No	DATE	OPPONENTS	H/A	RESULT	SADLER	WOODIFIELD	ROBSON	COURTNEY	WERNER	MASON	KENNETT
1	18/4	Arena-Essex	A	W46-44	4+1(4)	0(0)	7+1(5)	12+1(5)	1(4)	8(5)	14+1(7)
2	19/4	Arena-Essex	H	L44-46	2+1(4)	R/R	10(5)	12(6)	8+1(5)	6(5)	6+2(5)
3	23/5	Arena-Essex (R)	A	L40-55	3(4)	2+1(3)	9(5)	6+2(4)	9+1(5)	0(3)	11+1(6)
4	26/5	Arena-Essex (R)	H	L44-46	4(4)	8+1(4)	8+2(5)	6+1(4)	5+2(4)	4(3)	9+2(6)

(R) = Replay

GOLDEN DOUBLE/TACTICAL JOKER RIDES:

Match No. 3: Scott Robson's total includes 4 points from a tactical joker ride; Edward Kennett's total includes 4 points from a tactical joker ride; Brent Werner's total includes 2 points from a tactical joker ride.

OTHER MEETINGS

26 March: A10 Trophy (first-leg)

King's Lynn 60 Rye House 36 (Scott Robson 11; Nigel Sadler 8+1; Brent Werner 8; Brett Woodifield 5+1; David Mason 3+2; Edward Kennett 1; Mark Courtney 0).

29 March: A10 Trophy (second-leg)

Rye House 53 (Brent Werner 11+2; Nigel Sadler 10+2; David Mason 8+1; Edward Kennett 7; Scott Robson 6+1; Mark Courtney 6; Brett Woodifield 5+2) King's Lynn 39 – King's Lynn won 99-89 on aggregate.

28 June: Home Counties Cup

Rye House 44 (David Mason 14+1; Scott Robson 9+1; Brent Werner 7+1; Brett Woodifield 6+1; Nigel Sadler 5+1; Mark Courtney 2+1; Joel Parsons 1+1) Eastbourne 43.

20 July: Challenge

Rye House 60 (Brent Werner 15; Edward Kennett 12; Nigel Sadler 9+2; Scott Robson 8+3; David Mason 7+1; Brett Woodifield 6+3; Mark Courtney 3) Reading 30.

9 August: Premier League International

England 43 (Chris Harris 15+1; Andrew Moore 10+3; Scott Robson 10+1; Ricky Ashworth 4; Andrew Appleton 2; Barrie Evans 2; James Brundle 0) Australia 47 (Craig Watson 12; Nigel Sadler 7+1; Lee Herne 7; Joel Parsons 6+2; Brett Woodifield 6+1; Rory Schlein 6+1; Frank Smart 3+1).

INDIVIDUAL MEETING

25 October: Ace of Herts Championship

1st Brent Werner (after run-off) 14; 2nd Steve Masters 14; 3rd Chris Neath (after run-off) 11; Leigh Lanham 11; Chris Harris 10; Nigel Sadler 10; Edward Kennett 9; Joonas Kylmakorpi 8; Brett Woodifield 8; Scott Robson 8; Steve Boxall 6; David Mason 3; Joel Parsons 2; Mark Courtney 2; James Cockle (res) 2; Barrie Evans 1; Adam Allott 1.

SHEFFIELD PIRTEK TIGERS

NOTE: The information below relates only to the main Sheffield team. For details of the second side, please refer to the Conference League section.

ADDRESS: Owlerton Sports Stadium, Penistone Road, Owlerton, Sheffield, South Yorkshire.
PROMOTERS: Neil Machin & Malcolm Wright.
TRACK LENGTH: 361 metres.
FIRST MEETING: 30 March 1929.
YEARS OF OPERATION: 1929 English Dirt-track League; 1930-31 Northern League; 1932 Speedway National Association Trophy; 1933 National League; 1938-39 National League Division Two; 1945 Open; 1946 Northern League; 1947-50 National League Division Two; 1951-52 Open; 1960-64 Provincial League; 1965-67 British League; 1968-74 British League Division One; 1975-88 British League; 1991-94 British League Division Two; 1995-03 British Premier League.

CLUB HONOURS

BRITISH SPEEDWAY CUP (DIVISION TWO) WINNERS: 1947.
KNOCK-OUT CUP WINNERS: 1974, 2002.
FOUR-TEAM CHAMPIONS: 1999, 2000.
LEAGUE CHAMPIONS: 1999, 2002.
YOUNG SHIELD WINNERS: 1999, 2002.
PREMIERSHIP WINNERS: 2000.

RIDER ROSTER 2003

ASHWORTH, Ricky   b. 17 August 1982, Salford, Greater Manchester.
    BRITISH CAREER: (2001) Sheffield (CL); (2002) Sheffield (PL & CL); (2003) Sheffield (PL), Poole.
BIRKINSHAW, James   b. 6 March 1980, Sheffield, South Yorkshire.
    BRITISH CAREER: (1996) Owlerton, Sheffield, Hull; (1997) Sheffield, Belle Vue (AL), Newcastle; (1998) Newcastle, St Austell; (1999) Workington, Edinburgh, Linlithgow, Berwick, Sheffield, Stoke; (2000) Sheffield (PL & CL), Glasgow; (2001) Newcastle, Sheffield (CL), Isle of Wight; (2002) Sheffield (PL), Boston, Wolverhampton (CT); (2003) Sheffield (PL).
BRADY, Ross   b. 17 February 1981, Winchburgh, Broxburn, Scotland.
    BRITISH CAREER: (1997) Lathallan, Peterborough (AL); (1998) Mildenhall, Peterborough (PL), Berwick; (1999-00) Edinburgh; (2001) King's Lynn, Hull; (2002) Hull; (2003) Glasgow, Sheffield (CL & PL).
COMPTON, André   b. 15 May 1977, Dewsbury, West Yorkshire.
    BRITISH CAREER: (1993) Bradford, Newcastle; (1994) Stoke, Newcastle, Buxton; (1995-96) Buxton; (1997) Newcastle, Berwick; (1998-99) Sheffield; (2000) Peterborough, Newcastle; (2001) Newcastle; (2002) Newcastle, Poole; (2003) Sheffield, Poole.
COMPTON, Benji   b. 17 September 1986, Tenerife, Spain.
    BRITISH CAREER: (2002) Newcastle (CL); (2003) Sheffield (CL & PL), Swindon (PL),

Hull (BLC), Mildenhall (KOC), Exeter.

HALL, Richard   b. 23 August 1984, Northallerton, North Yorkshire.
BRITISH CAREER: (2001) Newcastle; (2002) Newcastle (PL & CL), Trelawny, Glasgow; (2003) Sheffield (CL & PL), Stoke (PL), Coventry (BLC), Hull (BLC), Newport (PL), Boston (KOC & CT), Exeter, Reading, Workington, Somerset.

MOORE, Andrew   b. 6 October 1982, Lincoln, Lincolnshire.
BRITISH CAREER: (1998) Skegness, Norfolk; (1999) Mildenhall, Sheffield, Arena-Essex; (2000) Sheffield (CL & PL), Berwick; (2001) Sheffield (PL & CL); (2002-03) Sheffield (PL).

PRIEST, Luke   b. 18 June 1985, Birmingham, West Midlands.
BRITISH CAREER: (2000) Ashfield, Owlerton; (2001) Sheffield (CL), Boston; (2002) Sheffield (CL), Wolverhampton (CT); (2003) Sheffield (CL & PL), Stoke (CT & PL), Workington, Exeter, Newport (BLC), Arena-Essex, Wolverhampton (BLC), Belle Vue (BLC).

SMITH, Scott A.   b. 29 September 1972, Sheffield, South Yorkshire.
BRITISH CAREER: (1990-95) Cradley Heath; (1996-99) Sheffield; (2000) Berwick; (2001-03) Sheffield.

WILSON, Ben   b. 15 March 1986, Sheffield, South Yorkshire.
BRITISH CAREER: (2001) Sheffield (CL); (2002) Sheffield (CL & PL), Glasgow; (2003) Sheffield (PL & CL), Buxton (CT).

WILSON, Sean   b. 7 November 1969, York, Yorkshire.
BRITISH CAREER: (1986-88) Sheffield; (1989) Coventry; (1990) Coventry, King's Lynn; (1991-93) Bradford; (1995-96) Bradford; (1997) Coventry; (1998) Belle Vue; (1999-03) Sheffield.

PREMIER LEAGUE

(* Denotes bonus-point victory)

No	DATE	OPPONENTS	H/A	RESULT	S. WILSON	MOORE	SMITH	BIRKINSHAW	A. COMPTON	ASHWORTH	B. WILSON	HALL	B. COMPTON	BRADY	OTHERS
1	5/4	King's Lynn	A	L44-46	–	7+1(4)	7(4)	5+3(4)	4+1(4)	10+2(6)	1+1(3)	–	–	–	10(5)
2	10/4	King's Lynn	H	W57-33*	7(4)	7(4)	11(5)	5+3(4)	15(5)	7(4)	5+2(4)	–	–	–	–
3	12/4	Workington	A	L44-45	2(4)	11+1(5)	8(4)	5(4)	9(5)	4+1(4)	5+3(4)	–	–	–	–
4	26/4	Berwick	A	W53-37	13(5)	9+2(5)	7+2(5)	R/R	6+1(4)	13+2(6)	5(5)	–	–	–	–
5	9/5	Edinburgh	A	L28-62	9(6)	7(5)	0(4)	1+1(3)	4(4)	6(4)	1(4)	–	–	–	–
6	18/5	Newcastle	A	L41-48	14(5)	8+1(6)	2(3)	0(3)	11(5)	1(4)	5+2(4)	–	–	–	–
7	22/5	Newcastle	H	W61-29*	12+2(5)	7+2(4)	14(5)	7+3(4)	12(4)	9+2(5)	0(3)	–	–	–	–
8	25/5	Glasgow	A	L42-47	16(6)	9+1(6)	2(3)	3(4)	7(4)	4+1(4)	1(3)	–	–	–	–
9	29/5	Swindon	H	W54-36	11(5)	10+1(5)	5(4)	4+1(4)	11+1(4)	12+3(5)	–	1(3)	–	–	–
10	1/6	Swindon	A	L40-50*	12(6)	6+3(5)	4(4)	2+1(3)	13+1(6)	3(3)	–	0(3)	–	–	–
11	5/6	Workington	H	W49-40*	15(5)	4+1(4)	9+1(4)	3(4)	7(5)	9(5)	–	–	2+1(3)	–	–
12	8/6	Newport	A	L40-50	15+1(6)	6(4)	0(3)	0(3)	8+1(6)	8(5)	3+1(3)	–	–	–	–
13	12/6	Isle of Wight	H	W47-42	9+1(5)	4(4)	6+1(4)	3+2(3)	6+2(4)	19(7)	0(3)	–	–	–	–
14	15/6	Rye House	A	W46-44	17+1(6)	11(4)	R/R	2(5)	12+2(5)	2+1(5)	2(5)	–	–	–	–
15	19/6	Berwick	H	W53-36*	12+1(5)	6(4)	R/R	8+2(6)	12(5)	13+2(5)	1+1(4)	1(1)	–	–	–
16	3/7	Arena-Essex	H	W49-41	16+1(6)	14(6)	–	7(5)	R/R	8(5)	4+2(4)	–	–	0(4)	–
17	10/7	Newport	H	W57-33*	14+1(5)	9(4)	–	6+2(4)	6(4)	12+3(5)	5+1(4)	–	–	5+2(4)	–
18	17/7	Rye House	H	W56-34*	9+1(4)	11(4)	–	3+1(4)	14+1(5)	11+1(5)	4(4)	–	–	4+2(4)	–

SHEFFIELD TIGERS: back row, left to right: Ben Wilson, André Compton, Ricky Ashworth, Scott A. Smith, Andrew Moore, James Birkinshaw. Front, on bike: Sean Wilson.

PREMIER LEAGUE continued

No	DATE	OPPONENTS	H/A	RESULT	S.WILSON	MOORE	SMITH	BIRKINSHAW	A.COMPTON	ASHWORTH	B.WILSON	HALL	B.COMPTON	BRADY	OTHERS
19	18/7	Arena-Essex	A	L36-53	11(6)	13(6)	–	2(4)	8+1(5)	0(0)	1(4)	–	–	1(5)	–
20	22/7	Isle of Wight	A	L42-49	14+1(6)	6(4)	–	4+1(3)	12+2(6)	5+2(5)	0(3)	–	–	1(3)	–
21	24/7	Somerset	H	W64-26	14+1(5)	8+1(4)	–	8+2(4)	14+1(5)	11+1(4)	2+1(4)	–	–	7+2(4)	–
22	28/7	Exeter	A	W46-44	14(5)	4(4)	–	2(4)	8(5)	9(4)	2+1(4)	–	–	7+2(4)	–
23	29/7	Trelawny	A	L33-57	10(6)	3(4)	–	0(3)	9+2(6)	4+1(4)	2+1(3)	–	–	5+2(4)	–
24	31/7	Glasgow	H	W52-38*	13+1(5)	R/R	–	5+1(4)	9+2(5)	11(5)	6+2(6)	–	–	8+1(5)	–
25	2/8	Stoke	A	W48-42	13(5)	10(4)	–	–	11+1(5)	4+1(4)	0(3)	–	–	4(4)	6+1(5)
26	4/8	Reading	A	L42-47	15+1(6)	2(3)	–	–	12+1(6)	3(4)	0(0)	–	–	7(5)	3(5)
27	7/8	Stoke	H	W55-35*	12+1(5)	9+1(5)	–	4+1(5)	3(3)	9(4)	–	8+2(4)	–	10(4)	–
28	14/8	Exeter	H	W51-39*	18(6)	10(5)	–	2(4)	R/R	11+1(6)	–	–	2(4)	8+3(5)	–
29	21/8	Reading	H	W58-32*	18(6)	14+1(5)	–	9+2(4)	R/R	10+3(5)	–	–	2+1(4)	5(4)	0(2)
30	3/9	Hull	A	L43-47	12(5)	7+2(4)	–	0(3)	–	10(5)	–	5(6)	–	0(3)	9(4)
31	11/9	Trelawny	H	W55-34	12(6)	8+1(5)	–	8+1(4)	R/R	13+1(6)	–	6+3(5)	–	8+1(4)	–
32	12/9	Somerset	A	W53-37*	13+2(5)	8+3(4)	–	2(4)	–	10(4)	0(4)	–	–	6(4)	14+1(5)
33	18/9	Hull	H	W58-32*	16(6)	13+2(5)	–	6(4)	R/R	12+3(5)	2+1(4)	2+1(2)	–	7+1(4)	–
34	2/10	Edinburgh	H	W58-32	15(5)	14+1(6)	–	11+3(6)	–	5+1(4)	–	3+1(4)	–	R/R	10+2(4)

DETAILS OF OTHER RIDERS:

Match No. 1: Craig Watson 10(5); Match No. 25: Adam Allott 6+1(5); Match No. 26: Adam Allott 3(5); Match No. 29: Luke Priest 0(2); Match No. 30: Scott Robson 9(4); Match No. 32: Brent Werner 14+1(5); Match No. 34: Paul Pickering 10+2(4).

GOLDEN DOUBLE RIDES:

Match No. 20: André Compton's total includes 4 points from a golden double ride.

PREMIER LEAGUE AVERAGES

Rider	Mts	Rds	Pts	Bon	Tot	Avge	Max
Sean Wilson	33	176	423	16	439	9.98	4 Full; 4 Paid
André Compton	26	125	241	20	261	8.35	2 Full; 3 Paid
Ricky Ashworth	34	156	278	32	310	7.95	5 Paid
Andrew Moore	33	151	275	25	300	7.95	2 Paid
Scott A. Smith	13	52	75	4	79	6.08	–
Ross Brady	18	74	93	16	109	5.89	–
James Birkinshaw	31	123	127	30	157	5.11	–
Richard Hall	7	28	26	7	33	4.71	–
Ben Wilson	25	92	57	19	76	3.30	–
Benji Compton	3	11	6	2	8	2.91	–
Luke Priest	1	2	0	0	0	0.00	–
Guests	6	28	52	4	56	8.00	2 Paid

NOTE: André Compton's totals include one golden double ride (4 points), modified to the normal score i.e. 2 points.

BRITISH LEAGUE CUP

(* Denotes bonus-point victory)

No	DATE	OPPONENTS	H/A	RESULT	S. WILSON	MOORE	SMITH	BIRKINSHAW	COMPTON	ASHWORTH	B. WILSON	BRADY	OTHERS
1	27/3	Hull	H	W55-35	–	7(4)	6(4)	9+2(4)	13+1(5)	4(4)	4(4)	–	12+1(5)
2	3/4	Belle Vue	H	W50-42	–	2+1(4)	12+1(5)	3+1(4)	11+1(4)	4(4)	5+3(4)	–	13(5)
3	18/4	Stoke	H	W50-40	13(5)	8+3(5)	9(4)	2+1(4)	4+1(4)	11(5)	3+1(3)	–	–
4	19/4	Stoke	A	W46-44*	4+1(4)	11+1(6)	5+3(4)	R/R	9+1(5)	13(7)	4+1(4)	–	–
5	8/5	Coventry	H	W47-43	5+1(4)	3+1(4)	7+1(4)	7+1(4)	11(5)	8(5)	6+3(4)	–	–
6	17/5	Coventry	A	L42-48	9(5)	12+1(6)	1+1(3)	1(3)	12(6)	6+2(4)	1(3)	–	–
7	9/7	Hull	A	W51-39*	15(5)	5+1(4)	–	3(4)	12+2(5)	6+1(4)	3+1(4)	7(4)	–
8	14/7	Belle Vue	A	L35-55	5(4)	3(4)	–	1(3)	15(6)	4+1(5)	3+1(5)	4+1(4)	–
9	25/9	Eastbourne	H	L43-47	18(7)	6+3(5)	–	5+1(4)	R/R	9+1(6)	3(3)	2+1(4)	0(1)
10	27/9	Eastbourne	A	L31-59	5+1(4)	2+1(4)	–	2(4)	–	9(5)	2+2(5)	3+1(3)	8(5)

DETAILS OF OTHER RIDERS:

Match No. 1: Peter Carr 12+1(5); Match No. 2: Simon Stead 13(5); Match No. 9: Richard Hall 0(1); Match No. 10: Chris Neath 8(5).

BRITISH LEAGUE CUP AVERAGES

Rider	Mts	Rds	Pts	Bon	Tot	Avge	Max
André Compton	8	40	87	6	93	9.30	1 Paid
Sean Wilson	8	38	74	3	77	8.11	1 Full
Scott A. Smith	6	24	40	6	46	7.67	–
Ricky Ashworth	10	49	74	5	79	6.45	–
Andrew Moore	10	46	59	12	71	6.17	–
Ross Brady	4	15	16	3	19	5.07	–
Ben Wilson	10	39	34	12	46	4.72	–
James Birkinshaw	9	34	33	6	39	4.59	–
Richard Hall	1	1	0	0	0	0.00	–
Guests	3	15	33	1	34	9.07	–

KNOCK-OUT CUP

(* Denotes aggregate victory)

No	DATE	OPPONENTS	H/A	RESULT	S. WILSON	BIRKINSHAW	SMITH	MOORE	COMPTON	ASHWORTH	B. WILSON	BRADY	HALL	OTHERS
1	15/5	Hull	H	W56-43	9(4)	5(4)	12+2(5)	12+2(5)	7+1(4)	7+1(4)	4+1(4)	–	–	–
2	28/5	Hull	A	W48-41*	11(4)	3(5)	R/R	11(6)	11+2(6)	12+4(7)	0(0)	–	–	–
3	26/6	King's Lynn	H	W50-48	10(5)	10+1(4)	–	3+2(4)	6+1(4)	8+3(5)	6+3(4)	7(4)	–	–
4	2/7	King's Lynn	A	W49-48*	13+1(5)	2(4)	–	19(6)	–	5+1(4)	1+1(3)	3+1(4)	–	6(4)
5	4/9	Arena-Essex	H	W57-41	17+1(6)	8+1(4)	–	7(5)	R/R	9(5)	–	12+1(6)	4+1(4)	–
6	19/9	Arena-Essex	A	L43-55*	13(6)	3(4)	–	8(4)	–	5+1(4)	0(3)	3(4)	–	11(5)
7	7/10	Isle of Wight	A	L44-49	10(5)	5+2(6)	–	8+1(5)	–	5+1(4)	–	R/R	4+1(5)	12(5)
8	16/10	Isle of Wight	H	W47-46	7(5)	11+2(6)	–	9+2(5)	–	8+1(5)	–	R/R	8+2(5)	4+2(4)

DETAILS OF OTHER RIDERS:

Match No. 4: Rusty Harrison 6(4); Match No. 6: Brent Werner 11(5); Match No. 7: Brent Werner 12(5); Match No. 8: Brent Werner 4+2(4).

GOLDEN DOUBLE/TACTICAL JOKER RIDES:

Match No. 4: Andrew Moore's total includes 4 points from a tactical joker ride and 6 points from a golden double outing; Sean Wilson's total includes 4 points from a tactical joker ride; Rusty Harrison's total includes 0 points from a tactical joker ride; Match No. 6: Sean Wilson's total includes 2 points from a golden double ride and 6 points from a tactical joker outing; Andrew Moore's total includes 6 points from a tactical joker ride; Brent Werner's total includes 2 points from a tactical joker ride; Match No. 7: Brent Werner's total includes 6 points from a tactical joker ride.

OTHER MEETINGS

16 March: Easy-Rider/Pirtek Cup (first-leg)
   Sheffield 45 (André Compton 12; Nicki Pedersen 11+1; Ricky Ashworth 8+1; Scott A. Smith 6+1; James Birkinshaw 5+1; Andrew Moore 2; Ben Wilson 1) Stoke 45.
29 March: Easy-Rider/Pirtek Cup (second-leg)
   Stoke 52 Sheffield 38 (Andrew Moore 7+1; Scott A. Smith 7; Ricky Ashworth 7; Phil Morris 6; Ben Wilson 5+3; André Compton 4+1; James Birkinshaw 2+2) – Stoke won 97-83 on aggregate.

INDIVIDUAL MEETING

23 October: Teng Tools Northern Riders' Championship
   (Qualifying scores: Sean Wilson 15; Gary Havelock 14; Ricky Ashworth 12; Paul Pickering 12; Adam Shields 10; Sam Ermolenko 9; Andrew Moore 8; Chris Harris 7; Carl Stonehewer 7; Joe Screen 6; James Birkinshaw 5; Scott A. Smith 5; Rory Schlein 4; Ben Wilson 2; Richard Hall (res) 2; Shane Parker 1; Norbert Magosi 1) Semi-Final: 1st Shields; 2nd Ermolenko; 3rd Ashworth; 4th Pickering; Final: 1st Wilson; 2nd Havelock; 3rd Ermolenko; 4th Shields.

SOMERSET ORCHARD FM REBELS

ADDRESS: Oak Tree Arena, Edithmead, Highbridge, Somerset.
PROMOTERS: Andy Hewlett.
TRACK LENGTH: 300 metres.
FIRST MEETING: 2 June 2000.
YEARS OF OPERATION: 2000-01 British Conference League; 2002-03 British Premier League.

CLUB HONOURS

CONFERENCE TROPHY WINNERS: 2001.
KNOCK-OUT CUP WINNERS: 2001.

RIDER ROSTER 2003

BISHOP, Steve   *b. 28 November 1963, Bristol, Avon.*
BRITISH CAREER: (1981) Swindon, Canterbury; (1982–83) Swindon, Exeter; (1984) Stoke, Exeter; (1985) Exeter; (1986) Exeter, Swindon; (1987) Arena-Essex; (1988) Poole, Long Eaton; (1989) Long Eaton, Exeter; (1990) Exeter; (1995) Oxford; (1997–98) St Austell; (1999) Swindon; (2000–02) Somerset; (2003) Somerset, Hull.

BRANNEY, Craig   *b. 31 July 1982, Whitehaven, Cumbria.*
BRITISH CAREER: (2000) Ashfield; (2001) Workington, Buxton, Isle of Wight, Newport (PL); (2002) Newcastle (CL), Hull; (2003) Newcastle (PL & CL), Armadale (CT), Workington, Swindon (PL), Hull, Somerset.

CANDY, Paul   *b. 4 February 1980, Basingstoke, Hampshire.*
BRITISH CAREER: (2003) Carmarthen, Somerset, Exeter.

CUNNINGHAM, Glenn   *b. 10 June 1975, Bristol, Avon.*
BRITISH CAREER: (1991–92) Oxford; (1993–96) Swindon; (1997) Reading; (1998) Peterborough; (1999) Swindon; (2000) Peterborough, Belle Vue; (2001) Newport; (2002) Somerset; (2003) Somerset, Eastbourne.

DYMINSKI, Simon   *b. 18 October 1983, Swindon, Wiltshire.*
BRITISH CAREER: (2002) Swindon (CT & PL), Edinburgh, Peterborough (CL); (2003) Swindon (CL), Somerset.

FINLOW, Rob   *b. 27 May 1984, Bromsgrove, Hereford & Worcester.*
BRITISH CAREER: (1999) Newport (CL); (2000) Newport (CL), Buxton; (2001) Newport (CL & PL); (2002) Newport (CL & PL), Wolverhampton (CT), Somerset; (2003) Wolverhampton (CL), Somerset, Stoke (KOC), Buxton (CT).

GIFFARD, Daniel   *b. 10 November 1984, Eastbourne, East Sussex.*
BRITISH CAREER: (2000) Rye House; (2001) Rye House, Reading, Berwick, Newport; (2002) Isle of Wight, Rye House (CL & PL), Edinburgh; (2003) Wimbledon, Eastbourne (BLC), Somerset, Stoke.

GORDON, Graeme   *b. 16 June 1976, Rosehill, Sutton, Surrey.*
BRITISH CAREER: (1993) Exeter; (1994) Swindon; (1995) Devon, Exeter; (1996) Devon, Buxton, Exeter; (1997–00) Exeter; (2001) Trelawny; (2002) Wimbledon, Somerset; (2003) Somerset.

GOUGH, David   *b. 11 January 1986, Newport, South Wales.*
BRITISH CAREER: (2001) Newport (CL); (2002) Carmarthen; (2003) Carmarthen, Somerset (BLC), Newport (CL).

GROEN, Maik   *b. 3 June 1975, Netherlands.*
BRITISH CAREER: (2003) Somerset (BLC).

HALL, Richard   *b. 23 August 1984, Northallerton, North Yorkshire.*
BRITISH CAREER: (2001) Newcastle; (2002) Newcastle (PL & CL), Trelawny, Glasgow; (2003) Sheffield (CL & PL), Stoke (PL), Coventry (BLC), Hull (BLC), Newport (PL), Boston (KOC & CT), Exeter, Reading, Workington, Somerset.

HODGSON, Lee   *b. 19 February 1985, Preston, Lancashire.*
BRITISH CAREER: (2000) Sheffield (CL); (2001) Sheffield (PL & CL), Arena-Essex, Swindon; (2002) Stoke, Workington, Mildenhall; (2003) Mildenhall, Somerset, Workington.

HOLMES, Jamie *b. 19 November 1979, Exeter, Devon.*
BRITISH CAREER: (1999) Newport (CL); (2000) Newport (CL), Swindon, Stoke; (2001) Somerset; (2002) Newport (CL); (2003) Somerset (BLC), Trelawny (CT & BLC), Swindon (CL).

JAMES, Scott *b. 25 May 1984, Adelaide, South Australia.*
BRITISH CAREER: (2002) Workington, Mildenhall; (2003) Mildenhall, Workington, Somerset (KOC), Coventry (BLC).

JIROUT, Mario *b. 21 July 1976, Pardubice, Czech Republic.*
BRITISH CAREER: (1995-97) Peterborough; (1999) Peterborough; (2001) Peterborough; (2002-03) Somerset.

KATT, Stephan *b. 15 September 1979, Kiel, Germany.*
BRITISH CAREER: (2003) Somerset.

LAMB, Jessica *b. 5 February 1977, Poole, Dorset.*
BRITISH CAREER: (2001) Boston; (2003) Somerset (BLC), Trelawny (CT).

LEMON, Mark *b. 12 February 1973, Brainsdale, Victoria, Australia.*
BRITISH CAREER: (1990) Poole; (1991) Poole, Middlesbrough; (1992) Long Eaton, Middlesbrough; (1996) Oxford; (1997-98) Poole; (1999) Eastbourne, Hull; (2000) Oxford; (2002) Oxford; (2003) Somerset, Belle Vue.

McCABE, Shane *b. 3 May 1974, Townsville, Queensland, Australia.*
BRITISH CAREER: (2002) Peterborough (CL), Edinburgh, Somerset, Trelawny, Rye House, Newport, Stoke; (2003) King's Lynn, Boston, Peterborough (CL, ELKOC & BLC), Somerset.

MACKAY, Brendon *b. 14 August 1980, Darwin, Northern Territory, Australia.*
BRITISH CAREER: (2001-02) Reading; (2003) Somerset, Trelawny (CT), Newport (BLC), Exeter (BLC), Mildenhall.

MANCHESTER, Chris *b. 28 June 1973, St Louis, Missouri, USA.*
BRITISH CAREER: (1994-97) Belle Vue; (1999) Belle Vue; (2003) Belle Vue, Somerset.

MANN, James *b. 25 October 1983, Bolton, Greater Manchester.*
BRITISH CAREER: (1999) Buxton; (2000) Buxton, Workington, Stoke, Ipswich; (2001) Workington, Buxton; (2002) Workington, Buxton; (2003) Somerset, Mildenhall.

MEAKINS, Gordon *b. 18 March 1974, Aylesbury, Buckinghamshire.*
BRITISH CAREER: (1999) King's Lynn (CL); (2000) Peterborough (CL); (2001) Buxton; (2002) Carmarthen; (2003) Carmarthen, Somerset (BLC).

PRYER, Adam *b. 14 April 1983, King's Lynn, Norfolk.*
BRITISH CAREER: (1999) King's Lynn (CL); (2000) Peterborough (CL), Berwick; (2001) Peterborough (EL & CL); (2002) Peterborough (CL), Rye House (PL); (2003) Somerset, Peterborough (CL).

READ, Matt *b. 5 August 1981, Maidstone, Kent.*
BRITISH CAREER: (1997) Anglian Angels, King's Lynn; (1998-99) Arena-Essex; (2000) Arena-Essex, Reading; (2002) Isle of Wight; (2003) Eastbourne (BLC), Somerset.

THOMPSON, Mark *b. 8 July 1979, Orsett, Essex.*
BRITISH CAREER: (1996) Sittingbourne, Linlithgow, Mildenhall, Eastbourne (CL); (1997) Anglian Angels; (1998) Mildenhall, Newport, Stoke; (1999) King's Lynn (CL); (2000-01) Mildenhall; (2002) King's Lynn (CL), Mildenhall, Arena-Essex, Workington, Stoke; (2003) Boston, Stoke (PL), Newport (BLC), Somerset, Peterborough (BLC), Coventry (BLC), King's Lynn, Arena-Essex.

SOMERSET REBELS: back row, left to right: Glenn Cunningham, Mark Lemon, Andy Hewlett (Promoter), Graeme Gordon, Stephan Katt, Ray Dickson (Team Manager). On bike: Steve Bishop. Front, kneeling: James Mann, Scott James.

WALKER, Simon *b. 19 February 1980, Bristol, Avon.*
BRITISH CAREER: (2001) Newport (CL); (2002) Newport (CL), Arena-Essex, Swindon (CT), Trelawny; (2003) Swindon (CL), Trelawny (CT), Reading, Somerset (BLC), Poole (BLC), Exeter (BLC), Newport.

PREMIER LEAGUE

(* Denotes bonus-point victory)

No	DATE	OPPONENTS	H/A	RESULT	CUNNINGHAM	GORDON	KATT	BISHOP	LEMON	HODGSON	MANN	DYMINSKI	READ	FINLOW	MACKAY	CANDY	MANCHESTER	JIROUT	OTHERS
1	9/4	Hull	A	W46-44	8(4)	5+1(4)	5+1(4)	11(5)	11(5)	3(4)	3+1(4)								
2	18/4	Swindon	H	L42-48	11+2(6)	3(4)	8+2(4)	5+1(5)	12+1(5)	0(2)	3(4)								
3	9/5	Berwick	H	D45-45	13+1(5)	8+1(4)	4(4)	8+1(4)	10+2(5)										1(3)
4	30/5	Exeter	H	W48-42	8+1(4)	11+1(5)	4(4)		7+2(4)			6+2(5)	12+2(5)						0(3)
5	3/6	Isle of Wight	A	L36-54	3+3(4)	2(3)	5(5)					2+1(3)	14(6)						0(3)
6	6/6	Glasgow	H	W46-44	10(5)	6(4)	9(4)		9+1(4)			2(4)	7+2(4)						
7	20/6	Newcastle	H	W47-43	9+1(4)	6+1(4)	6(4)		12(5)				8+2(5)	3+1(5)					
8	21/6	Rye House	A	L33-57	11+1(6)	1(3)	5(4)		9(6)				4+1(5)	5+1(5)					2(3)
9	22/6	Stoke	A	L35-55	3(3)	10(6)	5+1(4)		9+3(6)				5+1(4)	2(3)					1(3)
10	27/6	Isle of Wight	H	L37-53	11(6)	3+1(4)	3+2(4)		12(5)				4+2(5)	2+2(4)					0(3)
11	30/6	Exeter	A	L35-55	9(6)	4+2(4)	5(4)		15(6)				1(4)	1(3)	0(3)				1+1(3)
12	3/7	Swindon	A	L30-60	7(6)	5+2(4)	4+2(4)		9(6)				4(4)	3(4)					
13	4/7	Reading	H	W46-45	7(4)	3(4)	7(4)		15+1(6)				10+2(5)	1(3)					
14	11/7	Arena-Essex	A	L34-56	5(5)	5(5)	1(3)	4+1(4)	15(6)				3+1(4)	1+1(3)					
15	13/7	Newcastle	A	L38-52	11(6)	5(5)	R/R	1+1(4)	17(6)				4+1(6)	1+1(3)					
16	24/7	Sheffield	A	L26-64	8+1(6)	1(3)	3(4)	5+1(5)	6(6)				2(3)	6+1(4)	0(3)				
17	25/7	Stoke	H	W58-32*	14+1(5)	8+2(4)	8+2(4)	5(4)	9+1(5)				8+1(4)	1(3)					
18	6/8	Edinburgh	A	L44-46	8+2(5)	8+1(4)	3(4)	7+1(5)	12+1(5)				5+1(4)	0(3)					
19	8/8	Edinburgh	H	L35-55	10+1(6)	6(4)	0(3)	1(3)	11+1(6)				7+3(5)	1+1(3)					
20	9/8	Berwick	A	L32-58	2(4)	1(4)	4(4)	2(3)	14+1(6)				8+1(6)	0(3)					
21	15/8	Workington	H	D46-46	8(4)	7+3(4)			18+1(6)			1(4)	6+2(5)	2(4)		6(4)			
22	18/8	Reading	A	L36-54	5(4)	3(4)			10(6)			1+1(3)	5+3(5)	5(3)		10(5)			
23	29/8	King's Lynn	H	L38-52	14(6)	4+1(4)			6+1(4)			1(2)	8+2(6)	9+3(5)		3(4)			
24	2/9	Trelawny	A	L38-52	11+1(6)	4+1(4)			11(6)				2+2(4)	3(3)	1(3)	4+1(4)	3+2(4)		1(3)
25	5/9	Newport	H	L44-46	7(4)	8(5)			10+1(5)				6+1(4)	0(3)			8(4)		0(3)
26	6/9	Workington	A	L30-60	5+1(5)	4(5)			8(5)				2+1(5)	5+1(3)			6+1(4)		1(3)
27	7/9	Glasgow	A	L35-55	8+1(4)	8(6)			8+1(6)				4+1(4)	7+2(5)			2+1(4)		2+1(3)
28	12/9	Sheffield	H	L37-53	6(5)	11(6)			5(4)				6+2(5)	3(4)			5+2(4)		0(3)
29	19/9	Trelawny	H	W46-44	7(4)	8+1(4)			11(5)				8+1(5)	1(3)			9+1(4)		4+1(8)
30	26/9	Hull	H	W52-38*	13+1(5)	7+1(4)			10(5)				9+2(4)	0(0)	1(4)			3(3)	
31	1/10	Arena-Essex	A	L42-48	7(4)	7+1(4)			9+1(5)				12(6)						
32	8/10	King's Lynn	A	L31-59	4(4)	2+2(4)			10(6)				3+3(5)	1(3)	0(5)				11(5)
33	12/10	Newport	A	L39-50	7+1(4)	1(3)			12+2(6)				6+1(5)	0(5)					13(6)
34	17/10	Rye House	H	W50-40	6+2(4)	8(4)			7(4)				9+2(5)						20+1(13)

DETAILS OF OTHER RIDERS:

Match No. 3: Daniel Giffard 1(3); Match No. 4: Shane McCabe 0(3); Match No. 5: Mark Thompson 0(3); Match No. 10: Jamie Holmes 2(3); Match No. 11: Tom Brown 1(3); Match No. 12: Tom Brown 0(3); Match No. 13: Tom Brown 1+1(3); Match No. 24: Simon Walker 1(3); Match No. 26: Simon Walker 0(3); Match No. 27: Simon Walker 1(3); Match No. 28: Craig Branney 2+1(3); Match No. 29: Tommy Allen 0(3); Match No. 30: Simon Walker 3(4); Craig Branney 1+1(4); Match No. 32: Craig Watson 11(5); Match No. 33: Brent Werner 13(6); Match No. 34: Craig Watson 15(5); Simon Walker 4+1(5); Richard Hall 1(3).

GOLDEN DOUBLE RIDES:

Match No. 12: Mark Lemon's total includes 0 points from a golden double ride; Match No. 13: Mark Lemon's total includes 2 points from a golden double ride; Match No. 21: Mark Lemon's total includes 4 points from a golden double ride.

PREMIER LEAGUE AVERAGES

Rider	Mts	Rds	Pts	Bon	Tot	Avge	Max
Mark Lemon	34	182	356	21	377	8.29	–
Glenn Cunningham	34	163	276	21	297	7.29	1 Paid
Matt Read	30	141	188	42	230	6.52	–
Mario Jirout	7	27	36	7	43	6.37	–
Graeme Gordon	34	143	183	21	204	5.71	–
Chris Manchester	4	17	23	1	24	5.65	–
Stephan Katt	19	75	89	10	99	5.28	–
Steve Bishop	10	42	49	6	55	5.24	–
Rob Finlow	26	91	69	15	84	3.69	–
James Mann	2	8	6	1	7	3.50	–
Craig Branney	2	7	3	2	5	2.86	–
Simon Dyminski	7	26	14	4	18	2.77	–
Jamie Holmes	1	3	2	0	2	2.67	–
Simon Walker	5	18	9	1	10	2.22	–
Lee Hodgson	2	6	3	0	3	2.00	–
Brendon Mackay	3	9	3	1	4	1.78	–
Daniel Giffard	1	3	1	0	1	1.33	–
Richard Hall	1	3	1	0	1	1.33	–
Paul Candy	6	21	2	0	2	0.38	–
Shane McCabe	1	3	0	0	0	0.00	–
Mark Thompson	1	3	0	0	0	0.00	–
Guests	9	35	44	3	47	5.37	1 Full

NOTE: Mark Lemon's totals include three golden double rides (6 points), modified to the normal score i.e. 3 points.

BRITISH LEAGUE CUP

No	DATE	OPPONENTS	H/A	RESULT	CUNNINGHAM	GORDON	KATT	BISHOP	LEMON	MANN	FINLOW	GROEN	DYMINSKI	READ	JIROUT	OTHERS
1	28/3	Exeter	H	L43-47	4+2(4)	9(4)	5+1(4)	12+1(5)	10(5)	1(4)	–	–	–	–	–	–
2	4/4	Trelawny	H	L42-49	7+1(4)	5(4)	5+1(4)	10+1(5)	10+1(6)	4+2(4)	1+1(3)	–	–	–	–	–
3	7/4	Exeter	A	L36-54	11(6)	3+3(4)	3(4)	5+1(4)	13(6)	1(3)	–	–	–	–	–	0(3)
4	14/4	Wolverhampton	A	L33-57	11(6)	4+1(4)	4+2(4)	5(4)	8(6)	1(3)	–	–	–	–	–	–
5	23/5	Wolverhampton	H	L33-57	6+1(5)	3+1(4)	3(4)	3+1(3)	9(5)	–	–	5+2(4)	4(5)	–	–	–

BRITISH LEAGUE CUP continued

No	DATE	OPPONENTS	H/A	RESULT	CUNNINGHAM	GORDON	KATT	BISHOP	LEMON	MANN	FINLOW	GROEN	DYMINSKI	READ	JIROUT	OTHERS
6	27/5	Trelawny	A	L31-59	9+1(6)	9+2(7)	7(5)	R/R	5(5)	–	–	–	–	–	–	1(7)
7	6/7	Newport	A	L31-59	R/R	12+1(7)	–	–	13(7)	–	5+1(6)	–	–	–	–	1(10)
8	18/7	Newport	H	L42-48	9+2(6)	6(4)	5+3(4)	7(3)	9+2(6)	–	4+1(3)	–	–	2(4)	–	–
9	1/8	Poole	H	L39-50	10(6)	–	3+2(4)	5+2(4)	13(6)	–	–	–	–	–	5+2(4)	3+1(6)
10	25/8	Poole	A	L39-51	9(6)	7+2(4)	4+3(4)	–	11+1(6)	–	1(3)	–	DNA	–	7+1(4)	–

DETAILS OF OTHER RIDERS:

Match No. 1: Jamie Holmes 2(4); Match No. 3: Tom Brown 0(3); Match No. 4: Gordon Meakins 0(3); Match No. 6: David Gough 0(1); Paul Candy 1(6); Match No. 7: Brendon Mackay 1(4); Jessica Lamb 0(3); Simon Walker 0(3); Match No. 9: Paul Candy 2(3); Jamie Holmes 1+1(3).

GOLDEN DOUBLE RIDES:

Match No. 2: Mark Lemon's total includes 2 points from a golden double ride.

BRITISH LEAGUE CUP AVERAGES

Rider	Mts	Rds	Pts	Bon	Tot	Avge	Max
Steve Bishop	7	28	47	6	53	7.57	–
Mario Jirout	2	8	12	3	15	7.50	–
Mark Lemon	10	58	100	4	104	7.17	–
Glenn Cunningham	9	49	76	7	83	6.78	–
Graeme Gordon	9	42	58	10	68	6.48	–
Stephan Katt	9	37	39	12	51	5.51	–
Maik Groen	2	7	6	2	8	4.57	–
Rob Finlow	3	12	10	3	13	4.33	–
Simon Dyminski	1	5	4	0	4	3.20	–
James Mann	4	14	7	2	9	2.57	–
Jamie Holmes	2	7	3	1	4	2.29	–
Matt Read	1	4	2	0	2	2.00	–
Paul Candy	2	9	3	0	3	1.33	–
Brendon Mackay	1	4	1	0	1	1.00	–
David Gough	1	1	0	0	0	0.00	–
Jessica Lamb	1	3	0	0	0	0.00	–
Gordon Meakins	1	3	0	0	0	0.00	–
Simon Walker	1	3	0	0	0	0.00	–
Guest	1	3	0	0	0	0.00	–

NOTE: Mark Lemon's totals include one golden double ride (2 points), modified to the normal score i.e. 1 point.

KNOCK-OUT CUP

No	DATE	OPPONENTS	H/A	RESULT	LEMON	GORDON	KATT	CUNNINGHAM	BISHOP	MANN	JAMES
1	6/4	Newport	A	L35-61	11(5)	6+2(4)	2(4)	8(5)	4(4)	2+2(4)	2(4)
2	11/4	Newport	H	L43-49	15(6)	5+1(4)	7+1(4)	7+1(5)	6+3(4)	1+1(3)	2(4)

GOLDEN DOUBLE/TACTICAL JOKER RIDES:

Match No. 1: Mark Lemon's total includes 4 points from a tactical joker ride; Graeme Gordon's total includes 4 points from a tactical joker ride; Glenn Cunningham's total includes 4 points from a tactical joker ride; Match No. 2: Mark Lemon's total includes 4 points from a golden double ride.

OTHER MEETINGS

19 March: International Club Challenge

> Somerset 51 (Steve Bishop 13+1; Mark Lemon 13+1; Glenn Cunningham 6+1; Graeme Gordon 6; Stephan Katt 6; Jamie Holmes 4+1; Adam Pryer 3+1) Kaparna 39 (Magnus Karlsson 12+1; Jaroslaw Hampel 11+1; Kim Jansson 6; Tomasz Gapinski 4+1; Sebastian Bengtsson 4+1; Joonas Kylmakorpi 2; Norvy Brandin 0).

26 April: Premier League

> Stoke 1 Somerset 5 (Mark Lemon 3; Graeme Gordon 2+1; Glenn Cunningham DNR; Stephan Katt DNR; James Mann DNR; Simon Dyminski DNR; Steve Bishop R/R) – meeting abandoned after heat one.

11 July: Paul Gladwin Memorial Four-Team Tournament

> Weymouth 26 (Justin Elkins 8; Wayne Barrett 7; Ben Barker 6; Nathan Irwin 5), Swindon 17 (Malcolm Holloway 6; Simon Walker 6; Nick Lee 3; Lee Smart 2), Bristol 15 (Jamie Holmes 7; Paul Candy 5; Brendon Mackay 2; Andy Carfield 1; Jessica Lamb 0), Newport 14 (Tom Brown 7; Dan Warwick 5; David Minall 1; Oliver Hackett 1).

22 August: Conference Challenge (first-leg)

> Bristol 43 (Rob Finlow 16; Simon Dyminski 8; Simon Walker 6+2; Lee Smart 6+1; Matthew Cross 6; Paul Candy 1; Oliver Hackett 0) Weymouth 47.

25 August: Conference Challenge (second-leg)

> Weymouth 53 Bristol 36 (Graeme Gordon 12; Matthew Cross 10; Simon Walker 5+2; Paul Candy 5+1; Lee Smart 4+1; Oliver Hackett 0; Jamie Holmes R/R) – Weymouth won 100-79 on aggregate.

3 October: Conference Challenge

> Bristol 67 (Simon Walker 16+1; Lee Smart 14; Matthew Cross 10+2; Paul Candy 9+4; Andy Carfield 9+3; Darren Hatton 9+3; Rob Finlow R/R) Newport 23.

INDIVIDUAL MEETINGS

13 June: Somerset Open

> (Qualifying scores: David Ruud 14; Adam Shields 12; Michael Coles 11; Craig Boyce 11; Mark Lemon 10; Brent Werner 10; Olly Allen 10; Andy Smith 8; Davey Watt 7; Glenn Cunningham 7; Claus Kristensen 5; Graeme Gordon 4; Matt Read 4; Stephan Katt 4; Steve Masters 2; Malcolm Holloway 1) Final: 1st Ruud; 2nd Shields; 3rd Coles; 4th Boyce.

10 October: Graeme Gordon Testimonial

(Qualifying scores: Mark Lemon 10; Magnus Zetterstrom 10; Craig Boyce 10; Scott Nicholls 10; David Ruud 10; Chris Harris 9; Danny Bird 8; Carl Stonehewer 8; Shane Parker 6; Matt Read 5; Adam Shields 3; Krister Marsh 3; Adam Allott 2; Glenn Cunningham 1; Daniel Davidsson 1; Matthew Cross (res) 0; Gary Phelps 0) Semi-Final: 1st Boyce; 2nd Nicholls; 3rd Harris; 4th Ruud; Final: 1st Nicholls; 2nd Zetterstrom; 3rd Lemon; 4th Boyce.

STOKE EASY-RIDER POTTERS

NOTE: The information below relates only to the main Stoke team. For details of the second side, please refer to the Conference League section.

ADDRESS: Newcastle-under-Lyme Stadium, Loomer Road, Chesterton, Staffordshire.
PROMOTER: Dave Tattum.
TRACK LENGTH: 312 metres.
FIRST MEETING: 12 April 1973.
YEARS OF OPERATION: 1972 Training; 1973-74 British League Division Two; 1975-90 National League; 1991-92 British League Division Two; 1994 British League Division Three; 1995 British Academy League; 1996-03 British Premier League
NOTES: (1) The team rode under the name of 'Chesterton' in 1973; (2) The team rode under the name of 'Cradley Heath & Stoke' in 1996.

PREVIOUS VENUE: HANLEY Stadium, Sun Street, Hanley, Staffordshire.
YEARS OF OPERATION: 1929 English Dirt-track League & Open; 1939 National League Division Two; 1947-49 National League Division Three; 1950-53 National League Division Two; 1960-63 Provincial League.

CLUB HONOURS

LEAGUE CHAMPIONS: 1949.
PAIRS CHAMPIONS: 1984, 1988, 1989.
FOUR-TEAM CHAMPIONS: 1990.

RIDER ROSTER 2003

ALLOTT, Adam   b. 19 March 1983, Stockport, Greater Manchester.
BRITISH CAREER: (1998) Norfolk, Buxton; (1999) Buxton, Sheffield; (2000) Sheffield, Owlerton; (2001) Sheffield; (2002) Sheffield (CL), Swindon, Somerset; (2003) Buxton, Stoke (BLC), King's Lynn.
ARMSTRONG, Jon   b. 1 August 1974, Manchester.
BRITISH CAREER: (1992-93) Belle Vue; (1994) Coventry; (1996) Buxton, Sheffield; (1997)

Buxton, Belle Vue (AL), Swindon, Stoke; (1998) Newport (CL & PL); (1999) Belle Vue, Stoke; (2000) Newport (PL); (2001) Stoke; (2002) Buxton, Stoke; (2003) Stoke.

BUNYAN, Jason   b. 9 March 1979, Milton Keynes, Buckinghamshire.
BRITISH CAREER: (1995) Poole; (1996) Eastbourne (CL); (1997) Oxford, Isle of Wight, Peterborough (AL); (1998) Isle of Wight; (1999-01) Ipswich; (2002) Reading; (2003) Coventry, Stoke (BLC).

COOK, Joe   b. 24 December 1983, King's Lynn, Norfolk.
BRITISH CAREER: (2002) King's Lynn (CL), Arena-Essex, Newport (PL), Isle of Wight; (2003) Stoke (PL & CT), Oxford (BLC & CL).

FINLOW, Rob   b. 27 May 1984, Bromsgrove, Hereford & Worcester.
BRITISH CAREER: (1999) Newport (CL); (2000) Newport (CL), Buxton; (2001) Newport (CL & PL); (2002) Newport (CL & PL), Wolverhampton (CT), Somerset; (2003) Wolverhampton (CL & BLC), Somerset, Stoke (KOC), Buxton (CT).

GIFFARD, Daniel   b. 10 November 1984, Eastbourne, East Sussex.
BRITISH CAREER: (2000) Rye House; (2001) Rye House, Reading, Berwick, Newport; (2002) Isle of Wight, Rye House (CL & PL), Edinburgh; (2003) Wimbledon, Eastbourne (BLC), Somerset, Stoke.

GRANT, Rob   b. 10 June 1984, Newcastle-upon-Tyne, Tyne & Wear.
BRITISH CAREER: (1999) Linlithgow; (2000) Ashfield, Newcastle; (2001) Newcastle; (2002) Newcastle, Boston, Stoke; (2003) Berwick, Sheffield (CL), Stoke.

HALL, Richard   b. 23 August 1984, Northallerton, North Yorkshire.
BRITISH CAREER: (2001) Newcastle; (2002) Newcastle (PL & CL), Trelawny, Glasgow; (2003) Sheffield (CL & PL), Stoke (PL), Coventry (BLC), Hull (BLC), Newport (PL), Boston (KOC & CT), Exeter, Reading, Workington, Somerset.

KESSLER, Robbie   b. 5 April 1973, Neuwied, Germany.
BRITISH CAREER: (1994) Sheffield; (1996-97) Sheffield; (1999) King's Lynn; (2000-01) Sheffield; (2002) Hull; (2003) Stoke.

MACKLIN, Paul   b. 10 October 1975, Manchester.
BRITISH CAREER: (1994) Stoke; (1996-99) Buxton; (2000) Berwick, Stoke & Newcastle; (2001) Newcastle; (2002) Boston; (2003) Stoke (CT & PL)

MOGRIDGE, Alan   b. 6 November 1963, Westminster, London.
BRITISH CAREER: (1981) Wimbledon; (1982-83) Crayford, Wimbledon; (1984) Canterbury, Wolverhampton; (1985) Hackney; (1986) Canterbury, Rye House, Ipswich, Hackney; (1987) Hackney; (1988) Hackney, Sheffield, Bradford; (1989-90) Ipswich; (1991-92) Arena-Essex; (1993) Peterborough; (1994) Middlesbrough, Sheffield; (1995) Arena-Essex; (1996) London, Eastbourne; (1997) Eastbourne; (1999-00) Berwick; (2001) Swindon; (2002-03) Stoke.

PICKERING, Paul   b. 15 February 1966, Hartlepool, Cleveland.
BRITISH CAREER: (1992) Middlesbrough; (1993) Middlesbrough, Bradford; (1994-96) Bradford; (1997) Reading; (1998-03) Stoke.

PRIEST, Luke   b. 18 June 1985, Birmingham, West Midlands.
BRITISH CAREER: (2000) Ashfield, Owlerton; (2001) Sheffield (CL), Boston; (2002) Sheffield (CL), Wolverhampton (CT); (2003) Sheffield (CL), Stoke (CT & PL), Workington, Exeter, Newport (BLC), Arena-Essex, Wolverhampton (BLC), Belle Vue (BLC).

SIMMONS, Nick   b. 24 July 1981, Leamington Spa, Warwickshire.
BRITISH CAREER: (1997) Shuttle Cubs, Ryde; (1998) Newport (CL & PL), Isle of

STOKE POTTERS: back row, left to right: Jon Armstrong, Nick Simmons, Jan Staechmann, Daniel Giffard, Alan Mogridge. Front, on bike: Paul Pickering.

Wight, Exeter; (1999) Isle of Wight, Stoke, Newport (CL); (2000) Arena-Essex; (2001) Newport (PL & CL), Somerset; (2002) Isle of Wight; (2003) Stoke, Reading, Mildenhall, Workington, King's Lynn, Exeter.

SMITH, Scott   *b. 4 February 1980, Brisbane, Queensland, Australia.*
BRITISH CAREER: (2001-02) Newport; (2003) Reading, Stoke.

STAECHMANN, Jan   *b. 5 June 1966, Kolding, Denmark.*
BRITISH CAREER: (1985-90) Wolverhampton; (1991-94) Long Eaton; (1995-96) Hull; (1997) Peterborough; (1998-99) Oxford; (2000) Oxford, Belle Vue; (2001-02) Stoke; (2003) Stoke, Oxford.

THOMPSON, Mark   *b. 8 July 1979, Orsett, Essex.*
BRITISH CAREER: (1996) Sittingbourne, Linlithgow, Mildenhall, Eastbourne (CL); (1997) Anglian Angels; (1998) Mildenhall, Newport, Stoke; (1999) King's Lynn (CL); (2000-01) Mildenhall; (2002) King's Lynn (CL), Mildenhall, Arena-Essex, Workington, Stoke; (2003) Boston, Stoke (PL), Newport (BLC), Somerset, Peterborough (BLC), Coventry (BLC), King's Lynn, Arena-Essex.

WRIGHT, James   *b. 13 June 1986, Stockport, Greater Manchester.*
BRITISH CAREER: (2002) Buxton; (2003) Buxton, Belle Vue (BLC), Newcastle (PL), Stoke (PL), Workington, Hull, King's Lynn.

PREMIER LEAGUE

(* Denotes bonus-point victory)

No	DATE	OPPONENTS	H/A	RESULT	PICKERING	ARMSTRONG	KESSLER	MOGRIDGE	STAECHMANN	SIMMONS	GIFFARD	COOK	PRIEST	SMITH	GRANT	OTHERS
1	27/4	Glasgow	A	L40-50	–	5(4)	6+1(4)	8+1(6)	5+1(4)	1+1(3)	–	–	–	–	–	15+2(9)
2	6/5	Isle of Wight	A	L35-54	–	2+2(3)	6+1(5)	6(4)	12(6)	0(3)	–	–	–	–	–	9+1(9)
3	12/5	Reading	A	L43-47	–	2(3)	9(4)	4+1(4)	12+2(6)	1+1(4)	–	–	–	–	–	15+2(9)
4	24/5	Rye House	H	W57-32	13+2(5)	6+1(4)	–	6+1(4)	15(5)	4(4)	–	–	–	–	–	13+1(8)
5	25/5	Rye House	A	W54-35*	7(5)	7+1(4)	–	6+1(4)	13+1(5)	2+1(4)	8+1(4)	–	–	–	–	11(4)
6	31/5	Glasgow	H	L44-46	5(4)	4(4)	–	6+2(4)	12(5)	2(3)	4+3(5)	–	–	–	–	11+1(5)
7	5/6	Swindon	A	L35-55	5(4)	1+1(3)	–	6+5(6)	8(5)	0(3)	1(3)	–	–	–	–	14(6)
8	13/6	Edinburgh	A	L35-55	2(3)	2(3)	–	4+2(5)	13(6)	0(3)	1(4)	–	–	–	–	13(6)
9	15/6	Berwick	H	W53-37	10(5)	5+1(4)	–	7+2(4)	15(5)	5+1(5)	–	–	–	–	–	11(7)
10	22/6	Somerset	H	W55-35	10+1(5)	4+1(4)	–	9+3(4)	15(5)	3(4)	–	2+1(4)	–	–	–	12(4)
11	25/6	King's Lynn	A	L37-52	12(6)	4+3(4)	–	7(4)	7+1(5)	1(3)	–	0(3)	–	–	–	6+1(5)
12	29/6	Reading	H	L44-46	14(6)	3+1(4)	–	R/R	9+1(5)	2+1(5)	–	3+1(5)	–	–	–	13(5)
13	1/7	Trelawny	A	L34-55	12+1(7)	1(4)	–	R/R	12(6)	0(5)	–	3(4)	–	–	–	6(4)
14	6/7	Swindon	H	W46-44	11(5)	8+3(5)	–	R/R	11+1(5)	–	1(5)	2(5)	–	–	–	13(5)
15	12/7	King's Lynn	H	W46-44	16(6)	6+2(5)	–	R/R	11(5)	–	1(1)	7+3(7)	–	–	–	5(4)
16	20/7	Arena-Essex	H	L44-48	12+1(6)	4+1(5)	–	R/R	15(6)	–	–	1(4)	5+1(5)	–	–	7(4)
17	25/7	Somerset	A	L32-58	13(7)	5(6)	–	R/R	9(6)	–	–	0(3)	1(3)	–	–	4+1(5)
18	2/8	Sheffield	H	L42-48	10(5)	3+2(3)	–	4+1(4)	12(6)	–	–	2(3)	3+2(4)	–	–	8+2(5)
19	7/8	Sheffield	A	L35-55	11(6)	1(3)	–	4+2(5)	13(6)	–	–	1(3)	1(4)	–	–	4(3)
20	9/8	Hull	H	W60-32	13+1(5)	7+1(4)	–	8+3(4)	9+1(4)	–	–	7+1(4)	–	11+2(5)	5+3(4)	–

PREMIER LEAGUE continued

No	DATE	OPPONENTS	H/A	RESULT	PICKERING	ARMSTRONG	KESSLER	MOGRIDGE	STAECHMANN	SIMMONS	GIFFARD	COOK	PRIEST	SMITH	GRANT	OTHERS
21	16/8	Exeter	H	W55-35	10+1(4)	3(4)	–	8+2(4)	14+1(5)	–	–	2(3)	–	6+1(4)	12+2(6)	–
22	23/8	Workington	H	D45-45	12+2(5)	R/R	–	4(4)	16+1(6)	–	–	0(3)	–	8(5)	–	5(7)
23	25/8	Workington	A	L35-54	9(6)	R/R	–	8+1(5)	13+1(6)	–	–	1(3)	–	2+1(4)	–	2+1(5)
24	30/8	Edinburgh	H	L44-46	12(5)	R/R	–	4(4)	15+1(6)	–	–	–	1(4)	8(5)	–	4(6)
25	31/8	Newport	A	L41-48	12(6)	R/R	–	1+1(3)	10+2(6)	–	–	–	1(3)	12(6)	–	5+2(6)
26	12/9	Arena-Essex	A	L30-60	1(4)	R/R	–	4(4)	8(6)	–	–	2+2(5)	–	8(5)	–	7+1(6)
27	13/9	Newcastle	H	L43-47	12+1(5)	R/R	–	8+1(4)	10+2(5)	–	–	0(7)	–	0(1)	–	13(7)
28	22/9	Exeter	A	W46-44*	17(6)	R/R	–	8(4)	10+3(5)	–	–	0(4)	–	7+1(5)	4+2(6)	–
29	24/9	Hull	A	L41-49*	16(6)	R/R	–	5+1(5)	10+2(6)	–	–	0(4)	–	8(5)	2(4)	–
30	27/9	Berwick	A	L32-58	12(6)	R/R	–	3(6)	10(5)	–	–	1+1(4)	–	–	2(5)	4(6)
31	5/10	Newcastle †	A	L29-43	8(4)	R/R	–	0(3)	7(4)	–	–	2+1(3)	–	10(5)	2(5)	–
32	12/10	Trelawny	H	L42-49	8(4)	2(3)	–	6+1(4)	13(6)	–	–	4(4)	–	8+1(5)	1+1(4)	–
33	14/10	Newport	H	W46-44	7(5)	7+3(4)	–	3+1(4)	13(5)	–	–	4+1(4)	–	6(4)	6(4)	–
34	18/10	Isle of Wight	H	L43-47	9+1(5)	4(4)	–	7+2(4)	8(5)	–	–	1(3)	–	5(4)	9+1(5)	–

† Meeting abandoned after twelve heats, with the result standing.

DETAILS OF OTHER RIDERS:

Match No. 1: Andrew Appleton 12+1(6); Richard Hall 3+1(3); Match No. 2: Davey Watt 9+1(6); Paul Macklin 0(3) Match No. 3: Davey Watt 12+1(5); Mark Thompson 3+1(4); Match No. 4: Garry Stead 11(4); James Wright 2+1(4); Match No. 5: Davey Watt 11(4); Match No. 6 Chris Harris 11+1(5); Match No. 7: Garry Stead 14(6); Match No. 8: Kevin Little 13(6); Match No. 9: Frede Schott 11(4); James Wright 0(3); Match No. 10: Chris Neath 12(4); Match No. 11: Jason Bunyan 6+1(5); Match No. 12: Frede Schott 13(5); Match No. 13: Mark Simmonds 6(4); Match No. 14: Chris Harris 13(5); Match No. 15: Glenn Cunningham 5(4); Match No. 16: Mark Lemon 7(4); Match No. 17: Andrew Moore 4+1(5); Match No. 18: Frank Smart 8+2(5); Match No. 19: Adrian Rymel 4(3); Match No. 22: Simon Cartwright 5(7); Match No. 23: Simon Cartwright 2+1(5); Match No. 24: Adam Allott 4(6); Match No. 25: Kauko Nieminen 5+2(6); Match No. 26: Mark Courtney 7+1(6); Match No. 27: Simon Cartwright 13(7); Match No. 30: Kevin Doolan 4(6).

GOLDEN DOUBLE RIDES:

Match No. 16: Jan Staechmann's total includes 6 points from a golden double ride; Match No. 32: Jan Staechmann's total includes 2 points from a golden double ride.

PREMIER LEAGUE AVERAGES

Rider	Mts	Rds	Pts	Bon	Tot	Avge	Max
Jan Staechmann	34	182	381	21	402	8.84	3 Full; 1 Paid
Paul Pickering	31	161	321	11	332	8.25	1 Paid
Robbie Kessler	3	13	21	2	23	7.08	–
Scott Smith	14	63	99	6	105	6.67	–
Alan Mogridge	28	120	154	34	188	6.27	1 Paid
Richard Hall	1	3	3	1	4	5.33	–
Jon Armstrong	24	94	96	23	119	5.06	–
Rob Grant	9	43	43	9	52	4.84	–
Mark Thompson	1	4	3	1	4	4.00	–
Daniel Giffard	6	22	16	4	20	3.64	–

Rider	Mts	Rds	Pts	Bon	Tot	Avge	Max
Luke Priest	6	23	12	3	15	2.61	–
Joe Cook	23	92	45	11	56	2.43	–
Nick Simmons	13	49	21	5	26	2.12	–
James Wright	2	7	2	1	3	1.71	–
Paul Macklin	1	3	0	0	0	0.00	–
Guests	26	133	222	12	234	7.04	1 Full

NOTE: Jan Staechmann's totals include two golden double rides (8 points), modified to the normal score i.e. 4 points.

BRITISH LEAGUE CUP

(* Denotes bonus-point victory)

No	DATE	OPPONENTS	H/A	RESULT	PICKERING	ARMSTRONG	KESSLER	MOGRIDGE	STAECHMANN	SIMMONS	COOK	ALLOTT	GIFFARD	SMITH	OTHERS
1	2/4	Hull	A	L41-49	9(5)	R/R	9+1(5)	6+1(4)	13+2(6)	2(3)	0(4)	2+1(3)	–	–	–
2	12/4	Hull	H	W54-36*	10(4)	4+1(4)	5+1(4)	14+1(5)	15(5)	2(4)	4(4)	–	–	–	–
3	18/4	Sheffield	A	L40-50	6(4)	2(4)	8(4)	5+2(4)	15(6)	0(3)	4(4)	–	–	–	–
4	19/4	Sheffield	H	L44-46	5(4)	2(3)	15(5)	5+2(4)	13+1(5)	4(5)	0(0)	–	–	–	–
5	7/6	Coventry	H	D45-45	8(4)	4+2(4)	–	2(4)	13(5)	3+1(4)	–	–	6+3(4)	–	9(5)
6	28/6	Coventry	A	L31-59	3+1(5)	3+1(3)	–	–	9(6)	4+1(3)	1(3)	–	–	–	11+2(10)
7	30/7	Belle Vue	H	L35-55	13(6)	4+1(4)	–	2+1(4)	8(5)	–	2+1(4)	–	–	–	6(7)
8	15/9	Belle Vue	A	W46-44	6+1(4)	R/R	–	–	10(5)	–	7+3(5)	8+1(6)	–	11(6)	4+2(4)

DETAILS OF OTHER RIDERS:

Match No. 5: Andrew Moore 9(5); Match No. 6: Andrew Moore 6+1(6); Tony Atkin 5+1(4); Match No. 7: Jason Bunyan 5(4); Luke Priest 1(3); Match No. 8: Kevin Doolan 4+2(4).

BRITISH LEAGUE CUP AVERAGES

Rider	Mts	Rds	Pts	Bon	Tot	Avge	Max
Jan Staechmann	8	43	96	3	99	9.21	1 Full
Daniel Giffard	1	4	6	3	9	9.00	–
Robbie Kessler	4	18	37	2	39	8.67	1 Full
Scott Smith	1	6	11	0	11	7.33	–
Paul Pickering	8	36	60	2	62	6.89	–
Alan Mogridge	6	25	34	7	41	6.56	1 Paid
Adam Allott	2	9	10	2	12	5.33	–
Jon Armstrong	6	22	19	5	24	4.36	–
Joe Cook	7	24	18	4	22	3.67	–
Nick Simmons	6	22	15	2	17	3.09	–
Luke Priest	1	3	1	0	1	1.33	–
Guests	5	23	29	4	33	5.74	–

NOTE: Adam Allott's figures include one match as a guest.

KNOCK-OUT CUP

No	DATE	OPPONENTS	H/A	RESULT	KESSLER	ARMSTRONG	MOGRIDGE	STAECHMANN	SIMMONS	FINLOW	OTHERS
1	10/5	Newcastle	H	W51-44	9(4)	4+1(4)	8+3(4)	11+2(5)	3+1(4)	3+2(4)	13(5)
2	11/5	Newcastle	A	L40-50	7(4)	3(4)	6(4)	10(5)	3+1(5)	0(3)	11+1(5)

DETAILS OF OTHER RIDERS:

Match No. 1: Andrew Moore 13(5); Match No. 2: Scott Robson 11+1(5).

OTHER MEETINGS

16 March: Easy-Rider/Pirtek Cup (first-leg)

Sheffield 45 Stoke 45 (Jan Staechmann 11; Paul Pickering 9; Alan Mogridge 8+2; Robbie Kessler 8+1; Jon Armstrong 4+1; Nick Simmons 3+1; Joe Cook 2+2).

22 March: International Club Challenge

Stoke 47 (Jan Staechmann 12+1; Alan Mogridge 8; Robbie Kessler 7+1; Joe Cook 7+1; Jon Armstrong 5+2; Paul Pickering 4+1; Nick Simmons 4+1) Kaparna 43 (Andrew Moore 11+1; Joonas Kylmakorpi 11; Kim Jansson 7+3; Sebastian Bengtsson 7+1; Scott A. Smith 4+3; Jonas Davidsson 3; Norvy Brandin 0).

29 March: Easy-Rider/Pirtek Cup (second-leg)

Stoke 52 (Jan Staechmann 13+1; Paul Pickering 11+2; Robbie Kessler 9+2; Joe Cook 9+1; Alan Mogridge 8; Adam Allott 1+1; Nick Simmons 1) Sheffield 38 – Stoke won 97-83 on aggregate.

26 April: Premier League

Stoke 1 (Jon Armstrong 1; Paul Pickering 0; Robbie Kessler DNR; Alan Mogridge DNR; Jan Staechmann DNR; Nick Simmons DNR; Lee Hodgson DNR) Somerset 5 – meeting abandoned after heat one.

3 June: Youth International

Great Britain 48 (Chris Johnson 14; Jamie Westacott 9+1; Jamie Rodgers 7; Lee Smart 7; Jack Hargreaves 6+1; Shane Waldron 3+1; Adam Roynon 2+1) Germany 41 (Alexander Lieschke 13+1; Tobias Busch 11; Soenke Peterson 7; Richard Speiser 6; Frank Facher 4+1; Stefan Kurtz 0; Kevin Woelbert 0). Decided on aggregate race points, Great Britain won the series 90-88, with the first match at King's Lynn not counting, due to being abandoned after heat seven.

23 July: British League Cup

Belle Vue 13 Stoke 11 (Jason Bunyan 3; Joe Cook 2+2; Mark Lemon 2; Jan Staechmann 2; Luke Priest 2; Jon Armstrong 0; Paul Pickering 0) – meeting abandoned after heat four.

20 September: Premier League

Stoke 34 (Paul Pickering 9; Alan Mogridge 6; Rob Grant 6; Joe Cook 5; Scott Smith 4+4; Jan Staechmann 4+1; Jon Armstrong R/R) Isle Of Wight 26 – meeting abandoned after heat ten.

INDIVIDUAL MEETINGS

5 April: Loomer Road 30-Year Meeting

(Qualifying scores: Paul Pickering 11; Garry Stead 9; Jamie Smith 9; Robbie Kessler 9; Alan Mogridge 8; Tony Atkin 8; Jan Staechmann 6; Lee Complin 3; Joe Cook 2; Peter Carr 2; Jon Armstrong 2; Adam Allott 1; Nick Simmons 1) Final: 1st Pickering; 2nd Kessler; 3rd Stead; 4th Smith.

26 October: Pride of The Potteries

1st Mark Lemon 12; 2nd Carl Stonehewer (after run-off) 11; 3rd Ricky Ashworth 11; Jan Staechmann 10; Andy Smith 9; Paul Thorp 7; Adam Allott 7; Kristian Lund 6; Scott Smith 6; Alan Mogridge 5; James Wright 4; Rob Grant 4; Wayne Carter 3; Joe Cook 1; Luke Priest 0; Jon Armstrong 0; Jonathan Bethell (res) 0.

PEBLEY BEACH SWINDON ROBINS

NOTE: The information below relates only to the main Swindon team. For details of the second side, please refer to the Conference League section.

ADDRESS: Abbey Stadium, Blunsdon, nr. Swindon, Wiltshire.
PROMOTER: Peter Toogood.
TRACK LENGTH: 361.2 metres.
FIRST MEETING: 23 July 1949.
YEARS OF OPERATION: 1949 Open & National League Division Three; 1950-51 National League Division Three; 1952-53 Southern League; 1954-56 National League Division Two; 1957-64 National League; 1965-67 British League; 1968-74 British League Division One; 1975-90 British League; 1991-92 British League Division One; 1993-94 British League Division Two; 1995-96 British Premier League; 1997-98 British Elite League; 1999-03 British Premier League.

CLUB HONOURS

LEAGUE CHAMPIONS: 1956, 1957, 1967.
PAIRS CHAMPIONS: 1994.
KNOCK-OUT CUP WINNERS: 2000.
YOUNG SHIELD WINNERS: 2000.
FOUR-TEAM CHAMPIONS: 2003.

RIDER ROSTER 2003

ALLEN, Olly b. 27 May 1982, Norwich, Norfolk.
BRITISH CAREER: (1997) Peterborough (AL); (1998) Mildenhall, Norfolk, Peterborough, Arena-Essex; (1999-01) Swindon; (2002) Swindon, Peterborough; (2003) Swindon, Wolverhampton.
ALLEN, Tommy b. 4 September 1984, Norwich, Norfolk.
BRITISH CAREER: (2002) Swindon (CT & PL), Mildenhall (CL); (2003) Swindon (PL & CL).
BRANNEY, Craig b. 31 July 1982, Whitehaven, Cumbria.
BRITISH CAREER: (2000) Ashfield; (2001) Workington, Buxton, Isle of Wight, Newport (PL); (2002) Newcastle (CL), Hull; (2003) Newcastle (PL & CL), Armadale (CT), Workington, Swindon (PL), Hull, Somerset.

COMPTON, Benji   b. 17 September 1986, Tenerife, Spain.
BRITISH CAREER: (2002) Newcastle (CL); (2003) Sheffield (CL), Swindon (PL), Hull (BLC), Mildenhall (KOC), Exeter.

FRY, Paul   b. 25 October 1964, Ledbury, Hereford & Worcester.
BRITISH CAREER: (1984) Newcastle, Cradley Heath, Arena-Essex; (1986-87) Cradley Heath; (1988) Stoke; (1989-90) Long Eaton; (1991) King's Lynn; (1992-96) Exeter; (1997-98) Newport; (1999) Stoke; (2000-02) Swindon; (2003) Swindon, Peterborough.

GJEDDE, Charlie   b. 28 December 1979, Holstebro, Denmark.
BRITISH CAREER: (1998) Swindon; (1999) Coventry, Wolverhampton; (2001) Reading; (2002) Swindon; (2003) Swindon, Oxford.

HAWKINS, Ritchie   b. 9 November 1983, Peterborough, Cambridgeshire.
BRITISH CAREER: (2000) Sheffield (CL); (2001) Swindon, Sheffield (CL); (2002) Swindon (PL & CT); (2003) Swindon (PL & CL), Peterborough (BLC).

NEATH, Chris   b. 29 January 1982, Worcester, Hereford & Worcester
BRITISH CAREER: (1998-99) Newport (CL & PL); (2000-01) Newport (PL); (2002-03) Swindon, Wolverhampton.

NORTON, Danny   b. 27 August 1986, Hull, East Yorkshire.
BRITISH CAREER: (2001-02) Peterborough (CL); (2003) Peterborough (CL & BLC), Armadale (CT), Swindon (PL), Reading, Mildenhall (KOC & CT), Poole (BLC), Oxford (BLC).

PAGET, Simon   b. 24 March 1975, Swindon, Wiltshire.
BRITISH CAREER: (1996) Swindon (CL); (1997) M4 Raven Sprockets; (2000) Newport (CL), Swindon; (2003) Swindon (PL & CL).

SMITH, Jamie   b. 20 July 1983, Peterborough, Cambridgeshire.
BRITISH CAREER: (1998) Norfolk; (1999) Eastbourne, Glasgow; (2000) Newcastle, Peterborough (CL), Hull, Somerset; (2001) Hull, Somerset; (2002) Hull; (2003) Swindon.

PREMIER LEAGUE

(* Denotes bonus-point victory)

No	DATE	OPPONENTS	H/A	RESULT	GJEDDE	SMITH	FRY	NEATH	O. ALLEN	T. ALLEN	HAWKINS	OTHERS
1	14/4	Exeter	A	L41-49	13+1(6)	2(3)	8+2(5)	6(4)	9(6)	0(3)	3(3)	-
2	17/4	Trelawny	H	W48-42	12+1(5)	4+1(4)	6+1(4)	8+1(4)	12(5)	2+1(4)	4(4)	-
3	18/4	Somerset	A	W48-42	6+1(4)	5+1(4)	9+1(5)	7+1(4)	12(5)	1+1(3)	8+1(5)	-
4	7/5	King's Lynn	A	W46-44	11+1(6)	2+1(3)	5+2(4)	12+1(5)	14+1(6)	1(3)	1(3)	-
5	8/5	Berwick	H	W57-26	14(5)	8+2(5)	7+1(4)	12(4)	9(4)	1+1(4)	6+1(4)	-
6	21/5	Hull	A	L42-48	9+1(5)	4(4)	4+1(4)	6(4)	12+1(5)	3(3)	4+1(5)	-
7	29/5	Sheffield	A	L36-54	-	7(5)	7(6)	1+1(3)	15(6)	1+1(3)	3(4)	2+2(3)
8	31/5	Rye House	A	W45½-44½	10(5)	5(4)	3(4)	10½(4)	11+1(5)	2+1(4)	4(4)	-
9	1/6	Sheffield	H	W50-40	11+1(5)	3(4)	10+1(4)	5+1(4)	13(5)	2(3)	6+2(5)	-
10	5/6	Stoke	H	W55-35	-	5(4)	10+1(4)	7+2(4)	11+1(5)	3(4)	4+1(4)	15(5)
11	10/6	Trelawny	A	L42-48	5(4)	3+2(4)	11+1(6)	8+1(5)	10(5)	3(3)	2+2(3)	-
12	12/6	Glasgow	H	W49-41	5(4)	6(4)	9+1(5)	7+3(4)	14(5)	2+1(2)	6(6)	-
13	19/6	Newcastle	H	W50-42	-	8+1(4)	11(5)	7+2(4)	8(4)	0(4)	5(4)	11+1(5)
14	26/6	Arena-Essex	H	W49-41	-	6+2(4)	6(4)	7+1(4)	13(5)	3(4)	-	14+3(9)

SWINDON ROBINS: back row, left to right: Peter Oakes (Team Manager), Charlie Gjedde, Ritchie Hawkins, Jamie Smith, Simon Dyminski, Olly Allen, Peter Toogood (Promoter). On bike: Paul Fry. Front, kneeling: Chris Neath, Tommy Allen.

PREMIER LEAGUE continued

No	DATE	OPPONENTS	H/A	RESULT	GJEDDE	SMITH	FRY	NEATH	O. ALLEN	T. ALLEN	HAWKINS	OTHERS
15	3/7	Somerset	H	W60-30*	14+3(6)	0(2)	17+1(6)	R/R	12(4)	8+3(7)	9+1(5)	–
16	6/7	Stoke	A	L44-46*	12(5)	R/R	6(5)	8(5)	8(4)	3+1(5)	–	7+3(7)
17	11/7	Edinburgh	A	L42-48	17(6)	R/R	4(6)	8+2(6)	–	0(1)	4(6)	9+1(5)
18	12/7	Berwick	A	L43-47*	13+1(6)	R/R	6+1(5)	4(5)	–	–	2(5)	18+2(9)
19	13/7	Glasgow	A	L44-46*	15+1(6)	R/R	9+1(5)	5+2(5)	–	–	3+1(5)	12+1(9)
20	17/7	Exeter †	H	W48-36*	12(4)	R/R	12+1(5)	10+1(4)	10+1(4)	4(7)	0(0)	0(2)
21	24/7	Edinburgh	H	W51-39*	14+1(5)	R/R	11+1(5)	9(4)	10+1(5)	1(5)	–	6+1(6)
22	9/8	Workington	A	L43-47	–	7+1(4)	8+1(4)	9(5)	2(1)	2+1(5)	–	15+2(11)
23	10/8	Newcastle	A	L37-53	–	3(4)	4(4)	7+1(5)	12+1(6)	0(3)	–	11(8)
24	14/8	Workington	H	W52-37*	14(5)	6(4)	7+2(4)	6(4)	14+1(5)	0(1)	–	5+3(7)
25	21/8	Isle of Wight	H	L43-47	14(5)	10(4)	9+1(5)	5(4)	0(1)	3(5)	–	2+1(6)
26	24/8	Newport	A	W50-40	8+1(4)	6+1(4)	9+2(5)	8(4)	–	3(4)	–	16+2(9)
27	25/8	Reading	A	W48-42	12(5)	5+2(4)	8+1(4)	9+1(5)	–	2+1(4)	–	12+3(8)
28	28/8	Hull	H	W56-34*	14+1(5)	5+1(4)	9+2(4)	11+1(5)	–	1(4)	–	16(8)
29	4/9	Rye House	H	W49-41*	11+1(5)	4+1(4)	11+1(5)	11(4)	–	0(4)	3(4)	9+1(4)
30	18/9	King's Lynn	H	W52-37*	12+2(5)	2(3)	8+2(4)	12+1(5)	11(4)	6+1(5)	–	1+1(4)
31	25/9	Newport	H	D45-45*	10+2(5)	R/R	13+1(6)	7(4)	–	6+2(6)	–	9(9)
32	30/9	Isle of Wight	A	L40-50	13+2(6)	R/R	8(6)	8(4)	–	2+1(5)	–	9(9)
33	2/10	Reading	H	W51-39*	12(5)	R/R	5(4)	11(5)	–	5+1(6)	–	18+3(10)
34	3/10	Arena-Essex	A	L42-51	19(6)	R/R	2(4)	10+1(6)	–	0(4)	–	11+1(10)

† Meeting abandoned after fourteen heats, with the result standing.

NOTE: The home match against Berwick originally ended in a 57-33 victory on track, however, the points scored by Lee Smethills were subsequently deducted from the Bandits total, as his inclusion in their side was deemed ineligible.

DETAILS OF OTHER RIDERS:

Match No. 7: Benji Compton 2+2(3); Match No. 10: Chris Harris 15(5); Match No. 13: Chris Harris 11+1(5); Match No. 14: Garry Stead 9(5); Malcolm Holloway 5+3(4); Match No. 16: Malcolm Holloway 7+3(7); Match No. 17: Kevin Little 9+1(5); Match No. 18: Frede Schott 16+1(6); Craig Branney 2+1(3); Match No. 19: Frede Schott 12+1(6); Danny Norton 0(3); Match No. 20: Simon Paget 0(2); Match No. 21: Malcolm Holloway 6+1(6); Match No. 22: Brent Werner 12+1(5); Malcolm Holloway 3+1(6); Match No. 23: Leigh Lanham 9(5); Malcolm Holloway 2(3); Match No. 24: Malcolm Holloway 5+3(7); Match No. 25: Carl Wilkinson 2+1(6); Match No. 26: Mark Lemon 11(5); Malcolm Holloway 5+2(4); Match No. 27: Chris Harris 8+1(4); Malcolm Holloway 4+2(4); Match No. 28: Simon Stead 12(4); Daniel King 4(4); Match No. 29: Chris Harris 9+1(4); Match No. 30: Malcolm Holloway 1+1(4); Match No. 31: Simon Stead 6(3); Simon Cartwright 3(6); Match No. 32: Antonio Lindback 6(4); Adam Allott 3(5); Match No. 33: Chris Harris 12+3(5); Malcolm Holloway 6(5); Match No. 34: Chris Harris 8(6); Malcolm Holloway 3+1(4).

GOLDEN DOUBLE RIDES:

Match No. 34: Charlie Gjedde's total includes 6 points from a golden double ride.

PREMIER LEAGUE AVERAGES

	Mts	Rds	Pts	Bon	Tot	Avge	Max
Charlie Gjedde	28	143	329	21	350	9.79	1 full; 2 paid
Olly Allen	23	105	242	8	250	9.52	1 full; 1 paid
Chris Neath	33	146	261.5	24	285.5	7.82	1 full
Paul Fry	34	160	272	30	302	7.55	1 paid
Jamie Smith	24	93	116	16	132	5.68	–
Benji Compton	1	3	2	2	4	5.33	–
Ritchie Hawkins	19	79	77	10	87	4.41	–
Craig Branney	1	3	2	1	3	4.00	–
Tommy Allen	32	128	70	17	87	2.72	–
Danny Norton	1	3	0	0	0	0.00	–
Simon Paget	1	2	0	0	0	0.00	–
Guests	31	152	224	28	252	6.63	2 full; 1 paid

NOTE: Charlie Gjedde's totals include one golden double ride (6 points), modified to the normal score i.e. 3 points.

BRITISH LEAGUE CUP

(* Denotes bonus-point victory)

No	DATE	OPPONENTS	H/A	RESULT	GJEDDE	SMITH	FRY	NEATH	O. ALLEN	HAWKINS	T. ALLEN	OTHERS
1	3/4	Isle of Wight	H	D45-45	6(5)	7+1(4)	8+2(4)	8(4)	10(5)	4(4)	2(4)	–
2	10/4	Oxford	H	W48-37	12(5)	5+1(4)	8+2(5)	8(4)	7(4)	5+2(4)	3+2(4)	–
3	15/4	Isle of Wight	A	L41-49	11(6)	4+1(4)	4(4)	4(4)	14(6)	3(3)	1+1(3)	–
4	18/5	Eastbourne	A	L37-52	14(6)	5+4(4)	2+1(4)	6(4)	6(5)	2+2(3)	2(4)	–
5	23/6	Reading	A	D45-45	7(4)	5+2(4)	6+1(4)	11(5)	11(5)	–	4(4)	1(4)
6	27/6	Oxford	A	L40-50*	–	7(5)	3+2(4)	12+1(6)	2+2(3)	–	3(3)	13+3(9)
7	10/7	Reading	H	W52-38*	15(5)	R/R	11+3(6)	10+1(4)	6(2)	6(7)	4+1(6)	–
8	7/9	Eastbourne	H	W51-39	13+2(5)	R/R	6(5)	8(3)	–	2+1(5)	7(7)	15(5)

NOTE: The home match against Oxford originally ended in a 48-41 victory on track; however, the points scored by Lukasz Jankowski were subsequently deducted from the Oxford's total, as his inclusion in their side was deemed ineligible.

DETAILS OF OTHER RIDERS:

Match No. 5: Malcolm Holloway 1(4); Match No. 6: Nigel Sadler 10+2(6); Malcolm Holloway 3+1(3); Match No. 8: Simon Stead 15(5).

BRITISH LEAGUE CUP AVERAGES

Rider	Mts	Rds	Pts	Bon	Tot	Avge	Max
Charlie Gjedde	7	36	78	2	80	8.89	1 Full; 1 Paid
Chris Neath	8	34	67	2	69	8.12	–
Olly Allen	7	30	56	2	58	7.73	–
Jamie Smith	6	25	33	9	42	6.72	–
Paul Fry	8	36	48	11	59	6.56	–

Rider	Mts	Rds	Pts	Bon	Tot	Avge	Max
Ritchie Hawkins	6	26	22	5	27	4.15	–
Tommy Allen	8	35	26	4	30	3.43	–
Guests	4	18	29	3	32	7.11	1 Full

KNOCK-OUT CUP

No	DATE	OPPONENTS	H/A	RESULT	GJEDDE	SMITH	FRY	NEATH	O. ALLEN	T. ALLEN	HAWKINS	OTHERS
1	13/5	Isle of Wight	A	L38-54	–	3+2(4)	8(4)	4(4)	7(5)	1(3)	3(4)	12(6)
2	15/5	Isle of Wight	H	L49-51	18+1(6)	8(4)	10+1(5)	6+2(4)	6(4)	1(3)	0(4)	–

DETAILS OF OTHER RIDERS:

Match No. 1: Leigh Lanham 12(6).

GOLDEN DOUBLE/TACTICAL JOKER RIDES:

Match No. 1: Leigh Lanham's total includes 4 points from a tactical joker ride and 0 points from a golden double outing; Match No. 2: Charlie Gjedde's total includes 4 points from a tactical joker ride and 6 points from a golden double outing; Jamie Smith's total includes 6 points from a tactical joker ride; Paul Fry's total includes 4 points from a tactical joker ride.

OTHER MEETINGS

20 March: M4 Trophy (first-leg)

Swindon 45 (Charlie Gjedde 11; Olly Allen 10; Jamie Smith 7+2; Paul Fry 7; Ritchie Hawkins 6+1; Chris Neath 2+1; Tommy Allen 2) Newport 45.

23 March: M4 Trophy (second-leg)

Newport 50 Swindon 40 (Paul Fry 14; Charlie Gjedde 8+2; Chris Neath 5; Olly Allen 4; Ritchie Hawkins 4; Jamie Smith 3+1; Tommy Allen 2+1) – Newport won 95-85 on aggregate.

24 March: M4 Trophy (first-leg)

Reading 45 Swindon 45 (Charlie Gjedde 13+1; Paul Fry 9+1; Olly Allen 8; Chris Neath 6; Jamie Smith 5+1; Tommy Allen 4; Ritchie Hawkins 0).

27 March: M4 Trophy (second-leg)

Swindon 55 (Charlie Gjedde 15; Chris Neath 11+3; Olly Allen 11+1; Paul Fry 9+1; Jamie Smith 5; Ritchie Hawkins 3; Tommy Allen 1+1) Reading 35 – Swindon won 100-80 on aggregate.

M4 TROPHY TABLE

Team	Mts	Won	Drn	Lst	For	Agn	Pts	Bon	Tot
Swindon	4	1	2	1	185	175	4	1	5
Newport	4	1	2	1	184	176	4	1	5
Reading	4	1	2	1	171	189	4	1	5

NOTE: With all three sides finishing level on 5 points, it was decided to replay the competition, although in the event this never took place.

1 October: Three-Team Tournament

King's Lynn 48, Swindon 32 (Brett Woodifield 8+1; Nigel Sadler 8; Chris Harris 6; Malcolm Holloway 5+2; Simon Walker 3; Tommy Allen 2+2), Hull 28.

INDIVIDUAL MEETINGS

1 May: Championship of Great Britain semi-final

   1st Danny Bird 12; 2nd Paul Fry 12; 3rd Chris Neath 12; Leigh Lanham 11; Michael Coles 11; Glenn Cunningham 11; Chris Harris 9; James Grieves 8; Olly Allen 7; Ray Morton 7; Simon Stead 4; Mark Simmonds 4; Shaun Tacey 4; Roger Lobb 2; Seemond Stephens 2; Simon Dyminski (res) 2; Ritchie Hawkins (res) 1; André Compton 0.

31 July: Leigh Adams Testimonial

   (Qualifying scores: Jason Crump 15; Joe Screen 13; Leigh Adams 12; Olly Allen 11; Jason Lyons 10; Steve Johnston 9; Carl Stonehewer 8; Travis McGowan 8; Dean Barker 7; Antonio Lindback 7; Sam Ermolenko 5; Magnus Zetterstrom 5; Frank Smart 4; Craig Watson 3; Paul Fry 2; Malcolm Holloway (res) 1; Tomasz Lukaszewicz 0; Cameron Woodward 0) First Semi-Final: 1st Lyons; 2nd Adams; 3rd Crump; 4th Stonehewer; Second Semi-Final: 1st McGowan; 2nd Screen; 3rd Allen; 4th Johnston; Final: 1st Adams; 2nd Lyons; 3rd Screen; 4th McGowan.

TRELAWNY JAG TIGERS

NOTE: The information below relates only to the main Trelawny team. For details of the second side, please refer to the Conference League section.

ADDRESS: Clay Country Moto Parc, Longstone Pit, nr. Nanpean, St Austell, Cornwall.
PROMOTER: Ray Purvis

   NOTE: Original promoter Godfrey Spargo resigned in April 2003.

TRACK LENGTH: 230 metres.
FIRST MEETING: 10 April 2001.
YEARS OF OPERATION: 2001–03 British Premier League.

CLUB HONOURS

PREMIER TROPHY WINNERS: 2002.

RIDER ROSTER 2003

BROWN, Tom   b. 19 June 1984, Panteg, Pontypool, Wales.
   BRITISH CAREER: (2000) Peterborough (CL), Newport (CL); (2001) Newport (CL & PL), Isle of Wight, Exeter; (2002) Workington, Newport (CL), Swindon (CT & PL), Isle of Wight, Edinburgh, Trelawny; (2003) Trelawny (PL & CT), Newport (CL).

HARRIS, Chris   b. 28 November 1982, Truro, Cornwall.
   BRITISH CAREER: (1998) St Austell; (1999–00) Exeter; (2001) Trelawny; (2002–03) Trelawny, Peterborough.

HOLLOWAY, Malcolm   b. 22 December 1956, Stratton St Margaret, Wiltshire.
   BRITISH CAREER: (1977) Swindon, Oxford; (1978–79) Milton Keynes, Swindon; (1980–83) Swindon; (1984–88) Reading; (1989) Mildenhall, Reading; (1996) Swindon (CL);

TRELAWNY TIGERS: back row, left to right: Steve Masters, Emiliano Sanchez, Tom Brown, Matej Zagar, Simon Phillips, Pavel Ondrasik. Front, on bike: Chris Harris.

(2000) Somerset, Reading; (2001–02) Somerset, Swindon (CT), Mildenhall (CL); (2003) Swindon (CL), Trelawny (CT & PL), Coventry (BLC).

HOLMES, Jamie   *b. 19 November 1979, Exeter, Devon.*
BRITISH CAREER: (1999) Newport (CL); (2000) Newport (CL), Swindon , Stoke; (2001) Somerset; (2002) Newport (CL); (2003) Somerset (BLC), Trelawny (CT & BLC).

HORTON, James   *b. 22 June 1985, Slough, Berkshire.*
BRITISH CAREER: (2001–02) Peterborough (CL); (2003) Peterborough (CL & BLC), Boston (CT), Trelawny (PL & CT).

MASTERS, Steve   *b. 6 December 1970, Eastbourne, East Sussex.*
BRITISH CAREER: (1989–91) Eastbourne; (1992–93) Swindon; (1994) Swindon, Cradley Heath, Reading, Poole; (1995) Poole; (1996–97) Swindon; (1998) Swindon, Isle of Wight; (1999) Swindon; (2000) King's Lynn; (2001) Newport; (2002) Trelawny; (2003) Trelawny, Oxford.

ONDRASIK, Pavel   *b. 10 December 1975, Prague, Czech Republic.*
BRITISH CAREER: (2001–03) Trelawny.

PHILLIPS, Simon   *b. 22 March 1974, St Austell, Cornwall.*
BRITISH CAREER: (1997) St Austell; (1998) Newport (CL), St Austell, Norfolk, Exeter; (1999) Mildenhall, Rye House; (2000) Somerset, Isle of Wight; (2001) Isle of Wight, Somerset, Trelawny; (2002) Trelawny; (2003) Trelawny (PL & CT).

PRYNNE, Jason   *b. 27 April 1974, Truro, Cornwall.*
BRITISH CAREER: (1997–99) St Austell; (2000) St Austell, Exeter; (2001) Exeter; (2002) Wimbledon, Exeter, Trelawny; (2003) Wimbledon, Trelawny.

SANCHEZ, Emiliano   *b. 9 December 1977, Buenos Aires, Argentina.*
BRITISH CAREER: (1999–01) Glasgow; (2002–03) Trelawny.

WOLFF, Richard   *b. 12 June 1976, Prague, Czech Republic.*
BRITISH CAREER: (2001–03) Trelawny.

WOLTER, Mirko   *b. 6 September 1976, Teterow, Germany.*
BRITISH CAREER: (1996–97) Sheffield; (2003) Trelawny.

ZAGAR, Matej   *b. 3 April 1983, Ljubljana, Slovenia.*
BRITISH CAREER: (2003) Trelawny.

PREMIER LEAGUE

(* Denotes bonus-point victory)

No	DATE	OPPONENTS	H/A	RESULT	SANCHEZ	ONDRASIK	ZAGAR	MASTERS	HARRIS	PHILLIPS	BROWN	PRYNNE	WOLTER	HOLLOWAY	WOLFF	OTHERS
1	17/4	Swindon	A	L42-48	0(3)	3(4)	10+2(6)	9+2(5)	16(6)	2(3)	2+1(3)	–	–	–	–	–
2	22/4	King's Lynn	H	L44-46	5+2(4)	8(4)	10(5)	3+2(4)	12(5)	5(4)	1(4)	–	–	–	–	–
3	6/5	Arena-Essex	H	W55-35	4+2(4)	10(4)	12+2(5)	8+1(4)	15(5)	5(4)	1(4)	–	–	–	–	–
4	20/5	Rye House	H	W60½-29½	8(4)	14+1(5)	10+2(4)	9+2(4)	13½(5)	2+1(4)	–	4+1(4)	–	–	–	–
5	26/5	Exeter	A	L37-53	11(5)	R/R	–	0(3)	12+1(6)	2+1(6)	–	3+2(5)	–	–	–	9+1(5)
6	3/6	Berwick	H	W53-37	12+2(5)	–	14(5)	12+3(5)	8(4)	7(7)	–	R/R	–	–	–	0(4)
7	4/6	King's Lynn	A	L38-54	2(2)	–	6(4)	11+2(7)	15+1(6)	2(6)	–	R/R	–	–	–	2+1(5)
8	10/6	Swindon	H	W48-42*	9+1(4)	–	11+3(5)	5(4)	15(5)	4(5)	0(3)	4(4)	–	–	–	–
9	17/6	Hull	H	W53-37	12+1(5)	–	8+3(4)	10+1(4)	11(5)	1(1)	3+1(7)	–	8+3(4)	–	–	–
10	22/6	Glasgow	A	L44-46	7(4)	–	–	5+3(4)	11+1(5)	–	2(4)	–	3+1(4)	2+1(4)	–	14(5)

PREMIER LEAGUE continued

No	DATE	OPPONENTS	H/A	RESULT	SANCHEZ	ONDRASIK	ZAGAR	MASTERS	HARRIS	PHILLIPS	BROWN	PRYNNE	WOLTER	HOLLOWAY	WOLFF	OTHERS
11	1/7	Stoke	H	W55-34	12(5)	–	11(5)	9+1(4)	9+1(4)	–	3+2(4)	–	7+1(4)	4(4)	–	–
12	7/7	Rye House	A	L38-52*	3(5)	–	5+1(4)	13+2(6)	10(6)	–	0(3)	–	5(4)	2+1(3)	–	–
13	8/7	Edinburgh	H	L44-46	6(4)	6+1(4)	14+1(6)	5+3(4)	5(5)	–	3(3)	–	–	5(4)	–	–
14	15/7	Workington	H	W52-38	7+1(4)	6+3(4)	12+2(5)	11+1(5)	8(4)	–	2+1(4)	–	–	6+1(4)	–	–
15	20/7	Newcastle	A	L38-52	2(3)	2+2(4)	14(6)	9(5)	8+3(6)	–	2(3)	–	–	1(3)	–	–
16	22/7	Glasgow	H	W59-31*	6+1(4)	13+2(5)	11+1(4)	7(4)	14+1(5)	–	4(3)	–	–	4+2(5)	–	–
17	26/7	Workington	A	W46-44*	0(3)	11(5)	11(4)	7+3(4)	13(5)	–	2(4)	–	–	2(5)	–	–
18	29/7	Sheffield	H	W57-33	6+1(4)	10+2(4)	12(5)	9(4)	12(5)	–	4+2(4)	–	–	4(4)	–	–
19	1/8	Edinburgh	A	L44-49	2+1(4)	2+2(3)	18+1(6)	10(5)	11+1(6)	–	0(3)	–	–	1(3)	–	–
20	2/8	Berwick	A	L42-48*	0(4)	7(4)	15(6)	3+1(4)	15+2(6)	–	2(3)	–	–	0(3)	–	–
21	5/8	Reading	H	W51-39	9+1(5)	10+1(4)	R/R	12+2(6)	13+1(6)	–	1(4)	–	–	6(5)	–	–
22	19/8	Newcastle	H	W47-46	–	10+3(5)	5(4)	5+1(4)	19(6)	–	2+1(3)	–	–	5(6)	1(2)	–
23	27/8	Hull	A	W50-40*	–	4+2(5)	8(4)	16+1(6)	12(5)	–	3(5)	–	–	7+1(5)	R/R	–
24	2/9	Somerset	H	W52-38	–	7+1(4)	14(5)	8+3(4)	12+1(5)	–	1(4)	–	–	4(4)	6(4)	–
25	9/9	Exeter	H	W62-28*	–	15(5)	13+1(5)	2+1(4)	9+2(4)	–	8(4)	–	–	7+2(4)	8+2(4)	–
26	11/9	Sheffield	A	L34-55*	–	7(5)	13(6)	0(3)	–	–	1(3)	–	–	2(3)	0(4)	11+1(6)
27	15/9	Reading	A	W48-42*	–	7+2(4)	14(5)	5+1(4)	9+1(5)	–	2+1(4)	–	–	6+1(5)	5+1(4)	–
28	16/9	Isle of Wight	H	W48-42	–	9+1(5)	8+1(4)	8+1(4)	14(5)	–	1(4)	–	–	2(4)	6+1(4)	–
29	19/9	Somerset	A	L44-46*	–	12+1(5)	9+1(4)	2(4)	14+1(6)	–	2+1(4)	–	–	2(3)	3(4)	–
30	21/9	Newport	A	L42-48	–	8(4)	9(5)	3+2(4)	10(5)	–	3+2(4)	–	–	5(4)	4(4)	–
31	23/9	Isle of Wight	A	L40-53	–	6+1(5)	12(6)	4+1(4)	14(6)	–	1+1(3)	–	–	2(3)	1(3)	–
32	7/10	Newport	H	W47-43	–	8+1(5)	3(2)	8(4)	15(5)	–	0(5)	–	–	5+1(5)	8+1(4)	–
33	12/10	Stoke	A	W49-42*	–	5(4)	–	0(1)	13(5)	–	4+2(5)	–	–	9+1(6)	6+1(4)	12(5)
34	17/10	Arena-Essex	A	L36-54*	–	0(3)	–	10(5)	8+1(6)	–	0(3)	–	–	2(3)	3(4)	13(6)

DETAILS OF OTHER RIDERS:

Match No. 5: Frank Smart 9+1(5); Match No. 6: Jamie Holmes 0(4); Match No. 7: James Horton 2+1(5); Match No. 10: Frede Schott 14(5); Match No. 26: Simon Stead 11+1(6); Match No. 33: Charlie Gjedde 12(5); Match No. 34: Charlie Gjedde 13(6).

GOLDEN DOUBLE RIDES:

Match No. 7: Chris Harris' total includes 4 points from a golden double ride; Match No. 19: Matej Zagar's total includes 6 points from a golden double ride; Match No. 22: Chris Harris' total includes 6 points from a golden double ride; Match No. 31: Chris Harris' total includes 6 points from a golden double ride.

PREMIER LEAGUE AVERAGES

Rider	Mts	Rds	Pts	Bon	Tot	Avge	Max
Matej Zagar	29	139	309	21	330	9.50	2 Paid
Chris Harris	33	173	387½	18	405½	9.38	3 Full; 1 Paid
Pavel Ondrasik	26	113	200	26	226	8.00	1 Full; 3 Paid
Steve Masters	34	146	238	40	278	7.62	1 Paid
Emiliano Sanchez	21	85	123	13	136	6.40	–
Mirko Wolter	5	20	27	5	32	6.40	–

Rider	Mts	Rds	Pts	Bon	Tot	Avge	Max
Richard Wolff	12	45	51	6	57	5.07	–
Jason Prynne	2	9	7	3	10	4.44	–
Malcolm Holloway	25	102	95	11	106	4.16	–
Simon Phillips	9	40	30	2	32	3.20	–
Tom Brown	30	114	60	15	75	2.63	–
James Horton	1	5	2	1	3	2.40	–
Jamie Holmes	1	4	0	0	0	0.00	–
Guests	5	27	59	2	61	9.04	–

NOTE: Chris Harris' figures include three golden double rides (16 points), modified to normal score i.e. 8 points; Matej Zagar's figures include one golden double ride (6 points), modified to normal score i.e. 3 points.

BRITISH LEAGUE CUP

(* Denotes bonus-point victory)

No	DATE	OPPONENTS	H/A	RESULT	SANCHEZ	ONDRASIK	ZAGAR	MASTERS	HARRIS	PHILLIPS	BROWN	WOLTER	HOLLOWAY	WOLFF	OTHERS
1	24/3	Exeter	A	L39-54	2(4)	9+2(5)	9+1(6)	0(3)	17(6)	2(3)	0(3)	–	–	–	–
2	25/3	Exeter	H	W63-27*	8+1(4)	8(4)	13+2(5)	13+2(5)	12(4)	7+2(4)	2+1(4)	–	–	–	–
3	1/4	Newport	H	D45-45	2+2(4)	10(5)	6(4)	5+1(4)	14(5)	5(4)	3+1(4)	–	–	–	–
4	4/4	Somerset	A	W49-42	5+1(4)	12(5)	8(4)	6+1(4)	12(5)	5(4)	1(4)	–	–	–	–
5	8/4	Wolverhampton	H	W48-42	3(4)	8(4)	13(5)	5+1(4)	14(5)	4+1(5)	1(4)	–	–	–	–
6	13/4	Newport	A	L44-46	9+2(6)	6+2(4)	–	3+1(4)	15(5)	DNR	5(6)	–	–	–	6+1(4)
7	15/4	Poole	H	L40-51	4+1(4)	6+2(4)	9(6)	4+1(4)	11+1(6)	–	2+1(3)	–	–	–	4+1(3)
8	23/4	Poole	A	L38-52	4+1(5)	8+1(5)	4+1(4)	6(4)	11(6)	2+1(3)	3(3)	–	–	–	–
9	27/5	Somerset	H	W59-31*	12(4)	–	14+1(5)	8+2(4)	10(4)	5+1(5)	–	5(4)	–	–	5(4)
10	8/9	Wolverhampton	A	L27-60	–	.5(4)	7(6)	5+1(4)	8+1(6)	–	0(3)	–	2(4)	0(3)	–

DETAILS OF OTHER RIDERS:

Match No. 6: Brent Werner 6+1(4); Match No. 7: Jason Prynne 4+1(3); Match No. 9: Jamie Holmes 5(4).

GOLDEN DOUBLE RIDES:

Match No. 2: Chris Harris' total includes 6 points from a golden double ride; Match No. 7: Chris Harris' total includes 4 points from a golden double ride.

BRITISH LEAGUE CUP AVERAGES

Rider	Mts	Rds	Pts	Bon	Tot	Avge	Max
Chris Harris	10	52	119	2	121	9.31	2 Full
Pavel Ondrasik	9	40	72	7	79	7.90	–
Matej Zagar	9	45	83	5	88	7.82	2 Paid
Jason Prynne	1	3	4	1	5	6.67	–
Steve Masters	10	40	55	10	65	6.50	1 Paid
Emiliano Sanchez	9	39	49	8	57	5.85	1 Full
Jamie Holmes	1	4	5	0	5	5.00	–

Rider	Mts	Rds	Pts	Bon	Tot	Avge	Max
Simon Phillips	7	28	30	5	35	5.00	–
Mirko Wolter	1	4	5	0	5	5.00	–
Tom Brown	9	34	17	3	20	2.35	–
Malcolm Holloway	1	4	2	0	2	2.00	–
Richard Wolff	1	3	0	0	0	0.00	–
Guest	1	4	6	1	7	7.00	–

NOTE: Chris Harris' figures include two golden double rides (10 points), modified to normal score i.e. 5 points.

KNOCK-OUT CUP

(* Denotes aggregate victory)

No	DATE	OPPONENTS	H/A	RESULT	SANCHEZ	ONDRASIK	ZAGAR	MASTERS	HARRIS	PHILLIPS	BROWN	WOLTER	HOLLOWAY	WOLFF	OTHERS
1	5/5	Reading	A	L45-51	2+1(4)	6(4)	8+1(4)	9+1(5)	14(5)	5(5)	1(3)	–	–	–	–
2	13/5	Reading	H	W65-30*	8+1(4)	14+1(5)	10(4)	10+3(5)	12(4)	6+1(4)	5+1(4)	–	–	–	–
3	21/6	Berwick	A	L42-55	8(5)	–	–	8(4)	20(6)	–	2(4)	1+1(3)	2+1(4)	–	1+1(4)
4	24/6	Berwick	H	W61-34*	11(4)	–	14+1(5)	9+1(4)	11+1(5)	–	3(4)	8+3(4)	5(4)	–	–
5	12/8	Isle of Wight	H	W49-43	–	9(4)	13(5)	8+4(5)	6(4)	–	3+1(4)	–	6+2(4)	4+1(4)	–
6	26/8	Isle of Wight	A	L45-54	–	10(5)	13(5)	5+1(5)	15(6)	–	0(4)	–	2(5)	R/R	–

DETAILS OF OTHER RIDERS:

Match No. 3: Les Collins 1+1(4).

GOLDEN DOUBLE/TACTICAL JOKER RIDES:

Match No. 1: Matej Zagar's total includes 6 points from a tactical joker ride; Chris Harris' total includes 6 points from a tactical joker ride; Match No. 3: Chris Harris' total includes 6 points from a tactical joker ride and 2 points from a golden double outing; Steve Masters' total includes 4 points from a tactical joker ride; Emiliano Sanchez's total includes 2 points from a tactical joker ride; Match No. 6: Chris Harris' total includes 6 points from a tactical joker ride and 2 points from a golden double outing; Matej Zagar's total includes 6 points from a tactical joker ride; Pavel Ondrasik's total includes 4 points from a tactical joker ride.

WORKINGTON J. EDGAR & SON COMETS

ADDRESS: Derwent Park Stadium, Workington, Cumbria.
PROMOTERS: Tony Mole & Ian Thomas.
TRACK LENGTH: 364 metres.
FIRST MEETING: 3 April 1970.
YEARS OF OPERATION: 1970–74 British League Division Two; 1975–81 National League; 1985 Open; 1987 National League; 1994 Demonstration; 1999–03 British Premier League (NOTE: In 1987, the track was occupied by 'Glasgow Tigers', who later became known as 'Workington Tigers').

CLUB HONOURS

PAIRS CHAMPIONS: 1999, 2000, 2001, 2003.
FOUR-TEAM CHAMPIONS: 2001.

RIDER ROSTER 2003

BRANNEY, Craig   b. 31 July 1982, Whitehaven, Cumbria.
  BRITISH CAREER: (2000) Ashfield; (2001) Workington, Buxton, Isle of Wight, Newport
  (PL); (2002) Newcastle (CL), Hull; (2003) Newcastle (PL & CL), Armadale (CT),
  Workington, Swindon (PL), Hull, Somerset.
COLLINS, Aidan   b. 21 April 1982, Stockport, Greater Manchester.
  BRITISH CAREER: (1998) Newport (CL); (1999) Buxton, Edinburgh; (2000) Glasgow,
  Ashfield; (2001) Glasgow; (2002) Buxton, Swindon, Edinburgh; (2003) Workington.
COLLINS, Chris   b. 18 July 1982, Manchester.
  BRITISH CAREER: (2001) Buxton, Newcastle, Stoke; (2002) Buxton, Newport (PL),
  Workington; (2003) Workington, Buxton.
HALL, Richard   b. 23 August 1984, Northallerton, North Yorkshire.
  BRITISH CAREER: (2001) Newcastle; (2002) Newcastle (PL & CL), Trelawny, Glasgow;
  (2003) Sheffield (CL & PL), Stoke (PL), Coventry (BLC), Hull (BLC), Newport (PL),
  Boston (KOC & CT), Exeter, Reading, Workington, Somerset.
HARRISON, Rusty   b. 11 October 1981, Adelaide, South Australia, Australia.
  BRITISH CAREER: (2000) Glasgow; (2001-03) Workington.
HODGSON, Lee   b. 19 February 1985, Preston, Lancashire.
  BRITISH CAREER: (2000) Sheffield (CL); (2001) Sheffield (PL & CL), Arena-Essex,
  Swindon; (2002) Stoke, Workington, Mildenhall; (2003) Mildenhall, Somerset, Workington.
JAMES, Scott   b. 25 May 1984, Adelaide, South Australia.
  BRITISH CAREER: (2002) Workington, Mildenhall; (2003) Mildenhall, Workington,
  Somerset (KOC), Coventry (BLC).
KARLSSON, Peter I.   b. 12 July 1976, Saffle, Sweden.
  BRITISH CAREER: (1999-03) Workington.
NIEMINEN, Kauko   b. 29 August 1979, Seinajoki, Finland.
  BRITISH CAREER: (2002-03) Workington.
PRIEST, Luke   b. 18 June 1985, Birmingham, West Midlands.
  BRITISH CAREER: (2000) Ashfield, Owlerton; (2001) Sheffield (CL), Boston; (2002)
  Sheffield (CL), Wolverhampton (CT); (2003) Sheffield (CL & PL), Stoke (CT & PL),
  Workington, Exeter, Newport (BLC), Arena-Essex, Wolverhampton (BLC), Belle Vue
  (BLC).
SCOTT, Blair   b. 14 May 1980, Edinburgh, Scotland.
  BRITISH CAREER: (1996) Linlithgow, Scottish Monarchs; (1997) Edinburgh, Lathallan;
  (1998-01) Edinburgh; (2002) Edinburgh, Belle Vue, Workington; (2003) Workington.
SIMMONS, Nick   b. 24 July 1981, Leamington Spa, Warwickshire.
  BRITISH CAREER: (1997) Shuttle Cubs, Ryde; (1998) Newport (CL & PL), Isle of
  Wight, Exeter; (1999) Isle of Wight, Stoke, Newport (CL); (2000) Arena-Essex; (2001)
  Newport (PL & CL), Somerset; (2002) Isle of Wight; (2003) Stoke, Reading, Mildenhall,
  Workington, King's Lynn, Exeter.

WORKINGTON COMETS: back row, left to right: Kauko Nieminen, Simon Stead, Peter I. Karlsson, Rusty Harrison. On bike: Carl Stonehewer. Front, kneeling: Blair Scott, Aidan Collins.

STEAD, Simon   *b. 25 April 1982, Sheffield, South Yorkshire.*
BRITISH CAREER: (1997) Peterborough (AL); (1998) Peterborough (PL), Buxton; (1999–01) Sheffield; (2002) Sheffield, Peterborough; (2003) Workington, Wolverhampton.

STONEHEWER, Carl   *b. 16 May 1972, Manchester.*
BRITISH CAREER: (1988–89) Belle Vue; (1990) Wolverhampton; (1991–93) Belle Vue; (1994) Peterborough; (1995–96) Long Eaton; (1997) Long Eaton, King's Lynn, Peterborough, Coventry, Eastbourne; (1998) Sheffield; (1999–02) Workington; (2003) Workington, Belle Vue.

WRIGHT, James   *b. 13 June 1986, Stockport, Greater Manchester.*
BRITISH CAREER: (2002) Buxton; (2003) Buxton, Belle Vue (BLC), Newcastle (PL), Stoke (PL), Workington, Hull, King's Lynn.

PREMIER LEAGUE

(* Denotes bonus-point victory)

No	DATE	OPPONENTS	H/A	RESULT	STONEHEWER	NIEMINEN	STEAD	A. COLLINS	HARRISON	C. COLLINS	SCOTT	KARLSSON	JAMES	OTHERS
1	12/4	Sheffield	H	W45-44	14+2(6)	4+1(4)	15(6)	3+2(3)	–	1(3)	6(5)	–	–	2+1(3)
2	26/4	Newcastle	H	W49-40	13+1(5)	8+1(4)	10(4)	4+1(4)	–	4+1(4)	1+1(4)	–	–	9+1(5)
3	27/4	Newcastle	A	W46-44*	8(4)	3+2(4)	9+1(5)	6(4)	–	4+1(4)	3+3(4)	–	–	13(5)
4	4/5	Newport	A	L41-49	15(6)	3(4)	–	2+1(3)	8(6)	5+1(4)	4+3(4)	–	–	4(3)
5	5/5	Rye House	A	L40-50	14(6)	4+3(6)	–	3(3)	6(5)	1(3)	8(4)	–	–	4(3)
6	10/5	Edinburgh	H	W46-44	14(5)	4+2(4)	–	5(4)	4+1(4)	2(3)	8(5)	9+1(5)	–	–
7	24/5	Berwick	A	L39-51	17(6)	0(3)	13(6)	2(4)	5+1(5)	0(3)	2(3)	–	–	–
8	26/5	Berwick	H	W46-44	14(5)	6+1(4)	10(5)	2(4)	8+1(4)	1+1(3)	5+1(5)	–	–	–
9	31/5	Hull	H	W50-40	12(5)	5(4)	10+1(5)	6+1(4)	7(4)	2(3)	8+2(5)	–	–	–
10	5/6	Sheffield	A	L40-49	11(5)	1+1(3)	9(5)	1(4)	7+2(4)	3+2(3)	8+1(6)	–	–	–
11	11/6	Hull	A	W46-44*	14+1(5)	3(4)	14(5)	0(3)	4+1(4)	1(3)	10(6)	–	–	–
12	20/6	Arena-Essex	A	L38-52	15+1(6)	2(5)	12(6)	1+1(3)	3(4)	2+1(3)	3+1(3)	–	–	–
13	28/6	Exeter	H	W50-39	11+3(5)	R/R	8(4)	9(7)	15(5)	3+1(4)	4(5)	–	–	–
14	30/6	Reading	A	L43-47	11+1(6)	0(3)	10+1(5)	4(3)	13+1(6)	–	5(4)	–	0(3)	–
15	1/7	Isle of Wight	A	L35-55	12(6)	1(3)	10(6)	5+1(4)	5+1(5)	–	0(3)	–	–	2(3)
16	6/7	Rye House	H	W54-36*	12+2(5)	9+1(4)	13+1(5)	7+3(6)	9(4)	–	4+1(3)	–	–	0(3)
17	12/7	Glasgow	H	W56-34	15(5)	5(4)	13+1(5)	8(5)	9(4)	–	2+1(4)	–	–	4+2(3)
18	14/7	Exeter	A	L30-59	11(6)	0(3)	9(6)	2+1(4)	7+1(5)	–	0(3)	–	–	1(3)
19	15/7	Trelawny	A	L38-52	15(6)	0(3)	13(6)	4+1(4)	4(5)	–	1+1(3)	–	–	1+1(3)
20	18/7	Edinburgh	A	L42-48	15(6)	1(3)	11+2(6)	4+2(4)	8+1(5)	–	3+1(4)	–	–	0(3)
21	20/7	Glasgow †	A	W38-34*	9(3)	4(4)	12(4)	2(5)	9(3)	–	0(2)	–	–	2(3)
22	26/7	Trelawny	H	L44-46	11(5)	5+2(4)	10+1(5)	11+2(6)	4+1(4)	–	2+1(4)	–	–	1(2)
23	2/8	Isle of Wight	H	W50-43	12+1(5)	7+3(5)	20(6)	4(4)	7+1(4)	–	0(3)	–	–	0(3)
24	9/8	Swindon	H	W47-43	9+1(5)	12+2(7)	14(5)	3(3)	4+2(4)	–	5+1(4)	–	–	0(3)
25	14/8	Swindon	A	L37-52	8+1(6)	7+2(4)	12(5)	0(3)	9(6)	–	0(3)	–	–	1(3)
26	15/8	Somerset	A	D46-46	13(5)	8+2(5)	13+2(6)	2+1(4)	6(4)	–	1(3)	–	–	3+1(3)
27	16/8	King's Lynn	H	W53-37	14(5)	10+3(5)	12(4)	4+1(4)	9(5)	–	4(4)	–	–	0(3)
28	23/8	Stoke	A	D45-45	9(5)	12+3(6)	11(5)	2(3)	4+1(4)	–	4(4)	–	–	3(3)
29	25/8	Stoke	H	W54-35*	9(4)	10(5)	14(5)	5+3(4)	6(4)	–	4+2(4)	–	–	6+2(4)

PREMIER LEAGUE continued

No	DATE	OPPONENTS	H/A	RESULT	STONEHEWER	NIEMINEN	STEAD	A. COLLINS	HARRISON	C. COLLINS	SCOTT	KARLSSON	JAMES	OTHERS
30	27/8	King's Lynn	A	L32-58	0(3)	9(7)	14(6)	2+1(3)	2+1(4)	–	4(4)	–	–	1+1(3)
31	30/8	Newport	H	W59-31*	13(5)	8(4)	15(5)	6+3(4)	10+2(4)	3+1(4)	4(4)	–	–	–
32	6/9	Somerset	H	W60-30*	10+2(4)	8+2(4)	15(5)	6(4)	14+1(5)	4(4)	3+1(4)	–	–	–
33	13/9	Arena-Essex	H	W56-34*	14+1(5)	6+1(4)	15(5)	4(4)	9(4)	2(3)	6+2(5)	–	–	–
34	4/10	Reading	H	W56-34*	12+2(5)	9+2(4)	–	10+1(4)	6(4)	2(4)	8+2(4)	9+1(5)	–	–

† Meeting abandoned after twelve heats, with the result standing.

DETAILS OF OTHER RIDERS:

Match No. 1: Kevin Little 2+1(3); Match No. 2: Andrew Appleton 9+1(5); Match No. 3: Andrew Moore 13(5); Match No. 4: Danny Bird 4(3); Match No. 5: Andrew Moore 4(3); Match No. 15: Tony Dart 2(3); Match No. 16: Craig Branney 0(3); Match No. 17: Lee Hodgson 4+2(3); Match No. 18: Tony Dart 1(3); Match No. 19: Tony Dart 1+1(3); Match No. 20: Nick Simmons 0(3); Match No. 21: Carl Shield 2(3); Match No. 22: Mark Thompson 1(2); Match No. 23: James Wright 0(3); Match No. 24: Lee Hodgson 0(3); Match No. 25: Luke Priest 1(3); Match No. 26: Nick Simmons 3+1(3); Match No. 27: Lee Hodgson 0(3); Match No. 28: James Wright 3(3); Match No. 29: Richard Hall 6+2(4); Match No. 30: Richard Hall 1+1(3).

GOLDEN DOUBLE RIDES:

Match No. 23: Simon Stead's total includes 6 points from a golden double ride.

PREMIER LEAGUE AVERAGES

Rider	Mts	Rds	Pts	Bon	Tot	Avge	Max
Carl Stonehewer	34	174	406	19	425	9.77	1 Full; 3 Paid
Simon Stead	30	156	363	10	373	9.56	5 Full
Peter I. Karlsson	2	10	18	2	20	8.00	–
Rusty Harrison	31	138	221	19	240	6.96	1 Full; 2 Paid
Kauko Nieminen	33	140	174	34	208	5.94	–
Richard Hall	2	7	7	3	10	5.71	–
Aidan Collins	34	135	139	26	165	4.89	–
Blair Scott	34	135	130	25	155	4.59	–
Chris Collins	17	58	40	9	49	3.38	–
Lee Hodgson	3	9	4	2	6	2.67	–
Carl Shield	1	3	2	0	2	2.67	–
Nick Simmons	2	6	3	1	4	2.67	–
Tony Dart	3	9	4	1	5	2.22	–
Mark Thompson	1	2	1	0	1	2.00	–
James Wright	2	6	3	0	3	2.00	–
Luke Priest	1	3	1	0	1	1.33	–
Craig Branney	1	3	0	0	0	0.00	–
Scott James	1	3	0	0	0	0.00	–
Guests	5	19	32	2	34	7.16	–

NOTE: Simon Stead's figures include one golden double ride (6 points), modified to normal score i.e. 3 points.

BRITISH LEAGUE CUP

(* Denotes bonus-point victory)

No	DATE	OPPONENTS	H/A	RESULT	STONEHEWER	NIEMINEN	STEAD	A. COLLINS	HARRISON	C. COLLINS	SCOTT	JAMES	OTHERS
1	15/3	Newcastle	H	W50-40	13(5)	0(3)	10(4)	3+1(4)	12+1(5)	2(3)	10(6)	–	–
2	16/3	Newcastle	A	L43-46*	11(5)	0(3)	10(4)	2+1(4)	10(5)	1(3)	9+1(6)	–	–
3	29/3	Edinburgh	H	D45-45	8(5)	8(4)	12+1(5)	0(3)	7+1(4)	6+2(5)	4(4)	–	–
4	30/3	Glasgow	A	W53-37	14(5)	2(3)	12(4)	4(4)	9+2(5)	–	10(6)	2+1(3)	–
5	5/4	Glasgow	H	W55-35*	12+1(5)	7+3(4)	11(5)	5+2(4)	10(4)	3+1(4)	7(4)	–	–
6	11/4	Edinburgh	A	L39-53	15(6)	1(3)	7(5)	6+1(5)	–	2(3)	4+1(4)	–	4(4)
7	18/4	Berwick	H	W50-40	14+1(5)	6(4)	11(5)	4+2(4)	–	2+1(4)	5(4)	–	8(4)
8	19/4	Berwick	A	W48-42*	14(5)	1+1(3)	14+1(5)	1(3)	–	0(3)	11+2(7)	–	7(4)
9	27/9	Poole	H	L40-50	10(5)	R/R	–	4+2(5)	10+1(6)	4+1(5)	4+1(5)	–	8(4)
10	8/10	Poole	A	L33-57	9(6)	5(4)	–	1+1(3)	3+1(4)	0(3)	4(4)	–	11+1(6)

DETAILS OF OTHER RIDERS:

Match No. 6: Shaun Tacey 4(4); Match No. 7: Pavel Ondrasik 8(4); Match No. 8: Pavel Ondrasik 7(4); Match No. 9: Frank Smart 8(4); Match No. 10: Chris Harris 11+1(6).

GOLDEN DOUBLE RIDES:

Match No. 6: Carl Stonehewer's total includes 4 points from a golden double ride.

BRITISH LEAGUE CUP AVERAGES

Rider	Mts	Rds	Pts	Bon	Tot	Avge	Max
Simon Stead	8	37	87	2	89	9.62	1 Full; 1 Paid
Carl Stonehewer	10	52	118	2	120	9.23	1 Paid
Rusty Harrison	7	33	61	6	67	8.12	–
Blair Scott	10	50	68	5	73	5.84	–
Kauko Nieminen	9	31	30	4	34	4.39	–
Aidan Collins	10	39	30	10	40	4.10	–
Scott James	1	3	2	1	3	4.00	–
Chris Collins	9	33	20	5	25	3.03	–
Guests	5	22	38	1	39	7.09	–

NOTE: Carl Stonehewer's figures include one golden double ride (4 points), modified to normal score i.e. 2 points.

KNOCK-OUT CUP

No	DATE	OPPONENTS	H/A	RESULT	STONEHEWER	NIEMINEN	STEAD	A. COLLINS	HARRISON	JAMES	C. COLLINS	SCOTT	OTHERS
1	22/3	King's Lynn	H	W46-43	12+1(5)	7+1(4)	6+1(4)	6(4)	10+1(5)	1(3)	4+1(5)	–	–
2	9/4	King's Lynn	A	L43-52	16(5)	3+2(4)	10+1(5)	4+1(4)	–	–	3+2(4)	1(4)	6(4)

DETAILS OF OTHER RIDERS:

Match No. 2: Michal Makovsky 6(4).

GOLDEN DOUBLE/TACTICAL JOKER RIDES:

Match No. 2: Carl Stonehewer's total includes 6 points from a tactical joker ride; Simon Stead's total includes 4 points from a tactical joker ride.

OTHER MEETINGS

21 May: Inter-League Challenge
Poole 56 Workington 37 (Carl Stonehewer 14; Simon Stead 10; Peter I. Karlsson 6+1; Kauko Nieminen 4+3; Aidan Collins 2; Blair Scott 1+1; Rusty Harrison 0).
7 June: Inter-League Challenge
Workington 46 (Rusty Harrison 11+2; Simon Stead 9; Peter I. Karlsson 8; Carl Stonehewer 7; Kauko Nieminen 5+1; Blair Scott 4; Chris Collins 2) Poole 44.

INDIVIDUAL MEETING

21 June: Cumberland Open Championship
(Qualifying scores: Rusty Harrison 12; Frede Schott 11; Carl Stonehewer 9; Andrew Moore 8; Kauko Nieminen 6; George Stancl 6; Garry Stead 5; Aidan Collins 5; Rory Schlein 4; Kevin Doolan 3; Blair Scott 2; Chris Collins 1; Karl Langley (res) 0) First Semi-Final: 1st Nieminen; 2nd Harrison; 3rd Moore; 4th A. Collins; Second Semi-Final: 1st Stonehewer; 2nd Schott; 3rd Stead; 4th Stancl; Final: 1st Stonehewer; 2nd Schott; 3rd Harrison; 4th Nieminen.

CONFERENCE LEAGUE 2003

RACING DIARY OF THE SEASON

MARCH

15 In Suffolk, Mildenhall swing into action with a Conference Trophy fixture against Wimbledon, and in a hard-fought match, it's the Fen Tigers who take victory by 48 points to 42, with Scott James racing to a superb 13+1 points.

23 Carmarthen begin their second season of activity in the sunshine, but it's a 45-43 league victory for visiting Wolverhampton, with the returning Graham Jones heading the Wolf Cubs' scoring on a massive 17 points. Mildenhall host the first-leg of a Three-Team Tournament, and coast to victory with a 52-point total against Boston (29) and Peterborough (26).

26 Wimbledon open up with an individual meeting for the Ronnie Moore Cup, and Boston's Darren Mallett sprints to a super 15-point maximum to take victory from the home pair of Wayne Barrett (13) and Chris Schramm (12).

28 Boston run the second-leg of the Three-Team Tournament against East Anglian rivals Mildenhall and Peterborough, with the Fen Tigers taking command of the contest courtesy of a 42-point tally, with the Barracuda-Braves scoring 36, and the Pumas 29.

30 Newport start their league campaign with a 52-37 success over Wimbledon, their main contributors being maximum men Scott Pegler (14+1) and Carl Wilkinson (12). The British Under-21 Championship qualifier is run on Grand Prix lines at Mildenhall, with Jason King victorious in the final as brother Daniel occupies third spot. Ben Wilson provides the sandwich filling in the runner-up position, with Chris Mills at the back in fourth place.

APRIL

2 In a tension-packed league meeting, Wimbledon scrape home 46-44 against a dogged Oxford septet.

4 Boston charge to a 55-35 success over Wimbledon in the Knock-Out Cup, led by a fabulous 16+3 points from seven starts from flying reserve Darren Mallett.

5 Mildenhall secure overall Three-Team Tournament victory, as they finish level on 42 points with home side Peterborough, while Boston score 24, giving an aggregate result of Mildenhall 136, Peterborough 97, Boston 89.

6 Buxton begin their tenth season of racing with a comfortable 52-37 Conference Trophy victory over Boston. Carmarthen suffer their second successive home league defeat at the hands of Swindon, going down 49-41 in an exciting clash, with Malcolm Holloway using all his experience to register a five-ride full house for the victorious Sprockets. Despite the efforts of Scott Pegler (16+1) and Tom Brown (11+1), Newport cannot stop Mildenhall from winning 47-43 in a league fixture at Queensway Meadows. Peterborough stage their second home meeting in two days, and manage to overcome Oxford 49-40 in a league fixture.

9 Spearheaded by a five-ride maximum from Daniel Giffard, plus 14+2 from Wayne Barrett and 13+1 from Gavin Hedge, Wimbledon cruise to a 55-35 league victory over Sheffield.

13 In the Conference Trophy, Mildenhall easily beat Buxton 59-31, with Scott James thundering to a paid maximum (14+1). A tight tussle at the East of England Showground eventually results in a 48-42 victory for Peterborough over Sheffield in the Conference League. Stoke Spitfires spring into Conference Trophy action, defeating Carmarthen 47-43 in a tight tussle, thanks largely to a 15-point maximum from Joe Cook.

14 Sheffield swamp Newport 63-27 in a one-sided league fixture, with both Richard Hall (14+1) and Ben Wilson (12) hitting maximums.

16 Overcoming a 20-point first-leg deficit, Wimbledon defeat Boston 55-35 in the Knock-Out Cup, thereby forcing a 90-90 draw on aggregate and necessitating a replay.

18 Boston quickly return to winning ways, with a comfortable 59-31 success over Carmarthen in their opening league match, the main scorer for the Barracuda-Braves being maximum-man Darren Mallett (13+2).

20 Despite lending the opposition two riders, Buxton still ease to a 56-34 win over Oxford, led by heavy scoring from James Wright (14) and paid full house man Chris Collins (13+2). Carmarthen suffer another home reverse, going down 50-41 at the hands of Mildenhall in the league. Despite being behind all through the first half of their Conference League match, Peterborough recover well to win 48-42 against Wimbledon, aided no end by an 18-point haul from Danny Norton, and 15+1 from Shane McCabe. The final league match of the day sees both Craig Branney (14+1) and Jamie Robertson (11+1) hit paid maximums, as Newcastle race to a 57-32 success over Newport, with William Lawson (14) also making a telling contribution.

21 Rye House begin their league campaign with a 51-40 victory over Mildenhall at Hoddesdon, with Edward Kennett scorching to a five-ride maximum, while Aussie Joel Parsons weighs in with 16+2 from seven starts.

22 Rare Tuesday-night action at Swindon sees the Sprockets defeat Sheffield 50-39 in an entertaining Conference League encounter, led handsomely by a full 15-pointer from Ritchie Hawkins. Trelawny Pitbulls start their Conference Trophy programme with a sound home defeat, going down 53-37 at the hands of Boston. Wolverhampton inflict a first league defeat of the season on Peterborough, winning a closely-fought contest 47-42, thanks in no small way to an unbeaten tally from Graham Jones (15).

23 Wimbledon crush an under-strength Stoke outfit 71-19 in the Conference Trophy, their points chart including no less than four maximum scorers in Wayne Barrett (14+1), Daniel Giffard (14+1), Gavin Hedge (10+2) and Andre Cross (9+3).

27 Following heavy overnight rain, Carmarthen chief Nigel Meakins calls off his side's league clash against Peterborough. Persistent rain causes Newport's league match against Rye House to be abandoned after thirteen heats, but at least the result stands, with the visitors taking a 44-34 victory back to Hoddesdon. Mildenhall suffer a 46-44 home reverse to Boston in an action-packed Conference Trophy derby meeting, with injuries to both Daniel King and James Mann playing a major part in their loss.

28 A heavy downpour causes Wolverhampton to postpone their attractive Conference League fixture against Wimbledon.

30 Wimbledon have no difficulty in swamping Trelawny 60-30 in a Conference Trophy encounter.

1 Frede Schott, so inspirational with Championship-winners Edinburgh, and the Premier League's top man of 2003.

2 Terrific action from the
European Grand Prix at Katowice,
Poland, as Krzysztof Cegielski
leads the way, with Lukas Dryml,
Jason Crump and Mikael Max in
close attendance.

3 Slovenian Matej Zagar enjoyed
a wonderful first season in British
speedway with Trelawny.

4 Cornish teenager Ben Barker came on in leaps and bounds with the Oxford Silver Machine Academy.

5 Super stuff from the Swedish Grand Prix at Avesta, as Bjarne Pedersen (20), Jason Crump (2) and Rune Holta (11) exit the corner.

6 Berwick's Michal Makovsky is sandwiched between the Allen brothers of Swindon, Tommy on the outside and Olly on the inside.

7 Racing at close quarters from left to right, as Chris Harris, Andre Compton, Nigel Sadler and Krzysztof Kasprzak enter the first bend at Peterborough.

8 Nicki Pedersen and Jason Crump battle for supremacy at the British Grand Prix, staged at Cardiff's magnificent Millennium Stadium.

9 Arms aloft, Nicki Pedersen takes the plaudits after winning the British Grand Prix. He is flanked by runner-up Jason Crump (left) and third-placed Tony Rickardsson.

10 A supreme racing family as brothers Peter Karlsson, Mikael Max and Magnus Karlsson display the 2003 Wolverhampton race jacket.

11 All smiles from a trio of fast-improving Newcastle Gems, namely Jamie Robertson (7) alongside brothers John and Craig Branney (6).

Opposite page:
12 Charismatic American Greg Hancock proved a great mid-season acquisition for Oxford.

Opposite page

13 An airborne Jason Crump entertains the crowd at the Danish Grand Prix in Copenhagen.

14 The final of the Slovenian Grand Prix, with Leigh Adams heading to victory from Nicki Pedersen, Scott Nicholls and Tomasz Gollob.

This page

15 Newcastle's flying Dane Kenneth Bjerre leads from the Swindon duo of Paul Fry and Chris Neath.

16 From left to right, Leigh Adams, Ryan Sullivan, Tony Rickardsson and Gary Havelock blast away to start another race.

17 Trelawny's Chris Harris enjoyed a tremendous campaign in what was the Tigers' last year of racing at the fabulous Clay Country Moto Parc.

18 The Wolverhampton pairing of Mikael Max (1) and Sam Ermolenko (2) appear to have the edge on Oxford's Charlie Gjedde as they charge to the first turn.

19 Scott Nicholls (13) and Greg Hancock (6) dice for position in the Scandinavian Grand Prix at Gothenburg.

20 The sensational Tomasz Gollob (7) leads from Hans N. Andersen (25) and Lee Richardson in the Polish Grand Prix at Bydgoszcz.

21 Tony Rickardsson (1) and Nicki Pedersen (12) in super action at the Prague-staged Czech Republic Grand Prix.

22 Swashbuckling Frank Smart bade farewell to British speedway in 2003.

23 Edinburgh's Frede Schott in combat with Berwick's Michal Makovsky

24 World Cup winners Sweden celebrate their triumph. Back row, left to right: Andreas Jonsson, Tony Olsson (Team Manager), Peter Karlsson. Front row, left to right: Peter Ljung, Mikael Max, David Ruud.

Opposite page

25 It was glory all the way for Poole in 2003, and here the riders and management celebrate winning the Sky Sports Elite League with many of their happy supporters.

26 Sean Wilson celebrates his triumph in the Premier League Riders' Championship along with Craig Watson (5), Adam Shields (12) and Carl Stonehewer.

27 Lee Richardson with the spoils of victory at the Elite League Riders' Championship, flanked by runner-up Andreas Jonsson (12) and third-placed Scott Nicholls (5).

This page

28 World Under-21 Champion Jaroslaw Hampel going through his paces for British club Ipswich.

29 Jason Crump (2) and Lee
Richardson (17) battle for the lead
in the Norwegian Grand Prix at
Hamar.

30 Nicki Pedersen is crowned as
speedway's thirtieth World
Champion, ahead of runner-up
Jason Crump (left) and third-
placed Tony Rickardsson (right).

MAY

1 Owlerton serves up a thriller, as Sheffield's league fixture with Peterborough ends all-square at 45-45.

3 Armadales's opening Conference Trophy meeting against Boston unfortunately falls victim to inclement weather. Rye House race to a convincing 53-37 league success over Oxford.

4 Buxton's eagerly-awaited league fixture with Mildenhall is called off due to the elements. Carmarthen again lose at home, going down 52-37 to a powerful Sheffield side, for whom Ben Wilson cards a paid maximum (17+1). Newcastle are beaten 48-41 by visiting Boston in a league fixture, despite a Herculean seven-ride stint from William Lawson, which nets 19+1 points. A third home defeat of the day occurs at Stoke, as Mildenhall run riot to win a Conference Trophy encounter 53-36.

6 Despite Graham Jones' 21-point maximum, which includes a golden double outing, Wolverhampton suffer a 51-42 reverse to visiting Newcastle.

7 Wimbledon narrowly beat Buxton 47-43 in an incident-packed Conference League encounter at Plough Lane.

11 Boston maintain their unbeaten league record, with an emphatic 58-32 success over Wimbledon. Knock-Out Cup action sees Buxton gain a 48-40 first-leg victory over Armadale, in the Scottish side's first-ever competitive match. Mildenhall canter to a huge 66-23 win against beleaguered Carmarthen in the Conference Trophy, with all but one of the homesters paid for double-figure tallies.

13 Wolverhampton's eagerly anticipated league fixture against Mildenhall unfortunately falls victim to heavy rainfall.

14 Wimbledon jump back to second place in the league table, thanks to a 60-30 mauling of Carmarthen, with Wayne Barrett (14+1) remaining undefeated.

16 The day's two scheduled fixtures are called off due to torrential rain: Oxford v. Mildenhall (Knock-Out Cup) and Boston v. Scunthorpe Select (Challenge).

18 In the first part of a double-header, Buxton battle their way to a 49-40 league win over Carmarthen. The second match is also against the Welsh outfit in the Conference Trophy, and with the homesters narrowly leading 37-35, rain causes the match to be abandoned after twelve heats, although thankfully with the result standing. Against a backdrop of dark skies, Mildenhall comfortably defeat Peterborough 56-33 in a league encounter at West Row. Newcastle jump to the head of the league table thanks to a 50-39 victory against Sheffield, the high-flying Gems' main points coming from Craig Branney (16) and William Lawson (15+1). Newport's Conference League match against Wolverhampton is washed away, following the earlier postponement of the senior Welsh side's Premier League fixture against Edinburgh.

20 Wolverhampton's return CL clash with Newport is also washed out after prolonged rain in the West Midlands.

21 Wimbledon are held to a hard-fought 45-45 draw by a dogged Wolverhampton side in a rain-affected league match at Plough Lane.

24 Rain again sees off Armadale's much-anticipated first home fixture versus Boston in the Conference Trophy. Rye House romp to a 57-33 league success over Wolverhampton.

25 Carmarthen gain their first point of a difficult campaign, drawing 45-45 with visiting Armadale in the Conference Trophy. Thanks to the sterling efforts of unsung hero and track curator Jerry Thompson, Mildenhall's league match against Buxton is completed, with the homesters winning 56-34.

26   Will Beveridge nets an 18-point maximum, as Buxton host the return league encounter with Mildenhall, and just hold on to win 47-43. It's individual action at Newcastle, and William Lawson shows his mettle to land first prize in the Chris Prime Memorial Trophy after netting 14 points. Meanwhile, the remaining podium positions are filled by Jamie Robertson and Ben Wilson.

27   With two unbeaten sides on track, it's visiting Boston who maintain their league record with a 46-43 success at Swindon. Mechanical problems prove costly as Wolverhampton suffer a 47-38 reverse at the hands of visiting Rye House. The second part of a double dose of league activity at Monmore Green sees the homesters quickly return to winning ways, however, by defeating Wimbledon 47-42.

28   Seventy-five years of speedway in Britain is celebrated in style at Wimbledon, with the staging of the London Best Pairs. Represented by Daniel Giffard and Jason Prynne, the home side emerge victorious on a tally of 19, ahead of nostalgic names from the past in Wembley (16), Hackney (15), Harringay (15), New Cross (14) and West Ham (11).

31   Armadale at last stage their first home match, defeating Buxton 55-34 in the Knock-Out Cup, with Barry Campbell's six-ride full house helping them through to the next round.

JUNE

1   Sittingbourne stages its first full-blown meeting in six years with a festival of speedway, and following semi-finals which see the elimination of the home side, plus both Norwich and Club Cradley Heath, the final results in a victory for Weymouth (26) over Lydd (16) and Belle Vue (12). Buxton is the venue for the second Youth International between Great Britain and Germany, with the tourists impressively racing to a 47-42 success. Carmarthen stage a double-header against Wimbledon, but lose both matches – 48-42 in the league, and 50-43 in the Conference Trophy. With no quarter asked or given, Mildenhall and Rye House engage in a high-energy tussle at West Row, with the homesters just shading a 48-44 success, in spite of a 19-point haul from top Raider Edward Kennett. Following delays caused by rain, Peterborough claim a 49-41 league win over Wolverhampton, with home number one Shane McCabe carding a 12-point maximum. Boston host a challenge match against a Scunthorpe Select, and comfortably compile a 54-35 victory. Showers hit Brough Park, but fail to dampen the riders' enthusiasm as Newcastle triumph 51-37 against Oxford in the Conference League. Stoke are pipped 49-41 by visiting Trelawny in the Conference Trophy, with veteran Malcolm Holloway posting an undefeated 15 points for the victorious Cornish outfit.

2   Sheffield Prowlers suffer their first home league defeat since 1996, as Tommy Allen's paid maximum (14+1) inspires Swindon to a 47-43 success.

3   Thrills and spills are the order of the day as Wimbledon jump to the top of the Conference League table, courtesy of a 58-32 win over Swindon.

6   Former Grand-Prix racer Andy Smith marks his Conference League debut with a six-ride maximum as Oxford overpower Carmarthen 57-33.

8   Buxton's league encounter with Wolverhampton is called off after heavy rain sets in on the Peak District. Following great work from the track staff, Carmarthen's double-header with Rye House is able to go ahead. The first match is in the Knock-Out Cup, with the visiting Raiders winning 50-40. The Hertfordshire side follow that up with an even bigger victory in a league fixture, their 54-36 success taking them above Wimbledon at the head of the table. Teenage wonder Edward Kennett rubs salt into the Dragons' wounds,

brilliantly plundering 15-point maximums in both matches. Newport race to an impressive 56-33 win over Sheffield in entertaining league action at Queensway Meadows. Mildenhall have no trouble in building up a 53-37 first-leg lead from their Knock-Out Cup tie against Oxford. Following the earlier postponement of Newcastle's PL match against Stoke, the Geordie side's Conference League encounter with Peterborough is obviously also called off, due to heavy rainfall.

9   Rye House march on in the Knock-Out Cup, with a 67-23 thrashing of Carmarthen in the second-leg of their tie. Three Raiders emerge unbeaten from the match, namely Edward Kennett (15), Barrie Evans (12+3) and Joel Parsons (10+2). Reading entertain local rivals Swindon in a Conference challenge, and in a thrilling battle, it's the visiting Sprockets who claim a narrow 47-46 success.

10 A Graham Jones 15-point maximum inspires Wolverhampton to a 48-41 league victory over a spirited Buxton outfit.

11 Wimbledon surrender their home record, going down 46-44 to bogey side Mildenhall in an entertaining league encounter.

15 Buxton dig deep for a 48-41 Conference Trophy victory over Wimbledon, the win only being assured in the final heat. Individual fare at Carmarthen sees Jamie Robertson retain his West Wales Championship, triumphing in the final from Chris Schramm, Steven Braidford and Matthew Wethers. Powerful Rye House dispense with Sheffield by a 58-31 scoreline in the league, with both Barrie Evans (14+1) and Edward Kennett (12) unbeaten by an opponent. Boston make it five league wins out of five, demolishing Newport 68-22, with three riders remaining unbeaten, namely Trevor Harding (17+1), Mark Thompson (15+3) and Luke Clifton (15+3). A delayed start doesn't stop Mildenhall from sprinting to a comfortable 58-32 league success over Swindon, as James Brundle hits a stylish paid full house (13+2).

17 A rather one-sided affair results in a 57-33 league victory for Wolverhampton against a depleted Swindon outfit, with both Matthew Wethers (18) and Graham Jones (15) carding maximums.

18 Injury-hit Wimbledon suffer a 47-42 reverse at the hands of league-leaders Rye House, as Edward Kennett nets a super paid maximum (17+1) for the Raiders.

20 Boston continue on their merry way, earning a hard-fought 51-39 win over a battling Trelawny in the Conference Trophy.

21 Afternoon action sees Armadale swamp Trelawny 65-24 in the Conference Trophy, with Trent Leverington remaining unbeaten from four starts (11+1). Staying with the Conference Trophy, Joe Cook returns from injury to plunder a four-ride full house, as Stoke defeat Wimbledon 51-39.

22 A Conference League double-bill at Peterborough sees the homesters defeat Newport 54-36, before the second match results in a 52-38 success for a rampant Boston outfit. Buxton have little difficulty in beating Sheffield 54-36 in the league, with James Wright thundering to a paid maximum (14+1). Mildenhall keep the pressure on pole-position club Rye House, easily beating Newport 65-25, with both Scott James (12) and James Brundle (11+1) unbeaten by an opponent.

23 Double-header league fare at Sheffield results in 53-37 victory for the Prowlers against Buxton, with the second match against Boston being curtailed due to Luke Clifton's nasty-looking twelfth-heat crash. With Boston leading 37-35 at the time, the result stands, thereby maintaining the Barracuda-Braves' 100 per cent record from seven matches.

24   Tom Brown surges to a wonderful six-ride maximum, as Trelawny thrash Wimbledon 60-30 in the Conference Trophy, but the Dons collect the bonus point when the Welshman grinds to a halt in a run-off.

25   Four-Team Tournament fare at Hull sees Buxton accumulate 29 points to take victory from Scunthorpe (25), Wolverhampton (23) and the home quartet (19).

28   It's a walk in the park as Armadale pile up the points to defeat Carmarthen 70-20 in the Conference Trophy, with no less than five men going through the card unbeaten by an opponent, namely Matthew Wethers (15), Barry Campbell (12+3), Trent Leverington (12), Craig Branney (10+2) and Carl Shield (10+2).

29   Newport have no answer as high-flying Newcastle comfortably win 52-37 in the league at Queensway Meadows. Trevor Harding (17+1) and Mark Thompson (15+3) record paid maximums, as Boston romp to a 62-30 success against under-fire Carmarthen in the Conference Trophy. Star-studded Mildenhall move to the top of the Conference League table, easily defeating Wolverhampton 55-34 at West Row, with all-action Aussie Scott James notching a paid maximum (9+3). Sittingbourne's second meeting of the year sees James Theobald triumph in the Vic Harding Memorial Trophy, with Nick Lee filling the runner-up spot ahead of James Clement and James Purchase. A nine-heat team match follows, with the home side being held to a 27-27 draw by Hackney.

JULY

1   Trelawny survive a testing time, before defeating Stoke 46-43 in the Conference Trophy. The day's other match between Wolverhampton and Boston in the league is postponed following heavy showers.

2   Rain unfortunately puts paid to Wimbledon's scheduled league fixture against Peterborough.

4   The much-anticipated league clash between unbeaten Boston and table-toppers Mildenhall is called off due to the effects of rain the previous day at Saddlebow Road.

6   It's real David-and-Goliath stuff in the Welsh hills, as Carmarthen finally win a league match, defeating the previously unbeaten Boston 45-43 in an edge-of-the-seat encounter. Mildenhall extend their lead at the head of the league table, narrowly winning 46-44 at Newcastle, as Ben Howe scorches to an 18-point maximum.

8   Tom Brown's unbeaten tally (14+1) helps Trelawny to a 55-35 win against Armadale in the Conference Trophy.

9   Oxford comprehensively defeat Peterborough 53-37 in the Conference League, with Joe Cook garnering a superb full house (15). Wimbledon's plush Plough Lane is the venue as Great Britain grab a 52-37 success over Sweden in an Under-21 international, with Chris Neath plundering a stylish 15-point maximum for the series victors.

11   Somerset's Oak Tree Arena plays host to a Four-Team Tournament in memory of Paul Gladwin, with Weymouth (26) taking victory from Swindon (17), Bristol (15) and Newport (14).

12   Armadale easily record a 57-33 win against Wimbledon in the Conference Trophy. Rye House have little difficulty in piling up a 57-32 victory over Newport in a Conference League encounter.

13   The first match of a double-header sees Carmarthen romp to a 64-26 success against Buxton in the league, as both Craig Taylor (15) and Ben Powell (12+3) hit maximums. The second fixture again brings the same sides face-to-face on Conference Trophy business, with the homesters having to work much harder for a 46-42 win. Injury-hit

Boston slump to a 58-32 reverse at the hands of visiting Sheffield, as both Ben Wilson (14+1) and Rob Grant (13+2) remain unbeaten for the South Yorkshire outfit. Thanks largely to a superb 17-point return from reserve Tony Dart, league leaders Mildenhall triumph 50-40 against a spirited Oxford side. Newcastle move up to third spot in the league, courtesy of a 51-39 victory over depleted Wimbledon.

15 A closely contested Conference Trophy encounter results in a 48-42 success for Mildenhall at Trelawny.

16 It's close throughout, with Wimbledon finally securing a 46-41 win against battling Buxton in the Conference Trophy at Plough Lane. The day's other fixture, a league match between Oxford and Newcastle, is called off due to excessive amounts of rainfall.

19 The inaugural Conference League Four-Team Championships are staged at Mildenhall, but with the homesters qualifying for the final, along with Peterborough, Rye House and Boston, the meeting is disappointingly abandoned due to a thunderstorm.

20 A solid team performance sees Buxton triumph 52-35 against Wolverhampton in the league. Carmarthen come up trumps in the battle of the Welsh sides, winning 49-40 at Newport in a cracking league encounter.

21 A double dose of league action at Owlerton sees Sheffield firstly demolish Wimbledon 64-25, with Richard Hall (15) and Rob Grant (11+1) remain unbeaten by an opponent. The second match results in an emphatic 62-28 success for the Prowlers against Newcastle, with Rob Grant again unbeaten on 15 points, while Ben Wilson (14+1) and Benji Compton (9+3) net paid maximums.

22 League activity sees Wolverhampton defeat Oxford 50-38, with both Matthew Wethers (15) and Graham Jones (14+1) unbeaten by an opponent.

23 Having initially finished all-square, the first-leg of the Knock-Out Cup replay results in a hard-fought 46-44 victory for Wimbledon over Boston, with Mark Burrows completing a scintillating six-ride paid maximum (17+1).

26 Power-packed Armadale romp to a 61-32 victory against Mildenhall in the Conference Trophy, with four teamsters plundering full-house tallies in Craig Branney (14+1), Matthew Wethers (12+3), Barry Campbell (12) and Trent Leverington (11+1).

27 Buxton come from behind to beat a depleted Mildenhall 53-37 in the Conference Trophy. Carmarthen race to a fifth successive league victory, defeating Peterborough 48-41 at their United Counties Showground raceway. The second-leg of the Knock-Out Cup replay results in a 50-39 victory for Boston over Wimbledon, with the Barracuda-Braves progressing to the next stage. Sittingbourne stage their third meeting of the season, and representing Hackney, it's Gareth Hickmott and Jon Stevens who take the accolades in the Best Pairs Championship.

30 Oxford claim a narrow 45-44 win over Mildenhall in the Knock-Out Cup, but it's the Fen Tigers who progress through on aggregate. 'Buzz' Burrows surges to a 15-point maximum as Wimbledon are taken to the wire before defeating Armadale 46-44 in the Conference Trophy.

AUGUST

1 Boston's much-anticipated league clash against Rye House is called off due to persistent rainfall.

2 Rye House comfortably beat Newcastle 53-36 in the league at Hoddesdon.

3 Buxton suffer their first home loss of the campaign, going down 49-41 to Boston in a

thrilling league match, with Trevor Harding yielding a full six-ride maximum for the victors. Mildenhall remain untroubled throughout, as they defeat Trelawny 52-36 in the Conference Trophy at West Row.

4   Challenge-match action at Smallmead sees Reading scorch to a 63-25 victory over Carmarthen, with Luke Priest gleaning a paid maximum (11+1) for the Ravens.

6   The Junior Championship at Belle Vue results in victory for Richard Hall, courtesy of a well-gained 15-point maximum, with James Wright (14) and Lee Derbyshire (12) filling the other podium positions. Knock-Out Cup action sees Stoke held to a 45-45 draw at by a battling Armadale outfit at Loomer Road. Wimbledon suffer a home reverse, going down 49-44 at the hands of league title-chasing Boston, despite Buzz Burrows' golden double inclusive 21-point full house.

7   Blunsdon plays host to a league double-header, with Swindon suffering a narrow 45-44 defeat in the first match against a Graham Jones-inspired Wolverhampton. Match number two versus Carmarthen is curtailed after heat thirteen due to the 10 p.m. curfew, but that doesn't stop the Sprockets from winning 48-29, with both Barry Campbell (11+1) and Simon Walker (10+2) unbeaten.

8   Trevor Harding (18) and Dean Garrod (11+4) hit maximums as Boston keep up their league challenge by romping to a 56-33 success over Newcastle. A double league feature at Oxford sees the homesters beat Wimbledon 57-33, prior to hammering Newport 70-20. There are no maximums in the first match, but three of the Silver Machine Academy outfit are undefeated against the Mavericks, namely Joe Cook (17+1), Ricky Scarboro (14+1) and Chris Johnson (10+2).

9   Armadale cruise to a 58-31 victory over Stoke in the Knock-Out Cup to progress through, with Gary Beaton plundering a paid full-house (9+3).

10 Buxton dig deep to beat second-in-the-table Rye House 46-44 at their Hi-Edge raceway. A full 15-pointer from Craig Taylor inspires Carmarthen to a 57-31 Conference Trophy victory against Trelawny at the United Counties Showground. By walloping Peterborough 61-29 at Saddlebow Road, Boston displace Rye House in the league table, with Trevor Harding scoring another maximum (15). Mildenhall maintain top spot with an eighth successive league victory, their 63-26 win over Sheffield including an unbeaten performance from Wayne Broadhurst (12). Newcastle run riot to thrash an under-strength Swindon side 61-27 in the league, with John Branney (21) and brother Craig (16+2) thundering to maximum tallies.

11 Sheffield are held to a 45-45 draw by a determined Mildenhall side in a thrilling league encounter at Owlerton. Wolverhampton have little difficulty in racking up a 59-31 league success against Newport at Monmore Green.

12 Tuesday-night racing at Blunsdon results in a comfortable 54-36 victory for Swindon over Buxton, with Tommy Allen going through the card unbeaten (15). Wolverhampton chalk up an impressive 57-28 win against Sheffield, helped no end by maximums from Graham Jones (15) and Steven Braidford (13+2).

13 Inclusive of a golden-double heat success, Ben Howe nets a huge 23-point tally, but it doesn't prevent Mildenhall from losing 48-45 in a thrilling Conference Trophy fixture at Wimbledon.

15 After nineteen years in the speedway wilderness, Weymouth reopen with individual fare for the Wessex Rosebowl and, despite persistent drizzle, a crowd of around 2,500 witness Justin Elkins take victory with a 15-point maximum.

16 Armadale maintain their 100 per cent home record in the Conference Trophy, courtesy of a 48-42 victory against battling Boston.

17 Lee Derbyshire dashes to a first-ever full maximum (15), and Paul Sharples is also unbeaten (9+3), as Buxton romp to a 60-30 win over Conference League basement-club Newport. Carmarthen are caught cold as Stoke race to a 51-39 success at the Welsh venue, with Graham Jones grabbing a six-ride full house (18). A much-anticipated league clash finally results in a 50-39 win for Mildenhall against Boston, as the Fen Tigers retain the number one position in the table.

18 Both Barrie Evans (17+1) and Joel Parsons (15+3) score maximums as Rye House go second in the league standings, courtesy of a 58-30 victory over Carmarthen. Challenge-match action over thirteen heats at Reading sees local rivals Swindon steal away with a narrow 39-38 success under their belts.

19 Tommy Allen nets a four-ride full house as Swindon find little difficulty in posting a 54-36 league victory over Wimbledon. A thrilling league meeting finally results in a 47-43 home loss for depleted Wolverhampton against a spirited Carmarthen outfit.

20 Wimbledon crush Carmarthen 61-29 in the Conference Trophy, with Joel Parsons plundering the lot (15).

22 Somerset is the stage for the first-leg of an entertaining challenge match, with Bristol eventually going down 47-43 at the hands of Weymouth. Boston's scheduled double-header against Buxton, in the league and Conference Trophy, only gets as far as the fourth heat of the former before rain curtails the proceedings with the homesters leading 14-10.

23 Title-chasing Rye House race to a huge 64-26 victory over Boston, thereby consolidating second spot in the league table.

24 Buxton claim a hard-fought 49-41 success over Stoke in the Conference Trophy at Hi-Edge. Carmarthen suffer a 49-41 home reverse against Mildenhall in the Conference Trophy, with both Danny Norton (17+1) and Nick Simmons (17+1) remaining unbeaten for the Fen men. Newport suffer their tenth league defeat in a row, losing 49-41 to local rivals Swindon at Queensway Meadows. A last-heat 5-1 sees Stoke through to a narrow 45-44 win against Buxton, with the redoubtable Graham Jones carding a paid maximum (17+1).

25 Rye House move to the top of the league on race-points difference, courtesy of a 57-33 success over Peterborough. Before a large audience, Weymouth canter to a 53-36 win against Bristol in the second-leg of the challenge for an overall aggregate victory. League action at Brough Park sees Newcastle comfortably dispose of Buxton by a 57-33 scoreline.

26 Swindon stage a Conference League double-header and although both matches are curtailed by a time curfew, the Sprockets firstly defeat Newcastle 45-39, and then Peterborough 43-34. Depleted Trelawny suffer a 51-39 home reverse to Carmarthen in the Conference Trophy. Wolverhampton dig deep to inflict a 50-40 league defeat on Mildenhall, with both Graham Jones (18) and new signing Trent Leverington (17+1) posting maximums. The Fen Tigers claim the bonus point, however, to move back into pole position in the league standings.

27 League activity at Plough Lane sees Wimbledon triumph 53-37 over Newcastle as 'Buzz' Burrows zips to a six-ride full house (18).

29 Boston narrowly beat Stoke 46-44 in thrilling Conference Trophy action at Saddlebow Road.

30 Rye House host the prestigious Conference League Riders' Championship, and it's home man Barrie Evans who tallies 14 points to take the title, ahead of Newcastle's Jamie Robertson (11), with Boston's Trevor Harding (10) winning a four-man run-off for third spot.

31 Maximums from Chris Collins (18) and James Wright (15) lead the way as Buxton comfortably defeat Swindon 58-31 in the league. Mildenhall increase their lead at the top of the league, courtesy of a 54-36 victory against Wimbledon. Newcastle boast three maximum men in William Lawson (15), Jamie Robertson (13+2) and Craig Branney (12) as they easily register a 58-29 league success over Carmarthen.

SEPTEMBER

1 A double-header at Sheffield sees the Prowlers claim a brace of league victories against Carmarthen (67-22) and Oxford (54-35), with Richard Hall (15) and Gary Flint (11+4) gleaning maximums in the first match.

3 Both Mark Burrows (14+1) and Wayne Barrett (12) remain unbeaten as Wimbledon thunder to a 67-23 league win over Newport.

5 Oxford stage a double dose of league action, with the Silver Machine Academy claiming wins in both against Buxton (59-31) and local rivals Swindon (50-40). Terrific challenge-match action at Weymouth sees visiting Wimbledon secure a 46-44 success.

6 Armadale maintain their challenge at the top end of the Conference Trophy by beating Stoke 51-39, despite Graham Jones' fabulous 18-point maximum for the Spitfires.

7 At Sittingbourne, the homesters triumph 50-28 against Norwich in a challenge match as James Theobald (15) and Mark Baseby (13+2) post maximums. Newport claim their first win in twelve matches, defeating Oxford 46-43 in an exciting league clash at Queensway Meadows. League action at Hi-Edge results in a 57-33 success for Buxton against Peterborough, with Chris Collins gleaning a six-ride full house (18). William Lawson (14+1) is unbeaten by an opponent as Newcastle grab a 50-40 success over second-in-the-league Rye House. Boston score a huge 61-29 victory over Wimbledon in the Conference Trophy, with veteran Robert Hollingworth netting 18+1 points from seven starts. Handicapped pairs action at Mildenhall sees Tony Dart (18) and Paul Lee (14) take victory with a combined tally of 32 points.

8 Rye House move back to the head of the league table courtesy of a 50-39 win against a battling Buxton outfit. With the clock reaching 11 p.m., Wolverhampton's league encounter is curtailed, but with twelve heats run the result stands as a 40-31 victory to visiting Boston.

10 Conference Trophy action sees Boston grab a hard-fought 46-44 victory at Wimbledon's tight Plough Lane circuit.

11 Inclement weather abates in time for Blunsdon to stage its 1,500th speedway meeting, with Swindon playing hosts to both Newport and Mildenhall in a double dose of league action. The first match sees the Sprockets romp to a 61-29 success, with the highlight being Lee Smart's paid maximum (12+3). The Fen Tigers prove too powerful in the second fixture, with Paul Lee registering a five-ride full house (15) as his side claim a 48-42 win to regain top spot in the table.

12 Rye House record a significant 49-41 victory at third-in-the-table Boston and jump back to pole position in the standings. Weymouth narrowly defeat Swindon 46-43 in an entertaining challenge match, with Justin Elkins establishing a new track record of 54.8 seconds for the 223-metre raceway.

13   James Brundle (13+2), Lee Hodgson (11+1) and Paul Lee (10+2) remain undefeated as Mildenhall leap above Rye House at the head of the table, courtesy of a 68-22 drubbing of Carmarthen in the first part of a double-header. The second match results in a 55-35 success for the Fen Tigers over Boston in the first-leg of the Knock-Out Cup semi-final, with Paul Lee plundering a further paid maximum (13+2).

14   Buxton overcome an early deficit to beat Newcastle 59-31 in the league, helped on their way by maximum points from Chris Collins (15). Stoke gain a 50-40 victory against Boston in an exciting Conference Trophy match.

15   Knock-Out Cup semi-final fare sees solid-scoring Rye House race to a 59-31 first-leg win over Armadale.

16   In an effort to catch up with their league fixtures Peterborough stage a double-header at King's Lynn, with the first match resulting in a 55-32 loss to Rye House as the Raiders again return to the head of the table. The second meeting also results in defeat for the depleted Pumas, with James Wright netting a maximum (15) as Buxton win 48-41.

17   Away from the track, the result of the Swindon v. Mildenhall match is amended to a Sprockets' victory by a 42-41 scoreline, as Lee Hodgson is deemed ineligible to have appeared at reserve for the Fen Tigers, his 7 points in the match being deducted from their total. 'Buzz' Burrows plunders a paid full house (14+1) as Wimbledon complete their home league programme with a hard-earned 52-38 victory over a Peterborough side bolstered by the inclusion of guests Robert Hollingworth and Chris Johnson.

19   Boston are held to a 45-45 draw by visiting Mildenhall in the second-leg of the Knock-Out Cup semi-final as the Fen Tigers cruise through to the final. Oxford canter to a 61-31 success against Wolverhampton in the league, with Ben Barker netting a paid maximum (13+2) from the reserve berth. In their latest challenge match, non-league Weymouth suffer a 49-40 loss to visiting Belle Vue.

20   In the second-leg of their Knock-Out Cup semi-final tie, Armadale cannot prevent a powerful Rye House outfit from claiming a spot in the final, courtesy of a 50-40 scoreline. Another double dose of league action at King's Lynn sees Peterborough lose 46-43 to Newcastle, prior to being overwhelmed 65-25 by title-chasing Mildenhall. Matthew Wright (12+3), Paul Lee (12) and James Brundle (12) all remain unbeaten as the Fen Tigers again leapfrog Rye House to head the table.

21   Buxton have little difficulty in posting a 52-38 success over Trelawny in the Conference Trophy, with James Wright scorching to a five-ride full house (15). Carmarthen lose out to visiting Boston, going down 51-42 as Trevor Harding's paid maximum (17+1) helps the Barracuda-Braves jump above Mildenhall at the top of the Conference Trophy table, albeit temporarily. Bottom-of-the-league Newport claim only their fourth victory of the campaign, beating Peterborough 54-36. Paul Lee records maximum points (12) as Mildenhall oust Boston from top position in the Conference Trophy standings, courtesy of a 52-38 win against Stoke.

22   Rye House's chance of returning to the top of the table is scuppered as their meeting with Swindon is postponed due to torrential rain.

23   Trelawny complete their Conference Trophy fixtures, but go down 48-42 to visiting Buxton.

24   Both Wayne Barrett (14+1) and Mark Burrows (14+1) remain unbeaten as Wimbledon complete the double over non-league Weymouth in a challenge fixture at Plough Lane, winning 56-34.

26   Despite huge efforts, Boston can't prevent Mildenhall from collecting an important 46-44

league victory at Saddlebow Road. Crucially, the Fen Tigers' main challengers at the top of the league, Rye House, lose 63-25 at a rain-soaked Oxford, with Chris Schramm (15), Joe Cook (12) and Ben Barker (10+2) hitting maximums for the victorious Silver Machine Academy. The Wessex Stadium plays host to challenge match action as Weymouth defeat Norwich 51-38 before a crowd in excess of 1,000.

27 Craig Branney posts a fine five-ride maximum (15) as Armadale record a 50-40 success over Buxton in the Conference Trophy.

28 Sittingbourne stage their fifth and final public event of the season, with Hackney claiming a 47-42 victory over the Crusaders despite Nathan Irwin's brilliant 18-point full house. Carmarthen race to a convincing 54-35 win against Welsh rivals Newport in the league. Boston quickly return to winning ways with a 57-33 league success over Wolverhampton. Tony Dart (12+3), James Brundle (12), Wayne Broadhurst (11+1) and Paul Lee (11+1) romp to maximums as Mildenhall extend their advantage at the head of the league standings, crushing Newcastle 67-23.

OCTOBER

1 Wimbledon's challenge fixture versus a Conference League Select side is postponed when a burst water main in Colliers Wood means there is no water supply to the stadium.

3 A double dose of league fare at Oxford sees the Silver Machine Academy beat Sheffield 54-39 in the first match, with a 56-34 victory following against Newcastle. Darren Mallett (15), Mark Thompson (14+1), Robert Hollingworth (11+1) and James Horton (10+2) all return maximums as Boston cruise to the head of the Conference Trophy table by walloping Armadale 68-22. Challenge-match action at Somerset's Oak Tree Arena results in a 67-23 win for Bristol over Newport, with Andy Carfield scoring a paid maximum (9+3) for the Bulldogs.

4 With a huge 69-19 victory over an understrength Wimbledon outfit, Rye House enhance their league-title aspirations as Barrie Evans (14+1) and Luke Bowen (12+3) are paid for unbeaten tallies.

5 Buxton romp to a 61-26 success against Wimbledon in league activity, with Chris Collins (15), James Wright (14+1) and Jonathan Bethell (9+3) plundering maximums. Entertainment plus excitement is served up at the United Counties Showground as Carmarthen claim a hard-fought 47-43 league win over Newcastle. The restaging of the Four-Team Championship Final at Mildenhall sees Rye House just pip the host club to win their first trophy at Conference League level, the final scores being Rye House 30, Mildenhall 29, Peterborough 19, Boston 14.

6 Stoke complete their Conference Trophy fixtures by coming from behind to secure a 45-45 draw against a gritty Armadale side.

8 Oxford scorch to a 63-27 victory over Boston in a one-sided league match, with four riders hitting unbeaten tallies: Joe Cook (18), Chris Schramm (17+1), Chris Johnson (10+2) and Ben Barker (10+2). It takes a run-off to determine the outcome of the prestigious Laurels individual event at Wimbledon, with Wayne Barrett finally coming out on top from Mark Burrows.

9 Paul Lee shows his undoubted ability to win the OzChem Top Gun Championship at Sheffield, as Ben Wilson, Richard Hall and Mark Thompson fill the remaining podium positions in the final. The curtain comes down at Blunsdon with a double dose of Conference League action, but due to a number of alarming track spills and a 10 p.m.

curfew, both matches are curtailed after the magical twelve-heat mark has been reached, with the Sprockets firstly defeating title-aspirants Rye House 43-29, prior to losing 38-34 to local rivals Oxford.

10 Peterborough stage another double-header of league fare at King's Lynn and Danny Norton plunders a paid maximum (14+1) as the Pumas claim a narrow 46-44 success over Carmarthen in the first encounter. The following fixture sees visiting Swindon pull ahead from heat eight onwards to post an impressive 52-37 victory.

11 Injury-hit Rye House have to work hard to beat Swindon 47-43 in order to maintain their challenge for the League Championship, although the bonus point heads the way of the Wiltshire side.

12 Carmarthen wrap up their second season of racing with a comfortable 52-38 league win over Oxford. Newport romp to their biggest win of the year, beating Wolverhampton 63-25, with Danny Hughes (15+3), Scott Pegler (15) and Karl Mason (15) all remaining undefeated. Racing their fifth match in four days appears to have no effect on Swindon as they grab a 46-44 league victory at Boston, courtesy of a last-heat 5-1. Paul Lee hits another maximum as Mildenhall defeat a battling Armadale side 50-40 in the Conference Trophy at West Row.

13 Sheffield complete their league fixtures with a double-header at Owlerton. The first match sees Richard Hall (15) and Ben Wilson (13+2) register maximums as the Prowlers defeat Rye House 64-26 to end the Raiders' title hopes, thereby leaving Mildenhall as the Champions. In the second fixture, the Prowlers continue on their high-scoring way, thrashing Wolverhampton 62-28.

14 Boston entertain Buxton in a double dose of action, defeating the Hitmen 48-42 in the league and then winning their Conference Trophy encounter 50-40, with Richard Hall bagging an 18-point full house.

15 Oxford hosts the David Nix Memorial Trophy, with Craig Branney winning a rerun final from Newcastle team-mate Jamie Robertson and home favourite Chris Schramm. Wimbledon's season ends with Wayne Barrett (15) and Mark Burrows (13+2) posting maximums as the Dons defeat a Conference League Select side 48-42.

17 Boston slide to a 59-31 league reverse at Saddlebow Road as Oxford run riot, with Chris Schramm (18), Joe Cook (14+1) and Ben Barker (13+2) plundering unbeaten tallies.

18 Tremendous Knock-Out Cup final activity sees Edward Kennett return to the track and help Rye House to a first-leg 46-43 success over Mildenhall at Hoddesdon.

19 Bottom-of-the-table Newport go down 48-42 to visiting Boston in the league. The Knock-Out Cup final reaches a tremendous climax at West Row, with Mildenhall's hard-fought 48-41 win giving them an aggregate victory by just 4 points over Rye House.

22 Boston produce an excellent display to beat Mildenhall 50-40, with the victory making the Barracuda-Braves winners of the Conference Trophy competition.

24 Oxford defeat Champions Mildenhall 53-37 to secure third position in the final Conference League table.

26 Newport and Buxton complete the Conference League programme for the season with a thrilling 45-45 draw at Queensway Meadows, with Scott Pegler bagging a faultless 18-point maximum for the Mavericks. Following the earlier staging of the George English Memorial Trophy, Newcastle are held to a 21-21 draw by a Sunderland outfit in a Conference-level staging of the Tyne-Wear Trophy at Brough Park.

CONFERENCE LEAGUE TABLE

	Mts	Won	Drn	Lst	For	Agn	Pts	Bon	Tot
Mildenhall	24	18	1	5	1236	917	37	10	47
Rye House	24	18	0	6	1178	936	36	9	45
Oxford	24	14	0	10	1179	960	28	11	39
Boston	24	15	0	9	1103	1017	30	8	38
Swindon	24	14	0	10	1042	1036	28	5	33
Buxton	24	12	1	11	1095	1054	25	7	32
Newcastle	24	13	0	11	1072	1070	26	5	31
Sheffield	24	10	2	12	1115	1016	22	8	30
Wimbledon	24	9	1	14	1028	1126	19	5	24
Wolverhampton	24	10	1	13	1005	1116	21	2	23
Carmarthen	24	8	0	16	957	1177	16	4	20
Peterborough	24	6	1	17	950	1187	13	3	16
Newport	24	5	1	18	895	1243	11	1	12

CONFERENCE TROPHY TABLE

	Mts	Won	Drn	Lst	For	Agn	Pts	Bon	Tot
Boston	14	11	0	3	703	561	22	5	27
Mildenhall	14	9	0	5	675	587	18	5	23
Armadale	14	7	2	5	676	586	16	6	22
Buxton	14	8	0	6	624	610	16	4	20
Wimbledon	14	7	0	7	640	622	14	3	17
Stoke	14	5	1	8	590	667	11	2	13
Trelawny	14	4	0	10	568	686	8	1	9
Carmarthen	14	3	1	10	544	701	7	2	9

KNOCK-OUT CUP RESULTS

PRELIMINARY ROUND

Buxton	48	Armadale	40	
Armadale	55	Buxton	34	(Armadale won 95-82 on aggregate)

ROUND ONE

Boston	55	Wimbledon	35	
Wimbledon	55	Boston	35	(Boston and Wimbledon drew 90-90 on aggregate)
Carmarthen	40	Rye House	50	
Rye House	67	Carmarthen	23	(Rye House won 117-63 on aggregate)
Mildenhall	53	Oxford	37	
Oxford	45	Mildenhall	44	(Mildenhall won 97-82 on aggregate)

Stoke	45	Armadale	45	
Armadale	58	Stoke	31	(Armadale won 103-76 on aggregate)

REPLAY

Wimbledon	46	Boston	44	
Boston	50	Wimbledon	39	(Boston won 94-85 on aggregate)

SEMI-FINAL

Mildenhall	55	Boston	35	
Boston	45	Mildenhall	45	(Mildenhall won 100-80 on aggregate)
Rye House	59	Armadale	31	
Armadale	40	Rye House	50	(Rye House won 109-71 on aggregate)

FINAL

Rye House	46	Mildenhall	43	
Mildenhall	48	Rye House	41	(Mildenhall won 91-87 on aggregate)

ARMADALE DALE DEVILS

NOTE: The information below relates only to the second Edinburgh team. For details of the main side, please refer to the Premier League section.

ADDRESS: Armadale Stadium, Bathgate Road, Armadale, West Lothian.
PROMOTERS: John Campbell & Alex Harkess.
TRACK LENGTH: 280 metres.
FIRST MEETING: 31 May 2003.
YEARS OF OPERATION: 2003 Conference Trophy.

CLUB HONOURS

None.

RIDER ROSTER 2003

BEATON, Gary   b. 20 August 1986, Glasgow, Scotland.
    BRITISH CAREER: (2002) Newport (CL), Newcastle (CL); (2003) Wolverhampton (CL),
    Armadale (CT), Newcastle (CL), Glasgow.
BRANNEY, Craig   b. 31 July 1982, Whitehaven, Cumbria.
    BRITISH CAREER: (2000) Ashfield; (2001) Workington, Buxton, Isle of Wight, Newport
    (PL); (2002) Newcastle (CL), Hull; (2003) Newcastle (PL & CL), Armadale (CT),
    Workington, Swindon (PL), Hull, Somerset.

ARMADALE DEVILS: back row, left to right: Alan Robertson (Team Manager), Carl Shield, Andrew Tully, Matthew Wethers, Keith Maben. Front row, left to right: Gary Beaton, Sean Stoddart, Barry Campbell

CAMPBELL, Barry   b. 26 August 1979, Glasgow, Scotland.
BRITISH CAREER: (1995) Linlithgow, Swindon; (1996) Linlithgow, Edinburgh; (1997) Edinburgh, Lathallan; (1998) Edinburgh; (1999) Belle Vue, Workington; (2000-01) Workington; (2003) Edinburgh, Armadale (CT), Reading, Swindon (CL), Belle Vue (BLC).

DUNWORTH, Wayne   b. 20 January 1967, Nottingham, Nottinghamshire.
BRITISH CAREER: (1984) Boston; (1986) Mildenhall; (1987) Boston; (2002) Boston, Carmarthen; (2003) Trelawny (CT), Boston, Peterborough (CL), Armadale (CT).

LANGLEY, Karl   b. 2 June 1981, Whitehaven, Cumbria.
BRITISH CAREER: (2002) Workington; (2003) Newcastle (CL), Armadale (KOC), Mildenhall, Poole (BLC).

LEVERINGTON, Trent   b. 13 May 1980, Brisbane, Queensland, Australia.
BRITISH CAREER: (2003) Glasgow, Armadale (CT), Wolverhampton (CL).

MABEN, Keith   b. 24 December 1982, Edinburgh, Scotland.
BRITISH CAREER: (2003) Armadale (CT), Mildenhall (CT), Stoke (KOC).

NORTON, Danny   b. 27 August 1986, Hull, East Yorkshire.
BRITISH CAREER: (2001-02) Peterborough (CL); (2003) Peterborough (CL & BLC), Armadale (CT), Swindon (PL), Reading, Mildenhall (KOC & CT), Poole (BLC), Oxford (BLC).

ROYNON, Adam   b. 30 August 1988, Barrow-in-Furness, Cumbria.
BRITISH CAREER: (2003) Swindon (CL), Armadale (CT).

SHIELD, Carl   b. 27 June 1979, Bishop Auckland, County Durham.
BRITISH CAREER: (2002) Newcastle (CL), Sheffield (PLKOC); (2003) Berwick, Newcastle (CL), Armadale (CT), Edinburgh.

STODDART, Sean   b. 20 January 1987, Edinburgh, Scotland.
BRITISH CAREER: (2003) Armadale, Trelawny (CT), Carmarthen (CT), Newcastle (CL).

TULLY, Andrew   b. 26 May 1987, Douglas, Isle of Man.
BRITISH CAREER: (2003) Armadale (CT).

WETHERS, Matthew   b. 30 May 1985, Modbury, South Australia.
BRITISH CAREER: (2003) Armadale (CT), Wolverhampton (CL), Edinburgh.

WILDING, Rhys   b. 6 July 1982
BRITISH CAREER: (2003) Armadale (CT), Mildenhall.

CONFERENCE TROPHY

(* Denotes aggregate victory)

No	DATE	OPPONENTS	H/A	RESULT	LEVERINGTON	BEATON	CAMPBELL	STODDART	SHIELD	TULLY	WETHERS	BRANNEY	MABEN	ROYNON	OTHERS
1	25/5	Carmarthen	A	D45-45	R/R	2+1(4)	13(6)	2+1(4)	8+2(6)	0(3)	20(7)	–	–	–	–
2	21/6	Trelawny	H	W65-24	11+1(4)	5+1(4)	14(5)	–	9+2(4)	5+1(4)	12+2(5)	9+2(4)	–	–	–
3	28/6	Carmarthen	H	W70-20*	12(4)	6+3(4)	12+3(5)	–	10+2(4)	5+2(4)	15(5)	10+2(4)	–	–	–
4	6/7	Buxton	A	L43-47	R/R	5(5)	16+3(7)	3(3)	–	2(3)	14(7)	–	–	–	3(5)
5	8/7	Trelawny	A	L35-55*	R/R	0(3)	11+1(7)	3+2(5)	–	1(3)	7(5)	13+1(7)	–	–	–
6	12/7	Wimbledon	H	W57-33	R/R	10(4)	6(3)	4+2(4)	7+2(5)	11+2(6)	–	17(6)	2(3)	–	–
7	26/7	Mildenhall	H	W61-32	11+1(4)	7+1(4)	12(4)	4(4)	–	1(4)	12+3(5)	14+1(5)	–	–	–
8	30/7	Wimbledon	A	L44-46*	R/R	4(5)	7+1(5)	3(3)	–	1+1(3)	14+2(7)	15+1(7)	–	–	–

CONFERENCE TROPHY continued

No	DATE	OPPONENTS	H/A	RESULT	LEVERINGTON	BEATON	CAMPBELL	STODDART	SHIELD	TULLY	WETHERS	BRANNEY	MABEN	ROYNON	OTHERS
9	16/8	Boston	H	W48-42	6+4(4)	2(4)	10(4)	1+1(4)	–	5(4)	10(5)	14(5)	–	–	–
10	6/9	Stoke	H	W51-39	R/R	8(4)	9+3(5)	4(5)	–	–	13(6)	11+1(5)	0(1)	6+1(4)	–
11	27/9	Buxton	H	W50-40*	R/R	1(3)	10+1(5)	4+1(5)	–	4+1(6)	16+1(6)	15(5)	–	–	–
12	3/10	Boston	A	L22-68	R/R	5(6)	6(5)	7(7)	–	2(5)	–	–	1+1(4)	–	1(3)
13	6/10	Stoke	A	D45-45*	R/R	2(3)	12+2(6)	2+1(4)	–	1(4)	9+2(6)	19(7)	–	–	–
14	12/10	Mildenhall	A	L40-50*	R/R	1+1(4)	–	5(5)	–	0(4)	20(7)	14+1(7)	–	–	0(3)

DETAILS OF OTHER RIDERS:

Match No. 4: Danny Norton 3(5); Match No. 12: Wayne Dunworth 1(3); Match No. 14: Rhys Wilding 0(3).

CONFERENCE TROPHY AVERAGES

Rider	Mts	Rds	Pts	Bon	Tot	Avge	Max
Trent Leverington	4	16	40	6	46	11.50	1 Full; 2 Paid
Craig Branney	11	62	151	9	160	10.32	1 Full; 2 Paid
Matthew Wethers	12	71	162	10	172	9.69	1 Full; 1 Paid
Barry Campbell	13	67	138	14	152	9.07	1 Full; 1 Paid
Carl Shield	4	19	34	8	42	8.84	1 Paid
Adam Roynon	1	4	6	1	7	7.00	–
Gary Beaton	14	57	58	7	65	4.56	–
Sean Stoddart	12	53	42	8	50	3.77	–
Andrew Tully	13	53	38	7	45	3.40	–
Danny Norton	1	5	3	0	3	2.40	–
Keith Maben	3	8	3	1	4	2.00	–
Wayne Dunworth	1	3	1	0	1	1.33	–
Rhys Wilding	1	3	0	0	0	0.00	–

KNOCK-OUT CUP

(* Denotes aggregate victory)

No	DATE	OPPONENTS	H/A	RESULT	LEVERINGTON	BEATON	CAMPBELL	STODDART	LANGLEY	TULLY	WETHERS	MABEN	SHIELD	BRANNEY	ROYNON
1	11/5	Buxton	A	L40-48	R/R	6(6)	14+1(6)	1(4)	0(1)	2(5)	15+2(7)	2(1)	–	–	–
2	31/5	Buxton	H	W55-34*	R/R	4+1(4)	18(6)	3(4)	–	0(1)	12+1(6)	–	10+1(4)	8+1(5)	–
3	6/8	Stoke	A	D45-45	11(6)	5+2(5)	10(5)	4+3(4)	–	2(4)	R/R	–	–	13+1(6)	–
4	9/8	Stoke	H	W58-31*	8+2(5)	9+3(4)	9+1(4)	4+1(4)	–	5+3(4)	12(5)	–	–	11(4)	–
5	15/9	Rye House	A	L31-59	R/R	1(3)	5(5)	0(3)	–	1(2)	15+1(7)	–	–	8(7)	1(3)
6	20/9	Rye House	H	L40-50	11(4)	4+1(4)	6+2(6)	3(5)	–	5+2(4)	11(7)	–	–	R/R	–

BOSTON N.C. WILLIAMS & SON INSURANCE BARRACUDA-BRAVES

ADDRESS: Norfolk Arena, Saddlebow Road, King's Lynn, Norfolk.
PROMOTERS: Stephen Lambert & Malcolm Vasey.
TRACK LENGTH: 342 metres.
FIRST MEETING: 1 April 2000.
YEARS OF OPERATION: 2000–03 British Conference League.

PREVIOUS VENUE: Boston Sports Stadium, New Hammond Beck Road, Boston,
   Lincolnshire.
   YEARS OF OPERATION: 1970–74 British League Division Two; 1975–84 National League;
   1986–87 National League.

CLUB HONOURS

LEAGUE CHAMPIONS: 1973.
KNOCK-OUT CUP WINNERS: 1973, 2000.
PAIRS CHAMPIONS: 1977.
CONFERENCE TROPHY WINNERS: 2003.

RIDER ROSTER 2003

BOAST, Peter   *b. 11 April 1964, Louth, Lincolnshire.*
   BRITISH CAREER: (1994) Mildenhall; (1995) Mildenhall, Sheffield, Wolverhampton,
   Swindon; (1996) Mildenhall, Sheffield (1997) Sheffield; (1998) Skegness, Norfolk,
   Sheffield; (1999) Sheffield, King's Lynn (CL); (2000–02) Boston; (2003) Boston,
   Coventry (BLC), Hull.
CLIFTON, Luke   *b. 29 March 1982, Canterbury, Kent.*
   BRITISH CAREER: (1997) Anglian Angels; (1998) Skegness, Norfolk, King's Lynn (EL);
   (1999) King's Lynn (CL); (2000) Boston, Edinburgh, Arena-Essex; (2001) Arena-Essex,
   Boston; (2003) Boston.
DICKERSON, Roger   *b. 8 July 1965, Ipswich, Suffolk.*
   BRITISH CAREER: (2002) Wimbledon; (2003) Boston, Newport.
DUNWORTH, Wayne   *b. 20 January 1967, Nottingham, Nottinghamshire.*
   BRITISH CAREER: (1984) Boston; (1986) Mildenhall; (1987) Boston; (2002) Boston,
   Carmarthen; (2003) Trelawny (CT), Boston, Peterborough (CL), Armadale (CT).
GARROD, Dean   *b. 11 October 1975, Norwich, Norfolk.*
   BRITISH CAREER: (1993) Middlesbrough; (1994) Mildenhall; (1995–96) Mildenhall,
   Poole; (1997) Mildenhall, Newport; (1998) Mildenhall, Arena-Essex, Sheffield; (1999)
   Mildenhall, Buxton; (2000–03) Boston.
HALL, Richard   *b. 23 August 1984, Northallerton, North Yorkshire.*
   BRITISH CAREER: (2001) Newcastle; (2002) Newcastle (PL & CL), Trelawny, Glasgow;
   (2003) Sheffield (CL & PL), Stoke (PL), Coventry (BLC), Hull (BLC), Newport (PL),
   Boston (KOC & CT), Exeter, Reading, Workington, Somerset.

BOSTON BARRACUDA-BRAVES: back row, left to right: Malcolm Vasey (Co-Promoter/Team Manager), Peter Boast, Dean Garrod, Darren Mallett, Trevor Harding, Stephen Lambert (Co-Promoter). On bike: Mark Thompson. Front, kneeling: Luke Clifton, James Horton.

HARDING, Trevor   *b. 1 November 1986, Perth, Western Australia.*
   BRITISH CAREER: (2002) Sheffield (CL), Carmarthen; (2003) King's Lynn, Boston.
HOLLINGWORTH, Robert   *b. 31 December 1955, Boston, Lincolnshire.*
   BRITISH CAREER: (1973) Berwick; (1974) Boston; (1975) Boston, Hull, King's Lynn,
   Poole, Wolverhampton; (1976) Boston, Wolverhampton, White City; (1977) Boston,
   Wolverhampton; (1978) Edinburgh, Wolverhampton; (1979) Boston, King's Lynn; (1980–
   81) Boston, Coventry; (1982) Boston, King's Lynn; (1983) Scunthorpe; (1984) Boston;
   (1985) Mildenhall; (1986) Boston; (1999) King's Lynn (CL); (2000-02) Boston; (2003)
   Boston, Belle Vue (BLC), Poole (BLC).
HORTON, James   *b. 22 June 1985, Slough, Berkshire.*
   BRITISH CAREER: (2001-02) Peterborough (CL); (2003) Peterborough (BLC & CL),
   Boston (CT), Trelawny (PL & CT).
LOUTH, Karl   *b. 15 February 1987.*
   BRITISH CAREER: (2003) Newport (CL), Boston, Peterborough (CL), Wolverhampton.
McALLAN, David   *b. 20 June 1980, Edinburgh, Scotland.*
   BRITISH CAREER: (1996) Berwick; (1997) Berwick (PL & AL), Sheffield; (1998)
   Berwick, Newcastle; (1999) Edinburgh, Linlithgow; (2000) Ashfield, Stoke; (2001)
   Berwick, Boston, Stoke, Workington, Glasgow, Edinburgh, Newcastle; (2002) Glasgow,
   Sheffield (CL); (2003) Glasgow, Boston.
McCABE, Shane   *b. 3 May 1974, Townsville, Queensland, Australia.*
   BRITISH CAREER: (2002) Peterborough (CL), Edinburgh, Somerset, Trelawny, Rye
   House, Newport, Stoke; (2003) King's Lynn, Boston, Peterborough (CL, ELKOC &
   BLC), Somerset.
MALLETT, Darren   *b. 25 May 1986, Boston, Lincolnshire.*
   BRITISH CAREER: (2001) Somerset, Boston; (2002) Boston; (2003) Boston, King's Lynn.
ROLPH, Darren   *b. 17 May 1982, Braintree, Essex.*
   BRITISH CAREER: (2003) Boston.
THOMPSON, Mark   *b. 8 July 1979, Orsett, Essex.*
   BRITISH CAREER: (1996) Sittingbourne, Linlithgow, Mildenhall, Eastbourne (CL); (1997)
   Anglian Angels; (1998) Mildenhall, Newport, Stoke; (1999) King's Lynn (CL); (2000-01)
   Mildenhall; (2002) King's Lynn (CL), Mildenhall, Arena-Essex, Workington, Stoke;
   (2003) Boston, Stoke (PL), Newport (BLC), Somerset, Peterborough (BLC), Coventry
   (BLC), King's Lynn, Arena-Essex.
WOODHOUSE, Rodney   *b. 8 December 1960.*
   BRITISH CAREER: (2003) Boston.

CONFERENCE LEAGUE

(* Denotes bonus-point victory)

No	DATE	OPPONENTS	H/A	RESULT	THOMPSON	CLIFTON	HOLLINGWORTH	BOAST	HARDING	MALLETT	GARROD	McALLAN	DICKERSON	ROLPH	DUNWORTH	LOUTH
1	18/4	Carmarthen	H	W59-31	5+1(4)	8(4)	8+2(4)	10+1(4)	12+2(5)	13+2(5)	3+2(4)	–	–	–	–	–
2	4/5	Newcastle	A	W48-41	10+1(5)	3(3)	6+2(4)	9+1(5)	11+1(4)	8+4(6)	1(3)	–	–	–	–	–
3	11/5	Wimbledon	H	W58-32	12+1(5)	6+3(4)	9(4)	6+4(4)	10+1(5)	11+3(5)	4(3)	–	–	–	–	–
4	27/5	Swindon	A	W46-43	7(6)	5+2(4)	2+1(3)	–	15(6)	13(7)	4+3(4)	R/R	–	–	–	–
5	15/6	Newport	H	W68-22	15+3(6)	15+3(6)	5+1(3)	5+1(4)	17+1(6)	R/R	11+3(5)	–	–	–	–	–

CONFERENCE TROPHY continued

No	DATE	OPPONENTS	H/A	RESULT	THOMPSON	CLIFTON	HOLLINGWORTH	BOAST	HARDING	MALLETT	GARROD	McALLAN	DICKERSON	ROLPH	DUNWORTH	LOUTH
6	22/6	Peterborough	A	W52-38	8+3(6)	11+3(6)	4+1(4)	7+1(4)	16(6)	R/R	6+2(5)	–	–	–	–	–
7	23/6	Sheffield †	A	W37-35	10+1(4)	7+3(5)	1(3)	–	10(4)	R/R	1(4)	8(4)	–	–	–	–
8	6/7	Carmarthen	A	L43-45*	8(5)	11+1(7)	0(3)	11(6)	–	R/R	11+2(6)	–	2+2(3)	–	–	–
9	13/7	Sheffield	H	L32-58	9(7)	4(3)	9(6)	3(5)	0(1)	R/R	6+2(6)	–	1(2)	–	–	–
10	3/8	Buxton	A	W49-41	R/R	–	5(4)	9+1(6)	18(6)	–	9(6)	–	3+1(4)	5+3(4)	–	–
11	6/8	Wimbledon	A	W49-44*	–	8+3(6)	15(6)	9+2(6)	–	R/R	13+3(7)	–	3+3(3)	1+1(3)	–	–
12	8/8	Newcastle	H	W56-33 *	–	9+2(5)	12+2(5)	–	18(6)	R/R	11+4(5)	–	5(4)	–	1(4)	0(1)
13	10/8	Peterborough	H	W61-29*	–	2(3)	12+2(5)	11(4)	15(5)	–	10(5)	–	6+3(4)	5+3(4)	–	–
14	17/8	Mildenhall	A	L39-50	–	1(4)	6+1(5)	10+2(7)	13(7)	R/R	8(4)	–	1+1(3)	–	–	–
15	23/8	Rye House	A	L26-64	0(2)	3+2(6)	6(5)	13(7)	–	R/R	2(5)	–	2+1(5)	–	–	–
16	8/9	Wolverhampton ‡	A	W40-31	4(3)	5(3)	5+2(4)	7+1(3)	–	7+2(4)	6+3(4)	6+1(3)	–	–	–	–
17	12/9	Rye House	H	L41-49	7(5)	10(6)	7+2(5)	2(3)	R/R	10+1(6)	5+3(5)	–	–	–	–	–
18	26/9	Mildenhall	H	L44-46	7(4)	–	13+1(7)	–	13(5)	6+1(4)	1(3)	–	1+1(3)	3+1(4)	–	–
19	28/9	Wolverhampton	H	W57-33*	13(5)	–	9+2(5)	–	9(3)	13+1(5)	7+1(4)	–	3+2(4)	–	3(4)	–
20	8/10	Oxford	A	L27-63	1(3)	–	3(4)	–	–	R/R	10+1(7)	–	4+1(5)	9+2(7)	0(4)	–
21	12/10	Swindon	H	L44-46*	10+1(6)	–	9+2(5)	–	R/R	11+2(6)	8+1(5)	–	0(3)	6+1(5)	–	–
22	14/10	Buxton	H	W48-42*	14(6)	–	9+1(5)	–	R/R	12+1(6)	6+2(5)	–	4+2(4)	3(4)	–	–
23	17/10	Oxford	H	L31-59	5(6)	–	3+1(4)	2+1(4)	R/R	–	2+1(3)	–	6+2(5)	13(7)	–	0(1)
24	19/10	Newport	A	W48-42*	7+1(5)	–	12(5)	11+3(6)	R/R	10(5)	6+4(5)	–	–	–	–	2+1(4)

† Meeting abandoned after twelve heats, with the result standing.

‡ Meeting abandoned after twelve heats, with the result standing.

CONFERENCE LEAGUE AVERAGES

Rider	Mts	Rds	Pts	Bon	Tot	Avge	Max
Trevor Harding	14	69	177	5	182	10.55	3 Full; 2 Paid
Darren Mallett	11	59	114	17	131	8.88	1 Paid
David McAllan	2	7	14	1	15	8.57	–
Peter Boast	16	78	125	18	143	7.33	–
Robert Hollingworth	24	108	170	23	193	7.15	–
Mark Thompson	19	93	152	12	164	7.05	1 Paid
Luke Clifton	16	75	108	22	130	6.93	1 Paid
Dean Garrod	24	113	151	37	188	6.65	1 Paid
Darren Rolph	8	38	45	11	56	5.89	–
Roger Dickerson	14	52	41	19	60	4.62	–
Karl Louth	3	6	2	1	3	2.00	–
Wayne Dunworth	3	12	4	0	4	1.33	–

CONFERENCE TROPHY

(* Denotes bonus-point victory)

No	DATE	OPPONENTS	H/A	RESULT	THOMPSON	CLIFTON	HOLLINGWORTH	BOAST	HARDING	MALLETT	GARROD	DICKERSON	HORTON	DUNWORTH	McALLAN	OTHERS
1	6/4	Buxton	A	L37-52	1+1(3)	4(4)	2(3)	9+1(5)	5(5)	12+1(7)	4+1(3)	–	–	–	–	–
2	22/4	Trelawny	A	W53-37	8+1(5)	9+1(5)	9+1(4)	–	10(4)	8+2(4)	6+2(4)	3+2(4)	–	–	–	–
3	27/4	Mildenhall	A	W46-44	9(5)	1+1(3)	–	8+1(4)	13+2(5)	10+1(6)	0(3)	–	5+2(4)	–	–	–
4	20/6	Trelawny	H	W51-39*	5(5)	12+2(6)	8+2(5)	5+1(4)	15(5)	R/R	6+2(5)	–	–	–	–	–
5	29/6	Carmarthen	H	W62-30	15+3(6)	–	9+1(5)	9+1(4)	17+1(6)	R/R	7+3(5)	–	5+1(3)	0(1)	–	–
6	16/8	Armadale	A	L42-48	–	3+1(4)	9+1(6)	8+3(6)	–	R/R	3(4)	–	–	0(3)	19(7)	–
7	29/8	Stoke	H	W46-44	10(6)	4+1(3)	10(5)	9+1(6)	R/R	9+3(5)	4+1(5)	–	–	–	–	–
8	7/9	Wimbledon	H	W61-29	13+1(6)	8+2(4)	18+1(7)	7(4)	–	R/R	8+2(5)	7+3(4)	–	–	–	–
9	10/9	Wimbledon	A	W46-44*	6+2(5)	4+1(4)	11+1(6)	15(7)	–	R/R	8+2(5)	–	2+1(3)	–	–	–
10	14/9	Stoke	A	L40-50	R/R	1+1(2)	15(7)	–	–	8+1(6)	10(6)	–	3+1(4)	3+1(3)	–	–
11	21/9	Carmarthen	A	W51-42*	R/R	–	7+1(5)	6+1(5)	17+1(6)	14+2(6)	6+2(5)	–	–	–	–	1(3)
12	3/10	Armadale	H	W68-22*	14+1(5)	6+3(4)	11+1(4)	–	R/R	15(5)	7+4(4)	5(4)	10+2(4)	–	–	–
13	14/10	Buxton	H	W50-40	10+1(5)	–	9+1(5)	–	R/R	7+2(6)	2(3)	–	–	–	–	22+1(11)
14	22/10	Mildenhall	H	W50-40*	10+1(5)	–	7+2(4)	–	R/R	12+2(5)	1(3)	–	–	–	9+1(6)	11+1(7)

DETAILS OF OTHER RIDERS:

Match No. 11: Rodney Woodhouse 1(3); Match No. 13: Richard Hall 18(6); Darren Rolph 4+1(5); Match No. 14: Richard Hall 11+1(6); Darren Rolph 0(1).

CONFERENCE TROPHY AVERAGES

Rider	Mts	Rds	Pts	Bon	Tot	Avge	Max
Trevor Harding	6	31	77	4	81	10.45	1 Full; 3 Paid
Richard Hall	2	12	29	1	30	10.00	1 Full
David McAllan	2	13	28	1	29	8.92	–
Darren Mallett	9	50	95	14	109	8.72	1 Full
Robert Hollingworth	13	66	125	12	137	8.30	1 Paid
Mark Thompson	11	56	101	11	112	8.00	2 Paid
Peter Boast	9	45	76	9	85	7.56	–
Danny Norton	5	18	25	7	32	7.11	1 Paid
Luke Clifton	10	39	52	13	65	6.67	–
Roger Dickerson	3	12	15	5	20	6.67	–
Dean Garrod	14	60	72	19	91	6.07	–
Darren Rolph	2	6	4	1	5	3.33	–
Wayne Dunworth	3	7	3	1	4	2.29	–
Rodney Woodhouse	1	3	1	0	1	1.33	–

KNOCK-OUT CUP

(* Denotes aggregate victory)

No	DATE	OPPONENTS	H/A	RESULT	THOMPSON	CLIFTON	HOLLINGWORTH	BOAST	HARDING	MALLETT	HORTON	McCABE	McALLAN	GARROD	OTHERS
1	4/4	Wimbledon	H	W55-35	7+1(4)	7+1(4)	8(4)	5+1(4)	8+1(5)	16+3(7)	4+1(3)	–	–	–	–
2	16/4	Wimbledon	A	L35-55	3(4)	4+2(4)	9(6)	–	–		1(4)	1(2)	13(6)	4(3)	
3	23/7	Wimbledon (R)	A	L44-46	0(3)	15+2(7)	10+1(6)	12+1(6)	–	R/R	–	1+1(3)	–	6+3(5)	–
4	27/7	Wimbledon (R)	H	W50-39*	–	4(4)	14(5)	5+1(4)	–	R/R	–	–	–	11+3(7)	16(10)
5	13/9	Mildenhall	A	L35-55	1(4)	1(3)	*3(3)	4(4)	–	9+1(6)	–	–	–	4+2(4)	13(6)
6	19/9	Mildenhall	H	D45-45	4+1(3)	–	4+1(4)	2+2(4)	14(5)	7(4)	–	–	–	5(5)	9(5)

(R) = Replay

DETAILS OF OTHER RIDERS:

Match No. 4: Richard Hall 14(6); Darren Rolph 2(1); Roger Dickerson 0(3); Match No. 5: Richard Hall 13(6); Match No. 6: Richard Hall 9(6).

OTHER MEETINGS

23 March: Three-Team Tournament (first-leg)

Mildenhall 52, Boston 29, (Trevor Harding 8+1; Mark Thompson 7; Peter Boast 6+1; Darren Mallett 5+2; Robert Hollingworth 3+1; Luke Clifton 0) Peterborough 26.

28 March: Three-Team Tournament (second-leg)

Boston 36, (Trevor Harding 9+2; Mark Thompson 9; Robert Hollingworth 8; Darren Mallett 7+1; Peter Boast 2+1; Luke Clifton 1+1) Mildenhall 42, Peterborough 29.

5 April: Three-Team Tournament (third-leg)

Peterborough 42, Mildenhall 42, Boston 24 (Darren Mallett 6+1; Mark Thompson 5; Peter Boast 5; Luke Clifton 4+1; Dean Garrod 3; Robert Hollingworth 1+1). Aggregate result: Mildenhall 136 Peterborough 97, Boston 89.

1 June: Lincolnshire Cup

Boston 54 (Mark Thompson 13+1; Robert Hollingworth 11; Trevor Harding 10; Luke Clifton 7+1; Dean Garrod 5+1; Peter Boast 4+1; Darren Mallett 4+1) Scunthorpe Select 35 (Chris Collins 14+1; Benji Compton 9; Will Beveridge 8; Wayne Dunworth 2; Roger Dickerson 1+1; David Speight 1; Jamie Rodgers 0; Richard Hall R/R).

22 August: Conference League

Boston 14 (Dean Garrod 3+1; Luke Clifton 3; Mark Thompson 2; Robert Hollingworth 2; Peter Boast 2; Darren Rolph 1+1; Trevor Harding 1+1) Buxton 10 – meeting abandoned after heat four.

BUXTON HITMEN

ADDRESS: Buxton Raceway, Hi-Edge, off A53 Leek-to-Buxton Road, Buxton, Derbyshire.
PROMOTERS: Tim Jones & Mark Jenkins.
TRACK LENGTH: 240 metres.
FIRST MEETING: 19 May 1996.

YEARS OF OPERATION: 1996 British Conference League; 1997 British Amateur League; 1998-03 British Conference League.

PREVIOUS VENUE: Buxton Stadium, off A53 Leek-to-Buxton Road, Buxton, Derbyshire. YEARS OF OPERATION: 1994 British League Division Three; 1995 British Academy League.

CLUB HONOURS

KNOCK-OUT CUP WINNERS: 2002.

RIDER ROSTER 2003

ALLOTT, Adam   *b. 19 March 1983, Stockport, Greater Manchester.*
BRITISH CAREER: (1998) Norfolk, Buxton; (1999) Buxton, Sheffield; (2000) Sheffield, Owlerton; (2001) Sheffield; (2002) Sheffield (CL), Swindon, Somerset; (2003) Buxton, Stoke (BLC), King's Lynn.

BETHELL, Jonathan   *b. 18 March 1973, Kendal, Cumbria.*
BRITISH CAREER: (2003) Oxford (CL), Buxton.

BEVERIDGE, Will   *b. 9 September 1975, Hexham, Northumberland.*
BRITISH CAREER: (1992) Exeter; (1993) Middlesbrough, Newcastle, Sheffield, Exeter; (1994) Middlesbrough, Berwick, Cleveland; (1995) Berwick, Sheffield, Exeter, Oxford, Coventry, Swindon; (1996) Berwick; (1997-99) Glasgow; (2000) Newcastle, Edinburgh; (2001) Berwick, Boston, Glasgow, Reading, Stoke; (2002) Stoke, Buxton; (2003) Buxton.

BRANNEY, John   *b. 7 November 1985, Whitehaven, Cumbria.*
BRITISH CAREER: (2002) Rye House (CL), Newcastle (CL); (2003) Newcastle (CL), Wimbledon (CT), Mildenhall (CT), King's Lynn, Exeter, Newport (PL), Buxton (CT).

BROWN, Alan   *b. 19 February 1959, Stoke-on-Trent, Staffordshire.*
BRITISH CAREER: (2002) Buxton; (2003) Oxford (CL), Buxton, Newport (CL), Trelawny (CT).

BURNETT, Paul   *b. 24 October 1981, Bradford, West Yorkshire.*
BRITISH CAREER: (1997) Buxton, Belle Vue (AL), Western Warriors; (1998-03) Buxton.

COLLINS, Chris   *b. 18 July 1982, Manchester.*
BRITISH CAREER: (2001) Buxton, Newcastle, Stoke; (2002) Buxton, Newport (PL), Workington; (2003) Workington, Buxton.

DERBYSHIRE, Lee   *b. 3 December 1981, Stockport, Greater Manchester.*
BRITISH CAREER: (2002) Buxton; (2003) Buxton, Hull, King's Lynn, Belle Vue (BLC).

FINLOW, Rob   *b. 27 May 1984, Bromsgrove, Hereford & Worcester.*
BRITISH CAREER: (1999) Newport (CL); (2000) Newport (CL), Buxton; (2001) Newport (CL & PL); (2002) Newport (CL & PL), Wolverhampton (CT), Somerset; (2003) Wolverhampton (CL & BLC), Somerset, Stoke (KOC), Buxton (CT).

FLINT, Gary   *b. 5 May 1982, Ashington, Durham.*
BRITISH CAREER: (1999) Berwick, Linlithgow, St Austell; (2000) Ashfield, Berwick; (2001) Buxton, Newcastle, Exeter, Sheffield (PL), Berwick; (2002) Newcastle (CL), Somerset, Rye House (PL), Isle of Wight, Glasgow; (2003) Buxton, Sheffield (CL), Reading, Stoke (CT).

BUXTON HITMEN: back row, left to right: Jack Lee (Team Manager), Chris Collins, Paul Burnett, Jonathan Bethell, John Oliver, James Wright. Front row, left to right: Alan Brown, Paul Sharples, Lee Derbyshire, Martin McDermott.

KNOWLES, Phil   b. 10 May 1978, Bradford, West Yorkshire.
  BRITISH CAREER: (1994) Buxton; (1995) Belle Vue; (1996) Sheffield (CL), Belle Vue; (1997) Belle Vue (AL & EL); (1998) Buxton; (1999–01); (2003) Buxton.

McDERMOTT, Martin   b. 13 January 1988, Manchester.
  BRITISH CAREER: (2003) Buxton.

OLIVER, John   b. 22 July 1987, Melbourne, Victoria, Australia.
  BRITISH CAREER: (2003) Carmarthen (CL), Buxton, King's Lynn.

PICKERING, Phil   b. 25 October 1963, Hull, East Yorkshire.
  BRITISH CAREER: (1996) Peterborough (CL), Sheffield (CL); (1998) Buxton; (1999) Berwick, Buxton; (2000) Buxton, Newcastle, Berwick, Hull; (2001) Berwick, Boston, Newport (PL), Trelawny; (2003) Buxton.

SHARPLES, Paul   b. 25 April 1974, Manchester.
  BRITISH CAREER: (2002) Belle Vue; (2003) Buxton.

TUTTON, Matt   b. 19 June 1982, Newport, South Wales.
  BRITISH CAREER: (2000) Rye House; (2002) Swindon (CT), Wimbledon; (2003) Mildenhall, Buxton, Carmarthen (CT), Newport (CL).

WILSON, Ben   b. 15 March 1986, Sheffield, South Yorkshire.
  BRITISH CAREER: (2001) Sheffield (CL); (2002) Sheffield (CL & PL), Glasgow; (2003) Sheffield (PL & CL), Buxton (CT).

WRIGHT, James   b. 13 June 1986, Stockport, Greater Manchester.
  BRITISH CAREER: (2002) Buxton; (2003) Buxton, Belle Vue (BLC), Newcastle (PL), Stoke (PL), Workington, Hull, King's Lynn.

CONFERENCE LEAGUE

(* Denotes bonus-point victory)

No	DATE	OPPONENTS	H/A	RESULT	BEVERIDGE	KNOWLES	WRIGHT	COLLINS	FLINT	DERBYSHIRE	BURNETT	BETHELL	TUTTON	SHARPLES	OLIVER	OTHERS
1	20/4	Oxford	H	W56-34	9(4)	4+2(3)	14(5)	13+2(5)	8+3(5)	5(4)	–	–	–	–	–	3+1(4)
2	7/5	Wimbledon	A	L43-47	15(6)	1(3)	6(4)	14+1(6)	1(3)	5+1(5)	–	–	–	–	–	1(3)
3	18/5	Carmarthen	H	W49-40	5+2(4)	7(4)	13(5)	10+2(5)	1+1(4)	–	0(1)	13+3(7)	–	–	–	–
4	25/5	Mildenhall	A	L34-56	9(5)	1+1(4)	10+1(6)	12(6)	–	–	–	2+1(3)	0(3)	–	–	0(3)
5	26/5	Mildenhall	H	W47-43	18(6)	2+1(4)	12(6)	R/R	1+1(3)	–	–	9(7)	5+1(4)	–	–	–
6	10/6	Wolverhampton	A	L41-48	9+1(5)	–	10+2(5)	9+1(5)	–	8+1(6)	–	3+1(4)	2(4)	0(1)	–	–
7	22/6	Sheffield	H	W54-36	9(4)	–	14+1(5)	13(5)	–	10+1(6)	–	5+2(4)	2(3)	1+1(3)	–	–
8	23/6	Sheffield	A	L37-53*	12(6)	–	14(6)	7(5)	0(3)	4+1(4)	–	–	0(3)	0(3)	–	–
9	13/7	Carmarthen	A	L26-64	–	–	7(6)	R/R	–	12(7)	2(4)	4+1(5)	1(4)	–	–	0(4)
10	20/7	Wolverhampton	H	W52-35*	–	6+3(4)	16(6)	R/R	–	7+1(4)	6+2(4)	8+2(4)	–	3+1(4)	6+2(4)	–
11	3/8	Boston	H	L41-49	–	1(3)	18(7)	R/R	–	10+2(7)	7+2(6)	5+2(4)	–	–	0(3)	–
12	10/8	Rye House	H	W46-44	–	–	16(6)	R/R	–	10+1(6)	6+2(5)	5+1(4)	–	–	8+1(5)	1(4)
13	12/8	Swindon	A	L36-54	–	–	15(7)	R/R	–	12(7)	6+3(6)	–	1(3)	1(3)	1+1(4)	–
14	17/8	Newport	H	W60-30	–	–	13+1(5)	R/R	–	15(5)	7+3(4)	8+1(4)	2(4)	9+3(4)	6+3(4)	–
15	25/8	Newcastle	A	L33-57	–	–	19(7)	R/R	–	3(3)	4+2(6)	1(4)	–	3(5)	3(5)	–
16	31/8	Swindon	H	W58-31*	–	–	15(5)	18(6)	–	R/R	8+2(5)	10+3(5)	0(3)	–	7+1(5)	0(1)
17	5/9	Oxford	A	L31-59	–	–	18(7)	10(7)	–	R/R	1+1(4)	1(5)	0(3)	–	1(4)	–
18	7/9	Peterborough	H	W57-33	–	–	16(6)	18(6)	–	R/R	10+3(5)	6+3(3)	–	–	3(5)	4+1(5)

CONFERENCE LEAGUE continued

No	DATE	OPPONENTS	H/A	RESULT	BEVERIDGE	KNOWLES	WRIGHT	COLLINS	FLINT	DERBYSHIRE	BURNETT	BETHELL	TUTTON	SHARPLES	OLIVER	OTHERS
19	8/9	Rye House	A	L39-50	–	–	12+1(7)	18(7)	–	R/R	2+1(3)	–	–	5+1(5)	0(4)	2(4)
20	14/9	Newcastle	H	W59-31*	–	–	12(5)	15(5)	–	4+2(4)	2(1)	5+2(4)	–	9+4(5)	12+2(6)	–
21	16/9	Peterborough	A¶	W48-41*	–	–	15(5)	8+1(4)	–	13+1(5)	–	5+1(4)	–	3+1(4)	3(4)	1(4)
22	5/10	Wimbledon	H	W61-26*	–	–	14+1(5)	15(5)	–	10+1(4)	5+3(4)	9+3(4)	–	4(4)	4+1(4)	–
23	14/10	Boston	A	L42-48	–	–	10(5)	13+1(6)	–	11+2(6)	0(3)	2(3)	–	2+1(3)	4+2(4)	–
24	26/10	Newport	A	D45-45*	–	–	10(5)	10(5)	–	3+2(4)	9(4)	5+2(4)	–	6+3(5)	–	2+2(3)

¶ Match raced at King's Lynn.

DETAILS OF OTHER RIDERS:

Match No. 1: Phil Pickering 3+1(4); Match No. 2: Alan Brown 1(3); Match No. 4: Phil Pickering 0(3); Match No. 9: Alan Brown 0(4); Match No. 12: Alan Brown 1(4); Match No. 16: Martin McDermott 0(1); Match No. 18: Martin McDermott 4+1(5); Match No. 19: Martin McDermott 2(4); Match No. 21: Martin McDermott 1(4); Match No. 24: Martin McDermott 2+2(3).

CONFERENCE LEAGUE AVERAGES

Rider	Mts	Rds	Pts	Bon	Tot	Avge	Max
Chris Collins	16	88	203	8	211	9.59	4 Full; 1 Paid
James Wright	24	136	319	7	326	9.59	2 Full; 2 Paid
Will Beveridge	8	40	86	3	89	8.90	1 Full
Lee Derbyshire	17	87	142	16	158	7.26	1 Full
Jonathan Bethell	19	82	106	28	134	6.54	1 Paid
Paul Burnett	16	65	75	24	99	6.09	–
Paul Sharples	13	49	46	15	61	4.98	1 Paid
John Oliver	14	61	58	13	71	4.66	–
Phil Knowles	7	25	22	7	29	4.64	–
Gary Flint	5	18	11	5	16	3.56	–
Martin McDermott	5	17	9	3	12	2.82	–
Phil Pickering	2	7	3	1	4	2.29	–
Matt Tutton	10	34	13	1	14	1.65	–
Alan Brown	3	11	2	0	2	0.73	–

CONFERENCE TROPHY

(* Denotes bonus-point victory)

No	DATE	OPPONENTS	H/A	RESULT	BEVERIDGE	COLLINS	WRIGHT	ALLOTT	FLINT	DERBYSHIRE	BURNETT	KNOWLES	TUTTON	BETHELL	WILSON	OTHERS
1	6/4	Boston	H	W52-37	13(5)	10+2(5)	9(4)	10+1(4)	2(3)	3+2(5)	5(4)	–	–	–	–	–
2	13/4	Mildenhall	A	L31-59	11(6)	10(6)	2(4)	3(4)	0(3)	1(3)	–	–	–	–	–	4+1(3)
3	18/5	Carmarthen †	H	W37-35	9(3)	9(3)	8(3)	–	0(2)	–	–	1(3)	3+2(4)	7(6)	–	–
4	15/6	Wimbledon	H	W48-41	4(3)	12+1(5)	13+1(5)	–	–	13+2(6)	–	1+1(3)	3+1(4)	2+1(4)	–	–
5	6/7	Armadale	H	W47-43	3(3)	R/R	14(6)	–	–	13+1(7)	–	–	1(3)	7+3(5)	9+2(6)	–
6	13/7	Carmarthen	A	L42-46	–	R/R	16(7)	–	–	10+2(7)	4(3)	–	1(3)	11+3(7)	–	0(3)
7	16/7	Wimbledon	A	L41-46*	–	R/R	12+2(6)	–	–	6(6)	1+1(4)	–	–	4(4)	–	18+2(11)

CONFERENCE TROPHY continued

No	DATE	OPPONENTS	H/A	RESULT	BEVERIDGE	COLLINS	WRIGHT	ALLOTT	FLINT	DERBYSHIRE	BURNETT	KNOWLES	TUTTON	BETHELL	WILSON	OTHERS
8	27/7	Mildenhall	H	W53-37	–	R/R	15+2(6)	–	–	13(5)	6+1(4)	–	0(3)	–	12(6)	7+3(6)
9	24/8	Stoke	H	W49-41	–	R/R	15(6)	–	–	10(6)	10+4(6)	–	–	9+1(5)	–	5+2(7)
10	24/8	Stoke	A	L44-45*	–	R/R	14(6)	–	–	10(6)	8+1(5)	–	–	5+1(6)	–	7+3(7)
11	21/9	Trelawny	H	W52-38	–	13+1(5)	15(5)	–	–	8+1(4)	3+2(4)	–	–	6+1(4)	–	7+2(8)
12	23/9	Trelawny	A	W48-42*	–	15(6)	13+1(6)	–	–	R/R	0(1)	–	–	9+1(7)	–	11+5(10)
13	27/9	Armadale	A	L40-50	–	R/R	9+1(6)	–	–	14+1(7)	–	–	–	12(6)	–	5+2(11)
14	14/10	Boston	A	L40-50*	–	14+1(6)	12+1(6)	–	–	8(5)	0(3)	–	–	2+1(3)	–	4+2(7)

† Meeting abandoned after twelve heats, with the result standing.

DETAILS OF OTHER RIDERS:

Match No. 2: Phil Pickering 4+1(3); Match No. 6: Alan Brown 0(3); Match No. 7: Rob Finlow 15(7); Paul Sharples 3+2(4); Match No. 8: Rob Finlow 4+1(4); John Oliver 3+2(2); Match No. 9: Paul Sharples 4+2(4); John Oliver 1(3); Match No. 10: John Oliver 6+2(4); Paul Sharples 1+1(3); Match No. 11: John Oliver 6+2(5); Martin McDermott 1(3); Match No. 12: John Oliver 7+3(5); Paul Sharples 4+2(5); Match No. 13: John Oliver 3+1(5); Paul Sharples 1+1(3); John Branney 1(3); Match No. 14: John Oliver 4+2(4); Paul Sharples 0(3).

CONFERENCE TROPHY AVERAGES

Rider	Mts	Rds	Pts	Bon	Tot	Avge	Max
Chris Collins	7	36	83	5	88	9.78	–
James Wright	14	76	167	8	175	9.21	1 Full
Will Beveridge	5	20	40	0	40	8.00	–
Ben Wilson	2	12	21	2	23	7.67	–
Rob Finlow	2	11	19	1	20	7.27	–
Lee Derbyshire	12	67	109	9	118	7.04	–
Adam Allott	2	8	13	1	14	7.00	–
Phil Pickering	1	3	4	1	5	6.67	–
John Oliver	7	28	30	12	42	6.00	–
Jonathan Bethell	12	60	74	12	86	5.73	–
Paul Burnett	9	34	37	9	46	5.41	–
Paul Sharples	6	22	13	8	21	3.82	–
Matt Tutton	4	14	8	3	11	3.14	–
Phil Knowles	2	6	2	1	3	2.00	–
John Branney	1	3	1	0	1	1.33	–
Martin McDermott	1	3	1	0	1	1.33	–
Gary Flint	3	8	2	0	2	1.00	–
Alan Brown	1	3	0	0	0	0.00	–

KNOCK-OUT CUP

No	DATE	OPPONENTS	H/A	RESULT	BEVERIDGE	BROWN	KNOWLES	WRIGHT	COLLINS	FLINT	DERBYSHIRE	TUTTON	BETHELL
1	11/5	Armadale	H	W48-40	11(5)	1(3)	2+1(4)	11(4)	14+1(5)	6+1(5)	3(4)	–	–
2	31/5	Armadale	A	L34-55	13+1(7)	–	–	10+1(7)	R/R	0(3)	6(6)	1+1(3)	4+1(4)

OTHER MEETINGS

1 June: Youth International

Great Britain 42 (Lee Smart 11+2; Harland Cook 11+1; Jamie Westacott 10+2; Adam Roynon 5; Charles Wright 3; Andrew Tully 2+2) Germany 47 (Alexander Lieschke 15+2; Tobias Busch 11; Kevin Woelbert 7; Richard Speiser 6; Stefan Kurtz 5+2; Frank Facher 3; Soenke Peterson 0).

25 June: Conference Four-Team Tournament

Hull 19, Buxton 29 (Chris Collins 10; James Wright 9; Lee Derbyshire 7; Jonathan Bethell 3), Scunthorpe 25, Wolverhampton 23 – staged at Hull.

22 August: Conference League

Boston 14 Buxton 10 (Lee Derbyshire 6; John Oliver 3; James Wright 1; Paul Burnett 0; Paul Sharples 0; Jonathan Bethell 0; Chris Collins R/R) – meeting abandoned after heat four.

KEN MOSS – A TRIBUTE

Born in July 1937, Ken Moss created his own little piece of speedway history, when, on 8 May 1968, he was a member of the newly-formed Belle Vue 'Colts' side, which raced against Canterbury on the old Hyde Road circuit in the very first British League Division Two match. He was on the winning side too, since the Colts claimed a 55-23 success, and Ken, riding as reserve, netted 3+2 points from his two programmed starts. Ken, along with his great mate Ken Eyre, were both Buxton-based grass-track riders, who had previously joined the Belle Vue Training School, run by Dent Oliver during the winter of 1967. The idea of a Second Division had been agreed to by the BSPA as a way of giving young riders opportunities to make good, and the training sessions at the famous Manchester venue proved most successful. In actual fact, no less than six of the Colts' winning combination in that first match had come via the school, the one exception being a young Australian named John Woodcock, although even he duly took advantage of the training facilities to become a valued member of the Colts line-up. In the main, Ken rode as a reserve for Belle Vue's second side, but was surely one of the best in the business, as he accumulated 50 points from thirteen league matches for an average of 6.82. Indeed, with a final figure like that, he would have filled the role of a heat-leader in at least three other teams, while being a solid second-string in all of the rest. Small wonder then that the Colts became Division Two Champions, winning all their home matches, and losing just four on their travels. Ken was still on board with the side in 1969, when he became a most consistent rider, racking up 166 league points from twenty-nine matches for a 7.71 average, as the Colts retained their League Championship. On top of that, he also played a full part in the Colts' completion of a magnificent double, when they gained a 91-65 aggregate victory over Crewe to lift the Knock-Out Cup. Although Ken had been rather late in deciding to take up speedway, he was a marvellous rider to have in the Belle Vue team, being ever-willing to help and encourage the number of excellent youngsters who flocked to the Manchester venue for racing opportunities. In 1969, Ken had secured his first paid maximum (8+4) in a Knock-Out Cup tie against Ipswich at Hyde Road on 16 July, but in 1970, when the Colts moved their operation to Rochdale at a cost of £42,000, he recorded his first full maximum in a home league match versus Rayleigh on 4 October. By contrast to the sweeping bends of the Belle Vue circuit, the 418-yard Rochdale racing strip was constructed around a rugby pitch, and with 142 points to his name from twenty-eight matches, the track's uncompromising shape was no doubt a contributory factor in Ken's league average falling slightly to 6.60. Despite this, he was happy to remain with the Hornets the following season (when a young man by the name of Peter Collins burst into the side, and really made folk sit up and take notice). All told, Ken raced in thirty league matches, scoring 143 points for an average of 5.42, and when Rochdale closed down at the end of the campaign, he was temped to link up with Ellesmere Port in time for their opening in 1972. Unfortunately, things didn't work out for him at Thornton Road, and after completing just two league matches, he was forced to retire through injury. During his time in the saddle, Ken had also made fleeting appearances in the main Belle Vue Aces side during 1968 and 1969, but with his career over, he concentrated on building up his dairy business. He also kept an eagle eye on the sport, and particularly future British Champion Andy Smith, whom he generously sponsored and encouraged. Later on, after the highly regarded former Belle Vue rider Chris Morton had established a track in the Conference League, Ken again became involved in the sport with his hometown team, Buxton. He spent hour upon hour working on track maintenance and, in 1996, was responsible for the building of a purpose-built 240-metre raceway, adjacent to the original one, which had been housed within a stock-car stadium. Ken became sole promoter at Buxton in 1998, and the track he had built was a real credit to him, being smooth-surfaced with an ideal shape for youngsters to learn their craft. It's fair to say that facilities are sparse at the venue, but it is a cheerful little setting, with wonderful hillside views. Sadly, before Christmas in 2002, Ken learned he had terminal cancer, but so typically of the man, he took the news in his stride, and made sure everything at the Buxton circuit was in perfect order, before reaching agreement with Tim Jones and Mark Jenkins to take over as promoters for the 2003 season. Ken subsequently passed away in March, having put untold monies into his track, and although he naturally never told anyone just how much, the week-on-week improvements remain for all to see. Ken's contribution to Buxton speedway simply cannot be explained in mere words, for he gave opportunities to many youngsters, and thankfully the club lives on for others to enjoy from either side of the superbly constructed safety fence.

CARMARTHEN DRAGONS

ADDRESS: United Counties Showground, Nantyci, Carmarthen, West Wales.
PROMOTERS: Nigel Meakins & Gordon Meakins.
TRACK LENGTH: 242 metres.
FIRST MEETING: 21 April 2002.
YEARS OF OPERATION: 2002-03 British Conference League.

CLUB HONOURS

None.

RIDER ROSTER 2003

ANDREWS, Darren   *b. 19 January 1977, Banbury, Oxfordshire.*
    BRITISH CAREER: (1993) Coventry, Oxford; (1994) Coventry, Oxford, Mildenhall; (1995) Sittingbourne; (1996) Reading (CL); (1997) Berwick, Hull, Long Eaton, Oxford (PL & AL), Isle of Wight; (2000) St Austell; (2001) Rye House; (2002) Mildenhall, Hull; (2003) Oxford (CL & BLC), Carmarthen (CT).

BLACKMAN, Corey   *b. 30 April 1977, Perth, Western Australia.*
    BRITISH CAREER: (2002) Carmarthen, Reading, Edinburgh, Glasgow, Exeter, Wolverhampton (CT), Sheffield (CL), Trelawny; (2003) Exeter, Carmarthen.

CANDY, Paul   *b. 4 February 1980, Basingstoke, Hampshire.*
    BRITISH CAREER: (2003) Carmarthen, Somerset, Exeter.

CROSS, Matthew   *b. 26 August 1968, Taunton, Somerset.*
    BRITISH CAREER: (1987) Swindon; (1988) Poole; (1989) Swindon, Peterborough; (1990-92) Swindon; (1993) Swindon, Poole; (1994) Reading; (2000-01) Somerset; (2002-03) Carmarthen.

DAVIES, Chris   *b. 16 January 1976, Caerphilly, Mid Glamorgan.*
    BRITISH CAREER: (2003) Carmarthen.

EVANS, Dyfed   *b. 27 February 1970, Aberystwyth, Ceredigion, Mid Wales*
    BRITISH CAREER: (2002) Rye House (CL), Carmarthen, Wimbledon; (2003) Carmarthen.

FELTON, Dean   *b. 18 August 1969, Wolverhampton, West Midlands.*
    BRITISH CAREER: (1994) Buxton, Oxford, Ipswich; (1995-96) Buxton; (1997) Buxton, Stoke, Edinburgh, Skegness, Long Eaton, Shuttle Cubs; (1998) Stoke; (1999) Berwick, Glasgow; (2000) Buxton, Berwick; (2001) Stoke, Buxton, Edinburgh, Berwick; (2002) Carmarthen; (2003) Carmarthen, Belle Vue (BLC), Poole (BLC), Eastbourne (BLC), Wolverhampton (BLC).

GOUGH, David   *b. 11 January 1986, Newport, South Wales.*
    BRITISH CAREER: (2001) Newport (CL); (2002) Carmarthen; (2003) Carmarthen, Somerset (BLC), Newport (CL).

HATTON, Darren   *b. 31 March 1982, Cardiff, South Glamorgan, Wales.*
    BRITISH CAREER: (1999) King's Lynn (CL), Newport (CL); (2000) Rye House, Ashfield; (2002-03) Carmarthen.

HODGSON, Daniel   *b. 21 January 1982, Bradford, West Yorkshire.*
    BRITISH CAREER: (1998) Buxton; (1999) King's Lynn (CL); (2000) Buxton, Hull; (2001) Somerset, Sheffield (PL), Newport (CL); (2003) Carmarthen, King's Lynn (BLC).

MEAKINS, Gordon   *b. 18 March 1974, Aylesbury, Buckinghamshire.*
    BRITISH CAREER: (1999) King's Lynn (CL); (2000) Peterborough (CL); (2001) Buxton; (2002) Carmarthen; (2003) Carmarthen, Somerset (BLC).

NETTLESHIP, Scott   *b. 16 May 1984, Newcastle, Tyne & Wear.*
    BRITISH CAREER: (2003) Newcastle (CL), Mildenhall, Swindon (CL), Carmarthen, Peterborough.

OLIVER, John   *b. 22 July 1987, Melbourne, Victoria, Australia.*
    BRITISH CAREER: (2003) Carmarthen (CL), Buxton, King's Lynn.

POWELL, Ben   *b. 29 November 1984, Helensvale, Gold Coast, Queensland, Australia.*
    BRITISH CAREER: (2002) Sheffield (CL), Edinburgh, Trelawny, Glasgow; (2003) Carmarthen, Exeter.

CARMARTHEN DRAGONS: back row, left to right: Gordon Meakins, Corey Blackman, Nigel Meakins (Co-Promoter/Team Manager), Dean Felton, Darren Hatton. On bike: Craig Taylor. Front, kneeling: Ben Powell, David Gough.

ROWLETT, Thomas   *b. 22 January 1979, Wisbech, Cambridgeshire.*
    BRITISH CAREER: (1999) King's Lynn (CL); (2000-01) Mildenhall; (2002) Mildenhall, Wimbledon; (2003) Mildenhall, Carmarthen (CT), Oxford (CLKOC), Newport (CL).

STODDART, Sean   *b. 20 January 1987, Edinburgh, Scotland.*
    BRITISH CAREER: (2003) Armadale, Trelawny (CT), Carmarthen (CT), Newcastle (CL).

TAYLOR, Craig   *b. 31 January 1974, Dudley, West Midlands.*
    BRITISH CAREER: (1993) Wolverhampton; (1994) Stoke, Wolverhampton, Cradley Heath, Berwick; (1995) Stoke, Wolverhampton, Long Eaton, Belle Vue; Cradley Heath, Oxford; (1996) Buxton, Wolverhampton; (1997) Stoke, Wolverhampton; (1998) Berwick, Stoke; (1999) Wolverhampton; (2000) Newport; (2001) Buxton; (2002) Carmarthen; (2003) Carmarthen, Poole (BLC).

TUTTON, Matt   *b. 19 June 1982, Newport, South Wales.*
    BRITISH CAREER: (2000) Rye House; (2002) Swindon (CT), Wimbledon; (2003) Mildenhall, Buxton, Carmarthen (CT), Newport (CL).

CONFERENCE LEAGUE

(* Denotes bonus-point victory)

No	DATE	OPPONENTS	H/A	RESULT	FELTON	HATTON	CROSS	CANDY	TAYLOR	GOUGH	MEAKINS	HODGSON	BLACKMAN	POWELL	OTHERS
1	23/3	Wolverhampton	H	L43-45	10(5)	3+2(4)	6(4)	2+1(3)	9(5)	8+1(5)	5+2(4)	–	–	–	–
2	6/4	Swindon	H	L41-49	7+1(5)	7+1(5)	8(4)	2+2(3)	10(5)	–	6+1(5)	–	–	–	1(3)
3	18/4	Boston	A	L31-59	5(4)	1(6)	R/R	3+1(4)	12(6)	–	5(4)	5(6)	–	–	–
4	20/4	Mildenhall	H	L41-50	6(5)	4+1(4)	14+1(6)	2+2(3)	10(6)	–	3(3)	–	–	–	2+1(3)
5	4/5	Sheffield	H	L37-52	10(7)	3(3)	11+1(7)	–	R/R	8+1(5)	2(3)	3+2(5)	–	–	–
6	14/5	Wimbledon	A	L30-60	10(7)	1(3)	R/R	–	10+1(6)	–	2(3)	0(4)	7(7)	–	–
7	18/5	Buxton	A	L40-49	7+1(4)	2+2(4)	–	–	1(4)	–	1(3)	7(5)	13(5)	9(5)	–
8	1/6	Wimbledon	H	L42-48	5+1(4)	5+1(4)	–	–	9(5)	4+1(5)	3(3)	–	7+2(4)	9+1(5)	–
9	6/6	Oxford	A	L34-57	4+2(5)	4(4)	–	–	6(3)	3(3)	2(3)	–	9+1(6)	6+1(6)	–
10	8/6	Rye House	H	L36-54	12+1(5)	3(3)	4+2(4)	–	R/R	1+1(3)	–	–	9(6)	5(6)	2+1(3)
11	6/7	Boston	H	W45-43	4+1(4)	7(5)	6(4)	1+1(3)	13+1(5)	–	–	3+1(4)	–	11(5)	–
12	13/7	Buxton	H	W64-26*	8+3(4)	8+2(4)	8+3(4)	–	15(5)	–	–	2(4)	11(4)	12+3(5)	–
13	20/7	Newport	A	W49-40	7+1(5)	3+2(4)	8+2(5)	–	12+1(6)	–	–	4+2(4)	R/R	15+1(6)	–
14	27/7	Peterborough	H	W48-41	9+3(5)	8+2(6)	9+1(5)	–	5(3)	–	2+1(2)	3(4)	R/R	12(5)	–
15	7/8	Swindon †	A	L29-48	3(4)	2+1(5)	8+2(5)	–	5+1(4)	–	–	2(3)	R/R	9(5)	–
16	18/8	Rye House	A	L30-58	11(7)	7+3(7)	–	–	2(4)	–	3+2(3)	1+1(3)	R/R	6(6)	–
17	19/8	Wolverhampton	A	W47-43*	10(4)	4+1(4)	–	5+1(4)	11+2(5)	–	3+1(4)	2+1(4)	–	12(5)	–
18	31/8	Newcastle	A	L29-58	10+1(6)	2(5)	–	–	–	–	1+1(3)	1(5)	R/R	13(7)	2(4)
19	1/9	Sheffield	A	L22-67	3(5)	3(6)	–	–	–	–	2+1(5)	2(4)	R/R	9(6)	3(4)
20	13/9	Mildenhall	A	L22-68	4+1(6)	2(5)	–	3(6)	–	–	1(3)	0(3)	R/R	12(7)	–
21	28/9	Newport	H	W54-35*	9(4)	7+2(4)	8(4)	8+4(5)	–	–	6(4)	4+1(4)	–	12(5)	–
22	5/10	Newcastle	H	W47-43	13(6)	8+2(5)	R/R	6+2(5)	–	–	6+2(4)	2(4)	–	12(6)	–
23	10/10	Peterborough	A ¶	L44-46*	6(6)	8+2(5)	–	6+2(5)	–	-3+1(3)	11+1(5)	R/R	10(6)	–	
24	12/10	Oxford	H	W52-38	11(5)	8+3(6)	13+2(6)	–	–	–	0(3)	4+1(4)	R/R	16(6)	–

    † Meeting abandoned after thirteen heats, with the result standing.

    ¶ Match raced at King's Lynn.

DETAILS OF OTHER RIDERS:

Match No. 2: Chris Davies 1(3); Match No. 4: Dyfed Evans 2+1(3); Match No. 10: John Oliver 2+1(3); Match No. 18: Scott Nettleship 2(4); Match No. 19: Michael Mitchell 3(4).

GOLDEN DOUBLE RIDES:

Match No. 4: Matthew Cross' total includes 4 points from a golden double ride; Match No. 9: Ben Powell's total includes 2 points from a golden double ride.

CONFERENCE LEAGUE AVERAGES

Rider	Mts	Rds	Pts	Bon	Tot	Avge	Max
Matthew Cross	12	58	101	14	115	7.93	–
Ben Powell	18	102	189	6	195	7.65	1 Paid
Craig Taylor	15	72	130	6	136	7.56	1 Full
Corey Blackman	6	32	56	3	59	7.38	–
Dean Felton	24	122	184	16	200	6.56	–
David Gough	5	21	24	4	28	5.33	–
Paul Candy	10	41	38	16	54	5.27	–
Darren Hatton	24	111	110	27	137	4.94	–
Gordon Meakins	19	65	56	12	68	4.18	–
Dyfed Evans	1	3	2	1	3	4.00	–
John Oliver	1	3	2	1	3	4.00	–
Daniel Hodgson	18	75	56	10	66	3.52	–
Michael Mitchell	1	4	3	0	3	3.00	–
Scott Nettleship	1	4	2	0	2	2.00	–
Chris Davies	1	3	1	0	1	1.33	–

NOTE: (1) The figures for Matthew Cross include one golden double ride (4 points), modified to normal score i.e. 2 points;

(2) The figures for Ben Powell include one golden double ride (2 points), modified to normal score i.e. 1 point.

CONFERENCE TROPHY

(* Denotes bonus-point victory)

No	DATE	OPPONENTS	H/A	RESULT	FELTON	CANDY	CROSS	ANDREWS	TAYLOR	HATTON	MEAKINS	HODGSON	BLACKMAN	POWELL	GOUGH	OTHERS
1	13/4	Stoke	A	L43-47	13+1(6)	0(3)	6(3)	3+1(4)	13+2(6)	2+1(4)	6+1(4)	–	–	–	–	–
2	11/5	Mildenhall	A	L23-66	2+1(5)	–	R/R	3(6)	10(6)	2(5)	1+1(3)	5(5)	–	–	–	0(0)
3	18/5	Buxton †	A	L35-37	4+2(3)	–	–	–	7(3)	3+1(3)	3+1(3)	7(4)	8+1(4)	3(4)	–	–
4	25/5	Armadale	H	D45-45	9(5)	–	6+3(4)	9(4)	10(5)	4(4)	–	2+2(3)	–	–	5(5)	–
5	1/6	Wimbledon	H	L43-50	2+2(4)	–	–	–	12(6)	4+4(4)	2(3)	–	13+1(6)	5+1(3)	5(4)	–
6	28/6	Armadale	A	L20-70	8(7)	1(4)	–	–	–	1+1(4)	1+1(3)	4(5)	R/R	4(6)	–	1(1)
7	29/6	Boston	A	L30-62	6+1(7)	1+1(4)	–	2+1(4)	–	2+1(4)	–	7(6)	R/R	12(6)	–	–
8	13/7	Buxton	H	W46-42*	8(4)	–	9+1(4)	–	7(4)	2+1(5)	–	1(3)	11(5)	8+1(5)	–	–
9	10/8	Trelawny	H	W57-31	9+2(5)	–	–	10+1(4)	15(5)	6+2(4)	3+1(4)	5+2(4)	R/R	9+1(4)	–	–
10	17/8	Stoke	H	L39-51	10+2(7)	–	–	1+1(4)	8(6)	2(3)	–	2(3)	R/R	16+1(7)	–	–
11	20/8	Wimbledon	A	L29-61	10(6)	0(4)	–	–	1(2)	4+1(5)	0(3)	2+1(4)	–	12(6)	–	–
12	24/8	Mildenhall	H	L41-49	7+1(5)	–	–	9+3(6)	–	8+1(6)	4+1(4)	–	R/R	10(6)	–	3+2(3)
13	26/8	Trelawny	A	W51-39*	9+1(5)	3+3(4)	10+1(4)	–	–	8(4)	5+2(4)	–	–	12+1(5)	–	4+1(4)
14	21/9	Boston	H	L42-51	16(6)	1(3)	8(4)	5+1(4)	–	5+2(5)	0(3)	–	–	7+1(5)	–	–

† Meeting abandoned after twelve heats, with the result standing.

DETAILS OF OTHER RIDERS:

Match No. 2: Thomas Rowlett 0(0); Match No. 6: Sean Stoddart 1(1); Match No. 12 Matt Tutton 3+2(3); Match No. 13: Matt Tutton 4+1(4).

GOLDEN DOUBLE RIDES:

Match No. 5: Corey Blackman's total includes 6 points from a golden double ride; Match No. 7: Ben Powell's total includes 4 points from a golden double ride; Match No. 14: Dean Felton's total includes 6 points from a golden double ride.

CONFERENCE TROPHY AVERAGES

Rider	Mts	Rds	Pts	Bon	Tot	Avge	Max
Matthew Cross	5	19	39	5	44	9.26	–
Corey Blackman	3	15	29	2	31	8.27	–
Craig Taylor	9	43	83	2	85	7.91	1 Full
Ben Powell	11	57	96	6	102	7.16	–
Dean Felton	14	75	110	13	123	6.56	–
Matt Tutton	2	7	7	3	10	5.71	–
Darren Andrews	8	36	42	8	50	5.56	–
Darren Hatton	14	60	53	15	68	4.53	–
David Gough	2	9	10	0	10	4.44	–
Daniel Hodgson	9	37	35	5	40	4.32	–
Sean Stoddart	1	1	1	0	1	4.00	–
Gordon Meakins	10	34	25	8	33	3.88	–
Paul Candy	6	22	6	4	10	1.82	–
Thomas Rowlett	1	0	0	0	0	0.00	–

NOTE: The figures for Corey Blackman include one golden double ride (6 points), modified to normal score i.e. 3 points; the figures for Dean Felton include one golden double ride (6 points), modified to normal score i.e. 3 points; the figures for Ben Powell include one golden double ride (4 points), modified to normal score i.e. 2 points.

KNOCK-OUT CUP

No	DATE	OPPONENTS	H/A	RESULT	POWELL	FELTON	BLACKMAN	CROSS	TAYLOR	GOUGH	MEAKINS	OLIVER	HATTON	CANDY
1	8/6	Rye House	H	L40-50	11(6)	8+2(5)	10+1(7)	4+2(4)	R/R	3+1(4)	3(3)	1(1)	–	–
2	9/6	Rye House	A	L23-67	4(5)	6(5)	R/R	–	–	–	2+2(4)	2(5)	3(5)	6+1(6)

OTHER MEETING

4 August: Conference Challenge

Reading 63 Carmarthen 25 (Ben Powell 12; Chris Schramm 8; Darren Hatton 3; Dean Felton 1+1; Gordon Meakins 1; Daniel Hodgson 0; Darren Andrews R/R).

INDIVIDUAL MEETING

15 June: West Wales Select Open Championship

(Qualifying scores: Matthew Wethers 13; Steven Braidford 12; Jamie Robertson 12; Craig Branney 11; Chris Schramm 10; Craig Taylor 9; Dean Felton 9; Mark Burrows 9; Tom Brown 7;

Corey Blackman 6; Rob Finlow 5; Ben Powell 5; Darren Andrews 4; John Branney 3; Shane McCabe 2; Darren Hatton 2) First Semi-Final: 1st Wethers; 2nd Schramm; 3rd C. Branney; 4th Felton; Second Semi-Final: 1st Braidford; 2nd Robertson; 3rd Taylor; 4th Burrows; Final: 1st Robertson; 2nd Schramm; 3rd Braidford; 4th Wethers.

MILDENHALL SUPERIOR EXTERIORS FEN TIGERS

ADDRESS: Mildenhall Stadium, Hayland Drove, West Row Fen, Mildenhall, Suffolk.
PROMOTERS: Graham Drury & Denise Drury.
TRACK LENGTH: 260 metres.
FIRST MEETING: 18 May 1975.
YEARS OF OPERATION: 1973 Training; 1974 Open & Training; 1975-89 National League; 1990-91 Training; 1992 British League Division Two; 1994 British League Division Three; 1995 British Academy League; 1996 British Conference League; 1997 British Amateur League; 1998-03 British Conference League.

CLUB HONOURS

LEAGUE CHAMPIONS: 1979, 2003.
FOUR-TEAM CHAMPIONS: 1984, 1987.
PAIRS CHAMPIONS: 1987.
LEAGUE CUP WINNERS: 2000.
CONFERENCE TROPHY WINNERS: 2002.
KNOCK-OUT CUP WINNERS: 2003.

RIDER ROSTER 2003

BALDWIN, Carl   b. 4 July 1964, Ipswich, Suffolk.
    BRITISH CAREER: (1980) Mildenhall, Hull; (1981) Mildenhall; (1982-84) Mildenhall, Ipswich; (1985) Mildenhall; (1986) Peterborough, King's Lynn; (1987) Peterborough, Boston; (1988-89) Milton Keynes; (2002) Ipswich, Arena-Essex, Mildenhall; (2003) Mildenhall, Ipswich (BLC).
BARNETT, Russell   b. 26 May 1987.
    BRITISH CAREER: (2003) Mildenhall (CT), Rye House (CL), Newport (CL), Oxford (CL).
BRANNEY, John   b. 7 November 1985, Whitehaven, Cumbria.
    BRITISH CAREER: (2002) Rye House (CL), Newcastle (CL); (2003) Newcastle (CL), Wimbledon (CT), Mildenhall (CT), King's Lynn, Exeter, Newport (PL), Buxton (CT).
BROADHURST, Wayne   b. 28 February 1967, Minsterley, Shropshire.
    BRITISH CAREER: (1987) Coventry; (1988) Coventry, Stoke; (1989) Coventry; (1999) Stoke, Workington; (2000) Stoke; (2001) Wolverhampton, Stoke; (2002) Mildenhall; (2003) Mildenhall, Wolverhampton, Poole (BLC), Belle Vue (BLC).

BRUNDLE, James   *b. 15 December 1986, King's Lynn, Norfolk.*
BRITISH CAREER: (2002) King's Lynn (CL), Mildenhall; (2003) King's Lynn (PL), Mildenhall.

COMPTON, Benji   *b. 17 September 1986, Tenerife, Spain.*
BRITISH CAREER: (2002) Newcastle (CL); (2003) Sheffield (CL & PL), Swindon (PL), Hull (BLC), Mildenhall (KOC), Exeter.

DART, Tony   *b. 2 September 1979, Ashford, Kent.*
BRITISH CAREER: (2003) Mildenhall, King's Lynn, Peterborough (BLC), Isle of Wight (KOC).

HODGSON, Lee   *b. 19 February 1985, Preston, Lancashire.*
BRITISH CAREER: (2000) Sheffield (CL); (2001) Sheffield (PL & CL), Arena-Essex, Swindon; (2002) Stoke, Workington, Mildenhall; (2003) Mildenhall, Somerset, Workington.

HOWARD, Lee   *b. 6 July 1976, Manchester.*
BRITISH CAREER: (1999) King's Lynn (CL), Linlithgow; (2000) Buxton; (2001) Buxton, Newport (CL); (2002) Newcastle (CL); (2003) Stoke (CT), Mildenhall.

HOWE, Ben   *b. 6 December 1974, Crawley, Surrey.*
BRITISH CAREER: (1991-96) Ipswich; (1997) Ipswich, Poole; (1998) King's Lynn; (1999) Ipswich, Hull; (2000) Newport; (2002) Newport; (2003) Ipswich (BLC), Mildenhall.

JACKSON, Andrew   *b. 12 July 1975, Manchester.*
BRITISH CAREER: (2002) Wolverhampton (CT), Carmarthen, Newport (CL); (2003) Wolverhampton (CL), Sheffield (CL), Mildenhall (CT), Belle Vue (BLC), Swindon (CL), Trelawny (CT), Newcastle (CL).

JAMES, Scott   *b. 25 May 1984, Adelaide, South Australia.*
BRITISH CAREER: (2002) Workington, Mildenhall; (2003) Mildenhall, Workington, Somerset (KOC), Coventry (BLC).

KING, Daniel   *b. 14 August 1986, Maidstone, Kent.*
BRITISH CAREER: (2001) Peterborough (CL); (2002) Peterborough (CL), Swindon (CT); (2003) Peterborough (CL), Ipswich (BLC), Reading, Mildenhall, Arena-Essex.

LANGLEY, Karl   *b. 2 June 1981, Whitehaven, Cumbria.*
BRITISH CAREER: (2002) Workington; (2003) Newcastle (CL), Armadale (CLKOC), Mildenhall, Poole (BLC).

LEE, Paul   *b. 21 March 1981, Nottingham, Nottinghamshire.*
BRITISH CAREER: (1996) Peterborough (CL); (1997) Long Eaton, Shuttle Cubs, Peterborough (EL), Coventry; (1998) Hull; (1999-00) Sheffield; (2001) Coventry; (2002) Swindon; (2003) Mildenhall.

MABEN, Keith   *b. 24 December 1982, Edinburgh, Scotland.*
BRITISH CAREER: (2003) Armadale, Mildenhall (CT), Stoke (KOC).

MACKAY, Brendon   *b. 14 August 1980, Darwin, Northern Territory, Australia.*
BRITISH CAREER: (2001-02) Reading; (2003) Somerset, Trelawny (CT), Newport (BLC), Exeter (BLC), Mildenhall.

MANN, James   *b. 25 October 1983, Bolton, Greater Manchester.*
BRITISH CAREER: (1999) Buxton; (2000) Buxton, Workington, Stoke, Ipswich; (2001) Workington, Buxton; (2002) Workington, Buxton; (2003) Somerset, Mildenhall.

NEEDS, Lawrence   *b. 1 December 1986, Shrewsbury, Shropshire.*
BRITISH CAREER: (2002) Wolverhampton (CT); (2003) Wolverhampton (CL), Mildenhall.

MILDENHALL FEN TIGERS: back row, left to right: James Brundle, Tony Dart, Lee Hodgson, Ben Howe. On bike: Wayne Broadhurst. Front, kneeling: Nick Simmons, Matthew Wright.

NETTLESHIP, Scott   *b. 16 May 1984, Newcastle, Tyne & Wear.*
BRITISH CAREER: (2003) Newcastle (CL), Mildenhall, Swindon (CL), Carmarthen, Peterborough (CL).

NEWITT, Jason   *b. 13 January 1978, Oxford, Oxfordshire.*
BRITISH CAREER: (1996) Peterborough (CL); (1997) Peterborough (AL), Oxford (AL & PL); (2000) Somerset; (2003) Oxford (CL), Mildenhall.

NORTON, Danny   *b. 27 August 1986, Hull, East Yorkshire.*
BRITISH CAREER: (2001-02) Peterborough (CL); (2003) Peterborough (CL & BLC), Armadale (CT), Swindon (PL), Reading, Mildenhall (KOC & CT), Poole (BLC), Oxford (BLC).

ROWLETT, Thomas   *b. 22 January 1979, Wisbech, Cambridgeshire.*
BRITISH CAREER: (1999) King's Lynn (CL); (2000-01) Mildenhall; (2002) Mildenhall, Wimbledon; (2003) Mildenhall, Carmarthen (CT), Oxford (CLKOC), Newport (CL).

SIMMONS, Nick   *b. 24 July 1981, Leamington Spa, Warwickshire.*
BRITISH CAREER: (1997) Shuttle Cubs, Ryde; (1998) Newport (CL & PL), Isle of Wight, Exeter; (1999) Isle of Wight, Stoke, Newport (CL); (2000) Arena-Essex; (2001) Newport (PL & CL), Somerset; (2002) Isle of Wight; (2003) Stoke, Reading, Mildenhall, orkington, King's Lynn, Exeter.

THEOBALD, James   *b. 31 December 1985, Ashford, Kent.*
BRITISH CAREER: (2002) Rye House (CL), Carmarthen; (2003) Rye House (CL), Mildenhall, Sheffield (CL), Newport (CL), Peterborough (CL).

TUTTON, Matt   *b. 19 June 1982, Newport, South Wales.*
BRITISH CAREER: (2000) Rye House; (2002) Swindon (CT), Wimbledon; (2003) Mildenhall, Buxton, Carmarthen (CT), Newport (CL).

WILDING, Rhys   *b. 6 July 1982.*
BRITISH CAREER: (2003) Armadale (CT), Mildenhall.

WRIGHT, Matthew   *b. 19 November 1985, Harlow, Essex.*
BRITISH CAREER: (2002) Boston, Mildenhall, Carmarthen, Wimbledon; (2003) Mildenhall, Ipswich (BLC), Arena-Essex (BLC), Reading, Peterborough (BLC).

CONFERENCE LEAGUE

(* Denotes bonus-point victory)

No	DATE	OPPONENTS	H/A	RESULT	BROADHURST	HODGSON	BRUNDLE	MANN	JAMES	WRIGHT	DART	KING	HOWE	SIMMONS	LEE	OTHERS
1	6/4	Newport	A	W47-43	11(4)	4(3)	9(5)	8+2(4)	8(4)	5+3(6)	2+1(4)	–	–	–	–	–
2	20/4	Carmarthen	A	W50-41	12(4)	–	4+2(4)	12+1(5)	9(4)	2(3)	11+1(7)	–	–	–	–	0(3)
3	21/4	Rye House	A	L40-51	12(6)	–	–	6+2(4)	3(4)	3+3(4)	2(3)	7+1(6)	–	–	–	7+1(3)
4	18/5	Peterborough	H	W56-33	5(4)	7+1(4)	–	–	10+1(4)	4(4)	6+2(4)	12+2(5)	12+2(5)	–	–	–
5	25/5	Buxton	H	W56-34	7+1(4)	5+1(4)	15(5)	–	8+1(5)	4(4)	8+2(5)	–	9(3)	–	–	–
6	26/5	Buxton	A	L43-47*	13+1(6)	1+1(3)	13(5)	–	3+1(4)	1(3)	9(6)	3+1(3)	–	–	–	–
7	1/6	Rye House	H	W48-44	10+2(5)	7+1(4)	10+1(6)	–	11+2(6)	6+1(5)	4+2(5)	–	R/R	–	–	–
8	11/6	Wimbledon	A	W46-44	4+1(4)	2(3)	–	–	6(5)	3+2(3)	15(7)	–	13+2(5)	–	–	3+1(3)
9	15/6	Swindon	H	W58-32	7+2(4)	9+1(4)	13+2(5)	–	11+1(5)	6(4)	4+1(4)	–	8+1(4)	–	–	–
10	22/6	Newport	H	W65-25*	9+2(5)	8+2(4)	11+1(4)	–	12(4)	7+4(5)	10(4)	8+2(4)	–	–	–	–
11	29/6	Wolverhampton	H	W55-34	9+2(4)	6(4)	8+1(4)	–	9+3(4)	2+1(4)	10+1(5)	–	11+1(5)	–	–	–

CONFERENCE LEAGUE continued

No	DATE	OPPONENTS	H/A	RESULT	BROADHURST	HODGSON	BRUNDLE	MANN	JAMES	WRIGHT	DART	KING	HOWE	SIMMONS	LEE	OTHERS
12	6/7	Newcastle	A	W46-44	6+2(6)	10(5)	–	–	R/R	3+2(4)	9+1(6)	–	18(6)	–	–	0(3)
13	13/7	Oxford	H	W50-40	14(6)	5+2(6)	11+1(5)	–	R/R	1(3)	17(7)	–	2+2(3)	–	–	–
14	10/8	Sheffield	H	W63-26	12(4)	8+2(4)	13+1(5)	–	–	5+2(4)	–	–	13+1(5)	6+2(4)	–	6+1(4)
15	11/8	Sheffield	A	D45-45*	10+2(5)	10+1(5)	10+1(6)	–	–	1+1(4)	–	–	R/R	12+1(6)	–	2(4)
16	17/8	Boston	H	W50-39	7+1(4)	10+2(6)	11(5)	–	–	3+1(4)	2+1(2)	–	11(5)	6+2(4)	–	–
17	26/8	Wolverhampton	A	L40-50*	7+4(6)	11+2(6)	11(6)	–	–	2+1(5)	–	–	R/R	9(6)	–	0(1)
18	31/8	Wimbledon	H	W54-36*	9+1(4)	5+3(4)	8+1(4)	–	–	9(5)	7+2(4)	–	–	3(4)	13(5)	–
19	11/9	Swindon	A	L41-42*	4+2(4)	7+3(5)	10(5)	–	–	1+1(4)	–	–	–	8+1(4)	15(5)	3(3)
20	13/9	Carmarthen	H	W68-22*	10+1(4)	11+1(4)	13+2(5)	–	–	10+2(5)	7+2(4)	–	–	7+3(4)	10+2(4)	–
21	20/9	Peterborough	A¶	W65-25*	10+1(4)	5+2(4)	12(4)	–	–	12+3(5)	9+1(5)	–	–	5+3(4)	12(4)	–
22	26/9	Boston	A	W46-44*	4(4)	2+1(4)	11+2(5)	–	–	0(3)	9+1(5)	–	–	6+2(4)	14(5)	–
23	28/9	Newcastle	H	W67-23*	11+1(4)	7+2(4)	12(4)	–	–	12+3(6)	12+3(5)	–	–	2+1(2)	11+1(4)	–
24	24/10	Oxford	A	L37-53	–	–	R/R	–	–	1(4)	16(7)	–	–	13+1(7)	–	7+4(12)

¶ Match raced at King's Lynn

NOTE: The away match at Swindon originally ended in a 48-42 on-track victory; however, the points scored by Lee Hodgson were subsequently deducted from Mildenhall's total as his inclusion at reserve was deemed ineligible.

DETAILS OF OTHER RIDERS:

Match No. 2: Matt Tutton 0(3); Match No. 3: Carl Baldwin 7+1(3); Match No. 8: James Theobald 3+1(3) ; Match No. 12: Scott Nettleship 0(3); Match No. 14: Nick Lee 6+1(4); Match No. 15: Karl Langley 2(4); Match No. 17: Lee Howard 0(1); Match No. 19: Brendon Mackay 3(3); Match No. 24: Rhys Wilding 4+2(6); Lawrence Needs 1+1(3); Jason Newitt 2+1(3).

GOLDEN DOUBLE RIDES:

Match No. 3: Daniel King's total includes 4 points from a golden double ride.

CONFERENCE LEAGUE AVERAGES

Rider	Mts	Rds	Pts	Bon	Tot	Avge	Max
Paul Lee	6	27	75	3	78	11.56	2 Full; 2 Paid
Carl Baldwin	1	3	7	1	8	10.67	–
Ben Howe	9	41	97	9	106	10.34	1 Full; 1 Paid
James Brundle	19	92	205	15	220	9.57	3 Full; 3 Paid
James Mann	3	13	26	5	31	9.54	–
Wayne Broadhurst	23	105	203	26	229	8.72	2 Full; 1 Paid
Scott James	11	49	90	9	99	8.08	1 Full; 1 Paid
Tony Dart	20	99	169	21	190	7.68	1 Paid
Nick Simmons	11	49	77	16	93	7.59	–
Daniel King	4	18	28	6	34	7.56	–
Lee Hodgson	20	85	133	25	158	7.44	1 Paid
Nick Lee	1	4	6	1	7	7.00	–
James Theobald	1	3	3	1	4	5.33	–
Matthew Wright	24	101	103	30	133	5.27	1 Paid
Brendon Mackay	1	3	3	0	3	4.00	–

Rider	Mts	Rds	Pts	Bon	Tot	Avge	Max
Jason Newitt	1	3	2	1	3	4.00	–
Rhys Wilding	1	6	4	2	6	4.00	–
Lawrence Needs	1	3	1	1	2	2.67	–
Karl Langley	1	4	2	0	2	2.00	–
Lee Howard	1	1	0	0	0	0.00	–
Scott Nettleship	1	3	0	0	0	0.00	–
Matt Tutton	1	3	0	0	0	0.00	–

NOTE: (1) The figures for Daniel King include one golden double ride (4 points), modified to normal score i.e. 2 points;

(2) Lee Hodgson's record in the away match at Swindon has been deducted as his inclusion at reserve was deemed ineligible.

CONFERENCE TROPHY

(* Denotes bonus-point victory)

No	DATE	OPPONENTS	H/A	RESULT	BROADHURST	HODGSON	BRUNDLE	JAMES	WRIGHT	DART	MANN	KING	HOWE	SIMMONS	LEE	OTHERS
1	15/3	Wimbledon	H	W48-42	12(5)	6+1(4)	4(4)	13+1(5)	5+2(5)	1+1(3)	–	–	–	–	–	7+1(4)
2	13/4	Buxton	H	W59-31	8(4)	8(4)	10+4(5)	14+1(5)	4(4)	5+1(4)	10(4)	–	–	–	–	–
3	27/4	Boston	H	L44-46	10+1(5)	–	12+2(5)	4+2(4)	4(5)	7+1(7)	4+1(2)	3(2)	–	–	–	–
4	4/5	Stoke	A	W53-36	9(4)	7+2(4)	–	12(5)	6+2(4)	5+1(4)	–	–	13(5)	–	–	1(4)
5	11/5	Carmarthen	H	W66-23	–	7+2(4)	11+1(4)	11+1(4)	8+3(5)	8+3(6)	–	11(4)	10+2(4)	–	–	–
6	15/7	Trelawny	A	W48-42	12+3(6)	0(1)	–	R/R	3+3(6)	8+2(6)	–	11(5)	–	14(6)	–	–
7	26/7	Armadale	A	L32-61	13(7)	–	–	R/R	5+2(5)	9+1(7)	–	–	–	–	–	5(11)
8	27/7	Buxton	A	L37-53*	10+1(6)	–	–	R/R	1+1(4)	10(6)	–	–	–	–	–	16+1(14)
9	3/8	Trelawny	H	W52-36*	8(4)	–	14(5)	–	4+1(4)	–	–	–	9(4)	9+2(5)	–	8+2(8)
10	13/8	Wimbledon	A	L45-48*	11+1(7)	–	R/R	–	1(3)	5(4)	–	–	23(7)	–	–	5+1(9)
11	24/8	Carmarthen	A	W49-41*	9+1(5)	–	–	–	6(6)	–	–	–	R/R	17+1(6)	–	17+1(9)
12	21/9	Stoke	H	W52-38*	5+1(4)	4+2(4)	9(5)	–	6+1(4)	8+3(4)	–	–	–	8+2(5)	12(4)	–
13	12/10	Armadale	H	W50-40	8+2(5)	6+1(4)	R/R	–	11+1(7)	6+3(6)	–	–	–	4+1(3)	15(5)	–
14	22/10	Boston	A	L40-50	–	–	R/R	–	4+1(4)	5(5)	–	–	–	5+1(4)	18(7)	8+1(10)

DETAILS OF OTHER RIDERS:

Match No. 1: Carl Baldwin 7+1(4); Match No. 4: Thomas Rowlett 1(4); Match No. 7: John Branney 5(5); Karl Langley 0(3); Keith Maben 0(3); Match No. 8: Benji Compton 8+1(6); Ricky Scarboro 6(5); Andrew Jackson 2(3); Match No. 9: Danny Norton 6+2(4); Thomas Rowlett 2(4); Match No. 10: Danny Norton 5+1(5); James Theobald 0(4); Match No. 11: Danny Norton 17+1(6); Russell Barnett 0(3); Match No. 14: Danny Norton 6+1(6); Benji Compton 2(4).

GOLDEN DOUBLE RIDES:

Match No. 7: Wayne Broadhurst's total includes 6 points from a golden double ride; Match No. 10: Ben Howe's total includes 6 points from a golden double ride.

CONFERENCE TROPHY AVERAGES

Rider	Mts	Rds	Pts	Bon	Tot	Avge	Max
Paul Lee	3	16	45	0	45	11.25	2 Full
Ben Howe	4	20	52	2	54	10.80	1 Paid
Scott James	5	23	54	5	59	10.26	2 Paid

Rider	Mts	Rds	Pts	Bon	Tot	Avge	Max
James Mann	2	6	14	1	15	10.00	–
James Brundle	6	28	60	7	67	9.57	1 Paid
Daniel King	3	11	25	0	25	9.09	–
Nick Simmons	6	29	57	7	64	8.83	1 Paid
Carl Baldwin	1	4	7	1	8	8.00	–
Wayne Broadhurst	12	62	112	10	122	7.87	–
Danny Norton	4	21	34	5	39	7.43	1 Paid
Lee Hodgson	7	25	38	8	46	7.36	–
Tony Dart	12	62	77	16	93	6.00	–
Matthew Wright	14	66	68	17	85	5.15	–
Ricky Scarboro	1	5	6	0	6	4.80	–
Benji Compton	2	10	10	1	11	4.40	–
John Branney	1	5	5	0	5	4.00	–
Andrew Jackson	1	3	2	0	2	2.67	–
Thomas Rowlett	2	8	3	0	3	1.50	–
Russell Barnett	1	3	0	0	0	0.00	–
Karl Langley	1	3	0	0	0	0.00	–
Keith Maben	1	3	0	0	0	0.00	–
James Theobald	1	4	0	0	0	0.00	–

NOTE: The figures for Wayne Broadhurst include one golden double ride (6 points), modified to normal score i.e. 3 points;

The figures for Ben Howe include one golden double ride (6 points), modified to normal score i.e. 3 points.

KNOCK-OUT CUP

(* Denotes aggregate victory)

No	DATE	OPPONENTS	H/A	RESULT	BROADHURST	HODGSON	HOWE	JAMES	WRIGHT	DART	SIMMONS	COMPTON	NORTON	LEE	BRUNDLE	OTHERS
1	8/6	Oxford	H	W53-37	9+1(4)	6+2(4)	12+2(5)	12(5)	8+2(5)	6(4)	–	–	–	–	–	–
2	30/7	Oxford	A	L44-45*	14(6)	–	–	R/R	6+2(7)	5+1(3)	2(3)	11+2(6)	6(3)	–	–	–
3	13/9	Boston	H	W55-35	7+1(4)	3+1(3)	–	–	9(4)	8+1(4)	6+1(4)	–	–	13+2(5)	9(5)	–
4	19/9	Boston	A	D45-45*	7+2(4)	–	–	–	4+1(4)	0(0)	5+1(4)	–	4(4)	12+1(5)	13(5)	–
5	18/10	Rye House	A	L43-46	5(5)	–	–	–	3+1(4)	–	5(4)	2+2(4)	–	13+1(6)	R/R	15+2(7)
6	19/10	Rye House	H	W48-41*	3(1)	–	–	–	4+1(5)	12+2(7)	5(4)	–	–	12(6)	R/R	12+3(7)

DETAILS OF OTHER RIDERS:

Match No. 1: Lee Howard DNA.

OTHER MEETINGS

23 March: Three-Team Tournament (first-leg)

Mildenhall 52 (Scott James 12; Carl Baldwin 11+1; Wayne Broadhurst 9+1; Lee Hodgson 9+1; James Brundle 8+2), Boston 29, Peterborough 26.

28 March: Three-Team Tournament (second-leg)

Boston 36, Mildenhall 42 (James Brundle 10; Wayne Broadhurst 9+2; Scott James 9; Lee Hodgson 8+1; Tony Dart 3+1; Matthew Wright 2+1; Carl Baldwin 1), Peterborough 29.

5 April: Three-Team Tournament (third-leg)

Peterborough 42, Mildenhall 42 (Scott James 9+1; Wayne Broadhurst 9; James Mann 8+1; Carl Baldwin 6+2; Matthew Wright 6+2; Lee Hodgson 4+2), Boston 24. Aggregate result: Mildenhall 136 Peterborough 97, Boston 89.

INDIVIDUAL MEETING

30 March: British Under-21 Championship Qualifying Round

(Meeting run on a Grand Prix-style format) Eliminated competitors: James Cockle, Matthew Wright, James Horton, Tom Brown, Chris Collins, Luke Priest, Simon Dyminski, James Mann, Daniel Giffard, Richard Hall, James Brundle, Tommy Allen, Chris Schramm, Edward Kennett, Joe Cook and Danny Hughes; First Semi-Final: 1st Jason King; 2nd Ben Wilson; 3rd Rob Finlow; 4th Scott Courtney; Second Semi-Final: 1st Chris Mills; 2nd Daniel King; 3rd Barrie Evans; 4th Lee Hodgson; Consolation Final: 1st Finlow; 2nd Evans; 3rd Hodgson; 4th Courtney; Final: 1st J. King; 2nd Wilson; 3rd D. King; 4th Mills.

PAIRS MEETING

7 September: Handicap Best Pairs

1st Tony Dart (18) & Paul Lee (14) 32; 2nd Brendon Mackay (16) & Wayne Broadhurst (11) 27; =3rd Lee Smart (11) & Luke Priest (9) 20 and Matthew Wright (17) & Nick Simmons (3) 20; Darren Smith (13) & Lee Hodgson (5) 18; Carl Baldwin (14) & Robert Henry (0) 14.

NEWCASTLE ULTRAFAST GEMS

NOTE: The information below relates only to the second Newcastle team. For details of the main side, please refer to the Premier League section.

ADDRESS: Brough Park Stadium, The Fossway, Byker, Newcastle-upon-Tyne, Tyne & Wear.
PROMOTERS: George English, Dave Rowland & Darryl Illingworth.
TRACK LENGTH: 300 metres.
FIRST MEETING: 7 April 2002.
YEARS OF OPERATION: 2002-03 British Conference League.

CLUB HONOURS

None.

RIDER ROSTER 2003

BEATON, Gary   b. 20 August 1986, Glasgow, Scotland.
BRITISH CAREER: (2002) Newport (CL), Newcastle (CL); (2003) Wolverhampton (CL), Armadale, Newcastle (CL), Glasgow.

NEWCASTLE GEMS: back row, left to right: Carl Shield, Phil Bragg, Kenny Smith (Team Manager), William Lawson, Jamie Robertson, Kriss Irving. On bike: Craig Branney. Front, kneeling: John Branney, Karl Langley.

BRAGG, Phil *b. 1 March 1968, Whitehaven, Cumbria.*
BRITISH CAREER: (2000) Ashfield; (2001) Edinburgh; (2002) Workington, Newcastle (CL); (2003) Newcastle (CL).

BRANNEY, Craig *b. 31 July 1982, Whitehaven, Cumbria.*
BRITISH CAREER: (2000) Ashfield; (2001) Workington, Buxton, Isle of Wight, Newport (PL); (2002) Newcastle (CL), Hull; (2003) Newcastle (PL & CL), Armadale (CT), Workington, Swindon (PL), Hull, Somerset.

BRANNEY, John *b. 7 November 1985, Whitehaven, Cumbria.*
BRITISH CAREER: (2002) Rye House (CL), Newcastle (CL); (2003) Newcastle (CL), Wimbledon (CT), Mildenhall (CT), King's Lynn, Exeter, Newport (PL), Buxton (CT).

HAIGH, David *b. 12 December 1984.*
BRITISH CAREER: (2002) Newcastle (CL); (2003) Wimbledon, Newcastle (CL), Peterborough (CL).

IRVING, Kriss *b. 3 April 1987, Cumbria.*
BRITISH CAREER: (2003) Newcastle (CL).

JACKSON, Andrew *b. 12 July 1975, Manchester.*
BRITISH CAREER: (2002) Wolverhampton (CT), Carmarthen, Newport (CL); (2003) Wolverhampton (CL), Sheffield (CL), Mildenhall (CT), Belle Vue (BLC), Swindon (CL), Trelawny (CT), Newcastle (CL).

JONES, Steven *b. 27 September 1979, Gateshead, Tyne & Wear.*
BRITISH CAREER: (1997) Lathallan; (1998) Edinburgh, Newcastle; (1999) Newcastle, Linlithgow; (2002-03) Newcastle (CL).

LANGLEY, Karl *b. 2 June 1981, Whitehaven, Cumbria.*
BRITISH CAREER: (2002) Workington; (2003) Newcastle (CL), Armadale (CLKOC), Mildenhall, Poole (BLC).

LAWSON, William *b. 27 February 1987, Auchterarder, Perthshire, Scotland.*
BRITISH CAREER: (2002-03) Newcastle (PL & CL), Belle Vue (BLC).

NETTLESHIP, Scott *b. 16 May 1984, Newcastle, Tyne & Wear.*
BRITISH CAREER: (2003) Newcastle (CL), Mildenhall, Swindon (CL), Carmarthen, Peterborough.

PICKERING, Michael *b. 28 October 1982, Hull, East Yorkshire.*
BRITISH CAREER: (1998) Buxton; (2000) Buxton; (2002) Newport (CL); (2003) Hull, Newcastle (CL).

ROBERTSON, Jamie *b. 8 October 1986, Berwick-upon-Tweed, Northumberland.*
BRITISH CAREER: (2002) Newcastle (CL); (2003) Newcastle (PL & CL).

SHIELD, Carl *b. 27 June 1979, Bishop Auckland, County Durham.*
BRITISH CAREER: (2002) Newcastle (CL), Sheffield (PLKOC); (2003) Berwick, Newcastle (CL), Armadale, Edinburgh.

STODDART, Sean *b. 20 January 1987, Edinburgh, Scotland.*
BRITISH CAREER: (2003) Armadale, Trelawny (CT), Carmarthen (CT), Newcastle (CL).

WARBURTON, Ben *b. 20 September 1986, Sheffield, South Yorkshire.*
BRITISH CAREER: (2002) Boston, Wolverhampton (CT); (2003) Newport (CL), Oxford (CL), Sheffield (CL), Newcastle (CL).

CONFERENCE LEAGUE

(* Denotes bonus-point victory)

No	DATE	OPPONENTS	H/A	RESULT	C. BRANNEY	J. BRANNEY	LAWSON	JONES	ROBERTSON	LANGLEY	BRAGG	SHIELD	IRVING	BEATON	PICKERING	OTHERS
1	6/4	Wolverhampton	H	W48-41	R/R	8+1(5)	14(6)	3(4)	14+1(6)	3+2(4)	6+3(5)	–	–	–	–	–
2	20/4	Newport	H	W57-32	14+1(6)	5(4)	14(5)	–	11+1(4)	5+1(6)	8+1(5)	0(1)	–	–	–	–
3	4/5	Boston	H	L41-48	10(5)	1(5)	19+1(7)	6(5)	R/R	2(3)	3+1(4)	–	–	–	–	–
4	6/5	Wolverhampton	A	W51-42*	11+1(6)	4+3(5)	16(6)	8+2(5)	R/R	6(4)	–	–	6+3(4)	–	–	–
5	18/5	Sheffield	H	W50-39	16(6)	7+2(7)	15+1(6)	7(5)	R/R	–	2(2)	–	–	–		3+1(4)
6	1/6	Oxford	H	W51-37	10+2(5)	7(5)	9(4)	7+2(4)	14(5)	1(3)	–	–	3+1(4)	–	–	–
7	29/6	Newport	A	W52-37*	9+2(4)	5+2(5)	14(5)	7(4)	9(5)	3+1(4)	–	5(3)	–	–	–	–
8	6/7	Mildenhall	H	L44-46	10+2(5)	6+1(5)	13(5)	5+2(4)	7(4)	2(3)	–	–	1(4)	–	–	–
9	13/7	Wimbledon	H	W51-39	11+1(5)	8+2(5)	9(3)	6+1(4)	10(4)	2+1(4)	–	–	–	5+2(4)	–	–
10	21/7	Sheffield	A	L28-62	10+1(6)	2+2(3)	6(5)	–	4+1(5)	4(5)	–	0(3)	–	2(3)	–	–
11	2/8	Rye House	A	L36-53	8(6)	6+2(4)	13(6)	–	7+1(5)	0(3)	0(3)	–	2(3)	–	–	–
12	8/8	Boston	A	L33-56	15+1(7)	2(5)	–	8+2(7)	R/R	2+1(3)	–	–	–	–	6(5)	0(3)
13	10/8	Swindon	H	W61-27	16+2(6)	21(7)	9(4)	7+3(5)	R/R	–	–	–	3+1(4)	5+2(5)	–	–
14	25/8	Buxton	H	W57-33	14+2(6)	15+2(6)	11+1(5)	8(5)	R/R	–	–	–	–	2+1(3)	7+3(6)	–
15	26/8	Swindon †	A	L39-45*	14(6)	9+2(7)	R/R	11+2(6)	3(3)	2(3)	–	–	–	0(3)	–	–
16	27/8	Wimbledon	A	L37-53	17+1(7)	6+1(6)	R/R	0(3)	10(7)	2+1(3)	–	–	–	2(4)	–	–
17	31/8	Carmarthen	H	W58-29	12(4)	8+1(4)	15(5)	2+1(4)	13+2(5)	4+1(4)	–	–	–	–	4+1(4)	–
18	7/9	Rye House	H	W50-40	9+1(4)	1+1(4)	14+1(5)	8+1(4)	11(5)	–	–	–	4+2(4)	3(4)	–	
19	14/9	Buxton	A	L31-59	–	7+1(6)	R/R	–	15(7)	1+1(4)	–	–	2(4)	2+1(4)	4(5)	–
20	20/9	Peterborough	A¶	W46-43	17(6)	3+1(4)	–	11+1(5)	0(1)	7(5)	–	–	2(4)	–	6(5)	–
21	28/9	Mildenhall	A	L23-67	4(4)	8(6)	–	–	3(4)	–	–	–	0(3)	4+1(5)	2+1(5)	2(3)
22	3/10	Oxford	A	L34-56	17(6)	–	–	5(5)	10+1(6)	2(4)	–	–	0(3)	–	0(3)	0(3)
23	5/10	Carmarthen	A	L43-47*	–	–	R/R	15+2(7)	17(6)	1+1(4)	–	–	4(5)	–	5(5)	1(3)
24	13/10	Peterborough	H	W51-39*	8(4)	11+2(5)	–	7+1(4)	15(5)	5+1(4)	–	–	1(4)	–	4+2(4)	–

† Meeting abandoned after fourteen heats, with the result standing.

¶ Match raced at King's Lynn.

DETAILS OF OTHER RIDERS:

Match No. 5: Scott Nettleship 3+1(4); Match No. 12: David Haigh 0(3); Match No. 21: Sean Stoddart 2(3); Match No. 22: Ben Warburton 0(3); Match No. 23: Andrew Jackson 1(3).

CONFERENCE LEAGUE AVERAGES

Rider	Mts	Rds	Pts	Bon	Tot	Avge	Max
William Lawson	15	77	191	4	195	10.13	1 Full; 1 Paid
Craig Branney	21	113	252	17	269	9.52	1 Full; 2 Paid
Jamie Robertson	18	87	173	7	180	8.28	1 Full; 2 Paid
Steven Jones	19	90	131	20	151	6.71	–
John Branney	22	113	150	26	176	6.23	1 Full
Phil Bragg	4	17	17	5	22	5.18	–
Michael Pickering	10	46	41	7	48	4.17	–
Gary Beaton	9	35	26	9	35	4.00	–

Rider	Mts	Rds	Pts	Bon	Tot	Avge	Max
Scott Nettleship	1	4	3	1	4	4.00	–
Karl Langley	19	73	54	11	65	3.56	–
Carl Shield	3	7	5	0	5	2.86	–
Kriss Irving	12	44	26	5	31	2.82	–
Sean Stoddart	1	3	2	0	2	2.67	–
Andrew Jackson	1	3	1	0	1	1.33	–
David Haigh	1	3	0	0	0	0.00	–
Ben Warburton	1	3	0	0	0	0.00	–

OTHER MEETING

26 October: Tyne-Wear Trophy

Newcastle 21 (Jamie Robertson 11; Gary Beaton 4+1; Karl Langley 3+2; Steven Jones 3)
Sunderland 21 (John Branney 10+1; Craig Branney 7+1; Michael Pickering 4; Kriss Irving 0).

INDIVIDUAL MEETING

26 May: Chris Prime Memorial Trophy

1st William Lawson 14; 2nd Jamie Robertson 12; 3rd Ben Wilson 12; Benji Compton 11; Danny Hughes 11; Matthew Wethers 11; Craig Branney 8; Steven Jones 7; Richard Hall 6; David Speight 6; Gary Beaton 5; Phil Bragg 4; Scott Nettleship 4; Andrew Tully 4; Michael Pickering 2; Kriss Irving 1.

NEWPORT GMB MAVERICKS

NOTE: The information below relates only to the second Newport team. For details of the main side, please refer to the Premier League section.

ADDRESS: Hayley Stadium, Plover Close, Longditch Road, Queensway Meadows, Newport, Gwent, South Wales.
PROMOTER: Tim Stone.
TRACK LENGTH: 285 metres.
FIRST MEETING: 30 May 1997.
YEARS OF OPERATION: 1997 British Amateur League; 1998-03 British Conference League.

CLUB HONOURS

LEAGUE CHAMPIONS: 1999.

RIDER ROSTER 2003

BARNETT, Russell   *b. 26 May 1987.*
BRITISH CAREER: (2003) Mildenhall (CT), Rye House (CL), Newport (CL), Oxford (CL).
BROWN, Alan   *b. 19 February 1959, Stoke-on-Trent, Staffordshire.*
BRITISH CAREER: (2002) Buxton; (2003) Oxford (CL), Buxton, Newport (CL), Trelawny (CT).
BROWN, Tom   *b. 19 June 1984, Panteg, Pontypool, Wales.*
BRITISH CAREER: (2000) Peterborough (CL), Newport (CL); (2001) Newport (CL &
PL), Isle of Wight, Exeter; (2002) Workington, Newport (CL), Swindon (CT & PL), Isle
of Wight, Edinburgh, Trelawny; (2003) Trelawny (PL & CT), Newport (CL).
BURCHATT, Barry   *b. 25 October 1987, Farnborough, Kent.*
BRITISH CAREER: (2003) Newport (CL), Rye House (CL), Wimbledon.
CAMBRIDGE, Matt   *b. 14 May 1981, Rugby, Warwickshire.*
BRITISH CAREER: (2000) Sheffield (CL); (2001-02) Sheffield (CL), Exeter; (2003)
Newport (PL & CL), Wimbledon, Poole (BLC).
DAY, Terry   *b. 26 February 1985, Poole, Dorset.*
BRITISH CAREER: (2002) Wimbledon; (2003) Newport (CL).
DICKERSON, Roger   *b. 8 July 1965, Ipswich, Suffolk.*
BRITISH CAREER: (2002) Wimbledon; (2003) Boston, Newport.
GOUGH, David   *b. 11 January 1986, Newport, South Wales.*
BRITISH CAREER: (2001) Newport (CL); (2002) Carmarthen; (2003) Carmarthen,
Somerset (BLC), Newport (CL).
HUGHES, Danny   *b. 2 September 1983, Manchester.*
BRITISH CAREER: (1999) Workington; (2000) Buxton, Belle Vue; (2001) Buxton,
Newport (CL); (2002) Newport (CL), Stoke, Workington, Edinburgh; (2003) Newport
(CL & PL), Belle Vue (BLC), Stoke (CT).
LOUTH, Karl   *b. 15 February 1987.*
BRITISH CAREER: (2003) Newport (CL), Boston, Peterborough (CL), Wolverhampton (CL).
MALLETT, Nick   *b. 12 May 1987, Newport, South Wales.*
BRITISH CAREER: (2002) Swindon (CT); (2003) Newport (CL), Peterborough (CL).
MASON, Karl   *b. 4 March 1986, Hillingdon, London.*
BRITISH CAREER: (2001) Buxton, Mildenhall, Somerset; (2002) Newport (CL), Reading;
(2003) Newport (CL & PL), Exeter (BLC).
MINALL, David   *b. 30 March 1987, Walsall, West Midlands.*
BRITISH CAREER: (2003) Newport (CL).
NIXON, Matthew   *b. 1 June 1988, Northampton, Northamptonshire.*
BRITISH CAREER: (2003) Newport (CL).
PAINTER, Rob   *b. 23 June 1978, Whipps Cross, Walthamstow, London.*
BRITISH CAREER: (2001) Newport (CL), Boston; (2002) Peterborough (CL); (2003)
Peterborough (CL & BLC), Newport (CL).
PEGLER, Scott   *b. 3 August 1973, Exeter, Devon.*
BRITISH CAREER: (1989-90) Exeter; (1992-94) Exeter; (1995) Exeter, Devon; (1996)
Swindon (PL & CL); (1997) Newport (PL); (1998) Newport (PL & CL); (1999)
Newport (PL); (2000-03) Newport (CL).
ROWLETT, Thomas   *b. 22 January 1979, Wisbech, Cambridgeshire.*
BRITISH CAREER: (1999) King's Lynn (CL); (2000-01) Mildenhall; (2002) Mildenhall,

NEWPORT MAVERICKS: back row, left to right: Karl Mason, Tom Brown, Nick Mallett, Matt Cambridge. Front row, left to right: Dan Warwick, Scott Pegler, Danny Hughes.

Wimbledon; (2003) Mildenhall, Carmarthen (CT), Oxford (CLKOC), Newport (CL).

THEOBALD, James *b. 31 December 1985, Ashford, Kent.*
BRITISH CAREER: (2002) Rye House (CL), Carmarthen; (2003) Rye House (CL), Mildenhall, Sheffield (CL), Newport (CL), Peterborough (CL).

TUTTON, Matt *b. 19 June 1982, Newport, South Wales.*
BRITISH CAREER: (2000) Rye House; (2002) Swindon (CT), Wimbledon; (2003) Mildenhall, Buxton, Carmarthen (CT), Newport (CL).

WARBURTON, Ben *b. 20 September 1986, Sheffield, South Yorkshire.*
BRITISH CAREER: (2002) Boston, Wolverhampton (CT); (2003) Newport (CL), Oxford (CL), Sheffield (CL), Newcastle.

WARWICK, Carl *b. 7 October 1981, Poole, Dorset.*
BRITISH CAREER: (2002-03) Newport (CL).

WARWICK, Dan *b. 21 November 1983, Poole, Dorset.*
BRITISH CAREER: (2002) Newport (CL), Reading; (2003) Newport (CL & PL), Poole (BLC), Exeter.

WESTACOTT, Jamie *b. 9 April 1988, Newport, South Wales.*
BRITISH CAREER: (2003) Newport (CL), Stoke (CT).

WILKINSON, Carl *b. 16 May 1981, Boston, Lincolnshire.*
BRITISH CAREER: (1997) Peterborough (AL); (1998) Norfolk; (1999) King's Lynn (CL); (2000) Boston, Newcastle, Glasgow; (2001) Boston, Newport (PL); (2002-03) Newport (PL & CL).

CONFERENCE LEAGUE

(* Denotes bonus-point victory)

No	DATE	OPPONENTS	H/A	RESULT	PEGLER	MINALL	CAMBRIDGE	D. WARWICK	WILKINSON	MASON	MALLETT	HUGHES	BROWN	WESTACOTT	C. WARWICK	NIXON	OTHERS
1	30/3	Wimbledon	H	W52-37	14+1(5)	2+1(4)	7(4)	9+2(5)	12(4)	8+1(6)	–	–	–	–	–	–	0(2)
2	6/4	Mildenhall	H	L43-47	16+1(6)	–	3(3)	5+1(4)	–	6+1(5)	0(2)	2+1(3)	11+1(6)	–	–	–	–
3	14/4	Sheffield	A	L27-63	–	0(3)	R/R	8+1(6)	–	10(7)	1+1(4)	–	–	5+1(6)	–	–	3(4)
4	20/4	Newcastle	A	L32-57	–	1(3)	R/R	7(6)	–	5+1(5)	0(3)	12(7)	–	7+1(6)	–	–	–
5	27/4	Rye House †	H	L34-44	13(5)	0(3)	–	4+1(4)	–	3+1(3)	2+1(2)	–	7+2(5)	5(4)	–	–	–
6	8/6	Sheffield	H	W56-33	14(5)	–	–	8(4)	–	5+2(5)	0(1)	8+2(4)	11+1(5)	10+3(6)	–	–	–
7	15/6	Boston	A	L22-68	R/R	2(5)	–	7+1(7)	–	0(1)	–	9(7)	–	–	–	–	4+1(10)
8	22/6	Peterborough	A	L36-54	15(6)	1(4)	–	–	R/R	–	–	11+1(7)	–	–	–	–	9+4(13)
9	22/6	Mildenhall	A	L25-65	14(6)	0(4)	–	–	R/R	–	–	8(7)	–	–	–	–	3(13)
10	29/6	Newcastle	H	L37-52	12+1(6)	6(6)	–	6(5)	R/R	–	–	0(1)	12+2(7)	–	–	–	1(5)
11	12/7	Rye House	A	L32-57	R/R	0(4)	–	12+1(7)	13+1(5)	–	–	–	–	–	1(5)	–	6+1(10)
12	20/7	Carmarthen	H	L40-49	–	1(4)	–	9(4)	12(4)	3(5)	–	–	–	11+1(6)	3+1(4)	–	1(3)
13	8/8	Oxford	A	L20-70	R/R	1(4)	–	8(6)	–	–	1(4)	–	–	5(6)	4+1(6)	1(4)	–
14	11/8	Wolverhampton	A	L31-59	R/R	3(5)	–	8(7)	17(6)	–	1+1(4)	–	–	2(4)	0(4)	–	–
15	17/8	Buxton	A	L30-60	–	3+1(5)	–	11(7)	R/R	–	1(3)	–	13(7)	–	0(4)	–	2(4)
16	24/8	Swindon	H	L41-49	14(6)	2(5)	–	–	R/R	9+1(5)	0(3)	–	14+1(6)	–	2(5)	–	–
17	3/9	Wimbledon	A	L23-67	R/R	1(5)	–	6(4)	–	3(6)	–	6(6)	–	–	6+1(6)	1(3)	–
18	7/9	Oxford	H	W46-43	17(6)	5(4)	–	–	R/R	5+1(6)	–	4+1(5)	15+2(6)	–	0(3)	–	–
19	11/9	Swindon	A	L29-61	19(7)	1(5)	–	–	–	6(7)	1(4)	–	R/R	–	1(4)	1(3)	–

CONFERENCE LEAGUE continued

No	DATE	OPPONENTS	H/A	RESULT	PEGLER	MINALL	CAMBRIDGE	D. WARWICK	WILKINSON	MASON	MALLETT	HUGHES	BROWN	WESTACOTT	C. WARWICK	NIXON	OTHERS
20	21/9	Peterborough	H	W54-36	9(4)	7+2(5)	–	–	9(3)	11+2(5)	–	7+1(4)	10(5)	–	1(4)	–	–
21	28/9	Carmarthen	A	L35-54	18(7)	5(6)	–	–	R/R	11+1(7)	–	1(4)	–	–	–	0(3)	0(3)
22	12/10	Wolverhampton	H	W63-25*	15(5)	11+3(6)	–	–	–	15(5)	3+1(4)	15+3(6)	R/R	–	–	4+1(4)	–
23	19/10	Boston	H	L42-48	–	1(4)	–	–	R/R	17(6)	0(2)	7(6)	15+1(7)	–	–	–	2(4)
24	26/10	Buxton	H	D45-45	18(6)	4(5)	–	–	R/R	–	–	13+1(6)	8+1(5)	–	–	–	2(8)

† Meeting abandoned after thirteen heats, with the result standing.

DETAILS OF OTHER RIDERS:

Match No. 1: Terry Day 0(2); Match No. 3: Ben Warburton 3(4); Match No. 7: Roger Dickerson 3+1(5); Karl Louth 1(5); Match No. 8: James Theobald 4+2(4); Rob Painter 4+1(4); Thomas Rowlett 1+1(5); Match No. 9: Thomas Rowlett 2(4); Rob Painter 1(6); James Theobald 0(3); Match No. 10: David Gough 1(5); Match No. 11: Rob Painter 4+1(6); Barry Burchatt 2(3); Match No. 12: Rob Painter 1(3); Match No. 15: Alan Brown 2(4); Match No. 21: Russell Barnett 0(3); Match No. 23: Russell Barnett 2(4); Match No. 24: Matt Tutton 2(4); Russell Barnett 0(4).

CONFERENCE LEAGUE AVERAGES

Rider	Mts	Rds	Pts	Bon	Tot	Avge	Max
Carl Wilkinson	5	22	63	1	64	11.64	2 Full
Scott Pegler	14	80	208	3	211	10.55	2 Full; 1 Paid
Tom Brown	10	59	116	11	127	8.61	–
Danny Hughes	14	73	103	10	113	6.19	1 Paid
Karl Mason	16	84	117	11	128	6.10	1 Full
Dan Warwick	14	76	108	7	115	6.05	–
Jamie Westacott	6	34	43	6	49	5.76	–
Matt Cambridge	2	7	10	0	10	5.71	–
James Theobald	2	7	4	2	6	3.43	–
Roger Dickerson	1	5	3	1	4	3.20	–
Ben Warburton	1	4	3	0	3	3.00	–
Barry Burchatt	1	3	2	0	2	2.67	–
David Minall	22	99	57	7	64	2.59	–
Rob Painter	4	19	10	2	12	2.53	–
Carl Warwick	8	36	18	3	21	2.33	–
Alan Brown	1	4	2	0	2	2.00	–
Matt Tutton	1	4	2	0	2	2.00	–
Thomas Rowlett	2	9	3	1	4	1.78	–
Nick Mallett	12	36	10	4	14	1.56	–
Matthew Nixon	8	30	9	1	10	1.33	–
David Gough	1	5	1	0	1	0.80	–
Karl Louth	1	5	1	0	1	0.80	–
Russell Barnett	3	11	2	0	2	0.73	–
Terry Day	1	2	0	0	0	0.00	–

OTHER MEETINGS

11 July: Paul Gladwin Memorial Four-Team Tournament
Weymouth 26, Swindon 17, Bristol 15, Newport 14 (Tom Brown 7; Dan Warwick 5; David Minall 1; Oliver Hackett 1) – staged at Somerset.
3 October: Conference Challenge
Bristol 67 Newport 23 (Karl Mason 13; Jack Gledhill 4; Nick Mallett 3; Matthew Nixon 2; David Minall 1; Russell Barnett 0; Scott Pegler R/R) – staged at Somerset.

OXFORD SILVER MACHINE ACADEMY

NOTE: The information below relates only to the second Oxford team. For details of the main side, please refer to the Elite League section.

ADDRESS: Oxford Stadium, Sandy Lane, Cowley, Oxford.
PROMOTER: Nigel Wagstaff.
TRACK LENGTH: 297 metres.
FIRST MEETING: 25 May 1997.
YEARS OF OPERATION: 1997 British Amateur League; 2003 British Conference League.

CLUB HONOURS

None.

RIDER ROSTER 2003

ANDREWS, Darren   b. 19 January 1977, Banbury, Oxfordshire.
BRITISH CAREER: (1993) Coventry, Oxford; (1994) Coventry, Oxford, Mildenhall; (1995) Sittingbourne; (1996) Reading (CL); (1997) Berwick, Hull, Long Eaton, Oxford (PL & AL), Isle of Wight; (2000) St Austell; (2001) Rye House; (2002) Mildenhall, Hull; (2003) Oxford (CL & BLC), Carmarthen (CT).
BARKER, Ben   b. 10 March 1988, Truro, Cornwall.
BRITISH CAREER: (2003) Oxford (CL), Trelawny (CT).
BARNETT, Russell   b. 26 May 1987.
BRITISH CAREER: (2003) Mildenhall (CT), Rye House (CL), Newport (CL), Oxford (CL).
BETHELL, Jonathan   b. 18 March 1973. Kendal, Cumbria.
BRITISH CAREER: (2003) Oxford (CL), Buxton.
BROWN, Alan   b. 19 February 1959, Stoke-on-Trent, Staffordshire.
BRITISH CAREER: (2002) Buxton; (2003) Oxford (CL), Buxton, Newport (CL), Trelawny (CT).
COOK, Joe   b. 24 December 1983, King's Lynn, Norfolk.
BRITISH CAREER: (2002) King's Lynn (CL), Arena-Essex, Newport (PL), Isle of Wight; (2003) Stoke, Oxford (CL & BLC).

OXFORD SILVER MACHINE ACADEMY: back row, left to right: Pete Chapman (Team Manager), Chris Johnson, Ricky Scarboro, Darren Andrews, Andy Smith. On bike: Chris Mills. Front, kneeling: Ben Barker, James Purchase.

DOWNS, Carl   b. 13 November 1983, Coventry, Warwickshire.
   BRITISH CAREER: (1999) King's Lynn (CL); (2000) Boston, Peterborough (CL), Sheffield (CL); (2001) Newport (CL), Mildenhall; (2002) King's Lynn (CL); (2003) Oxford (CL & BLC), Coventry (BLC), Stoke (CT), Isle of Wight.

JOHNSON, Chris   b. 13 October 1987, Chichester, Sussex.
   BRITISH CAREER: (2003) Oxford (CL), Trelawny (CT), Isle of Wight.

MILLS, Chris   b. 29 March 1983, Chelmsford, Essex.
   BRITISH CAREER: (2001) Arena-Essex; (2002) King's Lynn (CL), Wimbledon; (2003) Isle of Wight, Oxford (CL).

NEWITT, Jason   b. 13 January 1978, Oxford, Oxfordshire.
   BRITISH CAREER: (1996) Peterborough (CL); (1997) Peterborough (AL), Oxford (AL & PL); (2000) Somerset; (2003) Oxford (CL), Mildenhall.

PURCHASE, James   b. 21 October 1987, Southampton, Hampshire.
   BRITISH CAREER: (2003) Oxford (CL), Peterborough (CL & BLC).

ROWLETT, Thomas   b. 22 January 1979, Wisbech, Cambridgeshire.
   BRITISH CAREER: (1999) King's Lynn (CL); (2000-01) Mildenhall; (2002) Mildenhall, Wimbledon; (2003) Mildenhall, Carmarthen (CT), Oxford (CLKOC), Newport (CL).

SCARBORO, Ricky   b. 31 July 1966, Grunby, Lincolnshire.
   BRITISH CAREER: (1999) Mildenhall, King's Lynn (CL); (2000) Boston; (2001) Boston, Newport (PL); (2002) Boston, King's Lynn (CL); (2003) Oxford (CL & BLC), Stoke (CT), Newport (PL).

SCHRAMM, Chris   b. 30 May 1984, Maldon, Essex.
   BRITISH CAREER: (2000) Peterborough (CL), Berwick, Arena-Essex; (2001) Peterborough (EL & CL), Isle of Wight, Reading; (2002) Reading, Peterborough (CL); (2003) Newport (PL), Wimbledon (CT), Peterborough (CL), Oxford (CL).

SMITH, Andy   b. 25 May 1966, York, North Yorkshire.
   BRITISH CAREER: (1982-88) Belle Vue; (1989-90) Bradford; (1991) Swindon; (1992-95) Coventry; (1996) Bradford; (1997) Coventry; (1998) Belle Vue, Swindon; (1999-01) Belle Vue; (2003) Oxford (EL & CL).

WARBURTON, Ben   b. 20 September 1986, Sheffield, South Yorkshire.
   BRITISH CAREER: (2002) Boston, Wolverhampton (CT); (2003) Newport (CL), Oxford (CL), Sheffield (CL), Newcastle.

WARNES, Tim   b. 29 March 1982, King's Lynn, Norfolk.
   BRITISH CAREER: (2002) Newport (CL), King's Lynn (CL); (2003) Oxford (CL), Swindon (CL).

CONFERENCE LEAGUE

(* Denotes bonus-point victory)

No	DATE	OPPONENTS	H/A	RESULT	SCARBORO	DOWNS	ANDREWS	WARNES	MILLS	JOHNSON	BARKER	COOK	NEWITT	SCHRAMM	OTHERS
1	2/4	Wimbledon	A	L44-46	7(4)	6+1(4)	10(5)	0(3)	11(5)	5+3(5)	5+1(4)	–	–	–	–
2	6/4	Peterborough	A	L40-49	5+1(4)	3+1(3)	8+2(5)	–	8(6)	1+1(3)	1(3)	14(6)	–	–	–
3	20/4	Buxton	A	L34-56	5+2(6)	0(3)	11(6)	–	R/R	7+1(6)	–	–	–	–	11+1(9)
4	3/5	Rye House	A	L37-53	4+2(5)	12(7)	3+1(4)	1(2)	12(6)	5+1(4)	0(2)	R/R	–	–	–
5	1/6	Newcastle	A	L37-51	12(7)	–	5+1(5)	0(1)	10(7)	10+4(7)	–	R/R	0(3)	–	–
6	6/6	Carmarthen	H	W57-34	12+1(5)	–	8(4)	–	9+3(6)	10+1(7)	0(1)	R/R	–	–	18(6)

CONFERENCE LEAGUE continued

No	DATE	OPPONENTS	H/A	RESULT	SCARBORO	DOWNS	ANDREWS	WARNES	MILLS	JOHNSON	BARKER	COOK	NEWITT	SCHRAMM	OTHERS
7	9/7	Peterborough	H	W53-37*	9+3(5)	0(2)	7+1(4)	–	R/R	5+3(4)	6(4)	15(5)	–	11(6)	–
8	13/7	Mildenhall	A	L40-50	5+2(5)	–	7(5)	–	11(7)	3(3)	1+1(3)	13(7)	–	R/R	–
9	22/7	Wolverhampton	A	L38-50	8+1(6)	0(1)	4+1(3)	–	R/R	3+2(4)	5+1(4)	11(6)	–	7+1(6)	–
10	8/8	Wimbledon	H	W57-33*	15+1(6)	5+2(4)	8+2(4)	–	–	7+2(4)	9+3(5)	13(5)	0(2)	R/R	–
11	8/8	Newport	H	W70-20	14+1(5)	8+2(4)	10+3(5)	–	–	10+2(4)	11+2(5)	17+1(6)	0(1)	R/R	–
12	1/9	Sheffield	A	L35-54	–	0(3)	0(3)	–	14(6)	3+1(5)	7+1(5)	0(3)	–	11(5)	–
13	5/9	Buxton	H	W59-31*	–	3+1(4)	7+4(5)	–	9+1(5)	12+2(6)	14(5)	14(5)	–	R/R	–
14	5/9	Swindon	H	W50-40	–	3+2(4)	5(4)	–	10+3(6)	11(5)	6+1(4)	15(6)	0(1)	R/R	–
15	7/9	Newport	A	L43-46*	–	1+1(3)	5+2(4)	–	11(5)	11+2(6)	3(4)	6+1(4)	–	6(4)	–
16	19/9	Wolverhampton	H	W61-31*	–	5+2(4)	2(3)	–	11+1(5)	7+4(4)	13+2(5)	10(4)	–	13+1(5)	–
17	26/9	Rye House	H	W63-25*	–	7+2(5)	6+1(4)	–	4+1(4)	9+2(4)	10+2(4)	12(4)	–	15(5)	–
18	3/10	Sheffield	H	W54-39	–	3+2(4)	3+1(4)	–	11+2(5)	6+1(4)	9+2(4)	9(4)	–	13+1(5)	–
19	3/10	Newcastle	H	W56-34*	–	5+3(5)	5+2(4)	–	0(0)	11+3(6)	13+1(6)	11(5)	–	11(4)	–
20	8/10	Boston	H	W63-27	–	3(4)	5+2(4)	–	R/R	10+2(4)	10+2(4)	18(6)	0(2)	17+1(6)	–
21	9/10	Swindon †	A	W38-34*	–	2+1(3)	1+1(3)	–	R/R	3+1(4)	11+3(5)	10(4)	–	11(5)	–
22	12/10	Carmarthen	A	L38-52*	–	5+1(6)	3(4)	–	R/R	11+2(7)	18+1(7)	–	1(3)	–	0(3)
23	17/10	Boston	A	W59-31*	–	1(4)	6+1(5)	–	R/R	7+2(5)	13+2(5)	14+1(5)	–	18(6)	–
24	24/10	Mildenhall	H	W53-37*	–	4+2(4)	3(4)	–	R/R	11+1(5)	5+1(5)	16+1(6)	–	14+1(6)	–

† Meeting abandoned after twelve heats, with the result standing.

DETAILS OF OTHER RIDERS:

Match No. 3: Alan Brown 7(4); Ben Warburton 4+1(4); Jonathan Bethell 0(1); Match No. 6: Andy Smith 18(6); James Purchase 0(0); Match No. 22: Russell Barnett 0(3).

CONFERENCE LEAGUE AVERAGES

Rider	Mts	Rds	Pts	Bon	Tot	Avge	Max
Andy Smith	1	6	18	0	18	12.00	1 Full
Joe Cook	18	91	218	4	222	9.76	3 Full; 2 Paid
Chris Schramm	12	63	147	5	152	9.65	2 Full; 1 Paid
Ben Barker	22	94	170	26	196	8.34	4 Paid
Chris Mills	14	73	131	11	142	7.78	–
Chris Johnson	24	116	178	43	221	7.62	2 Paid
Ricky Scarboro	11	58	96	14	110	7.59	1 Paid
Alan Brown	1	4	7	0	7	7.00	–
Darren Andrews	24	101	132	25	157	6.22	–
Ben Warburton	1	4	4	1	5	5.00	–
Carl Downs	21	81	76	23	99	4.89	–
Tim Warnes	3	6	1	0	1	0.67	–
Jason Newitt	6	12	1	0	1	0.33	–
Russell Barnett	1	3	0	0	0	0.00	–
Jonathan Bethell	1	1	0	0	0	0.00	–
James Purchase	1	0	0	0	0	0.00	–

KNOCK-OUT CUP

No	DATE	OPPONENTS	H/A	RESULT	MILLS	COOK	SCARBORO	WARNES	ANDREWS	JOHNSON	ROWLETT	DOWNS	SCHRAMM	BARKER
1	8/6	Mildenhall	A	L37-53	16(7)	R/R	11(7)	0(3)	2(4)	6+1(6)	2+1(3)	–	–	–
2	30/7	Mildenhall	H	W45-44	R/R	–	10+2(6)	–	3(3)	3+1(4)	–	7(5)	16(7)	6+1(5)

INDIVIDUAL MEETING

15 October: David Nix Memorial Trophy
(Qualifying scores: Chris Schramm 15; Ritchie Hawkins 13; Joe Cook 12; Jamie Robertson 12; Craig Branney 10; Darren Andrews 10; Paul Burnett 8; Chris Johnson 8; Ben Barker 8; Darren Mallett 8; John Branney 6; Carl Downs 4; Gordon Meakins 3; Tim Warnes 2; Karl Langley 1; Daniel Hodgson 0) Semi-Final: 1st Robertson; 2nd C. Branney; 3rd Cook; 4th Andrews; Final: 1st C. Branney; 2nd Robertson; 3rd Schramm; 4th Hawkins.

PETERBOROUGH H & M PUMAS

NOTE: The information below relates only to the second Peterborough side. For details of the main team, please refer to the Elite League section.

ADDRESS: East of England Showground, Alwalton, Peterborough, Cambridgeshire.
PROMOTERS: Mick Horton & Jim Lynch, with the former assuming full control at the end of September 2003.
TRACK LENGTH: 337 metres.
FIRST MEETING: 5 July 1996.
YEARS OF OPERATION: 1996 British Conference League; 1997 British Amateur League; 2000-03 British Conference League.

CLUB HONOURS

LEAGUE CHAMPIONS: 1997, 2002.

RIDER ROSTER 2003

CLARKE, Steve   b. 14 January 1984, Aylesbury, Buckinghamshire.
BRITISH CAREER: (2002) King's Lynn (CL), Wolverhampton (CT); (2003) Wolverhampton (CL), Peterborough (CL & BLC).
COLLINS, Neil   b. 15 October 1961, Partington, Greater Manchester.
BRITISH CAREER: (1978) Ellesmere Port; (1979) Nottingham, Workington, Sheffield; (1980) Edinburgh, Sheffield; (1981) Edinburgh, Cradley Heath, Belle Vue; (1982-83) Leicester; (1984-88) Sheffield; (1989-90) Wolverhampton; (1991) Belle Vue; (1992) Glasgow; (1993-94) Long Eaton; (1995) Sheffield; (1996) Belle Vue; (1997) Glasgow;

(1998) Stoke; (1999-00) Swindon; (2001) Belle Vue, Workington; (2002) Somerset; (2003) Hull, Peterborough (BLC & CL 4 Team Champs), Belle Vue.

DENNIS, Richie   b. 16 April 1988, Boston, Lincolnshire.
BRITISH CAREER: (2003) Peterborough (CL).

DOWNES, Phil   b. 22 February 1979, Hull, East Yorkshire.
BRITISH CAREER: (2003) Peterborough (CL).

DUNWORTH, Wayne   b. 20 January 1967, Nottingham, Nottinghamshire.
BRITISH CAREER: (1984) Boston; (1986) Mildenhall; (1987) Boston; (2002) Boston, Carmarthen; (2003) Trelawny (CT), Boston, Peterborough (CL), Armadale (CT).

FISHER, Neil   b. 6 March 1984.
BRITISH CAREER: (2003) Peterborough (CL).

HAIGH, David   b. 12 December 1984.
BRITISH CAREER: (2002) Newcastle (CL); (2003) Wimbledon, Newcastle (CL), Peterborough (CL).

HILL, Thomas   b. 16 September 1986, Sheffield, South Yorkshire.
BRITISH CAREER: (2003) Peterborough (CL), Wolverhampton (CL).

HORTON, James   b. 22 June 1985, Slough, Berkshire.
BRITISH CAREER: (2001-02) Peterborough (CL); (2003) Peterborough (CL & BLC), Boston (CT), Trelawny (PL & CT).

HUNTER, Chris   b. 12 March 1984, Middlesbrough, Cleveland.
BRITISH CAREER: (2000) Berwick, Workington; (2001) Newcastle; (2002) Newcastle (CL); (2003) Peterborough (CL).

KING, Daniel   b. 14 August 1986, Maidstone, Kent.
BRITISH CAREER: (2001) Peterborough (CL); (2002) Peterborough (CL), Swindon (CT); (2003) Peterborough (CL), Ipswich (BLC), Reading, Mildenhall, Arena-Essex.

KING, Jason   b. 13 April 1985, Maidstone, Kent.
BRITISH CAREER: (2000) Peterborough (CL); (2001) Peterborough (CL), Newport (PL), Newcastle; (2002) Swindon (PL & CT), Peterborough (CL & ELKOC); (2003) Arena-Essex, Peterborough (CL).

LOUTH, Karl   b. 15 February 1987.
BRITISH CAREER: (2003) Newport (CL), Boston, Peterborough (CL), Wolverhampton (CL).

McCABE, Shane   b. 3 May 1974, Townsville, Queensland, Australia.
BRITISH CAREER: (2002) Peterborough (CL), Edinburgh, Somerset, Trelawny, Rye House, Newport, Stoke; (2003) King's Lynn, Boston, Peterborough (CL, ELKOC & BLC), Somerset.

MALLETT, Nick   b. 12 May 1987, Newport, South Wales.
BRITISH CAREER: (2002) Swindon (CT); (2003) Newport (CL), Peterborough (CL).

NETTLESHIP, Scott   b. 16 May 1984, Newcastle, Tyne & Wear.
BRITISH CAREER: (2003) Newcastle (CL), Mildenhall, Swindon (CL), Carmarthen, Peterborough (CL).

NORTON, Danny   b. 27 August 1986, Hull, East Yorkshire.
BRITISH CAREER: (2001-02) Peterborough (CL); (2003) Peterborough (CL & BLC), Armadale (CT), Swindon (PL), Reading, Mildenhall (KOC & CT), Poole (BLC), Oxford (BLC).

OAKEY, Steve   b. 21 December 1975.
BRITISH CAREER: (2003) Peterborough (CL).

PETERBOROUGH PUMAS: back row, left to right: Chris Schramm, James Horton, Rob Painter, Jason Taylor, Shane McCabe, Jason King, Richie Dennis. On bike: Adam Pryer. Front, kneeling: Kenny Parker, Daniel King.

PAINTER, Rob   b. 23 June 1978, Whipps Cross, Walthamstow, London.
  BRITISH CAREER: (2001) Newport (CL), Boston; (2002) Peterborough (CL); (2003) Peterborough (CL & BLC), Newport (CL).

PRYER, Adam   b. 14 April 1983, King's Lynn, Norfolk.
  BRITISH CAREER: (1999) King's Lynn (CL); (2000) Peterborough (CL), Berwick; (2001) Peterborough (EL & CL); (2002) Peterborough (CL), Rye House (PL); (2003) Somerset, Peterborough (CL).

PURCHASE, James   b. 21 October 1987, Southampton, Hampshire.
  BRITISH CAREER: (2003) Oxford (CL), Peterborough (CL & BLC).

SCHRAMM, Chris   b. 30 May 1984, Maldon, Essex.
  BRITISH CAREER: (2000) Peterborough (CL), Berwick, Arena-Essex; (2001) Peterborough (EL & CL), Isle of Wight, Reading; (2002) Reading, Peterborough (CL); (2003) Newport (PL), Wimbledon (CT), Peterborough (CL), Oxford (CL).

TAYLOR, John   b. 18 February 1944.
  BRITISH CAREER: (2003) Peterborough (CL).

THEOBALD, James   b. 31 December 1985, Ashford, Kent
  BRITISH CAREER: (2002) Rye House (CL), Carmarthen; (2003) Rye House (CL), Mildenhall, Sheffield (CL), Newport (CL), Peterborough (CL).

CONFERENCE LEAGUE

(* Denotes bonus-point victory)

No	DATE	OPPONENTS	H/A	RESULT	McCABE	PRYER	PAINTER	HILL	D. KING	NORTON	HORTON	HUNTER	J. KING	DENNIS	PURCHASE	OTHERS
1	6/4	Oxford	H	W49-40	14(5)	R/R	2(3)	1(3)	11+3(6)	11+1(6)	10+5(7)	–	–	–	–	–
2	13/4	Sheffield	H	W48-42	9(3)	R/R	2(3)	–	10(5)	8+2(5)	6+1(5)	6+2(5)	7+1(4)	–	–	–
3	21/4	Wimbledon	H	W48-42	15+1(6)	R/R	2(4)	–	–	18(7)	4(4)	2+1(4)	–	7+1(5)	–	–
4	22/4	Wolverhampton	A	L42-47	7(5)	R/R	3+2(2)	–	–	12(7)	3+3(5)	1+1(3)	–	6+1(5)	–	10(5)
5	1/5	Sheffield	A	D45-45*	7+1(4)	R/R	0(2)	–	–	12(5)	1(4)	–	12+1(6)	2+1(4)	–	11+1(5)
6	18/5	Mildenhall	A	L33-56	7+1(6)	R/R	4+1(4)	1(2)	–	0(3)	11(7)	–	6(3)	4+1(5)	–	–
7	1/6	Wolverhampton	H	W49-41*	12(4)	R/R	1+1(3)	–	–	8+1(6)	13+1(6)	5+3(5)	–	10(6)	–	–
8	22/6	Newport	H	W54-36	8(4)	R/R	–	–	–	14(5)	12(5)	5+1(4)	–	5(4)	3+2(4)	7+2(4)
9	22/6	Boston	H	L38-52	11(6)	R/R	–	–	–	14(6)	5+1(5)	0(3)	–	5(7)	–	3(3)
10	9/7	Oxford	A	L37-53	7+3(7)	–	–	–	–	17(7)	5+1(6)	3+1(4)	R/R	3(3)	–	2+1(3)
11	27/7	Carmarthen	A	L41-48	13(6)	–	–	0(4)	–	9+2(6)	–	2(4)	–	14(7)	–	3+1(3)
12	10/8	Boston	A	L29-61	–	–	–	3+1(3)	–	–	–	5(5)	R/R	5(7)	–	16(15)
13	25/8	Rye House	A	L33-57	–	–	–	–	14(7)	–	4(5)	3+2(5)	R/R	8(7)	2+1(3)	2+1(4)
14	26/8	Swindon †	A	L34-43	–	–	–	–	16(6)	–	4(2)	3(5)	R/R	10+1(7)	1(4)	0(2)
15	7/9	Buxton	A	L33-57	–	–	–	1(4)	–	10(6)	–	9+1(7)	R/R	12(7)	–	1+1(6)
16	16/9	Rye House	H¶	L32-55	–	–	–	3+3(4)	R/R	–	9(6)	2(6)	–	10(7)	–	8(7)
17	16/9	Buxton	H¶	L41-48	–	–	–	2+1(4)	R/R	–	9(6)	12(5)	–	12+4(7)	–	6(4)
18	18/9	Wimbledon	A	L38-52	–	–	–	–	–	–	3(5)	–	–	10+1(6)	0(3)	25+4(16)
19	20/9	Newcastle	H¶	L43-46	–	–	–	4+1(4)	–	–	10(6)	–	R/R	19+1(7)	3(4)	7(9)
20	20/9	Mildenhall	H¶	L25-65	–	–	–	3+1(6)	–	–	6(5)	–	R/R	10(6)	2(4)	4(6)
21	21/9	Newport	A	L36-54*	–	–	–	4+3(5)	–	–	2+1(4)	–	–	10(6)	9+1(6)	11(8)
22	10/10	Carmarthen	H¶	W46-44	–	–	–	3(4)	–	14+1(5)	–	6+1(5)	R/R	16+2(7)	7+2(6)	0(3)
23	10/10	Swindon	H¶	L37-52	–	–	–	5(4)	–	9+2(6)	–	6+1(5)	R/R	13+2(7)	4+1(5)	0(3)
24	13/10	Newcastle	A	L39-51	–	–	–	0(4)	–	12(6)	–	10+2(7)	R/R	14(6)	–	3+1(8)

† Meeting abandoned after thirteen heats, with the result standing.

¶ Match raced at King's Lynn.

DETAILS OF OTHER RIDERS:

Match No. 4: Chris Schramm 10(5); Match No. 5: Chris Schramm 11+1(5); Match No. 8: Steve Clarke 7+2(4); Match No 9: Steve Clarke 3(3); Match No. 10: Steve Clarke 2+1(3); Match No. 11: John Taylor 3+1(3); Neil Collins R/R; Match No. 12: Steve Clarke 13(7); Wayne Dunworth 2(4); Karl Louth 1(1); Neil Fisher 0(3); Match No. 13: Steve Clarke 2+1(4); Match No. 14: Steve Clarke 0(2); Match No. 15: Phil Downes 1+1(3); Steve Clarke 0(3); Match No. 16: Wayne Dunworth 5(4); Steve Clarke 3(3); Match No. 17: Wayne Dunworth 6(4); Steve Clarke DNR; Match No. 18: Robert Hollingworth 13(7); Chris Johnson 11+3(6); James Theobald 1+1(3); Steve Clarke R/R; Match No. 19: Wayne Dunworth 7(6); Steve Clarke 0(3); Match No. 20: Wayne Dunworth 4(6); Steve Clarke DNR; Match No. 21: Chris Schramm 10(4); Nick Mallett 1(4); Steve Clarke R/R; Match No. 22: Steve Oakey 0(3); Match No. 23: Neil Fisher 0(3); Match No. 24: Scott Nettleship 3+1(5); David Haigh 0(3).

GOLDEN DOUBLE RIDES:

Match No. 9: Danny Norton's total includes 2 points from a golden double ride.

CONFERENCE LEAGUE AVERAGES

Rider	Mts	Rds	Pts	Bon	Tot	Avge	Max
Chris Schramm	3	14	31	1	32	9.14	–
Daniel King	4	24	51	3	54	9.00	–
Jason King	3	13	25	2	27	8.31	–
Shane McCabe	11	56	110	6	116	8.29	1 Full
Danny Norton	15	86	167	9	176	8.19	1 Paid
Richie Dennis	22	133	205	15	220	6.62	–
James Horton	18	93	117	13	130	5.59	–
John Taylor	1	3	3	1	4	5.33	–
Chris Hunter	17	82	80	16	96	4.68	–
Steve Clarke	9	32	30	4	34	4.25	–
Wayne Dunworth	5	24	24	0	24	4.00	–
Karl Louth	1	1	1	0	1	4.00	–
James Purchase	9	39	31	7	38	3.90	–
Rob Painter	7	21	14	4	18	3.43	–
Scott Nettleship	1	5	3	1	4	3.20	–
Thomas Hill	13	51	30	10	40	3.14	–
Phil Downes	1	3	1	1	2	2.67	–
James Theobald	1	3	1	1	2	2.67	–
Nick Mallett	1	4	1	0	1	1.00	–
Neil Fisher	2	6	0	0	0	0.00	–
David Haigh	1	3	0	0	0	0.00	–
Steve Oakey	1	3	0	0	0	0.00	–
Guests	2	13	24	3	27	8.31	–

NOTES: (1) Danny Norton's figures include one golden double ride (2 points), modified to normal score i.e. 1 point;

(2) The figures for Chris Schramm include one match as a guest.

OTHER MEETINGS

23 March: Three-Team Tournament (first-leg)

Mildenhall 52, Boston 29, Peterborough 26 (Shane McCabe 7+1; Jason King 6; Daniel King 5; Adam Pryer 3; Danny Norton 3; James Horton 2; Rob Painter 0).

28 March: Three-Team Tournament (second-leg)

    Boston 36, Mildenhall 42, Peterborough 29 (Daniel King 9; Chris Schramm 8; Shane McCabe 5; James Horton 4+1; Danny Norton 2+1; Rob Painter 1; Strider Horton 0).

5 April: Three-Team Tournament (third-leg)

    Peterborough 42 (Jason King 12; Chris Schramm 9+3; Danny Norton 9; Daniel King 6; James Horton 4; Rob Painter 2), Mildenhall 42, Boston 24. Aggregate result: Mildenhall 136 Peterborough 97, Boston 89.

RYE HOUSE ELMSIDE RAIDERS

NOTE: The information below relates only to the second Rye House team. For details of the main side, please refer to the Premier League section.

ADDRESS: Rye House Stadium, Rye Road, Hoddesdon, Hertfordshire.
PROMOTER: Len Silver.
TRACK LENGTH: 271 metres.
FIRST MEETING: 1 April 2002.
YEARS OF OPERATION: 2002-03 British Conference League.

CLUB HONOURS

FOUR-TEAM CHAMPIONS: 2003.

RIDER ROSTER 2003

BARNETT, Russell *b. 26 May 1987.*
    BRITISH CAREER: (2003) Mildenhall (CT), Rye House (CL), Newport (CL). Oxford (CL).
BOWEN, Luke *b. 26 January 1986, Harlow, Essex.*
    BRITISH CAREER: (2002) Rye House (CL), Carmarthen; (2003) Rye House (CL).
BOXALL, Steve *b. 16 May 1987, Canterbury, Kent.*
    BRITISH CAREER: (2002) Rye House (CL); (2003) Rye House (CL), Ipswich (BLC), Reading (BLC), King's Lynn.
BURCHATT, Barry *b. 25 October 1987, Farnborough, Kent.*
    BRITISH CAREER: (2003) Newport (CL), Rye House (CL), Wimbledon.
COCKLE, James *b. 26 May 1986, Enfield, Middlesex.*
    BRITISH CAREER: (2001) Rye House; (2002) Rye House (CL & PL); (2003) Rye House (CL).
COOK, Harland *b. 6 August 1988, Watford, Hertfordshire.*
    BRITISH CAREER: (2003) Rye House (CL).
COURTNEY, Jamie *b. 22 April 1988, Ashington, Northumberland.*
    BRITISH CAREER: (2003) Rye House (CL), Trelawny (CT).
COURTNEY, Scott *b. 3 January 1983, Middlesbrough, Cleveland.*
    BRITISH CAREER: (1999) Glasgow, Linlithgow; (2000) Glasgow, Ashfield; (2001) Glasgow,

RYE HOUSE RAIDERS: back row, left to right: Len Silver (Promoter), Harland Cook, John Sampford (Team Manager), Steve Boxall, James Cockle. Front row, left to right: Barry Burchatt, Luke Bowen, Joel Parsons.

Buxton, Mildenhall, Trelawny, Arena-Essex, Newcastle; (2002) Arena-Essex, Rye House (CL); (2003) Poole, Eastbourne (BLC), Rye House (CL).

EVANS, Barrie *b. 16 April 1984, King's Lynn, Norfolk.*

BRITISH CAREER: (1999) Mildenhall; (2000) Arena-Essex, Mildenhall; (2001) Arena-Essex, Mildenhall, Exeter; (2002) Newport, Rye House (CL); (2003) Hull, Rye House (CL).

KENNETT, Edward *b. 28 August 1986, Hastings, Sussex.*

BRITISH CAREER: (2001) Rye House, Mildenhall; (2002-03) Rye House (CL & PL), Eastbourne.

MITCHELL, Michael *b. 21 April 1984, Halifax, West Yorkshire.*

BRITISH CAREER: (2000) Peterborough (CL), Newport (CL); (2001) Sheffield (CL), Newport (CL); (2002) Mildenhall, Sheffield (CL), Buxton; (2003) Sheffield (CL), Stoke (CT), Rye House (CL).

PARSONS, Joel *b. 24 July 1985, Broken Hill, New South Wales, Australia.*

BRITISH CAREER: (2003) Reading, Eastbourne (BLC), Rye House (CL & PL), Newport (PL), Wimbledon (CT), Arena-Essex, Peterborough (BLC), Hull.

THEOBALD, James *b. 31 December 1985, Ashford, Kent.*

BRITISH CAREER: (2002) Rye House (CL), Carmarthen; (2003) Rye House (CL), Mildenhall, Sheffield (CL), Newport (CL), Peterborough (CL).

CONFERENCE LEAGUE

(* Denotes bonus-point victory)

No	DATE	OPPONENTS	H/A	RESULT	KENNETT	THEOBOLD	S. COURTNEY	COCKLE	EVANS	BOWEN	PARSONS	J. COURTNEY	BOXALL	BURCHATT	COOK	OTHERS
1	21/4	Mildenhall	H	W51-40	15(5)	1(3)	3(2)	4(4)	10+1(4)	2(5)	16+2(7)	–	–	–	–	–
2	27/4	Newport †	A	W44-34	15(5)	–	R/R	4+2(4)	7+1(4)	4+2(4)	13(5)	1(4)	–	–	–	–
3	3/5	Oxford	H	W53-37	R/R	–	–	8+2(5)	15+1(6)	7+1(4)	11+3(7)	7(4)	5(4)	–	–	–
4	24/5	Wolverhampton	H	W57-33	R/R	3+1(4)	–	11(5)	16+1(6)	11+3(6)	–	4+3(3)	12+3(6)	–	–	–
5	27/5	Wolverhampton	A	W47-38*	15(5)	–	–	6+1(4)	5(4)	0(3)	11(7)	3+1(3)	7+1(4)	–	–	–
6	1/6	Mildenhall	A	L44-48*	19(6)	–	–	1(3)	12+2(6)	0(3)	8(5)	2+1(3)	2(4)	–	–	–
7	8/6	Carmarthen	A	W54-36	15(5)	–	–	3+2(4)	10+2(5)	8+1(4)	8(4)	6(4)	4(4)	–	–	–
8	15/6	Sheffield	H	W58-31	12(4)	–	–	9+2(5)	14+1(5)	3(4)	6+1(4)	6(4)	8+2(4)	–	–	–
9	18/6	Wimbledon	A	W47-42	17+1(6)	–	–	3(4)	R/R	6(4)	6(4)	10+3(6)	10+3(7)	1(3)	–	–
10	12/7	Newport	H	W57-32*	15(6)	0(0)	–	6+2(5)	R/R	16+2(7)	11+2(6)	–	9+4(5)	–	–	–
11	2/8	Newcastle	H	W53-36	R/R	–	–	8+1(5)	16+1(6)	2(4)	8+2(5)	–	15+1(6)	4+1(4)	–	–
12	10/8	Buxton	A	L44-46	R/R	1(3)	–	2+1(4)	–	10+2(7)	15(6)	–	11(6)	–	5(4)	–
13	18/8	Carmarthen	H	W58-30*	R/R	0(1)	–	4(4)	17+1(6)	6+3(4)	15+3(6)	–	9(5)	–	7(4)	–
14	23/8	Boston	H	W64-26	R/R	–	–	11+2(5)	16(6)	6+1(4)	9+1(5)	–	10+2(5)	–	12+1(5)	–
15	25/8	Peterborough	H	W57-33	R/R	–	–	6(4)	15+1(6)	10+2(5)	13(6)	–	8+1(5)	–	5+1(4)	–
16	7/9	Newcastle	A	L40-50*	R/R	–	–	5(5)	8+2(6)	4(3)	10+1(7)	–	13+1(6)	–	0(3)	–
17	8/9	Buxton	H	W50-39*	R/R	–	–	3+1(4)	6(4)	7+2(4)	10(6)	–	16+1(6)	0(1)	8+1(5)	–
18	12/9	Boston	A	W49-41*	R/R	–	–	6(4)	14(6)	2(4)	12+1(6)	–	15+2(7)	–	0(3)	–
19	16/9	Peterborough	A¶	W55-32*	R/R	–	–	6+1(4)	5+2(5)	11(5)	12+3(6)	–	15(6)	–	6(4)	–
20	26/9	Oxford	A	L25-63	R/R	–	–	2(3)	–	2+1(3)	14(7)	–	4(5)	0(5)	3+1(6)	0(1)
21	4/10	Wimbledon	H	W69-19*	R/R	–	–	13+4(6)	14+1(5)	12+3(5)	15+2(6)	–	9(4)	–	6+2(4)	–
22	9/10	Swindon ‡	A	L29-43	R/R	–	–	3(4)	10+1(5)	2(2)	8+1(5)	–	5(3)	–	1(5)	–
23	11/10	Swindon	H	W47-43	R/R	2(3)	–	9+1(6)	11+2(5)	–	14(6)	–	6+1(5)	–	5+2(5)	–
24	13/10	Sheffield	A	L26-64	–	1(5)	–	8(6)	R/R	–	7(3)	–	–	6+1(6)	1(4)	3+1(6)

† Meeting abandoned after thirteen heats, with the result standing.

‡ Meeting abandoned after twelve heats, with the result standing.

¶ Match raced at King's Lynn.

DETAILS OF OTHER RIDERS:

Match No. 20: Russell Barnett 0(1); Match No. 24: Michael Mitchell 3+1(6).

GOLDEN DOUBLE RIDES:

Match No. 6: Edward Kennett's total includes 4 points from a golden double ride.

CONFERENCE LEAGUE AVERAGES

Rider	Mts	Rds	Pts	Bon	Tot	Avge	Max
Edward Kennett	8	42	121	1	122	11.62	5 Full; 1 Paid
Barrie Evans	19	100	221	20	241	9.64	3 Paid
Joel Parsons	23	131	256	25	281	8.58	1 Paid
Steve Boxall	21	103	184	19	203	7.88	–
Luke Bowen	22	94	131	23	154	6.55	1 Paid
James Cockle	24	107	141	22	163	6.09	–
Scott Courtney	1	2	3	0	3	6.00	–
Jamie Courtney	8	32	39	8	47	5.88	–
Harland Cook	13	56	59	8	67	4.79	–
Barry Burchatt	4	16	10	2	12	3.00	–
Michael Mitchell	1	6	3	1	4	2.67	–
James Theobald	7	19	8	1	9	1.89	–
Russell Barnett	1	1	0	0	0	0.00	–

NOTE: Edward Kennett's totals include one golden double ride (4 points), modified to the normal score i.e. 2 points.

KNOCK-OUT CUP

(* Denotes aggregate victory)

No	DATE	OPPONENTS	H/A	RESULT	KENNETT	COCKLE	PARSONS	BOXALL	EVANS	J. COURTNEY	BOWEN	COOK	BURCHATT
1	8/6	Carmarthen	A	W50-40	15(5)	3(4)	10(4)	2+1(4)	12+2(5)	2+1(4)	6+2(4)	–	–
2	9/6	Carmarthen	H	W67-23*	15(5)	7+2(4)	10+2(4)	10(4)	12+3(5)	9+1(4)	4+2(4)	–	–
3	15/9	Armadale	H	W59-31	R/R	3+2(4)	11+2(5)	15+1(6)	14+1(6)	–	10+4(5)	6+2(4)	–
4	20/9	Armadale	A	W50-40*	R/R	2(4)	16+2(7)	11+1(6)	11(5)	–	5+2(4)	5(4)	–
5	18/10	Mildenhall	H	W46-43	14(5)	2(4)	9+1(5)	9+1(4)	8+2(4)	–	–	2(3)	2(5)
6	19/10	Mildenhall	A	L41-48	12(6)	2(3)	5+1(5)	14+1(6)	6+1(4)	–	–	2(3)	0(3)

SHEFFIELD PIRTEK PROWLERS

NOTE: The information below relates only to the second Sheffield team. For details of the main side, please refer to the Premier League section.

ADDRESS: Owlerton Sports Stadium, Penistone Road, Owlerton, Sheffield, South Yorkshire.
PROMOTERS: Neil Machin & Malcolm Wright.
TRACK LENGTH: 361 metres.
FIRST MEETING: 25 April 1996.

YEARS OF OPERATION: 1996 British Conference League; 2000–03 British Conference League.

CLUB HONOURS

LEAGUE CHAMPIONS: 2000, 2001.

RIDER ROSTER 2003

BRADY, Ross   *b. 17 February 1981, Winchburgh, Broxburn, Scotland.*
   BRITISH CAREER: (1997) Lathallan, Peterborough (AL); (1998) Mildenhall, Peterborough (PL), Berwick; (1999-00) Edinburgh; (2001) King's Lynn, Hull; (2002) Hull; (2003) Glasgow, Sheffield (CL & PL).

COMPTON, Benji   *b. 17 September 1986, Tenerife, Spain.*
   BRITISH CAREER: (2002) Newcastle (CL); (2003) Sheffield (CL & PL), Swindon (PL), Hull (BLC), Mildenhall (KOC), Exeter.

COOPER, Paul   *b. 7 June 1982, York, North Yorkshire.*
   BRITISH CAREER: (2003) Sheffield (CL).

FLINT, Gary   *b. 5 May 1982, Ashington, Durham.*
   BRITISH CAREER: (1999) Berwick, Linlithgow, St Austell; (2000) Ashfield, Berwick; (2001) Buxton, Newcastle, Exeter, Sheffield (PL), Berwick; (2002) Newcastle (CL), Somerset, Rye House (PL), Isle of Wight, Glasgow; (2003) Buxton, Sheffield (CL), Reading, Stoke (CT).

GRANT, Rob   *b. 10 June 1984, Newcastle-upon-Tyne, Tyne & Wear.*
   BRITISH CAREER: (1999) Linlithgow; (2000) Ashfield, Newcastle; (2001) Newcastle; (2002) Newcastle, Boston, Stoke; (2003) Berwick, Sheffield (CL), Stoke.

HALL, Richard   *b. 23 August 1984, Northallerton, North Yorkshire.*
   BRITISH CAREER: (2001) Newcastle; (2002) Newcastle (PL & CL), Trelawny, Glasgow; (2003) Sheffield (CL & PL), Stoke (PL), Coventry (BLC), Hull (BLC), Newport (PL), Boston (KOC & CT), Exeter, Reading, Workington, Somerset.

JACKSON, Andrew   *b. 12 July 1975, Manchester.*
   BRITISH CAREER: (2002) Wolverhampton (CT), Carmarthen, Newport (CL); (2003) Wolverhampton (CL), Sheffield (CL), Mildenhall (CT), Belle Vue (BLC), Swindon (CL), Trelawny (CT), Newcastle (CL).

MITCHELL, Michael   *b. 21 April 1984, Halifax, West Yorkshire.*
   BRITISH CAREER: (2000) Peterborough (CL), Newport (CL); (2001) Sheffield (CL), Newport (CL); (2002) Mildenhall, Sheffield (CL), Buxton, Boston; (2003) Sheffield (CL), Stoke (CT), Rye House (CL).

PRIEST, Luke   *b. 18 June 1985, Birmingham.*
   BRITISH CAREER: (2000) Ashfield, Owlerton; (2001) Sheffield (CL), Boston; (2002) Sheffield (CL), Wolverhampton (CT); (2003) Sheffield (CL & PL), Stoke (CT & PL), Workington, Exeter, Newport (BLC), Arena-Essex, Wolverhampton (BLC), Belle Vue (BLC).

RODGERS, Jamie   *b. 24 April 1987, Barnsley, South Yorkshire.*
   BRITISH CAREER: (2003) Sheffield (CL).

SPEIGHT, David   *b. 21 March 1980, Bradford, West Yorkshire.*
   BRITISH CAREER: (2000) Owlerton; (2001) Sheffield (CL), Exeter, Stoke; (2002) Hull, Sheffield (CL), Wolverhampton (CT); (2003) Sheffield (CL), Coventry (BLC).

SHEFFIELD PROWLERS: back row, left to right: Jamie Rodgers, Richard Hall, Luke Priest, David Speight. On bike: Ben Wilson. Front, kneeling: Benji Compton, Michael Mitchell.

THEOBALD, James   *b. 31 December 1985, Ashford, Kent.*
   BRITISH CAREER: (2002) Rye House (CL), Carmarthen; (2003) Rye House (CL),
   Mildenhall, Sheffield (CL), Newport (CL), Peterborough (CL).
WILSON, Ben   *b. 15 March 1986, Sheffield, South Yorkshire.*
   BRITISH CAREER: (2001) Sheffield (CL); (2002) Sheffield (CL & PL), Glasgow; (2003)
   Sheffield (PL & CL), Buxton (CT).
WARBURTON, Ben   *b. 20 September 1986, Sheffield, South Yorkshire.*
   BRITISH CAREER: (2002) Boston, Wolverhampton (CT); (2003) Newport (CL), Oxford
   (CL), Sheffield (CL), Newcastle.

CONFERENCE LEAGUE

(* Denotes bonus-point victory)

No	DATE	OPPONENTS	H/A	RESULT	HALL	PRIEST	SPEIGHT	COMPTON	WILSON	MITCHELL	RODGERS	BRADY	GRANT	FLINT	COOPER	OTHERS
1	9/4	Wimbledon	A	L35-55	13(6)	1+1(3)	0(3)	7(4)	7+1(6)	1(3)	6(5)	–	–	–	–	–
2	13/4	Peterborough	A	L42-48	8(6)	4+1(4)	1+1(3)	7+2(4)	17(6)	3(3)	2(4)	–	–	–	–	–
3	14/4	Newport	H	W63-27	14+1(5)	8+2(4)	8+2(4)	6(4)	12(4)	5+1(4)	10+2(5)	–	–	–	–	–
4	22/4	Swindon	A	L39-50	4+1(5)	5+2(4)	5+2(4)	4(4)	11(5)	2(4)	8+2(4)	–	–	–	–	–
5	1/5	Peterborough	H	D45-45	9+1(5)	8(4)	1+1(3)	4+2(4)	15(5)	0(3)	8+1(6)	–	–	–	–	–
6	4/5	Carmarthen	A	W52-37	11+2(6)	11(5)	R/R	8+1(5)	17+1(6)	4+1(4)	1+1(4)	–	–	–	–	–
7	18/5	Newcastle	A	L39-50	6+2(6)	4(3)	1(3)	8+1(5)	13(6)	2+1(3)	5(4)	–	–	–	–	–
8	2/6	Swindon	H	L43-47	9+1(7)	10+4(6)	3+1(3)	13(7)	R/R	2(3)	6(4)	–	–	–	–	–
9	8/6	Newport	A	L33-56*	11(6)	5+1(5)	3+1(5)	4(4)	9(5)	0(3)	–	–	–	–	–	1(2)
10	15/6	Rye House	A	L31-58	4(3)	5+1(5)	3+1(4)	8(6)	4(4)	5+1(5)	–	–	–	–	–	2+2(3)
11	22/6	Buxton	A	L36-54	11+1(6)	3+2(4)	2+1(4)	8+1(6)	10(4)	1(3)	–	–	–	–	–	1(3)
12	23/6	Buxton	H	W53-37	11+1(5)	5+3(4)	4+2(4)	6+2(4)	11(5)	5+2(4)	–	11(4)	–	–	–	–
13	23/6	Boston †	H	L35-37	7(3)	2+1(4)	4(3)	4+1(4)	5(3)	1+1(3)	–	12(4)	–	–	–	–
14	13/7	Boston	A	W58-32*	11(4)	7+3(4)	3+1(4)	8+1(4)	14+1(5)	2(4)	–	–	13+2(5)	–	–	–
15	21/7	Wimbledon	H	W64-25*	15(5)	8+2(4)	10+5(7)	10+2(5)	10+1(4)	0(0)	–	–	11+1(4)	–	–	–
16	21/7	Newcastle	H	W62-28*	9(4)	6+2(4)	9+2(6)	9+3(4)	14+1(5)	–	–	–	15(5)	–	–	–
17	10/8	Mildenhall	A	L26-63	9(7)	9(7)	0(3)	5+2(5)	R/R	1(3)	–	–	–	2(5)	–	–
18	11/8	Mildenhall	H	D45-45	15(6)	6+1(5)	8+1(5)	10(6)	R/R	0(1)	–	–	–	0(1)	6+1(6)	–
19	12/8	Wolverhampton	A	L28-57	9(7)	12(7)	2+1(3)	3+2(5)	R/R	–	–	–	–	2(5)	–	0(3)
20	1/9	Carmarthen	H	W67-22	15(6)	10+3(5)	13+1(5)	6+2(4)	R/R	–	–	–	–	11+4(5)	12+2(5)	–
21	1/9	Oxford	H	W54-35	17(6)	6+2(4)	10(5)	9+2(6)	R/R	2(1)	–	–	–	4+3(4)	6+1(4)	–
22	3/10	Oxford	A	L39-54*	18+1(6)	8+1(5)	6(4)	2+1(4)	4(4)	1(3)	–	–	–	0(4)	–	–
23	13/10	Rye House	H	W64-26*	15(5)	9+2(4)	5+2(4)	8+1(4)	13+2(5)	–	–	–	–	9+2(4)	5+1(4)	–
24	13/10	Wolverhampton	H	W62-28*	12+1(5)	8+3(4)	6+2(4)	10+1(4)	13(5)	–	–	–	–	6+1(4)	7+1(4)	–

† Meeting abandoned after twelve heats, with the result standing.

DETAILS OF OTHER RIDERS:

Match No. 9: Ben Warburton 1(2); Match No. 10: James Theobald 2+2(3); Match No. 11: Andrew Jackson 1(3); Match No. 19: Ben Warburton 0(3).

GOLDEN DOUBLE RIDES:

Match No. 22: Richard Hall's total includes 6 points from a golden double ride.

CONFERENCE LEAGUE AVERAGES

Rider	Mts	Rds	Pts	Bon	Tot	Avge	Max
Rob Grant	3	14	39	3	42	12.00	1 Full; 2 Paid
Ross Brady	2	8	23	0	23	11.50	1 Full
Ben Wilson	18	87	199	7	206	9.47	2 Full; 4 Paid
Richard Hall	24	130	260	12	272	8.37	2 Full; 1 Paid
Paul Cooper	5	23	36	6	42	7.30	–
Luke Priest	24	108	160	37	197	7.30	–
Benji Compton	24	112	167	27	194	6.93	1 Paid
Jamie Rodgers	8	36	46	6	52	5.78	–
David Speight	23	93	107	27	134	5.76	–
Gary Flint	8	32	34	10	44	5.50	1 Paid
James Theobald	1	3	2	2	4	5.33	–
Michael Mitchell	19	57	37	7	44	3.09	–
Andrew Jackson	1	3	1	0	1	1.33	–
Ben Warburton	2	5	1	0	1	0.80	–

NOTE: Richard Hall's totals include one golden double ride (6 points), modified to the normal score i.e. 3 points.

INDIVIDUAL MEETINGS

20 March: Steel City Challenge

(Qualifying scores: Ben Wilson 13; Trevor Harding 13; Adam Allott 12; Chris Collins 12; Graham Jones 10; Richard Hall 9; Lee Hodgson 9; James Brundle 9; Luke Priest 8; David Speight 7; Jamie Rodgers 6; James Wright 5; Benji Compton 3; Lee Derbyshire 2; Mark Thompson 2; Michael Mitchell 0; Ben Warburton (res) 0) Semi-Final: 1st Jones; 2nd Collins; 3rd Allott; 4th Hodgson; Final: 1st Collins; 2nd Harding; 3rd Wilson; 4th Jones.

9 October: OzChem Top Gun Championship

(Qualifying scores: Paul Lee 15; Richard Hall 13; Mark Thompson 12; Ben Wilson 12; Chris Collins 10; Lee Derbyshire 9; Benji Compton 8; Danny Norton 8; John Oliver 7; James Wright 7; Paul Cooper 5; Darren Mallett 5; Michael Mitchell 3; Jonathan Bethell 3; David Speight 2; Ben Warburton (res) 1; Luke Priest 0) Semi-Final: 1st Thompson; 2nd Wilson; 3rd Collins; 4th Derbyshire; Final: 1st Lee; 2nd Wilson; 3rd Hall; 4th Thompson.

STOKE EASY-RIDER SPITFIRES

NOTE: The information below relates only to the second Stoke team. For details of the main side, please refer to the Premier League section.

ADDRESS: Newcastle-under-Lyme Stadium, Loomer Road, Chesterton, Staffordshire.
PROMOTER: Dave Tattum.
TRACK LENGTH: 312 metres.
FIRST MEETING: 13 April 2003.
YEARS OF OPERATION: 2003 Conference Trophy.

CLUB HONOURS

None.

RIDER ROSTER 2003

BASEBY, Mark   *b. 28 February 1988, Pembury, Kent.*
BRITISH CAREER: Stoke (CT), Swindon (CL).

BURROWS, Mark   *b. 10 June 1964, Sheffield, South Yorkshire.*
BRITISH CAREER: (1984) Scunthorpe, Sheffield; (1985) Scunthorpe, Edinburgh; (1986) Edinburgh; (1987) Middlesbrough; (1992) Glasgow, Middlesbrough; (1993) Middlesbrough; (1994) Buxton, Cleveland, Middlesbrough, Belle Vue, Coventry; (1995) Buxton, Long Eaton, Middlesbrough, Hull; (1996) Buxton; (1997-01) Stoke; (2002) Stoke, Belle Vue; (2003) Stoke (CT), Wimbledon, Coventry (BLC), Wolverhampton (BLC), Eastbourne (BLC), Belle Vue (BLC).

COOK, Joe   *b. 24 December 1983, King's Lynn, Norfolk.*
BRITISH CAREER: (2002) King's Lynn (CL), Arena-Essex, Newport (PL), Isle of Wight; (2003) Stoke (PL & CT), Oxford (CL & BLC).

DOWNS, Carl   *b. 13 November 1983, Coventry, Warwickshire.*
BRITISH CAREER: (1999) King's Lynn (CL); (2000) Boston, Peterborough (CL), Sheffield (CL); (2001) Newport (CL), Mildenhall; (2002) King's Lynn (CL); (2003) Oxford (CL & BLC), Coventry (BLC), Stoke (CT), Isle of Wight.

FLINT, Gary   *b. 5 May 1982, Ashington, Durham.*
BRITISH CAREER: (1999) Berwick, Linlithgow, St Austell; (2000) Ashfield, Berwick; (2001) Buxton, Newcastle, Exeter, Sheffield (PL), Berwick; (2002) Newcastle (CL), Somerset, Rye House (PL), Isle of Wight, Glasgow; (2003) Buxton, Sheffield (CL), Reading, Stoke (CT).

HARTLEY, David   *b. 28 January 1982, Manchester.*
BRITISH CAREER: (2003) Stoke (CT).

HOWARD, Lee   *b. 6 July 1976, Manchester.*
BRITISH CAREER: (1999) King's Lynn (CL), Linlithgow; (2000) Buxton; (2001) Buxton, Newport (CL); (2002) Newcastle (CL); (2003) Stoke (CT), Mildenhall.

HUGHES, Danny   *b. 2 September 1983, Manchester.*
BRITISH CAREER: (1999) Workington; (2000) Buxton, Belle Vue; (2001) Buxton, Newport (CL); (2002) Newport (CL), Stoke, Workington, Edinburgh; (2003) Newport (CL & PL), Belle Vue (BLC), Stoke (CT).

JONES, Graham   *b. 5 May 1963, Oswestry, Shropshire.*
BRITISH CAREER: (1984-87) Stoke; (1988) Stoke, Belle Vue, Reading, Sheffield, Wolverhampton, King's Lynn, Ipswich; (1989-93) Wolverhampton; (1994) Middlesbrough; (1995) Hull; (1996) Hull, Middlesbrough; (2003) Wolverhampton (CL & BLC), Stoke (CT), Coventry (BLC), Belle Vue (BLC), Eastbourne (BLC), Poole (BLC).

MacPHAIL, John   *b. 13 April 1988.*
BRITISH CAREER: (2003) Stoke (CT).

MABEN, Keith   *b. 24 December 1982, Edinburgh, Scotland.*
BRITISH CAREER: (2003) Armadale, Mildenhall (CT), Stoke (KOC).

MACKLIN, Paul   *b. 10 October 1975, Manchester.*
BRITISH CAREER: (1994) Stoke; (1996-99) Buxton; (2000) Berwick, Stoke, Newcastle;

STOKE SPITFIRES: back row, left to right: Nigel Crabtree (Team Manager), Jamie Nicol, Lee Smart, Luke Priest, Mark Burrows. On bike: Joe Cook. Front, kneeling: Lee Howard, Paul Macklin.

(2001) Newcastle; (2002) Boston; (2003) Stoke (CT & PL).

MITCHELL, Michael   *b. 21 April 1984, Halifax, West Yorkshire.*
BRITISH CAREER: (2000) Peterborough (CL), Newport (CL); (2001) Sheffield (CL), Newport (CL); (2002) Mildenhall, Sheffield (CL), Buxton; (2003) Sheffield (CL), Stoke (CT), Rye House (CL).

NICOL, Jamie   *b. 10 September 1986.*
BRITISH CAREER: Stoke (CT).

PRIEST, Luke   *b. 18 June 1985, Birmingham, West Midlands.*
BRITISH CAREER: (2000) Ashfield, Owlerton; (2001) Sheffield (CL), Boston; (2002) Sheffield (CL), Wolverhampton (CT); (2003) Sheffield (CL & PL), Stoke (CT & PL), Workington, Exeter, Newport (BLC), Arena-Essex, Wolverhampton (BLC), Belle Vue (BLC).

SCARBORO, Ricky   *b. 31 July 1966, Grimsby, Lincolnshire.*
BRITISH CAREER: (1999) Mildenhall, King's Lynn (CL); (2000) Boston; (2001) Boston, Newport (PL); (2002) Boston, King's Lynn (CL); (2003) Oxford (CL & BLC), Stoke (CT), Newport (PL).

SMART, Lee   *b. 5 April 1988, Swindon, Wiltshire.*
BRITISH CAREER: (2003) Swindon (CL), Stoke (CT).

WESTACOTT, Jamie   *b. 9 April 1988, Newport, South Wales.*
BRITISH CAREER: (2003) Newport (CL), Stoke (CT).

CONFERENCE TROPHY

(* Denotes bonus-point victory)

No	DATE	OPPONENTS	H/A	RESULT	BURROWS	SMART	MACKLIN	HOWARD	COOK	HARTLEY	NICOL	PRIEST	JONES	WESTACOTT	DOWNS	OTHERS
1	13/4	Carmarthen	H	W47-43	8(4)	6+1(5)	7(3)	4+2(4)	15(5)	6(5)	1(4)	–	–	–	–	–
2	23/4	Wimbledon	A	L19-71	–	2+1(5)	0(4)	4(5)	R/R	0(4)	3(4)	9(7)	–	–	–	1(1)
3	4/5	Mildenhall	H	L36-53	–	2(4)	3(4)	4(3)	–	4+2(4)	–	–	16(6)	5(6)	–	2+1(3)
4	1/6	Trelawny	H	L41-49	12(6)	3+1(3)	8+1(5)	7+1(4)	–	1(3)	1+1(4)	9(5)	–	–	–	–
5	21/6	Wimbledon	H	W51-39	13+1(5)	3(4)	9+1(5)	4(4)	12(4)	–	2(4)	8+1(4)	–	–	–	–
6	1/7	Trelawny	A	L43-46	9(5)	7(5)	3+1(3)	1(4)	14(5)	–	4+1(4)	5+3(4)	–	–	–	–
7	17/8	Carmarthen	A	W51-39*	–	5(4)	R/R	5+1(4)	11(6)	–	–	9+2(5)	18(6)	3+2(5)	–	–
8	24/8	Buxton	A	L41-49	–	–	–	2(4)	16+1(6)	0(4)	0(3)	7(4)	12(5)	–	4+1(4)	–
9	24/8	Buxton	H	W45-44	–	–	–	0(4)	12+2(5)	1+1(2)	–	9(4)	17+1(6)	–	4(4)	2(5)
10	29/8	Boston	A	L44-46	–	0(3)	–	1(3)	11+3(6)	–	–	4(4)	16(6)	–	5+1(4)	7(4)
11	6/9	Armadale	A	L39-51	–	2+2(4)	–	–	–	–	–	8(5)	18(6)	–	7(5)	4(10)
12	14/9	Boston	H	W50-40*	–	4+1(4)	–	–	9(4)	–	–	10+2(5)	12(5)	–	6+1(4)	9(8)
13	21/9	Mildenhall	A	L38-52	–	4(5)	–	DNA	14(6)	–	–	4(4)	15+1(6)	–	1(3)	–
14	6/10	Armadale	H	D45-45	–	13+1(6)	–	5+1(4)	–	–	–	7(5)	6(3)	4+1(4)	5+3(4)	5+2(4)

DETAILS OF OTHER RIDERS:

Match No. 2: Mark Baseby 1(1); Match No. 3: Danny Hughes 2+1(3); Match No. 9: Michael Mitchell 2(5); Match No. 10: Ricky Scarboro 7(4); Match No. 11: Danny Hughes 3(4); Gary Flint 1(3); John MacPhail 0(3); Match No. 12: Danny Hughes 7(4); Gary Flint 2(4); Match No. 14: Danny Hughes 5+2(4).

CONFERENCE TROPHY AVERAGES

Rider	Mts	Rds	Pts	Bon	Tot	Avge	Max
Graham Jones	9	49	130	2	132	10.78	2 Full; 1 Paid
Joe Cook	10	51	119	7	126	9.88	2 Full
Mark Burrows	4	20	42	1	43	8.60	–
Ricky Scarboro	1	4	7	0	7	7.00	–
Luke Priest	12	56	89	8	97	6.93	–
Paul Macklin	6	24	30	3	33	5.50	–
Carl Downs	7	28	32	6	38	5.43	–
Danny Hughes	4	15	17	3	20	5.33	–
Lee Smart	12	52	51	7	58	4.46	–
Mark Baseby	1	1	1	0	1	4.00	–
Jamie Westacott	3	15	12	3	15	4.00	–
Lee Howard	10	39	32	4	36	3.69	–
David Hartley	6	22	12	3	15	2.73	–
Jamie Nicol	6	23	11	2	13	2.26	–
Gary Flint	2	7	3	0	3	1.71	–
Michael Mitchell	1	5	2	0	2	1.60	–
John MacPhail	1	3	0	0	0	0.00	–

KNOCK-OUT CUP

No	DATE	OPPONENTS	H/A	RESULT	JONES	HOWARD	MACKLIN	PRIEST	COOK	SMART	NICOL	MABEN
1	6/8	Armadale	H	D45-45	14(6)	2(3)	0(3)	7+1(4)	16+1(6)	5+1(4)	1(4)	–
2	9/8	Armadale	A	L31-58	16(6)	1+1(4)	0(0)	4(5)	–	8(7)	2(4)	0(4)

SWINDON PRO-FIT SPROCKETS

NOTE: The information below relates only to the second Swindon team. For details of the main side, please refer to the Premier League section.

ADDRESS: Abbey Stadium, Blunsdon, nr. Swindon, Wiltshire.

PROMOTER: Peter Toogood.

TRACK LENGTH: 361.2 metres.

FIRST MEETING: 12 May 1996.

YEARS OF OPERATION: 1996 British Conference League; 1997 British Amateur League (fixtures shared with Reading, under the banner of 'M4 Raven Sprockets'); 2002 British Conference Trophy; 2003 British Conference League.

CLUB HONOURS

None.

RIDER ROSTER 2003

ALLEN, Tommy   *b. 4 September 1984, Norwich, Norfolk.*
BRITISH CAREER: (2002) Swindon (CT & PL), Mildenhall (CL); (2003) Swindon (PL & CL).

BASEBY, Mark   *b. 28 February 1988, Pembury, Kent.*
BRITISH CAREER: Stoke (CT), Swindon (CL).

CAMPBELL, Barry   *b. 26 August 1979, Glasgow, Scotland.*
BRITISH CAREER: (1995) Linlithgow, Swindon; (1996) Linlithgow, Edinburgh; (1997) Edinburgh, Lathallan; (1998) Edinburgh; (1999) Belle Vue, Workington; (2000-01) Workington; (2003) Edinburgh, Armadale (CT), Reading, Swindon (CL), Belle Vue (BLC).

DYMINSKI, Simon   *b. 18 October 1983, Swindon, Wiltshire.*
BRITISH CAREER: (2002) Swindon (CT & PL), Edinburgh, Peterborough (CL); (2003) Swindon (CL), Somerset.

GLEDHILL, Jack   *b. 25 June 1986, Leamington Spa, Warwickshire.*
BRITISH CAREER: (2002) Swindon (CT), Newport (CL); (2003) Swindon (CL).

HAWKINS, Ritchie   *b. 9 November 1983, Peterborough, Cambridgeshire.*
BRITISH CAREER: (2000) Sheffield (CL); (2001) Swindon, Sheffield (CL); (2002) Swindon (PL & CT); (2003) Swindon (PL & CL), Peterborough (BLC).

HOLLOWAY, Malcolm   *b. 22 December 1956, Stratton St Margaret, Wiltshire.*
BRITISH CAREER: (1977) Swindon, Oxford; (1978-79) Milton Keynes, Swindon; (1980-83) Swindon; (1984-88) Reading; (1989) Mildenhall, Reading; (1996) Swindon (CL); (2000) Somerset, Reading; (2001-02) Somerset, Swindon (CT), Mildenhall (CL); (2003) Swindon (CL), Trelawny (CT & PL), Coventry (BLC).

HOLMES, Jamie   *b. 19 November 1979, Exeter, Devon.*
BRITISH CAREER: (1999) Newport (CL); (2000) Newport (CL), Swindon, Stoke; (2001) Somerset; (2002) Newport (CL); (2003) Somerset (BLC), Trelawny (CT & BLC), Swindon (CL).

JACKSON, Andrew   *b. 12 July 1975, Manchester.*
BRITISH CAREER: (2002) Wolverhampton (CT), Carmarthen, Newport (CL); (2003) Wolverhampton (CL), Sheffield (CL), Mildenhall (CT), Belle Vue (BLC), Swindon (CL), Trelawny (CT), Newcastle (CL).

LEE, Nick   *b. 3 January 1983, Swindon, Wiltshire.*
BRITISH CAREER: (2002) Swindon (CT); (2003) Swindon (CL), Isle of Wight.

LEGG, Billy   *b. 6 September 1988, Swindon, Wiltshire.*
BRITISH CAREER: (2003) Swindon (CL).

NETTLESHIP, Scott   *b. 16 May 1984, Newcastle, Tyne & Wear.*
BRITISH CAREER: (2003) Newcastle (CL), Mildenhall, Swindon (CL), Carmarthen, Peterborough (CL).

PAGET, Simon   *b. 24 March 1975, Swindon, Wiltshire.*
BRITISH CAREER: (1996) Swindon (CL); (1997) M4 Raven Sprockets; (2000) Newport (CL), Swindon; (2003) Swindon (PL & CL).

SWINDON SPROCKETS: back row, left to right: Kevin Hawkins (Reserve Team Manager), Tommy Allen, Simon Dyminski, Malcolm Holloway, Jack Gledhill, Peter Oakes (Team Manager). Front row, left to right: Lee Smart, Darren Smith, Ritchie Hawkins.

ROYNON, Adam *b. 30 August 1988, Barrow-in-Furness, Cumbria.*
BRITISH CAREER: (2003) Swindon (CL), Armadale (CT).

SMART, Lee *b. 5 April 1988, Swindon, Wiltshire.*
BRITISH CAREER: (2003) Swindon (CL), Stoke (CT).

SMITH, Darren *b. 19 May 1981, Peterborough, Cambridgeshire.*
BRITISH CAREER: (1996) Mildenhall; (1997) Peterborough (AL); (1998) Skegness, Norfolk; (1999) Newcastle, Glasgow, Peterborough; (2001) Somerset, Boston; (2002) Boston, Wolverhampton (CL); (2003) Swindon (CL).

WALKER, Simon *b. 19 February 1980, Bristol, Avon.*
BRITISH CAREER: (2001) Newport (CL); (2002) Newport (CL), Arena-Essex, Swindon (CT), Trelawny; (2003) Swindon (CL), Trelawny (CT), Reading, Somerset (BLC), Poole (BLC), Exeter (BLC), Newport.

WARNES, Tim *b. 29 March 1982, King's Lynn, Norfolk.*
BRITISH CAREER: (2002) Newport (CL), King's Lynn (CL); (2003) Oxford (CL), Swindon (CL).

CONFERENCE LEAGUE

(* Denotes bonus-point victory)

No	DATE	OPPONENTS	H/A	RESULT	HAWKINS	GLEDHILL	HOLLOWAY	DYMINSKI	ALLEN	WALKER	SMART	SMITH	CAMPBELL	LEE	PAGET	ROYNON	OTHERS
1	6/4	Carmarthen	A	W49-41	11+1(5)	2(4)	15(5)	6+1(4)	6(4)	5(4)	4(4)	-	-	-	-	-	-
2	22/4	Sheffield	H	W50-39	15(5)	2+1(4)	11+1(5)	9+2(4)	9(4)	-	3(4)	1(4)	-	-	-	-	-
3	27/5	Boston	H	L43-46	14(6)	-	4+1(3)	12(5)	7+2(5)	3(3)	2(5)	1(3)	-	-	-	-	-
4	2/6	Sheffield	A	W47-43*	-	1(3)	11+1(5)	5+1(4)	14+1(5)	7(5)	2+1(5)	-	7+1(4)	-	-	-	-
5	4/6	Wimbledon	A	L32-58	-	-	18(7)	8+1(7)	0(6)	3(4)	3+1(3)	-	R/R	0(3)	-	-	-
6	15/6	Mildenhall	A	L32-58	-	0(3)	15(7)	6+2(7)	-	3(3)	3+2(4)	-	5(6)	-	-	-	R/R
7	17/6	Wolverhampton	A	L33-57	-	1+1(1)	10(6)	-	-	1+1(3)	5+1(6)	1+1(4)	12+1(7)	3+1(3)	-	-	R/R
8	7/8	Wolverhampton	H	L44-45	-	5+3(4)	-	9(5)	11(5)	7(4)	1(4)	6+1(4)	5+1(4)	-	-	-	-
9	7/8	Carmarthen (a)	A	W48-29*	-	-	-	6(4)	11(4)	10+2(4)	3+2(3)	4(3)	11+1(4)	3+2(4)	-	-	-
10	10/8	Newcastle	A	L27-61	-	3(6)	-	-	R/R	6+2(5)	10(7)	-	R/R	-	6+1(7)	-	2(5)
11	12/8	Buxton	H	W54-36	-	1(4)	-	12+1(5)	15(5)	10+1(4)	-	-	7+2(4)	3+1(4)	6+1(4)	-	-
12	19/8	Wimbledon	H	W54-36	-	-	-	11(5)	12(4)	13(5)	6+3(4)	-	4+3(4)	-	7(6)	-	1(2)
13	24/8	Newport	A	W49-41	-	-	-	0(3)	14(5)	9+1(5)	7+2(4)	-	6+1(4)	4+3(4)	9+2(5)	-	-
14	26/8	Newcastle (b)	H	W45-39	-	-	-	5+1(3)	6(3)	10(4)	6+1(6)	-	8+3(4)	2(3)	8+2(5)	-	-
15	26/8	Peterborough (c)	H	W43-34	-	-	-	7+1(4)	R/R	6(5)	9+1(5)	-	13(5)	2(3)	6+1(4)	-	-
16	31/8	Buxton	A	L31-58	1+1(3)	-	-	-	R/R	3+1(5)	7+1(6)	-	12(7)	-	-	8+2(6)	0(3)
17	5/9	Oxford	A	L40-50	0(1)	-	-	R/R	15(7)	3+1(5)	2+1(4)	-	12(5)	-	4+1(4)	4+1(4)	-
18	11/9	Newport	H	W61-29*	5+2(5)	-	-	8(4)	11(4)	11(4)	12+3(5)	-	6+4(4)	-	-	8+2(5)	-
19	11/9	Mildenhall	H	W42-41	-	-	-	7+1(4)	16(6)	10+1(6)	5+2(4)	-	1(4)	-	1+1(3)	2(3)	-
20	9/10	Rye House (d)	H	W43-29	-	-	-	8(3)	9(3)	8(3)	4(4)	-	5+1(4)	-	1(1)	8+2(6)	-
21	9/10	Oxford (e)	H	L34-38	3+1(5)	-	-	2(3)	9(4)	8(3)	3(1)	-	4+1(4)	-	-	5(4)	-
22	10/10	Peterborough	A ¶	W52-37*	1(4)	-	-	-	15(5)	13+1(5)	-	11+1(6)	R/R	-	-	11+3(7)	1(3)
23	11/10	Rye House	A	L43-47 *	4+2(5)	-	-	-	16(7)	12(6)	-	R/R	-	-	-	9+3(6)	2+2(4)
24	12/10	Boston	A	W46-44	1+1(3)	-	-	19+1(7)	16+1(7)	1(4)	3+1(4)	R/R	-	-	-	6+1(5)	-

(a) Meeting abandoned after thirteen heats, with the result standing.

(b) Meeting abandoned after fourteen heats, with the result standing.

(c) Meeting abandoned after thirteen heats, with the result standing.

(d) Meeting abandoned after twelve heats, with the result standing.

(e) Meeting abandoned after twelve heats, with the result standing.

¶ Match raced at King's Lynn.

NOTES: (1) The home match against Mildenhall originally ended in a 48-42 defeat on track; however, the points scored by Lee Hodgson were subsequently deducted from the Fen Tigers' total as his inclusion at reserve was deemed ineligible; (2) Tommy Allen is not credited with a full maximum in the away match against Peterborough as he suffered a two-minute exclusion, missing heat 15 as a result.

DETAILS OF OTHER RIDERS:

Match No. 6: Mark Steel R/R; Match No. 7: Mark Steel R/R; Match No. 10: Scott Nettleship 2(5); Match No. 12: Jamie Holmes 1(2); Match No. 16: Andrew Jackson 0(3); Match No. 22: Tim Warnes 1(3); Match No. 23: Mark Baseby 2+2(3); Billy Legg 0(1).

CONFERENCE LEAGUE AVERAGES

Rider	Mts	Rds	Pts	Bon	Tot	Avge	Max
Ritchie Hawkins	3	16	40	1	41	10.25	1 Full
Tommy Allen	19	93	215	4	219	9.42	2 Full; 1 Paid
Malcolm Holloway	7	38	84	3	87	9.16	1 Full
Simon Walker	23	102	177	12	189	7.41	1 Paid
Barry Campbell	16	74	118	19	137	7.41	1 Paid
Simon Dyminski	17	74	121	11	132	7.14	–
Adam Roynon	9	46	61	14	75	6.52	–
Simon Paget	9	39	48	9	57	5.85	–
Mark Baseby	1	3	2	2	4	5.33	–
Lee Smart	21	92	98	21	119	5.17	1 Paid
Darren Smith	7	28	27	4	31	4.43	–
Nick Lee	7	24	17	7	24	4.00	–
Jack Gledhill	15	55	30	12	42	3.05	–
Jamie Holmes	1	2	1	0	1	2.00	–
Scott Nettleship	1	5	2	0	2	1.60	–
Tim Warnes	1	3	1	0	1	1.33	–
Andrew Jackson	1	3	0	0	0	0.00	–
Billy Legg	1	1	0	0	0	0.00	–

OTHER MEETINGS

9 June: Conference Challenge
  Reading 46 Swindon 47 (Ritchie Hawkins 17; Tommy Allen 12+2; Lee Smart 6+1; Simon Walker 6; Jack Gledhill 3+1; Nick Lee 3; Malcolm Holloway R/R).

11 July: Paul Gladwin Memorial Four-Team Tournament
  Weymouth 26, Swindon 17 (Malcolm Holloway 6; Simon Walker 6; Nick Lee 3; Lee Smart 2), Bristol 15, Newport 14 – staged at Somerset.

18 August: Conference Challenge
  Reading 38 Swindon 39 (Tommy Allen 15; Simon Dyminski 10+1; Lee Smart 8+1; Simon Paget 4+1; Nick Lee 2; Simon Walker R/R).

12 September: Conference Challenge
  Weymouth 46 Swindon 43 (Lee Smart 16+1; Luke Priest 8+1; Richie Dennis 8+1; Tommy Allen 5; Simon Walker 3+2; Adam Roynon 3; Paul Candy 0: Barry Campbell R/R).

TRELAWNY DAMERELL'S PITBULLS

NOTE: The information below relates only to the second Trelawny team. For details of the main side, please refer to the Premier League section.

ADDRESS: Clay Country Moto Parc, Longstone Pit, nr. Nanpean, St Austell, Cornwall.
PROMOTER: Ray Purvis
 NOTE: Original promoter Godfrey Spargo resigned in April 2003.
TRACK LENGTH: 230 metres.
FIRST MEETING: 3 June 1997.
YEARS OF OPERATION: 1997 British Amateur League; 1998-00 British Conference League; 2003 Conference Trophy (Note: Between 1997-00, the team rode as 'St Austell Gulls').

CLUB HONOURS

LEAGUE CHAMPIONS: 1998.
KNOCK-OUT CUP WINNERS: 1998, 1999.

RIDER ROSTER 2003

ANKERS, Dean *b. 2 August 1979, Exeter, Devon.*
 BRITISH CAREER: (2003) Trelawny (CT).
BARKER, Ben *b. 10 March 1988, Truro, Cornwall.*
 BRITISH CAREER: (2003) Oxford (CL), Trelawny (CT).
BREWER, Tristan *b. 26 February 1973, Truro, Cornwall.*
 BRITISH CAREER: (2002) Carmarthen; (2003) Trelawny (CT).
BROWN, Alan *b. 19 February 1959, Stoke-on-Trent, Staffordshire.*
 BRITISH CAREER: (2002) Buxton; (2003) Oxford (CL), Buxton, Newport (CL), Trelawny CT).
BROWN, Tom *b. 19 June 1984, Panteg, Pontypool, Wales.*
 BRITISH CAREER: (2000) Peterborough (CL), Newport (CL); (2001) Newport (CL & PL), Isle of Wight, Exeter; (2002) Workington, Newport (CL), Swindon (CT & PL), Isle of Wight, Edinburgh, Trelawny; (2003) Trelawny (PL & CT), Newport (CL).
COURTNEY, Jamie *b. 22 April 1988, Ashington, Northumberland.*
 BRITISH CAREER: (2003) Rye House (CL), Trelawny (CT).
DUNWORTH, Wayne *b. 20 January 1967, Nottingham, Nottinghamshire.*
 BRITISH CAREER: (1984) Boston; (1986) Mildenhall; (1987) Boston; (2002) Boston, Carmarthen; (2003) Trelawny (CT), Boston, Peterborough (CL), Armadale (CT).
FERROW, Alan *b. 28 April 1982, Ashington, Northumberland.*
 BRITISH CAREER: (2003) Trelawny (CT), Arena-Essex, Newport (PL).
GENT, Harry *b. 19 September 1987, Leicester, Leicestershire.*
 BRITISH CAREER: (2003) Trelawny (CT).
HACKETT, Oliver *b. 11 September 1979, Bristol, Avon.*
 BRITISH CAREER: (2000) St Austell; (2003) Trelawny (CT).
HOLLOWAY, Malcolm *b. 22 December 1956, Stratton St Margaret, Wiltshire.*
 BRITISH CAREER: (1977) Swindon, Oxford; (1978-79) Milton Keynes, Swindon; (1980-83) Swindon; (1984-88) Reading; (1989) Mildenhall, Reading; (1996) Swindon (CL);

TRELAWNY PITBULLS: back row, left to right: Johnny Orchard, Oliver Hackett, Jamie Holmes, Adrian Rowe, Tristan Brewer. Front row, left to right: Dean Ankers, Steve Damerell (Sponsor), Ray Purvis (Promoter/Team Manager), Gary Penfold (Co-Team Manager).

(2000) Somerset, Reading; (2001-02) Somerset, Swindon (CT), Mildenhall (CL); (2003) Swindon (CL), Trelawny (CT & PL), Coventry (BLC).

HOLMES, Jamie *b. 19 November 1979, Exeter, Devon.*
BRITISH CAREER: (1999) Newport (CL); (2000) Newport (CL), Swindon, Stoke; (2001) Somerset; (2002) Newport (CL); (2003) Somerset (BLC), Trelawny (CT & BLC), Swindon (CL).

HORTON, James *b. 22 June 1985, Slough, Berkshire.*
BRITISH CAREER: (2001-02) Peterborough (CL); (2003) Peterborough (CL & BLC), Boston (CT), Trelawny (PL & CT).

JACKSON, Andrew *b. 12 July 1975, Manchester.*
BRITISH CAREER: (2002) Wolverhampton (CT), Carmarthen, Newport (CL); (2003) Wolverhampton (CL), Sheffield (CL), Mildenhall (CT), Belle Vue (BLC), Swindon (CL), Trelawny (CT), Newcastle (CL).

JOHNSON, Chris *b. 13 October 1987, Chichester, Sussex.*
BRITISH CAREER: (2003) Oxford (CL), Trelawny (CT), Isle of Wight.

LAMB, Jessica *b. 5 February 1977, Poole, Dorset.*
BRITISH CAREER: (2001) Boston; (2003) Somerset (CLT), Trelawny (CT).

MACKAY, Brendon *b. 14 August 1980, Darwin, Northern Territory, Australia.*
BRITISH CAREER: (2001-02) Reading; (2003) Somerset, Trelawny (CT), Newport (BLC), Exeter (BLC), Mildenhall.

ORCHARD, Johnny *b. 22 February 1969, Truro, Cornwall.*
BRITISH CAREER: (2003) Trelawny (CT), Rye House (PL).

PHILLIPS, Simon *b. 22 March 1974, St Austell, Cornwall.*
BRITISH CAREER: (1997) St Austell; (1998) Newport (CL), St Austell, Norfolk, Exeter; (1999) Mildenhall, Rye House; (2000) Somerset, Isle of Wight; (2001) Isle of Wight, Somerset, Trelawny; (2002) Trelawny; (2003) Trelawny (PL & CT).

ROWE, Adrian *b. 19 November 1983, Truro, Cornwall.*
BRITISH CAREER: (2002) Carmarthen.

STODDART, Sean *b. 20 January 1987, Edinburgh, Scotland.*
BRITISH CAREER: (2003) Armadale, Trelawny (CT), Carmarthen (CT), Newcastle (CL).

STYLES, Kevin *b. 13 October 1962, Stafford, Staffordshire.*
BRITISH CAREER: (2003) Trelawny (CT).

WALKER, Simon *b. 19 February 1980, Bristol, Avon.*
BRITISH CAREER: (2001) Newport (CL); (2002) Newport (CL), Arena-Essex, Swindon (CT), Trelawny; (2003) Swindon (CL), Trelawny (CT), Reading, Somerset (BLC), Poole (BLC), Exeter (BLC), Newport.

CONFERENCE TROPHY

(* Denotes bonus-point victory)

No	DATE	OPPONENTS	H/A	RESULT	BROWN	ROWE	HOLMES	BREWER	ORCHARD	ANKERS	HOLLOWAY	PHILLIPS	BARKER	WALKER	MACKAY	OTHERS
1	22/4	Boston	H	L37-53	14(5)	3(4)	9+1(5)	1+1(4)	9(4)	0(4)	–	–	–	–	–	1(4)
2	30/4	Wimbledon	A	L30-60		0(3)	R/R	2(4)	1(3)	–	16(7)	7+2(7)	4(6)	–	–	–
3	1/6	Stoke	A	W49-41	–	3+1(4)	6(4)	3+1(4)	–	0(3)	15(5)	13(5)	9+1(5)	–	–	–
4	20/6	Boston	A	L39-51	12(6)	1+1(4)	9+1(7)	–	–	–	R/R	–	2(4)	–	–	15+2(9)

CONFERENCE TROPHY continued

No	DATE	OPPONENTS	H/A	RESULT	BROWN	ROWE	HOLMES	BREWER	ORCHARD	ANKERS	HOLLOWAY	PHILLIPS	BARKER	WALKER	MACKAY	OTHERS
5	21/6	Armadale	A	L24-65	11(7)	0(4)	7(5)	–	–	–	R/R	–	3(5)	–	–	3(9)
6	24/6	Wimbledon	H	W60-30	18(6)	7+1(5)	9+1(5)	–	–	–	–	R/R	7+3(5)	10(4)	9+1(5)	–
7	1/7	Stoke	H	W46-43*	14(5)	4(4)	8+1(5)	–	–	1+1(4)	–	–	11+1(5)	3(3)	5+1(4)	–
8	8/7	Armadale	H	W55-35	14+1(5)	6(4)	9+2(4)	–	–	–	–	–	9+1(4)	8(4)	8+1(5)	1(4)
9	15/7	Mildenhall	H	L42-48	15(6)	4+3(5)	7+1(6)	–	–	0(3)	–	–	10+1(6)	0(0)	6+1(4)	–
10	3/8	Mildenhall	A	L36-52	11(5)	1+1(4)	11(5)	–	–	0(3)	–	–	3+1(4)	6+2(5)	4(4)	–
11	10/8	Carmarthen	A	L31-57	–	1+1(5)	2(4)	–	–	1(4)	–	–	13(7)	–	R/R	14+1(7)
12	26/8	Carmarthen	H	L39-51	R/R	–	–	–	–	0(3)	–	–	17(7)	–	14+1(7)	8+1(13)
13	21/9	Buxton	A	L38-52	R/R	0(3)	–	–	–	–	–	–	11(7)	11(6)	–	16+3(13)
14	23/9	Buxton	H	L42-48	R/R	2(3)	–	–	–	1(4)	–	–	6(7)	17(6)	–	16+1(10)

DETAILS OF OTHER RIDERS:

Match No. 1: Oliver Hackett 1(4); Match No. 4: James Horton 10+1(5); Jamie Courtney 4+1(3); Wayne Dunworth 1(1); Match No. 5: Jamie Courtney 2(3); Sean Stoddart 1(2); Alan Ferrow 0(4); Match No. 8: Jessica Lamb 1(4); Match No. 11: Chris Johnson 14+1(7); Match No. 12: Chris Johnson 8+1(7); Harry Gent 0(3); Kevin Styles 0(3); Match No. 13: Chris Johnson 12(6); Andrew Jackson 2+2(4); Alan Brown 2+1(3); Match No. 14: Chris Johnson 15+1(7); Kevin Styles 1(3).

GOLDEN DOUBLE RIDES:

Match No. 12: Ben Barker's total includes 0 points from a golden double ride.

CONFERENCE TROPHY AVERAGES

Rider	Mts	Rds	Pts	Bon	Tot	Avge	Max
Malcolm Holloway	2	12	31	0	31	10.33	1 Full
Tom Brown	8	45	109	1	110	9.78	1 Full; 1 Paid
James Horton	1	5	10	1	11	8.80	–
Simon Walker	7	28	55	2	57	8.14	–
Chris Johnson	4	27	49	3	52	7.70	–
Simon Phillips	2	12	20	2	22	7.33	–
Brendon Mackay	6	29	46	5	51	7.03	–
Jamie Holmes	10	50	77	7	84	6.72	–
Ben Barker	13	72	105	8	113	6.28	–
Johnny Orchard	2	7	10	0	10	5.71	–
Jamie Courtney	2	6	6	1	7	4.67	–
Alan Brown	1	3	2	1	3	4.00	–
Wayne Dunworth	1	1	1	0	1	4.00	–
Andrew Jackson	1	4	2	2	4	4.00	–
Adrian Rowe	13	52	32	8	40	3.08	–
Tristan Brewer	3	12	6	2	8	2.67	–
Sean Stoddart	1	2	1	0	1	2.00	–
Oliver Hackett	1	4	1	0	1	1.00	–
Jessica Lamb	1	4	1	0	1	1.00	–
Kevin Styles	2	6	1	0	1	0.67	–

Rider	Mts	Rds	Pts	Bon	Tot	Avge	Max
Dean Ankers	8	28	3	1	4	0.57	–
Alan Ferrow	1	4	0	0	0	0.00	–
Harry Gent	1	3	0	0	0	0.00	–

NOTE: Ben Barker's figures include one golden double ride (0 points).

WIMBLEDON GMB DONS

ADDRESS: Wimbledon Stadium, Plough Lane, London.
PROMOTERS: Wimbledon Speedway PLC (Chairman Ian Perkin, plus David Croucher, Paul Coppin, Peter Gower, Graham Howell, Sue Jackson-Scott, Darren Leach, James Shore, Stuart Towner and Company Secretary Kevin Harbottle).
TRACK LENGTH: 250 metres.
FIRST MEETING: 28 May 1928.
YEARS OF OPERATION: 1928 Open; 1929-31 Southern League; 1932-33 National League; 1934 National League & Reserve League; 1935-36 National League; 1937-39 National League Division One; 1946 National League; 1947-56 National League Division One; 1957-64 National League; 1965-67 British League; 1968-74 British League Division One; 1975-84 British League; 1985-90 National League; 1991 British League Division One; 2002-03 British Conference League.

CLUB HONOURS

NATIONAL TROPHY WINNERS: 1938, 1950, 1951, 1953, 1956, 1959, 1960, 1962.
RAC CUP WINNERS: 1954.
LEAGUE CHAMPIONS: 1954, 1955, 1956, 1958, 1959, 1960, 1961.
BRITANNIA SHIELD WINNERS: 1959.
KNOCK-OUT CUP WINNERS: 1962, 1968, 1969, 1970.

RIDER ROSTER 2003

BARRETT, Wayne b. 22 March 1968, Redruth, Cornwall.
    BRITISH CAREER: (1984) Weymouth; (1986-87) Poole; (1997) St Austell, Newport; (1998) St Austell; (1999-00) St Austell, Exeter; (2001) Trelawny, Boston; (2002) Boston, Wimbledon, Trelawny; (2003) Wimbledon, Eastbourne (BLC).
BRANNEY, John b. 7 November 1985, Whitehaven, Cumbria.
    BRITISH CAREER: (2002) Rye House (CL), Newcastle (CL); (2003) Newcastle (CL), Wimbledon (CT), Mildenhall (CT), King's Lynn, Exeter, Newport (PL), Buxton (CT).
BURCHATT, Barry b. 25 October 1987, Farnborough, Kent.
    BRITISH CAREER: (2003) Newport (CL), Rye House (CL), Wimbledon.

BURROWS, Mark b. 10 June 1964, Sheffield, South Yorkshire.
   BRITISH CAREER: (1984) Scunthorpe, Sheffield; (1985) Scunthorpe, Edinburgh; (1986)
   Edinburgh; (1987) Middlesbrough; (1992) Glasgow, Middlesbrough; (1993)
   Middlesbrough; (1994) Buxton, Cleveland, Middlesbrough, Belle Vue, Coventry; (1995)
   Buxton, Long Eaton, Middlesbrough, Hull; (1996) Buxton; (1997-01) Stoke; (2002)
   Stoke, Belle Vue; (2003) Stoke (CT), Wimbledon, Coventry (BLC), Wolverhampton
   (BLC), Eastbourne (BLC), Belle Vue (BLC).
CAMBRIDGE, Matt b. 14 May 1981, Rugby, Warwickshire.
   BRITISH CAREER: (2000) Sheffield (CL); (2001-02) Sheffield (CL), Exeter; (2003)
   Newport (PL & CL), Wimbledon, Poole (BLC).
CLEMENT, James b. 29 August 1985, Crawley, West Sussex.
   BRITISH CAREER: (2003) Wimbledon, Arena-Essex (BLC).
COLLYER, Peter b. 2 December 1981, Frimley Green, Camberley, Surrey.
   BRITISH CAREER: (1999) Reading, Glasgow, Rye House, Newcastle; (2002) Wimbledon,
   Carmarthen, Reading; (2003) Wimbledon, Reading (BLC).
CROSS, Andre b. 12 June 1967, Norwich, Norfolk.
   BRITISH CAREER: (2002-03) Wimbledon.
GIFFARD, Daniel b. 10 November 1984, Eastbourne, East Sussex.
   BRITISH CAREER: (2000) Rye House; (2001) Rye House, Reading, Berwick, Newport;
   (2002) Isle of Wight, Rye House (CL & PL), Edinburgh; (2003) Wimbledon,
   Eastbourne (BLC), Somerset, Stoke.
HAIGH, David b. 12 December 1984.
   BRITISH CAREER: (2002) Newcastle (CL); (2003) Wimbledon, Newcastle (CL),
   Peterborough (CL).
HEDGE, Gavin b. 30 January 1971, Norwich, Norfolk.
   BRITISH CAREER: (1996) Peterborough (CL); (1997) Peterborough (AL), Ryde,
   Mildenhall, Skegness, Isle of Wight, Oxford; (1998) Skegness, Norfolk, Arena-Essex,
   Peterborough; (1999) Mildenhall, Glasgow; (2000-01) Mildenhall; (2002) Mildenhall,
   Reading, Wimbledon; (2003) Wimbledon.
HICKMOTT, Gareth (formerly Gareth Roberts) b. 28 May 1980.
   BRITISH CAREER: (2003) Wimbledon.
HUNT, Chris b. 15 February 1964, Wallingford, Oxfordshire.
   BRITISH CAREER: (1980) Exeter; (1981) Swindon; (1982) Exeter, Milton Keynes; (1983)
   Milton Keynes, Glasgow; (1984) Milton Keynes; (2001) Isle of Wight, Newport (CL);
   (2002-03) Wimbledon.
JONES, Ron b. 26 May 1957.
   BRITISH CAREER: (2003) Wimbledon.
McDERMOTT, Martin b. 13 January 1988, Manchester.
   BRITISH CAREER: (2003) Buxton, Wimbledon.
PARSONS, Joel b. 24 July 1985, Broken Hill, New South Wales, Australia.
   BRITISH CAREER: (2003) Reading, Eastbourne (BLC), Rye House (CL & PL), Newport
   (PL), Wimbledon (CT), Arena-Essex, Peterborough (BLC), Hull.
PRYNNE, Jason b. 27 April 1974, Truro, Cornwall.
   BRITISH CAREER: (1997-99) St Austell; (2000) St Austell, Exeter; (2001) Exeter; (2002)
   Wimbledon, Exeter, Trelawny; (2003) Wimbledon, Trelawny.

WIMBLEDON DONS: back row, left to right: Wayne Barrett, Gareth Hickmott, Gavin Hedge, Andre Cross. On bike: Chris Hunt. Front, kneeling: Daniel Giffard.

SCHRAMM, Chris   b. *30 May 1984, Maldon, Essex.*
BRITISH CAREER: (2000) Peterborough (CL), Berwick, Arena-Essex; (2001) Peterborough (EL & CL), Isle of Wight, Reading; (2002) Reading, Peterborough (CL); (2003) Newport (PL), Wimbledon (CT), Peterborough (CL), Oxford (CL).

STEVENS, Jon   b. *3 January 1983, Croydon, Surrey.*
BRITISH CAREER: (2000) Rye House; (2001) Sheffield (CL); (2002) Wimbledon, Carmarthen; (2003) Wimbledon, Wolverhampton (BLC).

CONFERENCE LEAGUE

(* Denotes bonus-point victory)

No	DATE	OPPONENTS	H/A	RESULT	BARRETT	HEDGE	CLEMENT	PRYNNE	HUNT	CROSS	COLLYER	GIFFARD	HICKMOTT	BURROWS	CAMBRIDGE	OTHERS
1	30/3	Newport	A	L37-52	10(6)	9(6)	3+2(3)	4(3)	3+2(4)	8+2(5)	–	–	–	–	–	0(3)
2	2/4	Oxford	H	W46-44	13(5)	6(4)	4+1(4)	–	4+1(4)	7+2(5)	2+2(3)	10+1(5)	–	–	–	–
3	9/4	Sheffield	H	W55-35	14+2(6)	13+1(6)	–	R/R	4(4)	2+2(4)	7+2(5)	15(5)	–	–	–	–
4	21/4	Peterborough	A	L42-48	7+3(4)	3+1(4)	–	8(5)	1+1(3)	7+2(6)	6(3)	10(5)	–	–	–	–
5	7/5	Buxton	H	W47-43	9(5)	10(5)	–	5+2(4)	11+3(7)	1(3)	2+2(2)	9(4)	–	–	–	–
6	11/5	Boston	A	L32-58	13(6)	2(4)	0(3)	8+2(6)	2(3)	–	0(3)	7(5)	–	–	–	–
7	14/5	Carmarthen	H	W60-30	14+1(5)	10+1(4)	4+2(4)	8(4)	6+1(4)	–	5+1(4)	13+1(5)	–	–	–	–
8	21/5	Wolverhampton	H	D45-45	13(6)	1+1(2)	3+2(4)	11+1(6)	7+1(5)	–	2(3)	8(4)	–	–	–	–
9	27/5	Wolverhampton	A	L42-47	9+1(6)	R/R	2(4)	10+1(5)	1(4)	–	7+1(5)	13(6)	–	–	–	–
10	1/6	Carmarthen	A	W48-42*	13(5)	–	2(4)	9(4)	6+1(5)	–	5+1(4)	13(5)	0(3)	–	–	–
11	4/6	Swindon	H	W58-32	13+1(5)	–	7+2(5)	10+2(5)	9+3(5)	–	6+2(4)	8(3)	–	5(3)	–	–
12	11/6	Mildenhall	H	L44-46	6+1(4)	–	4+1(4)	1(4)	4(4)	–	4+1(4)	12+1(5)	–	13(5)	–	–
13	18/6	Rye House	H	L42-47	11+1(7)	–	1(3)	R/R	6+3(5)	–	12+1(6)	–	0(3)	12+1(6)	–	–
14	13/7	Newcastle	A	L39-51	R/R	–	2+1(3)	–	6+1(5)	–	13(7)	–	2(5)	16(7)	–	0(3)
15	21/7	Sheffield	A	L25-64	6(5)	–	0(3)	–	2+1(4)	–	4(4)	–	1(3)	9+1(6)	3(5)	–
16	6/8	Boston	H	L44-49	12(5)	–	1(4)	–	3(5)	–	6(4)	–	1+1(4)	21(6)	0(2)	–
17	8/8	Oxford	A	L33-57	–	–	0(4)	–	1(3)	–	7+1(6)	R/R	2(5)	20(7)	3(5)	–
18	19/8	Swindon	A	L36-54*	5(4)	–	0(3)	–	3+1(6)	–	5+1(6)	R/R	–	19(7)	4(5)	–
19	27/8	Newcastle	H	W53-37*	11(6)	–	–	–	11+2(6)	1(3)	8+3(5)	R/R	–	18(6)	4+1(4)	–
20	31/8	Mildenhall	A	L36-54	13(7)	–	1+1(3)	–	2(6)	3(3)	2(4)	R/R	–	15(7)	–	–
21	3/9	Newport	H	W67-23*	12(4)	–	10+3(6)	–	9+3(5)	3(1)	12+2(5)	R/R	–	14+1(5)	7+1(4)	–
22	18/9	Peterborough	H	W52-38*	15(6)	–	1(3)	–	9+1(6)	–	9+2(5)	R/R	–	14+1(5)	4+1(5)	–
23	4/10	Rye House	A	L19-69	–	–	0(3)	–	6+1(7)	–	7(6)	R/R	–	4(6)	1(4)	1(3)
24	5/10	Buxton	A	L26-61	–	–	2(4)	–	2(5)	–	9(7)	R/R	–	9(6)	–	4(8)

DETAILS OF OTHER RIDERS:

Match No. 1: Jon Stevens 0(3); Match No. 14: David Haigh 0(3); Match No. 23: Barry Burchatt 1(3); Match No. 24: Martin McDermott 4(5); Ron Jones 0(3).

GOLDEN DOUBLE RIDES:

Match No. 16: Mark Burrows' total includes 6 points from a golden double ride.

CONFERENCE LEAGUE AVERAGES

Rider	Mts	Rds	Pts	Bon	Tot	Avge	Max
Daniel Giffard	11	52	118	3	121	9.31	1 Full
Mark Burrows	14	82	186	4	190	9.27	2 Full; 2 Paid
Wayne Barrett	20	107	219	10	229	8.56	1 Full; 1 Paid
Jason Prynne	10	46	74	8	82	7.13	–
Gavin Hedge	8	35	54	4	58	6.63	–
Peter Collyer	23	105	140	22	162	6.17	–
Andre Cross	8	30	32	8	40	5.33	–
Chris Hunt	24	115	118	26	144	5.01	–
Matt Cambridge	8	34	26	3	29	3.41	–
James Clement	20	74	47	15	62	3.35	–
Martin McDermott	1	5	4	0	4	3.20	–
Barry Burchatt	1	3	1	0	1	1.33	–
Gareth Hickmott	6	23	6	1	7	1.22	–
David Haigh	1	3	0	0	0	0.00	–
Ron Jones	1	3	0	0	0	0.00	–
Jon Stevens	1	3	0	0	0	0.00	–

NOTE: Mark Burrows' figures include one golden double ride (6 points), modified to normal score i.e. 3 points.

CONFERENCE TROPHY

(* Denotes bonus-point victory)

No	DATE	OPPONENTS	H/A	RESULT	BARRETT	HEDGE	GIFFARD	SCHRAMM	PRYNNE	HUNT	CROSS	COLLYER	HICKMOTT	CLEMENT	PARSONS	OTHERS
1	15/3	Mildenhall	A	L42-48	9(5)	3(4)	11+1(6)	5+1(4)	8+2(5)	3(3)	3+2(3)	–	–	–	–	–
2	23/4	Stoke	H	W71-19	14+1(5)	10+2(4)	14+1(5)	–	10(4)	8+2(4)	9+3(4)	6+3(4)	–	–	–	–
3	30/4	Trelawny	H	W60-30	13+1(5)	11(5)	11(4)	–	8+3(4)	7+2(4)	5+3(4)	5+1(4)	–	–	–	–
4	1/6	Carmarthen	A	W50-43	14+1(5)	–	13(5)	–	10(4)	5+1(5)	–	6+1(4)	2+1(4)	0(3)		
5	15/6	Buxton	A	L41-48	14(7)	–	9(3)	–	R/R	5(5)	–	8+1(7)	5+3(5)	0(3)		
6	21/6	Stoke	A	L39-51*	8+1(5)	–	–	13(7)	R/R	8(5)	–	10+1(7)	0(3)	0(3)		
7	24/6	Trelawny	A	L30-60*	11+1(7)	–	–	–	R/R	5+1(5)	–	6(5)	0(3)	0(3)	8(7)	–
8	12/7	Armadale	A	L33-57	R/R	–	–	–	–	9+1(7)	–	15(6)	4+1(5)	4+1(5)		1(7)
9	16/7	Buxton	H	W46-41	15(6)	–	R/R	–	–	6+1(4)	–	11+2(7)	1+1(3)	2+1(4)	11+2(6)	
10	30/7	Armadale	H	W46-44	4(3)	–	–	–	–	5(5)	–	4+1(6)	–	6+2(4)	9(5)	18+2(8)
11	13/8	Mildenhall	H	W48-45	–	–	R/R	–	–	6(5)	–	7+4(5)	–	4+1(4)	13+1(6)	18(10)
12	20/8	Carmarthen	H	W61-29*	13+1(5)	–	–	–	–	9+1(5)	–	5+2(4)	–	1+1(1)	15(5)	18+2(10)
13	7/9	Boston	A	L29-61	–	–	R/R	–	–	4(6)	0(1)	8(7)	–	1(4)	–	16(12)
14	10/9	Boston	H	L44-46	11(6)	–	R/R	–	–	7+1(5)	–	6+1(4)	–	2(4)	14+1(6)	4(5)

Details of other riders:

Match No. 8: John Branney 1(4); David Haigh 0(3); Match No. 10: Mark Burrows 15(5); Matt Cambridge 3+2(3); Match No. 11: Mark Burrows 14(6); Matt Cambridge 4(4); Match No. 12: Matt Cambridge 9+2(6); Mark Burrows 9(4); Match No. 13: Mark Burrows 15(7); Matt Cambridge 1(5); Match No. 14: Matt Cambridge 4(5).

CONFERENCE TROPHY AVERAGES

Rider	Mts	Rds	Pts	Bon	Tot	Avge	Max
Daniel Giffard	5	23	58	2	60	10.43	1 Paid
Jason Prynne	4	17	36	5	41	9.65	–
Mark Burrows	4	22	53	0	53	9.64	1 Full
Wayne Barrett	11	59	126	6	132	8.95	2 Paid
Joel Parsons	6	35	70	4	74	8.46	1 Full
Andre Cross	4	12	17	8	25	8.33	1 Paid
Gavin Hedge	3	13	24	2	26	8.00	1 Paid
Chris Schramm	2	11	18	1	19	6.91	–
Peter Collyer	13	70	97	17	114	6.51	–
Chris Hunt	14	68	87	10	97	5.71	–
Matt Cambridge	5	23	21	4	25	4.35	–
Gareth Hickmott	6	23	12	6	18	3.13	–
James Clement	11	38	20	6	26	2.74	–
John Branney	1	4	1	0	1	1.00	–
David Haigh	1	3	0	0	0	0.00	–

KNOCK-OUT CUP

No	DATE	OPPONENTS	H/A	RESULT	BARRETT	CLEMENT	HEDGE	COLLYER	GIFFARD	HUNT	CROSS	PRYNNE	CAMBRIDGE	BURROWS
1	4/4	Boston	A	L35-55	R/R	0(3)	14(7)	3+1(6)	14(6)	0(3)	4(5)	–	–	–
2	16/4	Boston	H	W55-35	17(6)	–	14+1(6)	3+1(5)	11+1(5)	5+1(4)	5+1(4)	R/R	–	–
3	23/7	Boston (R)	H	W46-44	16+1(6)	3+1(4)	–	0(2)	R/R	8(7)	–	–	2+1(5)	17+1(6)
4	27/7	Boston (R)	A	L39-50	15(7)	1(3)	–	4+2(6)	R/R	1+1(3)	–	–	3(4)	15+1(7)

(R) = Replay

OTHER MEETINGS

9 July: Under-21 International

Great Britain 52 (Chris Neath 15; Edward Kennett 11+1; Simon Stead 10+1; Chris Harris 7+3; Olly Allen 5+1; Daniel Giffard 4; Jason King 0) Sweden 37 (Antonio Lindback 8+2; Erik Andersson 8; Daniel Davidsson 6+1; Peter Ljung 5+1; Fredrik Lindgren 4+1; Mattias Nilsson 3+2; Jonas Davidsson 3). Great Britain won the series 3-0.

5 September: Autumn Challenge Cup (first-leg)

Weymouth 44 Wimbledon 46 (Mark Burrows 14; Matt Cambridge 13+1; Joel Parsons 8+1; Peter Collyer 3+2; James Clement 3+1; Chris Hunt 3+1; Andre Cross 2).

24 September: Autumn Challenge Cup (second-leg)

Wimbledon 56 (Wayne Barrett 14+1; Mark Burrows 14+1; Chris Hunt 8+1; Joel Parsons 8; Matt Cambridge 5+1; Peter Collyer 4+3; James Clement 3+1) Weymouth 34 – Wimbledon won 102-78 on aggregate.

15 October: Challenge

Wimbledon 48 (Wayne Barrett 15; Mark Burrows 13+2; Matt Cambridge 11; Peter Collyer 4+1;

James Clement 3+1; Chris Hunt 1; Jon Stevens 1) Conference League Select 42 (Dean Felton 10; Karl Mason 8+2; Robert Hollingworth 7; Lee Smart 6+1; Tom Brown 5+1; Richie Dennis 3+2; James Theobald 3).

INDIVIDUAL MEETINGS

26 March: Ronnie Moore Cup
   1st Darren Mallett 15; 2nd Wayne Barrett 13; 3rd Chris Schramm 12; Daniel Giffard 11; Robert Hollingworth 10; Gavin Hedge 9; Danny Hughes 8; Martin Williams 6; Joel Parsons 6; Luke Clifton 6; James Horton 5; Andre Cross 4; Danny Norton 4; Jon Stevens 4; Mark Thompson 3; Chris Hunt 3; Gareth Hickmott (res) 1; Luke Bowen (res) 0.
8 October: The Laurels
   1st Wayne Barrett (after run-off) 12; 2nd Mark Burrows 12; 3rd Joel Parsons (after run-off) 11; Tom Brown 11; Ben Howe 9; James Wright 9; Steve Boxall 8; Barrie Evans 7; Jamie Robertson 7; Peter Collyer 7; Dean Felton 6; Chris Hunt 5; James Clement 5; Craig Branney 4; Wayne Broadhurst 4; Richie Dennis 2.

PAIRS MEETING

28 May: London Best Pairs
   1st Wimbledon 19 (Daniel Giffard 14; Jason Prynne 5+3); 2nd Wembley 16 (Peter Collyer 8+2; Chris Schramm 8); 3rd (after run-off) Hackney 15 (Edward Kennett 12; James Cockle 3; Jon Stevens (res) 0); Harringay 15 (Joel Parsons 8+1; Corey Blackman 7+3); New Cross 14 (Dean Felton 8+1; Robert Hollingworth 6+1); West Ham 11 (Mark Thompson 6+1; Chris Hunt 5+2; James Clement (res) 0).

WOLVERHAMPTON CENTRAL MORTGAGES CUBS

NOTE: The information below relates only to the second Wolverhampton team. For details of the main side, please refer to the Elite League section.

ADDRESS: Monmore Green Stadium, Sutherland Avenue, Wolverhampton, West Midlands.
PROMOTERS: Chris Van Straaten, John Woolridge & Terry Gough.
TRACK LENGTH: 264 metres.
FIRST MEETING: 2 June 1997.
YEARS OF OPERATION: 1997 British Amateur League (fixtures shared with Long Eaton, under the banner of 'Shuttle Cubs'); 2002 Conference Trophy; 2003 British Conference League.

CLUB HONOURS

None.

RIDER ROSTER 2003

BEATON, Gary   *b. 20 August 1986, Glasgow, Scotland.*
  BRITISH CAREER: (2002) Newport (CL), Newcastle (CL); (2003) Wolverhampton (CL), Armadale, Newcastle (CL), Glasgow.

BLACKWELL, Scott   *b. 13 August 1982, Wolverhampton, West Midlands.*
  BRITISH CAREER: (2001) Sheffield (CL), Newport (CL); (2002) Wolverhampton (CT), Carmarthen; (2003) Wolverhampton (CL).

BRAIDFORD, Steven   *b. 31 December 1985, Maidstone, Kent.*
  BRITISH CAREER: (2002) Wolverhampton (CT), Isle of Wight, Wimbledon; (2003) Wolverhampton (CL & BLC), King's Lynn (BLC).

CLARKE, Steve   *b. 14 January 1984, Aylesbury, Buckinghamshire.*
  BRITISH CAREER: (2002) King's Lynn (CL), Wolverhampton (CT); (2003) Wolverhampton (CL), Peterborough (CL & BLC).

FINLOW, Rob   *b. 27 May 1984, Bromsgrove, Hereford & Worcester.*
  BRITISH CAREER: (1999) Newport (CL); (2000) Newport (CL), Buxton; (2001) Newport (CL & PL); (2002) Newport (CL & PL), Wolverhampton (CT), Somerset; (2003) Wolverhampton (CL & BLC), Somerset, Stoke (KOC), Buxton (CT).

HARGREAVES, Jack   *b. 28 May 1988.*
  BRITISH CAREER: (2003) Wolverhampton (CL).

HILL, Thomas   *b. 16 September 1986, Sheffield, South Yorkshire.*
  BRITISH CAREER: (2003) Peterborough (CL), Wolverhampton (CL).

HOWL, Michael   *b. 5 January 1985, Shrewsbury, Shropshire.*
  BRITISH CAREER: (2003) Wolverhampton (CL).

JACKSON, Andrew   *b. 12 July 1975, Manchester.*
  BRITISH CAREER: (2002) Wolverhampton (CT), Carmarthen, Newport (CL); (2003) Wolverhampton (CL), Sheffield (CL), Mildenhall (CT), Belle Vue (BLC), Swindon (CL), Trelawny (CT), Newcastle (CL).

JONES, Graham   *b. 5 May 1963, Oswestry, Shropshire.*
  BRITISH CAREER: (1984–87) Stoke; (1988) Stoke, Belle Vue, Reading, Sheffield, Wolverhampton, King's Lynn, Ipswich; (1989–93) Wolverhampton; (1994) Middlesbrough; (1995) Hull; (1996) Hull, Middlesbrough; (2003) Wolverhampton (CL & BLC), Stoke (CT), Coventry (BLC), Belle Vue (BLC), Eastbourne (BLC), Poole (BLC).

LEVERINGTON, Trent   *b. 13 May 1980, Brisbane, Queensland, Australia.*
  BRITISH CAREER: (2003) Glasgow, Armadale, Wolverhampton (CL).

LOUTH, Karl   *b. 15 February 1987.*
  BRITISH CAREER: (2003) Newport (CL), Boston, Peterborough (CL), Wolverhampton (CL).

MATLAK, Tom   *b. 10 January 1982, Krakow, Poland.*
  BRITISH CAREER: (2003) Wolverhampton (CL).

MORGAN, Allan   *b. 26 May 1978.*
  BRITISH CAREER: (2003) Wolverhampton (CL).

NEEDS, Lawrence   *b. 1 December 1986, Shrewsbury, Shropshire.*
  BRITISH CAREER: (2002) Wolverhampton (CT); (2003) Wolverhampton (CL), Mildenhall.

PESTELL, Jeremy   *b. 18 October 1984, Northampton, Northamptonshire.*
  BRITISH CAREER: (2001) Rye House; (2002) Rye House (CL), Wimbledon; (2003) Wolverhampton (CL).

WOLVERHAMPTON CUBS: back row, left to right: Rob Finlow, Scott Blackwell, Jeremy Pestell, Andrew Jackson, Lawrence Needs, Derek Bodley (Team Manager), Steven Braidford. Front, on bike: Graham Jones.

TAYLOR, Glyn b. 24 August 1953, Cardiff, South Wales.
  BRITISH CAREER: (1973) Peterborough, Crewe; (1977) Reading; (1983) Reading, Edinburgh; (1987) Long Eaton; (1993) Sheffield; (1994) Sheffield, Coventry, Poole, Berwick, Stoke; (1995) Stoke, Hull, Belle Vue, King's Lynn; (1996) Bradford, Berwick; (1997) Newcastle; (2003) Wolverhampton (CL).

WETHERS, Matthew b. 30 May 1985, Modbury, South Australia.
  BRITISH CAREER: (2003) Armadale (CT), Wolverhampton (CL), Edinburgh.

CONFERENCE LEAGUE

(* Denotes bonus-point victory)

No	DATE	OPPONENTS	H/A	RESULT	JONES	BLACKWELL	BRAIDFORD	CLARKE	FINLOW	PESTELL	NEEDS	JACKSON	WETHERS	OTHERS
1	23/3	Carmarthen	A	W45-43	17(6)	0(2)	8+1(4)	0(3)	11+3(6)	8(4)	1(3)	–	–	–
2	6/4	Newcastle	A	L41-48	18(7)	1(3)	R/R	1(3)	13(7)	5(5)	2+1(3)	–	–	1(2)
3	22/4	Peterborough	H	W47-42	15(5)	2(4)	8(4)	–	11+1(5)	10(5)	0(3)	1(4)	–	–
4	6/5	Newcastle	H	L42-51	21(6)	0(2)	6(6)	3(3)	5(5)	4(4)	3(3)	–	–	–
5	21/5	Wimbledon	A	D45-45	14(5)	3(4)	6+1(4)	–	7+2(4)	7+1(5)	0(3)	–	8+2(5)	–
6	24/5	Rye House	A	L33-57	14(6)	2+1(4)	8(6)	–	6+1(4)	3(4)	0(3)	–	–	0(3)
7	27/5	Rye House	H	L38-47	5(5)	3(3)	9+1(5)	–	5(5)	1(4)	2(3)	–	13+1(5)	–
8	27/5	Wimbledon	H	W47-42*	15(5)	5(4)	2(3)	–	3+1(4)	9+1(6)	3+1(3)	–	10+3(5)	–
9	1/6	Peterborough	A	L41-49	–	2(3)	R/R	–	10+3(7)	14+1(7)	0(3)	–	13(6)	2+1(4)
10	10/6	Buxton	H	W48-41	15(5)	1(3)	10+1(5)	–	4(4)	2(4)	0(3)	–	16(6)	–
11	17/6	Swindon	H	W57-33	15(5)	1(4)	13+2(5)	–	5+1(4)	4+1(4)	1+1(3)	–	18(6)	–
12	29/6	Mildenhall	A	L34-55	12(6)	2+1(4)	2+1(4)	–	4(4)	0(3)	0(3)	–	14(7)	–
13	20/7	Buxton	A	L35-52	18(7)	0(2)	–	–	8(6)	5(6)	2(6)	2(3)	R/R	–
14	22/7	Oxford	H	W50-38	14+1(5)	–	6+1(4)	–	7+2(4)	4(4)	1+1(3)	–	15(5)	3(5)
15	7/8	Swindon	A	W45-44*	16(7)	1(4)	14(6)	–	R/R	1+1(5)	1(2)	–	12+2(6)	–
16	11/8	Newport	H	W59-31	11+1(5)	8+3(4)	9+1(4)	–	8+3(4)	4(4)	6+2(4)	–	13(5)	–
17	12/8	Sheffield	H	W57-28	15(5)	9(4)	13+2(5)	–	4+2(3)	1(4)	5+2(5)	–	10(4)	–
18	19/8	Carmarthen	H	L43-47	14+1(6)	9+2(7)	R/R	–	14(7)	–	3(4)	2+2(3)	–	1(3)
19	26/8	Mildenhall	H	W50-40	18(6)	6+1(5)	–	–	9+1(5)	–	0(4)	0(4)	R/R	17+1(6)
20	8/9	Boston †	H	L31-40	9(3)	2(3)	–	–	DNR	–	2(5)	–	11+1(4)	7(6)
21	19/9	Oxford	A	L31-61	20(7)	–	–	–	–	3(6)	4+1(5)	0(4)	R/R	4(8)
22	28/9	Boston	A	L33-57	R/R	–	–	–	12(6)	6+1(7)	3(5)	1(4)	11(5)	0(3)
23	12/10	Newport	A	L25-63	R/R	–	–	–	DNR	10(7)	1+1(5)	5+1(5)	–	9+1(10)
24	13/10	Sheffield	A	L28-62	–	–	–	–	R/R	1(4)	2+1(4)	0(3)	8(7)	17(12)

† Meeting abandoned after twelve heats, with the result standing.

NOTE: Matthew Wethers is not credited with a paid maximum in the home match against Boston as the meeting was abandoned before his fifth programmed ride.

DETAILS OF OTHER RIDERS:

Match No. 2: Gary Beaton 1(2); Match No. 6: Michael Howl 0(3); Match No. 9: Thomas Hill 2+1(4); Match No. 14: Jack Hargreaves 3(5); Match No. 18: Michael Howl 1(3); Match No. 19: Trent Leverington 17+1(6); Match No. 20: Trent Leverington 7(3); Allan Morgan 0(3); Match No. 21: Jack Hargreaves 4(5); Tomek Matlak 0(3); Match No. 22: Karl Louth 0(3); Match No. 23: Jack Hargreaves 7+1(7); Allan Morgan 2(3); Match No. 24: Glyn Taylor 13(6); Jack Hargreaves 3(4); Tom Matlak 1(2).

GOLDEN DOUBLE RIDES:

Match No. 4: Graham Jones' total includes 6 points from a golden double ride; Match No. 18: Graham Jones' total includes 2 points from a golden double ride; Match No. 21: Graham Jones' total includes 4 points from a golden double ride.

CONFERENCE LEAGUE AVERAGES

Rider	Mts	Rds	Pts	Bon	Tot	Avge	Max
Trent Leverington	2	9	24	1	25	11.11	1 Paid
Graham Jones	20	112	290	3	293	10.46	7 Full; 1 Paid
Matthew Wethers	14	76	172	9	181	9.53	2 Full
Glyn Taylor	1	6	13	0	13	8.67	–
Steven Braidford	14	65	114	11	125	7.69	2 Paid
Rob Finlow	19	94	146	20	166	7.06	–
Jeremy Pestell	21	102	102	6	108	4.24	–
Scott Blackwell	19	69	57	8	65	3.77	–
Jack Hargreaves	4	21	17	1	18	3.43	–
Thomas Hill	1	4	2	1	3	3.00	–
Lawrence Needs	24	88	42	11	53	2.41	–
Gary Beaton	1	2	1	0	1	2.00	–
Andrew Jackson	8	30	11	3	14	1.87	–
Steve Clarke	3	9	4	0	4	1.78	–
Allan Morgan	2	6	2	0	2	1.33	–
Tom Matlak	2	5	1	0	1	0.80	–
Michael Howl	2	6	1	0	1	0.67	–
Karl Louth	1	3	0	0	0	0.00	–

NOTE: Graham Jones' figures include three golden double rides (12 points), modified to normal score i.e. 6 points.

OTHER MEETINGS

25 June: Conference Four-Team Tournament

Hull 19, Buxton 29, Scunthorpe 25, Wolverhampton 23 (Matthew Wethers 10; Rob Finlow 9; Steven Braidford 3; Scott Blackwell 1; Lawrence Needs 0) – staged at Hull.

ADDITIONAL TRACKS &
MAJOR BRITISH MEETINGS
2003

ADDITIONAL TRACKS 2003

SITTINGBOURNE

ADDRESS: The Old Gun Site, Old Ferry Road, Iwade, Sittingbourne, Kent.
PROMOTER: Graham Arnold.
TRACK LENGTH: 251 metres.
FIRST MEETING: 5 November 1972.
YEARS OF OPERATION: 1971 Training; 1972-93 Open & Training; 1994 British League
    Division 3; 1995 British Academy League; 1996 British Conference League; 1997-2003
    Open & Training.

CLUB HONOURS

None.

Following prolonged planning problems, and several years of legal debate, promoter Graham
Arnold finally gained permission from Swale Borough Council to stage a limited number of
public events on top of the regular training schools held at his Sittingbourne circuit. A crowd
of some 500 subsequently attended the first such meeting on 1 June 2003 – it being the first
public event at the track since 13 October 1996, when a Four-Team Tournament resulted thus:
Peterborough 38, Sittingbourne 24, Eastbourne 19, Reading 14.

2003 MEETINGS

1 June: Festival Of Speedway:
    First Semi-Final: Lydd 21 (Michael Pickering 8; Nathan Irwin 8; Keith Yorke 3+1; Lance Stott
    2+1; John Weeks 0) Belle Vue 19 (Danny Hughes 9; Paul Sharples 7; Richard Walsh 1; David
    Farley 1; Chris White 1) Norwich 14 (Roger Dickerson 5; Daniel Berwick 4+1; Ben Warburton 2;
    Phil Downes 2; Ben Gilbert 1). Second Semi-Final: Weymouth 26 (Justin Elkins 9; Paul Candy
    7+2; Jack Gledhill 6; Simon Paget 4+2) Club Cradley Heath 18 (David Chadburn 7; Jon Stevens
    5; James Theobald 3+1; David Baker 3+1) Sittingbourne 10 (James Purchase 5; Nathan Morton
    3; Matt Etherington 1+1; David Durham 1; Martin Elliott 0). Final: 1st Weymouth 26 (Justin
    Elkins 9; Jack Gledhill 8; Simon Paget 5+2; Paul Candy 4+2) 2nd Lydd 16 (Nathan Irwin 8;
    Michael Pickering 5; Lance Stott 2+1; Keith Yorke 1+1) 3rd Belle Vue 12 (Paul Sharples 5;
    Danny Hughes 5; Richard Walsh 1; David Farley 1).
29 June: Vic Harding Memorial Trophy
    (Qualifying scores: Nick Lee 15; James Theobald 15; James Clement 11; James Purchase 10;
    Darren Smith 8; Keith Yorke 6; Rob Painter 6; Karl Rushen 4; Thomas Hill 4; Jon Stevens (res) 4;
    Thomas Rowlett 3; Michael Holding 2; Adam Filmer (res) 1; Jason Taylor (res) 1) Final: 1st
    Theobald; 2nd Lee; 3rd Clement; 4th Purchase. Challenge Match: Sittingbourne 27 (Mark
    Baseby 10; Barry Burchatt 5+1; Keith Yorke 5; Adam Filmer 5; Ben Gilbert 2+1) Hackney 27
    (Jon Stevens 10; David Durham 8+3; Richard Harbud 6; Lance Stott 3; Jason Taylor 0).

27 July: Best Pairs Championship

Group A: Cradley Heath 24 (Nick Lee 14; Mark Baseby 10); Hackney 23 (Gareth Hickmott 13; Jon Stevens 10); Team Set Lighting 18 (Steven Braidford 16; Adam Filmer 2); Bristol 13 (Paul Candy 11; Oliver Hackett 2); Norwich 12 (Thomas Rowlett 10; Alan Fenn-Smith 2). Group B: Weymouth 26 (Nathan Irwin 15; James Purchase 11); Sittingbourne 18 (Steve Boxall 12; Ben Gilbert 6); Scunthorpe 18 (Martyn Sturgeon 10; Karl Rushen 8); Lydd 18 (Lance Stott 13; Keith Yorke 5); Leicester 8 (Wesley Sheasby 6; Sidney Higgins 2; Rory Caveill (res) 0). First Semi-Final: 1st Boxall; 2nd Lee; 3rd Baseby; 4th Gilbert; Second Semi-Final: 1st Irwin; 2nd Hickmott; 3rd Stevens; 4th Purchase; Third-Place Race-Off: 1st Boxall; 2nd Irwin; 3rd Gilbert; 4th Purchase; Final: 1st Hickmott; 2nd Lee; 3rd Stevens; 4th Baseby; Winners – Hackney.

7 September: Conference Challenge

Sittingbourne 50 (James Theobald 15; Mark Baseby 13+2; Karl Rushen 11; Adam Filmer 6+1; Keith Yorke 4+3; Ben Gilbert 1; Harland Cook R/R) Norwich 28 (Jon Stevens 12; Martyn Sturgeon 7; Alan Fenn-Smith 4+1; Russell Paine 3+2; Rory Caveill 2+1; John Taylor 0; Roger Dickerson R/R).

28 September: Conference Challenge

Sittingbourne 42 (Nathan Irwin 18; James Theobald 10; Mark Baseby 10; Keith Yorke 2; Ben Gilbert 1; Karl Rushen 1; Adam Filmer 0) Hackney 47 (Harland Cook 12; James Purchase 10+1; Jon Stevens 9+1; Martyn Sturgeon 7+3; Alan Fenn-Smith 5+4; James Clement 4+2; R/R at No. 2).

WEYMOUTH

ADDRESS: Wessex Stadium (2), Radipole Lane, Weymouth, Dorset.
PROMOTER: Brian White.
TRACK LENGTH: 223 metres.
FIRST MEETING: 15 August 2003.
YEARS OF OPERATION: 2003 Open.

PREVIOUS VENUE: Wessex Stadium (1), Radipole Lane, Weymouth, Dorset.
YEARS OF OPERATION: 1954 Open; 1955 National League Division 2; 1962-63 Open; 1964 Metropolitan League; 1965 Open; 1966-67 Training; 1968 British League Division 2; 1969-70 Training; 1971-73 Open & Training; 1974 British League Division 2; 1975-84 National League; 1985 Open & Training.

CLUB HONOURS

PAIRS CHAMPIONS: 1982, 1983.

Following the closure of Weymouth Speedway after the 1984 season, Brian White had long-since harboured the idea of bringing the sport back to Dorset. He initially looked at Portland in 2001, but the idea to run in a disused quarry never got to the planning stage as it was discovered the site was of special scientific interest. He then ran his ideas past the football club, who had built on the old speedway site at Weymouth, but after some initial hope, that idea faded too. Brian then considered the Clay Pigeon Raceway, situated on the A37, before trying a site at Buckland Ripers, near Dorchester. Sadly, his subsequent planning application was greeted with numerous letters of complaint, and he was forced to back down. However, there was light at the end of the tunnel, as Chickerell Town Council did agree for one of their councillors to meet with directors from Weymouth FC, regarding the possibility of speedway again being accommodated at the Wessex Stadium site. Happily, they agreed to meet with Brian, and the rest is history as, on 15 August 2003, in front of some 2,500 spectators, speedway returned on what had been the practice football pitch, extremely close to where it had last been staged some nineteen years previously!

2003 MEETINGS

15 August: Wessex Rosebowl
> 1st Justin Elkins 15; 2nd Dan Warwick 13; 3rd Ben Barker (after run-off) 12; Dean Felton 12; Tom Brown 12; Chris Johnson 9; Brendon Mackay 7; Nick Lee 7; Jamie Holmes 7; Peter Collyer 7; Paul Candy 5; Harland Cook 4; Jack Gledhill 3; James Purchase 3; Simon Paget 2; Nathan Irwin 1.

22 August: Conference Challenge (first-leg)
> Bristol 43 Weymouth 47 (Justin Elkins 13+1; Ben Barker 11+1; Chris Johnson 11; Nathan Irwin 5+2; Dan Warwick 4+2; Brendon Mackay 3; Matt Cambridge R/R) – staged at Somerset.

25 August: Conference Challenge (second-leg)
> Weymouth 53 (Chris Johnson 18+1; Justin Elkins 12; Dan Warwick 11+3; Ben Barker 6+2; Nathan Irwin 6+1; Brendon Mackay 0; Matt Cambridge R/R) Bristol 36 – Weymouth won 100-79 on aggregate.

5 September: Autumn Challenge Cup (first-leg)
> Weymouth 44 (Brendon Mackay 11; Karl Mason 10+2; Dean Felton 9+1; Justin Elkins 9; Nathan Irwin 3+3; James Purchase 2; Dean Ankers 0) Wimbledon 46.

12 September: Conference Challenge
> Weymouth 46 (Brendon Mackay 13+1; Justin Elkins 12; Chris Johnson 7+3; Dean Felton 6; Ben Barker 5; Karl Mason 2+1; Nathan Irwin 1) Swindon 43.

19 September: Conference Challenge
> Weymouth 40 (Ben Powell 11; Justin Elkins 11; Dean Felton 6+1; Gordon Meakins 5+1; Paul Candy 4+2; Nathan Irwin 3; Matt Cambridge 0) Belle Vue Colts 49.

24 September: Autumn Challenge Cup (second-leg)
> Wimbledon 56 Weymouth 34 (Dean Felton 11+1; Chris Johnson 10; Lee Smart 8+1; Nathan Irwin 4; Ben Barker 1; Justin Elkins 0; Brendon Mackay R/R) – Wimbledon won 102-78 on aggregate.

26 September: Conference Challenge
> Weymouth 51 (Ben Powell 10; Dean Felton 10; Nathan Irwin 9; Paul Candy 8+3; Karl Mason 6+3; Justin Elkins 5+1; Gordon Meakins 3+3) Norwich 38 (Luke Priest 15+1; Lee Smart 10+2; Tom Brown 10; Matt Tutton 1; Alan Fenn-Smith 1; Mark Baseby 1; Nathan Morton R/R).

MAJOR BRITISH MEETINGS

BRITISH UNDER-21 CHAMPIONSHIP FINAL
24 APRIL, SHEFFIELD

1st	Simon Stead
2nd	Olly Allen
3rd	Edward Kennett
4th	Andrew Appleton

PRELIMINARY
Heat one: Edward Kennett, Ritchie Hawkins, Jason King, Shane Colvin.
Heat two: Lee Smethills, Glen Phillips, Ben Wilson, Lee Hodgson (ret).
Heat three: Barrie Evans, Aidan Collins, Rob Grant, Daniel King.
Heat four: (Rerun) Adam Allott, Rob Finlow, Ricky Ashworth (ret), Chris Mills (f, ex).
Heat five: (Rerun) Chris Mills, Rob Grant, Jason King (ret), Lee Hodgson (n.s.).
Heat six: Ricky Ashworth, Shane Colvin, Daniel King, Ben Wilson (f, rem).
Heat seven: (Rerun) Glen Phillips, Edward Kennett, Barrie Evans (f, rem), Rob Finlow (f, ex).
Heat eight: Lee Smethills, Ritchie Hawkins, Aidan Collins, Adam Allott (ret).
Heat nine: (Rerun – Awarded) Adam Allott, Shane Colvin, Chris Mills (f, ex), Barrie Evans (n.s.).
Heat ten: Ricky Ashworth, Aidan Collins, Rob Grant, Rob Finlow (n.s.).

SUPER SIXTEEN
Heat eleven: Glen Phillips, David Howe, Ritchie Hawkins, Jamie Smith (ret).
Heat twelve: (Rerun) Simon Stead, Edward Kennett, Andrew Moore (fell), Lee Smethills (f, ex).
Heat thirteen: Chris Harris, Aidan Collins, Adam Allott, Chris Neath (ret).
Heat fourteen: Ricky Ashworth, Olly Allen, Andrew Appleton, Shane Colvin (n.s.).
Heat fifteen: Ritchie Hawkins, Adam Allott, Lee Smethills, Shane Colvin (n.s.).
Heat sixteen: Andrew Appleton, Jamie Smith, Chris Neath, Andrew Moore (fell).
Heat seventeen: Olly Allen, Chris Harris, Glen Phillips, Edward Kennett.
Heat eighteen: (Rerun) Simon Stead, Aidan Collins, Ricky Ashworth (f, ex), David Howe (f, ex).
Heat nineteen: Ritchie Hawkins, Jamie Smith, Glen Phillips (ret), Ricky Ashworth (ex, two mins.).
Heat twenty: Edward Kennett, Andrew Appleton, Adam Allott, David Howe (n.s.).

SEMI-FINALS
Heat twenty-one: Olly Allen, Andrew Appleton, Chris Collins, Ritchie Hawkins.
Heat twenty-two: (awarded) Simon Stead, Edward Kennett, Jamie Smith, Chris Harris (f, ex).

'B' FINAL
Heat twenty-three: Chris Harris, Aidan Collins, Jamie Smith, Ritchie Hawkins.

'A' FINAL
Heat twenty-four: Simon Stead, Olly Allen, Edward Kennett, Andrew Appleton.

NOTE: Eliminated riders are underlined throughout

ROLL OF HONOUR

NOTE: Became known as the British Under-21 Championship in 1987, having previously been called the Junior Championship of Great Britain.

YEAR	FIRST	SECOND	THIRD
1969	Graham Plant	Geoff Ambrose	Mick Bell
1970	Barry Thomas	Dave Jessup	Mick Bell
1971	Ian Turner	Dave Jessup	Peter Ingram
1972	Allen Emmett	Gordon Kennett	Tony Davey
1973	Peter Collins	Barney Kennett	David Gagen
1974	Chris Morton	Steve Bastable	Neil Middleditch
1975	Neil Middleditch	Steve Weatherley	Joe Owen
1976	Michael Lee	Steve Weatherley	Colin Richardson
1977	Les Collins	Phil Collins	Colin Richardson
1978	Phil Collins	Ian Gledhill	Bob Garrad
1979	Kenny Carter	Nigel Flatman	Mel Taylor
1980	Mark Courtney	Kevin Smith	John Barker
1981	Rob Lightfoot	Peter Carr	Neil Evitts
1982	Peter Carr	Martin Hagon	Simon Cross
1983	Keith Millard	Simon Cross	Kenny McKinna
1984	Marvyn Cox	Simon Cross	Andy Smith
1985	Carl Blackbird	David Mullett	Andy Smith
1986	Gary Havelock	Andrew Silver	Daz Sumner
1987	Daz Sumner	David Biles	Mark Loram
1988	Mark Loram	Andy Phillips	Martin Dugard
1989	Martin Dugard	Chris Louis	Dean Barker
1990	Joe Screen	Mark Loram	Chris Louis
1991	*Not Staged*		
1992	Scott A. Smith	Mark Loram	Joe Screen
1993	Joe Screen	Carl Stonehewer	David Norris
1994	Paul Hurry	Ben Howe	James Grieves
1995	Ben Howe	Paul Hurry	Savalas Clouting
1996	Savalas Clouting	Scott Nicholls	Paul Hurry
1997	Leigh Lanham	Lee Richardson	Scott Nicholls
1998	Scott Nicholls	Lee Richardson	Paul Lee
1999	Scott Nicholls	Lee Richardson	David Howe
2000	David Howe	Lee Richardson	Paul Lee
2001	Simon Stead	David Howe	Paul Lee
2002	Simon Stead	Ross Brady	Olly Allen
2003	Simon Stead	Olly Allen	Edward Kennett

CHAMPIONSHIP OF GREAT BRITAIN FINAL
5 JULY, EASTBOURNE

1st	Scott Nicholls
2nd	Dean Barker
3rd	David Norris
4th	Joe Screen

	QUALIFYING SCORES					TOTAL
David Norris	3	3	3	3	3	15
Scott Nicholls	3	3	3	3	2	14
Dean Barker	2	3	2	3	3	13
Joe Screen	3	2	1	2	3	11
Leigh Lanham	1	2	2	3	2	10
David Howe	0	2	3	1	2	8
Carl Stonehewer	3	1	1	2	1	8
Olly Allen	2	F	2	0	3	7
Chris Neath	0	3	0	1	2	6
Stuart Robson	1	1	3	0	1	6
Glenn Cunningham	1	0	2	2	F	5
Chris Harris	0	2	0	2	1	5
Paul Hurry	2	1	1	1	X	5
James Grieves	2	0	X	F	1	3
Paul Fry	1	1	0	1	0	3
Danny Bird	0	0	X	0	0	0

RACE DETAILS:
Heat one: Joe Screen, Paul Hurry, Glenn Cunningham, Danny Bird.
Heat two: Carl Stonehewer, James Grieves, Paul Fry, Chris Harris.
Heat three: Scott Nicholls, Dean Barker, Stuart Robson, Chris Neath.
Heat four: David Norris, Olly Allen, Leigh Lanham, David Howe.
Heat five: Dean Barker, Joe Screen, Carl Stonehewer, Olly Allen (fell).
Heat six: David Norris, Chris Harris, Stuart Robson, Glenn Cunningham.
Heat seven: Scott Nicholls, David Howe, Paul Hurry, James Grieves.
Heat eight: Chris Neath, Leigh Lanham, Paul Fry, Danny Bird.
Heat nine: Scott Nicholls, Leigh Lanham, Joe Screen, Chris Harris.
Heat ten: David Howe, Glenn Cunningham, Carl Stonehewer, Chris Neath.
Heat eleven: (Rerun) David Norris, Dean Barker, Paul Hurry, Paul Fry.
Heat twelve: (Rerun) Stuart Robson, Olly Allen, Danny Bird (ex, obstructing track), James Grieves (ex, not under power).
Heat thirteen: David Norris, Joe Screen, Chris Neath, James Grieves (fell).
Heat fourteen: Scott Nicholls, Glenn Cunningham, Paul Fry, Olly Allen.
Heat fifteen: Leigh Lanham, Carl Stonehewer, Paul Hurry, Stuart Robson (f, rem).
Heat sixteen: Dean Barker, Chris Harris, David Howe, Danny Bird.
Heat seventeen Joe Screen, David Howe, Stuart Robson, Paul Fry.

Heat eighteen: Dean Barker, Leigh Lanham, James Grieves, Glenn Cunningham (fell).

Heat nineteen: (Rerun) Olly Allen, Chris Neath, Chris Harris, Paul Hurry (f, ex).

Heat twenty: David Norris, Scott Nicholls, Carl Stonehewer, Danny Bird.

Final: Scott Nicholls, Dean Barker, David Norris, Joe Screen.

ROLL OF HONOUR

NOTE: Became known as the Championship of Great Britain in 2002, having previously been called the British Final.

YEAR	FIRST	SECOND	THIRD
1961	Barry Briggs	Peter Craven	Ronnie Moore
1962	Peter Craven	Barry Briggs	Ronnie Moore
1963	Peter Craven	Barry Briggs	Leo McAuliffe
1964	Barry Briggs	Ken McKinlay	Ron How
1965	Barry Briggs	Nigel Boocock	Ken McKinlay
1966	Barry Briggs	Ivan Mauger	Colin Pratt
1967	Barry Briggs	Ivan Mauger	Eric Boocock
1968	Ivan Mauger	Barry Briggs	Eric Boocock
1969	Barry Briggs	Nigel Boocock	Ronnie Moore
1970	Ivan Mauger	Ronnie Moore	Roy Trigg
1971	Ivan Mauger	Barry Briggs	Tony Lomas
1972	Ivan Mauger	Nigel Boocock	Barry Briggs
1973	Ray Wilson	Bob Valentine	Peter Collins
1974	Eric Boocock	Terry Betts	Dave Jessup
1975	John Louis	Peter Collins	Malcolm Simmons
1976	Malcolm Simmons	Chris Morton	Doug Wyer
1977	Michael Lee	Dave Jessup	Doug Wyer
1978	Michael Lee	Dave Jessup	Malcolm Simmons
1979	Peter Collins	Michael Lee	Dave Jessup
1980	Dave Jessup	Michael Lee	Phil Collins
1981	Steve Bastable	Kenny Carter	John Louis
1982	Andy Grahame	Alan Grahame	Kenny Carter
1983	Chris Morton	Michael Lee	Andy Grahame
1984	Kenny Carter	Andy Grahame	Dave Jessup
1985	Kenny Carter	John Davis	Kelvin Tatum
1986	Neil Evitts	Phil Collins	Jeremy Doncaster
1987	Kelvin Tatum	Neil Evitts	Simon Wigg
1988	Simon Wigg	Kelvin Tatum	Chris Morton
1989	Simon Wigg	Kelvin Tatum	Alan Grahame
1990	Kelvin Tatum	Simon Cross	Jeremy Doncaster
1991	Gary Havelock	Kelvin Tatum	Chris Louis
1992	Gary Havelock	Martin Dugard	Andy Smith
1993	Andy Smith	Joe Screen	Gary Havelock
1994	Andy Smith	Joe Screen	Steve Schofield
1995	Andy Smith	Joe Screen	Dean Barker
1996	Joe Screen	Chris Louis	Carl Stonehewer

YEAR	FIRST	SECOND	THIRD
1997	Mark Loram	Chris Louis	Sean Wilson
1998	Chris Louis	Joe Screen	Paul Hurry
1999	Mark Loram	Joe Screen	Chris Louis
2000	Chris Loius	Paul Hurry	Martin Dugard
2001	Mark Loram	Stuart Robson	Martin Dugard
2002	Scott Nicholls	Lee Richardson	David Howe
2003	Scott Nicholls	Dean Barker	David Norris

PREMIER LEAGUE PAIRS CHAMPIONSHIP
19 JULY, WORKINGTON

1st	Workington
2nd	Newport
3rd	Isle of Wight
4th	King's Lynn

GROUP A

	QUALIFYING SCORES				TOTALS
Isle of Wight 24					
Adam Shields	4	4	3	4	15
Danny Bird	2	0	4	3	9
Newport 21					
Niels-Kristian Iversen	4	3	4	3	14
Frank Smart	2	2	3	F	7
Edinburgh 19					
Peter Carr	4	4	2	4	14
Rory Schlein	0	3	0	2	5
Glasgow 17					
George Stancl	3	3	4	2	12
Les Collins	2	0	3	0	5
Somerset 9					
Mark Lemon	3	2	2	2	9
Glenn Cunningham	0	0	0	0	0

GROUP B

	QUALIFYING SCORES				TOTALS
King's Lynn 21					
Shane Parker	2	3	3	2	10
Tomas Topinka	3	4	4	0	11

	QUALIFYING SCORES continued				TOTALS
Workington 21					
Carl Stonehewer	4	4	4	4	16
Simon Stead	0	0	2	3	5
Swindon 20					
Charlie Gjedde	2	4	2	4	12
Olly Allen	3	2	0	3	8
Trelawny 19					
Matej Zagar	4	0	0	4	8
Chris Harris	3	2	3	3	11
Arena Essex 9					
Henning Bager	0	0	0	2	2
Leigh Lanham	2	3	2	X	7

RACE DETAILS

Heat one: Peter Carr, George Stancl, Les Collins, Rory Schlein.

Heat two: Carl Stonehewer, Tomas Topinka, Shane Parker, Simon Stead.

Heat three: Adam Shields, Mark Lemon, Danny Bird, Glenn Cunningham.

Heat four: Matej Zagar, Chris Harris, Leigh Lanham, Henning Bager.

Heat five: Niels-Kristian Iversen, George Stancl, Frank Smart, Les Collins.

Heat six: Carl Stonehewer, Olly Allen, Charlie Gjedde, Simon Stead.

Heat seven: Peter Carr, Rory Schlein, Mark Lemon, Glenn Cunningham.

Heat eight: Tomas Topinka, Shane Parker, Chris Harris, Matej Zagar.

Heat nine: Adam Shields, Niels-Kristian Iversen, Frank Smart, Danny Bird.

Heat ten: Charlie Gjedde, Leigh Lanham, Olly Allen, Henning Bager.

Heat eleven: George Stancl, Les Collins, Mark Lemon, Glenn Cunningham.

Heat twelve: Carl Stonehewer, Chris Harris, Simon Stead, Matej Zagar.

Heat thirteen: Danny Bird, Adam Shields, Peter Carr, Rory Schlein.

Heat fourteen: Tomas Topinka, Shane Parker, Leigh Lanham, Henning Bager.

Heat fifteen: Niels-Kristian Iversen, Frank Smart, Mark Lemon, Glenn Cunningham.

Heat sixteen: Matej Zagar, Chris Harris, Charlie Gjedde, Olly Allen.

Heat seventeen: Adam Shields, Danny Bird, George Stancl, Les Collins.

Heat eighteen: (Rerun) Carl Stonehewer, Simon Stead, Henning Bager, Leigh Lanham (ex, crossed white line).

Heat nineteen: Peter Carr, Niels-Kristian Iversen, Rory Schlein, Frank Smart (fell).

Heat twenty: Charlie Gjedde, Olly Allen, Shane Parker, Tomas Topinka.

First Semi-Final: Danny Bird, Carl Stonehewer, Simon Stead, Adam Shields.

Second Semi-Final: Tomas Topinka, Frank Smart, Niels-Kristian Iversen, Shane Parker.

Consolation Final: Danny Bird, Adam Shields, Tomas Topinka, Shane Parker.

Grand Final: Carl Stonehewer, Simon Stead, Frank Smart, Niels-Kristian Iversen.

ROLL OF HONOUR

NOTE: Became known as the Premier League Pairs Championship in 1997, having previously been known as the National League Pairs Championship (1975-90) and Division Two Pairs Championship (1994)

YEAR	FIRST	SECOND
1975	Newcastle	Ellesmere Port
	(Tom Owen & Brian Havelock)	(John Jackson & Colin Goad)
1976	Ellesmere Port	Newcastle
	(John Jackson & Chris Turner)	(Joe Owen & Tom Owen)
1977	Boston	Newport
	(Robert Hollingworth & Colin Cook)	(Jim Brett & Brian Woodward)
1978	Ellesmere Port	Newcastle
	(John Jackson & Steve Finch)	(Tom Owen & Robbie Blackadder)
1979	Milton Keynes	Ellesmere Port
	(Andy Grahame & Bob Humphreys)	(John Jackson & Steve Finch)
1980	Middlesbrough	Boston
	(Mark Courtney & Steve Wilcock)	(Robert Hollingworth & Gary Guglielmi)
1981	Canterbury	Berwick
	(Mike Ferreira & Denzil Kent)	(Wayne Brown & Steve McDermott)
1982	Weymouth	Long Eaton
	(Martin Yeates & Simon Wigg)	(Alan Molyneux & Dave Perks)
1983	Weymouth	Glasgow
	(Martin Yeates & Simon Cross)	(Jim McMillan & Steve Lawson)
1984	Stoke	Berwick
	(Nigel Crabtree & Tom Owen)	(Bruce Cribb & Steve McDermott)
1985	Ellesmere Port	Poole
	(Joe Owen & Louis Carr)	(Martin Yeates & Stan Bear)
1986	Edinburgh	Hackney
	(Les Collins & Doug Wyer)	(Barry Thomas & Andy Galvin)
1987	Mildenhall	Peterborough
	(Dave Jessup & Mel Taylor)	(Ian Barney & Kevin Hawkins)
1988	Stoke	Poole
	(Graham Jones & Steve Bastable)	(Steve Schofield & David Biles)
1989	Stoke	Mildenhall
	(Nigel Crabtree & Eric Monaghan)	(Preben Eriksen & Peter Glanz)
1990	Hackney	Exeter
	(Steve Schofield & Andy Galvin)	(Steve Regeling & Peter Jeffery)
1991-93	*Not Staged*	
1994	Swindon	Glasgow
	(Tony Olsson & Tony Langdon)	(Nigel Crabtree & David Walsh)
1995-96	*Not Staged*	
1997	Long Eaton	Reading
	(Martin Dixon & Carl Stonehewer)	(David Mullett & Lee Richardson)
1998	Peterborough	Exeter
	(Glenn Cunningham & Brett Woodifield)	(Frank Smart & Michael Coles)

YEAR	FIRST	SECOND
1999	Workington	Arena-Essex
	(Carl Stonehewer & Brent Werner)	(Colin White & Leigh Lanham)
2000	Workington	Isle of Wight
	(Carl Stonehewer & Mick Powell)	(Ray Morton & Danny Bird)
2001	Workington	Newcastle
	(Carl Stonehewer & Peter I. Karlsson)	(Bjarne Pedersen & Jesper Olsen)
2002	Isle of Wight	Newport
	(Adam Shields & Danny Bird)	(Frank Smart & Craig Watson)
2003	Workington	Newport
	(Carl Stonehewer & Simon Stead)	(Frank Smart & Niels-Kristian Iversen)

CONFERENCE LEAGUE FOUR-TEAM CHAMPIONSHIP
19 JULY, MILDENHALL

NOTE: Unfortunately, due to a thunderstorm, this inaugural Conference League Four-Team Championship was abandoned before the final could take place. The final was subsequently rescheduled and took place at Mildenhall on 5 October.

FIRST SEMI-FINAL

Mildenhall 15			TOTAL
Wayne Broadhurst	3	2	5
Nick Simmons	2	F	2
Ben Howe	2	1	3
James Brundle	2	3	5

Peterborough 13			
Neil Collins	3	3	6
James Horton	2	2	4
Danny Norton	0	2	2
Shane McCabe	0	1	1

Wimbledon 11			
Mark Burrows	3	3	6
Peter Collyer	X	3	3
Wayne Barrett	1	F	1
Chris Hunt	1	–	1
Matt Cambridge (res)	F	–	0

Newcastle 9			TOTAL
Jamie Robertson	3	0	3
Steven Jones	F	2	2
Craig Branney	1	1	2
John Branney	1	1	2

RACE DETAILS

Heat one: Wayne Broadhurst, James Horton, Chris Hunt, Steven Jones (fell).

Heat two: Mark Burrows, Nick Simmons, Craig Branney, Danny Norton.

Heat three: (Rerun) Neil Collins, Ben Howe, John Branney, Peter Collyer (f, ex).

Heat four: Jamie Robertson, James Brundle, Wayne Barrett, Shane McCabe.

Heat five: (Rerun) Neil Collins, Wayne Broadhurst, Craig Branney, Wayne Barrett (fell).

Heat six: James Brundle, Danny Norton, John Branney, Matt Cambridge.

Heat seven: Mark Burrows, James Horton, Ben Howe, Jamie Robertson.

Heat eight: Peter Collyer, Steven Jones, Shane McCabe, Nick Simmons (fell).

SECOND SEMI-FINAL

Rye House 22			TOTAL
Edward Kennett	3	3	6
Barrie Evans	3	3	6
Joel Parsons	2	3	5
Steve Boxall	2	3	5

Boston 13			
Peter Boast	3	2	5
Luke Clifton	3	1	4
Mark Thompson	2	X	2
Roger Dickerson	1	1	2

Sheffield 10			
Richard Hall	1	2	3
Benji Compton	1	2	3
Ben Wilson	1	1	2
Rob Grant	X	2	2

Buxton 3			
Lee Derbyshire	2	0	2
Phil Knowles	0	1	1
Jonathan Bethell	0	0	0
Paul Burnett	0	0	0

RACE DETAILS

Heat one: Edward Kennett, Mark Thompson, Benji Compton, Paul Burnett.

Heat two: (Rerun) Barrie Evans, Lee Derbyshire, Roger Dickerson, Rob Grant (ex, foul riding).

Heat three: Peter Boast, Joel Parsons, Richard Hall, Phil Knowles.

Heat four: Luke Clifton, Steve Boxall, Ben Wilson, Jonathan Bethell.

Heat five: Edward Kennett, Richard Hall, Luke Clifton, Lee Derbyshire.

Heat six: (Rerun) Steve Boxall, Rob Grant, Phil Knowles, Mark Thompson (f, ex).

Heat seven: Joel Parsons, Benji Compton, Roger Dickerson, Jonathan Bethell.

Heat eight: Barrie Evans, Peter Boast, Ben Wilson, Paul Burnett.

PREMIER LEAGUE FOUR-TEAM CHAMPIONSHIP
27 JULY, SWINDON

1st	Swindon	
2nd	Trelawny	
3rd	Newport	
4th	Glasgow	

FIRST SEMI-FINAL

Swindon 15			TOTAL
Olly Allen	3	R	3
Charlie Gjedde	3	3	6
Chris Neath	3	0	3
Paul Fry	3	X	3

Glasgow 12			
George Stancl	1	2	3
Les Collins	0	2	2
Christian Henry	2	3	5
Kevin Doolan	0	2	2

Edinburgh 10			
Wayne Carter	1	1	2
Theo Pijper	2	0	2
Magnus Karlsson	1	2	3
Matthew Wethers	0	3	3

Isle of Wight 10			
Ray Morton	1	3	4
Adam Shields	2	X	2
Danny Bird	F	1	1
Sebastian Tresarrieu	2	1	3

RACE DETAILS

Heat one: Chris Neath, Adam Shields, Wayne Carter, Kevin Doolan.

Heat two: Paul Fry, Theo Pijper, George Stancl, Danny Bird (fell).

Heat three: Olly Allen, Sebastian Tresarrieu, Magnus Karlsson, Les Collins.

Heat four: Charlie Gjedde, Christian Henry, Ray Morton, Matthew Wethers.

Heat five: Ray Morton, George Stancl, Wayne Carter, Olly Allen (ret).

Heat six: (Rerun twice) Matthew Wethers, Les Collins, Paul Fry (f, ex), Adam Shields (f, ex).

Heat seven: Christian Henry, Magnus Karlsson, Danny Bird, Chris Neath.

Heat eight: Charlie Gjedde, Kevin Doolan, Sebastian Tresarrieu, Theo Pijper (f, rem).

SECOND SEMI-FINAL

Newport 15			TOTAL
Craig Watson	3	2	5
Niels-Kristian Iversen	3	3	6
Frank Smart	1	2	3
Tony Atkin	1	0	1
Trelawny 13			
Matej Zagar	1	3	4
Steve Masters	2	1	3
Chris Harris	3	3	6
Pavel Ondrasik	0	0	0
King's Lynn 11			
Trevor Harding	0	1	1
Davey Watt	2	1	3
Tomas Topinka	2	1	3
Shane Parker	2	2	4
Arena-Essex 9			
Lee Herne	0	0	0
Leigh Lanham	1	3	4
Henning Bager	0	0	0
Kelvin Tatum	3	2	5

RACE DETAILS

Heat one: Niels-Kristian Iversen, Shane Parker, Matej Zagar, Henning Bager.

Heat two: Kelvin Tatum, Steve Masters, Frank Smart, Trevor Harding.

Heat three: Chris Harris, Davey Watt, Tony Atkin, Lee Herne.

Heat four: Craig Watson, Tomas Topinka, Leigh Lanham, Pavel Ondrasik.

Heat five: Matej Zagar, Craig Watson, Trevor Harding, Lee Herne.

Heat six: Niels-Kristian Iversen, Kelvin Tatum, Davey Watt, Pavel Ondrasik.

Heat seven: Chris Harris, Frank Smart, Tomas Topinka, Henning Bager.

Heat eight: Leigh Lanham, Shane Parker, Steve Masters, Tony Atkin.

FINAL

Swindon 25

				TOTAL
Charlie Gjedde	3	3	3	9
Olly Allen	1	2	3	6
Chris Neath	2	1	1	4
Paul Fry	1	3	2	6

Trelawny 22

Matej Zagar	3	2	3	8
Steve Masters	1	0	3	4
Chris Harris	3	3	2	8
Pavel Ondrasik	0	1	1	2

Newport 21

Tony Atkin	2	0	2	4
Frank Smart	3	1	2	6
Craig Watson	2	2	1	5
Niels-Kristian Iversen	2	3	1	6

Glasgow 4

George Stancl	1	1	0	2
Les Collins	0	0	0	0
Christian Henry	R	-	-	0
Kevin Doolan	0	2	0	2
Trent Leverington (res)	0	0	-	0

RACE DETAILS

Heat one: Chris Harris, Tony Atkin, Olly Allen, Kevin Doolan.

Heat two: Frank Smart, Chris Neath, George Stancl, Pavel Ondrasik.

Heat three: Matej Zagar, Craig Watson, Paul Fry, Les Collins.

Heat four: Charlie Gjedde, Niels-Kristian Iversen, Steve Masters, Christian Henry (ret).

Heat five: Charlie Gjedde, Matej Zagar, George Stancl, Tony Atkin.

Heat six: Niels-Kristian Iversen, Olly Allen, Pavel Ondrasik, Les Collins.

Heat seven: Chris Harris, Craig Watson, Chris Neath, Trent Leverington.

Heat eight: Paul Fry, Kevin Doolan, Frank Smart, Steve Masters.

Heat nine: Olly Allen, Tony Atkin, Pavel Ondrasik, Trent Leverington.

Heat ten: Steve Masters, Frank Smart, Chris Neath, Les Collins.

Heat eleven: Matej Zagar, Paul Fry, Craig Watson, George Stancl.

Heat twelve: Charlie Gjedde, Chris Harris, Niels-Kristian Iversen, Kevin Doolan.

ROLL OF HONOUR

NOTE: This became known as the Premier League Four-Team Championship in 1997, having previously been known as the National League Four-Team Championship (1976-90) and the Division Two Four-Team Championship (1991-94).

YEAR	FIRST	SECOND	THIRD	FOURTH
1976	Newcastle	Eastbourne	Ellesmere Port	Workington
1977	Peterborough	Canterbury	Eastbourne	Stoke
1978	Peterborough	Stoke	Canterbury	Ellesmere Port
1979	Ellesmere Port	Mildenhall	Peterborough	Berwick
1980	Crayford	Rye House	Ellesmere Port	Stoke
1981	Edinburgh	Newcastle	Middlesbrough	Wolverhampton
1982	Newcastle	Mildenhall	Middlesbrough	Rye House
1983	Newcastle	Mildenhall	Milton Keynes	Long Eaton
1984	Mildenhall	Stoke	Milton Keynes	Boston
1985	Middlesbrough	Peterborough	Hackney	Stoke
1986	Middlesbrough	Arena-Essex	Hackney	Mildenhall
1987	Mildenhall	Arena-Essex	Eastbourne	Wimbledon
1988	Peterborough	Mildenhall	Eastbourne	Poole
1989	Peterborough	Stoke	Exeter	Eastbourne
1990	Stoke	Poole	Hackney	Ipswich
1991	Arena-Essex	Long Eaton	Edinburgh	Milton Keynes
1992	Peterborough	Edinburgh	Rye House	Glasgow
1993	Edinburgh	Swindon	Long Eaton	Rye House
1994	Oxford	Long Eaton	Peterborough	Edinburgh
1995-96	*Not Staged*			
1997	Long Eaton	Edinburgh	Oxford	Berwick
1998	Peterborough	Edinburgh	Hull	Reading
1999	Sheffield	Newport	Isle of Wight	Arena-Essex
2000	Sheffield	Isle of Wight	Swindon	Berwick
2001	Workington	Newcastle	Sheffield	Isle of Wight
2002	Berwick	Arena-Essex	Newport	Hull
2003	Swindon	Trelawny	Newport	Glasgow

CONFERENCE LEAGUE RIDERS' CHAMPIONSHIP
30 AUGUST, RYE HOUSE

1st	Barrie Evans
2nd	Jamie Robertson
3rd	Trevor Harding
4th	Joel Parsons

	QUALIFYING SCORES					TOTAL
Barrie Evans	3	3	3	2	3	14
Jamie Robertson	3	2	2	3	1	11
Trevor Harding	1	3	2	1	3	10
Joel Parsons	R	2	3	3	2	10
Tom Brown	3	0	2	2	3	10
Craig Branney	2	3	3	2	X	10
Rob Finlow	2	1	0	3	3	9
Chris Mills	2	3	1	3	0	9
Richard Hall	0	2	2	2	2	8
James Brundle	0	2	1	1	2	6
James Wright	1	1	1	1	2	6
Joe Cook	3	X	0	-	-	3
Tommy Allen	2	1	X	-	-	3
Ben Powell	R	1	M	1	1	3
Mark Burrows	X	R	3	F	R	3
Danny Norton	1	R	0	0	1	2
Dean Garrod (res)	1	0	-	-	-	1
Gordon Meakins (res)	0	1	-	-	-	1

RACE DETAILS

Heat one: Tom Brown, Chris Mills, Trevor Harding, Richard Hall.

Heat two: Barrie Evans, Craig Branney, Joel Parsons (ret), Ben Powell (ret).

Heat three: Jamie Robertson, Tommy Allen, James Wright, James Brundle.

Heat four: (Rerun) Joe Cook, Rob Finlow, Danny Norton, Mark Burrows (f, ex).

Heat five: (Rerun) Chris Mills, Joel Parsons, Tommy Allen, Joe Cook (f, ex).

Heat six: Craig Branney, Richard Hall, James Wright, Mark Burrows (ret).

Heat seven: Barrie Evans, Jamie Robertson, Rob Finlow, Tom Brown.

Heat eight: Trevor Harding, James Brundle, Ben Powell, Danny Norton (ret).

Heat nine: Craig Branney, Jamie Robertson, Chris Mills, Danny Norton.

Heat ten: Joel Parsons, Richard Hall, James Brundle, Rob Finlow.

Heat eleven: (Rerun twice) Mark Burrows, Tom Brown, Dean Garrod, Tommy Allen (f, ex), Ben Powell (ex, two mins.).

Heat twelve: Barrie Evans, Trevor Harding, James Wright, Joe Cook.

Heat thirteen: Chris Mills, Barrie Evans, James Brundle, Mark Burrows (fell).

Heat fourteen: Jamie Robertson, Richard Hall, Ben Powell, Joe Cook.

Heat fifteen: Joel Parsons, Tom Brown, James Wright, Danny Norton.

Heat sixteen: Rob Finlow, Craig Branney, Trevor Harding, Gordon Meakins.

Heat seventeen: Rob Finlow, James Wright, Ben Powell, Chris Mills.

Heat eighteen: Barrie Evans, Richard Hall, Danny Norton, Dean Garrod.

Heat nineteen: (Rerun) Tom Brown, James Brundle, Gordon Meakins, Craig Branney (ex, dislodged kickboard).

Heat twenty: Trevor Harding, Joel Parsons, Jamie Robertson, Mark Burrows (ret).

3rd-Place Run-Off: (Rerun) Trevor Harding, Joel Parsons, Tom Brown (f, rem), Craig Branney (f, ex).

ROLL OF HONOUR

NOTE: Previously also known as Division Three Riders' Championship (1994), Academy League Riders' Championship (1995) and Amateur League Riders' Championship (1997).

YEAR	FIRST	SECOND	THIRD
1994	Andy Howe	Kevin Little	Colin Earl
1995	Kevin Little	Chris Cobby	André Compton
YEAR	FIRST	SECOND	THIRD
1996	Mike Hampson	Justin Elkins	Graeme Gordon
1997	Jon Armstrong	Bobby Eldridge	David Howe
1998	Steve Bishop	Andrew Appleton	Seemond Stephens
1999	Jonathan Swales	Steve Camden	Scott Courtney
2000	Scott Pegler	Steve Bishop	Adam Allott
2001	David Mason	Scott Pegler	Simon Wolstenholme
2002	James Birkinshaw	Edward Kennett	Jamie Robertson
2003	Barrie Evans	Jamie Robertson	Trevor Harding

PREMIER LEAGUE RIDERS' CHAMPIONSHIP
28 SEPTEMBER, SHEFFIELD

1st	Sean Wilson
2nd	Adam Shields
3rd	Carl Stonehewer
4th	Craig Watson

	QUALIFYING SCORES					TOTAL
Carl Stonehewer	3	3	3	3	3	15
Adam Shields	3	3	3	2	3	14
Sean Wilson	3	2	3	3	1	12
Craig Watson	2	3	2	2	2	11
Chris Harris	R	2	3	1	3	9
Garry Stead	2	0	2	3	2	9
Shane Parker	3	0	0	3	2	8
Kenneth Bjerre	1	3	0	2	1	7
Frede Schott	2	2	1	1	1	7
Joonas Kylmakorpi	1	1	1	0	3	6
Michal Makovsky	1	2	2	0	1	6
Paul Fry	F	1	1	1	2	5
Andrew Appleton	1	1	2	1	0	5
Mark Lemon	2	1	0	R	0	3
Jan Staechmann	0	X	1	2	0	3
James Grieves	0	0	0	0	0	0

RACE DETAILS

Heat one: Shane Parker, Garry Stead, Michal Makovsky, Jan Staechmann.

Heat two: Sean Wilson, Craig Watson, Joonas Kylmakorpi, Chris Harris (ret).

Heat three: Adam Shields, Mark Lemon, Kenneth Bjerre, James Grieves.

Heat four: Carl Stonehewer, Frede Schott, Andrew Appleton, Paul Fry (fell).

Heat five: Craig Watson, Michal Makovsky, Andrew Appleton, James Grieves.

Heat six: Carl Stonehewer, Sean Wilson, Mark Lemon, Shane Parker.

Heat seven: Kenneth Bjerre, Chris Harris, Paul Fry, Garry Stead.

Heat eight: (Rerun) Adam Shields, Frede Schott, Joonas Kylmakorpi, Jan Staechmann (f, ex).

Heat nine: Sean Wilson, Michal Makovsky, Frede Schott, Kenneth Bjerre.

Heat ten: Adam Shields, Craig Watson, Paul Fry, Shane Parker.

Heat eleven: Carl Stonehewer, Garry Stead, Joonas Kylmakorpi, James Grieves.

Heat twelve: Chris Harris, Andrew Appleton, Jan Staechmann, Mark Lemon.

Heat thirteen: Carl Stonehewer, Adam Shields, Chris Harris, Michal Makovsky.

Heat fourteen: Shane Parker, Kenneth Bjerre, Andrew Appleton, Joonas Kylmakorpi.

Heat fifteen: Garry Stead, Craig Watson, Frede Schott, Mark Lemon (ret).

Heat sixteen: Sean Wilson, Jan Staechmann, Paul Fry, James Grieves.

Heat seventeen: Joonas Kylmakorpi, Paul Fry, Michal Makovsky, Mark Lemon.

Heat eighteen: Chris Harris, Shane Parker, Frede Schott, James Grieves.

Heat nineteen: Adam Shields, Garry Stead, Sean Wilson, Andrew Appleton.

Heat twenty: Carl Stonehewer, Craig Watson, Kenneth Bjerre, Jan Staechmann.

Semi-Final: Sean Wilson, Craig Watson, Garry Stead, Chris Harris (fell).

Final: Sean Wilson, Adam Shields, Carl Stonehewer, Craig Watson.

ROLL OF HONOUR

NOTE:: Became known as the Premier League Riders' Championship in 1997, having previously been known as Division Two Riders' Championship (1968-74 and 1991-94) and National League Riders' Championship (1975-90).

YEAR	FIRST	SECOND	THIRD
1968	Graham Plant	Ken Eyre	Graeme Smith
1969	Geoff Ambrose	Mick Bell	Ross Gilbertson
1970	Dave Jessup	Barry Crowson	Gary Peterson
1971	John Louis	Malcolm Shakespeare	Hugh Saunders
1972	Phil Crump	Arthur Price	Bob Coles
1973	Arthur Price	Bobby McNeil	Lou Sansom
1974	Carl Glover	Ted Hubbard	Phil Herne
1975	Laurie Etheridge	Brian Collins	Arthur Browning
1976	Joe Owen	John Jackson	Ted Hubbard
1977	Colin Richardson	Martin Yeates	Tom Owen
1978	Steve Koppe	John Jackson	Ted Hubbard
1979	Ian Gledhill	Steve Wilcock	Andy Grahame
1980	Wayne Brown	Martin Yeates	Steve Finch
1981	Mike Ferreira	Simon Wigg	Bruce Cribb
1982	Joe Owen	Steve Lomas	Bob Garrad
1983	Steve McDermott	Richard Knight	Martin Yeates

YEAR	FIRST	SECOND	THIRD
1984	Ian Barney	Dave Perks	Martin Yeates
1985	Neil Middleditch	Kevin Hawkins	Trevor Banks
1986	Paul Thorp	Steve Schofield	Les Collins
1987	Andrew Silver	Nigel Crabtree	David Blackburn
1988	Troy Butler	Mark Loram	Kenny McKinna
1989	Mark Loram	Kenny McKinna	David Blackburn
1990	Andy Grahame	Chris Louis	Craig Boyce
1991	Jan Staechmann	David Bargh	Troy Butler
1992	Robert Nagy	Mick Poole	Richard Green
1993	Gary Allan	Mick Poole	Tony Langdon
1994	Paul Bentley	Tony Olsson	Tony Langdon
1995-96	*Not Staged*		
1997	Peter Carr	Glenn Cunningham	Robert Eriksson
1998	Glenn Cunningham	Carl Stonehewer	Peter Carr
1999	Sean Wilson	Jesper Olsen	Craig Watson
2000	Carl Stonehewer	Peter Carr	Paul Pickering
2001	Carl Stonehewer	Sean Wilson	Bjarne Pedersen
2002	Adam Shields	Craig Watson	Phil Morris
2003	Sean Wilson	Adam Shields	Carl Stonehewer

CONFERENCE LEAGUE FOUR-TEAM CHAMPIONSHIP
5 OCTOBER, MILDENHALL

1st	Rye House
2nd	Mildenhall
3rd	Peterborough
4th	Boston

FINAL

Rye House 30

					TOTAL
Barrie Evans	3	1	3	1	8
Joel Parsons	3	X	R	3	6
Steve Boxall	2	2	3	2	9
Luke Bowen	2	1	2	2	7

Mildenhall 29

Nick Simmons	2	3	1	X	6
Wayne Broadhurst	2	3	2	X	7
James Brundle	0	X	–	–	0
Paul Lee	3	2	3	3	11
Matthew Wright (res)	2	3	–	–	5

Peterborough 19

					TOTAL
Daniel King	1	X	1	3	5
Jason King	3	3	3	F	9
Danny Norton	1	0	0	–	1
James Horton	1	0	2	–	3
Richie Dennis (res)	X	1	–	–	1

Boston 14

Darren Mallett	1	2	1	2	6
Mark Thompson	0	1	1	2	4
Luke Clifton	0	–	–	–	0
Peter Boast	X	0	R	0	0
Roger Dickerson (res)	3	0	1	–	4

RACE DETAILS

Heat one: Paul Lee, Luke Bowen, Daniel King, Mark Thompson.

Heat two: Jason King, Steve Boxall, Darren Mallett, James Brundle.

Heat three: (Rerun three times) Barrie Evans, Wayne Broadhurst, James Horton, Luke Clifton.

Heat four: (Rerun) Joel Parsons, Nick Simmons, Danny Norton, Peter Boast (f, ex).

Heat five: Jason King, Paul Lee, Barrie Evans, Peter Boast.

Heat six: (Rerun twice – awarded) Roger Dickerson, Daniel King (f, ex), Joel Parsons (f, ex), James Brundle (f, ex), No Time.

Heat seven: Wayne Broadhurst, Darren Mallett, Luke Bowen, Danny Norton.

Heat eight: Nick Simmons, Steve Boxall, Mark Thompson, James Horton.

Heat nine: Paul Lee, James Horton, Darren Mallett, Joel Parsons (ret).

Heat ten: (Rerun) Barrie Evans, James Wright, Mark Thompson, Richie Dennis (ex, foul riding).

Heat eleven: Steve Boxall, Wayne Broadhurst, Daniel King, Peter Boast (ret).

Heat twelve: Jason King, Luke Bowen, Nick Simmons, Roger Dickerson.

Heat thirteen: (Rerun) Matthew Wright, Luke Bowen, Richie Dennis, Peter Boast.

Heat fourteen: Paul Lee, Steve Boxall, Roger Dickerson, Danny Norton.

Heat fifteen: (Rerun) Joel Parsons, Mark Thompson, Jason King (fell), Wayne Broadhurst (f, ex).

Heat sixteen: (Rerun) Daniel King, Darren Mallett, Barrie Evans, Nick Simmons (f, ex).

ROLL OF HONOUR

	FIRST	SECOND	THIRD	FOURTH
2003	Rye House	Mildenhall	Peterborough	Boston

ELITE LEAGUE RIDERS' CHAMPIONSHIP
18 OCTOBER COVENTRY

1st Lee Richardson
2nd Andreas Jonsson
3rd Scott Nicholls
4th Jason Crump

	QUALIFYING SCORES					TOTAL
Jason Crump	2	3	2	3	3	13
Scott Nicholls	3	0	3	3	2	11
Dean Barker	3	2	3	3	0	11
Lee Richardson	2	3	2	2	2	11
Andreas Jonsson	3	0	3	3	1	10
Billy Janniro	2	3	2	2	1	10
Mark Loram	3	1	1	0	3	8
Todd Wiltshire	1	2	1	1	2	7
Tony Rickardsson	0	2	3	1	0	6
Mikael Max	1	3	0	2	0	6
Leigh Adams	2	2	1	0	1	6
Peter Karlsson	0	1	0	1	3	5
Charlie Gjedde	0	1	2	2	0	5
Joe Screen	1	1	0	0	2	4
Jason Lyons	1	R	0	1	1	3
Chris Harris (res)	3	–	–	–	–	3
David Norris	R	0	1	R	–	1

RACE DETAILS

Heat one: Mark Loram, Lee Richardson, Joe Screen, Peter Karlsson.
Heat two: Scott Nicholls, Jason Crump, Jason Lyons, Tony Rickardsson.
Heat three: Andreas Jonsson, Leigh Adams, Mikael Max, David Norris (ret).
Heat four: Dean Barker, Billy Janniro, Todd Wiltshire, Charlie Gjedde.
Heat five: Jason Crump, Dean Barker, Mark Loram, David Norris.
Heat six: Billy Janniro, Leigh Adams, Joe Screen, Scott Nicholls.
Heat seven: Mikael Max, Todd Wiltshire, Peter Karlsson, Jason Lyons (ret).
Heat eight: Lee Richardson, Tony Rickardsson, Charlie Gjedde, Andreas Jonsson.
Heat nine: Scott Nicholls, Charlie Gjedde, Mark Loram, Mikael Max.
Heat ten: Andreas Jonsson, Jason Crump, Todd Wiltshire, Joe Screen.
Heat eleven: Tony Rickardsson, Billy Janniro, David Norris, Peter Karlsson.
Heat twelve: Dean Barker, Lee Richardson, Leigh Adams, Jason Lyons.
Heat thirteen: Andreas Jonsson, Billy Janniro, Jason Lyons, Mark Loram.
Heat fourteen: Dean Barker, Mikael Max, Tony Rickardsson, Joe Screen.
Heat fifteen: Jason Crump, Charlie Gjedde, Peter Karlsson, Leigh Adams.
Heat sixteen: Scott Nicholls, Lee Richardson, Todd Wiltshire, David Norris (ret).
Heat seventeen: Mark Loram, Todd Wiltshire, Leigh Adams, Tony Rickardsson.
Heat eighteen: Chris Harris, Joe Screen, Jason Lyons, Charlie Gjedde.
Heat nineteen: Peter Karlsson, Scott Nicholls, Andreas Jonsson, Dean Barker.
Heat twenty: Jason Crump, Lee Richardson, Billy Janniro, Mikael Max.
Semi-Final: Andreas Jonsson, Lee Richardson, Billy Janniro, Dean Barker.
Final: Lee Richardson, Andreas Jonsson, Scott Nicholls, Jason Crump (ret).

ROLL OF HONOUR

NOTE:: Became known as the Elite League Riders' Championship in 1997, having previously been known as British League Riders' Championship (1965-67 and 1975-90), Division One Riders' Championship (1968-74 and 1990-94) and Premier League Riders' Championship (1995-96).

YEAR	FIRST	SECOND	THIRD
1965	Barry Briggs	Jimmy Gooch	Cyril Maidment
1966	Barry Briggs	Olle Nygren	Norman Hunter
1967	Barry Briggs	Nigel Boocock	Ray Wilson
1968	Barry Briggs	Eric Boocock	Ivan Mauger
1969	Barry Briggs	Ivan Mauger	Jim Airey
1970	Barry Briggs	Anders Michanek	Eric Boocock
1971	Ivan Mauger	Barry Briggs	Jim McMillan
1972	Ole Olsen	Martin Ashby	Ronnie Moore
1973	Ivan Mauger	Ray Wilson	Anders Michanek
1974	Peter Collins	Ivan Mauger	Phil Crump
1975	Peter Collins	Phil Crump	Martin Ashby
1976	Ole Olsen	Peter Collins	John Louis
1977	Ole Olsen	Peter Collins	Michael Lee
1978	Ole Olsen	Peter Collins	Steve Bastable
1979	John Louis	Bruce Penhall	Michael Lee
1980	Les Collins	Bruce Penhall	Larry Ross
1981	Kenny Carter	Chris Morton	Shawn Moran
1982	Kenny Carter	Shawn Moran	Hans Nielsen
1983	Erik Gundersen	Michael Lee	Hans Nielsen
1984	Chris Morton	Hans Nielsen	Erik Gundersen
1985	Erik Gundersen	Peter Collins	Chris Morton
1986	Hans Nielsen	Erik Gundersen	Shawn Moran
1987	Hans Nielsen	Chris Morton	Kelly Moran
1988	Jan O. Pedersen	Erik Gundersen	Hans Nielsen
1989	Shawn Moran	Hans Nielsen	Brian Karger
1990	Hans Nielsen	Kelly Moran	Ronnie Correy
1991	Sam Ermolenko	Hans Nielsen	Joe Screen
1992	Joe Screen	Per Jonsson	Gary Havelock
1993	Per Jonsson	Henrik Gustafsson	Chris Louis
1994	Sam Ermolenko	Hans Nielsen	Martin Dugard
1995	Gary Havelock	Billy Hamill	Jason Crump
1996	Sam Ermolenko	Jason Crump	Leigh Adams
1997	Greg Hancock	Tony Rickardsson	Chris Louis
1998	Tony Rickardsson	Jason Crump	Joe Screen
1999	Jason Crump	Todd Wiltshire	Jason Lyons
2000	Ryan Sullivan	Greg Hancock	Nicki Pedersen
2001	Jason Crump	Scott Nicholls	Nicki Pedersen
2002	Tony Rickardsson	Nicki Pedersen	Jason Crump
2003	Lee Richardson	Andreas Jonsson	Scott Nicholls

GRAND PRIX 2003

GRAND PRIX 2003

	EUROPE	SWEDEN	BRITAIN	DENMARK	SLOVENIA	SWEDEN	CZECH REP.	POLAND	NORWAY	TOTAL
NICKI PEDERSEN	20	8	25	16	20	7	18	18	20	152
JASON CRUMP	11	5	20	25	11	16	25	20	11	144
TONY RICKARDSSON	25	13	18	20	13	6	20	6	6	127
LEIGH ADAMS	11	18	13	11	25	18	11	11	8	126
GREG HANCOCK	8	16	16	18	11	13	6	8	25	121
TOMASZ GOLLOB	16	8	3	13	16	11	8	25	11	111
SCOTT NICHOLLS	6	2	13	11	18	20	6	13	13	102
RUNE HOLTA	13	11	11	13	8	5	16	8	13	98
RYAN SULLIVAN	6	25	7	8	8	25	5	3	7	94
ANDREAS JONSSON	–	2	11	7	7	13	13	7	16	76
PIOTR PROTASIEWICZ	13	6	8	6	2	3	4	16	5	63
LUKAS DRYML	18	20	8	7	5	–	–	–	–	58
MIKAEL MAX	7	13	5	1	3	8	7	5	3	52
BJARNE PEDERSEN	2	7	4	5	–	3	8	4	18	51
TOMASZ BAJERSKI	4	11	7	6	13	5	2	1	2	51
LEE RICHARDSON	7	1	4	–	–	8	7	11	7	45
HANS N. ANDERSEN	3	4	–	–	–	11	11	6	6	41
MARK LORAM	5	–	–	–	7	4	4	7	5	32
TODD WILTSHIRE	2	5	5	2	1	6	3	3	3	30
JASON LYONS	1	6	2	8	3	2	1	2	4	29
PETER KARLSSON	1	3	6	4	6	–	2	4	2	28
BOHUMIL BRHEL	5	3	1	5	–	1	5	5	1	26
RONNI PEDERSEN	–	4	6	3	–	1	–	1	8	23
KRZYSZTOF CEGIELSKI	8	7	–	–	–	–	–	–	–	15
TOMAS TOPINKA	–	–	–	–	–	–	13	–	–	13
JAROSLAW HAMPEL	–	–	–	–	–	–	–	13	–	13
DAVID HOWE	–	–	2	–	6	–	–	–	–	8
PETER LJUNG	–	–	–	–	–	7	–	–	–	7
ROMAN POVAZHNY	–	–	–	2	4	–	–	–	–	6
MATEJ ZAGAR	–	–	–	–	5	–	–	–	–	5
SEBASTIAN ULAMEK	4	–	–	–	–	–	–	–	–	4
CHARLIE GJEDDE	–	–	–	4	–	–	–	–	–	4
IZAK SANTEJ	–	–	–	–	4	–	–	–	–	4
DAVID RUUD	–	–	–	–	–	4	–	–	–	4
LARS GUNNESTAD	–	–	–	–	–	–	–	–	4	4
RAFAL KURMANSKI	3	–	–	–	–	–	–	–	–	3
SIMON STEAD	–	–	3	–	–	–	–	–	–	3
ROBERT DADOS	–	–	–	3	–	–	–	–	–	3
ALES DRYML	–	–	–	–	–	–	3	–	–	3
JOONAS KYLMAKORPI	–	–	–	–	–	2	–	–	1	3
SANDOR TIHANYI	–	–	–	–	2	–	–	–	–	2
RAFAL SZOMBIERSKI	–	–	–	–	–	–	–	2	–	2
MAGNUS ZETTERSTROM	–	1	–	–	–	–	–	–	–	1
CHRIS HARRIS	–	–	1	–	–	–	–	–	–	1
JESPER B. JENSEN	–	–	–	1	–	–	–	–	–	1
DENIS STOJS	–	–	–	–	1	–	–	–	–	1
JOSEF FRANC	–	–	–	–	–	–	1	–	–	1

GRAND PRIX OF EUROPE (ROUND ONE)
17 MAY, SLASKI STADIUM, KATOWICE, POLAND

The ninth Grand Prix series got underway at Poland's Slaski Stadium, the scene of Peter Collins' great World Final triumph of 1976, and also the place where Ivan Mauger landed his record-breaking sixth World title in 1979. With five Championships to his name, it was somewhat ironic that this would be the place where Tony Rickardsson began his quest to equal the legendary Kiwi's achievement, and anyone who thought the phlegmatic Swede might be complacent was very much mistaken. To say he breezed through the meeting would be an understatement, as he charged to a twelfth GP victory, defeating Nicki Pedersen, Lukas Dryml and Tomasz Gollob in the grand final. Prior to that, the brilliant Swede had comfortably won his heat in the pre-main event, defeating Mikael Max and Leigh Adams, with Mark Loram being a non-starter, having been ruled out of action by the FIM jury. Although England's last World Champion was prepared to give it a go, in their wisdom, the jury decided he hadn't sufficiently recovered from the broken arm he sustained while riding for Eastbourne on 18 April. Anyway, that win took King Tony safely into the main event, and a routine heat-thirteen victory over Rune Holta, Ryan Sullivan (returning to action after a broken collarbone sustained just eleven days previously in a Swedish Elite League match at Gothenburg) and Scott Nicholls followed. Then, in heat nineteen, another wheel-perfect effort took the multi-Champion to the flag from Nicki Pedersen, Krzysztof Cegielski and Greg Hancock, with the second-placed Dane looking the most likely challenger to Tony R's crown on this evidence. Into the semi-final, and a super-fast getaway gave him his fourth straight win of the night, with Gollob, Piotr Protasiewicz and Adams trailing in his wake. Yes indeed, he was truly up for it, and the delight was there for everyone to see, etched all over his face on the presentation podium. Of the others, Nicki Pedersen recovered from a fourth-heat exclusion after fellow Dane and namesake Bjarne had come down on the fourth turn. Referee Tony Steele adjudged the Oxford racer to be the cause of his compatriot's fall, but the excluded rider immediately recovered his composure to take the fifth-heat eliminator, and never ran anything less than a second for the rest of the evening. Meanwhile, with a good night's work, Czech ace Dryml continued his rapid rise up the rankings, and he most definitely had the fastest straight-line speed throughout the meeting. Fourth-placed Gollob put together another fine display, including a good recovery when an early bath looked a possibility after a last place in heat twenty. The always-exciting Pole bounced back with a win in the very next race to keep the majority of the 30,000 crowd happy, looking resplendent in his all-new yellow and blue racing suit too!

PRE-MAIN EVENT
Heat one: Hans N. Andersen, Lee Richardson, Krzysztof Cegielski, Sebastian Ulamek (ret).
Heat two: Bohumil Brhel, Lukas Dryml, Rafal Kurmanski, Todd Wiltshire (ret).
Heat three: Rune Holta, Piotr Protasiewicz, Jason Lyons, Peter Karlsson.
Heat four: (Rerun) Tomasz Bajerski, Scott Nicholls, Bjarne Pedersen, Nicki Pedersen (ex, foul riding).
Heat five: Nicki Pedersen, Krzysztof Cegielski, Todd Wiltshire, Jason Lyons.
Heat six: Rafal Kurmanski, Sebastian Ulamek, Bjarne Pedersen, Peter Karlsson.
Heat seven: Scott Nicholls, Lukas Dryml, Hans N. Andersen, Rune Holta (ex, two mins.).
Heat eight: Piotr Protasiewicz, Bohumil Brhel, Tomasz Bajerski, Lee Richardson.

Heat nine: Tony Rickardsson, Mikael Max, Leigh Adams, Mark Loram (n.s.).

Heat ten: Tomasz Gollob, Greg Hancock, Jason Crump, Ryan Sullivan.

Heat eleven: (Rerun) Nicki Pedersen, Lee Richardson, Sebastian Ulamek, Hans N. Andersen (f, ex).

Heat twelve: Krzysztof Cegielski, Rune Holta, Tomasz Bajerski, Rafal Kurmanski.

MAIN EVENT

Heat thirteen: (Rerun) Tony Rickardsson, Rune Holta, Ryan Sullivan, Scott Nicholls.

Heat fourteen: Piotr Protasiewicz, Greg Hancock, Lee Richardson, Leigh Adams.

Heat fifteen: Krzysztof Cegielski, Jason Crump, Lukas Dryml, Mikael Max.

Heat sixteen: (Rerun) Tomasz Gollob, Nicki Pedersen, Bohumil Brhel, Mark Loram (n.s.).

Heat seventeen: Lukas Dryml, Leigh Adams, Ryan Sullivan, Mark Loram (n.s.).

Heat eighteen: Lee Richardson, Mikael Max, Scott Nicholls, Bohumil Brhel (ret).

Heat nineteen: Tony Rickardsson, Nicki Pedersen, Krzysztof Cegielski, Greg Hancock.

Heat twenty: Jason Crump, Piotr Protasiewicz, Rune Holta, Tomasz Gollob.

Heat twenty-one: Tomasz Gollob, Lukas Dryml, Krzysztof Cegielski, Mikael Max.

Heat twenty-two: Rune Holta, Leigh Adams, Greg Hancock, Lee Richardson.

SEMI-FINALS

Heat twenty-three: Tony Rickardsson, Tomasz Gollob, Piotr Protasiewicz, Leigh Adams.

Heat twenty-four: Nicki Pedersen, Lukas Dryml, Rune Holta, Jason Crump.

GRAND FINAL

Heat twenty-five: Tony Rickardsson, Nicki Pedersen, Lukas Dryml, Tomasz Gollob.

NOTE: Eliminated riders are underlined throughout

GRAND PRIX OF SWEDEN (ROUND TWO)
31 MAY, MOTOR STADIUM, AVESTA

The second GP of the 2003 series was scheduled to take place at the Olympic Stadium in Stockholm; however, with public-sector workers on strike in many Swedish communities, including the capital, a late change saw the meeting switched to the Avesta home of Masarna, coincidentally Tony Rickardsson's team! Having aggravated his collarbone injury in an Elite League match at Peterborough just five days beforehand, Ryan Sullivan bounced back with a performance of bravery and spirit to claim his third Grand Prix success in a rerun final, ahead of the fast-emerging Lukas Dryml and the always-there-or-thereabouts Leigh Adams. The first attempt to run the race had seen Greg Hancock excluded for unfair riding after driving inside Adams on the pits bend, with both the Aussie and Dryml going down. Prior to that, 'Flyin' Ryan' had first taken to the track in heat four, when he rode well to go from fourth to second in a race that also saw British hope Lee Richardson crash heavily. The Englishman battled on in the fifth-heat eliminator, but a last-place finish saw him head out with just a single GP point to his name. Sullivan marched on in heat seven, when he brilliantly swept around Hancock for a fine win, and sailed into the main event. Jason Crump is always a leading GP contender, but his night went awry in heat sixteen, when he was beset by mechanical gremlins and ran a last. His participation ended abruptly in the next race, when he again finished at the rear, behind Rune Holta, Mikael Max and Bjarne Pedersen. So, what of Tony Rickardsson? Well, the World number one was a routine winner of heats nine and thirteen, with a further success following in heat nineteen over Adams, surprise-package Tomasz Bajerski, and Max. That saw him safely through to the semi-final stage, and he was joined by Sullivan after an epic heat-twenty effort took the determined Australian to the flag, having sensationally passed all three of his opponents in Holta, Dryml and Hancock. The latter American continued on, along with the thrilling Bajerski, in heat twenty-one, with Max and Dryml doing likewise over the next four thunderous laps. That was the race which put paid to Gollob's hopes, but not before the brilliant Pole had produced another of his full-throttle daredevil specials, only to face an earlier than hoped for exit, having finished in third spot. There was a shock in the first semi-final, when Hancock and Dryml got the drop on Rickardsson, and despite the Swede's frantic efforts, he was unable to get on terms. The other semi-final saw Sullivan charge away to win, while Adams shone brightly to pass both Bajerski and Max for a place in the final. All in all, it added up to an excellent Grand Prix, at what was a stand-in venue, the outcome leaving the overall standings nicely poised with both Rickardsson and Dryml heading the way on thirty-eight points apiece.

PRE-MAIN EVENT

Heat one: Greg Hancock, Tomasz Bajerski, Bohumil Brhel, Magnus Zetterstrom.

Heat two: Krzysztof Cegielski, Hans N. Andersen, Ronni Pedersen, Peter Karlsson.

Heat three: (Rerun) Mikael Max, Todd Wiltshire, Andreas Jonsson, Scott Nicholls (ex, tapes).

Heat four: Bjarne Pedersen, Ryan Sullivan, Jason Lyons, Lee Richardson (fell).

Heat five: Bohumil Brhel, Peter Karlsson, Andreas Jonsson, Lee Richardson.

Heat six: Jason Lyons, Ronni Pedersen, Scott Nicholls, Magnus Zetterstrom.

Heat seven: Ryan Sullivan, Greg Hancock, Mikael Max, Hans N. Andersen.

Heat eight: Krzysztof Cegielski, Bjarne Pedersen, Todd Wiltshire, Tomasz Bajerski.

Heat nine: Tony Rickardsson, Leigh Adams, Tomasz Gollob, Rune Holta.

Heat ten: (Rerun) Jason Crump, Lukas Dryml, Piotr Protasiewicz, Nicki Pedersen (ex, tapes).

Heat eleven: Mikael Max, Tomasz Bajerski, Ronni Pedersen, Bohumil Brhel.

Heat twelve: Jason Lyons, Todd Wiltshire, Hans N. Andersen, Peter Karlsson.

MAIN EVENT

Heat thirteen: Tony Rickardsson, Ryan Sullivan, Nicki Pedersen, Todd Wiltshire.

Heat fourteen: Lukas Dryml, Tomasz Bajerski, Tomasz Gollob, Krzysztof Cegielski.

Heat fifteen: Leigh Adams, Greg Hancock, Piotr Protasiewicz, Jason Lyons.

Heat sixteen: Rune Holta, Mikael Max, Bjarne Pedersen, Jason Crump.

Heat seventeen: Nicki Pedersen, Krzysztof Cegielski, Piotr Protasiewicz, Jason Crump.

Heat eighteen: Tomasz Gollob, Bjarne Pedersen, Jason Lyons, Todd Wiltshire.

Heat nineteen: Tony Rickardsson, Leigh Adams, Tomasz Bajerski, Mikael Max.

Heat twenty: Ryan Sullivan, Rune Holta, Lukas Dryml, Greg Hancock.

Heat twenty-one: Greg Hancock, Tomasz Bajerski, Nicki Pedersen, Bjarne Pedersen.

Heat twenty-two: Mikael Max, Lukas Dryml, Tomasz Gollob, Krzysztof Cegielski.

SEMI-FINALS

Heat 23: Greg Hancock, Lukas Dryml, Tony Rickardsson, Rune Holta.

Heat 24: Ryan Sullivan, Leigh Adams, Mikael Max, Tomasz Bajerski.

GRAND FINAL

Heat 25: (Rerun) Ryan Sullivan, Lukas Dryml, Leigh Adams, Greg Hancock (ex, foul riding).

NOTE: Eliminated riders are underlined throughout

GRAND PRIX OF GREAT BRITAIN (ROUND THREE)
14 JUNE, MILLENNIUM STADIUM, CARDIFF

The sun was beating down, and it was another speedway carnival-style day in Cardiff, with an official crowd of 36,676 converging on the magical Millennium Stadium for a third dose of 'Theatre Speedway'. There was great news too, as a further three-year deal had been struck to continue at the venue until 2006. British 'young-guns' David Howe and Simon Stead were the grateful recipients of wildcards, with Chris Harris also joining the action as a replacement for unfortunate injury victim Hans N. Andersen. In a meeting which included no less than three Pedersens, it was Nicki who again looked the man most likely to push Tony Rickardsson for the crown. The Dane started well, with an 'all the way' win from Jason Crump in the second heat, but he then faced an eliminator after Peter Karlsson had brilliantly swooped around him and Andreas Jonsson in the eighth race. The action was fast and furious as the colourful kevlar-clad gladiators left the traps in heat twelve, and referee Mick Posselwhite had a difficult decision to make when excluding Tomasz Gollob following Ronni Pedersen's first-bend tumble. The three Pedersens came to the line for the restart, and Ronni's brother Nicki remained cool to take the flag after shaking off the close attentions of both his sibling and the unrelated Bjarne on the opening lap. Into the main event, Nicki P's next outing occurred in race fifteen, when he unceremoniously bit the dust in the tussle for first-bend supremacy. Mercifully, the meeting official allowed a full quota of participants back for an exciting rerun, in which Crump surged from behind to win, while Leigh Adams eventually secured second spot after trading places with Pedersen. That left the gritty Dane facing another 'trapdoor' race in heat seventeen, but he again emerged with flying colours to cross the line ahead of Lukas Dryml, brother Ronni, and Mikael Max. Prior to that, Rickardsson had entered the fray in heat nine, only to suffer the ignominy of a tapes exclusion. The Swede was back at his best next time out, however, sprinting to victory from Scott Nicholls in heat sixteen, and he followed it up with a twentieth-race win over the impressive Rune Holta. The next heat brought Pedersen back into the limelight, and a good second place behind the fast-starting Greg Hancock took him and the American into the semis. Heat twenty-two resulted in a win for Jonsson over Adams, with pre-meeting joint-leader Dryml heading out, along with all-action Pole Tomasz Bajerski. World Champion of 1997 Hancock duly grabbed a place in the final with a win from Crump, as Adams and Holta headed for the dressing room. An incident-packed second semi-final then required three attempts before being resolved, the first running ending abruptly as Rickardsson was thrown from his steed, with Jonsson adjudged to be at fault. The rerun only lasted slightly longer, before Nicholls hit one of the ruts that had appeared in the one-off 280-metre circuit, and inadvertently sent Pedersen thudding into the safety fence. With just two battered and bruised speedsters left, it was a stroll into the final for Pedersen and Rickardsson as the race was eventually completed. Pedersen, incidentally making his twelfth start of the evening due to a plethora of reruns, powered to victory from the inside grid in the final, while all interest centred on the intriguing battle behind. Crump finally got the better of a ding-dong scrap for second place, while Rickardsson edged out Hancock for third spot. As in 2001 and 2002, the atmosphere at Cardiff was electric, with the result leaving Rickardsson at the head of the pile on fifty-six points, just three ahead of deserved British-GP victor Nicki Pedersen.

PRE-MAIN EVENT

Heat one: Todd Wiltshire, Simon Stead, Chris Harris, Tomasz Gollob.

Heat two: Nicki Pedersen, Jason Crump, Bohumil Brhel, David Howe.

Heat three: Scott Nicholls, Peter Karlsson, Lee Richardson, Jason Lyons.

Heat four: (Rerun) Andreas Jonsson, Bjarne Pedersen, Piotr Protasiewicz, Ronni Pedersen.

Heat five: Lee Richardson, Ronni Pedersen, David Howe, Chris Harris (fell).

Heat six: Tomasz Gollob, Piotr Protasiewicz, Jason Lyons, Bohumil Brhel (ret).

Heat seven: Todd Wiltshire, Jason Crump, Scott Nicholls, Bjarne Pedersen.

Heat eight: Peter Karlsson, Andreas Jonsson, Nicki Pedersen, Simon Stead.

Heat nine: (Rerun) Tomasz Bajerski, Ryan Sullivan, Greg Hancock, Tony Rickardsson (ex, tapes).

Heat ten: Mikael Max, Lukas Dryml, Leigh Adams, Rune Holta (ret).

Heat eleven: Scott Nicholls, Piotr Protasiewicz, Lee Richardson, Simon Stead.

Heat twelve: (Rerun) Nicki Pedersen, Ronni Pedersen, Bjarne Pedersen, Tomasz Gollob (ex, foul riding).

MAIN EVENT

Heat thirteen: (Rerun) Tomasz Bajerski, Rune Holta, Ronni Pedersen, Todd Wiltshire (f, ex).

Heat fourteen: Greg Hancock, Piotr Protasiewicz, Peter Karlsson, Lukas Dryml.

Heat fifteen: (Rerun) Jason Crump, Leigh Adams, Nicki Pedersen, Ryan Sullivan.

Heat sixteen: Tony Rickardsson, Scott Nicholls, Andreas Jonsson, Mikael Max.

Heat seventeen: Nicki Pedersen, Lukas Dryml, Ronni Pedersen, Mikael Max.

Heat eighteen: Andreas Jonsson, Ryan Sullivan, Peter Karlsson, Todd Wiltshire.

Heat nineteen: Jason Crump, Scott Nicholls, Piotr Protasiewicz, Tomasz Bajerski.

Heat twenty: Tony Rickardsson, Rune Holta, Leigh Adams, Greg Hancock.

Heat twenty-one: Greg Hancock, Nicki Pedersen, Piotr Protasiewicz, Ryan Sullivan.

Heat twenty-two: Andreas Jonsson, Leigh Adams, Lukas Dryml, Tomasz Bajerski.

SEMI-FINALS

Heat twenty-three: Greg Hancock, Jason Crump, Leigh Adams, Rune Holta.

Heat twenty-four: (Rerun twice) Nicki Pedersen, Tony Rickardsson, Scott Nicholls (ex, foul riding), Andreas Jonsson (ex, foul riding).

GRAND FINAL

Heat twenty-five: Nicki Pedersen, Jason Crump, Tony Rickardsson, Greg Hancock.

NOTE: Eliminated riders are underlined throughout

GRAND PRIX OF DENMARK (ROUND FOUR)
28 JUNE, PARKEN, COPENHAGEN

The GP roadshow moved on to Denmark, with the event being staged for the first time at Parken – a magnificent smaller version of Cardiff's Millennium Stadium. The change of venue from Vojens, which had been used for all of the previous eight Danish Grand Prix, clearly went down well with the speedway public, as 24,280 good folk filed through the Parken entrance gates. Having appeared a little subdued at the first two rounds of the season, Jason Crump had looked more like himself at Cardiff, and he kept the momentum going in Copenhagen to record the seventh GP win of his career. Much was naturally expected from the home contingent, but wildcard entrant Jesper B. Jensen literally fell by the wayside in heat five, to be followed by fellow wildcard man and Grand Prix debut-maker Charlie Gjedde in heat eleven, with Ronni Pedersen departing the scene after crashing in the very next race. When namesake Bjarne Pedersen became the next home man to go in heat seventeen, it left just Ronni's younger brother Nicki to do battle at the sharp end of the meeting. Crump showed little sign of what was to come, when he started with a third-place finish behind Rune Holta and the redoubtable Tony Rickardsson in heat ten. The gritty Australian really got going in heat fifteen however, winning all the way from Greg Hancock, while Tomasz Gollob occupied third spot after trading places with Jason Lyons, before almost snatching the runner-up position in a last-ditch sprint for the line. Crump next appeared in heat nineteen, but he was unable to do anything bar follow lone-British contestant Scott Nicholls and fellow Australian Leigh Adams home. That meant facing an eliminator next time out in heat twenty-one, but he showed his mettle to scorch away from the inside grid and defeat Hancock, with Lyons and the fallen Lukas Dryml exiting the scene. Safely through to the semi-finals, Crump competed in the first one, which had to be rerun after Nicholls had hit the deck. Gollob was leading Crump at the time of Nicholls' fall, and was clearly none too pleased that he had to do it all again. The Pole's displeasure was even more obvious when he missed out at the second attempt, Crump taking the flag ahead of home-favourite Nicki Pedersen. The other semi went the way of Rickardsson, and, with Hancock getting ahead of Holta and Adams in the early stages, it amazingly meant the exact same four speedsters would contest the final as at Cardiff! The question was, would they all finish in the same order again? Obviously, the Danes hoped it would be another win for Nicki P, but the intense pressure finally got to their man, as he lunged into the tapes for a shattering exclusion. After seeing off the close attentions of Rickardsson through the first corner, Crump sped to victory in the restart, leaving the Swede to mop-up second place and take his total to seventy-six points in the overall standings. That increased his lead to seven points over the unfortunate Pedersen, while Crump enhanced his chances no end, jumping up to third position with a tally of sixty-one.

PRE-MAIN EVENT
Heat one: (Rerun) Lukas Dryml, Bjarne Pedersen, Robert Dados, Charlie Gjedde.
Heat two: Piotr Protasiewicz, Tomasz Gollob, Todd Wiltshire, Jesper B. Jensen.
Heat three: Ryan Sullivan, Jason Lyons, Roman Povazhny, Peter Karlsson.
Heat four: Tomasz Bajerski, Bohumil Brhel, Mikael Max, Ronni Pedersen (f, rem).
Heat five: (Rerun twice) Robert Dados, Ronni Pedersen, Roman Povazhny (f, ex), Jesper B. Jensen (f, ex).
Heat six: Peter Karlsson, Charlie Gjedde, Todd Wiltshire, Mikael Max.

Heat seven: Lukas Dryml, Tomasz Gollob, Ryan Sullivan, Bohumil Brhel.

Heat eight: (Rerun) Piotr Protasiewicz, Bjarne Pedersen, Jason Lyons, Tomasz Bajerski.

Heat nine: Nicki Pedersen, Greg Hancock, Leigh Adams, Andreas Jonsson.

Heat ten: Rune Holta, Tony Rickardsson, Jason Crump, Scott Nicholls.

Heat eleven: Ryan Sullivan, Tomasz Bajerski, Charlie Gjedde, Robert Dados.

Heat twelve: (Rerun) Jason Lyons, Bohumil Brhel, Peter Karlsson, Ronni Pedersen (f, ex).

MAIN EVENT

Heat thirteen: (Rerun) Scott Nicholls, Nicki Pedersen, Lukas Dryml, Bohumil Brhel (f, ex).

Heat fourteen: Tony Rickardsson, Leigh Adams, Piotr Protasiewicz, Tomasz Bajerski.

Heat fifteen: Jason Crump, Greg Hancock, Tomasz Gollob, Jason Lyons.

Heat sixteen: Ryan Sullivan, Rune Holta, Andreas Jonsson, Bjarne Pedersen.

Heat seventeen: Lukas Dryml, Tomasz Gollob, Tomasz Bajerski, Bjarne Pedersen.

Heat eighteen: Andreas Jonsson, Jason Lyons, Piotr Protasiewicz, Bohumil Brhel.

Heat nineteen: Scott Nicholls, Leigh Adams, Jason Crump, Rune Holta.

Heat twenty: Tony Rickardsson, Nicki Pedersen, Ryan Sullivan, Greg Hancock.

Heat twenty-one: Jason Crump, Greg Hancock, Jason Lyons, Lukas Dryml (fell).

Heat twenty-two: Rune Holta, Tomasz Gollob, Ryan Sullivan, Andreas Jonsson.

SEMI-FINALS

Heat twenty-three: (Rerun) Jason Crump, Nicki Pedersen, Tomasz Gollob, Scott Nicholls (f, ex).

Heat twenty-four: Tony Rickardsson, Greg Hancock, Rune Holta, Leigh Adams.

GRAND FINAL

Heat twenty-five: (Rerun) Jason Crump, Tony Rickardsson, Greg Hancock, Nicki Pedersen (ex, tapes).

NOTE: Eliminated riders are underlined throughout

GRAND PRIX OF SLOVENIA (ROUND FIVE)
12 JULY, MATIJE GUBCA STADIUM, KRSKO

The GP series moved on to Slovenia, as the world's leading riders got back to a conventional race track in front of a crowd believed to be around the 10,000 mark. Having not raced since breaking an arm in April, the event marked the return of Britain's most recent World Champion Mark Loram and, considering his obvious rustiness, the Maltese-born racer put up a great show. However, the meeting centred around two Australians, namely Jason Crump and Leigh Adams. The former had thrown down the gauntlet by winning the previous round in Denmark, but his meeting was to end in heartbreak, when his steed ran out of fuel in the first semi-final, with a place in the last four beckoning. Adams, meanwhile, had only tasted victory in one previous Grand Prix (at Gothenburg in 2002), but he produced the goods when it mattered to become the fifth different winner in the five rounds thus far. The leading protagonists entered the fray in heat nine, when a rerun was called after a ferocious first turn. The restart saw Nicki Pedersen gain some unwanted grip on the second corner, and run into an unsuspecting Tomasz Gollob, sending the Pole hurtling into the fence. With Pedersen excluded, the race was finally completed as Crump led the battle-scarred Gollob home. The tenth heat brought Adams to the line and, despite being off gate four, he reacted quickly to outpace Tony Rickardsson and Greg Hancock for a fine win. Crump was back out in heat thirteen, and had to settle for a second-place finish behind the talented Tomasz Bajerski. Multi-World Champion Rickardsson was a clear winner of the next race, before heat fifteen ended in disaster for Lukas Dryml. The race saw Gollob leading from Hancock, when the chasing Czech ace was thrown down the home straight after his footrest had caught the airfence. It was a sickening incident, and Dryml was rushed off to hospital suffering from a broken nose and facial injuries. Gollob duly took the rerun from Hancock and Loram, with Adams then defeating Pedersen in a restarted heat sixteen, after Peter Karlsson had crashed out in the initial running. Bajerski led home his more illustrious Polish compatriot Gollob in heat nineteen, with Scott Nicholls keeping Pedersen at the rear. Then, in heat twenty, Hancock came from the outside grid to swoop around the pack on the first corner, and win with aplomb from Crump, Rickardsson and Adams. Heat twenty-one might have been an eliminator, but Adams didn't panic and a great ride saw him overhaul Rune Holta to follow Nicholls across the line for a place in the semis. Rickardsson then made sure of his place in the last eight, when a trademark start took him to victory from Pedersen. So, to that dramatic first semi-final, when Nicholls led from start to finish, while Crump worked his way past Bajerski and Pedersen, only to stop on the last lap. Gollob jetted to success in the other semi-final, with Adams holding second position throughout to eliminate both Rickardsson and Hancock. Amid great excitement, Adams made the gate from the inside to lead the final for three laps, before Pedersen darted through the smallest of gaps, and that seemed to be that. However, the Aussie sensationally cut-back, coming off the second bend, before outdriving the Dane up the back straight to take a deserved victory. Having passed the halfway mark, the result left Rickardsson and Pedersen level at the top of the chart on eighty-nine points apiece, with Adams in third place on seventy-eight, and Crump in fourth spot on seventy-two.

PRE-MAIN EVENT

Heat one: (Rerun) Ryan Sullivan, David Howe, Izak Santej, Peter Karlsson (ex, tapes).

Heat two: Matej Zagar, Jason Lyons, Denis Stojs, Todd Wiltshire.

Heat three: Lukas Dryml, Mark Loram, Mikael Max, Tomasz Bajerski.

Heat four: Andreas Jonsson, Roman Povazhny, Piotr Protasiewicz, Sandor Tihanyi.

Heat five: Mikael Max, Izak Santej, Sandor Tihanyi, Todd Wiltshire (ret).

Heat six: Tomasz Bajerski, Peter Karlsson, Piotr Protasiewicz, Denis Stojs (ret).

Heat seven: (Rerun) Ryan Sullivan, Lukas Dryml, Roman Povazhny, Jason Lyons (ex, tapes).

Heat eight: Matej Zagar, Andreas Jonsson, Mark Loram, David Howe.

Heat nine: (Rerun twice) Jason Crump, Tomasz Gollob, Scott Nicholls, Nicki Pedersen (ex, foul riding).

Heat ten: Leigh Adams, Tony Rickardsson, Greg Hancock, Rune Holta.

Heat eleven: Peter Karlsson, David Howe, Roman Povazhny, Mikael Max.

Heat twelve: Mark Loram, Tomasz Bajerski, Izak Santej, Jason Lyons.

MAIN EVENT

Heat thirteen: Tomasz Bajerski, Jason Crump, Ryan Sullivan, Rune Holta.

Heat fourteen: Tony Rickardsson, Scott Nicholls, David Howe, Matej Zagar.

Heat fifteen: (Rerun) Tomasz Gollob, Greg Hancock, Mark Loram, Lukas Dryml (f, ex).

Heat sixteen: (Rerun) Leigh Adams, Nicki Pedersen, Andreas Jonsson, Peter Karlsson (f, ex).

Heat seventeen: Mark Loram, Ryan Sullivan, Peter Karlsson, Matej Zagar.

Heat eighteen: Andreas Jonsson, Rune Holta, David Howe, Lukas Dryml (n.s.).

Heat nineteen: Tomasz Bajerski, Tomasz Gollob, Scott Nicholls, Nicki Pedersen.

Heat twenty: Greg Hancock, Jason Crump, Tony Rickardsson, Leigh Adams.

Heat twenty-one: Scott Nicholls, Leigh Adams, Rune Holta, Mark Loram.

Heat twenty-two: Tony Rickardsson, Nicki Pedersen, Ryan Sullivan, Andreas Jonsson.

SEMI-FINALS

Heat twenty-three: Scott Nicholls, Nicki Pedersen, Tomasz Bajerski, Jason Crump (ret).

Heat twenty-four: Tomasz Gollob, Leigh Adams, Tony Rickardsson, Greg Hancock.

GRAND FINAL

Heat twenty-five: Leigh Adams, Nicki Pedersen, Scott Nicholls, Tomasz Gollob.

NOTE: Eliminated riders are underlined throughout

GRAND PRIX OF SCANDINAVIA (ROUND SIX)
30 AUGUST, ULLEVI STADIUM, GOTHENBURG

After a six-week break, the GP series got back underway at the Ullevi Stadium on 23 August. Unfortunately, the event saw just three races completed as the man-made track became badly rutted and the competitors had great difficulty in simply remaining upright. Indeed, for such a prestigious meeting, it was incredible for the crowd of 26,250 (not to mention all those viewing on Sky television), to witness the cream of the sport two-wheeling around the turns. SVEMO, the Swedish federation, publicly accepted responsibility for the poor condition of the track, although there had been mitigating circumstances, including rainfall on the Thursday and Friday before the meeting. So the riders and supporters went home early, with the meeting quickly rescheduled to take place seven days later, when Ole Olsen and his team were brought in to rectify the racing circuit. To their credit, they did just that and the meeting went ahead satisfactorily, albeit before a greatly reduced audience of 12,130. Those present saw the title chase tighten-up dramatically, and at the end of it all there were three riders at the top of the pile all within a single point of each other, while several others still had a realistic shout of lifting the sport's premier prize. The evening itself belonged to flying Australian Ryan Sullivan, who took victory in the first and last races of the night to register the fourth GP success of his career. In between, Peterborough's ace in the pack posted a seventh heat win over Todd Wiltshire, ran a second to Leigh Adams in heat thirteen and a third behind Jason Crump and Scott Nicholls in heat twenty. Showing great composure, he then reeled off wins in heat twenty-two (from Greg Hancock) and in the second semi-final (ahead of Jason Crump) to claim a much-sought place in the showdown race. The final pitched Sullivan against Nicholls, Adams and Crump, but a super start and first turn took him clear of the opposition, with the resulting twenty-five points hauling him back into the title chase on the seventy-nine-point mark. For Crump, however, the final was a disaster as his machine barely left the gate, having suffered a broken rocker arm. It could have been a whole lot worse for the Belle Vue star, but in bagging sixteen precious points he still moved on to a total of eighty-eight, and in retaining fourth spot in the standings he was in just the right position to pounce should any of those above slip up in rounds seven to nine of the series. Making the most of Crump's misfortune, top Brit Nicholls held off Adams to finish a highly creditable second, with the twenty points earned taking him up to a total of seventy. Adams' third place meanwhile, gave him eighteen points and a share of the overall lead with Nicki Pedersen, their tally of ninety-six putting them just one ahead of previous leader Tony Rickardsson. For Pedersen, disappointment came in heat twenty-two, when the disadvantageous outside gate proved his downfall as he ran a last, thereby only collecting seven points. However, for Rickardsson it was simply one of those meetings best forgotten quickly, as he ran two lasts (in heats nine and sixteen), before a seventeenth race third place sent him through the dreaded exit door with just six points to his name. However, to be fair to the multi-Champion, he hadn't been 100 per cent fit since suffering concussion in a Swedish domestic meeting on 22 July, whilst riding for Masarna at Valsarna.

PRE-MAIN EVENT
Heat one: Ryan Sullivan, Bjarne Pedersen, Piotr Protasiewicz, Peter Ljung.
Heat two: Rune Holta, Todd Wiltshire, David Ruud, Jason Lyons.
Heat three: Mark Loram, Mikael Max, Hans N. Andersen, Joonas Kylmakorpi.
Heat four: Andreas Jonsson, Lee Richardson, Ronni Pedersen, Bohumil Brhel.
Heat five: Hans N. Andersen, Piotr Protasiewicz, Jason Lyons, Bohumil Brhel (ex, two mins).
Heat six: David Ruud, Peter Ljung, Joonas Kylmakorpi, Ronni Pedersen.
Heat seven: Ryan Sullivan, Todd Wiltshire, Mark Loram, Lee Richardson.
Heat eight: Rune Holta, Mikael Max, Andreas Jonsson, Bjarne Pedersen.
Heat nine: Leigh Adams, Tomasz Gollob, Greg Hancock, Tony Rickardsson.
Heat ten: Jason Crump, Scott Nicholls, Nicki Pedersen, Tomasz Bajerski.
Heat eleven: Peter Ljung, Hans N. Andersen, Mark Loram, Bjarne Pedersen (fell).
Heat twelve: Lee Richardson, Andreas Jonsson, David Ruud, Piotr Protasiewicz (ret).

MAIN EVENT
Heat thirteen: Leigh Adams, Ryan Sullivan, Andreas Jonsson, Tomasz Bajerski.
Heat fourteen: Scott Nicholls, Hans N. Andersen, Greg Hancock, Rune Holta.
Heat fifteen: Tomasz Gollob, Lee Richardson, Nicki Pedersen, Todd Wiltshire.
Heat sixteen: Jason Crump, Mikael Max, Peter Ljung, Tony Rickardsson.
Heat seventeen: Andreas Jonsson, Nicki Pedersen, Lee Richardson, Rune Holta.
Heat eighteen: Greg Hancock, Peter Ljung, Todd Wiltshire, Tomasz Bajerski.
Heat nineteen: Leigh Adams, Tomasz Gollob, Hans N. Andersen, Mikael Max.
Heat twenty: Jason Crump, Scott Nicholls, Ryan Sullivan, Lee Richardson (ret).
Heat twenty-one: Hans N. Andersen, Andreas Jonsson, Lee Richardson, Peter Ljung.
Heat twenty-two: Ryan Sullivan, Greg Hancock, Mikael Max, Nicki Pedersen.

SEMI-FINALS

Heat twenty-three: Leigh Adams, Scott Nicholls, Greg Hancock, Hans N. Andersen (fell).

Heat twenty-four: Ryan Sullivan, Jason Crump, Andreas Jonsson, Tomasz Gollob.

GRAND FINAL

Heat twenty-five: Ryan Sullivan, Scott Nicholls, Leigh Adams, Jason Crump (ret).

NOTE: Eliminated riders are <u>underlined</u> throughout

GRAND PRIX OF THE CZECH REPUBLIC (ROUND SEVEN)
6 SEPTEMBER, MARKETA STADIUM, PRAGUE

The world's top riders assembled in Prague for round seven, and on a conventional circuit at the Marketa Stadium they served up a spectacle that many folk felt was the best of the series thus far. It was real cut-and-thrust stuff, culminating in a leader board with just eight points dividing four title-chasing speedsters. It was Jason Crump who showed a typically high level of determination to defy another dose of misfortune and win on the night, thereby taking his overall tally of Grand Prix victories to eight. The Aussie began well in a rerun heat nine, after an over-anxious Greg Hancock had nudged the tapes and suffered exclusion at the hands of referee Tony Steele. The restart saw Crump race away to defeat his compatriot Ryan Sullivan, with Hans N. Andersen unchallenged in third spot. That moved 'Crumpie' forward to the first race of the Main Event, namely heat thirteen, and he made no mistake to finish ahead of reigning World Champion Tony Rickardsson, plus the British duo of Scott Nicholls and Lee Richardson. Everything seemed to be going along smoothly... that was until his next appearance in heat nineteen, when his clutch decided to malfunction and dragged him into the tapes. However, like the good 'un that he is, Crump bounced back in heat twenty-two, when he surged from the traps and pulled away to beat Nicki Pedersen, Tomasz Gollob and Mikael Max, the latter two heading out as a result. That saw him through to the second semi-final, when he emerged ahead from a closely-contested first bend and went on to inflict his second defeat of the meeting over Rickardsson, with the host country's exciting wildcard entrant Tomas Topinka holding out Leigh Adams for third place. That set up another showdown between Crump and Rickardsson in the final, but Belle Vue's main man, and indeed the number one rider in the entire Elite League averages, remained right in the groove as he got the drop and took command to again lead the Swede home, with Nicki Pedersen and the ever-improving Rune Holta in the third and fourth positions respectively. That gave Crump twenty-five GP points and took his overall tally to 113, but perhaps more significantly, he also carried forward to the last couple of rounds a psychological advantage over Rickardsson, having registered three straight successes in their races against each other. For Tony Rickardsson it wasn't an absolute disaster though, as he had been written off in some quarters after his showing in the Scandinavian Grand Prix, yet came back with a strong performance, and the twenty GP points gained took him back to the top of the tree on a total of 115. Breathing right down the Swede's neck, Nicki Pedersen was but a single digit behind, and just one ahead of Crump, after a characteristically full-blooded performance had left him in third place and earned him eighteen points. Clearly the series was set to go right to the wire between the main protagonists, not forgetting Adams, whose eleven points on the night took him up to 107 in total, just eight behind leader Rickardsson.

PRE-MAIN EVENT

Heat one: Mikael Max, Mark Loram, Tomasz Bajerski, Josef Franc.

Heat two: Rune Holta, Ales Dryml, Piotr Protasiewicz, Tomas Topinka.

Heat three: (Rerun) Bjarne Pedersen, Todd Wiltshire, Lee Richardson, Bohumil Brhel (f, ex).

Heat four: Nicki Pedersen, Tony Rickardsson, Peter Karlsson, Jason Lyons.

Heat five: Tomas Topinka, Lee Richardson, Tomasz Bajerski, Jason Lyons.

Heat six: Bohumil Brhel, Piotr Protasiewicz, Peter Karlsson, Josef Franc.

Heat seven: Tony Rickardsson, Mikael Max, Bjarne Pedersen, Ales Dryml.

Heat eight: Nicki Pedersen, Rune Holta, Mark Loram, Todd Wiltshire.

Heat nine: (Rerun) Jason Crump, Ryan Sullivan, Hans N. Andersen, Greg Hancock (ex, tapes).

Heat ten: Tomasz Gollob, Leigh Adams, Andreas Jonsson, Scott Nicholls.

Heat eleven: Bjarne Pedersen, Tomas Topinka, Piotr Protasiewicz, Todd Wiltshire (ret).

Heat twelve: Bohumil Brhel, Lee Richardson, Mark Loram, Ales Dryml.

MAIN EVENT

Heat thirteen: Jason Crump, Tony Rickardsson, Scott Nicholls, Lee Richardson.

Heat fourteen: Hans N. Andersen, Leigh Adams, Nicki Pedersen, Tomas Topinka.

Heat fifteen: (Rerun) Andreas Jonsson, Mikael Max, Ryan Sullivan, Bohumil Brhel (f, ex).

Heat sixteen: Rune Holta, Bjarne Pedersen, Greg Hancock, Tomasz Gollob.

Heat seventeen: Tomas Topinka, Tomasz Gollob, Scott Nicholls, Ryan Sullivan.

Heat eighteen: Nicki Pedersen, Lee Richardson, Greg Hancock, Bohumil Brhel.

Heat nineteen: (Rerun) Andreas Jonsson, Leigh Adams, Bjarne Pedersen, Jason Crump (ex, tapes).

Heat twenty: Tony Rickardsson, Rune Holta, Mikael Max, Hans N. Andersen.

Heat twenty-one: Hans N. Andersen, Tomas Topinka, Bjarne Pedersen, Lee Richardson.

Heat twenty-two: Jason Crump, Nicki Pedersen, Tomasz Gollob, Mikael Max.

SEMI-FINALS

Heat twenty-three: (Rerun) Rune Holta, Nicki Pedersen, Andreas Jonsson, Hans N. Andersen (ret).

Heat twenty-four: Jason Crump, Tony Rickardsson, Tomas Topinka, Leigh Adams.

GRAND FINAL

Heat twenty-five: Jason Crump, Tony Rickardsson, Nicki Pedersen, Rune Holta.

NOTE: Eliminated riders are underlined throughout

GRAND PRIX OF POLAND (ROUND EIGHT)
20 SEPTEMBER, POLONIA STADIUM, BYDGOSZCZ

With four riders in contention for the World Championship, combined with the brilliant Bydgoszcz raceway and Tomasz Gollob on his home patch, this eighth Grand Prix of the 2003 series had all the right ingredients to make it a classic. And that man Gollob certainly didn't disappoint his legion of partisan fans, producing a masterful display of five straight wins to post the eighth GP success of his career. The superstar Pole first entered the arena for heat nine, and amid an audible increase in volume from the packed terraces he swooped around Rune Holta on the opening lap, before charging away to win in style from the Norwegian, with the title-chasing Jason Crump surprisingly in third spot. That took Gollob straight through to the opening race of the Main Event (heat thirteen), and after drifting off-line on the first corner, a superb back-straight pass took him ahead of both Lee Richardson and Hans N. Andersen for his second success, with Bohumil Brhel eventually nicking third spot from the Dane. So the galloping Gollob moved on to heat nineteen when he again faced Crump, with Leigh Adams and Greg Hancock also thrown into the melting pot for good measure. This saw the Pole at his brilliant racing best after Hancock had got underneath him entering the back straight. Firstly, 'Atomic Tomasz' repelled a thrust from Adams, prior to decisively reeling in the American and charging past as they entered the last lap of the superb Bydgoszcz circuit. Sadly for Hancock, his machine faltered on the final turn, leaving Crump and Adams to fill the minor positions – Crump having earlier ousted his fellow countryman. The first semi-final brought Gollob face-to-face with compatriots Piotr Protasiewicz and newly-crowned World Under-21 Champion Jaroslaw Hampel, plus (for a second successive time) Adams. When the tapes lifted, wildcard entrant Hampel began strongly, only for Gollob to cruise by on the back straight for win number four. Meanwhile, after trading places, Protasiewicz and Hampel combined to make it a Polish 1-2-3, comfortably keeping Adams at the rear. While Gollob was on his charge to the final, the Championship protagonists going into this round – Tony Rickardsson, Nicki Pedersen and the previously mentioned Crump – had enjoyed a mix of fortunes. Rickardsson took a single-point advantage over Pedersen into the meeting and began in fine style too, registering a 'from-the-back' tenth-heat victory over the man who was breathing down his neck in the overall standings. Pedersen re-emerged in heat fourteen, which had to be rerun after Hampel was adjudged to have fouled the tapes. The Dane dashed off to win at the second attempt, while Crump and Mikael Max engaged in a ding-dong scrap with the Australian finally getting the better of the duel. Two heats later Rickardsson was back on track for his second outing, and with the riders in close proximity for the duration, the Swede ended up in last place behind race winner Andreas Jonsson, as Hancock and Mark Loram occupied the middle-order positions. That sent Rickardsson to an eliminator in the very next race and, amazingly, he could do no better than pass Brhel for third position, behind the first two of Scott Nicholls and Hampel. With the five-time Champion Rickardsson spiralling out with just six GP points to his name, the opportunity was there for Nicki Pedersen and Crump to put some distance between themselves and the Swede going into the concluding round at the Viking Stadium in Hamar, Norway. Crump marched on in the aforementioned heat nineteen behind Gollob, while Pedersen was dramatically beaten into third place by battling Brit Richardson and popular Pole Protasiewicz in heat twenty. The Dane therefore had to compete in a dreaded eliminator two races later, but remaining cool he sped to the flag ahead of Hampel, Hancock and Loram for a slot in the second semi-final. That saw Pedersen take Crump in the latter stages, only for the redoubtable Aussie to hit back and cross the line ahead as both speedsters safely headed into the final. Enter Gollob again and he capped a wonderful performance to win the most important race of the night with aplomb. Behind him, Crump thwarted the ever-pressing Pedersen, while Protasiewicz brought up the rear. With all to play for in Norway, that took Crump to top spot in the GP standings on 133 points, with Pedersen a single point behind on 132. Meanwhile in third place, although perhaps a tad too far behind on 121 points, was the previous Championship leader Rickardsson. But it was Gollob who rightly took all the plaudits for this showing, leaving speedway folk to wonder just what this man could achieve if he could only master the man-made stadium circuits?

PRE-MAIN EVENT
Heat one: Mark Loram, Bjarne Pedersen, Bohumil Brhel, Rafal Szombierski.
Heat two: Jaroslaw Hampel, Piotr Protasiewicz, Ryan Sullivan, Ronni Pedersen.
Heat three: Scott Nicholls, Mikael Max, Peter Karlsson, Todd Wiltshire.
Heat four: Greg Hancock, Lee Richardson, Tomasz Bajerski, Jason Lyons.
Heat five: Peter Karlsson, Bohumil Brhel, Jason Lyons, Ronni Pedersen (ret).
Heat six: Todd Wiltshire, Ryan Sullivan, Rafal Szombierski, Tomasz Bajerski.
Heat seven: Lee Richardson, Scott Nicholls, Mark Loram, Piotr Protasiewicz.
Heat eight: Jaroslaw Hampel, Greg Hancock, Bjarne Pedersen, Mikael Max.
Heat nine: Tomasz Gollob, Rune Holta, Jason Crump, Andreas Jonsson.
Heat ten: Tony Rickardsson, Nicki Pedersen, Leigh Adams, Hans N. Andersen.
Heat eleven: Mark Loram, Mikael Max, Peter Karlsson, Ryan Sullivan (ex, two mins.).
Heat twelve: Piotr Protasiewicz, Bohumil Brhel, Bjarne Pedersen, Todd Wiltshire.

MAIN EVENT
Heat thirteen: Tomasz Gollob, Lee Richardson, Bohumil Brhel, Hans N. Andersen.
Heat fourteen: (Rerun) Nicki Pedersen, Jason Crump, Mikael Max, Jaroslaw Hampel (ex, tapes).
Heat fifteen: Leigh Adams, Piotr Protasiewicz, Scott Nicholls, Rune Holta.
Heat sixteen: Andreas Jonsson, Greg Hancock, Mark Loram, Tony Rickardsson.
Heat seventeen: Scott Nicholls, Jaroslaw Hampel, Tony Rickardsson, Bohumil Brhel.
Heat eighteen: Mark Loram, Rune Holta, Hans N. Andersen, Mikael Max (ret).
Heat nineteen: Tomasz Gollob, Jason Crump, Leigh Adams, Greg Hancock (ret).
Heat twenty: Lee Richardson, Piotr Protasiewicz, Nicki Pedersen, Andreas Jonsson.
Heat twenty-one: Leigh Adams, Scott Nicholls, Rune Holta, Andreas Jonsson.
Heat twenty-two: Nicki Pedersen, Jaroslaw Hampel, Greg Hancock, Mark Loram.

SEMI-FINALS
Heat twenty-three: Tomasz Gollob, Piotr Protasiewicz, Jaroslaw Hampel, Leigh Adams.
Heat twenty-four: Jason Crump, Nicki Pedersen, Scott Nicholls, Lee Richardson.

GRAND FINAL
Heat twenty-five: Tomasz Gollob, Jason Crump, Nicki Pedersen, Piotr Protasiewicz.

NOTE: Eliminated riders are underlined throughout

GRAND PRIX OF NORWAY (ROUND NINE)
4 OCTOBER, VIKING SHIP STADIUM, HAMAR

The dramatic 2003 Grand Prix series reached its conclusion in Norway's impressive Viking Ship Stadium. With the outcome of the World Championship poised on a knife-edge there was bound to be yet more incident to go with that already witnessed over the previous eight rounds. Having ducked out early in Poland two weeks beforehand, reigning champion Tony Rickardsson began his quest as early as the fourth heat, when he made sure that first-bend supremacy was sufficient to carry him home from Andreas Jonsson, Jason Lyons and Tomasz Bajerski. The brilliant Swede was next out in the eighth race of the evening, which turned into something of a drawn-out affair. A hard first corner saw Hans N. Andersen come down, with all four competitors deemed eligible for a second attempt. Poole's Bjarne Pedersen fell on lap two in the rerun after appearing to have his line taken away by the aforementioned Andersen, but it was the Pirate who was rather unluckily excluded. Then, Ryan Sullivan produced a forceful first bend before leading home Rickardsson in the second restart. So the title holder had safely negotiated the first hurdle to join his chief rivals in the Main Event. In the very next heat Piotr Protasiewicz showed a clean pair of heels to defeat Scott Nicholls, Tomasz Gollob and all-American racer Greg Hancock. Next up was a much-anticipated meeting of the leading protagonists Jason Crump and Nicki Pedersen, who entered the meeting separated by a single point at the top of the leader board. Showing he meant business, Crump moved out from gate one and clashed with Pedersen as they made ready for the initial corner, with Lee Richardson efficiently slipping through to second place. With the positions seemingly set, Pedersen lost power and drifted wide on the last bend, allowing Leigh Adams through to third spot, although this was later revealed to be more of a clever tactical ploy than anything of a mechanical nature. Bjarne Pedersen claimed a tapes-to-flag success over 2000 World Champion Mark Loram in heat eleven, and with Todd Wiltshire exiting the fray at the back, the Australian went on an emotional lap bidding farewell to the supporters, having decided to retire at the end of the season. Nicki Pedersen marched on with a comfortable heat-thirteen win, with Norwegian Rune Holta keeping the patriotic home fans happy in second position. The next big race occurred in heat sixteen, when Crump jumped away from the gate only to hit a rut entering the back straight and head out towards the fence, with Bjarne Pedersen quickly taking over pole position from Hancock and Rickardsson. The Aussie's reaction was immediate as he stormed back into contention and brilliantly surged between Rickardsson and Hancock exiting the fourth turn. There was no catching Pedersen, however, with Crump eventually having to hold off a battling Hancock for second place. Rickardsson's last-place finish meant an eliminator appearance in the very next heat, but with Jonsson gating ahead and Gollob taking the multi-Champion wide into the first corner, there was no way back other than to pass Piotr Protasiewicz for third spot on lap three. Hancock and Adams proceeded on by filling the major positions in heat eighteen, immediately prior to the second meeting of the title-chasing duo of Crump and Nicki Pedersen. The spectacular Dane surged into the lead, while Crump and Richardson came down in a heap on the second bend, with the British rider deemed at fault having caught the Australian's front wheel. Nicholls trapped ahead in the rerun, with Crump and Pedersen again brushing together on the entry to the first turn. On the second lap Pedersen was sent out of shape by a rut and, after lifting alarmingly, he wrestled with his machine before crashing to the ground, with Crump only just avoiding the melee by riding right out by the fence. With Pedersen excluded, the resultant match race gave Nicholls and Crump automatic qualification for the semi-finals – the Brit taking an 'all the way' victory. With tension gripping the stadium, the battered and bruised Nicki Pedersen returned to the line for a crucial heat twenty-one and, showing remarkable composure, he gated alongside Jonsson before pulling away to win after the challenging Swede had caught a rut. That sent the third and fourth-placed Australian twosome of Adams and Sullivan through the exit door, leaving the former a frustrating one point off a podium position in the overall standings. The last race before the semi-finals saw Richardson excluded in the first running after a rut had sent him into the path of Gollob, with both speedsters taking an unwanted close inspection of the circuit. Hancock sped away to take the rerun, while a typical third-lap surge took Gollob inside Ronni Pedersen for a place among the last eight. Bjarne Pedersen duly made a sweet start to lead the first semi-final from Gollob, until a hard final-lap shake-up saw Nicki Pedersen come through to not only follow his namesake into the most coveted race of the night, but also put Crump under the most almighty pressure to follow suit. Considering the tension, it was hardly surprising that the title-chasing Australian failed to start on level terms, with Hancock setting the pace up front from Holta and Jonsson. 'Crumpie' soon ousted the Swede, however, to enter the back straight in hot pursuit of the second-placed Holta, and after making up ground at a fast rate of knots, he daringly rushed inside entering the third bend. Down came the Norwegian, with the television evidence showing that the Belle Vue linchpin had indeed hit his opponent's leg. There were audible yelps of joy from the Nicki Pedersen camp when Crump's exclusion light flashed on as the sport proclaimed a new World Champion and the thirtieth since the inaugural staging way back in 1936. In fact, Pedersen took the total of Danish victors to five, tagging his name under the illustrious list of Ole Olsen, Erik Gundersen, Hans Nielsen and Jan O. Pedersen. Back to the second semi-final, and Hancock went on to take victory from Jonsson in the rerun, while the chasing Holta unluckily tumbled down on the fourth lap. That left just one race to complete a gripping series and, emphasizing just how good it had been, the destination of the title hadn't been decided until the last but one heat, or put another way after an amazing 224 out of 225 races! With the final purely academic as far as the Championship was concerned, there was still the prestige of winning a GP up for grabs, so there was no let up from those participating as was demonstrated when Jonsson fell on the first bend after making contact with Nicki Pedersen. Much to his annoyance, Jonsson found himself excluded by referee Marek Wojaczek and there were many who felt the decision might have gone the other way, thereby showing consistency with Crump's exit from the previous race. Anyway, Hancock took full advantage of the second running to roar around the field on the first turn and joyfully canter to the sixth Grand Prix victory of his career from the unrelated Pedersens, Nicki and Bjarne respectively. Briefly looking at the overall totals for the series, although Nicki Pedersen had only enjoyed a solitary GP success at Cardiff on 14 June, he had accumulated 152 points from the nine rounds to finish ahead of the valiant Crump, whose 144-point tally remarkably gave him second place for a third year on the bounce! Outgoing champion Rickardsson was third on 127 points, just a single digit ahead of the stylish Adams. Three other riders also topped the 100-point mark and are worthy of mention for playing a full part in a fabulous series, namely Greg Hancock (121), Tomasz Gollob (111) and Scott Nicholls (102).

PRE-MAIN EVENT

Heat one: Rune Holta, Bjarne Pedersen, Joonas Kylmakorpi, Bohumil Brhel (ret).

Heat two: Ryan Sullivan, Mark Loram, Mikael Max, Lars Gunnestad.

Heat three: Ronni Pedersen, Hans N. Andersen, Todd Wiltshire, Peter Karlsson.

Heat four: Tony Rickardsson, Andreas Jonsson, Jason Lyons, Tomasz Bajerski.

Heat five: Todd Wiltshire, Lars Gunnestad, Tomasz Bajerski, Joonas Kylmakorpi.

Heat six: Mikael Max, Jason Lyons, Peter Karlsson, Bohumil Brhel.

Heat seven: Rune Holta, Ronni Pedersen, Mark Loram, Andreas Jonsson.

Heat eight: (Rerun twice) Ryan Sullivan, Tony Rickardsson, Hans N. Andersen, Bjarne Pedersen (f, ex).

Heat nine: Piotr Protasiewicz, Scott Nicholls, Tomasz Gollob, Greg Hancock.

Heat ten: Jason Crump, Lee Richardson, Leigh Adams, Nicki Pedersen.

Heat eleven: Bjarne Pedersen, Mark Loram, Jason Lyons, Todd Wiltshire.

Heat twelve: Andreas Jonsson, Hans N. Andersen, Lars Gunnestad, Mikael Max (fell).

MAIN EVENT

Heat thirteen: Nicki Pedersen, Rune Holta, Piotr Protasiewicz, Hans N. Andersen.

Heat fourteen: Ryan Sullivan, Lee Richardson, Mark Loram, Tomasz Gollob.

Heat fifteen: Scott Nicholls, Ronni Pedersen, Andreas Jonsson, Leigh Adams.

Heat sixteen: Bjarne Pedersen, Jason Crump, Greg Hancock, Tony Rickardsson.

Heat seventeen: Andreas Jonsson, Tomasz Gollob, Tony Rickardsson, Piotr Protasiewicz.

Heat eighteen: Greg Hancock, Leigh Adams, Hans N. Andersen, Mark Loram (f, rem).

Heat nineteen: (Rerun twice) Scott Nicholls, Jason Crump, Nicki Pedersen (f, ex), Lee Richardson (f, ex).

Heat twenty: Rune Holta, Bjarne Pedersen, Ronni Pedersen, Ryan Sullivan.

Heat twenty-one: Nicki Pedersen, Andreas Jonsson, Leigh Adams, Ryan Sullivan.

Heat twenty-two: (Rerun) Greg Hancock, Tomasz Gollob, Ronni Pedersen, Lee Richardson (ex, foul riding).

SEMI-FINALS

Heat twenty-three: Bjarne Pedersen, Nicki Pedersen, Scott Nicholls, Tomasz Gollob.

Heat twenty-four: (Rerun) Greg Hancock, Andreas Jonsson, Rune Holta (fell), Jason Crump (ex, foul riding).

GRAND FINAL

Heat twenty-five: (Rerun) Greg Hancock, Nicki Pedersen, Bjarne Pedersen, Andreas Jonsson (f, ex).

NOTE: Eliminated riders are underlined throughout

WORLD CHAMPIONSHIP ROLL OF HONOUR

NOTE: Run as a one-off World Final from 1936-94, and as the Grand Prix from 1995-2003

YEAR	FIRST	SECOND	THIRD
1936	Lionel Van Praag	Eric Langton	Bluey Wilkinson
1937	Jack Milne	Wilbur Lamoreaux	Cordy Milne
1938	Bluey Wilkinson	Jack Milne	Wilbur Lamoreaux
1939-48	*Not Staged*		
1949	Tommy Price	Jack Parker	Louis Lawson
1950	Freddie Williams	Wally Green	Graham Warren
1951	Jack Young	Split Waterman	Jack Biggs
1952	Jack Young	Freddie Williams	Bob Oakley
1953	Freddie Williams	Split Waterman	Geoff Mardon
1954	Ronnie Moore	Brian Crutcher	Olle Nygren
1955	Peter Craven	Ronnie Moore	Barry Briggs
1956	Ove Fundin	Ronnie Moore	Arthur Forrest
1957	Barry Briggs	Ove Fundin	Peter Craven
1958	Barry Briggs	Ove Fundin	Aub Lawson
1959	Ronnie Moore	Ove Fundin	Barry Briggs
1960	Ove Fundin	Ronnie Moore	Peter Craven
1961	Ove Fundin	Bjorn Knutsson	Gote Nordin
1962	Peter Craven	Barry Briggs	Ove Fundin
1963	Ove Fundin	Bjorn Knutsson	Barry Briggs
1964	Barry Briggs	Igor Plechanov	Ove Fundin
1965	Bjorn Knutsson	Igor Plechanov	Ove Fundin
1966	Barry Briggs	Sverre Harrfeldt	Antoni Woryna
1967	Ove Fundin	Bengt Jansson	Ivan Mauger
1968	Ivan Mauger	Barry Briggs	Edward Jancarz
1969	Ivan Mauger	Barry Briggs	Soren Sjosten
1970	Ivan Mauger	Pawel Waloszek	Antoni Woryna
1971	Ole Olsen	Ivan Mauger	Bengt Jansson
1972	Ivan Mauger	Bernt Persson	Ole Olsen
1973	Jerzy Szczakiel	Ivan Mauger	Zenon Plech
1974	Anders Michanek	Ivan Mauger	Soren Sjosten
1975	Ole Olsen	Aanders Michanek	John Louis
1976	Peter Collins	Malcolm Simmons	Phil Crump
1977	Ivan Mauger	Peter Collins	Ole Olsen
1978	Ole Olsen	Gordon Kennett	Scott Autrey
1979	Ivan Mauger	Zenon Plech	Michael Lee
1980	Michael Lee	Dave Jessup	Billy Sanders
1981	Bruce Penhall	Ole Olsen	Tommy Knudsen
1982	Bruce Penhall	Les Collins	Dennis Sigalos
1983	Egon Muller	Billy Sanders	Michael Lee
1984	Erik Gundersen	Hans Nielsen	Lance King
1985	Erik Gundersen	Hans Nielsen	Sam Ermolenko

YEAR	FIRST	SECOND	THIRD
1986	Hans Nielsen	Jan O. Pedersen	Kelvin Tatum
1987	Hans Nielsen	Erik Gundersen	Sam Ermolenko
1988	Erik Gundersen	Hans Nielsen	Jan O. Pedersen
1989	Hans Nielsen	Simon Wigg	Jeremy Doncaster
1990	Per Jonsson	Shawn Moran	Todd Wiltshire
1991	Jan O. Pedersen	Tony Rickardsson	Hans Nielsen
1992	Gary Havelock	Per Jonsson	Gert Handberg
1993	Sam Ermolenko	Hans Nielsen	Chris Louis
1994	Tony Rickardsson	Hans Nielsen	Craig Boyce
1995	Hans Nielsen	Tony Rickardsson	Sam Ermolenko
1996	Billy Hamill	Hans Nielsen	Greg Hancock
1997	Greg Hancock	Billy Hamill	Tomasz Gollob
1998	Tony Rickardsson	Jimmy Nilsen	Tomasz Gollob
1999	Tony Rickardsson	Tomasz Gollob	Hans Nielsen
2000	Mark Loram	Billy Hamill	Tony Rickardsson
2001	Tony Rickardsson	Jason Crump	Tomasz Gollob
2002	Tony Rickardsson	Jason Crump	Ryan Sullivan
2003	Nicki Pedersen	Jason Crump	Tony Rickardsson

NOTE: In 1990, Shawn Moran was subsequently stripped of second place, having tested positive in a drugs test at the Overseas Final.

WORLD CHAMPIONSHIP QUALIFYING
(FOR THE 2004 GRAND PRIX SERIES)

ROUND ONE: 26 April, Lonigo, Italy

1st Lee Richardson 14; 2nd Billy Janniro 13; 3rd Ryan Fisher 11; Tomas Topinka 11; Piotr Protasiewicz 11; Sebastian Ulamek 10; Theo Pijper 10; Matej Zagar 10; Sebastian Tresarrieu 7; Joachim Kugelmann 6; Mirko Wolter 5; Scott Smith 4; Jernej Kolenko 4; Simone Terenzani 3; Christian Miotello 1; Marko Vlah 0.

ROUND TWO: 1 May, Debrecen, Hungary

1st Peter Karlsson 13; 2nd Rafal Dobrucki 13; 3rd Jesper B. Jensen 12; Attila Stefani 11; David Howe 11; Sandor Tihanyi 10; Sergei Darkin 9; Jacek Rempala 8; Laszlo Szatmari 8; Oleg Kurguskin 8; Josef Franc 5; Norbert Magosi 4; Ronni Pedersen 4; Izak Santej 3; Manuel Hauzinger 1; Tomas Suchanek 0.

ROUND THREE: 4 May, Elgane, Norway

1st Grzegorz Walasek 13; 2nd Bjarne Pedersen 12; 3rd David Ruud 12; Charlie Gjedde 11; Stefan Andersson 10; Kaj Laukkanen 9; Hans N. Andersen 9; Peter I. Karlsson 9; Brent Werner 9; Chris Harris 8; Bjorn G. Hansen 8; Olly Allen 4; Samuel Taylor 3; Mikke Bjerk 2; Carl Raugstad 1; Remi Ueland 0.

ROUND FOUR: 8 June, Huesden-Zolder, Belgium

1st Lukas Dryml 12; 2nd Bohumil Brehel 12; 3rd Ales Dryml 11; Chris Slabon 11; Peter Ljung 10; Joonas Kylmakorpi 10; Roman Povazhny 8; Simon Stead 8; Kenneth Bjerre 7; Matthias Schultz 7; Mark Lemon 6; Magnus Zetterstrom 6; Craig Watson 5; Leigh Lanham 5; Henk Bos 2; Warren Meier 0.

FIRST SEMI-FINAL: 21 June, Terenzano, Italy

1st Peter Karlsson 13; 2nd David Howe 13; 3rd Billy Janniro 12; Ales Dryml 10; Piotr Protasiewicz 9; Tomas Topinka 9; Theo Pijper 8; Charlie Gjedde 8; Mataj Zagar 7; Chris Slabon 6; Peter Ljung 6; Laszlo Szatmari 4; Grzegorz Walasek 4; Jacek Rempala 4; David Ruud 3; Andrea Maida 3; Sandor Tihanyi 0.

SECOND SEMI-FINAL: 22 June, Rybnik, Poland

1st Roman Povazhny 12; 2nd Jesper B. Jensen 12; 3rd Bjarne Pedersen 12; Bohumil Brhel 11; Rafal Dobrucki 10; Lukas Dryml 10; Kaj Laukkanen 10; Sebastian Ulamek 8; Joonas Kylmakorpi 7; Sergei Darkin 6; Peter I. Karlsson 6; Jaroslaw Hampel 5; Attila Stefani 4; Simon Stead 3; Ryan Fisher 3; Lee Richardson 1; Brent Werner 0; Stefan Andersson 0.

FINAL: 17 August, Poole

	QUALIFYING SCORES					TOTAL
Piotr Protasiewicz	2	3	3	3	3	14
Bohumil Brhel	3	3	2	2	3	13
Bjarne Pedersen	2	2	2	3	3	12
Kaj Laukkanen	3	3	1	2	2	11
Ales Dryml	X	3	3	3	1	10
Jesper B. Jensen	1	R	3	3	2	9
Joonas Kylmakorpi (res)	3	2	0	1	1	7
Simon Stead	1	R	3	2	X	6
Rafal Dobrucki	3	0	1	1	1	6
Billy Janniro	2	2	1	1	0	6
Charlie Gjedde	F	1	0	2	2	5
Tomas Topinka	2	2	1	0	X	5
Roman Povazhny	X	1	F	1	3	5
Matej Zagar (res)	1	2	M	2	–	5
Sebastian Ulamek	1	1	2	F	–	4
Theo Pijper	0	0	0	0	1	1
Peter Karlsson	R	–	–	–	–	0
Lukas Dryml	n	–	–	–	–	0

RACE DETAILS

Heat one: (Rerun) Kaj Laukkanen, Bjarne Pedersen, Simon Stead, Ales Dryml (f, ex).

Heat two: (Rerun) Bohumil Brhel, Piotr Protasiewicz, Sebastian Ulamek, Charlie Gjedde (fell).

Heat three: (Rerun twice) Joonas Kylmakorpi, Tomas Topinka, Peter Karlsson (ret), Roman Povazhny (f, ex), Lukas Dryml (f, n.s.).

Heat four: Rafal Dobrucki, Billy Janniro, Jesper B. Jensen, Theo Pijper.

Heat five: Ales Dryml, Joonas Kylmakorpi, Charlie Gjedde, Theo Pijper.

Heat six: Kaj Laukkanen, Tomas Topinka, Sebastian Ulamek, Rafal Dobrucki.

Heat seven: Bohumil Brhel, Bjarne Pedersen, Roman Povazhny, Jesper B. Jensen (ret).

Heat eight: Piotr Protasiewicz, Billy Janniro, Matej Zagar, Simon Stead (f, rem, ret).

Heat nine: Ales Dryml, Sebastian Ulamek, Billy Janniro, Roman Povazhny (fell).

Heat ten: Jesper B. Jensen, Matej Zagar, Kaj Laukkanen, Charlie Gjedde.

Heat eleven: Piotr Protasiewicz, Bjarne Pedersen, Rafal Dobrucki, Joonas Kylmakorpi.

Heat twelve: Simon Stead, Bohumil Brhel, Tomas Topinka, Theo Pijper.

Heat thirteen: Ales Dryml, Bohumil Brhel, Rafal Dobrucki, Matej Zagar (ex, two mins).

Heat fourteen: Piotr Protasiewicz, Kaj Laukkanen, Roman Povazhny, Theo Pijper.

Heat fifteen: Bjarne Pedersen, Charlie Gjedde, Billy Janniro, Tomas Topinka.

Heat sixteen: Jesper B. Jensen, Simon Stead, Joonas Kylmakorpi, Sebastian Ulamek (fell).

Heat seventeen: (Rerun) Piotr Protasiewicz, Jesper B. Jensen, Ales Dryml, Tomas Topinka (f, ex).

Heat eighteen: Bohumil Brhel, Kaj Laukkanen, Joonas Kylmakorpi, Billy Janniro.

Heat nineteen: Bjarne Pedersen, Matej Zagar, Theo Pijper, Sebastian Ulamek (n.s.).

Heat twenty: (Rerun) Roman Povazhny, Charlie Gjedde, Rafal Dobrucki, Simon Stead (f, ex).

NOTE: Piotr Protasiewicz, Bohumil Brhel, Bjarne Pedersen, Kaj Laukkanen, Ales Dryml and Jesper B. Jensen qualified for the 2004 GP series.

MAJOR INTERNATIONAL MEETINGS
2003

MAJOR INTERNATIONAL MEETINGS 2003

WORLD CUP

NOTE: Formerly known as the World Team Cup (1960-2000)

QUALIFYING ROUND
11 MAY, DAUGAVPILS, LATVIA.
GERMANY 65 (Mirko Wolter 19; Christian Hefenbrock 14; Ronny Weis 12; Matthias Schultz
  12; Thomas Stange 8);
SLOVENIA 62 (Izak Santej 17; Matej Zagar 15; Jernej Kolenko 12; Ales Dolinar 12; Denis
  Stojs 6);
LATVIA 62 (Andrei Korolev 17; Vladimir Voronkov 13; Nikolai Kokin 13; Denis Popovich 11;
  Alexander Biznia 8)
ITALY 40 (Armando Castagna 15; Emiliano Sanchez 13; Simone Terenzani 7; Christian
  Miotello 5; Alessandro Dalla Valle 0);
AUSTRIA 19 (Fritz Wallner 10; Markus Pichler 5; Rene Pfeiffer 2; Ivan Nagar 1; Oliver Ozelt 1).

  NOTE: Matej Zagar subsequently defeated Andrei Korolev in a run-off to take Slovenia through to the latter stages alongside Germany.

ROUND ONE
3 AUGUST, HOLSTED, DENMARK
The Danish-staged World Cup Finals began at Holsted, and the first event was dominated by
the home nation. Nicki Pedersen began the proceedings with a fine win from Ales Dryml,
with subsequent Danish victories following, courtesy of Niels-Kristian Iversen, so hugely
impressive in the Premier League with Newport, and Bjarne Pedersen. The Dane's run of
success was briefly broken by a scintillating win from Finland's Joonas Kylmakorpi, who passed
both Kenneth Bjerre and Tomas Topinka on his way to the flag in heat four. Denmark
responded quickly, with victories from Hans N. Andersen and Nicki Pedersen, before
Kylmakorpi produced another Finnish success ahead of Iversen, who himself brilliantly came
through from fourth position. Four more wins followed for the Danes, through Bjarne
Pedersen, Bjerre, Andersen and Nicki Pedersen, while all the time the Czechs were filling vital
scoring positions to leave the scores after eleven heats at Denmark 30, Czech Republic 18,
Finland 14, Germany 4. The Czech charge continued in the next two heats, as Topinka and
Bohumil Brhel swept home, before normal service was resumed by the homesters, with
successive victories from Bjerre, Andersen, Nicki Pedersen and Iversen. With Denmark holding
a commanding 16-point lead from nearest challengers the Czech Republic, the classy
Kylmakorpi raced to his third win for Finland in heat eighteen. The Czechs then consolidated
their position in second spot, as Brhel and Topinka produced a brace of successes. Despite their
big lead, the homesters were relentless as Nicki Pedersen wrapped up a sparkling 15-point
maximum in heat twenty-one. Brhel's victory in the next race proved to be the last for any
other country, as the Danes closed out the meeting with a hat-trick of first places from Bjarne
Pedersen, Bjerre and Andersen, thereby cruising through to the final, with the Czech's heading
to the race-off.

DENMARK 62

	RACE SCORES						TOTAL
Nicki Pedersen	3	3	3	3	3	–	15
Niels-Kristian Iversen	3	2	R	3	2	–	10
Bjarne Pedersen	3	3	2	1	3	–	12
Kenneth Bjerre	1	3	3	2	3	–	12
Hans N. Andersen	3	3	3	1	3	–	13

CZECH REPUBLIC 51

Ales Dryml	2	2	2	2	1	1	10
Lukas Dryml	2	1	2	2	2	–	9
Bohumil Brhel	2	2	2	3	3	3	15
Tomas Topinka	2	R	3	3	4	–	12
Josef Franc	2	1	2	–	–	–	5

FINLAND 32

Kaj Laukkanen	1	2	1	2	2	1	9
Kauko Nieminen	0	1	1	1	0	–	3
Tomi Reima	0	0	1	–	–	–	1
Joonas Kylmakorpi	3	4	3	1	3	2	16
Juha Hautamaki	0	1	2	0	0	-	3

GERMANY 10

Mirko Wolter	0	0	1	1	2	–	4
Martin Smolinski	1	R	0	0	0	–	1
Ronny Weis	1	0	1	0	0	–	2
Matthias Schultz	0	0	0	0	1	–	1
Christian Hefenbrock	1	1	0	0	0	–	2

RACE DETAILS

Heat one: Nicki Pedersen, Ales Dryml, Kaj Laukkanen, Mirko Wolter.

Heat two: Niels-Kristian Iversen, Lukas Dryml, Martin Smolinski, Kauko Nieminen.

Heat three: Bjarne Pedersen, Bohumil Brhel, Ronny Weis, Tomi Reima.

Heat four: Joonas Kylmakorpi, Tomas Topinka, Kenneth Bjerre, Matthias Schultz.

Heat five: Hans N. Andersen, Josef Franc, Christian Hefenbrock, Juha Hautamaki.

Heat six: Nicki Pedersen, Joonas Kylmakorpi (tactical joker), Christian Hefenbrock, Tomas Topinka (ret).

Heat seven: Joonas Kylmakorpi, Niels-Kristian Iversen, Josef Franc, Mirko Wolter.

Heat eight: Bjarne Pedersen, Ales Dryml, Juha Hautamaki, Martin Smolinski (ret).

Heat nine: Kenneth Bjerre, Kaj Laukkanen, Lukas Dryml, Ronny Weis.

Heat ten: Hans N. Andersen, Bohumil Brhel, Kauko Nieminen, Matthias Schultz.

Heat eleven: Nicki Pedersen, Bohumil Brhel, Joonas Kylmakorpi, Martin Smolinski.

Heat twelve: Tomas Topinka, Juha Hautamaki, Ronny Weis, Niels-Kristian Iversen (ret).

Heat thirteen: Bohumil Brhel, Bjarne Pedersen, Kaj Laukkanen, Matthias Schultz.

Heat fourteen: Kenneth Bjerre, Ales Dryml, Kauko Nieminen, Christian Hefenbrock.

Heat fifteen: Hans N. Andersen, Lukas Dryml, Mirko Wolter, Tomi Reima.

Heat sixteen: Nicki Pedersen, Ales Dryml, Kauko Nieminen, Ronny Weis.

Heat seventeen: Niels-Kristian Iversen, Kaj Laukkanen, Ales Dryml, Matthias Schultz.

Heat eighteen: Joonas Kylmakorpi, Lukas Dryml, Bjarne Pedersen, Christian Hefenbrock.

Heat nineteen: Bohumil Brhel, Kenneth Bjerre, Mirko Wolter, Juha Hautamaki.

Heat twenty: Tomas Topinka, Kaj Laukkanen, Hans N. Andersen, Martin Smolinski.

Heat twenty-one: Nicki Pedersen, Lukas Dryml, Matthias Schultz, Juha Hautamaki.

Heat twenty-two: Bohumil Brhel, Niels-Kristian Iversen, Kaj Laukkanen, Christian Hefenbrock.

Heat twenty-three: Bjarne Pedersen, Tomas Topinka (tactical joker), Mirko Wolter (tactical joker), Kauko Nieminen.

Heat twenty-four: Kenneth Bjerre, Josef Franc, Tomi Reima, Martin Smolinski (f, rem).

Heat twenty-five: Hans N. Andersen, Joonas Kylmakorpi, Ales Dryml, Ronny Weis.

(Points: 1st = 3; 2nd = 2; 3rd = 1; 4th = 0; tactical joker = double points)

ROUND TWO
4 AUGUST, OUTRUP, DENMARK

The second round at Outrup saw Italy step in to replace the USA, who had pulled out of the competition due to the non-availability of their European-based riders, and the excessive costs of flying replacements over from their homeland. As things turned out, Australia, Champions of the previous two years, and Team Great Britain became embroiled in an epic tussle for top spot, and a place in the World Cup Final itself. Great Britain boss Neil Middleditch's selection raised more than a few eyebrows in the lead-up to the meeting, but those who questioned his judgement were forced to swallow hard and admit that his choices were spot on. Matej Zagar, such an immediate hit in the Premier League with Trelawny, set the ball rolling by winning the opening race from Scott Nicholls and Todd Wiltshire. Wins followed for Lee Richardson and Leigh Adams, but with David Norris following the classy Aussie over the line in heat three, Great Britain took an unexpected lead. It didn't last for long, however, as a fourth-heat victory for Jason Crump brought the Roos level on the nine-point mark. The Aussies collected wins in each of the next four races through Jason Lyons, Adams, Crump and Lyons again, but just when it looked like they might pull away decisively, back came the British boys with successes from Richardson and Norris. Australia countered that thanks to Crump and Lyons, with the tit for tat continuing as Dean Barker and Nicholls then collected further victories for Team Great Britain. So to heat fifteen, which saw Adams defeat Richardson to remain unbeaten, with his nation holding pole position on thirty-eight points, just three ahead of the chasing Brits at the interval stage. Meanwhile, despite Zagar's sterling efforts, Slovenia trailed on thirteen points, while Italy had just four on the scoreboard. That man Zagar stylishly took heat sixteen, but with Adams, Crump and Lyons racking up successive wins for Australia, it was beginning to look bleak for Britain. Trailing by seven points, GB manager 'Middlo' gave Richardson the nod for a 'tactical joker' ride in heat twenty, with both Slovenia and Italy following suit. In a dramatic race, Richardson took advantage as Wiltshire and Zagar battled on the first turn, driving through on the inside to lead. Wiltshire took up the pursuit, only to stop on the second lap, leaving Richardson to claim six points, and reduce his side's arrears to just a single point at one fell swoop. The heroic Richardson was out again in the very next race, when a victory over Lyons amazingly levelled things up at fifty-one points each, with just four heats to go. A win for Norris ahead of Wiltshire put GB ahead in the next, but that was straightaway cancelled out by Sullivan's 'from-the-back' triumph over Gary Havelock. With four victories out of four to his name, Adams held his nerve to defeat Barker in the penultimate race and complete a fabulous maximum, with Crump also finishing off a five-ride full house when beating Nicholls in the final heat. That gave the Aussies a total of sixty-two points, and their final spot was guaranteed, with the gallant Brits facing the prospect of having to do it all over again in the race-off.

AUSTRALIA 62

	RACE SCORES						TOTAL
Todd Wiltshire	1	2	2	R	2	–	7
Ryan Sullivan	2	2	2	2	3	–	11
Leigh Adams	3	3	3	3	3	–	15
Jason Crump	3	3	3	3	3	–	15
Jason Lyons	3	3	3	3	2	–	14

TEAM GREAT BRITAIN 60

Scott Nicholls	2	2	3	2	2	–	11
Lee Richardson	3	3	2	2	6	3	19
David Norris	2	3	2	2	3	–	12
Gary Havelock	2	2	2	2	–	–	8
Dean Barker	2	2	3	1	2	–	10

SLOVENIA 28

Matej Zagar	3	1	1	3	4	1	13
Izak Santej	1	0	1	1	1	–	4
Jernej Kolenko	R	1	1	1	1	–	4
Ales Dolinar	1	1	0	1	1	–	4
Denis Stojs	1	1	0	1	–	–	3

ITALY 6

Andrea Maida	0	1	1	0	0	–	2
Simone Terenzani	0	0	0	0	–	–	0
Christian Miotello	1	0	R	0	2	0	3
Daniele Tessari	R	0	0	0	0	–	0
Simone Muratelli	0	0	1	0	0	–	1

RACE DETAILS

Heat one: Matej Zagar, Scott Nicholls, Todd Wiltshire, Andrea Maida.
Heat two: Lee Richardson, Ryan Sullivan, Izak Santej, Simone Terenzani.
Heat three: Leigh Adams, David Norris, Christian Miotello, Jernej Kolenko (ret).
Heat four: Jason Crump, Gary Havelock, Ales Dolinar, Daniele Tessari (ret).
Heat five: Jason Lyons, Dean Barker, Denis Stojs, Simone Muratelli.
Heat six: Leigh Adams, Gary Havelock, Matej Zagar, Simone Muratelli.
Heat seven: Jason Crump, Dean Barker, Andrea Maida, Izak Santej.
Heat eight: Jason Lyons, Scott Nicholls, Jernej Kolenko, Simone Terenzani.
Heat nine: Lee Richardson, Todd Wiltshire, Ales Dolinar, Christian Miotello.
Heat ten: David Norris, Ryan Sullivan, Denis Stojs, Daniele Tessari.

Heat eleven: Jason Crump, David Norris, Matej Zagar, Simone Terenzani.

Heat twelve: Jason Lyons, Gary Havelock, Izak Santej, Christian Miotello.

Heat thirteen: Dean Barker, Todd Wiltshire, Jernej Kolenko, Daniele Tessari.

Heat fourteen: Scott Nicholls, Ryan Sullivan, Simone Muratelli, Ales Dolinar.

Heat fifteen: Leigh Adams, Lee Richardson, Andrea Maida, Denis Stojs.

Heat sixteen: Matej Zagar, Ryan Sullivan, Dean Barker, Christian Miotello (f, rem).

Heat seventeen: Leigh Adams, Scott Nicholls, Izak Santej, Daniele Tessari (f, rem).

Heat eighteen: Jason Crump, Lee Richardson, Jernej Kolenko, Simone Muratelli.

Heat nineteen: Jason Lyons, David Norris, Ales Dolinar, Andrea Maida.

Heat twenty: Lee Richardson (tactical joker), Matej Zagar (tactical joker), Christian Miotello (tactical joker), Todd Wiltshire (ret).

Heat twenty-one: Lee Richardson, Jason Lyons, Matej Zagar, Daniele Tessari.

Heat twenty-two: David Norris, Todd Wiltshire, Izak Santej, Simone Muratelli.

Heat twenty-three: Ryan Sullivan, Gary Havelock, Jernej Kolenko, Andrea Maida.

Heat twenty-four: Leigh Adams, Dean Barker, Ales Dolinar, Simone Muratelli (f, rem).

Heat twenty-five: Jason Crump, Scott Nicholls, Denis Stojs, Christian Miotello.

(Points: 1st = 3; 2nd = 2; 3rd = 1; 4th = 0; tactical joker = double points)

ROUND THREE
5 AUGUST, HOLSTED, DENMARK

The third round of the World Cup always looked likely to develop into a battle for supremacy between Poland and Sweden, and so it proved. First blood went to the Swedes when World number one Tony Rickardsson, despite a crash while riding for Masarna at Valsarna on 22 July, posted an opening-heat victory over the swashbuckling Tomasz Gollob. The Poles hit straight back, however, with Tomasz Bajerski taking the chequered flag ahead of Hungarian Norbert Magosi in the very next race. Courtesy of wins from Andreas Jonsson and Peter Karlsson, Sweden moved into the lead, but back came Poland again with a victory from Jaroslaw Hampel to tie the two leading teams up at twelve points apiece. By the end of heat ten, the Swedes appeared to have taken a grip on proceedings following further wins from David Ruud, Rickardsson, Jonsson and Karlsson, interspersed by a solitary Polish success from Hampel in the eighth heat. That left the scores standing at Sweden 26, Poland 22, Russia 8 and Hungary 4. The gritty Poles replied once more with Piotr Protasiewicz, Hampel, Gollob and Bajerski posting victories in turn to give them a single-point advantage at the head of the scoreboard. Needless to say, the Swedes didn't take that lying down, and wins from Rickardsson and Jonsson put them back in front by a point in what had developed into an enthralling ding-dong contest. Sebastian Ulamek then took heat seventeen to level things up, before the Russians briefly interrupted the two leading protagonists by nominating Sergei Darkin for a tactical joker outing. The Russian sped from the tapes to lead from a chasing Protasiewicz, while significantly, Ruud ground to a halt on the last lap. A final bid from the Pole saw him and the Russian clash, with the leading man spectacularly hitting the deck as he crossed the finish line. The result was allowed to stand, however, and that proved to be Russia's only win of the meeting, while Protasiewicz's second place gave Poland a two-point cushion over the Swedes. That proved to be the turning point, and with Poland in the ascendancy, Hampel rode a brilliant race to repel Rickardsson in heat eighteen, before a Gollob victory over Mikael Max increased their lead to four points. Sweden hit back with wins by Karlsson and Rickardsson either side of another Gollob triumph, but when Ulamek beat Max in the penultimate race, victory was assured for the proud Poles. The meeting was to end bizarrely though, with the final heat having to be rerun three times before being completed with a solitary rider! At the first attempt, Hungary's Csaba Hell was excluded, having collided with Jonsson and fallen on the first turn. In the rerun, Russian Renat Gafarov was excluded after coming to grief and taking the unfortunate Jonsson with him on the fourth corner. Battered and bruised, Jonsson then lined up for a match race against Protasiewicz, but with the Pole leading the way, he suddenly lifted, lost control and careered across the track to become the heat's third excluded rider. That left Jonsson on his own for the fourth running of the race, and unsurprisingly he completed it in the slowest time of the meeting. With Poland on fifty-eight points, they moved straight through to the World Cup Final, while just two points adrift, the Swedes went into the race-off, along with the plucky Russians.

POLAND 58

	RACE SCORES						TOTAL
Tomasz Gollob	2	2	3	3	3	–	13
Tomasz Bajerski	3	2	3	2	2	–	12
Sebastian Ulamek	2	1	2	3	3	–	11
Piotr Protasiewicz	2	2	3	2	X	–	9
Jaroslaw Hampel	3	3	3	3	1	–	13

SWEDEN 56

Tony Rickardsson	3	3	3	2	3	–	14
Mikael Max	1	2	2	2	2	–	9
Andreas Jonsson	3	3	2	3	3	–	14
Peter Karlsson	3	3	2	2	3	–	13
David Ruud	2	3	1	R	0	–	6

RUSSIA 28

Sergei Darkin	1	0	2	0	6	–	9
Renat Gafurov	0	1	1	2	X	–	4
Semen Vlasov	1	1	1	1	2	–	6
Roman Povazhny	1	2	1	1	1	1	7
Denis Gizatulin	1	0	1	0	–	–	2

HUNGARY 9

Zoltan Adorjan	0	0	0	0	0	–	0
Norbert Magosi	2	1	0	1	1	2	7
Sandor Tihanyi	0	1	0	1	0	0	2
Szablocs Vida	0	0	0	–	–	–	0
Csaba Hell	0	0	0	0	X	–	0

RACE DETAILS
Heat one: Tony Rickardsson, Tomasz Gollob, Sergei Darkin, Zoltan Adorjan.
Heat two: Tomasz Bajerski, Norbert Magosi, Mikael Max, Renat Gafurov.
Heat three: Andreas Jonsson, Sebastian Ulamek, Semen Vlasov, Sandor Tihanyi.

Heat four: Peter Karlsson, Piotr Protasiewicz, Roman Povazhny, Szablocs Vida.

Heat five: Jaroslaw Hampel, David Ruud, Denis Gizatulin, Csaba Hell.

Heat six: David Ruud, Roman Povazhny, Sebastian Ulamek, Zoltan Adorjan.

Heat seven: Tony Rickardsson, Piotr Protasiewicz, Norbert Magosi, Denis Gizatulin.

Heat eight: Jaroslaw Hampel, Mikael Max, Sandor Tihanyi, Sergei Darkin.

Heat nine: Andreas Jonsson, Tomasz Gollob, Renat Gafurov, Szablocs Vida.

Heat ten: Peter Karlsson, Tomasz Bajerski, Semen Vlasov, Csaba Hell.

Heat eleven: Piotr Protasiewicz, Mikael Max, Semen Vlasov, Zoltan Adorjan.

Heat twelve: Jaroslaw Hampel, Andreas Jonsson, Roman Povazhny, Norbert Magosi.

Heat thirteen: Tomasz Gollob, Peter Karlsson, Denis Gizatulin, Sandor Tihanyi.

Heat fourteen: Tomasz Bajerski, Sergei Darkin, David Ruud, Szablocs Vida.

Heat fifteen: Tony Rickardsson, Sebastian Ulamek, Renat Gafurov, Csaba Hell.

Heat sixteen: Andreas Jonsson, Tomasz Bajerski, Roman Povazhny, Zoltan Adorjan.

Heat seventeen: Sebastian Ulamek, Peter Karlsson, Norbert Magosi, Sergei Darkin.

Heat eighteen: Sergei Darkin (tactical joker), Piotr Protasiewicz, Sandor Tihanyi, David Ruud (ret).

Heat nineteen: Jaroslaw Hampel, Tony Rickardsson, Semen Vlasov, Sandor Tihanyi.

Heat twenty: Tomasz Gollob, Mikael Max, Roman Povazhny, Csaba Hell.

Heat twenty-one: Peter Karlsson, Renat Gafurov, Jaroslaw Hampel, Zoltan Adorjan.

Heat twenty-two: Tomasz Gollob, Semen Vlasov, David Ruud, Norbert Magosi.

Heat twenty-three: Tony Rickardsson, Tomasz Bajerski, Roman Povazhny, Sandor Tihanyi.

Heat twenty-four: Sebastian Ulamek, Mikael Max, Norbert Magosi (tactical joker), Denis Gizatulin.

Heat twenty-five: (Rerun three times) Andreas Jonsson, Piotr Protasiewicz (f, ex), Renat Gafurov (f, ex), Csaba Hell (f, ex).

(Points: 1st = 3; 2nd = 2; 3rd = 1; 4th = 0; tactical joker = double points)

RACE-OFF

7 AUGUST, OUTRUP, DENMARK

Five teams and five-man races were the order of the day, as Outrup hosted the World Cup Race-Off, with two places up for grabs in the final itself. For Team Great Britain, it was a chance to go one better, having gone through the exit door at this stage in the previous two World Cup contests. It was third-time lucky too, as an awesome performance saw them pummel the opposition to score a magnificent 80 points. The fact that World Champion Tony Rickardsson didn't represent Sweden shouldn't be allowed to detract from this showing either, as the British boys thoroughly deserved their success. Rickardsson did briefly appear in the pre-meeting practice, but decided against further participation due to the dizziness he was suffering as a result of the track spill in his homeland on 22 July. Although without their top man, the Swedes stuck to their task, and grittily just saw off a battling Czech Republic quintet to join Great Britain in the final. Despite only taking victory in the second heat through Tomas Topinka, the meeting began well for the Czechs and they led after three heats. Great Britain too were doing well, however, and following wins for Scott Nicholls in the opening race and Gary Havelock in heat three, Lee Richardson's subsequent success put them in the ascendancy. The Swedes motored back into the picture following a triple of first places from David Ruud, Peter Ljung and Peter Karlsson, to leave the scores intriguingly poised at Great Britain 20, Sweden 18, Czech Republic 15, Russia 9, Finland 8. The eighth heat was the cue for the brave Brits to up the pace, and Nicholls' second victory of the meeting was followed up with wins from Dean Barker, Havelock and Richardson, interspersed only by a Swedish success from Mikael Max in heat ten, which was rerun after Ales Dryml had been excluded for a tapes offence. Andreas Jonsson posted another Swedish win in heat thirteen, prior to Nicholls completing a personal hat-trick in the next race, as Great Britain proudly led the way by 8 points overall. Things then started to go badly wrong for Sweden, putting their very qualification in jeopardy, as Czech veteran Bohumil Brhel raced home in heat fifteen, ahead of Roman Povazhny and Barker, with Peter Ljung in fourth spot. Brhel duly completed a quick-fire double in a rerun sixteenth race, after Max (taking a tactical joker ride), had lifted and collected Sergei Darkin, sending the Russian sprawling and earning an exclusion. Compounding matters for the Swedes, Nicholls then sprinted to another win from Ales Dryml, and with Ljung at the back, the scoreboard made bleak reading for the Scandinavians: Great Britain 54, Czech Republic 40, Sweden 38, Russia 20, Finland 19. That picture soon changed as Barker took the next race from Karlsson, and with Ales Dryml in fourth position, the two sides chasing the flying Great Britain lads were locked together. The Swedish supporters breathed more easily when Jonsson posted three victories in the next four races, his run only interrupted by a Barker win in heat twenty-one. Despite Jonsson's excellent efforts, the Swedes were only a couple of points ahead of their nearest challengers in that all-important second position, with the Czechs giving Tomas Topinka the opportunity of turning that situation around, courtesy of a tactical joker ride. Although the brilliant Richardson sped away to take the chequered flag for the dominant Brits, Topinka did a great job to thwart the charging Max, and his double score put the Czechs a couple of points ahead of the Swedes as just two heats remained. After Darkin had been excluded for impeding Ales Dryml, the rerun penultimate race was won by David Norris from Karlsson and a somewhat subdued Joonas Kylmakorpi, but with Dryml in fourth place, it set up a tense grand finale with Sweden and the Czech Republic standing on tallies of 59 points apiece. The phlegmatic Karlsson proved the man for the occasion as he jetted from the start and completed the necessary laps in perfect unison with his machine, thereby inflicting the only defeat of the meeting on Nicholls. That was that. Sweden accompanied Team Great Britain through to the World Cup Final, but what heartache for the courageous Czechs, who were so near and yet so far from qualification. Meanwhile, for the Finns and the Russians it was a bridge too far, although in fairness, this was effectively their World Cup Final.

TEAM GREAT BRITAIN 80

	RACE SCORES						TOTAL
Scott Nicholls	4	4	4	4	3	–	19
Dean Barker	0	4	2	4	4	–	14
Gary Havelock	4	3	4	2	2	–	15
Lee Richardson	4	3	4	3	4	–	18
David Norris	3	2	2	3	4	–	14

SWEDEN 63

Andreas Jonsson	1	3	4	4	4	4	20
Mikael Max	3	4	3	X	2	–	12
Peter Ljung	0	4	1	0	–	–	5
Peter Karlsson	2	4	2	3	3	4	18
David Ruud	4	1	2	1	–	–	8

CZECH REPUBLIC 61

Ales Dryml	3	T	3	3	1	1	11
Tomas Topinka	4	2	1	3	6	2	18
Lukas Dryml	3	0	2	2	3	–	10
Bohumil Brhel	1	3	3	4	4	3	18
Toni Svab	2	2	–	–	–	–	4

FINLAND 26

Kauko Nieminen	0	1	0	1	1	–	3
Joonas Kylmakorpi	2	2	R	0	2	0	6
Juha Hautamaki	1	1	0	–	–	–	2
Kaj Laukkanen	3	2	3	2	1	2	13
Tomi Reima	1	0	0	0	1	–	2

RUSSIA 24

Sergei Darkin	2	1	1	2	F	X	6
Renat Gafurov	1	3	1	2	X	–	7
Denis Gizatulin	2	0	0	–	–	–	2
Semen Vlasov	0	0	1	0	0	–	1
Roman Povazhny	0	1	3	2	1	1	8

RACE DETAILS

Heat one: Scott Nicholls, Ales Dryml, Sergei Darkin, Andreas Jonsson, Kauko Nieminen.

Heat two: Tomas Topinka, Mikael Max, Joonas Kylmakorpi, Renat Gafurov, Dean Barker.

Heat three: Gary Havelock, Lukas Dryml, Denis Gizatulin, Juha Hautamaki, Peter Ljung (f, rem).

Heat four: Lee Richardson, Kaj Laukkanen, Peter Karlsson, Bohumil Brhel, Semen Vlasov.

Heat five: David Ruud, David Norris, Toni Svab, Tomi Reima, Roman Povazhny.

Heat six: Peter Ljung, Lee Richardson, Tomas Topinka, Sergei Darkin, Tomi Reima.

Heat seven: Peter Karlsson, Renat Gafurov, David Norris, Kauko Nieminen, Lukas Dryml.

Heat eight: Scott Nicholls, Bohumil Brhel, Joonas Kylmakorpi, David Ruud, Denis Gizatulin.

Heat nine: Dean Barker, Andreas Jonsson, Toni Svab, Juha Hautamaki, Semen Vlasov.

Heat ten: (Rerun) Mikael Max, Gary Havelock, Kaj Laukkanen, Roman Povazhny, Ales Dryml (ex, tapes).

Heat eleven: Gary Havelock, Bohumil Brhel, Peter Karlsson, Sergei Darkin, Joonas Kylmakorpi (ret).

Heat twelve: Lee Richardson, Ales Dryml, David Ruud, Renat Gafurov, Juha Hautamaki.

Heat thirteen: Andreas Jonsson, Kaj Laukkanen, David Norris, Tomas Topinka, Denis Gizatulin.

Heat fourteen: Scott Nicholls, Mikael Max, Lukas Dryml, Semen Vlasov, Tomi Reima.

Heat fifteen: Bohumil Brhel, Roman Povazhny, Dean Barker, Peter Ljung, Kauko Nieminen.

Heat sixteen: (Rerun) Bohumin Brhel, David Norris, Sergei Darkin, Kaj Laukkanen (tactical joker), Mikael Max (tactical joker – ex, foul riding).

Heat seventeen: Scott Nicholls, Ales Dryml, Renat Gafurov, Kaj Laukkanen, Peter Ljung.

Heat eighteen: Dean Barker, Peter Karlsson, Roman Povazhny, Ales Dryml, Tomi Reima.

Heat nineteen: Andreas Jonsson, Tomas Topinka, Gary Havelock, Kauko Nieminen, Semen Vlasov.

Heat twenty: Andreas Jonsson, Lee Richardson, Lukas Dryml, Roman Povazhny, Joonas Kylmakorpi.

Heat twenty-one: Dean Barker, Lukas Dryml, Kaj Laukkanen, David Ruud, Sergei Darkin (fell).

Heat twenty-two: (Rerun) Andreas Jonsson, Bohumil Brhel, Gary Havelock, Tomi Reima, Renat
Gafurov (ex, foul riding).

Heat twenty-three: Lee Richardson, Tomas Topinka (tactical joker), Mikael Max, Kauko Nieminen,
Semen Vlasov.

Heat twenty-four: (Rerun) David Norris, Peter Karlsson, Joonas Kylmakorpi, Ales Dryml, Sergei Darkin
(tactical joker – ex, impeding opponent).

Heat twenty-five: Peter Karlsson, Scott Nicholls, Tomas Topinka, Roman Povazhny, Joonas Kylmakorpi.

(Points: 1st = 4; 2nd = 3; 3rd = 2; 4th = 1; 5th = 0; tactical joker = double points)

FINAL

9 AUGUST, VOJENS, DENMARK

The Vojens Speedway Centre was the venue for the World Cup Final, and on a difficult track
surface, it was a Tony Rickardsson-less Sweden who surprised everyone to take the crown.
Prior to the meeting few would have tipped the Swedes, instead probably going for the
Australians to complete a hat-trick of titles, although in fairness, all five teams were fairly
evenly matched. The Aussies, in the shape of Jason Crump, started like a house on fire as the
Belle Vue linchpin thundered to an opening heat success in a new track-record time. The wins
were certainly spread around in the first few races, with Mikael Max (Sweden), Bjarne
Pedersen (Denmark) and Sebastian Ulamek (Poland) leaving Great Britain as the only side
who hadn't taken the chequered flag. Either side of an unexpected Swedish success from Peter
Ljung in heat six, stylish Australian Leigh Adams recorded a brace of victories to give his
country the lead on 19 points, ahead of Sweden on 17, Poland 16, Denmark 13 and Team
Great Britain 5. The track had begun to get rutted early on, although its only victim had been
Jason Lyons in the initial running of the third heat. Crump notched a fourth win for the
Aussies in heat eight, and it looked as if the Antipodeans were well on course to retain their
trophy. The British boys had found it hard going, mustering just 8 points from as many starts,
but they came roaring back in heat nine when Lee Richardson doubled that total courtesy of
an excellent tactical joker outing. That was at the second time of asking after the circuit had
caught out cheery Dane Charlie Gjedde. Lyons suffered a similar fate in the next heat, which
was eventually won by Max. The Swede's victory was a telling one too, for it brought his
country level with Australia at the head of the leader board, with the other three sides sitting
nicely on 18 points apiece. Amazingly, Lyons' night didn't get any better when he took a third
fall in heat eleven, with Gjedde providing the home fans with something to cheer in the
restart, while Peter Karlsson's fourth-place point saw the Swedes sneak in front overall. That
soon changed when Jaroslaw Hampel won the next race from Ryan Sullivan, whose second
place again gave Australia the lead on 28 points from Sweden on 26, Poland 25, Denmark 23
and Great Britain 22. With things balanced on a knife-edge, Australia made significant strides
through successive victories from Adams, Crump and the fast-starting Todd Wiltshire. That gave
them a 9-point cushion over nearest challengers Sweden, and it was difficult to envisage
anything other than an Aussie success. A brief revival saw Max canter home for the Swedes in
heat sixteen, but this was immediately countered by more Australian flag-taking from both
Crump and Wiltshire, which put them 13 points to the good. Little did anyone know at the
time, but the Roos would only collect 7 more points from as many heats as the Swedes stepped
on the gas, beginning with a significant 8-point tactical joker ride from Max, while the

unfortunate Lyons retired in last place. After Bjarne Pedersen had come to grief, Andreas Jonsson took a rerun heat twenty, with the fallen Dane recovering his composure to take the subsequent race ahead of Tomasz Gollob, who was playing the tactical joker card. Just four heats remained and all five countries theoretically still had a chance of lifting the World Cup, with the scores standing at Australia 54, Sweden 50, Denmark 40, Great Britain 39, Poland 38. Nicki Pedersen certainly boosted Danish hopes when he sped away to defeat Hampel and collect double points in the first of those races, while Jonsson passed Dean Barker for third position to take the Swedes within 2 points of Australia, for whom Lyons' last place was his only finish of the meeting. Gollob won heat twenty-three from a pressing Max, and with Sullivan unable to oust the third-placed Gjedde, the two leading sides were tied on 55 points each. Incredibly, Ljung made a jet-propelled start to win the penultimate race, while Adams had to settle for just a single point after being unable to get on terms with Nicki Pedersen and Richardson in the higher-scoring positions. Having remained cool when it mattered in the race-off at Outrup, Peter Karlsson was the right man to have in the deciding heat as far as the Swedes were concerned, and he didn't disappoint as he followed Hampel home to give them an unlikely, but deserved, World Cup success.

SWEDEN 62

	RACE SCORES						TOTAL
Andreas Jonsson	0	3	3	4	2	–	12
Mikael Max	4	4	2	4	8	3	25
Peter Ljung	2	4	0	0	4	–	10
Peter Karlsson	2	2	1	2	3	–	10
David Ruud	3	1	0	1	–	–	5

AUSTRALIA 57

Jason Crump	4	4	4	4	1	–	17
Todd Wiltshire	3	2	4	4	2	–	15
Jason Lyons	X	X	X	R	0	–	0
Ryan Sullivan	3	1	3	2	1	–	10
Leigh Adams	4	4	4	2	1	–	15

DENMARK 53

Nicki Pedersen	3	3	1	3	8	3	21
Hans N. Andersen	1	2	2	2	0	–	7
Bjarne Pedersen	4	0	1	X	4	–	9
Ronni Pedersen	1	2	1	–	–	–	4
Charlie Gjedde	2	X	4	1	3	2	12

POLAND 49

Tomasz Gollob	2	3	3	6	4	–	18
Tomasz Bajerski	2	0	3	2	1	0	8
Jaroslaw Hampel	1	1	4	0	3	4	13
Sebastian Ulamek	4	1	0	1	–	–	6
Piotr Protasiewicz	1	3	X	0	–	–	4

TEAM GREAT BRITAIN 44

Gary Havelock	1	0	2	X	–	–	3
Dean Barker	0	1	2	2	1	–	6
David Norris	3	3	1	1	0	–	8
Lee Richardson	0	8	3	1	2	–	14
Scott Nicholls	0	2	3	3	3	2	13

RACE DETAILS

Heat one: Jason Crump, Nicki Pedersen, Tomasz Gollob, Gary Havelock, Andreas Jonsson.

Heat two: Mikael Max, Todd Wiltshire, Tomasz Bajerski, Hans N. Andersen, Dean Barker.

Heat three: (Rerun) Bjarne Pedersen, David Norris, Peter Ljung, Jaroslaw Hampel, Jason Lyons (f, ex).

Heat four: Sebastian Ulamek, Ryan Sullivan, Peter Karlsson, Ronni Pedersen, Lee Richardson.

Heat five: Leigh Adams, David Ruud, Charlie Gjedde, Piotr Protasiewicz, Scott Nicholls.

Heat six: Peter Ljung, Piotr Protasiewicz, Hans N. Andersen, Ryan Sullivan, Gary Havelock.

Heat seven: Leigh Adams, Tomasz Gollob, Peter Karlsson, Dean Barker, Bjarne Pedersen.

Heat eight: Jason Crump, David Norris, Ronni Pedersen, David Ruud, Tomasz Bajerski.

Heat nine: (Rerun) Lee Richardson (tactical joker), Andreas Jonsson, Todd Wiltshire, Jaroslaw Hampel, Charlie Gjedde (f, ex).

Heat ten: (Rerun) Mikael Max, Nicki Pedersen, Scott Nicholls, Sebastian Ulamek, Jason Lyons (f, ex).

Heat eleven: (Rerun) Charlie Gjedde, Tomasz Bajerski, Gary Havelock, Peter Karlsson, Jason Lyons (f, ex).

Heat twelve: Jaroslaw Hampel, Ryan Sullivan, Dean Barker, Nicki Pedersen, David Ruud.

Heat thirteen: Leigh Adams, Andreas Jonsson, Hans N. Andersen, David Norris, Sebastian Ulamek.

Heat fourteen: (Rerun) Jason Crump, Lee Richardson, Mikael Max, Bjarne Pedersen, Piotr Protasiewicz (f, ex).

Heat fifteen: Todd Wiltshire, Scott Nicholls, Tomasz Bajerski, Charlie Gjedde, Peter Ljung.

Heat sixteen: Mikael Max, Scott Nicholls, Leigh Adams, Ronni Pedersen, Jaroslaw Hampel.

Heat seventeen: Jason Crump, Charlie Gjedde, Dean Barker, Sebastian Ulamek, Peter Ljung.

Heat eighteen: Todd Wiltshire, Nicki Pedersen, Peter Karlsson, David Norris, Piotr Protasiewicz.

Heat nineteen: Mikael Max (tactical joker), Tomasz Gollob, Hans N. Andersen, Lee Richardson, Jason Lyons (ret).

Heat twenty: (Rerun) Andreas Jonsson, Scott Nicholls, Ryan Sullivan, Tomasz Bajerski, Bjarne Pedersen (f, ex).

Heat twenty-one: (Rerun) Bjarne Pedersen, Tomasz Gollob (tactical joker), Todd Wiltshire, David Ruud, Gary Havelock (f, ex).

Heat twenty-two: Nicki Pedersen (tactical joker), Jaroslaw Hampel, Andreas Jonsson, Dean Barker, Jason Lyons.

Heat twenty-three: Tomasz Gollob, Mikael Max, Charlie Gjedde, Ryan Sullivan, David Norris (f, rem).

Heat twenty-four: Peter Ljung, Nicki Pedersen, Lee Richardson, Leigh Adams, Tomasz Bajerski.

Heat twenty-five: Jaroslaw Hampel, Peter Karlsson, Scott Nicholls, Jason Crump, Hans N. Andersen.

(Points: 1st = 4; 2nd = 3; 3rd = 2; 4th = 1; 5th = 0; tactical joker = double points)

ROLL OF HONOUR

YEAR	FIRST	SECOND	THIRD	FOURTH
1960	Sweden	Great Britain	Czechoslovakia	Poland
1961	Poland	Sweden	Great Britain	Czechoslovakia
1962	Sweden	Great Britain	Poland	Czechoslovakia
1963	Sweden	Czechoslovakia	Great Britain	Poland
1964	Sweden	Soviet Union	Great Britain	Poland
1965	Poland	Sweden	Great Britain	Soviet Union
1966	Poland	Soviet Union	Sweden	Great Britain
1967	Sweden	Poland	Great Britain & Soviet Union	–
1968	Great Britain	Sweden	Poland	Czechoslovakia
1969	Poland	Great Britain	Soviet Union	Sweden
1970	Sweden	Great Britain	Poland	Czechoslovakia
1971	Great Britain	Soviet Union	Poland	Sweden
1972	Great Britain	Soviet Union	Poland	Sweden
1973	Great Britain	Sweden	Soviet Union	Poland
1974	England	Sweden	Poland	Soviet Union
1975	England	Soviet Union	Sweden	Poland
1976	Australia	Poland	Sweden	Soviet Union
1977	England	Poland	Czechoslovakia	Sweden
1978	Denmark	England	Poland	Czechoslovakia
1979	New Zealand	Denmark	Czechoslovakia	Poland
1980	England	USA	Poland	Czechoslovakia
1981	Denmark	England	West Germany	Soviet Union
1982	USA	Denmark	West Germany	Czechoslovakia
1983	Denmark	England	USA	Czechoslovakia
1984	Denmark	England	USA	Poland
1985	Denmark	USA	England	Sweden
1986	Denmark	USA	England	Sweden
1987	Denmark	England	USA	Czechoslovakia
1988	Denmark	USA	Sweden	England
1989	England	Denmark	Sweden	USA
1990	USA	England	Denmark	Czechoslovakia
1991	Denmark	Sweden	USA	England
1992	USA	Sweden	England	Denmark
1993	USA	Denmark	Sweden	England
1994	Sweden	Poland	Denmark	Australia
1995	Denmark	England	USA	Sweden
1996	Poland	Russia	Denmark	Germany
1997	Denmark	Poland	Sweden	Germany
1998	USA	Sweden	Denmark	Poland
1999	Australia	Czech Republic	USA	England
2000	Sweden	England	USA	Australia
2001	Australia	Poland	Sweden	Denmark
2002	Australia	Denmark	Sweden	Poland
2003	Sweden	Australia	Denmark	Poland

WORLD UNDER-21 CHAMPIONSHIP

NOTE: Formerly known as the European Junior Championship (1977-87)

QUALIFYING ROUNDS

ROUND ONE; 3 MAY, TERENZANO, ITALY

1st Jamie Smith 14; 2nd Thomas Stange 13; 3rd Robert Miskowiak 12; Ryan Fisher 11; Rinat Gafurov 11; Tom Suchanek 11; Rafal Kurmanski 9; Primoz Klenovsek 8; Daniele Tessari 7; Rene Schaefer 6; Patrik Linhart 4; Szabolcs Vida 4; Primoz Legan 3; Mate Szegedi 2; Mattia Carpanese 2; Marco Gregnanin 2; Denis Gizatullin 0.

ROUND TWO; 4 MAY, WIENER NEUSTADT, AUSTRIA

1st Jaroslaw Hampel 15; 2nd David Howe 14; 3rd Krzysztof Kasprzak 13; Jernej Kolenko 11; Andrew Appleton 10; Fredrich Wallner 9; Jan Jaros 8; Miroslav Fencl 8; Marko Vlah 7; Matthias Schultz 6; Andrej Karpov 5; Ivan Vargek 4; Christian Hefenbrock 3; Jan Halabrin 2; Jaye Stevens 1; Manuel Hauzinger 1.

ROUND THREE; 24 MAY, AVESTA, SWEDEN

1st Kenneth Bjerre 15; 2nd Jonas Davidsson 12; 3rd Peter Ljung 11; Fredrik Lindgren 11; Niels-Kristian Iversen 11; Daniel Davidsson 10; Steven Andersen 8; Rune Sola 8; Mads B. Petersen 8; Charlie Moller 8; Antonio Lindback 6; Mico Brotkin 4; Andreas Lekander 3; Marius Rokeberg 3; Juha Hautamaki 1; Mikke Bjerk 1.

ROUND FOUR; 25 MAY, POOLE, ENGLAND

1st Chris Harris 14; 2nd Rafal Szombierski 13; 3rd Miroslaw Jablonksi 12; Simon Stead 12; Lukasz Romanek 11; Edward Kennett 10; Olly Allen 9; Rory Schlein 8; Aidan Collins 8; Bryan Yarrow 5; Cameron Woodward 4; Mathieu Tresarrieu 4; Kyle Legault 3; Eric Carillo 3; Martin Malek 2; Ritchie Hawkins 2; Aurillien Lamarque 0.

FIRST SEMI-FINAL; 9 JUNE, ABENSBERG, GERMANY

1st Chris Harris 13; 2nd Niels-Kristian Iversen 13; 3rd Krzysztof Kasprzak 12; Jaroslaw Hampel 12; Fredrik Lindgren 10; Robert Miskowiak 9; David Howe 7; Ryan Fisher 7; Martin Smolinski 7; Rinat Gafurov 6; Andrew Appleton 6; Simon Stead 6; Tomas Suchanek 4; Rory Schlein 3; Fritz Wallner 3; Rune Sola 2.

SECOND SEMI-FINAL; 29 JUNE, LJUBLJANA, SLOVENIA

1st Peter Ljung 12; 2nd Matej Zagar 12; 3rd Kenneth Bjerre 11; Rafal Kurmanski 10; Rafal Szombierski 10; Jamie Smith 9; Jonas Davidsson 9; Olly Allen 9; Edward Kennett 7; Lukasz Romanek 7; Miroslaw Jablonski 7; Jernej Kolenko 6; Steven Andersen 4; Daniel Davidsson 3; Jan Jaros 3; Primoz Klenovsek 1.

WORLD UNDER-21 CHAMPIONSHIP FINAL
13 SEPTEMBER, KUMLA, SWEDEN

1st	Jaroslaw Hampel
2nd	Chris Harris
3rd	Rafal Szombierski
4th	Fredrik Lindgren

	RACE SCORES					TOTAL
Jaroslaw Hampel	3	3	3	3	2	14
Chris Harris	3	2	3	3	2	13
Rafal Szombierski	2	2	2	2	3	11
Fredrik Lindgren	0	3	2	3	3	11
Matej Zagar	2	3	1	1	3	10
Niels-Kristian Iversen	R	3	3	0	3	9
Rafal Kurmanski	2	1	3	1	1	8
Kenneth Bjerre	1	1	R	3	2	7
David Howe	0	1	2	2	1	6
Peter Ljung	3	2	X	1	0	6
Jonas Davidsson	3	0	0	2	1	6
Robert Miskowiak	1	1	1	2	1	6
Jamie Smith	1	0	2	0	2	5
Ryan Fisher	2	2	R	R	–	4
Martin Smolinski	1	0	1	0	0	2
Olly Allen	R	X	1	1	0	2
Lukasz Romanek (Res)	0	–	–	–	–	0

RACE DETAILS

Heat one: Peter Ljung, Ryan Fisher, Kenneth Bjerre, David Howe.

Heat two: Jonas Davidsson, Rafal Szombierski, Martin Smolinski, Olly Allen (ret).

Heat three: Chris Harris, Matej Zagar, Robert Miskowiak, Fredrik Lindgren.

Heat four: Jaroslaw Hampel, Rafal Kurmanski, Jamie Smith, Niels-Kristian Iversen (ret).

Heat five: Fredrik Lindgren, Rafal Szombierski, David Howe, Jamie Smith.

Heat six: Jaroslaw Hampel, Chris Harris, Kenneth Bjerre, Jonas Davidsson.

Heat seven: Niels-Kristian Iversen, Ryan Fisher, Robert Miskowiak, Martin Smolinski.

Heat eight: (Rerun) Matej Zagar, Peter Ljung, Rafal Kurmanski, Olly Allen (f, ex).

Heat nine: Rafal Kurmanski, David Howe, Robert Miskowiak, Jonas Davidsson.

Heat ten: Niels-Kristian Iversen, Rafal Szombierski, Matej Zagar, Kenneth Bjerre (ret).

Heat eleven: Jaroslaw Hampel, Fredrik Lindgren, Olly Allen, Ryan Fisher (ret).

Heat twelve: (Rerun) Chris Harris, Jamie Smith, Martin Smolinksi, Peter Ljung (f, ex).

Heat thirteen: Jaroslaw Hampel, David Howe, Matej Zagar, Martin Smolinski.

Heat fourteen: Kenneth Bjerre, Robert Miskowiak, Olly Allen, Jamie Smith.

Heat fifteen: Chris Harris, Rafal Szombierski, Rafal Kurmanski, Ryan Fisher (ret).

Heat sixteen: Fredrik Lindgren, Jonas Davidsson, Peter Ljung, Niels-Kristian Iversen.

Heat seventeen: Niels-Kristian Iversen, Chris Harris, David Howe, Olly Allen.

Heat eighteen: Fredrik Lindgren, Kenneth Bjerre, Rafal Kurmanski, Martin Smolinski.

Heat nineteen: Matej Zagar, Jamie Smith, Jonas Davidsson, Lukasz Romanek.

Heat twenty: Rafal Szombierski, Jaroslaw Hampel, Robert Miskowiak, Peter Ljung.

Third-Place Run-Off: Rafal Szombierski, Fredrik Lindgren.

ROLL OF HONOUR

YEAR	FIRST	SECOND	THIRD
1977	Alf Busk	Joe Owen	Les Collins
1978	Finn Jensen	Kevin Jolly	Neil Middleditch
1979	Ron Preston	Airat Faljzulin	Ari Koponen
1980	Tommy Knudsen	Tony Briggs	Dennis Sigalos
1981	Shawn Moran	Toni Kasper	Jiri Hnidak
1982	Toni Kasper	Mark Courtney	Peter Ravn
1983	Steve Baker	David Bargh	Marvyn Cox
1984	Marvyn Cox	Neil Evitts	Steve Lucero
1985	Per Jonsson	Jimmy Nilsen	Ole Hansen
1986	Igor Marko	Tony Olsson	Brian Karger
1987	Gary Havelock	Piotr Swist	Sean Wilson
1988	Peter Nahlin	Henrik Gustafsson	Brian Karger
1989	Gert Handberg	Chris Louis	Niklas Karlsson
1990	Chris Louis	Rene Aas	Tony Rickardsson
1991	Brian Andersen	Morten Andersen	Jason Lyons
1992	Leigh Adams	Mark Loram	Joe Screen
1993	Joe Screen	Mikael Karlsson	Rune Holta
1994	Mikael Karlsson	Rune Holta	Jason Crump
1995	Jason Crump	Dalle Anderson	Ryan Sullivan
1996	Piotr Protasiewicz	Ryan Sullivan	Jesper B. Jensen
1997	Jesper B. Jensen	Rafal Dobrucki	Scott Nicholls
1998	Robert Dados	Krzysztof Jablonski	Matej Ferjan
1999	Lee Richardson	Ales Dryml	Nigel Sadler
2000	Andreas Jonsson	Krzysztof Cegielski	Jaroslaw Hampel
2001	David Kujawa	Lukas Dryml	Rafal Okoniewski
2002	Lukas Dryml	Krzysztof Kasprzak	David Howe
2003	Jaroslaw Hampel	Chris Harris	Rafal Szombierski

EUROPEAN CHAMPIONSHIP

QUALIFYING ROUNDS

FIRST SEMI-FINAL; 6 JUNE, OUTRUP, DENMARK

1st Niels-Kristian Iversen 13; 2nd Hans N. Andersen 11; 3rd Magnus Zetterstrom 11; Charlie Gjedde 11; Peter I. Karlsson 11; David Ruud 10; Nicki Pedersen 10; Kenneth Bjerre 9; Peter Karlsson 9; Peter Ljung 7; Ronni Pedersen 5; Kristian Lund 5; Bjorn G. Hansen 4; Tobias Johansson 2; Mikke Bjerk 1; Steven R. Andersen 1; Ola Rosland 0.

SECOND SEMI-FINAL; 7 JUNE, LONIGO, ITALY

1st Matej Zagar 15; 2nd Slawomir Drabik 14; 3rd Krzysztof Jablonski 13; Attila Stefani 11;

Sebastian Tresarrieu 10; Andrea Maida 8; Janusz Kolodziej 8; Josef Franc 8; Denis Gizatullin 7; Joachim Kugelmann 6; Rinat Gafurov 6; Izak Santej 4; Tomas Suchanek 4; Marco Muller 2; Daniele Tessari 2; Vladimir Visvader 1; Simone Tadiello 1.

EUROPEAN CHAMPIONSHIP FINAL
30 AUGUST, SLANY, CZECH REPUBLIC

1st	Krzysztof Kasprzak
2nd	Slawomir Drabik
3rd	Magnus Zetterstrom
4th	Matej Zagar

	RACE SCORES					TOTAL
Krzysztof Kasprzak	3	2	1	3	3	12
Slawomir Drabik	3	3	2	1	3	12
Magnus Zetterstrom	0	3	3	3	2	11
Matej Zagar	2	3	1	2	2	10
Igor Marko	2	1	3	3	0	9
Rafal Szombierski	3	3	2	1	0	9
Charlie Gjedde	1	2	1	3	2	9
Sebastian Tresarrieu	0	2	2	1	3	8
Andrzej Huszcza	2	1	R	2	3	8
Peter I. Karlsson	3	0	1	2	1	7
Toni Svab	1	2	3	0	0	6
Krzysztof Jablonski	0	X	3	2	1	6
Niels-Kristian Iversen	2	1	2	F	1	6
Richard Wolff	1	0	0	0	2	3
Attila Stefani	1	1	0	1	R	3
Andrea Maida	0	0	0	0	1	1

RACE DETAILS
Heat one: Slawomir Drabik, Niels-Kristian Iversen, Toni Svab, Andrea Maida.
Heat two: Peter I.Karlsson, Igor Marko, Richard Wolff, Krzysztof Jablonski.
Heat three: Krzysztof Kasprzak, Andrzej Huszcza, Charlie Gjedde, Magnus Zetterstrom.
Heat four: Rafal Szombierski, Matej Zagar, Attila Stefani, Sebastian Tresarrieu.
Heat five: Slawomir Drabik, Sebastian Tresarrieu, Andrzej Huszcza, Peter I. Karlsson.
Heat six: Matej Zagar, Charlie Gjedde, Igor Marko, Andrea Maida.
Heat seven: Rafal Szombierski, Krzysztof Kasprzak, Niels-Kristian Iversen, Richard Wolff.
Heat eight: (Rerun) Magnus Zetterstrom, Toni Svab, Attila Stefani, Krzysztof Jablonski (f, ex).
Heat nine: Igor Marko, Slawomir Drabik, Krzysztof Kasprzak, Attila Stefani.
Heat ten: Magnus Zetterstrom, Rafal Szombierski, Peter I. Karlsson, Andrea Maida.
Heat eleven: Krzysztof Jablonski, Niels-Kristian Iversen, Matej Zagar, Andrzej Huszcza (ret).
Heat twelve: Toni Svab, Sebastian Tresarrieu, Charlie Gjedde, Richard Wolff.
Heat thirteen: Magnus Zetterstrom, Matej Zagar, Slawomir Drabik, Richard Wolff.
Heat fourteen: Krzysztof Kasprzak, Krzysztof Jablonski, Sebastian Tresarrieu, Andrea Maida.

Heat fifteen: Charlie Gjedde, Peter I. Karlsson, Attila Stefani, Niels-Kristian Iversen (fell).

Heat sixteen: Igor Marko, Andrzej Huszcza, Rafal Szombierski, Toni Svab.

Heat seventeen: Slawomir Drabik, Charlie Gjedde, Krzysztof Jablonski, Rafal Szombierski.

Heat eighteen: Andrzej Huszcza, Richard Wolff, Andrea Maida, Attila Stefani (ret).

Heat nineteen: Sebastian Tresarrieu, Magnus Zetterstrom, Niels-Kristian Iversen, Igor Marko.

Heat twenty: Krzysztof Kasprzak, Matej Zagar, Peter I. Karlsson, Toni Svab.

First-Place Run-Off: Krzysztof Kasprzak, Slawomir Drabik.

ROLL OF HONOUR

YEAR	FIRST	SECOND	THIRD
2001	Bohumil Brhel	Mariusz Staszewski	Krzysztof Cegielski
2002	Magnus Zetterstrom	Krzysztof Kasprzak	Rafal Szombierski
2003	Krzysztof Kasprzak	Slawomir Drabik	Magnus Zetterstrom

If you are interested in purchasing other books published by Tempus,
or in case you have difficulty finding any Tempus books in your local bookshop,
you can also place orders directly through our website

www.tempus-publishing.com

or from

BOOKPOST, Freepost, PO Box 29, Douglas, Isle of Man IM99 1BQ
Tel 01624 836000   email bookshop@enterprise.net